Project Finance in Theory and Practice

Project Finance in Theory and Practice

Designing, Structuring, and Financing Private and Public Projects

Stefano Gatti

AMSTERDAM • BOSTON • HEIDELBERG • LONDON
NEW YORK • OXFORD • PARIS • SAN DIEGO
SAN FRANCISCO • SINGAPORE • SYDNEY • TOKYO

Academic Press is an imprint of Elsevier

ELSEVIER

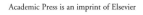

Academic Press is an imprint of Elsevier
30 Corporate Drive, Suite 400, Burlington, MA 01803, USA
525 B Street, Suite 1900, San Diego, California 92101-4495, USA
84 Theobald's Road, London WCIX 8RR, UK

This book is printed on acid-free paper.

Library of Congress Cataloging-in-Publication Data
Application Submitted

British Library Cataloguing-in-Publication Data
A catalogue record for this book is available from the British Library.

ISBN 13: 978-0-12-373699-4 $\cup$

For information on all Academic Press publications
visit our Web site at www.books.elsevier.com

Printed in the United States of America
07 08 09 10   9 8 7 6 5 4 3 2 1

Abbreviated Contents

Case Studies

Contents

Foreword

William L. Megginson

This is a timely book examining an extremely timely topic. During the past three decades, project finance has emerged as an important method of financing large-scale, high-risk domestic and international business ventures. This is usually defined as limited or nonrecourse financing of a new project to be developed through the establishment of a vehicle company (separate incorporation). Thus the distinguishing features of project finance (PF) are, first, that creditors share much of the venture's business risk and, second, that funding is obtained strictly for the project itself without an expectation that the corporate or government sponsor will coinsure the project's debt—at least not fully. PF is most commonly used for capital-intensive projects, with relatively transparent cash flows, in riskier-than-average countries, using relatively long-term financing, and employing far more detailed loan covenants than will conventionally financed projects. (Stefano Gatti and his collaborators have written an excellent and comprehensive survey of project finance techniques, processes, and practices, which practitioners and researchers should both value as a key resource.)

Project finance has grown very rapidly in the recent past. Esty and Sesia (2007) report that a record $328 billion in PF funding was arranged in 2006, up from $165 billion in 2003 and substantially above the previous record $217 billion in 2001. A key reason why project finance has emerged so spectacularly recently is that the world economy is now growing at very nearly its fastest pace ever. Since 2003, global GDP has grown at a compound annual growth rate of almost 5%, with growth in developing countries approaching 7% on average. Rapid growth demands even greater-than-average investment in infrastructure, such as ports, bridges, roads, telecommunications networks, electric power generation and distribution facilities, airports, intra- and intercity rail networks, and water and sewerage facilities. The OECD predicts that the world will need to spend almost 4% of national and global GDP on infrastructure each year to support accelerating growth—around $1.6 trillion annually—yet governments are ill-placed to fund more than a fraction of these investments. The remainder must come from private sources, either as stand-alone projects or as public-private cooperative ventures. Project finance is certain to figure prominently in meeting the world's infrastructure investment needs, especially in emerging markets.

PF has also been gaining global financing market share, especially as a vehicle for channeling development capital to emerging markets. Gatti, Kleimeier, Megginson, and Steffanoni (2007) report that over 60% of the value (and 68% of the number) of project finance loans extended between 1991 and 2005 were arranged for borrowers located outside of North America and western Europe, with over 40% of the total being arranged for Asian projects.

Project finance is very good at funding specific investments in certain industries. Typically, PF is used for capital-intensive infrastructure investments that employ established technology and generate stable returns, preferably returns that are denominated in or can be easily converted to hard currencies. PF is not good at funding high-risk investments with uncertain returns, so it is rarely used to fund research and development spending, new product introductions, advertising campaigns, or other potentially high-return intangible investments. PF is used only for tangible, large projects with known construction risks and well-established operating technology. Brealey, Cooper, and Habib (1996) also stress that one of the key comparative advantages of project finance is that it allows the allocation of specific project risks (i.e., completion and operating risk, revenue and price risk, and the risk of political interference or expropriation) to those parties best able to manage them. PF is especially good at constraining governments from expropriating project cash flows after the project is operating, when the temptation to do so is especially great. At this stage, all the investments have been made and the project cash flows are committed to paying off the heavy debt load.

The key players in project finance are the project sponsors who invest in the special-purpose vehicle (SPV); the host government and often state-owned enterprises; the construction and engineering firms responsible for actually constructing the project; legal specialists who design the contracts essential to allocating project risks and responsibilities; accounting, financial, and risk assessment professionals who advise the principal actors and assess project risks; lead arranging banks that organize and lead the banking syndicate that funds the project loan; and participating banks that are part of the loan syndicate. Governments typically play a much larger and more direct role in project finance than in any other form of private funding. State-owned enterprises are especially important as counterparties to project vehicle companies, since these state companies often have privileged or monopoly positions as providers of telecom, electricity, water, and sewerage services in the host countries.

Project finance is not really true corporate finance; in fact, PF can be defined in contrast to standard corporate finance, as clearly discussed in the first chapter of this book. A touchstone of corporate capital investment is the separation of investment and financing decisions, with corporate managers assessing all investment projects using a firm-wide weighted average cost of capital required rate of return, accepting all positive NPV projects, and then funding the capital budget with internal cash flow (retained earnings) and external securities issues (mostly debt). Project finance is the exact antithesis of this investment method. In PF, each major investment project is organized and funded separately from all others, and the discretion of the SPV over project cash flows is explicitly minimized. Whereas the essence of corporate finance is to provide funding for limited-liability corporations with perpetual life and complete discretion over internal capital investment, project finance involves the creation of an entirely new vehicle company, with a strictly limited life, for each new investment project. A cardinal objective of PF contracting is to minimize the ability of project sponsors and, especially, host governments to expropriate project cash flows after the capital-intensive investment has been made and begins generating high free cash flows.

Though creation of a vehicle company is the seminal step in all project financings, the work of the syndicated loan lead arranging bank is arguably the most crucial. The bank selected by the project sponsors must perform three vital and difficult tasks. First, this bank must perform the classic task of performing due diligence on the vehicle company and the project itself to ensure that all potential adverse inside information is revealed before loan syndication. This is especially difficult because the sponsor need not be concerned about reputational effects—it will arrange but a single financing before expiring—and thus has great incentive to hide adverse information about the project and the sponsor's own motives. Second, the lead arranger must attract a sufficient number and diversity of participating banks to fund the PF loan(s) at a price that is both low enough to ensure project solvency and high enough to compensate the banks adequately for the (known and unknown) risks they are taking by extending long-term, illiquid financing.

The lead arranger must also design an optimal loan syndicate that will deter strategic defaults (Chowdry, 1991; Esty and Megginson, 2003) but allow for efficient renegotiation in the event of liquidity defaults. Finally, the lead arranger must spearhead monitoring of the borrower after the loan closes and discourage the sponsor (or the project's host government) from strategically defaulting or otherwise expropriating project cash flows. This is especially difficult in project finance, since many such projects have extremely high up-front costs but then generate large free cash low streams after the project is completed (Bolton and Scharfstein, 1996; Esty and Megginson, 2003). Furthermore, the lenders, represented by the lead arranger, typically have little or no power to seize assets or shut down project operations in project host countries, so deterrence must be expressed through some other mechanism. Surprisingly, Kleimeier and Megginson (2000) show that PF loans have lower spreads than many other types of syndicated loans, despite being riskier nonrecourse credits with longer maturities, suggesting that the unique contractual features of project finance in fact reduce risk.

This book analyzes clearly and in detail all of the issues I have raised. The reader will find answers to many questions related to the design, organization, and funding of these complex and fascinating project finance deals in the pages of this excellent volume.

William L. Megginson
Professor and Rainbolt Chair in Finance
Price College of Business
The University of Oklahoma
Norman, Oklahoma

Preface

I started working in the project finance field in 1993, when I was assistant professor at the Institute of Financial Markets and Financial Intermediation at SDA Bocconi School of Management in Milan. My initial involvement was due to the launch of a new research project investigating the development of project finance techniques in Italy. At that time, Europe had just started to see the use of this technique in the private sector, particularly for the development and subsequent exploitation of offshore crude reserves (the Forties Fields, off the coast of Scotland). The Italian project finance market was still in its infancy.

From that point on, the most absorbing field of interest on my research agenda and in my professional activity has been project finance. In the past few years, I've organized several teaching activities, both at a graduate level and in MBA programs, in Italy and abroad, in order to disseminate knowledge on this important field of finance.

If we look at the numbers, the growth of the market is impressive: From 1994 to 2004, project finance loans grew at a 24% annual compounded rate, and today this technique accounts for more than 5% of the total market for syndicated loans. Yet despite these numbers, this topic has received little attention from the academic or practitioners' press. Not many books and no corporate finance international handbooks deal with project finance. Academic journals that have hosted papers on the subject are very few.

This is why I decided to collect a large part of the teaching notes, reports, and case studies I have developed over the past few years and organize them into a book. My objective is to provide the reader with a complete view on how a deal can be organized—from industrial, legal, and financial standpoints—and the alternatives for funding it. But what must never be forgotten is that project finance is a highly leveraged transaction where two principles are key to its success: (1) Cash is king; (2) lenders control the destiny of the project. In fact, lender satisfaction is just as important as the legitimate claim of project sponsors for a satisfactory return on capital.

This book requires no previous experience in the field, and most of the concepts are explained for readers who are approaching this subject for the first time. Yet the complete coverage of all aspects involved in structuring deals makes it suitable for professionals as well as graduate/MBA/EMBA students.

Chapter 1 opens the book with a description of the rationale underpinning project finance deals and a discussion of the difference between corporate finance and project finance.

Chapter 2 is dedicated to the analysis of the market at an international level. Trends clearly demonstrate that project finance loans are a rapidly growing segment of the syndicated loan market and that the destination of funds is quickly changing. In particular, the largest portion of loans is beginning to flow into PPPs (public-private partnerships) and into projects where public administrative bodies play the role of concession awarder to private sponsors. In Europe, PPP projects account for more than 36% of total project finance loans; in Asia this percentage stands at a remarkable 25%.

Chapter 3 focuses on risk analysis and risk management. The chapter considers project contracts as risk management tools. Together with insurance policies, in fact, they are the most powerful instruments of this kind for reducing a deal's cash flow volatility, to the benefit of both lenders and sponsors.

Chapter 4 presents a rare discussion of the role of external consultants in project finance transactions. Here we also describe what legal advisors, independent technical advisors, and insurers are required to do in the overall process of deal design, implementation and funding.

In Chapter 5 we discuss how to appraise the bankability of the deal. Since cash is king, two topics are of particular relevance: (1) the analysis of cash flows generated by the venture and (2) the optimal capital structure. The analysis of cover ratios (which represent the balance between cash generation and cash needs for debt service) and sensitivity and scenario analysis completes the financial analysis of the transaction.

Chapter 6 presents an overview of financing options. Since the book targets an international readership, we address the role played by multilateral and bilateral institutions in developing countries. Syndicated loans, equity and mezzanine/subordinated loans, and leasing and project bonds are all included and analyzed from the economic and financial points of view.

Chapter 7 is dedicated to the legal aspects of project finance. After examining the special-purpose vehicle, we provide a thorough description of the finance, security, and project documents. Although we take the lawyers' perspective, constant attention is given to the implications for the finance profession.

Finally, Chapter 8 explores some recent developments in the literature on project finance, brought about by the forthcoming adoption of the new Basel II rules. The chapter looks at Basel II requirements for lenders in terms of credit risk analysis of specialized lending deals (which encompasses project finance) and discusses the as-yet-unresolved issue of how to measure the value at risk of a project finance transaction.

The book includes three case studies. The aim of the first, "Cogeneration," is to describe the setup of the contractual network of a deal and to identify the weak points of a project and possible available solutions. The second, "Italy Water System," is an Excel-based case study that can be used as a business game. The aim here is to develop negotiating skills in the participants, who must maximize the trade-off of conflicting utility functions (of sponsors, lenders, and public administration). The third case is a reprint of a classic article by Benjamin Esty, from Harvard Business School; it discusses the syndication process of the Hong Kong Disney Park.

Acknowledgments

This book has taken me more than a year and a half to finish. I hope that the reader will appreciate all the effort put into making an updated and complete handbook.

This result wouldn't have been possible without the continuous support provided by Karen Maloney, Jay Donahue, and Roxana Boboc at Elsevier. My special thanks go to Karen, who from the very beginning enthusiastically supported my proposal to publish a book on the topic with her publisher and followed the progress of the work step by step.

Acknowledgments go to all the people who have worked with me these past years, both scholars and professionals, to disseminate knowledge on this subject. For their suggestions and encouragement I would like to thank Andrea Sironi, Francesco Saita, Alvaro Rigamonti, Mauro Senati, Giancarlo Forestieri, Emilia Garcia-Appendini, Andrea Resti, Ben Esty, Bill Megginson (who was so kind to dedicate his time to write the presentation), Stefanie Kleimeier, Marco Sorge, Blaise Gadanecz, Ian Cooper, Michel Habib, Giuseppe Cappellini, Sergio Ferraris, Issam Hallak.

Special thanks to my contributors in this volume Alessandro Steffanoni and Daniele Corbino (for the release of the excel file supporting the Italy Water Case), Massimo Novo (for the legal part of the book), Fabio Landriscina and Mark Pollard (for the insurance section).

Alessandro Steffanoni is the head of project finance team in Interbanca, the Italian merchant bank of Banca Antonveneta- ABN AMRO Group, and jointed the bank in 2006 as deputy head of the team. He has been involved in advisory and structuring roles in PFI, waste to energy and renewable energy Project financing. From 2000 to 2006 he was member of project finance team in Banca Intesa focused on domestic and international PFI and Energy transactions. Alessandro has been collaborating in L. Bocconi University and in Bocconi Business School since 1998.

Daniele Corbino has been working for the project finance desk of Intesa Sanpaolo since 2004, in different industries like power and energy, media and telecom, infrastructures and shipping finance. He serves as lecturer in investment banking and structured finance at Universitá Bocconi and SDA Bocconi School of Management.

Massimo Novo is an Italian qualified lawyer and a partner at Clifford Chance, Milan. He studied at the University of Turin (JD), the Scuola Superiore Enrico Mattei (MBA) and at Columbia University Law School (LLM). He specializes in Project Finance, Acquisition Finance and Real Estate Finance and is a regular contributor to the post-graduate courses at the Bocconi University Business School.

Fabio Landriscina is Head of Project Financing Team of Marsh SpA in Italy and he is in charge of Banks Insurance Advisory co-ordination and development for the Italian market. He has been working in the Project Financing field for eight years and has been involved in the great majority of the main PFI/PPP projects in Italy acting both as Insurance Advisor and Placing Broker both for Lenders and/or for the Project Companies. He joined Marsh in 2004 from another major international broker, where he was Senior Account Executive with particular involvement in the Project Financing activity. Fabio holds an Economics degree from Brescia University.

Mark Pollard is Head of Industry Practices for Marsh Europe, Middle East and Africa, and the Managing Director of Marsh Inc. Since the late '90s, he has been responsible for Project Financing consulting in Italy, and has project managed a number of innovative programmes. Before joining Marsh, Mark worked as underwriter on international technological and infrastructure risks for a major European insurance company. Mark holds a Master of Arts degree from Oxford University, graduating in 1982 in Classics, and is a Fellow of the Chartered Insurance Institute.

Thanks also to Jill Connelly and Peter De Hunt for their help in translating the manuscript and Lorenzo Marinoni for the valuable support in preparing the instructors' material.

Finally, thanks to all my friends and relatives who I have taken time and attention away from while spending days (and sometimes nights) writing the pages of this book. I want to dedicate it to my mother Graziella, whose love her son is one of the most precious jewels in his life.

Stefano Gatti, Milan, June 2007

About the Author

Stefano Gatti is Professor of Banking and Finance at Bocconi University in Milan, where he is also the Director of the BSc of Economics and Finance and Director of the ITP-International Teachers' Program at SDA Bocconi School of Management. He has published a large number of books and papers related to financial intermediation, investment banking, and structured finance. He also serves as a consultant for industrial and financial firms and sits on several boards of directors of Italian and multinational firms.

CHAPTER 1

Introduction to the Theory and Practice of Project Finance

Introduction

This chapter introduces the theory and practice of project finance. It provides a general overview of everything that will be analyzed in greater detail in subsequent chapters. We believe it is useful to start with a chapter describing the salient features of a project finance deal, essential project finance terminology, the basics of the four steps of risk management (identification, analysis, transfer, and residual management), together with the theory that financial economics has developed on this topic. This chapter also helps to understand the reasons for using project finance as compared with more traditional approaches employed by companies to finance their projects.

Section 1.1 provides an exact definition of the term *project finance* so as to avoid confusion with other, apparently similar contractual structures. The impression is, in fact, that all too often corporate loans issued directly to the party concerned are confused with true project finance structures.

Section 1.2 analyzes the reasons why project finance is used by sponsoring firms and the advantages it can bring to sponsors and lenders, and it highlights the main differences between corporate financing and project financing.

Section 1.3 reviews the main categories of project sponsors and clarifies the different reasons why each category is interested in designing and managing a new project finance deal.

Section 1.4 introduces the basic terminology of project finance and illustrates the key contracts used in the deal to manage and control the risks involved in the project. This section is an introduction to the topic of risk management, which is discussed in greater detail in Chapter 3.

Finally, Section 1.5 reviews the theory of project finance and the most important concepts associated with the financial economics of project finance:

1

contamination risk, the coinsurance effect and wealth expropriation of lenders by sponsoring firms.

1.1   What Is Project Finance?

A huge body of literature is available today on the subject of structured finance in general and project finance in particular. The majority of authors agree on defining *project finance* as financing that as a priority does not depend on the soundness and creditworthiness of the sponsors, namely, parties proposing the business idea to launch the project. Approval does not even depend on the value of assets sponsors are willing to make available to financers as collateral. Instead, it is basically a function of the project's ability to repay the debt contracted and remunerate capital invested at a rate consistent with the degree of risk inherent in the venture concerned.

Project finance is the structured financing of a specific economic entity—the SPV, or special-purpose vehicle, also known as the project company—created by sponsors using equity or mezzanine debt and for which the lender considers cash flows as being the primary source of loan reimbursement, whereas assets represent only collateral.

The following five points are, in essence, the distinctive features of a project finance deal.

1. The debtor is a project company set up on an ad hoc basis that is financially and legally independent from the sponsors.
2. Lenders have only limited recourse (or in some cases no recourse at all) to the sponsors after the project is completed. The sponsors' involvement in the deal is, in fact, limited in terms of time (generally during the setup to start-up period), amount (they can be called on for equity injections if certain economic-financial tests prove unsatisfactory), and quality (managing the system efficiently and ensuring certain performance levels). This means that risks associated with the deal must be assessed in a different way than risks concerning companies already in operation.
3. Project risks are allocated equitably between all parties involved in the transaction, with the objective of assigning risks to the contractual counterparties best able to control and manage them.
4. Cash flows generated by the SPV must be sufficient to cover payments for operating costs and to service the debt in terms of capital repayment and interest. Because the priority use of cash flow is to fund operating costs and to service the debt, only residual funds after the latter are covered can be used to pay dividends to sponsors.
5. Collateral is given by the sponsors to lenders as security for receipts and assets tied up in managing the project.

1.2   Why Do Sponsors Use Project Finance?

A sponsor can choose to finance a new project using two alternatives:

1. The new initiative is financed on balance sheet (corporate financing).
2. The new project is incorporated into a newly created economic entity, the SPV, and financed off balance sheet (project financing).

Alternative 1 means that sponsors use all the assets and cash flows from the existing firm to guarantee the additional credit provided by lenders. If the project is not successful, all the remaining assets and cash flows can serve as a source of repayment for all the creditors (old and new) of the combined entity (existing firm plus new project).

Alternative 2 means, instead, that the new project and the existing firm live two separate lives. If the project is not successful, project creditors have no (or very limited) claim on the sponsoring firms' assets and cash flows. The existing firm's shareholders can then benefit from the separate incorporation of the new project into an SPV.

One major drawback of alternative 2 is that structuring and organizing such a deal is actually much more costly than the corporate financing option. The small amount of evidence available on the subject shows an average incidence of transaction costs on the total investment of around 5–10%. There are several different reasons for these high costs.

1. The legal, technical, and insurance advisors of the sponsors and the loan arranger need a great deal of time to evaluate the project and negotiate the contract terms to be included in the documentation.
2. The cost of monitoring the project in process is very high.
3. Lenders are expected to pay significant costs in exchange for taking on greater risks.

On the other hand, although project finance does not offer a cost advantage, there are definitely other benefits as compared to corporate financing.

1. Project finance allows for a high level of risk allocation among participants in the transaction. Therefore the deal can support a debt-to-equity ratio that could not otherwise be attained. This has a major impact on the return of the transaction for sponsors (the equity IRR), as we explain in Chapter 5.
2. From the accounting standpoint, contracts between sponsors and SPVs are essentially comparable to commercial guarantees. Nonetheless, with project finance initiatives they do not always appear "off balance sheet" or in the notes of the directors.
3. Corporate-based financing can always count on guarantees constituted by personal assets of the sponsor, which are different from those utilized for the investment project. In project finance deals, the loan's only collateral refers to assets that serve to carry out the initiative; the result is advantageous for sponsors since their assets can be used as collateral in case further recourse for funding is needed.
4. Creating a project company makes it possible to isolate the sponsors almost completely from events involving the project if financing is done on a no-recourse (or more often a limited-recourse) basis. This is often a decisive point, since corporate financing could instead have negative repercussions on riskiness (therefore cost of capital) for the investor firm if the project does not make a profit or fails completely.

The essential major differences between project financing and corporate financing are summarized in Table 1-1.

TABLE 1-1   Main Differences Between Corporate Financing and Project Financing

Factor	Corporate Financing	Project Financing
Guarantees for financing	Assets of the borrower (already-in-place firms)	Project assets
Effect on financial elasticity	Reduction of financial elasticity for the borrower	No or heavily reduced effect for sponsors
Accounting treatment	On balance sheet	Off-balance sheet (the only effect will be either disbursement to subscribe equity in the SPV or for subordinated loans)
Main variables underlying the granting of financing	Customer relations Solidity of balance sheet Profitability	Future cash flows
Degree of leverage utilizable	Depends on effects on borrower's balance sheet	Depends on cash flows generated by the project (leverage is usually much higher)

1.3   Who Are the Sponsors of a Project Finance Deal?

By participating in a project financing venture, each project sponsor pursues a clear objective, which differs depending on the type of sponsor. In brief, four types of sponsors are very often involved in such transactions:

- **Industrial sponsors,** who see the initiative as upstream or downstream integrated or in some way as linked to their core business
- **Public sponsors** (central or local government, municipalities, or municipalized companies), whose aims center on social welfare
- **Contractor/sponsors,** who develop, build, or run plants and are interested in participating in the initiative by providing equity and/or subordinated debt
- **Purely financial investors**

1.3.1   Industrial Sponsors in Project Finance Initiatives Linked to a Core Business

Let's use an example to illustrate the involvement of sponsors who see project finance as an initiative linked to their core business. For instance, a major project involving IGCC (integrated gasification combined cycle) cogeneration includes outputs (energy and steam) generated by fuels derived from refinery by-products. The residue resulting from refining crude oil consists of heavy substances such as tar; the disposal of this toxic waste represents a cost for the producer.

The sponsors of these project finance deals are often oil companies that own refineries. In fact, an IGCC plant allows them to convert the tar residue into energy by means of eco-compatible technologies. The by-product is transformed into fuel for the plant (downstream integration). The sponsor, in turn, by supplying feedstock for the power plant, converts a cost component into revenue, hence a cash inflow.

Lenders in this kind of project carefully assess the position of the sponsor, since the SPV should face a low supply risk. The sponsor/supplier has every interest in selling the tar promptly to the SPV. If this does not happen, the supplier not only will forfeit related revenue but will be subject to penalties as well.

1.3.2 Public Sponsors with Social Welfare Goals

Historically, project finance was first used in the oil extraction and power production sectors (as later detailed in Chapter 2). These were the more appropriate sectors for developing this structured financing technique because they were marked by low technological risks, a reasonably predictable market, and the possibility of selling what was produced to a single buyer or a few large buyers based on multiyear contracts (like take-or-pay contracts, which are discussed in detail in Chapter 7).

So project finance initially was a technique that mainly involved parties in the private sector. Over the years, however, this contractual form has been used increasingly to finance projects in which the public sector plays an important role (governments or other public bodies). As we see in the next chapter, governments in developing countries have begun to encourage the involvement of private parties to realize public works.

From this standpoint, it is therefore important to distinguish between projects launched and developed exclusively in a private context (where success depends entirely on the project's ability to generate sufficient cash flow to cover operating costs, to service the debt, and to remunerate shareholders) from those concerning public works. In the latter cases success depends above all on efficient management of relations with the public administration and, in certain cases, also on the contribution the public sector is able to make to the project.

Private-sector participation in realizing public works is often referred to as **PPP** (public–private partnership). In these partnerships the role of the public administration is usually based on a concession agreement that provides for one of two alternatives.

In the first case, the private party constructs works that will be used directly by the public administration itself, which therefore pays for the product or service made available. This, for instance, is the case of public works constructing hospitals, schools, prisons, etc.

The second possibility is that the concession concerns construction of works in which the product/service will be purchased directly by the general public. The private party concerned will receive the operating revenues, and on this basis (possibly with an injection in the form of a public grant) it will be able to repay the investment made. Examples of this type of project are the construction of toll roads, the creation of a cell phone network, and the supply of water and sewage plants.

Various acronyms are used in practice for the different types of concession. Even if the same acronyms often refer to different forms of contract, the following are very common:

- BOT (build, operate, and transfer)
- BOOT (build, own, operate, and transfer)
- BOO (build, operate, and own)

In a BOT framework, the public administration delegates planning and realization of the project to the private party together with operating management of the facility for a given period of time. During this period the private party is entitled to retain all receipts generated by the operation but is not the owner of the structure concerned. The facility will then be transferred to the public administration at the end of the concession agreement without any payment being due to the private party involved.

A BOOT framework differs from the BOT framework in that the private party owns the works. At the end of the concession term the works are transferred to the public administration, and in this case a payment for them can be established.

Lastly, the BOO framework has characteristics in common with the other two. The private party owns the works (as in the BOOT case), but ownership is not transferred at the end of the concession agreement. Therefore the residual value of the project is exploited entirely by the private sector.

The country that first launched a systematic program of such projects was the UK, where these PPPs formed part of what was known as the PFI, or Private Finance Initiative. The PFI (Private Finance Initiative) is a strategic economic policy introduced in the United Kingdom in 1992 to migrate the public administration from being the owner of assets and infrastructures to becoming a purchaser of services from private parties. Every year a special department of the Treasury Ministry establishes general plans for ventures involving private capital, subdivided into three categories: (1) completely self-financed works (not requiring any public sector capital); (2) joint ventures (works for which the public sector provides grants while operations remain in the hands of private parties); (3) contracted sale of services to the public sector (where private parties bear the cost of the necessary structures to provide the services purchased).

1.3.3   Contractor/Sponsors Who Develop, Build, or Run the Plant

Clearly, in this case a contractor is interested in supplying plants, materials, and services to the SPV. This aim of this player is to participate in the project finance deal:

1. in the initial phase by handling design and construction of the plant;
2. during the operational phase, as shareholder of the SPV.

This interest is entirely possible, and is in fact legitimate, in private projects. However, PPPs involving the public administration are normally subject to more rigid procurement procedures. These rules serve to safeguard the public's interest and ensure that sponsors win contracts for a given project only after undergoing a more or less complex public tender.

When the contractor is also a shareholder in the SPV, there is an additional advantage: The contractor will benefit directly if the project succeeds. As builder, this company will be highly motivated to finish the plant on time, within budget, and in accordance with the performance specifications set down in the contract. In fact, in this way operations can be activated as planned, the project will begin to generate cash flows, and, as a shareholder in the SPV, the contractor will start earning dividends after having collected down payments for construction.

It is quite common to find contractors who also offer to run the plant once it is operational. Plant managers have a clear interest in sponsoring a project finance deal because they would benefit both from cash flows deriving from the operation and maintenance (O&M) contract as well as from dividends paid out by the SPV during the operational phase.

1.3.4 The "Purely" Financial Investor

The purely financial investor plays the part of sponsor of a project finance initiative with a single goal in mind: to invest capital in high-profit deals. These players seek substantial returns on their investments and have a high propensity for risk; as such they are similar in many ways to venture capitalists. Their involvement in a structured finance deal is seen (from the perspective of the banks providing financial backing) as a private equity activity in which purely financial investors play a passive role. In other words, they have no say in the industrial policies of the SPV. In practice, cases in which purely financial investors are shareholders in the SPV are still few, but the number is growing.

In Chapter 6, we will see that along with traditional loans, almost all multilateral development banks implement investment plans in the equity capital of the project companies. What is more, private banks are also developing private equity alternatives to granting loans for project finance deals. In the UK, for instance, with various project finance ventures in the health field, banks have opted to finance projects with equity rather than loans, in particular in cases where project finance could not sustain sufficient debt-to-equity ratios.

1.4 Overview of the Features of Project Finance

A project finance deal can always be viewed as a contractual network that revolves around the SPV. In fact, each counterparty sets up contracts with the SPV that refer to specific phases or parts of the project. The deal is successful when all the interests of the parties involved (though not always entirely compatible) are satisfied at the same time. Every contract, in turn, can include subcontracts with third parties and the provision of collateral guarantees.

Figure 1-1 provides a graphic representation of a typical contract framework used in projects involving cogeneration of electrical power.

Some clarifications are called for regarding the model illustrated in Figure 1-1. First, a single participant in a project finance deal can take on a number of roles. In cogeneration projects, for example, the contractor can be sponsor, builder, and operator of a plant at the same time, either alone or in a joint venture with others. In waste-to-energy facilities, the city administration or a consortium of communities or a municipalized company might act as supplier of solid waste to burn as fuel as well as shareholder in the SPV. Banks can be sponsors and lenders simultaneously. It should also be said that in project finance transactions, the fact that only a few players (i.e., the sponsors) participate in a variety of ways is perfectly natural. In fact, the primary interest of sponsors is to appropriate the highest share of cash flows generated by the project. By playing many different roles, they will gain from greater flows (in terms of both higher revenue and lower costs, for example, if the sponsor also buys the SPV's output at particularly advantageous conditions).

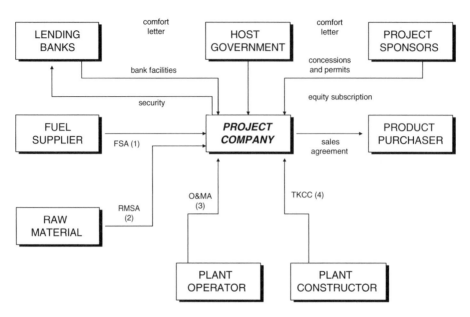

FIGURE 1-1   Typical Contract Structure of a Project Finance Deal [(1) fuel supply agreement; (2) raw material supply agreement; (3) operating and maintenance agreement; (4) turnkey construction contract]

Second, not all the organizations shown in Figure 1-1 are necessarily involved in a project finance deal. For example, with domestic ventures, there is no foreign host government, and a deal with exclusively private actors would not count sponsors belonging to the public administration.

The third point has to do with the financing structure. Figure 1-1 assumes that credit is granted directly in favor of the SPV. However, financing may also be structured through leasing plants (see Section 6.10), or with a bond issue on the stock market (see Section 6.11).

Figure 1-1 indicates that the success of the deal depends on the network of contracts that the SPV sets up with all the different counterparties. A quick overview of such contracts can help in introducing the risk management process in project finance, which is analyzed further in Chapter 3.

1.4.1   The Contractor and the Turnkey Construction Contract (TKCC)

The contractor is the company (or consortium of companies) that wins the tender for the design and construction of a given plant on the basis of a fixed-price turnkey contract, often known as EPC—Engineering, Procurement, and Construction. Contract obligations are taken on by the main contractor (who commits directly to the SPV) and are later passed on to consortium members. Among these players, there may also be an operator or operation and maintenance contractor who steps in after construction is complete.

The main contractor is normally responsible for damages resulting from delays in completing the facilities but may also receive an early completion bonus if the project is finished ahead of schedule. In addition, the contractor is required to pay penalty fees (*liquidated damages*) if the plant does not pass performance tests on certain key variables at guaranteed levels. For example, with a power plant, the minimum performance standard refers to the production of energy and steam, emissions, and heat rate, as certified by an independent technical advisor (see Section 4.2). On the other hand, the contractor again can earn a bonus if the certified performance of the power plant is better than that established in the contract with the SPV.

1.4.2   Operations and Maintenance Contractor and the O&M Agreement

The operator is the counterparty who takes over the plant after the construction phase is complete. This company handles maintenance for a set number of years, guaranteeing the SPV that the plant is run efficiently in keeping with the preestablished output parameters. Therefore, the operator plays a key role during the postcompletion phase of the project finance initiative.

The operator may be an already-in-place company (perhaps even one of the sponsors) or a joint venture created to serve as operator by the shareholders of the SPV. In these cases, two or more sponsors constitute an ad hoc service company and grant equity. The ownership structure of the service company may or may not be the same as in the SPV.

1.4.3   Purchasers and Sales Agreements

These are the counterparties to whom the SPV sells its output. Purchasers of goods or services produced by the plant might be generic, which means not defined ex ante (i.e., a retail market) or a single buyer who commits to buying all the project company's output. In this case, purchasers are called *offtakers,* who buy output wholesale based on long-term purchase contracts often signed on a take-or-pay basis (see Chapters 3 and 7 for more details).

Examples of the first case can be found in the supply of drinking water, traffic flow on a toll road, and tourist flow in a hotel or leisure park. Other examples are public services managed on the basis of concession contracts, such as cemeteries, parking lots, and sports facilities.

A case of wholesale supply would be projects in the power sector. With cogeneration plants, for example, power is sold to industrial users or utilities along with steam. In this case, it is not uncommon for SPVs to set up a leasing contract with the steam buyer for the land facing the buyer's industrial facility. Similar circumstances can be seen in the oil and gas and mining sectors, where output of a given oil field or deposit is sold on a long-term basis to one buyer or a few buyers. In the PPP sector there are also cases of wholesale supply. In the health field, for example, users do not pay for hospital services; instead, relative costs are covered directly by a branch of the public administration.

1.4.4   Suppliers and Raw Material Supply Agreements (RMSAs)

These companies supply input to the SPV to run the plant on the basis of long-term contracts that include arrangements for transporting and stocking raw materials.

In practice, in various cases of project finance ventures there are rarely more than a few suppliers. In fact, preference is generally given to only one supplier, often a sponsor, with which long-term RMSAs are closed (see Chapters 3 and 7 for more details). Examples of projects with a sole supplier are biogas production plants. In these circumstances, the solid waste for composting is supplied by a local body or a consortium of local organizations that provide trash for the landfill (i.e., the raw material for biogas production).

1.4.5   *Project Finance as a Risk Management Technique*

The process of risk management is crucial in project finance, for the success of any venture and is based on four closely related steps:

1. Risk identification
2. Risk analysis
3. Risk transfer and allocation of risks to the actors best suited to ensure coverage against these risks
4. Residual risk management

Risks must be identified in order to ascertain the impact they have on a project's cash flows; risks must be allocated, instead, to create an efficient incentivizing tool for the parties involved. If a project participant takes on a risk that may affect performance adversely in terms of revenues or financing, this player will work to prevent the risk from occurring.

From this perspective, project finance can be seen as a system for distributing risk among the parties involved in a venture. In other words, effectively identifying and allocating risks leads to minimizing the volatility of cash inflows and outflows generated by the project. This is advantageous to all participants in the venture, who earn returns on their investments from the flows of the project company.

Risk allocation is also essential for another reason. This process, in fact, is a vital prerequisite to the success of the initiative. In fact, the security package (contracts and guarantees, in the strict sense) is set up in order to obtain financing, and it is built to the exclusive benefit of original lenders. Therefore, it is impossible to imagine that additional guarantees could be given to new investors if this were to prove necessary once the project was under way.

Figure 1-2 provides a model of the risk management process, highlighting the critical steps and the ways risks can be managed. These are discussed in greater detail in Chapter 3 (allocation through contracts with relevant counterparties of the SPV) and Chapter 4 (allocation through insurance policies).

1.5   The Theory of Project Finance

Up to now attention has been focused on introducing the basic components of a project finance transaction as they are known in practice. This section completes the picture and looks at the same concepts from the standpoint of financial economics theory. The aim is to provide a theoretical rationale for the use of project finance in the broader context of corporate finance theory.

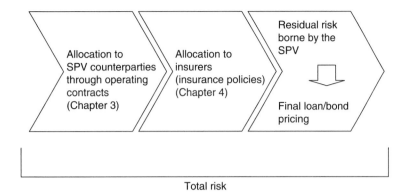

FIGURE 1-2   The Risk Management Process in Project Finance

1.5.1   Separate Incorporation and Avoidance of Contamination Risk

Under normal circumstances, an already-in-place company that wants to launch a new investment project would finance it on balance sheet. As a result, the project will be incorporated in the company's business and the relative increase in the value of its assets will depend on the size of the new project as compared with the rest of the company's assets.

Once the project is up and running it will generate cash flows and will be able to provide a return on the capital employed, which it is assumed equals r.

But because this is a new project, company management is faced with the problem of financing the new venture. In an already-in-place company, coverage would first and foremost come from cash flow generated by already-existing business or by recourse to new debt or by raising fresh equity. On the contrary, as seen in Section 1.2, project finance involves the separation between an existing company (or more than one, as is often the case) and a new industrial project.

Naturally each option has a cost for the company. In the case of self-financing and equity this will be cost of equity (k_e), whereas in the case of debt the cost of this is (k_d).

The difference between the two financing strategies is shown in Figure 1-3.

We assume that the cost of equity can be estimated using the standard CAPM (capital asset pricing model):

$$k_e = r_f + (r_m - r_f) \times \beta$$

In the equation, the excess return for the stock market is measured by the expression ($r_m - r_f$), in which r_m is the return for a general stock exchange index calculated over a long period and r_f is the risk-free rate for government securities. So, for instance, if it is assumed that the effective return for 5-year government securities is 4.5%, the excess return for the stock market is 5%, and stock risk (β) equals 0.8, then the net cost of capital will be 8.5%, that is, 4.5 points of risk-free return and a 4-point risk premium.

The cost of debt (k_d) can be calculated as the weighted average of the effective cost of the various loan facilities used by the company on which interest is explicitly

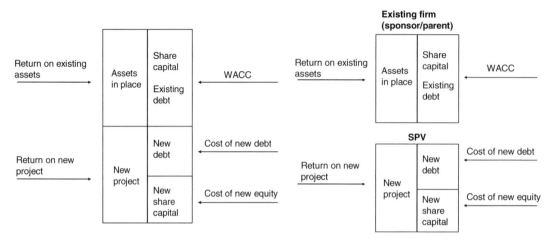

FIGURE 1-3   Comparison of Corporate Financing and Project Financing Strategies

charged. If, for instance, the company utilizes only an overdraft facility with an effective cost of 10% and a mortgage loan with a cost of 8% and the respective percentages of the company's total borrowings are 70% and 30%, then k_d can be calculated as follows:

$$k_d = \lfloor k_{cof} \times p_{cof} + k_{mort.} \times p_{mort.} \rfloor \times (1 - t)$$
$$= (10\% \times 70\% + 8\% \times 30\%) \times (1 - 0.33) = 6.30\%$$

The weighted average is multiplied by (1 − 0.33), where 0.33 is the corporate income tax rate given the tax deductibility of interests.

Given the weight of debt and equity in the company's liabilities, a new investment project concerning the company's core business will cost it a weighted average of the cost of debt and cost of equity (or WACC—weighted average cost of capital):

$$WACC = k_e \times \frac{NC}{NC + D} + k_d \times (1 - t) \times \frac{D}{NC + D}$$

For our firm, the WACC using values for k_d and k_e, respectively, of 6.30% net of tax and 8.5%, and a supposed weight of 50% for both equity and debt capital is 7.40%.

Assuming management intends to maximize the value of the company, it will go ahead with the new project if the return on the new initiative (r) is greater than the cost of resources required to finance it (WACC), or $r \geq$ WACC.

It is reasonable to assume that when a company finances a new project on balance sheet (corporate financing), creditors and shareholders will establish the cost of new debt or cost of new equity based on two factors:

1. The soundness and profitability of the venture that management intends to launch
2. The soundness and profitability of the company that will realize the new venture (often the more important factor)

This second assessment is the most critical for creditors. In fact, if the new venture were to fail and thus were unable to repay capital and interest, creditors could demand reimbursement from cash flows generated by other, already-existing business. This would still be the case even if creditors were guaranteed by the new project's assets and cash flow. Certainly such a guarantee would give them a preferential right with respect to other company creditors. But it is also true that if the new project's cash flow and assets were insufficient to repay capital and interest, then they could still demand repayment from the remaining cash flows produced by other company assets.

There are, however, cases in which the corporate finance–based lending approach is not the best solution for realizing new projects.

Let's suppose now that the new project shows features that are distinctive to project finance deals:

1. It is very large compared to the company's current size.
2. It has a higher degree of risk than the average risk level for the asset portfolio in the balance sheet.
3. It is linked to the company's own core business.

Factor 1 indicates that once the project comes on stream it will have a considerable weight in terms of total assets (the sum of assets existing before embarking on the project and those concerning the project itself). In other words, the larger the project, the greater will be the increase in assets on the balance sheet. If the new project were to fail, its sheer size would jeopardize continuation of the company's other business and value of remaining assets. This risk (often overlooked in financial theory) can be considered the *contamination risk*.

Factors 2 and 3 can be understood by using a classic principle of financial theory. Suppose two projects (A and B) were to be recorded on the same balance sheet, each with a certain measure of risk. (Normal financial practice is to utilize the standard deviation of expected returns for the two projects.) Then it is possible to establish the overall risk for the combination of these two projects. It is assumed that r, the return on the project, is measured by ROI (return on investment, that is, the ratio between NOPAT—net operating profit after taxes—and total assets employed by each of the two projects), respectively ROI_A and ROI_B for Projects A and B.

The return for the combination of Projects A and B is equal to the sum of the average returns for the two projects weighted by the respective value of assets for each project in terms of total company assets. This would mean that

$$r_{A+B} = \frac{ROI_A \times A_A}{A_A + A_B} + \frac{ROI_B \times A_B}{A_A + A_B}$$

where r_{A+B} indicates the return on the company's business asset portfolio, A_A and A_B, the value of assets invested, respectively, in Project A and in Project B. For example, if Project A has a value of 1,000 euros and Project B a value of 4,000 euros and an ROI_A of 10% and an ROI_B of 20%, then the return for the company's asset portfolio will be

$$r_P = \frac{10\% \times 1,000}{1,000 + 4,000} + \frac{20\% \times 4,000}{1,000 + 4,000} = 18\%$$

Instead the risk underlying the A + B portfolio is not the weighted average of risks for the two investments (which can be measured, for instance, using the standard deviation for returns r_A and r_B over an appropriate period). In effect, if A and B concern operations in two very different sectors (as, for instance, in the case of conglomerates with loosely linked strategies and very weak business synergies), the correlation between the two operations will be very low indeed. This means the trend for results of one project shed little or no light on the trend for the other.

In financial theory the risk for a two-operation portfolio can be calculated via the following equation:

$$\sigma_P = \sqrt{\sigma_A^2 \times w_A^2 + \sigma_B^2 \times w_B^2 + 2\sigma_A \times w_A \times \sigma_B \times w_B \times \rho_{A,B}}$$

in which w_A and w_B are, respectively, the weights of Projects A and B in the asset portfolio (in the example it is 20% for Project A and 80% for Project B), σ_A^2 and σ_B^2 are the variances for returns of the two investments, and $\rho_{A,B}$ is the correlation between the risk levels for A and for B.

For purposes of the example it is assumed that σ_A and σ_B are, respectively, 5% and 20% and that the two businesses are negatively correlated by a factor of 0. (Statistically, it is said that the two projects are *independent* of each other.) In this case the portfolio risk is less than the simple weighted average of the two business risks:

$$\sigma_P = \sqrt{5^2 \times 0.2^2 + 20^2 \times 0.8^2 + 2 \times 5 \times 20 \times 0.2 \times 0.8 \times 0} = \pm 16.03\%$$

However, the third assumption indicates that the diversification effect is not present. The new project is linked to the core business, and therefore the correlation between existing assets and new assets is very strong and positive.

At this point the three factors will be considered simultaneously, with the help of Table 1-2, which shows that Project B is large, has a higher risk than that of already-existing assets, but also has a higher return than on assets already available to management.

TABLE 1-2   Returns and Risks for Asset Portfolios with Varying Degrees of Correlation Between Projects

	Existing Assets (Project A)	New Assets (Project B)			
Market value	1,000	4,000			
% on total value	20.0%	80.0%			
Expected Return	10%	20%			
Standard deviation (+/−)	5%	20%			
	Correlation Coefficient				
	−1	0	0.4	0.8	1
Expected return	18.0%	18.0%	18.0%	18.0%	18.0%
Risk (std deviation)	15.0%	16.03%	16.4%	16.8%	17.0%

If we examine this case ex ante (that is, review the case before the new project is realized), we see that the company's overall return will rise to 18%, an increase of 8 percentage points over the initial level of 10%. The forecast average return is the weighted average of returns for Projects A and B and is not affected by any correlation between the two projects.

Instead as regards ex ante forecast risk, correlation has an important impact. In the example, a potential range was assumed from a correlation coefficient of -1 to a coefficient of $+1$. The negative extreme would represent projects diversifying from the core business, whereas the positive extreme would indicate projects that are perfectly synchronized with the trend for returns of Project A (the core business).

Observing the results, it is quite obvious that Factor 3 forces toward extreme results. Given a constant average return for the combination of Projects A and B of 18%, management will see company risk (standard deviation of returns) rise from 5% for Project A alone to 15% (correlation -1) or 17% (correlation $+1$) for combined Projects A + B.

The significant result caused by contamination risk should also be noted. Even if it were management's intention to launch a new venture to diversify from the company's core business (in which case the new project will have a negative correlation coefficient), the risk for combination A + B will be higher than the original 5% for Project A alone. This is easily understood, given that Project B is four times the size of Project A (contamination risk).

In effect (still from an ex ante standpoint), if management wants to launch a new Project B and finances it on balance sheet, therefore combined with Project A, these company directors will have to bear in mind that financers and shareholders will see the Project A + B combination as being riskier. They will be prepared to finance the new venture but not at k_e and k_d levels existing before embarking on the new project. The values of k_e and k_d will go up in order to compensate creditors and shareholders for the greater ex ante risk for the company incorporating the new project.

If the increase for the weighted average cost of capital (that is, the weighted average of k_e and k_d) is greater than the increase for the company's expected return (8%), then the strategy to finance the new venture on balance sheet will lead to a reduction and not an increase in the value of the company.

This conclusion is why large, risky projects are isolated by the sponsors in an ad hoc vehicle company, that is, off balance sheet. Separation avoids the risk that Project B contaminates Project A, thereby increasing the weighted average cost of capital for both. Because project finance is indeed an off-balance-sheet solution, it achieves this important result.

1.5.2 Conflicts of Interest Between Sponsors and Lenders and Wealth Expropriation

Everything presented in the previous section assumed that management was reasoning ex ante, that is, before the new project was effectively realized. A further assumption was that there were already-existing assets (in the example, Project A assets).

It was stated that separating the two projects can be the optimum solution to avoid contamination risk, that is, a situation in which default of the new project also leads to default of already-existing assets.

However, separation is not necessarily always the best solution from the standpoint of creditors. Let's assume that, for simplicity's sake, management finances already-existing assets and those required for the new project with a single debt with a value at maturity of 100. Furthermore, it is assumed to be a zero-coupon debt and that the difference between 100 and the present value of the debt at the start of the project is financed by equity capital.

Management can decide to finance existing assets (Project A) and new project assets (Project B) separately by using a project finance approach, or they could finance the combined projects using a corporate finance approach.

Now future cash flows for existing and new project assets will be considered according to six possible scenarios. The situation is summarized in the Table 1-3.

In Solution 1 (corporate finance), cash flows from Projects A and B are used jointly to repay the debt contracted for existing and new venture assets. As can be seen, the company defaults in Scenarios 1, 2, and 3, whereas it manages to make a positive payoff to shareholders in the remaining ones.

In Solution 2 (project finance), cash flows for Project B are only used to repay debts for that project. If there is a positive difference, then Project B can pay dividends to Project A (its parent company).

As can be seen in Table 1-3, Project B is in default in Scenarios 1, 3, and 5; it manages to pay dividends to its parent company in the remaining scenarios.

TABLE 1-3   Example of Trade-off Between Contamination Risk and Loss of Coinsurance Effect

	Scenario					
Hypothesis	1	2	3	4	5	6
Debt Project A (assets in place)	100	100	100	100	100	100
Debt Project B (new project)	100	100	100	100	100	100
Expected cash flows Project A (assets in place)	50	50	130	130	300	300
Expected cash flows Project B (new project)	50	130	50	130	50	130
Solution 1: on-balance-sheet financing						
Total cash flows Project A + B	100	180	180	260	350	430
Total debt Project A + B	200	200	200	200	200	200
Payoff creditors	100	180	180	200	200	200
Payoff shareholders	default	default	default	60	150	230
Solution 2: off-balance-sheet financing						
Total cash flows Project B	50	130	50	130	50	130
Total debt Project B	100	100	100	100	100	100
Payoff creditors Project B	50	100	50	100	50	100
Payoff for shareholders Project A (dividends)	default	30	default	30	default	30
Dividends from Project B (X)	0	30	0	30	0	30
Total cash flows 1 (Y)	50	50	130	130	300	300
Total cash flow (X + Y)	50	80	130	160	300	330
Total debt Project A	100	100	100	100	100	100
Payoff creditors	50	80	100	100	100	100
Payoff shareholders sponsors	default	default	30	60	200	230

Source: Adapted from Brealey, Cooper, and Habib (1996).

Project A (the parent company) can count on its own cash flows and dividends paid by Project B to repay its own debts. Table 1-3 shows that Project A is only in default in the two unfavorable Scenarios, 1 and 2.

The following conclusions can therefore be drawn.

1. In Scenario 2, project financing is the optimum solution because it avoids the damaging effect of contamination risk from Project A. (Project A defaults but not the new project.)

2. In Scenario 3, project financing is still the optimum solution, but for the opposite reason. In this case damage to existing assets as a result of contamination risk from Project B is avoided. (Project B is in default but not Project A.)

3. In Scenario 5, the project financing solution is still optimal from the standpoint of Project A shareholders (the payoff is 200 instead of 150 in the corporate finance solution), however, *not* from the point of view of creditors, since Project A shareholders extract a value of 50 from lenders. In fact, if the project had been financed on balance sheet, the remaining Project A cash flows would have avoided default of the project and enabled full repayment of creditors. In other words, in Scenario 5 there is no longer a coinsurance effect of the company as regards the project, and vice versa.

To summarize, in our example, separation of the company and the project is always the optimum solution from the shareholders' standpoint and can cause wealth expropriation from creditors. However, management must always assess the trade-off between the benefits gained by separating the two projects and the disadvantages due to the loss of the coinsurance effect created between company and project. While from a purely theoretical standpoint it will always be useful for sponsors to separate new projects from existing companies, if a new venture defaults it will have a significant impact on the sponsors' reputation and could lead to negative consequences with regard to the cost of new debt contracted (k_d) to finance additional new projects. In certain situations, therefore, the coinsurance effect might be preferable to benefits for shareholders as a result of company–project separation.

CHAPTER ◆ 2

The Market for Project Finance: Applications and Sectors

Introduction

The focus of this chapter is the project finance market. Here we present:

1. The historical evolution of the sector and of market segments in an international context, distinguishing between various macro areas at a global level
2. A detailed look at the European market and public–private partnerships (PPPs)

The data presented here are taken from the Thomson One Banker databank, and they refer to loans granted for project finance transactions. Bond issues, which are specifically addressed in Section 6.11, are not included.

Section 2.1 focuses on the historical evolution of project finance worldwide; Section 2.2 presents market data. Details on the European context and PPP initiatives are given in Sections 2.2.1 and 2.2.2, respectively.

2.1   Historical Evolution of Project Finance and Market Segments

It's been said that project finance is a technique that was already common during the Roman Empire. It was used to finance imports and exports of goods moving to and from Roman colonies. Nonetheless, modern project finance dates back to the development of railroads in America from 1840 to 1870. In the 1930s, the technique was used to finance oil field exploration and later well drilling in Texas and Oklahoma.

Funding was provided on the basis of the ability of producers to repay principal and interest through revenues from the sale of crude oil, often with long-term supply contracts serving as counterguarantees.

In the 1970s, project finance spread to Europe as well, again in the petroleum sector. It became the financing method used for extracting crude off the English coast. Moreover, in the same decade, power production regulations were passed in the United States (PURPA—the Public Utility Regulatory Policy Act of 1978). In doing so, Congress promoted energy production from alternative sources and required utilities to buy all electric output from qualified producers (IPPs, or independent power producers). From that point on, project finance began to see even wider application in the construction of power plants for traditional as well as alternative or renewable sources.

From a historical perspective, then, project finance came into use in well-defined sectors having two particular characteristics:

1. A captive market, created by means of long-term contracts at preset prices signed by big, financially solid buyers (offtakers)
2. A low level of technological risk in plant construction

In these sectors, the role of project sponsor has always been taken on by large international contractors/developers and multinationals in the petroleum industry.

In the 1980s and 1990s, in contrast, the evolution of project finance followed two different development trends. The first involved exporting the financing technique to developing countries; this was promoted by the same developers. Since room in the market in their home countries was gradually diminishing, these entrepreneurs offered project finance to governments in developing countries as a quick way to reach a decent level of basic infrastructure with a greater contribution of private capital. The support offered by export credit agencies (see Chapter 6) in the home countries of contractors and multinationals played a key role in the process of developing the project finance technique.

The second trend in the project finance market emerged in those industrialized countries that initially tested the technique in more traditional sectors. In fact, these nations began to use project finance as an off-balance-sheet technique for realizing:

• Projects with less (or less effective) market risk coverage; examples can be found in sectors where there is no single large buyer, such as toll roads, leisure facilities, and city parking lots.
• Projects in which the public administration participates in promoting works for the public good. In many cases, such works cannot repay investment costs or cover operating expenses or debt service at market prices. This is why such projects have to be subsidized to some degree by public grants. In some countries (the UK is front-runner in Europe), project finance is very often applied when carrying out public works through a program called the Private Finance Initiative (PFI).

Figure 2-1 summarizes these points. Cell II refers to the best example project finance initiatives; in fact, this is where the technique originated. The two arrows pointing toward Cell I and Cell III indicate market trends that are under way. Note that Cell IV shows a risk combination that is not suited to project financing. In fact, high uncertainty, an extremely rigid contract structure, and high financial leverage

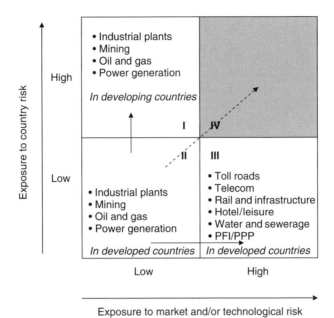

FIGURE 2-1   Evolution of the Project Finance Market by Type of Market and Underlying Risks
Source: Adaptation of Esty (2002a).

make it difficult for management to respond quickly or to adapt to change. In these cases a corporate finance loan is a more appropriate solution.

The matrix in Figure 2-1 is also significant from another perspective: It enables us to pinpoint the sectors in which project finance is applied, depending on the capacity of the initiative to cover associated costs and investments with its cash inflows. Specifically, note that in the sectors listed in Cells II and I, the product in question can be sold at market prices on the basis of long-term contracts (take or pay agreements or offtake agreements; see Chapter 3). For the projects in Cell III, on the other hand (with the exception of the hotel and leisure facilities and telecom), setting a market price that can generate adequate profits for sponsors is usually complicated. These initiatives pertain to goods/services with major externalities (such as water system management or urban and social development of areas where roads are to be built) or to those associated with the needs of the general population that have costs that dramatically impact lower-income segments (health care, for example). In these situations, entrusting a project completely to the private sector could make it impossible for some people to exploit the service offered through the realization of the initiative in question. This gives rise to the need for public funding in the form of contributions on works that can mitigate the investment costs for private sponsors and consequently the level of prices or fees paid by end users as well.

In this regard, a classification is quite widely used among operators that draws a distinction between project finance initiatives that are fully self-financed (i.e., project finance in the strict sense) and those that are partially self-financed. For the former, the assessment is based on the soundness of the contractual framework and the counterparties. In the latter case, in addition to these factors, bankability depends a great deal on the level of public grants conferred.

2.2   The Global Project Finance Market

The observations made in the previous section are confirmed by market data on the value of initiatives undertaken with project finance.[1] In this section, we briefly review the project finance situation at a global level and then examine the European context. We also provide a summary of the PPP market worldwide. The time frame considered here is 2003–2006. Table 2-1 illustrates the market breakdown for project finance by geographic macro area; Table 2-2, in contrast, shows the sectors in which this technique is applied.

In quantitative terms, the data from the Thomson One Banker databank indicate steady growth in the project finance market at a global level. This type of financing has expanded from US$73.5 billion in 2003 to nearly 132 billion in 2006, with a CAGR at 21% (see Table 2-1). The increase in the value of project finance initiatives differs in various geographic macro areas. The Americas, Central Asia/Asia Pacific, and, in particular, Europe absorb the majority of loans. However, Africa accounts for a total of around 18% of total financing in the four-year period.

This last figure confirms what Figure 2-1 reveals regarding the market trends for project finance (a shift from Cell II to Cell I). The macro regions with a higher concentration of developing countries show a stronger growth rate in the application of project finance than that found in countries where this instrument is traditionally used. The case of Africa, with a 54% CAGR in the four-year period, clearly exemplifies the trends described in Section 2.1

In Table 2-2 we can measure the intensity of the use of project finance in various sectors. The picture quite clearly shows a high concentration in certain sectors. Specifically, the energy and power sector absorbs nearly 50% of all loans granted from 2003 to 2006, followed by industrials (which includes transportation and infrastructure), with around 25% of the total, and telecom and media, with just over 6.5%. Even health care, a sector where PPPs are typically applied, accounts for a respectable 1.5% of the market total for the time frame in question. In this case, too, an analysis of the growth rates shows the existence of the market trends illustrated in Figure 2-1.

If we consider the growth rates for government and health care (sectors linked to the development of project finance in the context of PPPs), we can see that the increase here is among the strongest in the four-year period, with +18% and +47% respectively. The energy and power sector shows a major upswing (+25%), in line with expansion in industrials, transportation, and infrastructure. This seems to demonstrate that while traditional sectors of application continue to expand in terms of volume, other sectors where project finance has been more recently introduced show even more pronounced growth rates, in particular in developed countries. So the shift from Cell II to Cell III is also substantiated by statistics.

---

1. The data referred to in this entire chapter should be considered in light of the limitations of the database. To be more specific, the transactions surveyed by Thomson One Banker do not represent the entire universe of project finance initiatives realized in a certain year in a given sector/country, since the databank sources information provided on a voluntary basis by the intermediaries involved in these projects. Generally, the vast assortment of smaller projects set up at a local level (some of which may not even be syndicated because they are handled directly by the sponsoring bank) are not captured in this collection of data. Furthermore, this limitation becomes even more critical the more closely we examine an individual country or a specific geographical area.

TABLE 2-1 Breakdown of Global Value of Project Finance Initiatives by Geographical Area

Region	2003 Amount (US$ mil.)	2003 %	2003 Number	2004 Amount (US$ mil.)	2004 %	2004 Number	2005 Amount (US$ mil.)	2005 %	2005 Number	2006 Amount (US$ mil.)	2006 %	2006 Number	Total 2003–2006 Amount (US$ mil.)	Total 2003–2006 %	Total 2003–2006 Number	CAGR 2003–2006
Africa/Middle East	7,751.10	10.50	16	17,485.10	15.00	31	30,040.20	21.60	48	28,345.40	21.50	30	83,621.80	18.11	125	**54.1%**
Americas	13,167.90	17.90	76	28,933.90	24.70	111	26,127.70	18.80	104	34,743.60	26.30	71	102,973.10	22.30	362	**38.2%**
Central Asia/Asia Pacific	11,341.30	15.40	60	31,453.80	26.90	84	23,064.70	16.60	88	13,952.60	10.60	43	79,812.40	17.29	275	7.2%
Europe	38,297.60	52.10	151	32,990.70	28.20	204	56,534.40	40.60	248	51,205.30	38.80	136	179,028.00	38.78	739	**10.2%**
Japan	2,979.70	4.00	14	5,970.80	5.10	35	3,408.60	2.40	24	3,706.30	2.80	24	16,065.40	3.48	97	7.5%
Unknown	36.80	0.10	1	77.90	0.10	3	51.70	—	1				166.40	0.04	5	
Industry total	73,574.50	100.00	318	116,912.10	100.00	468	139,227.30	100.00	513	131,953.10	100.00	304	461,667.00	100.00%	1,603	21.5%

Source: Thomson One Banker.

TABLE 2-2 Breakdown of Project Finance Initiatives Worldwide by Sector

Sector	2003			2004			2005			2006			Total 2003–2006			CAGR 2003–2006
	Amount (US$ mil.)	%	Number	Amount (US$ mil.)	%	Number	Amount (US$ mil.)	%	Number	Amount (US$ mil.)	%	Number	Amount (US$ mil.)	%	Number	
Consumer products and services	623.30	0.80	14	1,982.80	1.70	25	4,100.40	2.90	25	1,656.20	1.30	14	8,362.70	1.81	78	**38.5%**
Consumer staples	405.00	0.60	3	656.70	0.60	2	674.00	0.50	1	257.10	0.20	2	1,992.80	0.43	8	−14.1%
Energy and power	35,686.40	48.50	128	58,553.50	50.10	191	67,044.90	48.20	247	67,114.10	50.90	161	228,398.90	49.47	727	23.4%
Financials	6,506.20	8.80	13	5,090.10	4.40	30	6,367.70	4.60	26	4,029.20	3.10	9	21,993.20	4.76	78	−14.8%
Government and agencies	589.90	0.80	8	367.10	0.30	4	789.00	0.60	6	963.20	0.70	5	2,709.20	0.59	23	17.8%
Healthcare	638.20	0.90	9	1,994.10	1.70	29	2,077.30	1.50	17	2,009.50	1.50	12	6,719.10	1.46	67	**46.6%**
High technology	66.30	0.10	1	1,400.90	1.20	5	155.70	0.10	2	750.00	0.60	1	2,372.90	0.51	9	**124.5%**
Industrials	19,378.00	26.30	92	24,510.40	21.00	100	34,176.00	24.50	107	38,445.80	29.10	61	116,510.20	25.24	360	25.7%
Materials	4,081.10	5.50	23	12,805.70	11.00	56	10,629.60	7.60	45	9,573.60	7.30	25	37,090.00	8.03	149	**32.9%**
Media and entertainment	1,689.30	2.30	9	4,498.30	3.80	11	3,759.70	2.70	11	2,313.40	1.80	4	12,260.70	2.66	35	11.0%
Real estate	745.60	1.00	7	177.30	0.20	4	1,828.40	1.30	14	988.20	0.70	4	3,739.50	0.81	29	9.8%
Retail										1,543.10	1.20	1	1,543.10	0.33	1	
Telecommunications	3,165.10	4.30	11	4,875.10	4.20	11	7,624.60	5.50	12	2,309.90	1.80	5	17,974.70	3.89	39	−10.0%
Industry total	73,574.50	100.00	318	116,912.10	100.00	468	139,227.30	100.00	513	131,953.10	100.00	304	461,667.00	100.00	1,603	21.5%

Source: Thomson One Banker.

The telecom sector, conversely, shows a downslide in the last year of our time frame. There may be several different explanations for this phenomenon. First, we should keep in mind that the technological acceleration seen in the sector in recent years is gradually slowing. The second explanation may be linked to the transformation that has taken place in the telephony market in several western European countries. In fact, UMTS technology has come to the fore in the four-year period considered here. Many operators financed tenders to win bids for UMTS licenses using project finance logic on the basis of future revenues generated from exploiting these permits. That at present no more licenses are supposedly being issued and the progressive consolidation seen in the sector provide a convincing explanation for the downward trend starting in 2005.

Lastly, Table 2-3 gives the percentage breakdown of the use of project finance by sector in the different geographic macro areas. The reference data relate to the entire four-year period from 2003 to 2006. The information shown in the table indicates the percentage weight of financing granted in a given geographical area with respect to the total financing conferred worldwide in the same time frame.

The breakdown by sector is quite heterogeneous within different geographic areas. Note specifically the two zones that most clearly exemplify this disparity: Africa and the Middle East. Here, in fact, the most substantial percentages cluster around the base sectors. (Energy, industrials, and materials alone make up 20% of the total of project financing worldwide for the period.) Sectors where the technique is still new, however, reflect much lower figures. Conversely, in Europe (which has a longer history of project finance) the sectors with the highest numbers are those that have recently evolved, shown in Cell III of Figure 2-1. In fact, telecom, government, health care, and, obviously, power and industrials/infrastructure account for around 20% of the total of initiatives funded with project finance in the period in question.

TABLE 2-3 Percentage Breakdown by Sector and Macro Area of the Global Value of Project Finance Initiatives

Sector	Africa and Middle East	Americas	Central Asia and Asia Pacific	Europe	Japan	Total 2003–2006	% of Total by Sector
Consumer products and services		0.04%	0.11%	1.61%	0.11%	1.87%	1.9%
Consumer staples	0.15%	0.08%	0.16%	0.04%	0.00%	0.43%	0.4%
Energy and power	**13.56%**	**13.71%**	**8.98%**	**12.80%**	0.38%	49.43%	49.4%
Financials	0.06%	1.34%	1.11%	2.12%	0.17%	4.81%	4.8%
Government and agencies	0.01%		0.11%	0.43%	0.04%	0.59%	0.6%
Health care		0.21%	0.03%	1.17%	0.05%	1.46%	1.5%
High technology		0.02%	0.37%	0.08%	0.05%	0.51%	0.5%
Industrials	1.40%	3.07%	**4.74%**	**15.74%**	0.17%	25.12%	25.1%
Materials	3.34%	1.58%	2.53%	0.60%	0.02%	8.07%	8.1%
Media and entertainment		0.08%	1.00%	0.81%	0.75%	2.66%	2.7%
Real estate	0.03%	0.17%	0.02%	0.40%	0.19%	0.81%	0.8%
Retail				0.33%		0.33%	0.3%
Telecommunications	1.27%	0.43%	0.10%	1.70%	0.40%	3.91%	3.9%
Percent of total by region	19.8%	20.8%	19.3%	37.8%	2.3%		

Source: Thomson One Banker.

2.2.1   A Closer Look at the European Market

Table 2-4 shows the breakdown of amounts financed in Europe, differentiated by Monetary Union member and nonmember states. It is immediately apparent that figures for countries that belong to the union are much higher than for nonmembers. The former, in fact, account for more than 95% of the total on the European market in the entire time frame analyzed. This is due to both the progressive expansion of the

TABLE 2-4   European Project Finance Market

Nation	2003 Amount (US$ mil)	%	2004 Amount (US$ mil)	%	2005 Amount (US$ mil)	%	2006 Amount (US$ mil)	%
European Union								
Belgium			30.40	0.10	187.40	0.36	331.70	0.68
Cyprus	134.60	0.36					942.40	1.94
Czech Republic	354.30	0.95			30.00	0.06	353.00	0.73
Denmark							818.70	1.69
Finland	2,419.40	6.48	59.80	0.19	362.30	0.69		
France	650.90	1.74	**2,467.10**	**7.92**	**5,491.80**	**10.46**	**16,178.20**	**33.38**
Germany	1,059.50	2.84	642.50	2.06	2,544.20	4.85	4,943.80	10.20
Greece			102.80	0.33			572.30	1.18
Hungary	284.60	0.76	1,745.50	5.60	1,241.10	2.36	23.40	0.05
Ireland-Rep	374.00	1.00	949.80	3.05	150.90	0.29	1,447.80	2.99
Italy	**9,460.20**	**25.33**	**4,342.70**	**13.94**	**8,983.50**	**17.11**	798.00	1.65
Lithuania					40.10	0.08		
Netherlands	3,959.00	10.60	737.50	2.37	1,388.80	2.65	483.60	1.00
Poland	435.30	1.17	281.00	0.90	169.80	0.32		
Portugal	981.80	2.63	2,506.00	8.05	2,047.60	3.90	1,496.50	3.09
Slovak Rep					493.30	0.94		0.00
Spain	**7,685.50**	**20.58**	**5,978.50**	**19.20**	**16,823.30**	**32.05**	**7,500.60**	**15.47**
Sweden			167.30	0.54				
United Kingdom	**9,542.40**	**25.55**	**11,132.70**	**35.75**	**12,542.40**	**23.89**	**12,582.40**	**25.96**
Total	37,341.50	100.00	31,143.60	100.00	52,496.50	100.00	48,472.40	100.00
Non–European Union								
Bulgaria			45.60	5.52	1,338.40	80.42	1,658.30	78.50
Croatia	77.50	11.39	379.10	45.89			16.70	0.79
Iceland	19.70	2.90						
Isle of Man	53.00	7.79						
Kazakhstan	60.00	8.82						
Norway	197.40	29.02	401.40	48.59			437.40	20.71
Romania	18.60	2.73			176.00	10.58		
Switzerland	254.10	37.35			149.90	9.01		
Total	680.30	100.00	826.10	100.00	1,664.30	100.00	2,112.40	100.00
Total European Union/Total EU + non-EU	98.21%		97.42%		96.93		95.82	

Source: Thomson One Banker.

number of union members and the greater use of the project finance technique in quantitative terms in the first group of nations.

We can see quite obvious "pockets" of project finance within the EU. While in some countries the instrument is almost completely nonexistent, as in Denmark, Lithuania, Malta, and Slovakia, other nations, such as the UK, Italy, Spain, and France, are the markets that account for the largest portion of the total, followed by Germany and Portugal. In these countries, where project finance is most common, laws exist that specifically regulate its use, in particular in the context of PPPs; moreover, the technique is extensively applied in a large number of sectors. In this regard, see Table 2-5, which gives an overview of the European situation with reference to project finance applied to PPPs set up by the European Investment Bank.

As we can observe in Table 2-5, project finance is most widely used in countries in which sectors of application for this technique are more numerous, and above all, where the institutional and legislative contexts are more advanced. These nations already have regulatory frameworks in place and project task forces in action. Moreover, the public administration here plays an active role in promoting the use of PPPs.

The final point in our discussion of the EU is that figures on countries from the former Soviet bloc do not prove very significant; in these nations it appears that project finance is used sporadically.

As regards the other non-EU countries in Europe, we immediately notice the limited scale of project finance. However, we should point out that in Europe, among member and nonmember states, various market development trends are under way. In examining Table 2-4, in fact, we can see a higher volatility in amounts in EU areas with respect to non-EU zones, where the tendency is toward more decisive growth. Though we can't refer to nonmembers as "developing nations" in the strict sense, this phenomenon is further proof of the shift from Cell II to Cell I highlighted in Figure 2-1.

2.2.2 PPP Development

A large fraction of project finance initiative is referred to projects involving the public administration. Such initiatives are run by the private sector on the basis of concession contracts. The goods or services in question are sold to end users (as in the case of toll roads) or to the public administration itself (hospitals or prisons, for example). One of the most obvious trends in the project finance market at a global level is the gradual shift from entirely private initiatives (Cell II) to projects involving the public administration (Cells III and IV in Figure 2-1), as indicated in Table 2-6.

The first key observation is the different level of dissemination of PPPs in the world. While in Europe and Central Asia/Asia Pacific, PPPs account for more than 25% of total loans granted—in the Americas the percentage is just above 14%. This figure is much lower in Japan and in Africa. The second factor to consider is the varying level of distribution of the technique among different sectors. Transportation and infrastructure make up nearly 80% of the total from 2003 to 2006, but sizeable percentages are also found in other sectors as well: water (around 8%), education (around 5%), and health care and hospitals (over 5%). Again, in examining distribution by sector, in Europe we note widespread use of PPPs in all sectors analyzed by Thomson One Banker. In the geographic areas where PPPs are less common, sectors of application are limited almost exclusively to transportation and water. Therefore, it seems that there is additional room for developing this technique in the coming years.

TABLE 2-5   Development of PPPs in the European Union in Terms of Sector, Institutional Level, and Legislation (2005 data)

	Austria	Belgium	Denmark	Finland	France	Germany	Greece	Ireland	Italy	Luxembourg	Netherlands	Portugal	Spain	Sweden	UK
Social housing	+		+		++	++	++	+	+		+		+		operation
Airports	+	++			++	+	operation		++	+		+	+		operation
Defense		+		+	+	+++				+				+	operation
Health care and hospitals	++			++	++	+		++	+++		+	++	++	+	operation
Ports and harbors			++		++				++		+	+	operation		
Prisons	+		+		++	++			+		+	+			operation
Light railway		+	++		traditional	+++		++	+++		+++	+++	++	+++	operation
Heavy railway	++	+	++		++	+++					+++	+	+	+	
Roads	++	++	++	++	traditional	+++	+++	++++	++++		+++	operation	operation	+	operation
Education and schools	+	+	++	++	+	+++		+++			++	+	+		operation
Sports and entertainment			++			++++	+++		++				+		operation
Water and sewerage	+	++			traditional	++++	+++		++		+++		+++		operation
PPP—Institutional level	ooo	o	oo		o	oo	ooo	ooo	ooo		ooo	ooo	oo		ooo
PPP legislation	**	*		*	**	**	**	***	***			***	*		***

Legend: (+) under discussion; (++) projects under tender auction; (+++) many awarded projects, some of them in financial close; (++++) many closed projects; **(operation)** many closed projects, most of them in operating phase; **(traditional)** many closed projects, most of them in operating phase (traditional concession agreements).

Legend: (°) project task force still missing; some actions taken and sometimes project task forces at regional level; (°°) project task force under way (or existing but only for consulting purposes); (°°°) existing project task forces heavily involved in promoting PPP; (*) proposed regulation; (**) draft regulation already proposed and satisfactory; regulation for specific sectors already available; (***) satisfactory regulation already available.

TABLE 2-6 Dissemination of PPPs by Sector and Geographic Area, 2003–2006

Sector	Africa and Middle East Amount (US$ mil.)	%	Number	Americas Amount (US$ mil.)	%	Number	Central Asia/Asia Pacific Amount (US$ mil.)	%	Number	Europe Amount (US$ mil.)	%	Number	Japan Amount (US$ mil.)	%	Number	Total sector 2003–2006	% of Total
City agency										81.70	0.1%	2				81.70	0.1%
Educational services							116.60	0.6%	2	4,481.00	6.9%	46	460.80	26.2%	14	5,058.40	4.6%
Health care provides services (HMOs)							136.70	0.7%	1	3,216.20	4.9%	45				3,352.90	3.0%
Hospitals				355.60	2.4%	1				2,171.80	3.3%	15	237.20	13.5%	2	2,764.60	2.5%
Motion pictures/ Audiovisual										113.80	0.2%	3				113.80	0.1%
National agency										445.70	0.7%	3				445.70	0.4%
National government	66.10	0.8%								175.00	0.3%	1	122.20	7.0%	1	297.20	0.3%
Public administration		0.0%	1	7.20	0.0%	1	320.10	1.6%	2	195.00	0.3%	3	40.00	2.3%	1	628.40	0.6%
Regional agency							181.70	0.9%	2	1,074.50	1.6%	6				1,256.20	1.1%
Transportation infrastructure	5,347.90	65.1%	18	13,646.30	92.2%	35	18,908.10	93.3%	55	49,470.40	76.0%	111	435.70	24.8%	3	87,808.40	79.7%
Water and waste management	2,799.60	34.1%	8	797.90	5.4%	7	606.20	3.0%	7	3,705.90	5.7%	27	461.90	26.3%	7	8,371.50	7.6%
Total PPPs	8,213.60	100.0%		14,807.00	100.0%		20,269.40	100.0%		65,131.00	100.0%		1,757.80	100.0%		110,178.80	100.0%
Total project finance deals	83,621.80			102,973.10			79,812.40			179,028.00			16,065.40				
PPP's/Total project finance deals	9.8%			14.4%			25.4%			36.4%			10.9%				

Source: Thomson One Banker.

CHAPTER • 3

Project Characteristics, Risk Analysis, and Risk Management

Introduction

A successful project financing initiative is based on a careful analysis of all the risks the project will bear during its economic life. Such risks can arise either during the construction phase, when the project is not yet able to generate cash, or during the operating phase.

Risk is a crucial factor in project finance since it is responsible for unexpected changes in the ability of the project to repay costs, debt service, and dividends to shareholders. Cash flows can be affected by risk, and if the risk hasn't been anticipated and properly hedged it can generate a cash shortfall. If cash is not sufficient to pay creditors, the project is technically in default.

Most of the time allocated to designing the deal before it is financed is, in fact, dedicated to analyzing (or mapping) all the possible risks the project could suffer from during its life. Above all, focus lies on identifying all the solutions that can be used to limit the impact of each risk or to eliminate it.

There are three basic strategies the SPV can put in place to mitigate the impact of a risk:

1. Retain the risk.
2. Transfer the risk by allocating it to one of the key counterparties.
3. Transfer the risk to professional agents whose core business is risk management (insurers).

The first strategy is quite common in a corporate finance setting. An industrial firm may retain a given risk because it considers risk allocation to third parties too expensive or the cost of insurance policies excessive compared to the effects determined by that risk. In this case the firm usually tries to implement internal procedures for the control and prevention of the risk. On the other hand, the same risk is likely to have a lower impact compared to a project finance setting. If a firm must close a plant that has caught fire, production can continue in other premises of the firm. Technically speaking, the risk is not idiosyncratic. This is not true for project financing. If the plant burns down, the SPV doesn't have other premises where production can continue, and the project is technically (and economically) in default. This explains why Strategy 1 is implemented in SPVs, but it is not enough. Lenders would never accept financing an SPV subject to risks that are completely internalized.

Strategy 2 is the cornerstone of the project finance design, a strategy that is implemented through extensive work performed by the legal advisors of sponsors and lenders. The principle is intuitive. Since the key contracts revolving around the SPV (construction, supply, purchase, O&M) allocate rights and obligations to the SPV and its respective counterparties, such agreements can be used as an effective risk management tool. Every counterparty will bear the cost of the risk it is best able to control and manage. In this way, each player has the incentive to respect the original agreement in order to avoid the negative effects determined by the emergence of the risk in question. If a risk arises and it has been allocated (transferred) to a third party, this same party will bear the cost of the risk without affecting the SPV or its lenders.

Finally, Strategy 3 is implemented as a residual mitigation policy. Some risks are so remote or so difficult to address that any one of the SPV counterparties is open to bear them. Insurers are in the best position to buy them from the SPV against the payment of an insurance premium. These companies can do so because they manage large risk portfolios where the joint probability of emergence of all the risks in the portfolio at the same time is very low.

Figure 3-1 summarizes these concepts and introduces the contents of the chapter. On the left-hand side, a classification of risks is proposed based on the different phases of the life cycle of the project. On the right-hand side, the most important methods for risk allocation are shown. It is particularly important to stress that the risks common to the pre- and postcompletion phase are hedged by an almost exclusive use of insurance contracts or derivative contracts.

This chapter is dedicated to risk analysis and risk allocation through Strategy 2. Risk coverage through insurance is dealt within Chapter 4. More precisely, Section 3.1 is dedicated to the process of risk analysis and proposes a classification of project risks based on the project life cycle. Section 3.2 covers the risk allocation phase and explains how risks can be allocated to the SPV counterparties by means of key contracts. Special attention is dedicated to market risk (the risk arising from a drop in sales) given the paramount importance of this risk in determining the future cash flow generation of a project. Mechanisms such as offtake agreements are analyzed, and information is also provided for the use of such contracts in PPPs.

3.1   Identifying Project Risks

Risks inherent to a project finance venture are specific to the initiative in question; therefore there can be no exhaustive, generalized description of such risks. This is why it is preferable to work with broader risk categories, which are common to various initiatives.

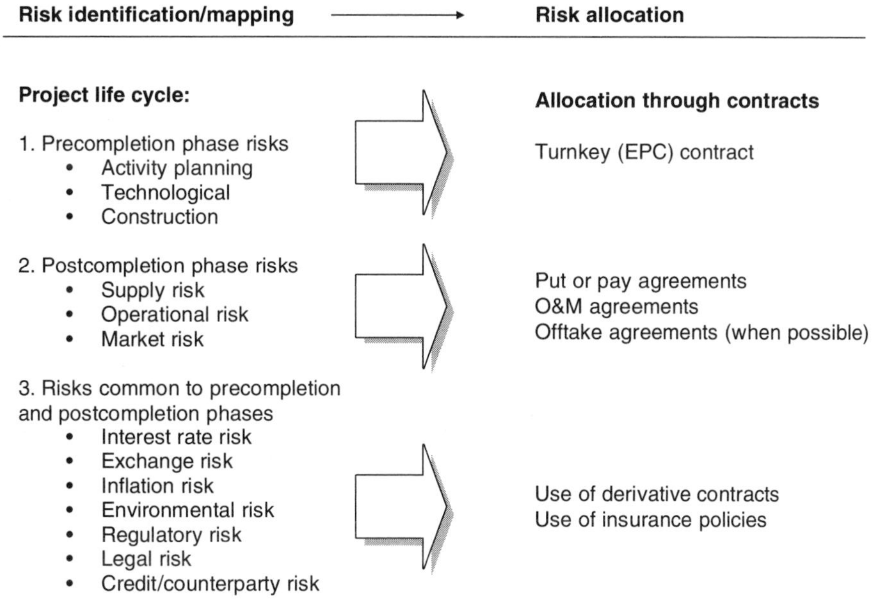

Risk identification/mapping ———————➤ **Risk allocation**

Project life cycle:

1. Precompletion phase risks
   - Activity planning
   - Technological
   - Construction

Allocation through contracts

Turnkey (EPC) contract

2. Postcompletion phase risks
   - Supply risk
   - Operational risk
   - Market risk

Put or pay agreements
O&M agreements
Offtake agreements (when possible)

3. Risks common to precompletion and postcompletion phases
   - Interest rate risk
   - Exchange risk
   - Inflation risk
   - Environmental risk
   - Regulatory risk
   - Legal risk
   - Credit/counterparty risk

Use of derivative contracts
Use of insurance policies

FIGURE 3-1   Classification of Risks and the Strategies for Their Allocation (Hedging)

The criterion used to identify risk is chronological, an intuitive choice, seeing as this parameter is generic enough to be usable across different sectors of application. A project goes through at least two phases in its economic life:

1. The construction, or precompletion, phase
2. The operational, or postcompletion, phase

These phases have very distinct risk profiles and impact the future outcome of the initiative in question in different ways. In keeping with our chosen criterion, the risks to allocate and to cover are:

- Precompletion phase risks
- Postcompletion phase risks
- Risks common to both phases

3.1.1   Precompletion Phase Risks

The phase leading up to the start of operations involves building the project facilities. This stage is characterized by a concentration of industrial risks, for the most part. These risks should be very carefully assessed because they emerge at the outset of the project, before the initiative actually begins to generate positive cash flows.

3.1.1.1   Activity Planning Risk

Project finance initiatives are carried out on the basis of a project management logic.[1] This involves delineating the timing and resources for various activities that are

1. See Project Management Institute Standard Committee (1996).

linked in a process that leads to a certain result within a preset time frame. The logical links among various activities are vital in order to arrive at the construction deadline with a plant that is actually capable of functioning. Grid analysis techniques (the critical path method—CPM—and the project evaluation and review technique—PERT), supported by software, make it possible to map out the timing of the project activities (Gantt chart). Delays in completing one activity can have major repercussions on subsequent activities. The risk is, in fact, that the structure on which the SPV depends to generate cash flows during the operations phase may not be available. This is known as *planning risk*.

For example, in a recent project in the cogeneration sector, a problem came up in coordinating the construction of a deasphalting plant (required to treat tar so that it can be used as fuel in the cogeneration plant) with the activation of the power station. The timing of the two activities (building the plant and initiating power production) was critical for the economic sustainability of the project. In fact, the deasphalting plant had to be completed on time in order for the power plant to be tested with fuel that was to be supplied by one of the sponsors. If the plant was not finished, the test would be run on an alternative feedstock, which the SPV's sponsor would have to supply for the entire duration of the project, with a sizeable increase in costs.

Additional effects of bad planning are possible repercussions on the SPV's other key contracts. For example, a delay in the completion of a facility could result in penalties to be paid to the product purchaser. As a worst-case scenario, the contract might even be canceled.

3.1.1.2   Technological Risk

In some sectors where project finance is applied, construction works can require the use of technologies that are innovative or not fully understood. Under normal circumstances, it is the contractor who decides on the most suitable technology, with the consent of the other sponsors; in this case the contractor will almost certainly opt for tried and tested technology. However, it is not uncommon for a contractor to find the technological choice made upstream by other sponsors. In this situation, the contractor and technology supplier do not coincide, and the risk arises that a specific license, valid in theory, proves inapplicable in a working plant. This is known as *technological risk*.

Examples of technological risk arise in projects involving innovative technologies that have not been adequately consolidated in the past. Almost all works in the sector of alternative power sources share the risk that the plant project may not pass performance tests, and only then it would become apparent that the project has failed from a technical standpoint.

Given the negative potential of technological risk, it is very hard to imagine that a project finance venture would be structured on the basis of *completely* unknown, untested technology. In fact, technological risk requires flexibility, while the aim of project finance is to foresee every possible future event ex ante in order to limit the behavior of management (i.e., the SPV) and block the use of project funds for different purposes.

3.1.1.3   Construction Risk or Completion Risk

This type of risk can take various forms, but the key aspect here is that the project may not be completed or that construction might be delayed. Some examples of construction risk pertain to:

- Noncompletion or delayed completion due to force majeure
- Completion with cost overruns
- Delayed completion
- Completion with performance deficiency

In a project finance transaction, construction risk is rarely allotted to the SPV or its lenders. As a result, it is the contractor or even the sponsors themselves who must assume this risk. Whether or not the banks are willing to accept construction risk also depends on the nature of the technology (innovative or consolidated) and the reputation of the contractor.

3.1.2 Postcompletion Phase Risks

The major risks in the postcompletion phase involve the supply of input, the performance of the plant as compared to project standards, and the sale of the product or service. These risks are as important as those faced by the project during its precompletion phase since their occurrence can cause a reduction of cash flows generated by the project during its economic life. If cash flows are lower than expected, lenders and sponsors can find it difficult to get repaid or to reach satisfying levels of internal rate of return.

Supply risk arises when the SPV is not able to obtain the needed production input for operations or when input is supplied in suboptimal quantity or quality as that needed for the efficient utilization of the structure. Or the SPV might find input, but at a higher price than expected. This situation is even more serious if negotiated prices exceed the retail price of the product or service or of the contracted price to the purchaser with long-term agreements with the SPV. The effects of supply risk are that the plant functions below capacity, margins shrink and supplemental costs accrue due to the need to tap additional sources for input.

The operating risk (or performance risk) arises when the plant functions but technically underperforms in postcompletion testing. In the power sector, for example, the input/output ratio of a plant might gradually deteriorate, or emission standards might not be met, or input consumption could be over budget. The effect of performance risk is lower efficiency and, in the end, unwelcome cost overruns.

Demand risk (or market risk) is the risk that revenue generated by the SPV is less than anticipated. This negative differential may be a result of overly optimistic projections in terms of quantity of output sold, sales price, or a combination of the two. This difference can also be due to unanticipated strategies put in place by competitors, particularly if the product can be easily substituted. The case of the strong competition following the construction of the Eurotunnel by air carriers and ferry operators is a good example of market risk due to cross elasticity between alternative sources of the same transportation service.

3.1.3 Risks Found in Both the Pre- and Postcompletion Phases

Risks found in both the construction and operational phases are those that might systematically arise during the life of the project, though with differing intensity depending on the phase in the life cycle of the initiative.

Many risks common to both phases pertain to key macroeconomic and financial variables (inflation, exchange rate, interest rate); consequently, any division between the categories of industrial and financial risk is actually somewhat arbitrary. For example, the exchange rate risk inherent in a construction contract in dollars with an SPV domiciled in a EMU country can be considered both an industrial risk (since it is linked to a nonfinancial contract) and a financial risk (because it would be covered by recourse to financial derivatives, if need be).

3.1.3.1 Interest Rate Risk

In project finance ventures, there is always the risk of fluctuations in interest rates. We will see in Chapter 6 that in this context credit is always granted with a variable rate, due to the long life of such projects. In addition, unlike exchange rate risk, interest rate risk indiscriminately strikes both domestic and international projects as well as ventures with multi-currency cash flows. Sponsors and their advisors have to decide whether or not to cover against this risk, a decision that is not exactly identical throughout the life of the project.

During the construction phase, the project does not generate revenues. However, drawdowns begin to produce interest payable, the amount of which depends on the level of interest rates during the years in which the project is under construction. Out of the total value of direct and indirect investments, clearly the interest on drawdowns cannot be precisely defined with certainty ex ante. Only a percentage of total investments consists of definite costs; this percentage certainly includes construction costs, which are defined on the basis of a turnkey contract. In addition, a reasonable estimate can be made of the cost of land; the same may be said for some development costs and for owner's costs. Interest payable, in contrast, depends on trends in the benchmark rate.

This cost item represents a significant percentage of total costs; in fact, the more intense the recourse to borrowed capital, the greater the weight of the interest component. The risk the SPV runs is that unexpected peaks in the benchmark rate to which the cost of financing is indexed can cause an increase in the value of the investments such as to drain project funds entirely. For this reason, a rather widely used strategy is comprehensive coverage of the variable-rate loan throughout the entire project construction phase.

The most difficult problem for the SPV's sponsors is to select the best strategy for covering floating-interest-rate loans during the postcompletion phase of the venture. Often advisors decide on the approach to adopt on a case-by-case basis, depending on the specific features of the project in question. Nonetheless, the key concept advisors focus on is *self-protection of cash flows*, i.e., valuing whether cash flows from operations are sustainable in the face of negative variations in the value of the debt service. A rise in interest rates impacts debt service value by increasing payouts to lenders. Clearly this effect will abate over time (given the same rate variation) due to the progressive reduction in the outstanding debt. In any case, the main point is to ascertain the capacity of operating cash flows, i.e., to verify how these flows move over time. Naturally, self-protection of cash flows depends on the underlying connection among variables that move industrial cash flows and interest payable. When this correlation is high and positive, any increase in interest rates is counterbalanced by variables that determine operating cash flows. The project, at least in part, will be "self-immunized" from rate risk. If there is no such correlation, an unexpected increase in the cost of financing would best be avoided because the project would not easily withstand such a contingency.

For example, consider a PPP project in the hospital sector, discussed further in Section 3.2.4.3. The periodic payments by the public administration to the SPV/ concession holder are linked specifically to the Consumer Price Index as a benchmark for the rate of inflation. This is a considerable advantage, because nominal rates move in relation to the inflation rate. As we know, nominal rates are made up of a real component and a premium requested by investors to protect their purchasing power. Ideally, therefore, the SPV would find itself in a situation where a variation in debt service would be compensated by an increase in revenues. The conditional must be used, however, since inflation can be determined with different parameters in terms of revenues and interest rates.

The only risk remaining for the SPV to face would be that the trends in actual interest rates may not be in line with the projections given in the financial model. The ideal strategy, then, would be to draw up a swap contract on the true interest rate or to use contracts that cover inflation risk (Section 3.1.3.4).

In practice, interest rate risk tends to be completely covered during the postcompletion phase: Percentages usually run from 70% to 90% of the outstanding debt; this gradually decreases as the outstanding debt diminishes. However, we must keep in mind that this coverage eliminates variability and in so doing prevents the SPV from taking advantage of possible drops in interest rates. Coverage strategies, in fact, are subject to a very considerable opportunity cost.

3.1.3.2   Exchange Rate Risk

Essentially this risk emerges when some financial flows from the project are stated in a different currency than that of the SPV. This often occurs in international projects where costs and revenues are computed in different currencies. However, a similar situation may arise in domestic projects when a counterparty wants to bill the SPV in foreign currency. Various industrial multinational groups, for example, customarily invoice in a hard currency, even if it is not that of the host country.

When possible, the best risk coverage strategy is *currency matching*. In other words, advisors of an SPV try to state as many flows as possible in the home currency, avoiding any use of foreign currency. If this is not possible (usually because counterparties have strong bargaining power), the following coverage instruments provided by financial intermediaries must be used:

- Forward agreements for buying or selling
- Futures on exchange rates
- Options on exchange rates
- Currency swaps

3.1.3.3   Derivatives Contracts for Managing Interest Rate Risk and Exchange Risk

Covering financial risk in a project finance venture does not differ greatly from policies on corporate treasury management. However, one major difference is clearly that the project life of such ventures is always longer than the time horizon for which these instruments are traded. In particular, this is the case regarding coverage instruments listed on stock exchanges and for some over-the-counter derivatives (such as futures on exchange rates). For this reason, structured finance transactions most often involve specific negotiated forms of coverage earmarked specifically for the project or use rollover strategies on standard contracts as they reach maturity.

Forward Contracts: A forward contract involves an exchange with a delayed settlement. Traders set down contract conditions (specifically the date of settlement and the price) upon signature of the contract, and the exchange is actually settled at a future, preagreed date. A forward contract might pertain to a currency exchange rate (on maturity, the traders sell each other one form of currency for another on the basis of an exchange rate set when the contract is drawn up), a financial asset, or an interest rate.

If the price is fixed when the contract is made and remains unchanged until settlement, any potential fluctuations in the quotation on exchange rates, interest rates, or the financial asset in question do not affect the two parties, so both are covered. Of course, when listed prices rise above the negotiated price level of the forward contract, the buyer is at an advantage; the reverse will occur if the listing falls below the agreed-on price level. (Naturally, for the seller the opposite is true.)

In project finance ventures, forward contracts are used for the most part as coverage against exchange rate risks. This is true despite the greatest complication, which lies in the fact that the forward exchange market is very liquid only for maturities up to 12 months but is practically nonexistent for time horizons spanning more than 18 months.

Forward Contracts on Interest Rates—The Forward Rate Agreement: Traders can also agree to exchange a future interest rate. The forward rate agreement (or FRA) is one of the most widely used futures written on interest rates. With an FRA, the buyer pledges to pay the seller interest accrued on a principal at a preagreed rate, starting at a future date, and for certain period of time. The seller, on the other hand, commits to paying a fixed interest rate on the principal based on the interest rate at the future date. So, for example, a 6–9 FRA means that for 3 months (the difference between 9 and 6) the buyer and the seller will calculate an interest differential 6 months after the contract term takes effect. Clearly, the contract expires in month 9 (6 + 3). The FRA buyer sets the future rate and is covered from interest rate risk. If in fact the future rate is higher than what was agreed on in the contract, the seller of the forward rate agreement pays the difference between the two rates to the buyer. Conversely, the buyer pays if the future rate proves to be lower than the preset rate.

In project finance deals, the SPV would buy forward rate agreements in order to fix the cost of financing. However, the FRA market also shows higher liquidity on maturities that are much shorter than the entire tenor of the loan.

Swaps: Swaps are contracts between two counterparties that stipulate reciprocal disbursement of payment streams at preestablished future dates for a set period of time. We can think of a swap as a combination of several forward transactions. In any case, the payment streams relate to interest calculated on given principal. When interest rates are stated in two different currencies, we refer to *currency swaps*, and the two streams can be either fixed rate or variable rate. When interest rates pertain to the same currency, obviously one of the flows is calculated at a fixed rate and the other at a variable rate. Contracts known as *interest rate swaps*, in their simplest form, are a periodic exchange of fixed-rate streams against variable-rate streams (usually indexed to LIBOR or Euribor) for a given time horizon.

Swaps are used to modify the conditions of a preexisting loan. A swap buyer, who agrees to pay a fixed interest rate (short position) and periodically receive a variable rate (long position), aims to cover against possible future increases in interest rates on the base loan. If a rate increase does in fact occur, then the heavier debt burden is counterbalanced by positive differentials between variable and fixed rates that the swap counterparty will have to pay.

Swaps are over-the-counter contracts handled by intermediaries on the basis of the specific needs of a trader. In this sense, they are contractual structures that are well suited to covering exchange and interest rate risk in project finance deals.

Futures: A future is a forward agreement in which all contractual provisions are standardized (the underlying asset, date of maturity and date of delivery of the instrument in question, minimum contract lot). This is done to facilitate and expedite the trade of these instruments on official exchanges. In futures markets, a clearing house serves to guarantee obligations resulting from futures exchanges. This organization requires traders to pay an initial margin as collateral and daily variation margins until the position closes (the *marking to market* and *variation margins* mechanisms). Due to this fact, futures differ from forward contracts in light of their lower risk for counterparties and greater market liquidity.

In project finance ventures, *interest rate futures* can be used to curb the negative repercussions of a rise in interest rates on a loan raised by the project company. However, more difficulties are involved in using this instrument. For example, coverage is comprehensive only if there is a future contract on the market that corresponds to the interest rate paid on the base loan. If this is not the case, the operator is exposed to *basis risk*; i.e., the risk that trends in the two interest rates (on the loan and on the future) diverge considerably. Instead, exchange rate risk coverage entails fewer problems: Futures markets, in fact, offer contracts written on the most widely exchanged currencies on an international level. Another drawback regarding the use of futures lies in the difficulty of finding contracts that last as long as the life span of the base transaction, as mentioned earlier. Of course, it may be possible continually to renew the contracts in question as they mature.

Options and Interest Rate Options (Caps, Floors, and Collars):   Options, which are either listed on the stock markets or negotiated over the counter, are contracts that allow (but do not oblige) the buyer to purchase (*call option*) or sell (*put option*) a commodity or a financial asset at a fixed price (*strike price*) at a future date in exchange for payment of a premium. Unlike all the contracts described previously, options let the buyer choose whether or not to settle the contract. The cost of this choice is the premium the buyer pays to the seller.

Having this alternative is very important for the buyer, who can minimize the negative effects of keeping a position while maximizing positive effects. So, for example, the buyer of a call will not exercise an option if the listing on the underlying security at the expiry date is lower than the strike price; in doing so he or she will only lose the premium. Instead, the higher the price of the asset on expiry as compared to the strike price, the greater the profits for the buyer will be. The opposite occurs when one buys a put option.

In project finance deals, options are used both for covering exchange rate risk and protecting an SPV's cash flows from interest rate risk. With regard to the latter case, in practice interest rate caps, floors, and collars are widely used.

With an interest rate cap, a buyer pays a premium in exchange for the right to receive the difference (if positive) between two interest rates: a variable rate (usually the rate stipulated for the base loan raised by the cap buyer) and a preset rate agreed on with the seller (strike rate or cap rate). The buyer and seller also establish relative maturities and time horizons in advance. If the difference between the variable interest rate and the cap rate is negative, the buyer simply pays the premium and receives nothing in return. The underlying asset that is the basis for flow calculations is fixed from the outset. If a cap buyer has already taken out a long-term loan, the reference principal coincides with the residual debt in each period in the amortization schedule.

An interest rate cap is an attractive instrument for companies who have variable-rate financing and fear an excessive increase in their debt burden. SPVs fall into this category. Coverage by means of a cap allows them to fix a quota on increases, though this instrument also intensifies the debt burden when rates fall.

With an *interest rate floor*, in contrast, a buyer pays a premium in exchange for the right to receive the difference (if negative) between two interest rates: a variable rate and a preset rate arranged with the seller (*strike rate* or *floor rate*). If the difference between the variable interest rate and the floor rate is positive, the floor buyer in this case simply pays the premium and receives nothing in return.

Interest rate floor buyers are usually investors dealing in variable-rate assets who anticipate a downturn in prices. With a floor, they set a lower limit to this downward trend, though forfeiting part of the yield, given the premium payment, if rates rise or remain stable.

Lastly, an *interest rate collar* is a combination of buying (selling) a cap and selling (buying) a floor. More specifically, a collar buyer is in the same position as a cap buyer and a floor seller. If the variable rate exceeds the cap rate, the collar buyer will be paid the difference by the counterparty; if instead the variable rate falls below the floor rate, the buyer will pay the difference to the counterparty. (Note that we are in the position of a floor seller.) If the variable rate lies between the cap rate and the floor rate, no exchange takes place.

Figure 3-2 illustrates how a collar works.

The two horizontal lines indicate the floor rate (lower bound) and the cap rate (upper bound). Consider for example time t_2. In this case the current level of interest rates is lower than the floor rate, so the SPV, having sold the floor to the hedging bank, will pay the difference. On the contrary, at time t_3 we find the opposite situation. The current level of interest rates is higher than the cap rate, so the SPV is entitled to receive the difference from the hedging counterparty. In this way, the risk of interest rate fluctuations is limited to the corridor represented by the difference between cap and floor rates.

Buying a collar is a common strategy among SPVs in project finance deals. Doing so allows the company to establish a "band" for rate fluctuation without having to bear the higher cost of buying a pure interest rate cap.

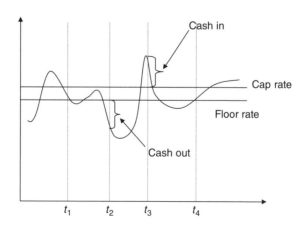

FIGURE 3-2   Model of How a Collar Works

3.1.3.4   Inflation Risk

Inflation risk arises when the cost dynamic is subject to a sudden acceleration that cannot be transferred to a corresponding increase in revenues. Inflation risk derives from the fact that most contracts between SPVs and their commercial counterparties are based on revision mechanisms for rates or installments based on the behavior of a given price index.

Both industrial and financial costs and revenues are impacted by inflation risk. Consider, for instance, the effects of inflation on floating-rate loans. It is only natural that in project finance this point is crucial, considering the long tenor of the relative loans and the multiplicative effect of the capitalization factor applied to real cash flows. When costs grow more rapidly than revenues, cash flows from operations used for debt service slow to a trickle.

Inflation risk is even more difficult to deal with in the framework of ventures in which the buyer is a public entity or a service is offered for public use, such as with public transportation. In this context, in fact, fee readjustments that take the inflation dynamic into account must be approved by means of administrative measures. Delays in this process can create the conditions for diseconomies in operations for periods of time that are not always predictable.

To cover against this risk, a swap contract is drawn up between a hedging bank and the SPV. This *Consumer Price Index swap* (CPI swap) serves to mitigate the effect that a drop in inflation would have on the capacity of nominal cash flows to service the debt, in any given period.[2]

When a hedging contract is signed, the benchmark inflation rate is quoted by the hedging bank for the entire tenor of the loan (henceforth *Fixed Swapped Index*, or FSI). From that time forward the debt service, in terms of capital and interest, is "immunized" from any possible future change in the rate of inflation. Figure 3-3 shows how a CPI works. The SPV receives indexed payments from the users (market) or from the offtaker, and payments are linked to a given Consumer Price Index (CPI_t). The CPI swap stipulates that the SPV pays the CPI to the hedging bank, which in turn pays the FSI to the project company. For any future level of CPI_t, the SPV bears no inflation risk.

In practice, the exchange of cash flows between the two counterparties coincides with each loan repayment after the scheduled revision of rates or periodic payments collected by the SPV. At this time, after agreeing to a base inflation rate to use for computing the coefficient for revising the payments, one of the two parties gives the other a certain sum of money depending on the differential between the real inflation rate (CPI) and the fixed rate (FSI) negotiated when the hedging contract was signed.

At every loan repayment date, the SPV can face three alternative scenarios:

1. $CPI_t <$ FSI: When this occurs, the inflation rate at t is less than the rate fixed when the hedging contract was signed. The drop in the nominal value of cash flows and the resulting emergence of inflation risk is counterbalanced by a corresponding amount paid by the hedging bank to the SPV.

2. $CPI_t >$ FSI: Here the inflation rate at t is higher than the rate fixed when the hedging contract was signed. The increase in the nominal value of cash flows is

---

2. Inflation risk coverage takes effect when the operational phase begins, because it is normally during this phase that financing is repaid.

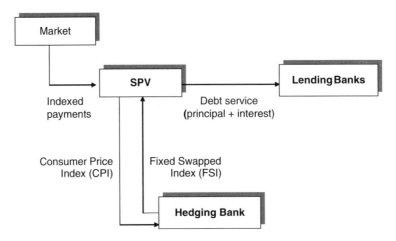

FIGURE 3-3   Counterparties and Cash Flows in a CPI Swap

counterbalanced by a corresponding amount paid by the SPV to the hedging bank.

3. CPI_t = FSI: In this circumstance, the real and fixed rates of inflation are exactly the same.

One can easily intuit that the use of a CPI swap is indispensable in certain situations. This is true, for example, when the sensitivity analysis carried out on the financial model reveals a strong correlation between variation in the estimated interest rate for defining the base case and the financial sustainability of the investment.

3.1.3.5 Environmental Risk

This risk has to do with any potential negative impact the building project could have on the surrounding environment. Such risk can be caused by a variety of factors, some of which are also linked to political risk. Here are some examples.

- Building or operating the plant can damage the surrounding environment.
- Change in law can result in building variants and an increase in investment costs.
- Public opposition to projects with major environmental impact could lead the host government to reconsider government support agreements (see Section 3.1.3.6) with the SPV and may create difficult operating conditions for the project.

Environmental issues are vital for many kinds of projects. Consider the transportation sector or road construction in an area with significant tourist flow or the energy sector and the problem of air pollution. Moreover, in recent years more restrictive legislation has been put in place to safeguard the environment. In Anglo-Saxon countries, for example, lenders are disinclined to ask for guarantees in the form of the plant itself, since the responsibility for possible environmental damage derives from the ownership (or actual control) of the project.

3.1.3.6 Regulatory Risk

There are various facets to regulatory risk; the most common are the following.

- The permits needed to start the project are delayed or canceled.
- The basic concessions for the project are unexpectedly renegotiated.
- The core concession for the project is revoked.

Delays are usually caused by inefficiency in the public administration or the complexity of bureaucratic procedures. If instead delays are the result of specific political intent to block the initiative, this situation would be more similar to political risk.

3.1.3.7 Political Risk and Country Risk

Political risk takes various forms, for instance, a lack of government stability, which for some projects may be critical. In energy production initiatives, for example, the SPV could be negatively impacted by a change of government if the new administration does not share the same views as the previous one. In addition, citizens themselves could completely reshape their national context through a referendum. An antinuclear referendum is an excellent example that gives an idea of the potential scope of political risk.

The following is a generally accepted classification of different types of political risk.

- **Investment risks:** These relate to limitations on the convertibility or transfer of currency abroad. Such restrictions are implemented for macroeconomic reasons, such as maintaining equilibrium in the balance of payments or defending the exchange rate. Other examples of investment risk are the host government's expropriating a plant without paying an indemnity, or nationalizing a plant, or the breakout of war, revolt, or civil war (political force majeure risk).
- **Change-in-law risks:** These include any modification in legislation that can hinder project operations.
- **Quasi-political risks:** This category encompasses a wide range of different circumstances. Normally, it includes all disputes and interpretations regarding contracts already in place (breach of contracts) that emerge from a political, regulatory, or commercial background. In some cases, these risks do depend not on the central government, but on the local administration empowered to implement its own laws and fiscal policies. If these public bodies are counterparties of the SPV and they default, the central government is under no obligation to provide any support; this results in "substate" or "subsovereign" risk. Lastly, quasi-political risks include so-called *creeping expropriation*, which refers to a combination of behaviors that a public body can adopt to "squeeze" project operations. Such actions do not constitute a formal act of breach of contract.

Political risks are especially important for lenders in project finance ventures located in developing countries. These nations, in fact, have legal structures that are not well defined, most have politically unstable governments, and there is little experience of private capital investments in strategic sectors.

There are two ways to cover against these risks. The first is to draw up an agreement with the government of the host country stating that the government will create a favorable (or at least nondiscriminatory) environment for the sponsors and the SPV. This kind of contract, called a *government support agreement*, can include provisions with the following intent:

1. To provide guarantees on key contracts (for example, the government provides guarantees that a key counterparty will fulfill its obligations as offtaker or input supplier)
2. To create conditions that would serve to prevent possible currency crises from adversely affecting the convertibility of the debt service and the repatriation of dividends (for example, the host country could set up ad hoc currency reserves through its central bank)
3. To facilitate the operational capacity of the SPV from a fiscal standpoint through tax relief or exemptions
4. To create favorable institutional conditions (for example, importation procedures exempt from customs duties, streamlined bureaucratic processes, service provision for the SPV, concessions for the use of public lands, or provisions for accepting international arbitration outside the host country to resolve legal disputes)

The second way to cover against political risks is through the insurance market. Insurance policies are available offering total or partial coverage against political risks. These policies are offered by multilateral development banks and export credit agencies (as we see in Section 6.5.2) as well as by private insurance companies (see Section 4.3).

3.1.3.8   Legal Risk

Legal risk centers primarily on the project's lenders, whose lawyers analyze and manage this risk (see Section 4.1). Their job is to ascertain whether the commercial law of the host country offers contract enforceability should problems emerge during the construction or postcompletion phases.

It should be noted that contract enforceability does not depend exclusively on the degree of economic development in a country. It also involves a series of other factors, such as a country's judicial tradition and the institutional conditions and context characteristics. As for the first variable, in countries where the rule of law is grounded in civil law, lenders find less protection than in nations where common law is in force. This is even true in countries with a solid level of economic development and consequently low political risk. Institutional conditions complicate matters, because they are linked to factors such as corruption and the tendency toward illicit behavior, which can often turn a decision against lenders. The magnitude this problem has reached has led various research organizations to compile indices that actually measure the degree of corruption and reliability of political and administrative institutions of a given country.

For example, the International Country Risk Guide (www.prsgroup.com) bases its analyses on corruption risk, expropriation risk for private property, and risk of contract repudiation. For each country, this guide compiles statistics on the level of exposure to said risks. It is easy to see that in these cases, contracts are likely to be evaded if the institutional system does not adequately safeguard the rights of lenders. Legal risk can be managed and covered by meticulous drafting of contracts. Calling in lawyers right from the initial setup phase of a venture clearly proves vital. The support of the host government also takes on major significance.

3.1.3.9 Credit Risk or Counterparty Risk

This risk relates to the parties who enter into contracts with the SPV for various intents and purposes. The creditworthiness of the contractor, the product buyer, the input supplier, and the plant operator is carefully assessed by lenders through an exhaustive due diligence process.

The financial soundness of the counterparties (or respective guarantors if the counterparties are actually SPVs) is essential for financers.

The significance of credit risk in project finance deals lies in the nature of the venture itself: off-balance-sheet financing with limited recourse to shareholders/sponsors and a very high level of financial leverage. These features form the basis of a different approach for determining minimum capital requirements that banks must respect with regard to project finance initiatives. This approach was established by the Basel Committee, the international body that counts representatives of banking supervisory authorities from several countries among its members (see Chapter 8).

3.2   Risk Allocation with Contracts Stipulated by the SPV

In the process of risk management, risk is identified and at the same time allocated to the parties involved in the transaction whenever possible. To ascertain that all risks are appropriately allocated to various players, lenders take a comprehensive look at the network of contracts with the SPV. Normally, when lenders are solicited for funds, the SPV has already configured risk allocation by means of a series of preliminary contracts and has covered the residual portion of risk with insurance policies. Depending on the method used for covering risk, lenders might ask to reconsider certain terms or renegotiate some contracts. In this case, renegotiations can also take the form of direct agreements between lenders (see Chapter 7) and some of the parties involved in the deal.

In any case, the most complex situation arises when the project analyses run by the banks reveal risks that were not initially addressed in the contracts. If these risks are critical to the success of the initiative, the following actions may be taken.

1. Closing on the financing is postponed until the problems in question are solved.
2. Problem solving is postponed until financial closing, as long as the credit agreement includes provisions that oblige the parties to implement an acceptable solution by a specified date. This requirement falls in the category of *covenants,* which are discussed in Chapters 6 and 7.

3.2.1   Allocation of Construction Risk: The Turnkey (or Engineering, Procurement, and Construction—EPC) Agreement

A turnkey agreement—also known as EPC (engineering, procurement, and construction)—is a construction contract by which the SPV transfers construction risk of the structure to the contractor. In exchange for a set fee, the contractor guarantees the SPV the following:

- The completion date
- The cost of the works
- Plant performance

In addition to these guarantees, there may be coverage against technological risk. Transferring this type of risk to third parties is always quite complex, in particular if the project's base license is extremely innovative. In concrete terms, the options available are the following:

- To ask independent technical advisors (see Section 4.2) their opinion on the effectiveness of the technology
- To oblige the technology supplier to pay penalties either in one lump sum or proportional to the patent value of the technology
- To oblige the contractor to provide performance guarantees on the technology that are incorporated in the construction contract (*wrapping* or *wraparound responsibility*).

Of course, the judgments of technical consultants do not constitute legally binding guarantees. Nonetheless, if a panel of experts unanimously supports the validity of the technology with initial due diligence of technological features, the project stands a greater chance of success than if the response is general skepticism.

Penalties paid by suppliers, whether lump sum or proportional, have a greater impact on the SPV's cash flows. However, it should be said that the amount of these penalties is always less than the overall value of the project. Therefore, lenders should not rely too heavily on these figures to recover their investments in case of setbacks.

Wrapping (or *wraparound responsibility*) is what provides lenders with a real guarantee. With this type of contract, the contractor is required to ensure that the plant corresponds exactly to design and technical specifications listed in the license agreement for use of know-how with the SPV. Of course, when contractors give this guarantee, presumably they are familiar with the technology to be developed, and as a result the SPV will clearly face higher construction costs.

When the technology in question is absolutely new, there is no wrapping. No contractor, however reliable, would be able to offer an SPV such a broad guarantee. In these cases, the venture can be financed only if the sponsors guarantee total recourse to lenders during the construction phase. Such recourse is eliminated only if the plant proves functional once construction is complete.

As far as guarantees on completion dates, when the preestablished construction time is up, one of two possible situations can occur:

1. The plant meets minimum performance standards.
2. The plant does not meet minimum performance standards.

Let's examine the two cases separately via Figure 3-4, which shows the crucial checkpoints the plant must pass before starting operations. The first test is performed by the independent technical engineer at the commercial operating date (COD), the date originally indicated in the construction contract as the deadline for the delivery of the facilities. The contractor is considered in compliance with contract obligations (and therefore does not face additional costs for delays in delivering the structure) if the plant meets minimum performance standards (MPS) in the initial test and is given a Provisional Acceptance Certificate (PAC). In power plants, for example, MPSs are

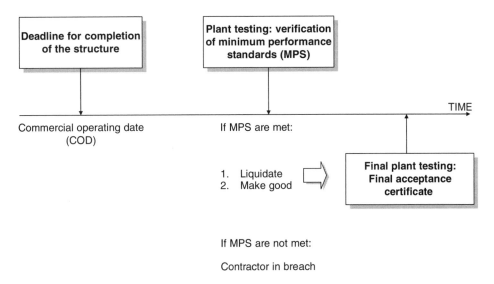

FIGURE 3-4   Contractor Guarantees on Project Completion Date and Performance: How They Work

set at 95% of the theoretical performance of the plant. These standards relate to electrical output, steam production, heat rate, and emissions.

If the plant meets the MPS but does not function at a 100% performance level as defined in the contract, the contractor is usually given two options:

- To liquidate
- To make good

In opting to liquidate, the contractor takes no steps to bring the plant up to the 100% performance level, but instead pays the SPV an amount referred to as *buydown damage,* which corresponds to the difference in actual revenue as compared to 100% yield. The buydown damage serves to ensure that the project satisfies debt service obligations, even in the event of a reduction in revenues caused by the plant's lower performance level. With the make-good option, the contractor pays the cost of bringing the plant up to 100% output within a set period of time.

Testing continues for a certain period of time, after which the plant is issued a Final Acceptance Certificate (FAC) (see Section 4.2.3) and is turned over to the SPV. The contractor guarantees that the facility is free of any pledges, claims, or mortgages. In addition, the terms of the construction contract include a commitment by the contractor to repair or substitute defective materials at no cost to the SPV for a preestablished warranty period starting from the date of the FAC.

Now let us return to Figure 3-4. If the plant does not pass the MPS test, the contractor is considered in breach of contract and in theory is obliged to reimburse the SPV for all down payments received during the construction phase. In actual practice, such a radical course of action is never taken. In fact, technically the project would be in default. However, with the consensus of lending banks, the SPV always attempts to negotiate the completion of the plant with the contractor or another counterparty, who pays the SPV damages in proportion to the revenue lost due to the delay.

The contractor is not in breach of contract if plant completion is delayed due to force majeure events. What exactly constitutes such an event is the subject of very intense negotiations between contractors, sponsors, and lenders. In addition, contractors always attempt to negotiate the following in the construction contract:

- Bonuses in their favor if the plant is completed ahead of schedule or if it functions more efficiently than specified in the contract (for example, with a lower level of input consumption)
- Clauses that limit their responsibility for paying damages, up to a maximum percentage of the turnkey price (guaranteed by a performance bond that contractors post in deposit until construction is complete)

3.2.2   Allocation of Supply Risk: Put-or-Pay Agreements

The coverage method for limiting or eliminating supply risk consists in drafting contracts for unconditional supply (*put-or-pay agreements* or *throughput agreements*). In these accords, the supplier sells the SPV preset volumes of input at preagreed prices (again, adjusted according to predicted trends of a given price index). If supply is lacking, normally the supplier is required to compensate for the higher cost incurred by finding another source of input. Figure 3-5 illustrates how this contract works.

A put-or-pay contract has the same criticality as a take-or-pay agreement (see Section 3.2.4). In the power sector, for example, one of the primary aims of a long-term fuel supply contract is to ensure that revision mechanisms for the input price are balanced with those relating to price adjustments for the sale of electricity.

If the Supplier is able to supply good or service

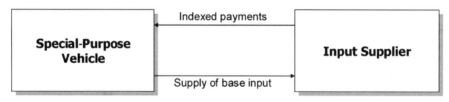

If the Supplier is not able to supply good or service

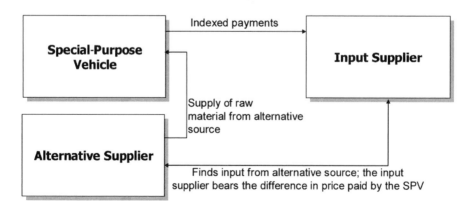

FIGURE 3-5   How a Put-or-Pay Contract Works

In this way, sales revenues and supply costs are synchronized. In cases where the input is not physically near the plant or the structure in question, the sponsors also negotiate contracts for transporting input from its production site to where it will actually be utilized.

3.2.3   Allocation of Operational Risk: Operations and Maintenance (O&M) Agreements

Operating risk can be mitigated by the experience and the reputation of the project operator. As far as O&M contracts are concerned, two solutions are possible:

- **Fixed-price contract:** Here the operator assumes risks relating to the fluctuations in operating costs and makes a profit only if the costs actually incurred are lower than the contract price for services rendered. See Figure 3-6.
- **Pass-through contract:** In this case, the operator receives a fixed payment and performance bonuses while the SPV covers operating costs. With this contract structure, the level of performance bonuses is crucial, as is determining penalties the operator would face if satisfactory output levels are not attained. See Figure 3-7.

As a supplemental guarantee, lenders also request a step-in right, which is the option to remove the original operator and substitute that company with another of the lender's choosing. This is one of the many direct agreements made between banks and the different counterparties of the SPV discussed in Chapter 7.

3.2.4   Allocation of Market Risk

Market risk coverage is crucial in project finance. This is because a reduction or cancellation of market risk allows the SPV to lock in the first line of cash flows or to reduce its volatility (and consequently the risk of a cash shortage).

FIGURE 3-6   Structure of a Fixed-Price Maintenance Contract

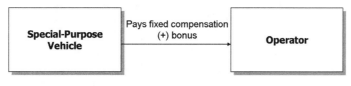

FIGURE 3-7   Structure of a Pass-Through Maintenance Contract

However, this coverage is not always possible. It is simpler if there is a single buyer of the good or service (the offtaker), but it becomes impossible when dealing with a retail market. For example, it is much easier to draw up long-term sales contracts with an industrial buyer or a utility, as occurs in the power sector. However, the situation becomes more complicated in the transportation sector (roads, tunnels, parking lots, etc.) or when dealing with building hotels or leisure facilities. In these fields, the variability of tourist or traffic flows can never be completely eliminated. Only minor remedies can be put in place by sponsors.

- They can conduct sensitivity analyses to estimate users' reactions to a (potentially substantial) fee reduction (always within a defined range of probability).
- They can attempt to limit demand fluctuations by drawing up contracts that ensure minimum use of the structure. An example might be contracts assigning some parking spaces to a specific counterparty; another example is the hotel and leisure sector, where tour operators can contract for guaranteed room availability in certain periods of the year for the business segment.
- They can force the public administration to guarantee a minimum level of revenues where there is a variable market. In this case, although it is improper to talk about offtaking agreements, the public administration can act as a wholesale buyer, reducing the level of market risk otherwise borne by project sponsors. Two examples related to the transportation sector and the hospital/health care services sector are discussed in Section 3.2.4.3.

3.2.4.1   Offtake Agreements

When the SPV sells goods or services to a single large counterparty, offtake agreements represent a very useful tool for structuring a project finance transaction. In fact, by mitigating market risk, such agreements decrease the volatility of future cash flows from operations, which are the basis of lenders' assessments as to the sustainability of the deal.

Offtake agreements are long-term contracts in which one counterparty (usually an SPV) commits to delivering certain volumes/quantities of a good or service. The other, called the offtaker, agrees to pay predefined sums of money or a set fee for a certain period of time in exchange for a good/service from the SPV. The price the offtaker pays is indexed to parameters that track trends in the rate of inflation for production prices and consumer prices.

The most common types of offtake agreements are set up on a take-or-pay basis. Figure 3-8 illustrates the functioning of such an agreement. The offtaker commits to buying a good or service produced by the SPV and is obligated to pay even if it does not actually take a good or service. This latter is true, however, only if the SPV is able to supply the good in question, i.e., only if the SPV's production output is available for delivery.

In contrast, as the lower part of Figure 3-8 shows, if output is unavailable, it is the SPV that commits to providing an alternative source for the product or service and must compensate for the greater costs incurred by the offtaker if and when the case may be. In this way, a take-or-pay duplicates a put-or-pay contract, discussed earlier in Section 3.2.2.

Offtake contracts take various names, depending on the sector in question and the business conducted by the SPV; these agreements have been used the longest in the power sector (see Section 3.2.4.2). In the telecom sector, for example, there are IRU

If the SPV is able to supply good or service

If the SPV is not able to supply good or service

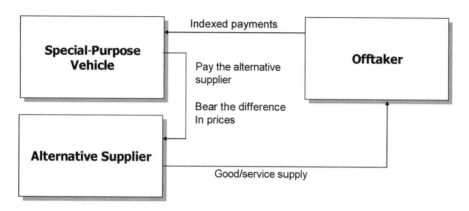

FIGURE 3-8   Structure of Take-or-Pay Contracts

contracts (indefeasible rights of use), which refer to the exclusive right to use a specific portion of the capacity of a communications cable for a set period of time. In exchange for this right, the beneficiary company (generally a service provider) pays fixed periodic sums to the owner of the network (often the SPV). Another example is in the shipping industry, where we find time charter contracts (which usually run from five to fifteen years). This tool enables ship owners to finance investment initiatives while employing a limited amount of their own financial resources. With a time charter, a third party (often a service company) pays a rental fee to the SPV, which is usually the owner of a fleet of ships, for the use of these vessels. In this way, the SPV curtails its market risk, e.g., finding no renters and leaving its fleet anchored in port.

3.2.4.2   Offtake Contracts in the Power Sector

The power sector is certainly the investment area in which such agreements have evolved the furthest and for the longest time. Today, in fact, various types of contract frameworks can satisfy the needs of the counterparties involved in an investment initiative while respecting the principle of correct risk allocation among project participants. The contract structures to which we refer are the following:

- PPA (power purchase agreement)
- tolling (based on a tolling agreement)

Power Purchase Agreement Structure: The contract model for distributing electrical power known as the PPA was the first to be used on a wide scale in the United States and various European countries to develop construction projects for private power plants. This contract structure is based on long-term agreements between private investors and a public counterparty or an entity linked to the public administration that essentially poses no credit risk.

With a PPA, the SPV undersigns contracts in two directions:

1. A fuel supply agreement (FSA) to ensure fuel supply and mitigate supply risk
2. A power purchase agreement (PPA), a supply contract for the long-term sale of all power generated by the plant to one or more wholesalers (offtakers) to mitigate the risk of selling energy output

Specifically, the PPA contract establishes that the project company will make a certain amount of electric power available daily; the offtaker, in turn, is obligated both to make a minimum purchase and to pay a fee, part of which is fixed and part variable.

The fixed component, also known as the capacity charge, serves to cover fixed costs of the plant, the return on investments of the sponsors, and debt service. The variable component, which can also be called the energy charge or energy fee, is indexed to the actual electric power produced; it goes to meeting both fuel costs and variable operation and maintenance (O&M) costs. Basically, every increment in fuel prices should translate into an increase in the electricity rate paid by the buyer (pass-through). Normally, the method for revising this rate is established at the outset and is linked to the revision mechanism for fuel costs. The rate is calculated by using the following equation:

$$\text{PPA rate} = \text{Cf} + \text{Ef}$$

where:

Cf = Capacity fee = fixed costs + debt service + sponsor reimbursement

Ef = Energy fee = fuel + variable O&M costs

Figure 3-9 illustrates how the PPA rate is determined.

In the energy sector, the PPA contract is the keystone for project finance initiatives. In this context, lenders' main concern should be to verify that the contract

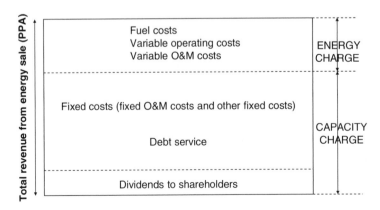

FIGURE 3-9   Determination of the PPA Rate

extends to the entire tenor of the loan and on the assessment of the offtaker creditworthiness. Specifically, banks focus on escape clauses that buyers reserve for themselves. In addition, banks tend to make buyers accept contract provisions allowing for an adequate amount of time to devise solutions that would prevent withdrawal from the contract.

There are two basic PPA contracts, the American model and the British model. In the first, federal and state authorities grant power producers the exclusive right to supply and distribute energy in a given area. As for power generation, this right is limited: Utilities can buy the energy generated by independent producers only if this power is cheaper than what they produce themselves.

In the UK, on the other hand, power producers sell their output on an energy exchange (the Power Pool), which then transmits this power to local distributors who buy from the same exchange. The Power Pool is run by the National Grid Company (NGC); producers offer energy to this company on the basis of set prices, specifying if the plant is operational or in standby. The NGC takes responsibility for periodically compiling a classification of power plants, based primarily on the bid price but also on the plant's capacity to respond rapidly to NGC demand and on its geographical location. Energy demand is conveyed to the NGC through regional electric companies (RECs), who base the purchase prices they offer on local needs. In the British model, producers do not know exactly what price they will receive for the power they supply. The same is true for the RECs, which do not know ahead of time what price they will pay for electric power supply. Therefore, this is a market model in which prices depend on supply meeting demand.

This uncertainty is dealt with by means of a mechanism known as a *contract on differences* between the independent producer and the REC. In this agreement, the parties set up a hedging fund on the basis of a strike price. If the price paid by the REC to the Pool exceeds the strike price, then the producer refunds the REC; if instead this price falls below the strike price, it is the REC who pays the difference to the producer. In reality, the contract on differences is an exact replica of the PPA contract in the American model.[3]

Tolling Structures: PPAs have gradually been replaced by other types of contract models. An example is *tolling,* which enables the energy producer (usually an SPV or an independent power producer—IPP) to generate sufficient cash flows to repay initial investments. At the same time, this setup allows for more efficient and rational risk allocation. Tolling contracts were first invented and developed in the petrochemical industry, in particular in the crude oil refining sector.

In the electric power sector, in contrast, tolling has been used in countries that first liberalized domestic markets for electricity and gas: the United States and the UK and later Spain and Italy.

This type of contract has basically evolved from the need for fuel suppliers to allocate risk in an innovative way while preserving the project's ability to raise capital on a nonrecourse basis. The base contract that typifies a tolling structure is called

---

3. A contract for differences is similar to a hedging contract between the SPV and a hedging counterparty. With hedging, an agreement is drawn up between the two parties for the sale of a commodity at a set price for a given period of time. At the same time, a lower bound and an upper bound are set to limit price variations for the commodity. If on the settlement date the price is between the lower and upper bounds, the SPV sells the product on the open market. If instead the price goes below the lower bound (above the upper bound), the SPV has the right to sell the commodity at the lower bound price to the hedging counterparty (and vice versa, the hedging counterparty has the right to buy at the upper bound price).

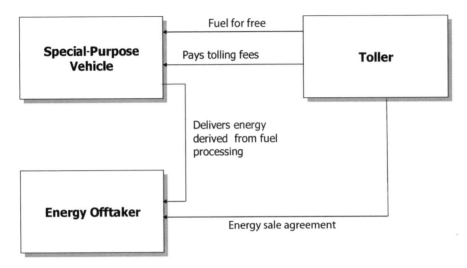

FIGURE 3-10   Functioning of the Tolling Agreement

a tolling agreement. According to this accord, on one hand a wholesale customer, called the toller, supplies fuel as a "free issue good" to the project company's plant and gives this company orders for converting the quantity of fuel delivered into energy. In exchange for services offered, the SPV, on the other hand, has the right to receive a tolling fee. Figure 3-10 shows the functioning of a standard tolling agreement.

The unique features of a tolling structure can be summarized as follows.

- All market risks, especially those relating to supply and the sales price of electric power, are taken on by the toller, who sets up agreements directly for fuel supply and transportation and for sale of electric power.
- The project company, in exchange for the tolling fee paid by the toller, offers its production capacity and provides the service of converting fuel into electricity.
- Only operating risk is taken on by the SPV.
- The project company can rely on readily predictable and constant cash flows for the duration of the tolling agreement, regardless of the fluctuations in the power market or in the price of fuel used to produce electricity.

The tolling fee paid by the toller to the project company for services rendered is one way to guarantee this final condition.

There are generally two approaches to building a tolling fee: financial and industrial. In both cases, per-unit fixed costs and variable costs of operations are taken as components of the fee, for they are essential to the functioning of the plant. The difference between the two calculation methods is the remuneration of factors taken into consideration: financial resources, loan capital, and equity in the financial approach, investment capital in the industrial approach.

According to the financial approach, the tolling fee can easily be compared to the capacity charge described earlier in relation to PPA structures. In fact, this fee is meant to cover fixed costs of the plant, return on investments for sponsors, and debt service. Following the industrial approach, in contrast, the tolling fee is seen as a source for remunerating the capital invested in the project. In addition to covering fixed costs of operations, the fee includes amortization for goods tied up in the investment initiative as well as the return on capital invested requested by lending institutions.

In some cases a variable-cost item may be factored into the tolling fee, which is indexed to contracted thermal efficiency criteria (*heat rate adjustment*). Nonetheless, the key component of the variable fee of a PPA—fuel costs—is absent, because fuel is supplied directly by the toller. The amount due is calculated by applying the following equations, depending on whether the financial or the industrial approach is used.

Financial Approach:

$$\text{Tolling fee} = Ds + Rs + Foc + Voc$$

where:

$$Ds = \text{Debt service}$$
$$Rs = \text{Remuneration of sponsors}$$
$$Foc = \text{Fixed operating costs}$$
$$Voc = \text{Variable operating costs}$$

Industrial Approach:

$$\text{Tolling fee} = Am + Rci + Foc + Voc$$

where:

$$Am = \text{Amortization}$$
$$Rci = \text{Remuneration of investment capital}$$
$$Foc = \text{Fixed operating costs}$$
$$Voc = \text{Variable operating costs}$$

Figures 3-11 and 3-12 show the structure of the tolling fee in the financial approach and the industrial approach, respectively.

This type of contract makes it possible to maximize the financial leverage of the SPV, since one of the cornerstones of project finance is fully actualized: Risk is allocated to players who, in each specific case, are in the best position to control it. Lastly, it should be emphasized that in tolling structures, risks are taken on primarily by the toller. For this reason, the toller must demonstrate to lenders sufficient technical/professional skills to handle both supplying fuel and selling electric power while maintaining a high credit standing for the entire tenor of the loan.

Take-and-Pay Contracts (Merchant Plants): In recent years, project finance ventures in the power sector have been structured much more aggressively as far as the risk assessed and allocated among various participants in the investment initiative. This trend can be attributed to a series of conditions that have emerged on the financial markets in the past few years. Examples are a high level of available liquidity, a growing tendency for commercial banks to assume greater risks in order to win market share while thwarting competitors, and high oil prices, which have allowed energy and oil companies to boost their profit margins.

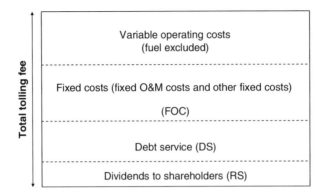

FIGURE 3-11   Structure of the Tolling Fee in the Financial Approach

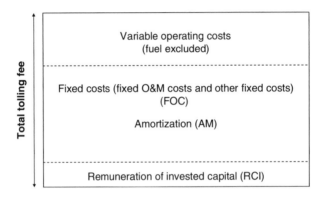

FIGURE 3-12   Structure of the Tolling Fee in the Industrial Approach

Among the financial models adopted in this context, which is characterized by intense speculation on financial markets, we find the *merchant structure*. Within this framework, the project company does not enter into any long-term contract guaranteeing fuel supply within a set price bracket or the sale of electricity generated by the plant. In fact, the offtaker pays for only what it actually buys (take and pay). As a result, the SPV's cash flows are exposed to operating risks, inherent in the ability to produce electric power efficiently and economically, supply risk, and market risk, i.e., the level of liquidity and volatility of the electric power market throughout the life of the project.

With merchant structures, in fact, fuel suppliers are forced to accept a considerable share of the price risk of electricity, leaving most of remuneration to the power producers. This particularly aggressive type of structure is called *merchant square*. It is distinctive both because there is no fuel supply agreement (FSA) to cover against supply risk or power purchase agreement (PPA) to cover against market risk in a strict sense. In this way, the SPV buys fuel and sells electric output daily and is completely exposed to market risk on both fronts.

Nonetheless, in practice, exposure to fuel supply risk is lower and is normally mitigated by implementing an FSA. Moreover, fuel sellers are often forced to accept price indexing for fuel that is linked to the actual sales price of electric power on regulated markets.

3.2.4.3 Offtake Agreements in PPP initiatives

Sponsors of projects falling in the PPP category often ask the public administration to cover at least a part of the market risk related to such initiatives. A PPP, in fact, is a way to transfer most of the risks of providing services to a retail public of end users to private parties, leaving the public sector only the role of director and supervisor of service provision to taxpayers. For this reason, it seems natural to ask the public administration for some form of subsidy in order to improve the attractiveness for the private sector and project profitability for sponsors.

Such subsidies are very similar to a take-or-pay agreement. They generally involve the payment of tariffs when the usage of the facility built by the SPV is below a certain predefined level or tariffs with a minimum floor amount that compensates the private sector for the availability of a given facility, regardless of the number of users. An example of the first type is the shadow toll system used in transportation facilities; the second type can be found in hospital and health care services.

Offtaking Contracts in the Transportation Sector—The Shadow Toll System: The shadow toll system is used in the context of building toll roads and upgrading preexisting roads. This contract mechanism facilitates awarding concessions for segments of roadways—either BOT or its variant, DBFO (design, build, finance, and operate)—to private operators. With this contract, the public administration pays an annual toll to the private concession holder based on the volume of traffic on the road and the service levels. The word *shadow* refers to the fact that the end user does not actually pay a toll to the operator; in fact, there are no tollgates for collecting money. The final cost of road construction is factored into the national budget and so is paid for by citizens through taxes.

The private concession holder pledges to raise capital to carry out the project and for a set time period has the right to collect shadow tolls (usually for around 30 years). This revenue allows the concession holder to recover the costs of upgrading or building the road and to earn a reasonable return on capital invested. When the concession expires, payments stop and the road is turned over to the public administration, which pays no additional fee to the concession holder.

During the term of the concession, the concession awarder pays the holder on the basis of the number of vehicles that travel on the road. Payments are based on a *banding system* linked to the use of the roadway. In the UK, a rather common formula is for potential concession holders to make an offer based on multiple banding, where every band covers a different project cost profile (see Figure 3-13). Band 1 is used to cover fixed O&M costs and senior debt service. Band 2 serves to cover variable management and O&M costs and to service the subordinate debt. Lastly, Band 3 is normally earmarked for paying out dividends. For traffic volumes above a given level (Band 4), as decided by the public administration and the concession holder, no shadow tolls are paid. As a result, there is a cap on costs for the public administration and revenue for sponsors.

There are several advantages to the shadow toll system.

- **Incentives for the concession holder:** Given that payments to this company are based on traffic volumes and service quality, it is in the concession holder's best interest to complete the road construction quickly and to avoid construction delays or inefficient management of the infrastructure.
- **Limitation of traffic risk:** This facilitates private partners in the search for financing for building new roads or upgrading existing ones. Moreover, a

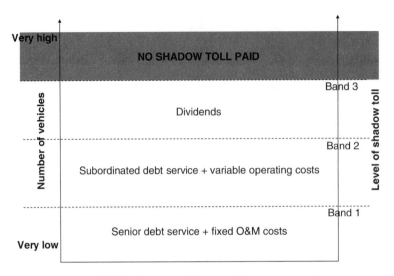

FIGURE 3-13   Banding Scheme in Transportation Projects

well-structured banding system can curb the adverse effects of a lower traffic flow than expected.

• **For the public administration:** The private concession holder assumes the risk of maintaining and operating the road; the public sector can set a maximum limit on its financial commitment by capping shadow toll payments. In this way, the risk of extra revenues to the private concession holder is eliminated.[4]

Offtaking Contracts in the Hospital and Health Care Services Sector: An interesting example of contract replicating a take-or-pay agreement is the payment of periodic sums to be made by the public administration for the use of services provided by an SPV that runs a hospital (but this holds true also for the use of prisons or schools, for example). This is the focal point in setting up a hospital construction venture structured through project finance. In fact, the periodic payment is the subject of lengthy negotiations between the public partner and the SPV (the private concession holder). Such a payment is made when the new structure opens; this amount is broken down into a number of fixed and/or variable components. With specific reference to England, a country with a long history of implementing project finance in the context of PPPs, the public body/principal (the NHS Trust) makes no down payment until the hospital actually opens. At this point, payment is based exclusively on services rendered and usually consists of the following three components:

1. *An availability payment* linked to accessible floor space, which is around 57% of the periodic payment
2. *A service fee*, determined by the level of service quality as compared to a benchmark specified in the contract, usually 35% of the periodic payment
3. *A volume fee*, proportional to the number of services performed (payment by usage, volume, or demand), around 8% of the periodic payment

---

4. More in-depth information and useful links on the use of DBFO systems in the roadway sector as well as data relating to the American and English situations can be found at www.innovativefinance.org.

The largest component of the annual installment, therefore, is the availability payment. In fact, the total income generated from service provision and commercial activities (for example, parking, shops) is insufficient to guarantee a satisfactory level of profitability to project sponsors. More specifically, these revenues are not enough to reimburse private investors for their financial commitment to build and operate a facility as technologically and operationally complex as a hospital, despite the fact that hospitals are setting aside more and more space for private enterprise.

For all these reasons, the availability payment becomes the key mechanism for market risk allocation between private investors and the public administration.

A further clarification is that the first two components of the periodic payment are not fixed during the concession period. Instead, they are subject to an evaluation system that may lead to performance deductions in the total amount of the quotas due. These deductions are calculated by starting with the level of service offered and then tallying penalty points if the facility is not available or if services are inadequate. Through this mechanism, the private operator takes on part of the operational risk associated with maintaining a level of efficiency for the facility in question (which is linked to construction and maintenance risks) and service provision (performance quality risk). The public administration does not share this risk.

The third item is also variable, proportional to the volume of services offered. This is a way to transfer a share of the project's "market risk" to the private player. In other words, if the hospital's capacity is not sufficiently filled, a smaller volume of services will be needed, so the private operator will perform and be paid for fewer services. In some cases, the last two items are calculated together in the service fee; in this case the periodic payment is made up of two components:

- Availability fee, again linked to the availability of the facility, subject to availability deductions
- Service fee, linked to service provision, subject to performance deductions

During the first PPP initiatives experience in the UK, certain drawbacks came to light when the periodic payment was split into two or more different items. These problems were basically caused by two factors:

- The need to redraft an ad hoc contract for every single project, due to the fact that the penalty point system was impossible to replicate for different projects
- The risk that once construction was complete, the provider would have little interest in operating the facility and would instead focus primarily on recovering the real estate investment by collecting the entire availability fee

This explains why, in the UK, the periodic payment is rarely itemized. Instead, it is combined in a single fee, especially when several services are provided by the concession holder. This fee includes both the availability of the facility ("hardware" services) and relative availability deductions as well as service performance and relative penalties if contract standards are not met. Service performance relating to the two categories is not taken separately, but instead becomes part of an overall assessment of performance points, which are the basis of the evaluation (and remuneration) of the private operator.

Risks found in both the pre- and postcompletion phases | | | | | | | Precompletion Phase Risks | | Postcompletion Phase Risks | | |

	Exchange Rate Risk	Interest Rate Risk	Inflation Risk	Environmental Risk	Regulatory Risk	Political Risk	Country Risk	Technological, Planning, or Design Risk	Construction Risk	Operational Risk	Supply Risk	Demand Risk
Special-purpose Vehicle	Currency matching							Sponsors' guarantees to lenders				
Contractor					Limited to obtaining building permits			Included in the construction agreement	Fixed-price turnkey agreement	Turnkey agreement (first test)		
Technology supplier								Penalties to be paid				
Operator										Penalty payments and removal of operator (later tests)		
Buyers			Establishing pre-agreed inflation adjustments									Take or pay
Suppliers			Establishing pre-agreed inflation adjustments								Put-or-pay agreement or throughput agreement	
Export credit agencies (ECAs)						Credit insurance programs	Credit insurance programs					
Banks	Derivative products and coverage instruments	Derivative products									Endorsement credit to back supplier's loans	Letter of credit to back buyer's loans
Insurance companies				Insurance policies		Insurance policies	Insurance policies		Insurance policies	Insurance policies		
Independent engineering firms								Assessments on technological validity		Certification of later testing		

FIGURE 3–14 Risk/Participant Matrix for a Project Finance Deal

3.3   Summary of the Risk Management Process

Here we briefly review the topics presented in this chapter by building a matrix (also known as a *risk matrix*), shown in Figure 3-14. The matrix (which represents only one possible example) is easy to read. Scanning horizontally, we can evaluate the contribution of each player in eliminating risks taken on by the SPV. Reading vertically instead, we can verify whether each of these risks has been identified and adequately covered. In other words, the matrix can be used ex ante by lenders (i.e., before actually providing funds and the closing of the credit agreement) to map risks and assess whether they have been assigned to at least one of the SPV's counterparties. The principle is rather intuitive: The greater the number of intersections between actors and risks where the SPV does not appear, the lower the project riskiness to be faced by the SPV's lenders.

identify risk and cover risk

CHAPTER • 4

The Role of Advisors in a Project Finance Deal[*]

Introduction

A project finance deal is destined to require the services of a whole host of advisors, specialists in unrelated disciplines whose activity has only one thing in common: All of their input is related to the same project that must then be assembled on paper. Sponsors and lenders are left with the rather complex task of coordinating all these various activities and contributions, making strategic decisions while putting together the project, even if at times inputs from advisors lead to divergent conclusions.

The number, specialization, and level of expertise of advisors required for a deal generate quite a significant overall cost for the project company. This is not a marginal factor. Project finance is a form of financing in which costs are particularly high in relation to the size of the deal in question. This is also why each project finance deal has a critical minimum-size threshold below which structuring costs become excessive in relation to its forecasted income and cash flows.

The team of project consultants includes various specialists who start working on the project at different stages of its development. The involvement of each specific advisor differs considerably in terms of quantity of work performed; this can also depend on the type of project concerned. To give just one of an endless list of possible examples, technical advisors would certainly be much more involved in a project based on innovative technology than more "routine" projects from a technological standpoint.

This chapter focuses on the roles of legal, technical, and insurance advisors. The involvement of these professionals in putting together a project finance deal is

---

* Section 4.1 is by Massimo Novo; Introduction and Section 4.2 are by Stefano Gatti; Section 4.3 by Fabio Landriscina and Mark Pollard.

essential for its success; their input helps to make it bankable for lenders. On the other hand, these advisory services are essential both for sponsors (who need to submit to arrangers a well-structured and credible operating and financial plan in every respect) and for banks involved in the venture (first and foremost for arrangers, but through them also for other banks called on to support the deal).

Lawyers, engineers, and insurers play a critical role in various stages of project finance. However, the approach adopted in the following pages will be to review the activities of each professional category separately. Activities performed by each of the sponsors' or banks' advisors will be outlined almost in isolation and, above all, without taking into account possible interaction with other professional roles. In real life, of course, the situation is much more complex because the advisors concerned often work in parallel throughout the structuring stage of the deal (and often during the operations phase, even though the intensity and importance of such activities may differ). This approach means that several ideas will recur in all of the following sections, though possibly seen from different perspectives.

Section 4.1 illustrates the activities of legal advisors, outlining the various tasks performed in chronological order. The same approach is used to review the tasks and objectives of independent engineers in Section 4.2. Lastly, insurance advisors are discussed in Section 4.3.

4.1   The Role of Legal Advisors in Project Finance Deals

One project advisor in particular—the legal advisor or, more correctly, advisors, as is seen later—plays a very special role, mainly because of the range of tasks performed and consequently their importance as regards the overall structuring of the project. For reasons described in the following pages, legal advisors are the project's first "pure" advisors (excluding financial advisors, who often act in this role before going on to become mandated lead arrangers, as we see in Chapter 6). They are appointed by sponsors and arrangers, and their task covers the entire process of structuring the deal (and beyond, as mentioned later).

In fact, the importance of the legal advisors' role in project finance is such that it would almost seem justified to consider them as being among the key players within the overall framework. In terms of importance and weight in strategic decisions, this role is entirely different from that played by other advisors, inasmuch as it is intimately linked with the very substance of the project.

But perhaps this is excessive: Legal advisors don't personally make, or shouldn't make, strategic decisions. However, their performance and technical/professional decisions (as expressed in the technical/legal advice given to clients) are of fundamental importance in structuring the project. This role is similar in many ways to that of an engineer, who establishes the foundations and realizes an industrial work's complex in detail on a turnkey basis.

The professionalism and prestige of a law firm involved in structuring the project are essential for the successful outcome of the project itself. The complexity of financing without recourse means there is no room for improvisation or an "amateurish" approach when preparing the legal documentation for the project itself. No serious sponsor (or, for that matter, serious lender) can run the risk of incurring the very high costs of structuring a deal that then turns out to be organized in an approximate, off-the-cuff manner. At worst this could lead to a cost for a deal that is then rejected by the banking system or that gets the "thumbs down" when tested by the bank credit market, thus denying the validity of the very project finance nature of the deal.

As we see in the next chapter, the financial model underlying project analysis is the first tool used to check the bankability of the project for lenders; in fact, from their point of view the business plan *is* the project. But it is also a fact that in project finance the sponsors sell a series of future incomes and cash flows to the banking system that exist only on paper when banks underwrite the deal.[1] It is legal advisors who guarantee that there is a sound link between current risks and future income/cash flows. They do so by constructing a contractual system that creates a reliable expectation as regards the effective achievement of the forecast income for the project and its distribution as indicated in the financial model. This is significant from the standpoint of sponsors' and lenders' investment decisions. To use an expression taken from the theory of contracts, the aim is to create a bilateral contract (better still, a system of contracts), not between parties seated around a negotiating table but between current costs and forecast profits. This is by no means a simple task, but one that sums up the nature of project finance or at least the nature of its legal framework.

4.1.1 Legal Advisor, Legal Advisors, and Law Firms: The International Part and Local Legal Counsel

Up to now we have used the term *legal advisor* in a rather loose manner. It is important to note, however, that there is never just one legal advisor (even if in certain cases some ingenuous sponsors, terrified by the estimated legal costs for the deal, think they can manage by appointing only one advisor, who is given a kind of "*super partes*" mandate to be the sole legal advisor for the project). A project, in fact, is developed in several stages, each of which sees lawyers involved in various aspects and who represent the different parties concerned. From now on, the term *lawyers* will be considered synonymous with *legal advisor*, even if the role of giving legal advice can, at least in principle, by played by internal legal advisors of companies involved in the project. In actual fact, however, this does not happen very often. It would be unusual for internal lawyers to have the necessary specialized knowledge and even rarer for them to be able to mobilize the quantity of resources necessary to follow the structuring of a project finance deal in an efficient and timely manner.

One other point needs to be clarified: When speaking of lawyers, the plural is used to emphasize that in a project there are indeed several lawyers involved representing each of the main parties implicated in the deal (lawyers would say, "representing each client"). In fact a project requires:

- Specialized expertise in many different fields (ranging from corporate to financial, real estate to administrative law). Realistically, no single professional can possess sufficient knowledge in such a wide range of fields, including an adequate knowledge of precedents. (By *precedents*, we refer to practical precedents and market practices as opposed to *jurisprudence*, namely, court decisions that can be read in specialist publications or, for quite some time now, downloaded from dedicated Internet sites.)

---

1. It is also true, however, that there are cases of project finance where realization of the works concerned is already under way at the time financing without or with limited recourse is finalized.

- A huge quantity of work concentrated in a given amount of time: This clearly concerns lawyers, but others as well.

When we speak of lawyers, therefore, this really means medium- to large-sized law firms that can dedicate a team of several professionals to a single project. Experience over the past few years has shown that a relatively small number of international or international-level law firms has the size (and the client base and the intention) to develop a project finance deal. While not necessarily exclusive, and certainly not "aristocratic," the project financing "club" does tend to have very few members.

As we see in greater detail in Chapters 6 and 7, bank lending is governed by a credit agreement or facility agreement, which is the hub around which the project finance contractual system rotates. And there are two legal systems that the project credit agreement (and numerous other documents related to it) normally refer to the British and U.S. systems. In the majority of cases, the latter means the law as interpreted in the State of New York; technically it is improper to refer to the law of the United States of America.

The choice of one or the other legal system depends on many factors, in the majority of cases determined by the nationality of sponsors, arranger banks, and location of works to be realized. Sometimes, for specific project contracts (typically construction contracts), it can be the management culture or the nationality of the counterpart that dictates the applicable law. Large multinational groups have specific, well-defined policies on such matters, which usually means they refuse to enter into contracts not governed by their own national legal system or by an internationally recognized legal system. In Europe, it is practice in the large majority of cases to refer to British law, although approaches in some European countries differ quite substantially. By now nations have developed refined, consolidated practices within a mature banking community and quite frequently adopt their national law. (It is difficult to give examples without running the risk of strenuous objections; however, a tentative list would include Germany, France, and the Netherlands.) Other countries are still experiencing a significant divergence between what is acceptable to the international banking community, which continues to prefer British law, and their national legal systems. But this gap seems to be narrowing.

This is why it is normal to separate the "international" legal input, which concerns the finance documents, from the "local" input, strictly linked to the law of the country in which the project is located. From a conceptual standpoint this distinction would seem clear; however, this is much less the case from the practical operations standpoint. Undoubtedly, there will be a team of lawyers who assist sponsors and arrangers in structuring a project finance deal, British or American lawyers (more exactly, those entitled to practice the legal profession under British law or that of the State of New York, although the right to practice almost always coincides with nationality) and local lawyers. In the following pages an attempt is made to describe the boundary for each of these areas of competence.

4.1.2   Project Financing Development Stages and Impacts on the Role of Legal Advisors

Our task now is to describe what lawyers do in order to structure a project. The first observation is that the various lawyers involved in structuring a project perform different tasks according to the project's development and, of course, depending on which client has retained them to work on the project.

It is probably advisable to follow a strictly chronological approach, as was used in the previous chapter when discussing project life cycle. We describe below the development stages of a project finance deal, classifying legal activities in each stage and for each of the parties concerned.

1. Forming the group of sponsors
2. Preparing the project documents
3. Defining the project financing
4. Maintaining the project financing during the building phase and in the following operating period

These distinct stages will now be reviewed one by one, in order to understand what legal advisors do in each particular stage. Readers can consult Table 4-1 for an overview of what lawyers do in each stage indicated and which parties are involved.

4.1.2.1 Forming the Group of Sponsors

It is very infrequent that a project finance venture be undertaken by a single party, for the reasons explained in previous chapters. Seen from a strictly cor-

TABLE 4-1 Stages in Structuring Project Finance Deals and the Roles of Lawyers

Stage	Activity Required	Lawyers Involved
1. Forming the group of sponsors	Organizing the project company	Sponsors' lawyers
	Articles of incorporation for the project company	Sponsors' lawyers
	Agreements between sponsors (joint ventures or whatever)	Sponsors' lawyers
	Check on bankability of the venture on a without or limited recourse basis	Sponsors' lawyers Project company lawyers
2. Industrial development of the project	Project documents	Project company lawyers
		Sponsors' lawyers (when the sponsors are a counterpart of the project company)
		Arrangers' lawyers (bankability analysis)
	Due diligence report	Arrangers' lawyers
	Legal opinions	Sponsors' lawyers Arrangers' lawyers
3. Project financing	Mandate letter and financing term sheet	Arrangers' lawyers Project company lawyers
	Finance documents	Arrangers' lawyers Project company lawyers
	Assistance during syndication phase	Arrangers' lawyers
4. Maintenance of project financing	Periodic contacts with agent bank and sponsors	Sponsors' lawyers Arrangers' lawyers

porate standpoint, it can be said that the initial stage of a project is more or less similar to a joint venture. The distinctive feature of a joint venture in relation to project finance is the need to ensure right from the early stages that the initiative has the necessary characteristics to be financed without or with limited recourse. The worst outcome for a venture of this nature is to discover, perhaps after many months' work, that the system doesn't consider it to be bankable, in which case sponsors are either forced to abandon the project or to finance it using their own resources.

In this preliminary phase and based on initial indications as to the nature and peculiarities of the deal (which lawyers receive directly from either sponsors or their advisors), the sponsors' legal advisors organize the project company, preparing the articles of incorporation and negotiating the necessary agreements between sponsors (normally incorporated in the shareholders' agreement, but they can also involve more detailed, complex contractual structures). These agreements will regulate relations between sponsors and distribution of project risks. It will be remembered, furthermore, that part of the project funding must be put up by sponsors, who, for this purpose, can be called on to sign agreements as regards their equity contribution in financing the project.

Because a number of sponsors are probably involved, normally each of them is assisted by a different legal advisor, given that at this stage each sponsor has two objectives (so necessary compromises between sponsors may not be easy to reach): (1) to create the best possible legal basis for developing the project so that future contractual partners (lenders but also the project company's suppliers and purchasers of goods or services) see it as a solid and cohesive venture, but also (2) to obtain the best result for itself in financial and contractual terms when structuring the project as a joint venture. This objective is not easily attained, for sometimes an advantage for one sponsor will be a disadvantage for another or perhaps all other potential partners. Nonetheless, this critical aspect cannot be overlooked (although it often is neglected by inexpert legal advisors or those inexperienced in project finance).

This means that once the preorganization phase between sponsors of the project company is complete, one legal advisor (normally, but not always, the main sponsor's lawyer) or sometimes a different legal firm is assigned the role of legal representative for the project company itself.

Sometimes in the initial stage a project is developed by a single sponsor who later (either by choice or out of necessity) invites other parties to participate as cosponsors. This can be achieved either by negotiation with a single party selected beforehand as a result of direct contacts or by means of a competitive bid. In the latter case the main concern of the sponsor organizing the bid (or embarking on negotiations) is the confidentiality of information that inevitably must be made available to the counterparty for negotiation purposes. Instead the counterparty instructs its lawyers to review the venture and its legal and contractual implications. This requires a due diligence investigation similar, from many standpoints, to that conducted for company acquisition purposes, but with two specific differences.

1. Unlike a corporate acquisition, it is an exercise conducted entirely on paper: The project, by definition, doesn't yet exist, and so the only aspects that can be verified are whether its development and resulting revenue are reasonable and likely to be achieved.

2. The overriding factor to check is the venture's bankability with or without limited recourse. The advisors asked to make an initial assessment of this essential condition are the lawyers.

4.1.2.2 Industrial Development of the Project—The Project Documents

The choice of project counsel (who, technically speaking, is the legal advisor of the project company, which appoints a law firm by granting a formal power of attorney) is a joint decision taken by the sponsors. As already mentioned, sometimes this is the law firm preferred by the main sponsor, who may be the one making the largest investment in the project (and therefore in the project company) or the one who more than any other characterizes and/or conditions the project itself. (For instance, it could be the sponsor that has the underlying technology for the project.)

So project counsel is the lawyer for the project. In the event of conflict of interest among sponsors, the aim of project counsel is to remain neutral (clearly an embarrassing situation) and to act in the best interests of the project, that is (subjectively), of the project company. This is by no means just a theoretical situation, especially when other fundamental players in structuring the financing—the arrangers—enter the scene. Suppose, for example, that the arrangers are not entirely convinced that the contractor for turnkey construction work is reliable and that the company in question is one of the sponsors or belongs to the same group. The arrangers will ask for greater coverage (a *mitigation*, another of the key words used in relation to project finance) for this risk. Who pays the bill, the sponsor concerned or all sponsors? The answer, if there is one, lies in the agreements between sponsors mentioned in the previous section; otherwise this opens a legal and negotiation parenthesis in the project development that is part of the previous stage in terms of structure, though not in terms of time. This, in turn, leads to a further consideration: Because of unforeseen issues arising during definition of the relevant project finance agreements, the agreements between sponsors can and/or must change. In extreme cases, this may even lead to a change in the original group of sponsors. In practice, this has happened in the past on a number of occasions.

When speaking of industrial development of the project, this in fact refers to making the necessary preparations to *begin construction work* but not construction itself. This is because the necessary financing is not yet available; in fact, work will begin when structuring the deal, as described in these pages, is complete.

Typically this development stage concerns the project documents: In this stage the project company sets up contracts and obtains permits and other legal papers required to realize the necessary works and to operate in accordance with the aims of the project. At this stage, the project company lawyers usually perform the task of drawing up a complete list of these documents and finalizing and/or obtaining them.

Following is a list of possible project documents, drawn up without reference to any specific deal.

Concessions from the Public Administration: This is a necessary element when public works or works of public interest subject to a government concession are realized using a project finance approach. As seen in Chapter 1 when speaking of the involvement of private capital in public works, this factor comes up frequently but not always in project finance. However, it is found in the UK, particularly in the case of PFIs realized as part of that government's PPP approach.[2]

Permits to Realize Project Works: Again these are not documents produced by the project company, although they are required to be able to realize the project. Their existence and validity is a necessary condition for launching the project, and so they are the subject of specific clauses in the credit agreement, which will normally contain an attachment listing the permits required to realize the project works. Town planning and building permits are particularly important, as are those relative to the environmental impact of the project itself.

Contracts for Use of Third-Party Assets or Rights: These are documents by means of which the project is assured tangible rights (for instance, the ownership of or right of access to the area where the project will be realized) or intangible rights (like those allowing the use of a given technology) necessary for its realization. Sometimes these rights are granted by the public administration, and so the relevant document assumes an importance (also) from the standpoint of administrative law.

Rights Relevant to the Area Where the Project Works Will Be Developed: The project company must ensure it has the necessary rights (normally rights of ownership or a building lease) as regards the site where the project will be realized. A legal complication concerning these rights comes up in BOT-based contracts, in which the works will be transferred to the public administration after a certain period. Such rights represent a considerable technical and legal complication in projects in which the nature of legal property rights as regards the project are more difficult to define, for example, projects such as the exploitation of oil fields under the North Sea (whether in territorial waters or otherwise) and the Channel Tunnel.

Contract for Realization of the Project Works and Relevant Subcontracts: This is the document that contains clauses regulating the area of the project subject to most risk and is probably the most important document project company lawyers have to prepare. It should be noted that one possible scenario that could significantly affect negotiation of this contract is whether the performing company is or is not linked to one of the sponsors.

Operation and Maintenance (O&M) Management Contracts and Technical Consultancy Contracts: Often this is covered by the O&M contract described in Chapters 1 and 3 and is the other essential project contract concerning the operating stage. Specific projects may have special characteristics that mean project company operation management is covered by several contracts. Again in this case, it is not infrequent that one of the sponsors is also the supplier of project management services. Also this contract is initially "managed" by the project company lawyers.

Bonds and Guarantees for Project Contracts: These are guarantees (bonds) from banks or financially sound third parties (normally the parent company or holding company of one of the parties to the project contract), the purpose of which is to render the responsibility of a given party bankable, usually as regards damages or

---

2. Data for the EU market prepared by the European Investment Bank show that PFI projects received support from the bank between 1990 and the end of 2003 amounting to around 15 billion euros, of which 25% went to the UK. These transactions were mainly in the form of a design, build, finance, and operate (DBFO) scheme that didn't produce a negative impact on national deficits or debt. See EIB, *Evaluation of PPP Projects Financed by the EIB*, March 2005.

repayment of advances received. In essence these are seen as accessories to the project documents, and the required forms for these guarantees are given in attachment. In reality these are rather well-known, standard forms in the financial market.

Insurance: Technically speaking, these are project contracts, even if normally advisors specialized in the insurance sector are assigned to prepare them, as is seen in Section 4.3. The project company must have adequate insurance coverage for risk exposure and is an aspect regulated in an extremely detailed manner in the credit agreement. The insurance element is vital when structuring a project finance deal; however, practices in the insurance field are extremely specialized and are therefore considered the domain of a separate profession. Insurance is handled by consultants and brokers with a considerable degree of separation from the rest of the legal and contractual activity in terms of structuring the project finance deal.

Procurement Contracts for Raw Materials Required for Project Operations: Fuel supply agreements (contracts for the purchase of fuel for projects in the power generation field) are particularly important in this category.

Sales Contracts: These contracts generate the project company's income. A detailed analysis of the nature and necessary features of these contracts can be found in Chapters 4 and 7.

4.1.2.3   Project Financing—The Finance Documents

The stage when the finance documents are defined (first and foremost, the credit agreement) is clearly central to a project finance deal.

While project contracts are normally prepared by project company lawyers and reviewed (and modified, if necessary) by the arrangers' lawyers, preparation of the finance documents is usually the responsibility of the arrangers' lawyers, who then negotiate them with the project company lawyers. So in this case the arrangers' lawyers lead the process by preparing and managing the documents concerned, whereas the project company lawyers come into the picture afterwards when they receive and review the documents.

At this stage the project is almost entirely in the hands of lawyers. More than any other document, the credit agreement is a contract that requires highly special-ized lawyering. Decisions of a business nature required from the principal actors (arrangers and project company's sponsors) are the guidelines around which the credit agreement is fashioned. This then becomes the control document for the entire project. In the early stages, a specific project finance deal is above all an industrial idea regulated by a financing contract, which will then provide most of the financial resources to realize the project itself. Bearing this in mind, it indeed makes sense to say that "on the starting grid" project financing is a legal product waiting to become an industrial and financial reality. If not, this concept would be difficult to accept.

The finance documents usually include the following.

- Documents by which the sponsors appoint one or more banks (the arrangers) to organize and grant the financing: These are normally referred to as *mandate documents* or *commitment documents*. These usually include a letter of appoint-ment (a mandate), in which the arrangers (as we see in Chapter 6, they are referred to as *mandated arrangers*—MAs—or even mandated lead arrangers—MLAs; a bit of emphasis at this stage doesn't do any harm and costs nothing) are appointed to organize the financing, or a letter of commitment, in which the arrangers commit themselves to sign (initially, i.e., before but with a view to syndication) a table summarizing the main financial and legal terms of the deal.

- The credit agreement
- The security documents, which constitute the package of collateral granted in relation to the financing
- The intercreditor agreement, which regulates some or all of the relations between lenders
- Some other ancillary documents relating to the credit agreement, for instance, fee letters that establish the commissions due to the arrangers
- Contracts concerning capital made available to the project company by sponsors, often known as the *equity contribution agreements.*
- Other documents concerning financing in the event the credit agreement and equity capital put up by sponsors are not the only sources of project financing
- Hedging agreements to cover the risk of swings in both interest and currency exchange rates
- Direct agreements, which pertain to an area lying between security documents and project contracts

An analysis of the credit agreements and other finance documents refers more to the legal nature of project finance as opposed to describing the role played by legal advisors; this analysis is found in Chapter 7.

4.1.2.4   The Due Diligence Legal Report

This document is a report prepared by the arrangers' lawyers for their clients giving a summary of the project and its formal and substantial bankability. Its content describes everything concerning the project assembled by the sponsors and project company.

- Nature and characteristics of the project company
- Project contracts
- Administrative concessions and permits
- The general regulatory setting for the project: Depending on the case, arrangers may want a description of other legal aspects concerning the project, for instance, the guarantee system and the administrative and concessionary system

This document normally constitutes one of the many conditions governing the project company's ability to utilize the financing granted under the credit agreement. This is a consolidated practice, to the point that no project company or sponsor raises any objection to the fact that from a formal standpoint this report is controlled entirely by the arrangers (who must unilaterally state that they are satisfied) and the arrangers' lawyers. In theory the due diligence legal report ought to be prepared months before the credit agreement is finalized. In practice, however, things are very different: The due diligence legal report is one of the many documents finalized by the lawyers and approved by the arrangers during the last few days before the financial close of the project.

4.1.2.5   Legal Opinions

The legal opinions are contained in yet another summary document used in the final stages of structuring the financing and again constitute a condition for releasing the financing itself.

The legal opinion document is very formal and extremely technical from a juridical standpoint; therefore, a detailed analysis of how it is structured is beyond the scope of this book. Suffice to say that the following points are ones that arrangers and lenders would expect to see covered by legal opinions concerning a project finance deal.

- That the project company has been formed and complies with laws in force.
- Validity of the finance documents and project contracts signed by the project company and other parties (normally the so-called "opinion documents," which collectively refer to documents that are subject to a legal opinion).
- Validity and conformity with laws in force of the opinion documents; under British law such documents are considered to be legal, valid, and binding.
- Validity of collateral that guarantees credit facilities lenders grant to the project company.
- Ownership of project assets by the project company.
- Validity (and sometimes the appropriate scope) of licenses, concessions, and other administrative permits.
- The existence of and any restrictions referring to convertibility of foreign exchange, tax withholdings on interest payments, other taxes due for concessions once the opinion documents are signed.
- Validity of specific clauses concerning damages, gross-up and calculation and payment of late-payment interest. Certain legal systems can create various obstacles as to the validity of such clauses; for this reason the international banking community is quite concerned about such issues.
- Legal status of the project company's bonds and existence under local law of regulations ensuring preferential treatment to given creditors (possibly the state for income taxes, social security agencies, employees, and, in certain cases, the national banking system).
- Whether according to local law a party can be sentenced to pay sums of money in other than the country's own local currency.
- Validity of provisions in the opinion documents as regards choice of other than local law in favor of foreign jurisdiction (or arbitration clauses).
- The existence of immunity from legal or executive action in favor of any parties involved in the project. These issues are clearly very important for projects to realize assets under a concessionary or similar regime.

The foregoing list is only given by way of example. It is difficult to imagine that the preceding points would not be covered in legal opinions foreseen in a project credit agreement; however, depending on the circumstances, there could well be several more issues that the arrangers would like to see covered by legal opinion.

When preparing and issuing legal opinions, the lawyers involved in the project are once again formally distinct from one another. Arrangers (and lenders) will certainly want to see a legal opinion from their own "local" legal advisors (namely, those legal advisors in the country where the project is to be developed) and one of its own advisors as regards (let's say) British law pertaining to those documents (normally the credit agreement and certain other finance documents) that are governed by other than local law, as mentioned in Section 4.1.1.

Normally project company lawyers also issue a legal opinion concerning local law However, the content of this is sometimes (but not always) rather "lightweight" by comparison to the one prepared by the arrangers' lawyers. Sometimes certain specific aspects concerning the project company or other parties, such as the existence of litigation or other agreements that could affect the project contracts, are covered by the internal legal staff of the sponsors or other parties. Less frequently (although it does happen), the project company's international lawyers are asked to give their legal opinion on the finance documents.

4.1.2.6 Syndicating the Financing

Once structuring of the project finance deal is complete, the arrangers and coarrangers face the delicate task of syndicating the transaction in the banking market. This is the moment when the deal is at the mercy of the open sea, so to speak, when a significant number of specialists from various banks (each with its own professional and company culture and opinions, and not only this) will examine the deal with a magnifying glass to decide whether or not to buy in.

As for the sponsors, for them, at least formally, this is a quiet moment ("their" objective has been achieved because the financing has been assured). They have every interest, and normally a formal obligation, to cooperate with the arrangers to ensure syndication goes well.

Once again the arrangers' lawyers play a fundamental role. To simplify matters (but not excessively), three things are presented to banks invited to participate in the pool.

1. **The project in terms of its industrial and technical nature.** This is, of course, a necessary aspect, although it is not expected to cause any surprises. It is difficult to imagine that sponsors with reliable industrial experience in the sector fail to convince potential lenders of the technical/industrial merits of what they are proposing to do and their ability to achieve it. But because of its very nature it is extremely unusual that an industrial project proposed for funding using a project financing approach is not actually reliable from a technical/industrial standpoint.
2. **The project in numbers.** The figures for the project can be especially positive or otherwise, however, again this aspect will not normally cause any surprises: The numbers have obviously been good enough to justify financing it (otherwise the arrangers themselves would have abandoned the deal long before). Usually specialized advisors are called in to audit the financial model used.
3. **Regulatory and contractual aspects of the project.** This is a task for the lawyers: At this point they prepare the summary report showing the transformation of an expected income into binding and reliable contractual relations. The lawyers must be able to demonstrate that they have turned the technical/industrial expectations (point 1) and figures from the financial model (point 2) into an effective value by means of a network of legal, company, and contractual relationships created so that lenders invited to participate can be convinced "to buy the project."

4.1.2.7 The Operating Period: Maintenance of the Project Financing

With the financial close (that is, when all conditions established have been met, thereby enabling initial disbursement of financing to build the plant or works), the project company is authorized to use the project financing facility. In theory this would coincide with the start of construction; however, in reality quite frequently construction of project works has already gotten under way by utilizing:

- Equity that in any event the sponsors are committed to assign (see Section 6.7)
- Subordinated loans made temporarily by sponsors to the project company and that are reimbursed to them simultaneous with the first utilization of the project financing facility (see Section 6.8)
- A temporary loan (bridge financing) that the project financing lenders (less often, other lenders, for obvious reasons) have granted to the project company, backed by collateral provided by the sponsors (see Section 6.9)

Whatever the scenario in which the project will be carried forward, the time when lawyers play an essential role has now come to an end. Also, the arrangers' task is technically and formally complete and the role of directing the deal passes to the agent. The agent and sponsors will consult with their lawyers from time to time in the event of problems concerning the project or financing if things aren't proceeding according to plan. However, this doesn't happen very often (unless the project hits rough water from a technical, industrial, and, therefore, financial standpoint), so relations normalize between the main parties involved in the deal and their advisors (legal or otherwise). The lawyers' moment of glory (for which they pay a high price in terms of stress and work hours, even though they are usually well paid for their efforts) comes to an end. The project now becomes a new chapter in their *cursus honorum* and, perhaps, in the leaflet describing the law firm and its track record in terms of the most important deals in which it has participated.

4.2   The Role of the Independent Engineer in Project Finance Deals

One of the most critical areas when structuring a project finance deal is the technical aspects involved. While the project's construction and engineering features may be clear to the sponsors, often this is not the case for lenders, who therefore need a specialized professional to help them evaluate the deal and decide whether to support it or not. On the other hand, as was seen in the previous section, technical aspects are also very important for the sponsors' and arrangers' lawyers when they are preparing the project documents and finance documents.

So the technical consultant's role—often known also as *independent engineer* or *independent technical advisor*—is extremely important in deals for project financed transactions. The independent engineer plays a *super partes* role and is asked to express an opinion as to the project's feasibility, make a survey to evaluate it, and act as the controller in order to safeguard the project and, above all, those who put up the money to finance it.

The independent engineer's role is useful not only for lender banks but also for the other parties involved. Activities concerning the project can be performed for the benefit of sponsor companies or the SPV itself, for instance, in a case where a reliable technical opinion is required as regards the possibility to use a given production technology developed by one of the sponsors in the deal.

So, in effect there will usually be not one but a number of "technical consultants." As we will see, the sponsors and the constructor's site manager also use third-party technical advice at various stages in the project—especially when works are nearing completion and the project will be moving into the test phase. At these times there will be a joint presence of the sponsors', constructors', and banks' independent engineers, each of whom is required to give an opinion to the party that has appointed them.

The more significant activities performed by independent engineers in a project finance deal can be subdivided into four basic phases:

1. Due diligence reporting
2. Monitoring realization of the project (engineering and construction)
3. Assistance during acceptance of the plant
4. Monitoring operations management

As mentioned, this is only a very rough classification and should therefore not be taken as either rigid or exclusive. Independent engineers will be involved more or less intensively, depending on the stage of the project—certainly they will have a more dominant role in innovative or highly complex technological projects.

But even though only a general guide, the categorization according to the phases just indicated is effectively that used normally at an international level to outline activities by major engineering companies. The objective is always to minimize the risks lenders run during a project finance deal.

Furthermore, the phase categorization constitutes a good starting point and framework for the analysis. Each phase will be analyzed in terms of:

- An independent engineer's objectives
- Expected benefits for banks
- Basic documentation necessary for the phase concerned
- Supplementary and accessory activities and services (as appropriate)
- Scope of activities for each phase and reports produced by the independent engineer

4.2.1 Initial Due Diligence Reporting

Seen from the position of an arranger or a bank that may finance a structured finance deal, even apparently simple projects can create problems in terms of evaluating technical factors, and in fact no bank has the necessary technical expertise on its staff. This is why involvement of an independent engineer is justified during the early stages of structuring the deal. The due diligence report the independent engineer will produce consists of a critical analysis of all technical aspects of the deal, with reference to project, contractual, and financial pictures that are usually already quite well defined.

A review of the technical and technological variables clearly constitutes the focus of this advisor's activity. In addition, banks often ask for an opinion as regards business and insurance aspects of the project; however, these assessments are only secondary to the basic activities outlined earlier.

Table 4-2 summarizes the main content of due diligence activities, covered in detail in the following pages.

A technical advisor's activities in this phase benefit lenders because they obtain an analysis made by an independent party. As part of the study, the independent engineer checks that the technical variables included in the financial model are acceptable; an opinion is then given as to the reasonableness of costs forecast to realize the project. If the independent engineer confirms that the fundamental project variables proposed by the sponsors are complete and reasonable, then this is already an important factor as regards the possible bankability of the deal under review.

TABLE 4-2   Summary of the Initial Due Diligence Phase

Phase	Independent Engineer's Activities	Documents Required	Documentation Produced
Initial due diligence	• Critical analysis of the project's technical aspects • Analysis of the project's business aspects • Analysis of the project's insurance aspects	1. Preliminary feasibility study with draft financial plan 2. Basic or detailed project outline 3. Market analysis 4. Information memorandum with indications of the main parties involved in the deal (sponsors, constructor, buyers and suppliers, banks, insurance companies, etc.) and financing term sheet 5. Supply and procurement contracts 6. Agreements 7. Authorizations, permits, licenses, and concessions 8. Any services and construction contracts 9. Security package	Initial due diligence report

The opinion of the independent engineer is, furthermore, a great help to the banks' lawyers when preparing the due diligence legal report discussed in Section 4.1.2.4.

4.2.1.1   Documents Required for the Due Diligence Activity

Preparing an accurate initial due diligence report requires the availability of various documents; following are those normally requested by an independent engineer.

- Preliminary feasibility study and draft financial plan
- Project outline or details
- Market analysis
- Information memorandum with indications of the main parties involved in the deal (sponsors, constructor, purchasers and suppliers, banks, insurance companies, etc.) and the financing term sheet
- Supply and purchase contracts
- Agreements
- Authorizations, permits, licenses, and concessions
- Any service and construction contracts
- Security package

4.2.1.2   Accessory Services

The independent engineer can even be asked to give an opinion when some of the documents indicated earlier are in a rough first draft or even lacking. Some engineering companies are also able to assist lenders during initial structuring of the deal. In this case they help banks complete the necessary documents to clearly define all aspects of the project for purposes of the feasibility study.

An independent engineer might provide an opinion on a wide range of issues, for instance:

- Market analysis for products, semifinished goods, and raw materials required to feed the production cycle and relevant simulations based on alternative scenarios
- Whether assumptions underlying the sponsors' sales plan—in terms of quantities and prices—are realistic
- Maturity of technology
- Appropriateness of planned technical choices
- Possible impacts as regards the choice of machinery and equipment
- Whether assumptions concerning plant system output are realistic
- Sensitivity analysis of the financial plan. The aim here is to evaluate the degree of robustness of cash flows once the project is operative, in the event a change in one or more variables might affect the venture (identified by means of risk assessment).

4.2.1.3   Documents Produced During the Due Diligence Activity Phase

During the due diligence exercise, already-available contractual documentation is reviewed in depth in order to identify critical points as regards relations between the parties involved in the deal, which mainly pertain to potential technical and technological problems. Once the study is complete, a due diligence report is prepared (first in a preliminary form as a collection of comments and then as a final report) in which the independent engineer gives an opinion on the following issues.

- Whether documentation is complete and the technologies are adequate and reliable based on a check of significant aspects of the project to ensure the start-up and functionality (potential, performance, utilization factor) of plant operations. The opinion also takes into account the frequency and duration of maintenance requirements.
- Analysis of the project's vulnerability if harmful events were to occur. This review is useful for quantifying the maximum probable loss (or MPL) as regards the works in the event of accidental damage. See also Section 8.7.3.
- Project data as regards plant safety. This requires a simulation of several possible emergency scenarios in order to assess the probability of catastrophic events and their impact in terms of damage to structures and the surrounding environment (Environmental Impact Assessment, or EIA).
- The soundness of financial assumptions concerning construction and management costs for the structures.
- The reasonableness of assumptions concerning the time schedule for construction and start-up of business operations.
- The organizational framework for the construction and management of the works, especially organizational and operational capabilities of companies involved in the construction stage.

4.2.2   Monitoring Realization of the Project (Engineering and Construction)

This is a particularly delicate phase in a project finance deal. In fact, the SPV has been financed based on the conditions laid out in the credit agreement and has started to draw funds made available by the financing banks.

The start of the project works requires careful progress monitoring. Consequently, periodic reports should be produced for lenders certifying that the venture is going ahead as planned. Thus independent engineers both monitor and certify the works.

In brief, these are the activities they perform:

- Monitor construction of the works
- Issue certified progress reports
- Validate mechanical completion (certify completion of works)

4.2.2.1 Monitoring Construction of the Works

The aim of monitoring construction by means of on-site inspections and assessments is to check that works are proceeding in accordance with specifications established at the time of initial planning. The check is all-inclusive and covers the construction site, works associated with it, and also procurement of materials. The independent engineer checks that everything is proceeding satisfactorily in terms of timing and cost. A summary of the activities and documentation produced in this phase is shown in Table 4-3.

Furthermore, this monitoring activity means assumptions concerning timing and cost to finish can be evaluated and, therefore, so can the effects of possible delays on the SPV's business plan. This last point is essential information for lenders. As a result of monitoring works periodically, they receive an updated picture of progress and can, if necessary, take timely corrective action as indicated in the credit

TABLE 4-3   Summary of the Engineering and Construction Phase—Monitoring Project Realization

Phase	Independent Engineer's Activities	Documents Required	Documentation Produced

Monitoring realization of the structure	• Check that progress for works corresponds to initial plans
	• Check procurement activities
		1. Contracts (EPC contract, civil works and relevant subcontracts)
		2. Detailed plans (data sheets, technical specifications, plans and diagrams, construction standards)
		3. Progress reports issued by the principal or the general contractor, together with:
		  • Schedule baseline and definition of project milestones
		  • Detailed construction schedules
		  • Any recovery plans
		  • Progress curves
		  • Site organization and relevant organization chart, plus subcontractor organization with S-curve for resources employed
		  • Safety plan and quality control
		  • Procurement plan with main item purchasing list
		  • List of lifting and handling equipment
		  • List of changes during course of works
		  • Permitting plan
			Progress monitoring reports

agreement to keep risk factors under control and limit the impact on the project's operating cash flow.

Documents Required to Monitor Works: The process of monitoring works is based on a wide range of very technical documents. While a detailed description of each of these falls outside the scope of this book, a list of them is given here for reference purposes.

1. Supply contracts (EPC contract, civil works and related subcontracts)
2. Detailed plans (data sheets, technical specifications, plans and drawings, construction standards)
3. Progress report issued by the SPV or the general contractor, accompanied by:

   - General plans for works (schedule baseline) and definition of project milestones
   - Detailed construction schedules
   - Recovery plans, if applicable
   - Progress curves for works
   - Construction site organization and relevant organization chart and, in addition, the organization of subcontractors with the S-curve for resources employed[3]
   - Safety plan and quality control system
   - Main item purchasing list
   - List of lifting and moving machinery and equipment
   - List of changes while work is in progress
   - Permitting plan

Accessory Services: In addition to monitoring works and construction sites, the independent engineer may be asked to provide support to prepare some of the documents mentioned previously:

   - Preparation of the overall works plan using project management techniques (CPM—critical path method, PERT—program evaluation and review technique, grid analysis, and WBS—work breakdown structure) and assistance for defining organizations responsible for safety and quality control (preparation of production, monitoring, and testing plans)
   - Study and preparation of recovery plans as a response to changes in operating conditions included in the works baseline, the aim of which is to bring the project back on track to achieve initial objectives and at the same time to limit potential damage
   - Assistance in the testing and acceptances phases for major equipment
   - As regards projects that have not yet reached the executive phase, a critical evaluation of choices made during the development phase and check for consistency with contractual terms

Documents Produced During the Construction of Works Phase: The independent engineer effectively acts as the project manager on behalf of lenders, and so the

---

3. S-curves represent the cumulative figures for resources employed on a project at a given time. They are obtained by adding up costs incurred to realize activities necessary to achieve an objective. Usually these activities are defined in detail at the start of works using what in project management are referred to as **WBS** (work breakdown structure) techniques, whereby tasks are listed alongside the resources required for their completion. The S-curve, in other words, indicates cumulative costs for resources over time and based on the concatenation in time of activities established by applying grid analysis (CPM, critical path method, and PERT, project evaluation and review technique). For detailed information on this subject, see Harrison (1985).

tasks performed in no way differ from those performed by the project manager appointed by the general contractor.

During the construction stage, various periodic monitoring reports are prepared that summarize analyses and valuations made:

- Physical progress made, evaluated using work breakdown structure techniques
- Time required to complete the works
- Actual and potential causes that have led or may lead to partial delays
- Forecast variances from the works baseline plan by evaluating time necessary for completion
- Changes while works are in progress and risks arising from these changes
- Status of authorizations and permits required to start or complete works
- Efficiency and effectiveness of the organizational and productive structures assigned to carry out the works
- Validity of business assumptions based on expected developments in the market

4.2.2.2 Issuing Progress Reports

From Chapter 3 we know that constructors are often paid based on the progress of works. So when predefined stages in the construction process are reached, the SPV pays a percentage of the total value of the works. Before such payments are made, a condition precedent (to be discussed in Chapter 7) is the issue of a specific certificate by the independent engineer. This is based on a check of effective execution of works and confirms that costs indicated in the construction contract correspond, also taking into account any changes during work in progress. A summary of the activities and documentation produced in this phase is shown in Table 4-4.

The works progress certificate is essential for lender banks inasmuch as it represents a guarantee that financing used by the SPV for works carried out by the general contractor to a given date is in line with contractual commitments.

Documents Required to Issue Works Progress Certificates: The independent engineer must have at least the following documents before issuing the works progress certificate:

- Supply contracts
- Plans, plus relevant size and volume calculations
- General ledger

TABLE 4-4   Summary of the Engineering and Construction Phase—Issue of Certified Progress Reports

Phase	Independent Engineer's Activities	Documents Required	Documentation Produced
Issue of certified progress reports	• Check that a tranche of the works has been executed • Check that costs are in line with the EPC contract and with changes during the course of works	1. Contracts 2. Plans together with relevant survey calculations and measurements 3. General ledger 4. Works accounts 5. Progress report signed by the site manager 6. Statement that works have been executed as planned, signed by the engineer and the site manager	Certificate stating that works have been executed in conformity with contractual conditions

- Works accounting records
- Progress of works status, countersigned by the site manager
- Declaration that works have been executed as prescribed, countersigned by the design engineer and site manager

Documents Produced: The independent engineer's certificate takes the form of a report attesting that the progress of works status signed by the site manager corresponds to works effectively realized.

4.2.2.3 Validation of Mechanical Completion (Works Completion Certificate)

Validation of mechanical completion represents the final review of all progress of works status; it includes a check, performed on a sample basis, that works have been executed and realized in a satisfactory manner. So the works completion certificate attests to the correctness of declarations made by the site manager and the sponsors' technical advisor. A summary of the activities and documentation produced in this phase is shown in Table 4-5.

Banks rely heavily on this certificate, which represents a guarantee given by the independent engineer as to the completeness and accuracy of certified data and in particular that the latter correspond to what was established contractually and included in the financial plan.

Documents Required to Issue the Mechanical Completion Certificate: The independent engineer can issue the mechanical completion certificate based on the same documentation indicated in the previous section. In effect, mechanical completion is a summary of all the works progress reports:

- Supply contracts with list of prices
- Construction plans with relevant size and volume calculations
- General ledger
- Works accounting records
- All progress of works status reports, countersigned by the site manager
- All declarations that works have been executed as prescribed, countersigned by the design engineer and the site manager
- Authorizations, permits, and concessions (as required for the case in point)

TABLE 4-5   Summary of the Engineering and Construction Phase—Validation of Mechanical Completion

Phase	Independent Engineer's Activities	Documents Required	Documentation Produced
Validation of mechanical completion	• Sample check that works have been completed • Check correctness of site manager's certifications	• Contracts, with list of prices • Construction plans, with relevant survey calculations and measurements • General ledger • Works accounts • *All* progress reports signed by the site manager • *All* statements that works have been executed as planned, signed by the engineer and the site manager • Authorizations, permits, and concessions (required for the purpose)	Certificate attesting to mechanical completion

Documents Produced: The site manager and sponsors' technical advisor together with the independent engineer check completion of the works and prepare the punch list (a document listing construction details not yet completed) to check that any problems that might have arisen during construction have been resolved. This activity leads to production of a certificate stating that everything covered by the contract as regards realization of the works has indeed been completed.

4.2.3 Assistance at the Time of Plant Acceptance

With mechanical completion, the site manager and the technical advisor certify that the construction phase has been completed. The completion of this stage overcomes certain risks typically found during the material realization stage reviewed in Chapter 3. However, lenders must now verify whether the plant has been realized in accordance with contractual specifications and, therefore, that output is in line with the performance assumptions initially included in the financial plan (and certified in the initial technical due diligence report prepared by the independent engineer).

Therefore the independent engineer also plays an important role during acceptance of the plant. In fact this expert's assistance will be requested:

- To validate the Provisional Acceptance Certificate, or PAC, for the plant
- During the test phase (between issue of the PAC and the Final Acceptance Certificate, or FAC)
- To validate the FAC for the plant

4.2.3.1 Validation of the Provisional Acceptance Certificate (PAC)

After evaluating the testing procedures as regards the plant, the banks' independent engineer then participates in acceptance testing itself. The first test the plant must pass is to meet the minimum performance standard. If this is not met, the general contractor is deemed to be in default and is required to pay liquidated damages. Furthermore, the independent engineer analyzes the results certified by a third-party organization and confirms their acceptability in terms of meeting contractual performance requirements. Participation in testing plus evaluation of the tests and the results constitute validation of the PAC for the plant (see Table 4-6).

Benefits for banks as a result of validation of the PAC are that they obtain certification as to the completeness and accuracy of certified data, particularly as regards their meeting standards established contractually and included in the financial plan.

Documents Required to Validate the PAC: In order to validate the PAC, the minimum documentation the independent engineer requires is the following:

- Supply contracts (EPC, civil works, subcontracts)
- Construction plans
- Operating manual
- Maintenance manual
- Safety plans
- Authorizations, permits, and concessions (required for the purpose concerned)
- Detailed plans covering commissioning, start-up, acceptance testing, and testing phases (an opinion must be given as regards validity of testing itself)

TABLE 4-6   Summary of Assistance During the Plant Acceptance Phase—Validation of the PAC

Phase	Independent Engineer's Activities	Documents Required	Documentation Produced
Validation of the Provisional Acceptance Certificate	• Participation in acceptance tests • Analysis of test standards adopted • Review of certificates issued by third parties	• Contracts (EPC contract, civil works, subcontracts) • Construction plans • Operating manual • Maintenance manual • Safety plans • Authorizations, permits, and concessions (required for the purpose) • Detailed schedule for the commissioning, start-up, acceptance test, and final testing phases (this is required in order to express an opinion on adequacy of testing) • List of resources used and relevant qualifications (with training plan, if required) • Acceptance procedure, with details of preliminary operations, raw materials requirements, parameters to be checked, methods of execution, and applicable test standards	Report on the adequacy of the provisional acceptance certificate

- List of human resources employed and relevant qualifications (with training plan, if necessary)
- Acceptance procedure, with details of preliminary operations, raw materials requirements, parameters to be checked, methods to be employed, and applicable testing standards

Documents Produced: As already mentioned, the independent engineer must first express an opinion on the testing methods as to their applicability, completeness, and adequacy of the standards indicated, highlighting any shortcomings in the testing procedures adopted. Participation in testing means the independent engineer can evaluate whether the procedures have been applied correctly and that parameters checked in fact corresponded to the standards and that certified performance data agree with contractual requirements. This also means that any variances can be identified and analyzed.[4]

As a result of the foregoing, the PAC for the plant certifying that standards have been reached and the required performance achieved are validated.

4.2.3.2   Monitoring the Testing Phase

The testing phase for the plant is usually never very short, and so quite some time can pass between issue and validation of the PAC and production of the Final Acceptance Certificate. During the time between the PAC and the FAC, the independent engineer must constantly inspect the plant and analyze periodic maintenance reports produced by the manager of the facility. It is very important that technical and operational variables for the plant be checked, together with the methods employed

---

4. If there is a variance between certified test values and those guaranteed, then it is not part of the independent engineer's task to provide a support service and assistance to the banks in order to evaluate the technical and financial impact of differences found and define strategies to minimize any negative effects of these. Such services are considered accessory to the PAC validation.

TABLE 4-7 Summary of Assistance During the Plant Acceptance Phase—Monitoring the Testing Phase

Phase	Independent Engineer's Activities	Documents Required	Documentation Produced
Monitoring the testing phase	• Periodic inspection of the plant • Review and check periodic maintenance reports issued by the manager • Check the correctness and application of safety measures	• Contracts (EPC contract, civil works, subcontracts) • As-built plans • Operating manual • Maintenance manual • Safety plans • Safety statistics • List of operations personnel and relevant qualifications • Periodic maintenance reports prepared by the manager • Historical records of alerts and breakdowns • Historical records of main operating parameters for plant system performance (to be defined based on type of production) • Accounts for consumption of raw materials, fuels, chemicals, consumables, service fluids (water, natural gas, etc.) • Accounts for production • Accounts for disposal of by-products	Periodic monitoring report; statement as to the correctness of maintenance activities

for carrying out maintenance activities; the independent engineer's task includes checking the facility's safety procedures and verifying that they are applied correctly by management. (See Table 4-7 for a summary of activities and documentation produced by the independent engineer.)

Careful monitoring of the testing phase is very helpful for lenders. Thanks to the participation of the independent engineer, they obtain certification from an independent party attesting that the operational management of the facility is proceeding in accordance with contractual standards and international good engineering safety standards and complies with environmental regulations. Conformity of these variables is a critical precondition to ensure operations can continue throughout the entire life of the project. On the other hand, periodic checks on maintenance reports means that the following aspects can be identified rapidly:

- Damage to machinery and systems due to bad management, defects in construction or assembly, lack of or inadequate maintenance
- Financial damage due to systems being down because of poor management or inadequate maintenance
- Catastrophic events and/or environmental catastrophes as a result of poor management of plant safety

Documents Required to Monitor the Testing Phase: The minimum documents that the independent engineer must have are the following:

- Supply contracts (EPC, civil works, subcontracts)
- Plans as built
- Operating manual

- Maintenance manual
- Safety plans
- Safety statistics
- List of operations staff and their qualifications
- Periodic maintenance reports prepared by management
- Historical report of alarms and breakdowns
- Historical report of main operating parameters concerning plant performance (to be defined according to type of production)
- Accounts for use of raw materials, fuels, chemicals, consumables, service fluids (water, gas, etc.)
- Production accounting records
- Accounts for disposal of by-products

Documents Produced: During the testing phase the independent engineer periodically produces a monitoring report that summarizes valuations of the variables indicated.

4.2.3.3   Validation of the Final Acceptance Certificate (FAC)

Validation of the FAC for the plant is carried out when periodic checks during the testing period have been completed. The bank's independent engineer participates in the final inspection of plant systems (which is an activity the site manager and sponsors' technical advisor are responsible for), analyzes historical operation and maintenance reports, analyzes results certified by the third-party organization, and confirms that the latter are correct in terms of meeting contractual requirements (Table 4-8).

TABLE 4-8   Summary of Assistance During the Plant Acceptance Phase—Validation of the FAC

Phase	Independent Engineer's Activities	Documents Required	Documentation Produced
Validation of the Final Acceptance Certificate	• Participation in final tests of the plant • Analysis of reports during the testing period	• Contracts (EPC contract, civil works, subcontracts) • Construction plans • Operating manual • Maintenance manual • Safety plans • Authorizations, permits, and concessions (required for the purpose) • Detailed schedule for the commissioning, start-up, acceptance test, and final testing phases • List of operations personnel and relevant qualifications • Maintenance reports • Historical records of alerts and breakdowns • Historical records of main operating parameters for plant system performance • Accounts for consumption of raw materials, fuels, chemicals, consumables, service fluids (water, natural gas, etc.) • Accounts for production • Accounts for disposal of by-products	Statement that standards established in the construction contract have been fully observed

During the final check the following aspects are considered:

- State of repair and maintenance of the works
- A checkup on the spare parts inventory and warehouse
- Any operating problems identified

Validation of the FAC is very important for banks. In fact, they will receive certification from their independent engineer that plant performance conforms with what was established contractually and included in the financial plan.

The validation of the FAC requires the same documents indicated for the test monitoring phase, and the result of this phase is a document attesting that plant performance fully conforms with the contractual terms.

4.2.4 Monitoring Operations Management

After the FAC has been issued, the plant is finally considered to be operative. From this moment onward the attention of participants in the deal (and among these, of course, the banks) is focused on checking that plant management and maintenance meet the standards defined in the operation and maintenance agreements. The task of the bank's independent engineer, therefore, is to carry out periodic inspections of plant systems and to analyze historical operation and maintenance reports prepared by management of the facility. The check made by the independent engineer concerns maintenance procedures, management of stocks and the spare parts warehouse, and management of safety systems (Table 4-9).

For banks, the advantage of the independent engineer's activities during the operations phase is that they obtain reports certifying the adequacy of maintenance

TABLE 4-9   Summary of the Operations Management Monitoring Phase

Phase	Independent Engineer's Activities	Documents Required	Documentation Produced
Operations management monitoring	• Make periodic checks of the plant • Check management of the materials and spare parts warehouse • Periodic check of validity of safety devices and equipment • Review historical maintenance reports issued by the manager	• As-built plans • Operating manual • Maintenance manual • Safety plans • Safety statistics • List of operations personnel, with relevant qualifications and costs • Maintenance reports • Historical records of alerts and breakdowns • Historical records of main operating parameters for plant system performance (to be defined based on type of production) • Warehouse accounts (materials and spare parts management) • Accounts for consumption of raw materials, fuels, chemicals, consumables, service fluids • Accounts for production • Accounts for disposal of by-products	Periodic monitoring reports

operations in terms of their being sufficient to ensure that the plant can continue to produce the cash flows indicated in the financial plan. Furthermore, the report means that any corrective action required can be taken (and the necessary costs quantified) if there are significant variances from predefined standards as a result of events listed in Section 4.2.3.2.

Documents Required for Periodic Monitoring: Periodic monitoring of operations requires availability of the following documentation:

- Plans as built
- Operating manual
- Maintenance manual
- Safety plans
- Safety statistics
- List of operations staff and their qualifications and cost
- Maintenance reports
- Historical report of alarms and breakdowns
- Historical report of main operating parameters concerning plant performance, depending on the type of facility realized
- Warehouse accounting records (materials and spare parts management)
- Accounts for use of raw materials, fuels, chemicals, consumables, service fluids
- Production accounting records
- Accounts for disposal of by-products

Documents Produced During the Operations Phase: During the operations phase, after each inspection the independent engineer prepares a periodic monitoring report that summarizes the valuations of technical variables indicated previously.

4.3   Role of Insurance Advisors and Insurance Companies in Project Finance Deals

Insurance advisors play an extremely important role in project finance deals. Seen from a bank's or an investor's standpoint, the insurance program established to mitigate risks can often make a difference in terms of a project's bankability and in certain cases may even be indispensable. The insurance program and bonding system are, in fact, an effective part of the security package, and the ability of insurance advisors involved in analyzing insurable aspects of the project is essential for the positive outcome of the project itself. The ability to place insurance coverage in domestic and international insurance and reinsurance markets is fundamental too.

Given that project finance is basically a credit problem and that credit risks absorb equity capital, banks have become particularly sensitive to risk issues. This would suggest that in the future insurance programs will play an even more important role in the various forms of the structured finance deal. In fact, they represent—together with project contracts—a way of allocating risks associated with a business venture in a more appropriate manner based on the type of project. Structuring a project finance deal presupposes that the negotiation of operational and financial contracts are coordinated with insurance contracts that, above all, take into account the effective capacity of the international insurance and reinsurance market to absorb at a reasonable cost the increased number of risks identified. Another important point is that structuring a deal includes the very important task of subdividing and allocating risks between all parties involved in the project. However, this allocation of risks must be based on an analysis of the effective possibility individual parties have to be able to purchase/negotiate appropriate insurance cover.

In this section, an attempt is made to identify how and to what extent banks use the insurance solution in deals, why they use it, and which parties banks work with to analyze insurance issues. Precise indications are also given as regards the more common types of insurance contracts structure.

4.3.1 Rationale for Using Insurance in Project Finance Deals

It must first be said that while insurance is an important contractual risk mitigation tool, quite often it is treated as an add-on as opposed to being a fully integrated part of project finance. This tends to reduce its effectiveness and credibility, and in quite a number of cases it can be an obstacle to the bankability of projects.

As mentioned in Chapter 3, the very essence of project finance is to understand and evaluate potential risks, both those directly linked to the venture and side effects of indirect risks that can have a negative impact on the project's performance. The skill of a structured finance advisor is to define all possible risks that may affect the successful outcome of a project by preparing a list of probabilities that the events concerned will indeed occur and their likely impact. After completing this initial exercise, the next step is to determine the optimum method to mitigate each risk wherever this is effectively possible. The result of this process should be to make the deal "bankable" and establish the cost of risks concerning the project.

Insurance should be seen as a risk mitigation tool on a par with other key contracts in the deal, such as an offtake (take-or-pay) contract. In effect take-or-pay contracts are considered very important because as they generate and stabilize cash flows that will service the debt. However, the validity of an offtake agreement in mitigating market risk is clearly a function of plant production, and this could be interrupted or blocked either directly or indirectly in many different ways and for various reasons.

So insurance is a tool that must be properly coordinated and linked to the project's contractual structure. Coordination also means taking into account the technical principles of insurance and the effective negotiating power of the individual parties involved. One of the main problems is to analyze the real capability of the insurance and reinsurance market to provide appropriate solutions. This analysis, which starts with the risk matrix (see Chapter 3) constructed by the financial advisor based on opinions given by the various independent advisors, must then be passed to insurance advisors specialized in nonrecourse or limited-recourse structured finance deals. It will then be the insurance advisors' task to check whether suitable insurance programs can be sourced in the markets. In fact any decision to invest or operate in a given market implies assuming a certain degree of risk, which can usually be evaluated in terms of market risk. However, further risk factors must be considered when a project concerns other than the domestic environment; political, legal, and business uncertainties of the country concerned play an important role. In many cases these uncertainties can be a critical factor as regards support (including financing) for the venture. If these additional risks can be minimized or controlled, frequently the project becomes not only bankable but also more attractive for lenders. So it is indispensable to use the services of an advisor who can evaluate the insurability of the types of risk identified for each specific project.

Because there isn't just one type of risk classification, certain factors or macro areas can instead be considered when defining insurability. Examples with definitions of those used more frequently in the insurance market follow.

- **Pure risks:** The characteristic feature of these risks is their unpredictability, inasmuch as they are linked to accidental causes, only generate losses, and normally include the majority of traditional insurable conditions.
- **Financial risks:** These risks can sometimes result in losses but can also produce gains. They are linked to financial planning and even though predictable can generate profits or losses.
- **Legal/contractual risks:** The source of these risks is contractual agreements. Damage will arise in the case of noncompliance with contractual terms and conditions, but an additional damage will occur where the contractual aspect generates a liability for the party involved.
- **Organizational risks:** These risks arise in cases where powers of decision and relevant responsibilities have not been properly allocated between parties involved in the project.
- **Strategic risks:** These risks are intimately linked to company strategies, as regards both determining relationships with other projects and development decisions.

4.3.2   When Should Insurance Products Be Used?

Insurance should be used when the SPV's cost of risk mitigation using insurance policies is less than the premium for risk expressed in interbank interest rates requested by banks if no coverage exists. Of course, there is a minimum acceptable level of risk allocation for lenders that will finance the deal, which must necessarily be taken into account when structuring the insurance plan. In the first instance it is the sponsors' financial advisor who must make this difficult evaluation. The advisor is responsible for ensuring that the deal is structured in the most favorable manner for the sponsors. Therefore, insurance coverage will be used only if it is the most cost-effective way to achieve the risk mitigation requested. In making this assessment the financial advisor must be assisted by the insurance advisor, who should check the terms and cost of insurability in the insurance markets. The greatest difficulty in making this evaluation is that information and documentation to be submitted to the insurance and/or reinsurance markets is incomplete at this stage. At the same time, the volatility of these markets in recent years, in terms of both pricing and risk underwriting capacity, has become a further issue to be carefully considered. So the financial advisor's position also has a significant effect as far as lenders at a later stage are concerned: The lower the nonfinancial costs incurred by the project and the wider the insurance coverage, the more likely it is that the project will be a success and so be able to service the debt. It is therefore vital that the financial model for the project be structured taking into account a realistic estimate for insurance costs both during the implementation stage of the project and after it becomes operative and for a sufficiently long period while at the same time attempting to make reasonably reliable forecasts as regards the viability of the insurance cost.

4.3.3 Areas Where the Insurance Advisor Is Involved

In the majority of cases, it is the bank acting as advisor and/or arranger of a deal that requests the services of an insurance advisor when structuring the security package. The request normally follows a standard outline, giving a description of the deal, indicating the requirements/previous experience necessary in order to formulate the proposal, requesting details of the project team/curricula of professionals involved, and summarizing the scope of work when the deal is being structured and as the project progresses. The scope of work to be performed by the advisor will of course follow the development of the project based on progress in structuring the financing. Following is an example of the scope of work for an insurance advisor as regards the construction and operation of a plant using a project finance approach.

4.3.3.1 Preliminary Insurance Report Phase

The preliminary insurance report and general risk plan cover the following points:

1. Analysis and comments concerning contractual documentation for the project as far as insurance coverage is concerned and also with reference to any environmental guarantees that must be given
2. Insurance identification, allocation, and possible protective mechanisms as regards major project risks; identification and comments on noninsurable risks
3. Analysis of insurance regulations and their implications for the project
4. Preparation of the contractual term sheet for the proposed insurance program
5. Gathering and analyzing information with reference to rendering the services, preparing, when requested, memoranda, notes, and documents for discussion
6. Assistance in preparing those sections of the financial documentation that directly or indirectly refer to the insurance coverage program
7. Summary of the contractual terms of the main policies, specifying risk covered, limits on claims, exclusion, tenor, and other major conditions in order to adequately safeguard the banks' interests, also bearing in mind market standards for similar projects

4.3.3.2 Final Insurance Report Phase—Construction Phase

The final insurance report is issued at the time of the financial close and in any event before the first drawdown of funds. This document will in fact constitute a condition precedent for disbursement. The report reviews the overall adequacy of the proposed insurance strategy, with a check on final documents that will be submitted to the insurance advisor. Specifically, it will pertain to:

- Checking the insurance program against the financial documentation for the project
- Indications of ratings for underwriting companies
- Checking the insurance documentation (letters and policies) against financial documentation for the project
- Preparing a final insurance report ascertaining that the insurance program stipulated is in conformity with indications in the preliminary due diligence report

4.3.3.3   Final Insurance Report Phase—Operations Phase

The final insurance report will be issued before start-up of each plant operation phase. Activities concerned will be as follows:

- Checking the insurance program for the operations phase against the financial documentation for the project
- Indications of ratings for underwriting companies
- Checking the insurance documentation (letters and policies) against financial documentation for the project
- Preparing a final insurance report ascertaining that the insurance program stipulated is in conformity with indications in the preliminary due diligence report

4.3.3.4   The Most Problematic Areas

In order to better understand the importance of the role of qualified insurance advisors, following is a brief outline of some of the major insurance-related problems encountered in project finance deals. Obviously these problems appear greater seen from the lenders' standpoint, whereas they seem acceptable to the project's sponsors. This difference in points of view can often cause a bottleneck in projects.

- The pricing of the insurance package from the very beginning of project planning (feasibility study), then for the project implementation phase and throughout the entire operating period required to repay the debt
- The soundness of insurers and/or, in certain cases, reinsurers and the possibility of knowing their rating for the entire tenor of the loan
- The possibility for insurers to cancel policies if certain conditions should arise (e.g., an unfavorable claims/premium ratio)
- The possibility that sponsors may not renew or might reduce the insurance program (reduction of claim limits or maximum sum insurable, elimination of certain guarantees, increasing exclusions)
- The possibility that reinsurance markets, and therefore insurance markets, reduce or even completely cancel underwriting capacity (for instance, this happened during the two years after 2001 as far as guarantees against terrorist attacks were concerned)
- The possibility that insurers claim they were not correctly informed of project risks when these were underwritten and that they therefore reduce or cancel the extent of contractual guarantees. This contingency means that intermediaries used must be able to satisfy market requests for further information.
- The possibility that sponsors do not pay for insurance coverage or fail to utilize any claim reimbursements to reconstruct the works
- The possibility that claim reimbursements are paid to parties that are not entitled to them and the latter do not make an appropriate use of them
- A further aspect to consider is that it isn't always possible for a single insurer to cover the entire insurance package. This means there will be different legal platforms for each insurable risk, and these must be interpreted and reconciled. It is to be hoped that with the help of specialized professional intermediaries, the current modus operandi of insurers will, in time, change radically. In fact, the situation could reach the point that a role of lead insurer will be recognized with a status similar to that of lead arrangers in syndicated loans. This would then create a single reference point for full insurance coverage.

4.3.4   Types of Conventional and Financial Insurance Products Available for Project Finance Deals

Following is a list of conventional insurance products and those providing financial insurance coverage used in project finance deals.

- **Nonpayment risks:** These are policies covering damage for the SPV due to political or business reasons. Such accords can concern both medium- and long-term receivables and also leasing contracts and documentary credits.
- **Investment risks:** These are policies that cover the SPV for risks of currency inconvertibility, expropriation without compensation, war, and other political upheavals.
- **Collateral deprivation risks:** These policies guarantee the SPV protection against risks of loss of assets and failure of the concession authority to repurchase the structure.
- **Contract frustration risks:** These policies cover wrongful calling of guarantees and failure to deliver parts or pieces that are functional for the implementation of the project.
- **Credit enhancement:** Insurance can be required to guarantee a credit from a third party and to make asset securitization transactions easier to set up.
- **Transfer risks:** These policies are very frequently used in international projects in countries where there is very little stability. They cover risks of failure to retransfer investments back home, to service the debt, or as regards payments for leasing contracts.
- **Political risks:** Coverage for political risks is a very specialized field of insurance (see Chapter 3). In fact, by definition in this case the project is implemented in a country marked by political uncertainty and instability or with a fragile legal structure. It is quite obvious that, compared to normal situations, the question of insuring an investment or the position of a lender becomes a much more significant insurance issue. Political risk insurance is available to cover various events, such as:

    - Confiscation, expropriation, and nationalization
    - Forced abandonment of the venture
    - Transfer risks
    - Host government's refusal to repurchase the structure
    - Unilateral rejection of contracts
    - War, civil war, internal revolts, acts of terrorism

There can, however, be parties interested in coverage for political risks even for projects implemented in countries that are not unstable. In effect, the need for political risk coverage is an issue not only when the project concerns emerging or developing countries; it can also depend on the specific features of a deal set up in industrialized countries in which a change in political situation or global economic trend could damage the venture concerned. The key point in this case is if the country has been given an acceptable credit rating by major international agencies in relation to the contractual terms proposed to lenders, particularly if the deal is not limited to banks or investors from a single country. Ratings for any one country can be revised and downgraded, sometimes even unexpectedly.

It is very difficult to fix parameters to determine if political risk coverage in one of its various forms is necessary or not. This is exemplified in the fact that today, for certain projects in several countries, even well-developed ones, insurance is required against acts of terrorism or revolts. A further example is based on the widespread conviction that a company in a given country cannot raise money at a lower interest rate than the corresponding sovereign debtor. Use of insurance-type risk mitigation that has the effect of achieving credit enhancement by removing part of the risks can easily lead to a lower cost of funding than would be required for the country risk in which the project is domiciled. In any event, insurance coverage can be very effective in this sense even in countries with very robust economies.

When speaking of coverage for conventional risks, a distinction must be made between the project implementation phase and the operations phase. While construction is under way, the most common forms of coverage used are as described next.

Transport Policy: This policy covers all materials, including plant, equipment, and spare parts, from the moment the material leaves the supplier's warehouse to be loaded onto the transport vehicle. Coverage continues during transit and includes any intermediate stocking, until such time as the material is delivered to the point where works are being executed.

Start-Up Delay Caused by Transport: This policy is closely linked to the previous one and is a solution for protecting the financial plan by guaranteeing the debt and project cash flow from damage or losses resulting from the transport policy. It provides coverage for loss or damage to project materials during transport that cause a delay in the date established for start-up of business operations.

Third-Party Liability and Accidental Pollution: This policy provides insurance coverage for claims against the insured made by third parties for physical damage, death, loss, or damage to third-party property, including unexpected and accidental pollution.

Employers' Third-Party Liability: This policy protects the insured from legal action that may be taken by their employees or by legal representatives or agents appointed by employees and, in general, by all contingent, temporary, or permanent workers following death or injury for which the insured is liable. Each party involved in the project must take out such a policy for its own employees working on the project.

All Assembly Risks Policy: The main purpose of this coverage is to guarantee project materials during stocking, construction, assembly, installation, commissioning, and testing up to the time ownership is transferred, enabling the parties involved to recover the repair or replacement costs for the goods damaged as a consequence of the event guaranteed. Coverage includes damage caused by preexisting works. The tenor of the policy will include the works period and all commissioning and testing activities up to the issuance of the provisional acceptance certificate and must also cover the extended maintenance period up to issue of the Final Acceptance Certificate.

Delay in Start-Up Due to Assembly: This covers financial losses caused by a delay in start-up of plant operations as a result of an interruption during the construction, assembly, installation, commissioning, or testing phases due to an event covered by the all assembly risks policy that gives rise to a loss of profits or payment of fixed costs.

All Site Equipment Risks Policy: This policy is usually part of the all assembly risks policy and covers equipment, machinery, and temporary buildings used on the construction site by the contractor, subcontractors, and suppliers during construction of the works.

Force Majeure: The aim of this policy is to protect the owner for interest due to lenders in the event of a delay in completing the project or if it is abandoned. This policy should supplement the policies covering all assembly risks and indirect damage caused by assembly in order to complete coverage by including events that don't cause material damage to project assets. The main events insured are:

- Fire and accessory guarantees occurring outside the place where works are being executed, including damage during transport during the construction phase of assets that will be supplied and in supplier plants
- Strikes/shutdowns
- Union disputes
- Changes in law after the policy becomes effective leading to additional costs for the project than those originally planned under the previously existing law

Furthermore, in general it covers all other causes not within the control of the owner, constructor, or other participants in the project.

Third-Party Liability of the Board of Directors and Executives: This policy protects administrators, directors, and statutory auditors of companies involved in the project from monetary consequences, expenses as a result of appointing legal representatives, and payment of damages for which the individuals concerned are personally exposed in the event of errors or omissions committed during the exercise of their functions.

In contrast, the following insurance policies concern the project operations phase.

All Risks—Material and Direct Damage: The aim of this policy is to guarantee the widest possible "all risks" coverage for all parties concerned. The main scope here is to indemnify the owner and lenders for material damage to plant components comprising the project, including spare parts and fuel, based on new replacement value. The operator must set up this policy, which should include the owner, lenders, and constructor as additional insured parties, at its own expense.

Indirect Damages (Business Interruption):   If an event of material damage concerning the project guaranteed by the all material and direct damage risk policy negatively affects the project's ability to generate a financial return, then the resulting financial loss will be covered by this policy.

General Third-Party Liability: This policy insures parties involved in operations for accidents and/or damage to assets and/or financial losses affecting third parties during plant operations, including third-party product liability. The operator must set up this policy, which should include the owner, lenders, and constructor as additional insured parties, at its own expense.

Employers' Third-Party Liability: This policy protects insured parties from legal action that may be taken against them by their employees or by legal representatives or agents appointed by employees and, in general, by all contingent, temporary, or permanent workers following death or injury for which the insured are liable. Each party involved in the project must take out such a policy for its own employees who are working on the project.

Third-Party Pollution Liability: The policy protects parties involved in plant operations for cases of third-party liability as regards accidents and/or damage to property and/or financial losses as a result of pollution (sudden or gradual) arising during operation of the plant. The operator must set up this policy, which should include the owner, lenders, and constructor as additional insured parties, at its own expense.

Third-Party Liability of the Board of Directors and Executives: This policy protects administrators, directors, and statutory auditors of companies involved in the project from monetary consequences, expenses as a result of appointing legal representatives, and payment of damages, for which the individuals concerned are personally exposed in the event of errors or omissions committed during the exercise of their functions.

4.3.4.1 Bonding

One of the fundamental factors in project finance is a complex structure of guarantees that must be set up in which the SPV is the recipient while contractors, suppliers, and operators are the committed parties, in order to safeguard down payments made based on stated performance and other contractual commitments. The strong need for guarantees is to a large extent covered by bank bonding, products that up to now have been those most widely used and appreciated by banks lending to the SPV. However, because sponsors today are finding it increasingly difficult to obtain this kind of guarantee, competition in the form of insurance guarantees is becoming more intense and effective.

The increasing use of guarantees provided by the insurance market is mainly due to the fact that bank guarantees affect the borrower's level of indebtedness and so indirectly lower credit capability, which in turn impacts general borrowing power. This negative effect associated with use of bank bonding has led to an ever-increasing use of insurance bonds. But one of the problems concerning use of insurance instead of banking bonds is that the insurance market, as a general rule, is unwilling to issue guarantees that are not linked to a specific negative event. However, insurance policies can be used to define precise conditions that would reasonably justify the enforcement of the guarantee.

Apart from the impossibility of issuing an insurance policy in the absence of a specific negative event, an insurance bonding offers some advantages for the borrower compared to bank bonding.

- Insurance doesn't have the negative effect of the borrower's level of indebtedness.
- An insurance guarantee doesn't affect bank credit facilities, which can therefore be reserved for other uses.
- An insurance guarantee can sometimes be less costly than bank bonding.
- Such a guarantee can be negotiated with insurers to develop a tailor-made guarantee that is more in line with the reasons for which it is provided to a third party and can only be enforced by the beneficiary based on specific events of default incurred by the party presenting the guarantee.

Apart from this, the two forms of guarantee (bank and insurance) are identical, except for that insurance bonding tends to define conditions determining the payment request in much more detail than in the case of bank bonding. When a beneficiary files a claim, the only difference from the bank bonding case is that in order to request payment the beneficiary must draw up a formal report referring to the specific event of default for its own insurer. This is done at the time the claim is submitted; if the claim is found to be unjustified, then the necessary procedures are activated to recover sums paid by the insurer. This means that beneficiaries must be more cautious at the time they file claims.

4.3.5   Integrated Insurance Solutions—Structure and Content

A recent trend seen in the insurance market for project finance policies is the diffusion of integrated insurance packages. Initially studied for the needs of the construction sector, integrated insurance programs are now used in many project finance applications. Integrated packages mean the SPV doesn't have to assemble an insurance package by shopping around for policies from a number of insurers, often based on different legal platforms.

Stipulating an integrated policy can offer some benefits for those participating in the deal, as summarized next.

- Coverage is based on a single policy structured around specific components relevant to the various aspects of risk and based on a single legal platform.
- Coverage concerns all aspects of project development (independent of the requested start date for the coverage); it is in place right from the start, with known costs, and is not subject to negative changes in the market for the entire development period.
- The integrated package has features not currently available in alternative schemes.
- Integration simplifies the negotiation process for the insurance package.
- Many difficulties concerning construction litigation (about 80%) can be avoided; this in turn substantially reduces the possibility of what can often be very lengthy legal disputes.
- The sales process is simplified considerably, and the need for additional documentation and negotiations is reduced to the minimum.
- Financing the deal is simpler and faster because banks don't need to worry about checking that all risks are adequately covered or the terms for the coverage concerned. An integrated scheme, in fact, provides a uniform, integrated insurance platform, with a single insurance underwriter who works with lender banks from the very start of the project.
- The cost is lower than the sum of costs that would be incurred by adopting a conventional system of coverage with no coordination of all parties involved, which also inevitably results in less pervasive coverage. All aspects of minimum premium and duplication of coverage are eliminated at the component level.
- Costs associated with coverage are defined and known right from the start.

Standard integrated insurance package often include the following policies.

- **Contractors "all risks":** This is the main insurance component during the construction period.
- **Financial risks:** This component refers to bonding as regards performance, bid/payment, maintenance/retention, and other business guarantees.
- **Advance loss of profits:** This is of particular interest for project finance, since in its basic form it guarantees debt service during the construction phase of the project.
- **Professional indemnity:** This coverage concerns legal and contractual liabilities arising from professional activities required by the project.
- **Public and product liability:** This coverage is for liabilities arising from damage to third-party goods or property or damage to persons as well as third-party financial losses.

- **All risks property damage:** This component provides complete coverage for risks of damage to the structure after completion certificates are issued, namely, risks not covered by the contractors "all risks" component. It provides a wide range of financial protection for structures that have been completed but not yet occupied, occupied by the developer, or leased to third parties.
- **Business interruption resulting from property damage:** This area covers risks arising because of direct material damage that negatively affects the project's ability to generate income; the sums insured include debt service, fixed costs, and, in certain cases, expected profits.

4.3.6   Classification of Insurance Underwriters

Having seen the main categories of insurance policies available on the market, it is now time to look at the parties who offer such products.

There are four main categories of insurance underwriter in the international insurance market as regards project finance deals. Of these, some only act as financial insurance companies, whereas others operate over a more conventional range of insurance coverage. However, in general terms the categories refer to either multilateral, commercial, group captive, or monoline underwriters. The characteristics of these types of underwriter are as follows.

- **Multilateral insurance underwriters:** As the name suggests, these are financial insurance companies controlled by multilateral development banks. The most famous is the Multilateral Insurance Guarantee Agency (MIGA) (see Section 6.4.1.1). This organization is part of the World Bank Group and operates on a nonprofit basis to provide insurance for project finance ventures based on guidelines established by the World Bank itself. The strength of multilateral agencies is that they can provide coverage not available on the market, especially as regards countries with very low income levels. They do, however, have weaknesses: It usually takes a very long time to obtain approval for an application, and the up-front fees requested tend to be rather high.
- **Commercial insurance underwriters:** This is the largest group and includes the numerous companies offering a complete range of conventional insurance services and that, in certain cases, also offer financial insurance products. In the field of structured finance the main underwriters are Lloyds of London and AIG. Lloyds covers the entire spectrum of insurance and is probably the best-known company in the structured finance segment because of its ability to take on very specific risks for each venture concerned. Its procedures are also faster and more flexible than other underwriters at the international level. AIG, on the other hand, has a very complete range of insurance products and is best known for its specialization in the political risk insurance field. AIG can also provide equity for projects either directly or through its own or third-party managed closed funds.
- **Group captive insurance underwriters:** These are insurers that operate only with companies that make subscription club payments to obtain their insurance services. The amount of coverage available is based on the level of contribution to the subscription club that each member is willing to make. Exporters Insurance Company of Bermuda is probably the best-known group captive under-

writer for trade and project finance deals; it provides a complete range of insurance coverage for export credit and political risks.

- **Monoline insurance underwriters:** Monoline insurers are global financial insurance companies, and financial insurance is their only line of business (hence the term *monoline*). These are specialized underwriters with a S&P, Moody's, and Fitch best rating that provide credit enhancement guarantees offering adequate support for project finance deals under certain conditions. In fact, they can issue lenders and certain other parties unconditional and irrevocable guarantees to pay capital and interest for debts at maturity. The fact that today compliance with capital coefficients is becoming a critical issue for banks in many countries has provided considerable impetus for insurance products focusing on increasing credit ratings for deals. A further factor for this growth has been the impressive development of asset-backed securitization transactions, which have many features in common with project finance deals.

CHAPTER ⋄ 5

Valuing the Project and Project Cash Flow Analysis

Introduction

In order to ascertain whether or not a project finance formula can be applied for a given initiative, an advisor builds a financial model. The technical/industrial, legal, and insurance considerations are compiled, collated, and translated into numbers. Some are obtained from objective data, and others are computed within the framework of a precise set of assumptions. The advisor's aim is to come up with estimates on cash flows, profit and loss, and the balance sheet, along with a series of ratios based on the same forecasts. The projected cash flow calculation is vital for valuing the ability of the initiative to generate enough cash to cover the debt service and to pay sponsors dividends that are in line with expected returns.

Any general discussion of financial modeling is always far too theoretical. This is why the present chapter is based on data relating to the Italy Water Case, which is included in this book together with the financial model provided on a CD ROM.

The financial model is a crucial component of any investment project that companies intend to develop with project finance. By analyzing technical, economic, financial, and fiscal variables, the sponsors' idea is carefully scrutinized to ascertain whether it is convenient from an economic and financial standpoint.

Setting up a financial model is also imperative when a company wants to bid on a public service concession or a BOT scheme. In PPP initiatives, the public administration very often provides public grants during the construction phase; in other situations, it periodically pays the concession holder an operating fee. In still other cases, the concession holder's only compensation comes from proceeds related to providing a public service or operating the facility in question.

Concessions are awarded on the basis of tenders; companies competing for concessions must specify the proposed tariff level for the service in question as part of the tender documentation. This tariff is the key factor considered by the concession authority in choosing who will win the bid among the competing firms. For this reason, a company vying for a BOT concession for a plant has to build a financial model in order to determine a tariff scheme ex ante that will adequately cover construction costs and/or plant operations as well as to guarantee a satisfactory return on the capital invested by lenders and sponsors.

For example, in the Italy Water Case, the sponsors have to make exact estimates of construction costs (construction, additional charges, and development costs) and operating expenses. These figures are used to establish the tariff to charge the public administration for every liter or gallon of treated water and the total public grants required to make the deal financially sustainable. Of course, this analysis must be as precise as possible. In fact, the company that wins the concession cannot charge a higher rate than that specified during the bidding process (unless extraordinary circumstances arise and only on approval of the public administration). If the company were to do so, it would be subject to penalties (normally quite costly), and the concession would be put up for public tender once again.

This chapter is structured as follows. In Section 5.1 we introduce the concepts of cash flow and the input variables needed to estimate it. Once operating cash flow is defined, Section 5.2 describes the uses for cash flow and clarifies how to find the optimal capital structure for the realization of the investment in question. This structure must be determined in terms of both its financial sustainability as well as its economic convenience for sponsors and lenders. Economic convenience (measured by the IRR for the project, sponsors, and lenders) is discussed in Section 5.2. Section 5.3 turns to financial viability and the cover ratios used to measure it. Section 5.4 concludes with a presentation of sensitivity and scenario analyses.

5.1   Analysis of Operating Cash Flows and Their Behavior in Different Project Life-Cycle Phases

Identifying the operative components of cash flow during the feasibility study is vital for various reasons.

1. Project finance is viable only in light of the size and volatility of flows generated by the initiative. In fact, it is with these operating cash flows that the project pays back its loans and pays out dividends to the SPV's shareholders.
2. Lenders can't count on sponsors to recover loans because limited-recourse clauses actually prevent any such action.

While these points represent two constants in initiatives where project finance logic is applied, building the financial model of the initiative can't be done without taking the peculiarities of this logic into consideration. The technological and operative aspects discussed in prior chapters are often very specific; because of this, the modeler needs to develop ad hoc models on a case-by-case basis.[1]

To design the financial model of a project finance initiative effectively, advisors must first identify the cash flow components of the project. In other words, they must

---

1. Consider two cases: building a section of a toll road and constructing a plant for incinerating waste or biomass and producing electric power. These projects have very little in common, beginning with two basic features: the end product and the input needed to obtain it.

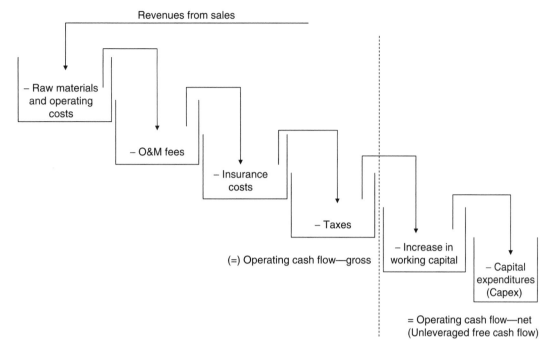

FIGURE 5-1   Waterfall Structure of the Operating Cash Flow

determine the difference between inflows and outflows *before* taking financial items into account (principal and interest payments, reserve account contributions, and dividends to sponsors). This difference is called the *operating cash flow*. See Figure 5-1, where the structure of cash flows is depicted as a "waterfall."

The operating cash flow takes on the configuration shown in Figure 5-1 in every year of the project's life. The waterfall structure shown in Figure 5-1 can be found in all corporate finance manuals labeled "unlevered free cash flow." However, this reflects the situation for ongoing concerns; for project finance things are different. In fact, Figure 5-1 shows that the weight of each category of items differs depending on the project's current phase. During construction, for example, the gross operating cash flow and the change in working capital items are zero, whereas the operating cash flow is sizeable (and negative). The explanation for this is that the Capex required for realizing the project is considerable.

Conversely, when operations are under way, Capex drops to zero. (In a project finance initiative, we have only one plant, which requires annual O&M costs only after construction is complete.) At the same time, we start to see positive flows from current operations as well as changes in working capital.

The fairly clear-cut separation between sustaining Capex and producing positive cash flows deriving from these capital expenditures is typical in project finance. For an ongoing concern that manages a portfolio of assets, the two types of cash flows can be found simultaneously in every year of the company's life.

The dynamic of operating cash flows can be illustrated as in Figure 5-2. The diagram shows the time from start-up to the end of the project life on the horizontal axis, and the value of cumulative net operating cash flows for each year of project life on the vertical axis. The first area (from time 0 to time *j* on the horizontal axis)

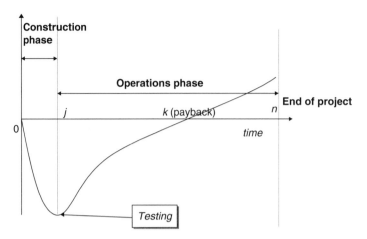

FIGURE 5-2   The Dynamic of Cumulative Operating Cash Flows for an Investment Project

represents the period in which the plant is under construction. From an economic standpoint, the project does not yet generate revenue, costs are incurred and paid over several years and are capitalized in the cost of construction. The income statement is "blank," and cost items refer solely to the SPV's balance sheet. From a financial viewpoint, during the construction phase the project can't generate revenue or cash inflows.[2]

The lack of revenues and inflows during the construction phase goes hand in hand with disbursements for Capex. Consequently, operating cash flows are negative, and cash requirements have to be covered by a pool of banks (brought together by the arranger) and by sponsors who begin to confer equity and subordinated debt. In the construction phase, therefore, lenders allow the project company to start drawing down the loans. At the same time, they count on the positive cash flows produced by the initiative, which will emerge only at some future point in time, i.e., at time *j* as shown in Figure 5-2.

After point *j,* the project moves into the operating phase and starts generating revenues (and therefore inflows) earmarked for paying operating costs. After the first few years in which operating cash flows are negative, the curve of cumulative flows reverses its course: Operating cash flows become positive, and this helps curtail the overall financial requirement.

On the graph, the distance between point *j* and point *k* (which represents the nondiscounted payback period on the investment) depends on the quantity of operating cash flows after construction is complete. More substantial flows correspond to a shorter *j–k* period, and vice versa.

As the project gradually moves forward in time toward year *n* (i.e., the last year of the project's life), the financing obtained from the sponsors is gradually paid back. In the final years of the project's life, revenues are earmarked solely for covering operating costs and financing increases in working capital, if required.

---

2. In certain situations, some plant tests can also result in output that can be sold on the market; however, this does not involve substantial flows. An example in the power sector is when plant testing produces electricity that can be sold to an offtaker.

As regards flows that emerge at the end of the project's life, two clarifications should be made. First, the amortization period for the loan granted to the project is shorter than the entire duration of the project life cycle. (In technical terms, this difference is called the *tail;* see also Section 5.2.2) In fact, circumstances may be such that at the end of its lifetime the project is not capable of generating the cash flows forecast by the arranger. This gives rise to the need for loan rescheduling, which would not be feasible if the duration of the operational phase and the amortization schedule were the same.

The second clarification has to do with the size and composition of the flow relating to the last year of operations. The terminal flow or terminal value (TV) depends on the type of investment project at hand. In cases of BOO concession schemes or investments in which the facility is legally owned by the SPV, the terminal value is either the payment the public administration makes at the end of the concession or the scrap value of the facilities and the current assets that are still on the SPV's books. Vice versa, with a BOT scheme, the concession authority already owns the plant and therefore makes no final payment to the SPV when the concession expires. The terminal flow in this case is negligible, amounting only to the liquidation of current assets.

5.1.1   Inputs for Calculating Cash Flows

From an operational standpoint, to come up with the estimate of expected future cash flows shown in Figure 5-1, first we have to define an extremely detailed set of input variables:

- The timing of the investment
- Initial investment costs
- The VAT dynamic
- Grants (when applicable), especially in PPP initiatives
- Analysis of sales revenues and purchasing costs
- Analysis of operating costs during the operating life of the project
- Fluctuations in working capital
- Taxes
- Macroeconomic variables

5.1.1.1   The Timing of the Investment

First, a thorough understanding of the time frame for the investment is needed. As an example, Table 5-1 shows the timing on the Italy Water Project, specifying the start and end dates, the duration of the concession, and the construction period (split into two work sections) and the operating period (again, divided into two work sections).

The length of the plant construction period impacts financial costs, especially interest and commitment fees, which accrue during construction. Legislation in many countries allows capitalization of these costs. In other words, they are not included in the profit and loss account and are added to plant costs and treated likewise during amortization. If the completion date set down in the contract is not respected, the contractor is subject to penalties, which must be factored into the financial model.

When the physical building of the plant is complete (i.e., mechanical completion), turnkey construction contracts usually call for successive testing and a commissioning period. If the plant has not achieved the preset minimum performance levels, the contractor is forced to pay the project company penalties proportional to the length

TABLE 5-1   Input Variables Underpinning the Timing on the Italy Water Project

Project Timing

Start date	Jan 1, 2006
End date	Dec 31, 2040
Concession duration	35.0 yr
Duration of entire operating phase	30.0 yr

Construction Period		**Operating Period**	
Total duration	5.0 yr	Start of operations	Jan 1, 2009
Section 1		1st Supply Level	
Start date	Jan 1, 2006	Start date	Jan 1, 2009
End date	Dec 31, 2008	End date	Dec 31, 2010
Duration of Section 1	3.0 yr	Duration	2.00 yr
Section 2		2nd Supply Level	
Start date	Jan 1, 2006	Start date	Jan 1, 2011
End date	Dec 31, 2010	End date	Dec 31, 2040
Total duration	5.0 yr	Duration	30.00 yr

of the delay in reaching these levels. The delay liquidated damages are also specified in the construction contract and must be included in the model. In fact, it is actually by analyzing the model that the sum of these damages is calculated; this figure is then incorporated into the construction contract. The model quantifies these penalties, which are normally expressed as a percentage of the contract value per week of delay with a maximum value, or cap, on these damages. This is computed on the basis of costs incurred every week that plant completion is postponed, naturally including financial charges.

Once minimal performance levels have been verified, the plant is tested to ascertain guaranteed levels (which, of course, are higher than minimum levels) corresponding to plant design. In some cases, the two types of testing are run simultaneously.

Table 5-2 shows the levels of water supplied by the Italy Water plant and the amount of power generated by the hydroelectric plants.

TABLE 5-2   Technical Inputs for the Italy Water Project

Nonpotable water supplied prior	209 Mln mc/yr	Energy produced at full capacity	106.111 GWh/yr
Potable water supplied prior	123 Mln mc/yr	Capacity in start-up phase	80%
1st Supply Level			
Nonpotable water: Supplementary volume supplied	30 Mln mc/yr		
Potable water: Supplementary volume supplied	90 Mln mc/yr		
2nd Supply level			
Nonpotable water: Supplementary volume supplied	40 Mln mc/yr		
Potable water: Supplementary volume supplied	170 Mln mc/yr		
Total water supplied at full capacity			
Nonpotable water	249 Mln mc/yr		
Potable water	293 Mln mc/yr		

Establishing a plant's functional life span depends on the projections relating to its technical or economic obsolescence. Generally, this time frame runs from 15 to 25 years. It should be noted that as regards to BOT or BOOT concession schemes, normally the period used in the relative models does not exceed the length of the contract itself. In fact, when the works in these cases are completed, the plant is transferred back to the public administration free of charge; therefore the concession holder no longer serves any useful purpose. The time horizon taken into consideration has a major impact on IRR (see Section 5.2.5). The longer the time period, the better the IRR, because once the debt has been completely paid off, in the final years of the project's life the venture produces cash flows earmarked exclusively for sponsors.

5.1.1.2 Initial Investment Cost

The price of the construction contract is only one of the components of the overall investment, and it is the simplest to quantify. In fact, this figure is specified in the turnkey construction contract. Seeing that this contract is normally signed only when the project development phase is complete, it is not unusual for the price to be changed in the interim. Along with the cost of the turnkey contract, other values that need to be estimated for the financial model are the following:

- Cost of purchasing the land where the facility will be built
- Owners' costs
- Development costs

In addition to these factors, which we can call the project's direct investments, the following indirect investments must also be taken into account:

- VAT on the value of direct investments
- The cost of guarantees and insurance policies (see Chapter 4)
- Capitalized interest

Figure 5-3 shows the logic behind the capital budgeting of the initial investment cost of a project finance initiative.

While the cost of plant construction (real estate and plant facilities) is not usually difficult to estimate, it is more complicated to identify all the cost items associated with plant construction. Usually all the outlay that derives from investments linked to building the plant are categorized under the heading "Owners' Costs," for example, the cost of excavating the land before beginning construction or of building access roads to the facility.

Development costs, in contrast, are related directly to realizing a project finance initiative. As we know, this form of financing is particularly onerous due to the high number of consultants needed for project development. The fees paid to these professionals are the most sizeable component of this cost category.

Beyond computing the absolute value of costs, it is also necessary to clarify the timing for each investment cost. For example, the construction contract normally stipulates that payments will be made when specific milestones are reached. These preset deadlines ensure that the construction plan is respected and verified. Clearly, the higher the concentration of costs in initial construction phases, the higher the interest that the project company will have to pay during the construction phase. Deferred installments can lead to significant benefits for the economy of the project.

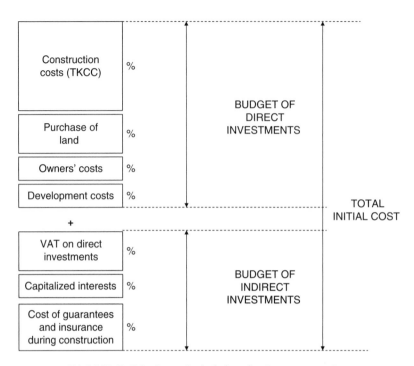

FIGURE 5-3   Items Included in the Construction Cost

In some cases, EPC contracts include terms for deferred or advanced payments that impact the project's financial needs. In fact, the following payment clauses are commonly found.

- **Advance payment**, which is usually 10% of the contract value. This is paid by the SPV to the contractor, who invoices this amount with later milestones.
- **Retention payment**, normally 5% of the contract value. The SPV withholds this sum from each milestone payment and makes it available only when the plant is successfully tested.
- **Final settlement**, which is a variable percentage of the contract value. This is paid by the SPV only when the testing phase is complete.

These advanced and/or deferred terms of payment may be included in an EPC contract, but they must be taken into account in the financial model when the cash flow analysis during the construction period is run. Table 5-3 shows the Capex figures on the Italy Water Project.

5.1.1.3   Vat—Value-Added Tax

As mentioned in the previous section, one of the factors the financial model has to estimate in order to quantify the initial investments of a project is VAT, which is an indirect investment. Since the direct investment items are quantified, the VAT rate that applies to these costs must also be determined. In many countries, refunds to taxpayers are often delayed. As a result, the reimbursement for VAT paid by the SPV during the construction period normally takes time. This is financed with a specific loan (VAT facility; see Section 6.9.4), the cost of which clearly impacts the project.

TABLE 5-3   Capex on the Italy Water Project

1st Section		
Capex 1	260,687 keuro	22.3%
Doubling YYYY	134,551 keuro	11.5%
Potable water system YYYY	143,332 keuro	12.3%
Design and other costs	64,445 keuro	5.5%
Expropriation	11,653 keuro	1.0%
TOTAL CAPEX 1st Section	**614,668 keuro**	**52.5%**
2nd Section		
Capex 2	80,417	6.9%
Doubling XXXX	91,414 keuro	7.8%
Potable water system XXXX	259,548 keuro	22.2%
Design and other costs	51,352 keuro	4.4%
Expropriation	23,337 keuro	2.0%
TOTAL CAPEX 2nd Section	**506,068 keuro**	**43.3%**
Total Capex	**1,120,736 keuro**	**95.8%**
Life-cycle cost	49,127 keuro	4.2%
Total Investment	**1,169,863 keuro**	**100.0%**

During the first year of construction, the project company will incur investment costs subject to VAT. Since the project company is not yet operational from a commercial standpoint, it cannot issue invoices and, consequently, collect VAT. For this reason, any VAT payments the SPV makes to suppliers are a credit toward the VAT Authority, and the SPV has to finance these expenditures until the VAT Office reimburses them or until VAT credits are offset by VAT debts from invoices to SPV customers.

The legislation of various countries allows for different options regarding VAT, and these alternatives impact the financial model in various ways.

1. A sponsor (holding at least 51% shares), which is normally in a position of debt toward the VAT Office due to its business, can offset the VAT credit of the controlled company on its own tax return. The SPV will have its VAT debt paid by the parent company, which will receive compensation in the form of a lower payment to the VAT Office when taxes fall due. Whenever possible, this is the optimal solution, since the SPV would not have to pay interest expenses to service the VAT facility.
2. When the VAT statement is compiled, the SPV requests immediate reimbursement for VAT credit, offering a suitable guarantee (for example, a letter of credit). Generally, this option implies that once the VAT reimbursement is requested, it would no longer be possible at a later date to compensate this credit with VAT debts that may arise in the interim (and that normally emerge when the company is operational).
3. The third option involves offsetting the SPV's VAT credits with VAT debts during the operating phase.

Some laws allow companies to compensate VAT credits with other debts toward certain public bodies. For example, in certain cases VAT debts collected on public grants awarded to the SPV can be deducted from VAT credits accrued during construction. In other situations, compensation can also be made between VAT and corporate income tax.

5.1.1.4   Public Grants

In PPP projects, public grants represent a key source of financing for building and operating facilities that serve the needs of the public. Legislation in several countries can establish the fee the concession authority pays to the concession holder/SPV as the concession price for partial funding of the project in question. The payment of this sum can be made contingent on milestones (in exchange for a guarantee provided by the shareholders of the concession holder/SPV for the amounts collected). Payment can also be made at the end of the construction phase, after plant testing, or according to other parameters based on the actual availability of funds.[3]

The different terms of payment are reflected in the project's financial model in various ways.

- **Testing grant:** When the public funding earmarked for a project is paid out at the end of the construction period, provisions are made for bridge financing, which is reimbursed in a bullet payment from the funds collected.
- **Milestone grant:** Here, loans are used on the basis of the milestones achieved, net of the portion of the grant received and the quota of equity conferred. The SPV's cash flows can be used to pay the contractor only after grants are collected during the construction phase.[4] In these cases, the shareholders and the SPV are often called on to provide bank guarantees or insurance coverage to the concession authority for reimbursement of the funds received. Fees incurred for this letter of credit, which has the same implicit risk as senior debt, are also included when the economic/financial plan is drawn up.

In the Italy Water Case, the public grant is calculated as a percentage of construction costs and paid out during the construction phase for each work section (see Table 5-4).

5.1.1.5   Analysis of the Sales Contract, the Supply Contract, and Operating Expenses

When the financial model is being built, contracts pertaining to the sale of the product, the supply of raw materials, and maintenance and operations are still in the drafting stage.

In terms of financial models, it is simple to verify how effective risk allocation can improve the inherent quality of a project. See Figure 5-4, where operating cash flows are illustrated along with the major forms of coverage for project risks.

When the advisor sets up the financial model and contract terms are not yet definitive, standard prices and conditions applied by the market for similar initiatives are included in the calculations. In the Italy Water case, the concession holder has to sign off taking contracts with a water supplier who buys the potable water and then

---

3. Some laws may oblige the concession authority to divest assets in order to source public grants. Therefore, the availability of funds for grants depends on the timing of the divestitures and the ability of the concession authority to carry out the public procedures required to sell off the assets in question.

4. When the percentage of grants is sizeable with respect to the project requirements, banks can issue a standby facility on a revolving basis that covers temporary lack of liquidity due to delays in grant disbursement by the concession authority.

TABLE 5-4   Payment of Public Grants in the Italy Water Case

	Year/Progr.							
	2006	2006	2007	2008	2009	2010	2011	2012
	1	2	3	4	5	6	7	8
Public Installments	**616,405**							
1st Section (keuro)	72,376	240,028	296,938	5,327	—	—	—	—
TOTAL CAPEX 1st Section	55%	55%	55%	55%	55%	55%	55%	55%
GRANT 1st Section (keuro)	**39,807**	**132,015**	**163,316**	**2,930**	—	—	—	—
2nd Section (keuro)	6,277	7,099	118,686	150,490	151,703	71,813	—	—
TOTAL CAPEX 2nd Section	55%	55%	55%	55%	55%	55%	55%	55%
GRANT 2nd Section (keuro)	**3,452**	**3,904**	**65,277**	**82,770**	**83,437**	**39,497**	—	—
Total Grants (keuro)	**43,259**	**135,920**	**228,593**	**85,699**	**83,437**	**39,497**	—	—

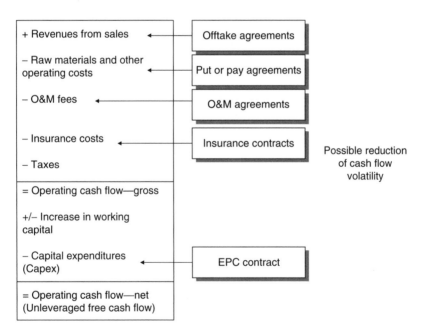

FIGURE 5-4   Operating Cash Flows and Contractual Agreements

pipes it through a water supply network to end users. The concession holder commits to delivering a certain quantity of water at preset contract prices, which are readjusted annually on the basis of prices indices (production or consumption). A similar situation applies for untreated water, which is sold to agricultural consortia on the basis of variable-length contracts with preset prices. Moreover, Italy Water will also

TABLE 5-5   Inputs Used to Quantify Revenues for the Italy Water Case

REVENUES FROM WATER	
Annual escalation	2.0%
REVENUES FROM POTABLE WATER	
Potable water already supplied (Min mc/yr)	123
Tariff Dec. 31, 2009 (Euro/000mc)	225.2
Additional potable water at full capacity (Min mc/yr)	170
Tariff Dec. 31, 2009 (Euro/000mc)	337.8
REVENUES FROM NONPOTABLE WATER	
Nonpotable water already supplied (Min mc/yr)	209
Tariff Dec. 31, 2009 (Euro/000mc)	0.0
Additional nonpotable water at full capacity (Min mc/yr)	40
Tariff Dec. 31, 2009 (Euro/000mc)	270.3
VAT	10%
REVENUES FROM POWER	
Annual escalation	1.5%
Tariff—flowing water	
Power at capacity (base calculation) (GWh/yr)	32.8
Tariff Dec. 31, 2009 (Euro (000)/GWh)	57
Tariff Dec. 31, 2009 (Euro (000)/GWh)	62
Tariff 25% F4	
Power at capacity (base calculation) (GWh/yr)	73.3
Tariff Dec. 31, 2009 (Euro (000)/GWh)	63
Tariff Dec. 31, 2009 (Euro (000)/GWh)	69
Green Certificate Tariff	
Power at capacity (base calculation) (GWh/yr)	106.1
Green Certificate Tariff (Dec. 31, 2009) (Euro (000)/GWh)	116
VAT	20%

be able to use the water for power production, which can be sold on the basis of long-term take-or-pay contracts with utilities operating in the power sector. In this regard, see the inputs at the basis of sales revenues on water and energy used for the Italy Water Case (Table 5-5).

An important feature in fixed-price contracts is the escalation mechanism that updates prices on the basis of inflation. Clearly, the project is subject to risk associated with the different formulae for cost and revenue indexation (which the model must be able to identify). Forecasts adopted in the Italy Water model index revenues on the sale of water to a cautious estimate of a 2% annual rate; revenues from power are escalated at 1.5% annually. The importance of these predictions derives from the fact that the concessions in question last a considerable length of time, and the multiplying effect of a high inflation rate, in the long run, could lead to an overestimation of the project's profitability potential.

As regards determining annual cost items, this process depends to a great extent on the choice of the plant operator. This may be an external company or the SPV itself (though less often). While in the latter case the project company will bear all types of costs inherent to plant operations and maintenance, in the former situation the key cost item for the project company is the O&M fee paid to the operator. At most, there may also be additional cost items such as insurance premiums and other costs for other, less important input used in the process.

However, it's rare that a definitive agreement already exists with the future operator when a project is initially being structured. So, from a financial modeling standpoint, it's best to detail all applicable categories of operating and maintenance costs, irrespective of the fact that some of these will be absorbed in the total remuneration paid to the third-party operator in the form of an O&M fee.

As regards the Italy Water Case, Tables 5-6, 5-7, and 5-8 respectively show inputs for estimating fixed costs, variable costs, and payments made to the public administration that assigns the concession.

A dummy item, general plant expenses, is often used. Normally calculated as a percentage of budgeted costs, it's slotted into the model under both annual costs and investment costs. This item, which is usually no more than 5% of the cost breakdown, serves as a "cushion" that can absorb small changes in cost or additional costs, when applicable.

TABLE 5-6   Inputs for Estimating Annual Fixed Costs for the Italy Water Case

		VAT
WATER		
1. Personnel costs		
Employees	130	0%
Annual cost (Euro (000))	60.48	
2. Ordinary maintenance (Euro (000))	5,355	20%
Percentage of investment	0.50%	
3. Other services (Euro (000))	2,066	20%
4. General plant expenses (Euro (000))	1,379	20%
Percentage of operating and personnel costs	5%	
POWER		
1. Operating cost of power plants (Euro (000))	1,350	20%

TABLE 5-7   Inputs for Calculating Annual Variable Costs for the Italy Water Case

		VAT
Water purification equipment		
Annual cost of potable water (mc) (Euro/000mc)	60	20%

TABLE 5-8   Costs Related to Annual Payments to the Public Administration for the Italy Water Case

Operating fee for existing aqueduct (euro)	2.5 million
Operating fee for the new aqueduct (euro)	5 million
Operating fee for exploitation of hydroelectric power (euro)	5 million

By detailing variable costs as a function of the quantity of raw material utilized, we can accurately estimate these costs as the level of operations of the plant varies. As a result, the model gives us correct values when simulating downside scenarios.

Lastly, in the case of public concessions, the concession authority may require that the concession holder pay an annual concession fee in exchange for the right to the economic exploitation of the plant. In the Italy Water Case, this fee is computed as shown in Table 5-8.

These fees are subject to annual revision; VAT is calculated for these amounts as a set percentage.

5.1.1.6   Trends in Working Capital

In light of estimates on operating costs and revenues, the financial model has to posit assumptions on inputs relating to the average collection period and the average payment period. These delays, in fact, have the effect of differentiating economic margins (computed on an accrual basis) from actual cash flows (computed on a cash basis).

Depending on the sign, variations in working capital represent an outlay or a source of cash. So these changes have to be estimated among the variables that determine operating cash flow. Nonetheless, we should remember that in numerous project finance initiatives, the weight of investments in working capital is not particularly heavy. In the power sector, for instance, there are no investments in inventories of finished products, and accounts receivable are fairly negligible given that big offtakers normally pay on a monthly basis. Another example is the transportation sector, where accounts receivable are even less relevant, since retail consumers pay for the service in cash. In PPP projects, the working capital requirement is linked to the average payment period of the public administration that granted the concession. However, if the contracts with various service providers include provisions for a perfect pass-through, working capital consists solely of paying the SPV's insurance policies. Therefore, this figure is very near zero.

In the Italy Water Case, the estimate of the average collection and payment periods is summed up in Table 5-9.

5.1.1.7   Taxes

The financial modeler has to collect a solid body of knowledge on the peculiarities of the various taxes that apply to the initiative. Table 5-10 shows the tax structure of the

TABLE 5-9   Variables Used for Estimating Working Capital for the Italy Water Case

	Term
Receivables	
Water revenues	60 days
Energy revenues	60 days
Existing water system	60 days
Payables	
Water opex (no personnel)	60 days
Authority fee	60 days
Energy opex	60 days

TABLE 5-10   Fiscal Variables in the Italy Water Case

TAXES	
IRES rate	33.00%
IRAP rate	4.25%
Substitute tax	0.25%

Italy Water Case. In Italy, IRES is the corporate income tax and IRAP is the regional tax on productive activities.

One of the key variables that must be studied to optimize the fiscal burden is the amortization policy for the plant. Tax law in various countries allows a certain margin of flexibility, which should be adequately exploited (length of the amortization period, accelerated amortization).

Depending on the type of project, there are various kinds of taxes to consider, such as the carbon tax, excises on natural gas, property taxes, and waste disposal taxes. For this reason, when operating in a given industrial sector it is advisable to get information from sponsors' management or other companies that work in the sector in question. The model also has to be able to identify accurately when taxes fall due. Consider the dynamic of advances and payments relating to various taxes; this can drastically alter the cash flows of a given operating period.

5.1.1.8   Macroeconomic Variables

Previously we pointed out that forecasting the inflation rate is vital for many projects. The structure of contracts tends to sterilize the impact of inflation on the project's profitability as far as possible. Nonetheless, is it nearly always inevitable that the project presents a certain level of risk in terms of variations in the rate of inflation.

Interest rate coverage policies usually tend to convert a significant portion of financing to a fixed rate. This practice itself is not without risks, in as much as the interest rate will remain unchanged even when benchmark market rates drop drastically; in other words, the weight of the fixed component of project costs increases. The other key macroeconomic variable is the level of and fluctuation in the exchange rate of the national currency with respect to one or more foreign currencies. This becomes significant when a part of the investments, costs, or revenues are stated in foreign currency.

The model should include macroeconomic forecasts developed by reputable research agencies. Variables typically studied are the expected trend in the interest rate, estimates of the national inflation rate, and, when applicable, forecasts of specific sector indices that impact costs and revenues of the project company. One should keep in mind that some classes of costs or revenues have different inflation dynamics. Consider, for example, price trends in crude oil with respect to employee wages. As far as possible, relevant inflation scenarios should be analyzed.

Another challenge for the advisor is deciding whether or not to define a correlation among macroeconomic variables. In this case, the decision centers on whether the model should automatically compute variations in interest rates given a certain change in the rate of inflation, based on an appropriate correlation coefficient.

5.2   Defining the Optimal Capital Structure for the Deal

Quantifying operating cash flows is crucial for defining the second key aspect of project finance initiatives: the optimal mix of debt and equity. In fact, financial models work on the basis of a logical framework that takes trends in operating cash flows as input; flows corresponding to financial items make up the other input. In the construction phase, such items consist of the use of bank loans, bond issues, and sponsor equity, and in the operations phase, reimbursement of the principal and interest to lenders and payment of dividends to the SPV's shareholders.

In Figure 5-5, the two key factors for setting up the optimal capital structure lie at the center of the diagram. Operating cash flow during the operating life represents cash available for debt service, while the financial structure and assumptions regarding loan repayment define the cash requirement.

During the construction phase the operating cash flow is negative. This results in a financial requirement to be covered with both share capital from sponsors and, more importantly, bank loans organized by the arranger. Conversely, during the postconstruction phase, operating cash flow becomes positive and has to be able to support the debt service (principal and interest), the obligation to create and maintain reserve accounts, and reimbursement on capital invested by sponsors. As a precautionary measure, flows relating to the debt service and deposits in a reserve account are subtracted from operating cash flow. If residual flows remain, they are made available to sponsors as dividends. See Figure 5-6.

As regards the reserve account, we should point out that this is established and maintained for the entire duration of the financing. The amount of funds to set aside in this account can be determined in various ways. However, a rather common practice is to decide on an account balance by applying the following formula:

$$B = DS \times n$$

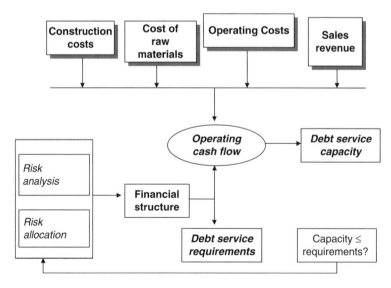

FIGURE 5-5   Process for Defining a Project's Capital Structure

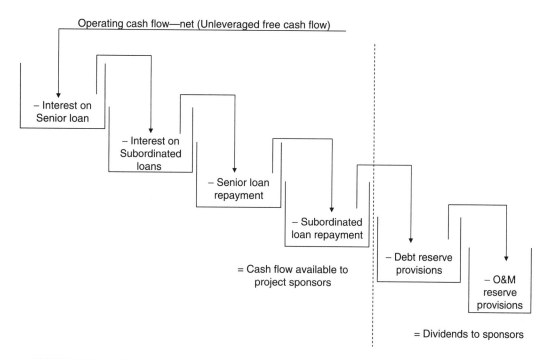

FIGURE 5-6   Waterfall Structure of the Possible Uses of Operating Cash Flows During Operations

where *B* is the minimum required balance, DS is the monthly debt service, and *n* is the number of months of debt service that the reserve account must cover. Naturally, over the years of operations of the initiative, the balance at any given moment could exceed the requirement expressed by the formula. In such a case, the cash can be freely withdrawn from the reserve account and earmarked for paying dividends to SPV shareholders.

In some projects, there may be a request for additional funds to be set aside in an O&M reserve account. For projects that require several rounds of extraordinary maintenance during their operating life cycle (also known as life-cycle costs), portions of cash flows available to shareholders are channeled into this account. In this way, lenders safeguard against behavior by the SPV that may be less than optimal by requesting that cash not be distributed so that the liquidity needed to carry out maintenance rounds is on hand when needed.

From the standpoint of the financial modeler, in order to complete Table 5-6, assumptions relating to the following points must be clarified:

1. *Equity:* the amount and the timing of contributions
2. *Senior debt:* the amount requested from lenders and the stipulated terms of repayment
3. *VAT facility:* the amount requested and terms of reimbursement
4. *Stand-by facility:* the amount requested and terms of reimbursement

The four sets of information are analyzed next.

5.2.1   Equity

Sponsors usually want to confer as little equity as possible and as late as possible. In the first version of the model, the financial advisor normally incorporates the sponsors' preliminary suggestions, allowing for possible changes when works are in progress. Establishing the debt/equity ratio is grounded in the following:

1. The degree of economic soundness of the project
2. The level of risk lenders are willing to accept
3. Precedents on the domestic or international financial market

Now we examine these factors individually.

1. The model's economic forecasts tend to worsen as the debt level rises. For this reason, modelers must verify the break-even point for indebtedness; once this point is exceeded, the initiative no longer has the credentials of economic viability needed to attract lenders.
2. The minimum level of economic viability that lenders demand depends, in turn, on their perception of the degree of risk. For example, potential investors may not believe that the contract structure surrounding an initiative affords adequate protection for the SPV. Or the contractual counterparties of the SPV or the sponsors themselves may not be considered entirely reliable in terms of respecting their contract obligations in the long run (performance guarantees, long-term supply, long-term purchase). In these cases, lenders will want to verify that the project has a more-than-satisfactory level of profitability in order to confront possible downside scenarios.
3. Once financing is underwritten by one or a few arrangers, it must then be presented to the market in order to be "resold" to participating banks or bond investors. The banks that are called on to study the economic convenience in underwriting the financing compare the features of the project with similar initiatives already introduced on the domestic market (or, when there are no projects of reference, on major foreign markets). Substantial differences with respect to existing projects normally elicit a cold reaction from banks, unless these disparities are justified by unique project characteristics that the arrangers will need to market effectively. This will be even more difficult if there is more than one factor deemed "aggressive" in a financing proposal, for instance, when a high debt/equity ratio is combined with long-term financing and margins lower than the market average.[5]

Sponsors have to inform the financial modeler as to the profit level they intend to achieve in order to ascertain that it can be reached. As we will see in Section 5.2.5, sponsors usually state their expectations in terms of internal rate of return (IRR).

---

5. There is a trade-off, which may also emerge irrespective of the project's level of profitability. Consider the fact that it's normal to find a certain degree of constructive "tension" in a bank on the appropriate level of financing parameters among the people who serve as arrangers (i.e., focused on valuing cash flows) and those who resell financing to participating banks (the so-called syndication desk), not to mention the credit committees themselves. On the other hand, there have been cases in which syndication transactions have failed and the arranger banks subsequently had to keep much more than the expected share of financing on their books. In these cases, sponsors suffer considerable damage to their image.

It's also worthwhile to include calculations of alternative profitability parameters in the model. If possible, these should be expressed in absolute terms as well and not as percentages, such as the net present value (NPV) or the payback period.[6]

It is also essential to define the timing of equity contributions. Capital can be conferred at the same time as drawdowns (pro quota) or before or after. This means that the first 100 euro of costs incurred by the project company will be financed in part with equity and in part with debt or only with equity or only with debt. Naturally, it is more convenient for sponsors to postpone equity payments, all other conditions being equal. For lenders the problem lies almost entirely in assessing the creditworthiness and the reliability of the SPV's shareholders.[7] On the other hand, equity invested in the project is seen by lenders as a sign of a strong sponsor commitment.

Sponsors enjoy some degree of freedom in choosing how to confer their share of equity. Along with pure equity, within certain limits they can normally make payments through subordinate loans (i.e., subordinate to the entire repayment of the senior debt) that involve an improvement in payout.

5.2.2 Senior Debt

The senior debt can be broken down into several parts (tranches or facilities), depending on the unique requirements and characteristics of the project. In the start-up phase of the model, all that needs to be considered is a loan to cover VAT payments (the VAT facility), one to cover design and construction costs, VAT excluded (base facility), and a stand-by facility to cover possible project cost increases. The technical details of these facilities are discussed in Section 6.9. As for the financial model, the analyst must provide a series of inputs to feed into it. The inputs for the base facility of the Italy Water Case are shown in Table 5-11.

The characteristics of the loan in terms of margins, tenor, minimum acceptable ratios, and so forth reflect the capacity to pay back project financing and the requests of the banks that may be interested in supporting the deal in a later, syndication phase.

A benchmark used to compute the tenor of financing for public concessions is the *tail*: the time remaining from loan maturity to the expiry date of the concession. A longer tail enables banks to mitigate the risk linked to the fact that during the life of the concession, obstacles that may come up could preclude the chance to refinance the outstanding debt. At the end of the concession, in fact, the concession holder no longer has the right to exploit the plant in question economically.

---

6. This allows us to avoid evaluating a project solely on the basis of a single index value, which can often lead to contradictory conclusions. There are, in fact, mathematical problems associated with profitability indices. (Simply consider that in some situations IRR gives more than one solution.) All of this aside, shareholders can be attracted by an exponential IRR growth in circumstances in which financial leverage is heavily used. They may even reach the point of losing sight of the convenience of investing a considerable portion of their available funds (even at the cost of curtailing the percentage return) when they have no other investment opportunities that are as lucrative (at the same level of risk, of course).

7. The risk is ending up with a partially built plant, with sources of financing dried up, and with shareholders who are no longer willing to confer equity. There may even be a negative economic scenario, which doesn't facilitate the task of finding new sponsors.

TABLE 5-11   Inputs for Estimating Senior Debt for the
Italy Water Case

SENIOR FACILITY	
Amount conferred (Euro (000))	361,720
Average tenor (years)	14.83
AVAILABILITY PERIOD	
First disbursement	Jan. 1, 2006
Last disbursement	Dec. 31, 2011
Duration (years)	6
PAYBACK PERIOD	
First repayment	Dec. 31, 2012
Last repayment	Dec. 31, 2026
Tenor (years)	15
Interest Expenses	
Base rate	4.50%
Margin	1.50%
Composite Rate	6.00%
Financial Fees	
Commitment fee	0.70%
Underwriting fees	1.00%

The interest rate consists of a benchmark rate (Libor or Euribor) plus a spread, which normally varies depending on the project phase. Financing is usually initiated with a variable rate but is covered for the most part by interest rate risk hedging contracts, such as swaps, collars, or interest rate options. Such agreements must be included in the financial model.

The dynamic of the debt principal repayment follows the evolution of the SPV's capacity to generate cash flows. This is initially weak—weighed down by plants that are not yet fully operational and by the increase in working capital—but growing stronger in the first years of operation. This growth is cut short abruptly at some point when taxes begin to increase once the plants are completely amortized. Finally, flows pick up again because progressive repayment of the debt results in fewer interest expenses. In the case of the Italy Water Project, the schedule repayment for the senior debt and the value of the annual debt service cover ratio (ADSCR; see Section 5.3) is shown in Figure 5-7.

In the Italy Water Case, the decision was made to include extraordinary maintenance costs (life-cycle costs) in calculating the ADSCR. These costs arise every two years during the entire concession period. This choice was also prompted by the absence of an O&M reserve earmarked especially for financing life-cycle costs, which impacts the debt repayment profile inasmuch as the flows available to service the debt also cover these costs.

In any case, there is room for flexibility in setting up the repayment plan, and it's only natural that the interests of lenders and of sponsors conflict. While sponsors benefit financially from a plan that would delay the largest debt installments (back-ended profile), lenders instead prefer to cut down on their exposure as quickly as possible.

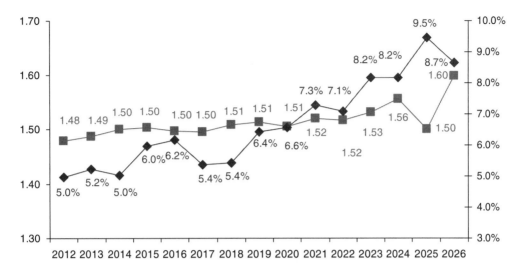

FIGURE 5-7   Percent Principal Repayment and the ADSCR of the Italy Water Case

The average loan life is one of the parameters used to draw up the debt repayment profile. It is calculated as follows:

$$\text{ALL} = \sum_{t=1}^{n} \text{RP} \times t$$

where:

ALL = Average loan life

RP = Repayment percentage referring to time period t

t = Time period in question (number of the year or the 6-month period being considered)

With maturities equal, the facility with a longer average life shows a higher level of risk, since repayment of the principal is more concentrated toward the end of the loan.

5.2.3   VAT Facility

Previously, we looked at various options that different legislation allows the SPV in terms of refunds on VAT. Usually an ad hoc credit line is set up that is drawn down at the same time VAT payments are made on initial investments. This credit normally involves a flexible repayment plan, since the installment is equal to net VAT collected by the project company in every period.

If the SPV can request reimbursement of VAT credit accrued during construction, repayment on the credit line takes the form of refunds from the VAT Office. Among the project's accounts, a VAT account might also be set up where net VAT flows collected every month are deposited. The balance on this account is utilized to pay back lenders at set intervals, typically every 3 or 6 months.

Albeit flexible, the loan amortization schedule essentially proves to be in line with that shown in the model. To establish, at the least, the maximum life of the loan, a termination date is usually set when the outstanding VAT credits are repaid by sourcing cash deposited in the SPV's accounts. It is important to notice—from the standpoint of the financial modeler—that even for interest payments on the VAT facility, the project company uses its own ability to generate cash, not the net VAT collected. The reason is that these funds can be earmarked for loan repayment as long as there is a VAT credit. After that, the net VAT collected is due to the VAT Office. This is why, unlike the base facility, the VAT facility does not include interest expenses related to the investment it has to finance; instead it is simply equal to the sum of the VAT disbursements.[8] In this regard, see Figure 5-8.

Due to the flexibility of the repayment schedule, the VAT facility is not generally converted to a fixed rate with swaps or other derivatives; it remains a variable-rate loan in every sense. Table 5-12 shows the input variables used for simulating the VAT facility in the Italy Water Case.

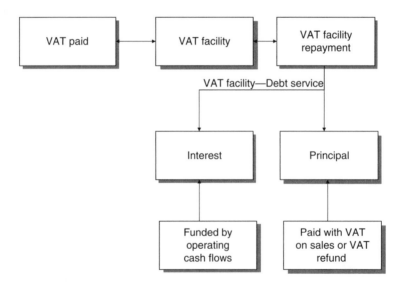

FIGURE 5-8   Logic Behind the VAT Facility

8. Lenders who finance the VAT facility essentially bear the same level of risk as those who finance the base facility. The assertion that the VAT facility basically represents a risk toward the state (i.e., the VAT Office) is false. Actually, a credit toward the VAT Office emerges only if the SPV requests a refund from the VAT Authority. In this case, the refund can be awarded as a guarantee to lenders, even though this allocation comes after the disbursement of the VAT facility. In addition, this credit offers adequate coverage for the amount disbursed but not for the interest accrued. If a termination date is set and the loan is still outstanding, at that time reimbursement comes from the operating cash flow of the company. If instead VAT is compensated, there is no formal VAT credit. Clearly, then, the VAT facility carries with it project risk rather than a state risk, and this is reflected in the application of an appropriate margin. Nonetheless, in light of the fact that the average loan life is much shorter than that of the base facility, the margin is lower and usually remains constant during the operating life of the project.

TABLE 5-12   Input Variables for the VAT Facility in the Italy Water Case

Average reimbursement period VAT Office	2 yr
Start date—VAT reimbursement	Jan 1, 2012
Terminal date—VAT reimbursement	Dec 31, 2013
IVA FACILITY	
Total amount (Euro (000))	**96,099**
AVAILABILITY PERIOD	
First disbursement	Jan 1, 2006
Final disbursement	Dec 31, 2011
Duration	6 yr
PAYBACK PERIOD	
First reimbursement	Dec 31, 2012
Final reimbursement	Dec 31, 2013
Duration	2 yr
Interest Charges	
Base rate	3.00%
Margin	1.00%
Composite Rate	4.00%
Financial fee	
Commitment fee	0.50%

5.2.4   Stand-by Facility

The construction contract has a fixed price, which means that the contractor can ask for price revisions only in exceptional cases. In addition, this type of agreement would, in theory, preclude any increase in the value of the total investments requested. We say "in theory" because the concession authority might want to modify the plant while work is in progress. Moreover, new laws that may come into effect could mean additional investments are needed, most often in the areas of environmental protection and workplace safety. These changes can be included in the contract, subject to prior agreement between the parties on the relative increase in the contract price and on approval of the banks and/or the independent engineer. Additional cost increases could result from investment items that, because they are not specified in the contract, are only estimated in the model.

To deal with these cost overruns, provisions are made for ad hoc financing to be tapped only if needed; this is usually called a *stand-by facility*. This facility is set up in such a way that when drawdowns are made, sponsors deposit additional equity at the same time. In this way, the debt/equity ratio remains constant. The loan agreement, then, must stipulate this commitment by sponsors. To discourage the use of this credit line unless absolutely necessary, margins are set higher than those of the base facility, normally over 10–15 basis points. The repayment schedule is exactly the same as that of the base facility.[9]

---

9. Even in cases of a stand-by facility, interest rate risk coverage policies can't be implemented because it isn't possible *a priori* to determine whether or not this credit line will actually be used and, if so, to what extent. At best, the project company can be obliged to cover interest rate risk on every drawdown it might make. However, this can't be foreseen when building the model.

5.2.5   Identifying Sustainable Debt/Equity Mixes for Sponsors and Lenders

Up to this point we have studied what operating cash flow is and where it can be channeled, but we haven't yet mentioned how to define the debt and equity mix to use to finance the structure. Clearly, without this information we can't evaluate whether the inequality in Figure 5-5 (Capacity > Requirements) is verified or determine the values on which the waterfall structure in Figure 5-6 is based.

What's more, from the perspective of financial models, the problem generates a circular calculation: The operating cash flow has to be used to pay the debt service and dividends, but we don't know how much this is until we work out the quantity of debt and capital conferred for the project. On the other hand, the amount of the loan actually drawn down, in turn, determines the total cash flow to cover in light of the capitalization of interest and fees on the same loan during the construction period.

This problem is solved through a process of trial and error. Basically, the arranger makes note of the variables that determine operating cash flow, along with project risks and relative coverage. A definite capital structure is then included in the model (usually the one the sponsors have in mind or suggest) and slotted into the framework of the spreadsheet. The proposed financial structure together with the hypothetical debt repayment plan give rise to the requirements for debt service for the principal and interest. By comparing the debt capacity (represented by operating cash flow) and debt requirements, we can see if the debt/equity mix is sustainable. If the former is larger than the latter, the hypothesis is technically feasible from a financial standpoint. If the opposite is true, the proposal is rejected. At this point the arranger will come up with another alternative with a lower debt component or with different contract terms with respect to the prior proposal.

By means of the simulations run through the financial model, the advisor/arranger can come up with a series of debt/equity mixes that in every year of the operating phase satisfy the condition:

$$\text{Operating cash flow} \ > \ \text{Debt service}$$

The final solution chosen lies in the logical scheme illustrated in Figure 5-9. The dotted lines in the work flowchart show a revision in the variables that determine operating cash flow; solid lines correspond to a change in the debt/equity mix or a modification in the terms of the loan agreement. The advisor's main concern is to set up the deal with a capital structure that can satisfy the demands of SPV shareholders as far as IRR. However, a necessary compromise between the needs of the sponsors and the interest of lenders must be found. If this doesn't happen, it will be impossible to raise the capital needed for the project.

5.2.5.1   Optimal Capital Structure for Project Sponsors

To ascertain which solution is actually chosen among the possible options, let's begin by saying that an advisor's first concern is to set up a deal that's consistent with the sponsors' mandate. Essentially, sponsors expect a return on the capital they've invested that is consistent with the degree of risk they've taken on in the project.

In finance literature on capital budgeting for investment projects, one of the most commonly used indicators for measuring the return on an investment is the internal rate of return (IRR). This is the interest rate that makes the net present value of a

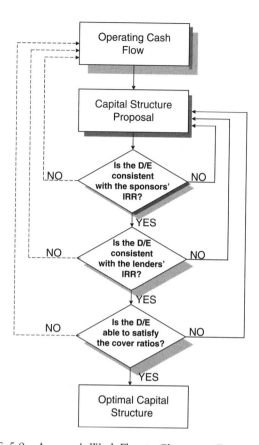

FIGURE 5-9   Arranger's Work Flow in Choosing a Financial Structure

project's positive operating cash flows equal to the net present value of its negative operating cash flows. With project finance, the former are generated during the operating phase; the latter are concentrated during the construction phase.

In other words, we have

$$\sum_{t=0}^{M} \frac{\text{OCF}_t}{(1 + \text{IRR}_{\text{project}})^t} = \sum_{t=M}^{n} \frac{\text{OCF}_t}{(1 + \text{IRR}_{\text{project}})^t}$$

The term on the left is the sum of the present value of negative cash flows from time 0 (project start-up) to M (end of the construction phase or COD, commercial operating date). The term on the right, in contrast, indicates the present value of positive flows produced by the project from M (again, the COD) to n (the last year of the project's life).

Consider the fact that the following is true of the operating cash flows.

- They are financed in part with debt and in part with equity during the construction phase.
- A portion is earmarked to repay the debt service, and another portion goes to paying dividends during the operating phase.

Keeping this in mind, it is also possible to calculate an IRR from the viewpoint of the sponsors and of the lenders. The IRR, in this case, represents the return on the operation for those who confer equity and the financing bank.

As for sponsors, future positive flows are represented by the dividends disbursed by the SPV or interest and principal repayments on the subordinate debt (see Chapter 6). Negative flows consist of equity injections for the initiative.[10]

In other words, we have

$$\sum_{t=0}^{M} \frac{C_t}{(1 + IRR_{equity})^t} = \sum_{t=M}^{n} \frac{D_t}{(1 + IRR_{equity})^t}$$

where:

C_t = Capital contribution in year t

M = Last year of equity contribution by sponsors

D_t = Dividends received by the sponsors in year t

IRR_{equity} = Internal rate of return for the sponsors

The term on the left side of the equation represents the discounting of all equity contributions, which offsets the right side, the current value of all dividends collected by sponsors starting from year M. Naturally, if $M = 0$, there would be only one equity payment at the start-up of construction and the left term would be simplified to C_0.

When sponsors commission the advisor/arranger to set up the deal, they already have a clear idea of the lowest acceptable IRR: This is their weighted average cost of capital (WACC) or a higher predefined threshold rate. Below this floor the initiative is of little interest to sponsors, and realizing it with project finance techniques is no longer economically convenient.

The calculation of WACC for the SPV must take into consideration both the cost of equity (k_e) and the cost of debt (k_d), with weights represented by the optimal debt-to-equity ratio selected on the basis of the work flow illustrated in Figure 5-9.

The cost of equity for the SPV (this equity being the sponsors' investment), in turn, reflects the WACC of each sponsor. Moreover, the cost of debt reflects the financial market's perception of the project's inherent risk as well as the intensity of competition on the financial markets. Therefore, this cost depends on project features, such as the economic/financial soundness of the initiative, the level of risk coverage provided by the contractual network surrounding the deal, and the standing of the counterparties to these contracts.

It follows that valuing the economic convenience of a project finance deal is more complicated than one involving an already-in-place company. This valuation must be done by comparing the project's IRR, calculated by using operating cash flows ($IRR_{Project}$) and the WACC of the SPV. This, in turn, is the weighted cost of the equity conferred by sponsors and the cost of the loans provided by creditors. The concepts are summarized in Figure 5-10.

---

10. Moreover, among other future benefits, there is interest on the cash in the SPV's accounts that was set aside during the operating phase. These are dividends that were not distributed for lack of economic "capacity" of net revenues of the vehicle company due to the weight of amortization during the project's first years of life. This is the effect of the "dividend trap," which is discussed in Section 6.8.

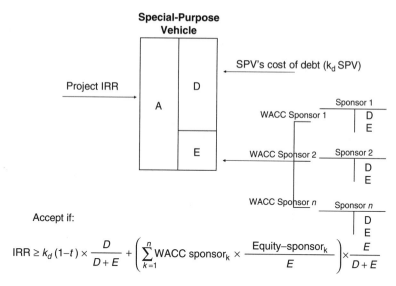

FIGURE 5-10   Calculation of WACC for an SPV

The term on the right side of the formula in Figure 5-10 is the WACC of the SPV, which, in turn, is given as the average of the cost funding on the debt (k_d) net of the fiscal effect $(1 - t)$ and the cost of equity. This latter factor is the WACC of each sponsor who participates in the deal.

In addition to the use of NPV and IRR for the valuation of the economic convenience of a project finance, many sponsors often also use the *payback period,* which is the moment in time when the project's outflows and inflows are equal. There are two variants of the payback period, one based on nominal flows and one based on discounted flows:

$$\textit{Nondiscounted payback}: \sum_{t=0}^{x} F_t = 0$$

$$\textit{Discounted payback}: \sum_{t=0}^{x} \frac{F_t}{(1+i)^t} = 0$$

where F_t are the cash inflows and outflows from the project, x is the payback period, and i is the selected discounting rate.

Although payback is not an accurate criterion for evaluating the economic convenience of investments projects, it is useful as a complementary indicator to the IRR. With equal rates of return, in fact, a project that can achieve payback more quickly is more attractive to a risk-averse investor.

5.2.5.2   Optimal Capital Structure for Lenders

An arranger or a participant in a project finance deal can frame an assessment of economic convenience in various ways.

The first is to calculate the net present value (NPV) by using the data contained in the financial model compiled by the advisor. Cash flows are discounted until the moment of assessment (realistically speaking, when the arranger asks the bank for the first disbursement of funds for the project) utilizing one's own cost of funding:

$$NPV = \sum_{t=M}^{M+n} \frac{DS_t}{(1 + c\_funding)^t} - \sum_{t=0}^{M} \frac{DU_t}{(1 + c\_funding)^t}$$

In the formula, M stands for the year when debt repayment begins, n is the terminal date for the last installment, DS is the debt service for each period t during the operating phase, and DU is the debt utilization during construction.

As we can see, the higher the NPV, the lower the cost of funding. Retail banks (i.e., banks that collect deposits from ordinary customers) can often earn lucrative margins because they can obtain a lower cost of funding than banks that would finance the deal by sourcing the interbank market. For these organizations, the initiative is only evaluated in terms of the margin over the benchmark rate.

The second way to value the economic convenience of a deal is to compute the IRR of the flows of lenders' fees, interest, and capital contributions/repayments, once again gleaned from the financial model drawn up by the advisor. Potential lenders evaluate whether the project's IRR is consistent with the degree of risk inherent to the initiative. The IRR for a lender who provides "pure" debt capital (that is, excluding the option of recourse to forms of mezzanine or subordinate debt) is influenced by the expected flows for debt service and the dynamic for the disbursement of funds during construction.

As a mathematical formula, we have

$$\sum_{t=0}^{M} \frac{D_t}{(1 + IRR_{debt})^t} = \sum_{t=M}^{M} \frac{K_t + I_t}{(1 + IRR_{debt})^t}$$

where:

$$D_t = \text{Drawdowns on funds in year } t$$

$$M = \text{Last drawdown period on loans}$$

$$M' = \text{Last payback period on funds}$$

$$K_t = \text{Principal repayment in year } t$$

$$I_t = \text{Interest repayment in year } t$$

$$IRR_{debt} = \text{IRR for lenders}$$

The sensitivity and expertise of the advisor/arranger lies in the ability to pinpoint an IRR that would elicit the interest of lenders' credit committees. Proposing an IRR that's too low would work to the sponsors' advantage but would involve the risk of taking on a sizeable portion of the financing. Advancing an IRR that's too high is no doubt appealing to the banking community, but it would jeopardize sponsors' satisfaction. A satisfactory level of IRR provides an additional filter to the advisor for the different debt/equity options for the initiative in question. In fact:

- If the proposed financial structure satisfies the sponsors but not the lenders, it has to be rejected.
- If there is no debt/equity mix that satisfies shareholders and lenders at the same time, estimates on operating cash flow should be revised. Then further attempts should be made to strike a balance between sponsors' and financers' interests.
- If the debt/equity mix satisfies both parties, the condition of economic convenience is guaranteed. The analysis should then be completed by calculating the cover ratios. If lenders find these acceptable too, then the project's financial structure has been found.

If the difference between the IRR and the cost of funding for an individual bank is positive, this signals that undertaking the initiative would be convenient because the NPV is positive. This difference, like the NPV, is not the same for all the banks because it depends on the cost of the funding sourced to participate in the initiative and on the fee level paid to each category of bank.

The limitation of the two methods just described lies in the basic assumption that the bank finances participation in the deal solely with capital collected from retail deposits (or from other banks if the funding is raised wholesale on the interbank market). In actual fact, lending also absorbs shareholders' equity. In fact, the riskier the loan, the greater this absorption should be. (In banking jargon, we say that the risk capital, or CaR—capital at risk, should be greater.) The shareholders' equity has a much higher opportunity cost than the cost of funding, and the two previous criteria could distort assessments on economic convenience.

There are a number of possible solutions to this crucial problem. The first is to calculate NPV by discounting the flows to a rate that represents a combination of risk capital and loan capital (intended as the marginal cost of funding based on an appropriate interbank rate) rather than only the cost of funding. The rate used for discounting can then be calculated as

$$\text{WMCF} = \text{IR} \times (1 - \text{RW} \times 8\%) \times (1 - t) + k_e \times \text{RW} \times 8\%$$

where:

$$\text{WMCF} = \text{Weighted marginal cost of funding}$$
$$\text{IR} = \text{Interbank rate}$$
$$\text{RW} = \text{Risk weight}$$
$$t = \text{Corporate tax rate}$$
$$k_e = \text{Cost of bank equity}$$
$$8\% = \text{Minimum capital requirement coefficient}$$

The weighting factors (RW) can be the percentages required by supervisory bodies in terms of capitalization (standardized approach), or they can be calculated internally by the bank using its internal rating systems (see Section 8.4). For example, suppose that the interbank rate is 4.5%, that k_e for the bank is 10%, and that the corporate tax rate is 40%. If the bank uses the risk weight proposed by the Basel

Committee for deals qualified as "strong" (70%), the deal is supposed to be financed with 70% × 8% = 5.6% equity and (100% – 5.6%) = 94.4% interbank deposits. The weighted marginal cost of funding would then be

$$\text{WMCF} = 4.5\% \times (1 - 0.70 \times 8\%) \times (1 - 0.40) + 10\% \times 0.7 \times 8\% = 4.81\%$$

The second solution would be to compare this same weighted marginal rate to the IRR of the initiative. If the difference between the IRR and the weighted marginal rate is positive, the deal is accepted; it's rejected if the opposite is true.

The third solution hinges on accounting parameters, although they are less accurate methodologically speaking. On the other hand, accounting data are immediately understandable by credit committees or the boards of directors of lending banks. Some banks take a criterion based on calculating the annual return on their equity absorbed by the project. They then compare it with a benchmark established by top management that represents the cost of funding for the bank (k_e). In some countries, banks refer to this with the acronym ROS (return on solvency).

A simplified calculation of the equity absorbed can be done by multiplying the outstanding debt at the end of every year (O) by the coefficient of the minimum capital requirement established by supervisory bodies. (For the portion of the loan that has actually been disbursed, this is 8%; for the portion that has been committed but not yet utilized, 6% is applied, i.e., 75% of an 8% coefficient.) The numerator of the quotient is represented by the margin with respect to the cost of funding (S, or spread) plus fees (F).

It would be convenient for the bank in question to participate in the initiative if:

$$\frac{S + F}{O \times 8\% + C \times 6\%} - k_e > 0$$

where C (committed) stands for the amount of financing that has not yet been utilized.

Table 5-13 provides an example showing this calculation with reference to a generic valuation date (December 31, 2005). Note that calculations are done on an actual/360 basis, and the return on equity absorbed is annualized under simple capitalization conditions. In this case, with a benchmark rate of 13%, the project generates an 11.91% return on solvency. Therefore, it should be rejected.

The last available option is based on the assumption that the bank can estimate value at risk (VaR), i.e., the unexpected loss on project finance initiative. This is done to quantify the maximum amount the bank could lose on a given time horizon and with a certain statistical level of confidence (usually 99%). As we'll see in Sections 8.4.1.1 and 8.4.1.2, some empirical tests show that the recovery rate on project finance deals is statistically higher than similar corporate exposures. So applying standard weighting factors (8% and 6%) could result in an overestimation of the equity absorbed.

Given historical data on the probability of default (PD) and the loss given default (LGD), if a bank can estimate the expected loss (EL) and its frequency distribution, a percentage value of unexpected loss can be computed within the chosen statistical level of confidence interval. While expected loss should be covered by the cost of funding (the margin), unexpected loss is a risk taken on by shareholders. They sustain this risk by utilizing their own equity, which has a cost of k_e. It follows that the

TABLE 5-13   Calculation of ROS for Banks for December 31, 2005

	Amount (euro/mil.)	Margin (b.p.)	Days in the Period	Margin (euro/mil.)
VAT loan—conferred at start of period	8,400	100	184	42,93
Base loan—conferred at start of period	40,791	150	184	312,73
Standby loan—conferred at start of period	—	160	184	—
Total margin				*355,66*

	Amount (euro/mil.)	Commitment Fee	Days in the Period	Commitment Fee (euro/mil.)
VAT loan—committed, not utilized	13,600	0.50%	184	34.76
Base loan—committed, not utilized	77,209	0.50%	184	197.31
Standby loan—committed, not utilized	7,000	0.60%	184	21.47
Total commitment fees				*253.53*
Total revenues				**609.20**

	Amount (euro/mil.)	Weighting Factor	Equity Absorbed (euro/mil.)
VAT loan—committed, utilized at end of period	11,350	8.00%	908.00
Base loan—committed, utilized at end of period	59,238	8.00%	4,739.04
Standby loan—committed, utilized at end of period	—	8.00%	—
VAT loan—committed, not utilized at end of period	10,650	6.00%	639.00
Base loan—committed, not utilized at end of period	58,762	6.00%	3,525.72
Standby loan—committed, not utilized at end of period	7,000	6.00%	420.00
Total equity absorbed			*10,231.76*
Return on equity absorbed (annualized)			*11.91%*
Benchmark rate			*13.00%*

interest rate the bank should charge on this deal in order to satisfy the expectations of shareholders must take the following into account:

- The internal transfer interest rate (IRT) used to finance the operation, usually close to an interbank rate
- The expected loss on project finance deals that are comparable to the case in question (EL)
- The value at risk of the deal (VaR)
- The difference between the k_e and the IRT (though the deal could be financed entirely with interbank loans, ideally, the project should absorb shareholders' equity as well)

So we have

$$R_r = \text{IRT} + \text{EL} + \text{VaR} \times (k_e - \text{IRT})$$

Rearranging this equation to express $(k_e - \text{IRT})$, we can get a measure of return corrected for risk, or risk-adjusted return on capital (RAROC).

TABLE 5-14   Example of a RAROC Calculation for December 31, 2005

	Amount (euro/mil.)	Margin (b.p.)	(days)	Margin (euro/mil.)
VAT loan—disbursed at the start of the period	8,400	100	184	42.93
Base loan—disbursed at the start of the period	40,791	150	184	312.73
Standby loan—disbursed at the start of the period	—	160	184	–
Total margin				*355.66*

	Amount (euro/mil.)	Commitment fee	Days	Commitment fee (euro/mil.)
VAT loan—committed, not utilized	13,600	0.50%	184	34.76
Base loan—committed, not utilized	77,209	0.50%	184	197.31
Standby loan—committed, not utilized	7,000	0.60%	184	21.47
Total commitment fees				*253.53*
Total revenues				**609.20**
Annualized return (including fees)				***2.48%***
Annualized return (including fees) (A)				2.48%
Expected loss (B)				1.50%
VaR (C)				5%
RAROC ((A−B)/C)				***19.54%***
Benchmark rate				**13.00%**

$$\text{RAROC} = \frac{R_r - \text{IRT} - \text{EL}}{\text{VaR}}$$

In fact, if we know the values of the spread ($R_r - \text{IRT}$) and the expected and unexpected loss, we can calculate the return on the project corrected for risk. This rate should be compared with the return expected on shareholders k_e to ascertain whether the operation is economically convenient.

Referring again to the previous example, the RAROC calculations are illustrated in Table 5-14. On the basis of available market data, we assume a default rate at one year of 2% and a recovery rate of 75%. This gives us an expected loss of 1.5%. We also posit that the unexpected loss (VaR) calculated at a 99% level of confidence is 5%. The actual annual rate is computed as the ratio of total revenues and (base + VAT + stand-by) loans utilized at the beginning of the period; annualization is done based on simple capitalization. Again, we set k_e at 13%. As we can see, in this case the RAROC is greater than the benchmark rate used, so the project should be financed.

5.3   Cover Ratios

The process illustrated in Figure 5-9 includes the verification of cover ratios in the decision-making process. In this section, we explain what these indices are and why they are used to value the bankability of project finance initiatives. An example will prove useful for introducing this topic.

We've seen that one of the discriminating criteria in various debt/equity mixes is the IRR level. One might ask then why the advisor doesn't stop at this stage in defining the financial structure.

Let's say that two project finance initiatives, A and B, have a total estimated cost of 1,000. Of this total, 800 is financed with bank loans organized by an arranger and 200 with shareholders' equity. Moreover, for simplicity's sake we'll suppose that construction will be finished on the two projects in the first working period (year 0) and that both begin to generate positive flows starting from year 1. The dynamic of the financial flows is represented in Tables 5-15 and 5-16, and the flow of the last year also includes the liquidation of any remaining assets.

TABLE 5-15   Project A—Financial Flows and Return Indicators

	Year					
	0	**1**	**2**	**3**	**4**	**5**
Operating cash flows	−1,000	50	150	850	1,800	2,100
Debt service	—	—	—	—	—	2,011
Dividends to sponsors	—	50	150	850	1,800	89
Investments—sponsors	200					
Investments—banks	800					

	Year					
	0	**1**	**2**	**3**	**4**	**5**
Financial flows—bank	−800	0	0	0	0	2,011
Financial flows—sponsors	−200	50	150	850	1,800	89
IRR—bank	20.2%					
IRR—sponsors	124%					

TABLE 5-16   Project B—Financial Flows and Return Indicators

	Year					
	0	**1**	**2**	**3**	**4**	**5**
Operating cash flows	−1,000	50	150	850	1,800	6,900
Debt service	0	35	110	600	730	0
Dividends to sponsors	0	15	40	250	1,070	6,900
Investments—sponsors	200					
Investments—banks	800					

	Year					
	0	**1**	**2**	**3**	**4**	**5**
Financial flows—bank	−800	35	110	600	730	—
Financial flows—sponsors	−200	15	40	250	1,070	6,900
IRR—bank	20.2%					
IRR—sponsors	124%					

As we can see, the same result emerges for both projects in terms of IRR, both for SPV shareholders and for a hypothetical lender. In the first case, however, the loan is reimbursed with a bullet payment at the end of the fifth year; in the second, capital is gradually collected and by the end of the fourth year the loan is paid in full.

The example reveals a simple conclusion, but not a trivial one: The same IRR can be obtained through different combinations of cash flows earmarked for debt service. Clearly, if the arranger is making forecasts and referring to expected flows, in the first case he or she will realize that payback to lenders depends exclusively on the fact that in year 5 the flow from Project A will be no less than the 2,011 debt service. If it were less, in fact, the project would have reached its last year of life and it wouldn't be possible to renegotiate the terms of repayment. In the case of Project B, in contrast, debt repayment is adapted, or "matched," to the dynamic of operating cash flows. When calculating the ratio between operating cash flow and the debt service (which shortly we will refer to as the *debt service cover ratio*), we note that this varies from a minimum of 1.36 in year 2 to 2.47 in year 4.

Basically, in Project B the arranger structured the financing so that in each year of the project's life, lenders collect on a part of their initial investment. Moreover, Project B's repayment plan finishes at the end of year 4, which also makes it possible to renegotiate the terms of repayment, taking advantage of the key terminal value of 6,900.

Summing up, then, with Project B there is a financial flow dynamic that is modulated according to the trend in operating cash flows. This match between the operational and financial aspects of the flows is exactly what cover ratios measure.

5.3.1   What Cover Ratios Can Tell Us and What They Can't

To make it easier to understand the meaning of cover ratios, it's helpful to look at what they *don't* do. They aren't indicators of the profitability for lenders in participating in a project. In fact, we have already seen that the financial model serves to compute the IRR for lenders and sponsors.

We have to remember that along with economic convenience, an initiative should also be valued in terms of financial sustainability. In other words, a project can be extremely lucrative (i.e., offer lenders an interesting IRR), yet it might not be financed if the timing for operating cash flows doesn't match the needs for debt service payment to lenders. Moreover, a project can generate a set IRR with various cash flow combinations, but these mixes are not always acceptable to lenders.

Cover ratios are indicators of financial sustainability. These parameters enable us to recognize the sustainability of the capital structure (and repayments on financing we've chosen) to realize a project finance deal. Put another way, cover ratios are indices that can show the extent to which a project's operating flows match those linked to the dynamic of financial items. A number of cover ratios are currently in use; two are particularly interesting.

5.3.1.1   Debt Service Cover Ratio (DSCR)

For each year of project operations[11] this ratio expresses the relationship between operating cash flow and the debt service on the principal and interest. So we have

---

11. Obviously, this ratio is meaningless during the construction phase, when by definition the numerator and denominator are both zero.

$$\text{DSCR} = \frac{\text{OCF}_t}{K_t + I_t}$$

where:

$$\text{OCF} = \text{Operating cash flow for year } t$$
$$K = \text{Payment on the principal in year } t$$
$$I = \text{Interest payment in year } t$$

The ratio tells us that in any given year of operations, the financial resources generated by the project (represented by the numerator) must be able to cover the debt service to lenders (the denominator of the quotient).

In theory, the lowest number the coefficient can be is 1. In this case, clearly the entire available cash flow can be used to the advantage of lenders to service the debt. We're speaking theoretically because it's equally clear that a DSCR sequence of 1 wouldn't be sustainable. This is true not so much for lenders, who would be completely satisfied (assuming for the moment there is no uncertainty regarding the outcome of the project), but for sponsors. In this situation, in fact, the flow of dividends would fall to zero for all the years earmarked for debt service. The end result in terms of the project's IRR for sponsors would be extremely unfavorable, to the point where the project would not be economically convenient.

The theoretical situation of a DSCR equal to 1 is not acceptable to lenders either, if we remove the unrealistic hypothesis of total certainty of the value of future cash flows generated by the project. The more lenders are risk-averse, the more they would insist that a safety margin be established to guard against unexpected circumstances that could shrink the project's cash flows and the greater than 1 the level of DSCR required for the initiative.

In this regard, the values gleaned from the project finance market are summed up in Table 5-17. As one would imagine, the level of cover ratios depends on the risk inherent to the project as perceived by lenders. This, in turn, is closely linked to the

TABLE 5-17   DSCRs in Various Sectors Where Project Finance Is Used

Project Sector	Average DSCR
Power:	
Merchant Plants (plants with no offtake agreement)	$2x$–$2.25x$
With a tolling agreement	$1.5x$–$1.7x$
In cases involving regulated business	$1.3x$–$1.5x$
Transportation/shipping	$1.25x$–$1.5x$
Telecom*	$1.2x$–$1.5x$
Water	$1.20x$–$1.30x$
Waste to energy	$1.35x$–$1.40x$
PFI**	$1.35x$–$1.40x$

* In the telecom sector, the average DSCR is determined by the security package. The data provided in Table 5-17 refer not only to project finance deals in the strict sense, but also to refinancing existing positions on a nonrecourse basis.

** As regards PFIs, one should consider the makeup of the base case used as a point of reference. The relevant data slotted into Table 5-17 do not take into account market risk due to revenue variables (parking lots, shopping centers, restaurants, etc.). Instead, they assess only counterparty risk and the transfer of project risk underwritten in the concession agreement to the concession awarder.

degree with which various cash flows are secured and therefore predictable. Projects in the transportation and telecommunications sectors, where long-term offtake contracts can't be implemented, can generally be financed only with higher cover ratios.

As far as the actual use of the DSCR, many loans require a specific average minimum level in addition to minimum cover ratios at set intervals (i.e., year by year). The average DSCR is nothing more than the average of the single DSCRs recorded in each year of operations:

$$\text{AVDSCR} = \frac{\dfrac{\text{OCF}_1}{K_1 + I_1} + \dfrac{\text{OCF}_2}{K_2 + I_2} + \cdots + \dfrac{\text{OCF}_n}{K_n + I_n}}{n} = \frac{\displaystyle\sum_{t=1}^{n} \dfrac{\text{OCF}_t}{K_t + I_t}}{n}$$

The symbols in this formula, besides those already explained, stand for the following:

$$\text{AVDSCR} = \text{Average debt service cover ratio}$$

$$n = \text{Length of the loan amortization plan in number of years}$$

Why is a coefficient for the AVDSCR required along with the yearly minimum? We can understand the reason by observing Figure 5-11. As we can see, both Project A and Project B have a minimum DSCR of 1.3; however, no bank would choose B over A. In fact, while A shows a coefficient for average debt service of 1.45 (which is higher than the minimum), the same figure for Project B corresponds exactly to the minimum. So preference would go to Project A due to the fact that during the operating phase, the initiative guarantees that in some years the DSCR is higher than the minimum accepted value. This is not the case with Project B.

5.3.1.2   Loan Life Cover Ratio (LLCR)

The second cover ratio is the quotient of the sum of the operating cash flows discounted to the moment of valuation (s) and the last scheduled year of debt repayment ($s + n$) (plus the available debt reserve, or DR) and the outstanding debt (O) at the time of valuation s. That is:

$$\text{LLCR} = \frac{\displaystyle\sum_{t=s}^{s+n} \dfrac{\text{OCF}_t}{(1 + i)^t} + \text{DR}}{O_t}$$

The meaning of this ratio is less intuitive than the DSCR, even though it's interpreted in a similar way.

To understand what this ratio tells us, we should explain that the LLCR is the relationship between two discounted sums. This is obvious at once for the numerator. For the denominator, simply consider that in financial mathematics, the outstanding debt at a given time s is nothing more than the discounting of the debt services that have yet to be paid by the borrower for the entire remainder of the loan itself. So we can say that

$$O_s = \sum_{t=s}^{s+n} \frac{\text{DS}_t}{(1 + i_{\text{loan}})^t}$$

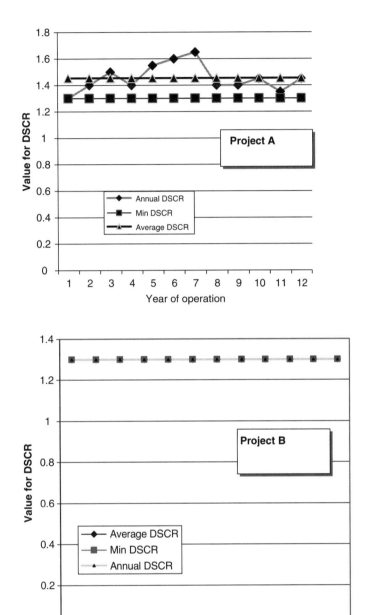

FIGURE 5-11   Significance of the AVDSCR

where DS represents the installment due at time t and i is the interest rate on the loan applied by the lender.

Secondly, consider that the LLCR is a ratio of the sums of two discounted flows. As such, an LLCR greater than 1 can be interpreted as a surplus of cash freely available to project sponsors if they were to opt to liquidate the initiative immediately. They could

TABLE 5-18   Determining the LLCR

Year	OCF	Debt Service	DSCR	NPV OCF (10%)	NPV (DS) (10%)	LLCR
0	—	—				
1	84,000,000	60,000,000	**1.40**	76,363,636	54,545,455	
2	37,500,000	25,000,000	**1.50**	30,991,736	20,661,157	
3	42,900,000	33,000,000	**1.30**	32,231,405	24,793,388	
		Average DSCR	**1.40**	*139,586,777*	*100,000,000*	**1.396**

reimburse the entire outstanding debt with the net revenue generated during the remaining loan repayment period. Let's look at Table 5-18 as an example.

In the table, we assume that the project generates the operating cash flows shown in the OCF column (during the years marked for repaying a 100 million loan with variable installments). Next is the debt service (DS) column. The relationship between the figures in the OCF and DS columns gives us the DSCR. The average DSCR over the time horizon considered here is 1.4.

The next two columns contain the NPV of operating cash flows (NPV OCF) and the debt service (NPV DS); both figures are calculated at a 10% rate. As one would expect, if we add the present values of the debt service, we immediately get the nominal value of the loan again (100 million). The discounted value of operating cash flows, in contrast, amounts to nearly 140 million. If we were to liquidate the investment project today, considering only flows freely generated in years 1, 2, and 3, the SPV would be able fully to reimburse the 100 million loan and could distribute around 40 million to its sponsors.

This simplified calculation is measured by the LLCR. For the project in question, this figure is 1.396 available euro for every single euro of outstanding debt at the time of valuation.

A third and final consideration regarding LLCR pertains to the rate utilized for discounting the numerator. As we saw in Section 5.2.5.2, the most accurate solution would be to calculate the marginal cost weighted for each participant bank in the initiative and to use this when discounting.

In practice, however, we use the nominal rate applied by lenders in a given year. If this is the case, then if discounted rate of the flows in the numerator is equal to that used to discount the flows in the denominator and all the DSCRs have the same value during the loan amortization period, then obviously the two cover ratios are equal. This is clearly illustrated in Table 5-19.

TABLE 5-19   Equivalency of DSCR and LLCR

Year	OCF	Debt Service	DSCR	NPV OCF (10%)	NPV (DS) (10%)	LLCR
0	—	—				
1	84,000,000	60,000,000	**1.40**	76,363,636	54,545,455	
2	35,000,000	25,000,000	**1.40**	28,925,620	20,661,157	
3	46,200,000	33,000,000	**1.40**	34,710,744	24,793,388	
		Average DSCR	**1.40**	*140,000,000*	*100,000,000*	**1.400**

TABLE 5-20   LLCR in Various Sectors Where Project Finance Is Utilized

Project Sector	Average LLCR
Power:	
Merchant plants (i.e., plants with no offtake agreement)	$2.25x–2.75x$
With tolling agreement	$1.5x–1.8x$
In cases involving regulated business	$1.3x–1.5x$
Transportation	$1.4x–1.6x$
Telecom	n.a.
Water	$1.30x–1.40x$
Waste to energy	$1.80x–1.90x$
PFI	$1.45x–1.50x$

We can see that the DSCRs in the three years are all 1.4, so they are all equal to the average DSCR. This figure, in turn, is exactly the same as the value of LLCR.[12] If instead, as happens in real life situations, the different DSCRs diverge over time, the average DSCR and the LLCR would not be equal. The latter can only be higher or lower as a function of the different distributions over time of the available cash flows during the loan amortization period.

In actual fact, as we saw with the DSCR, the minimum value of the requested LLCRs is a direct function of the project's inherent risk. In this regard, see Table 5-20.

5.3.2   Cover Ratios as an Application of the Certainty Equivalents Method

Up to this point, we've explained the need for cover ratios higher than 1 simply by referring to lenders' aversion to risk. We've said that the greater the margin of guarantee against unforeseen future events that lenders want, the higher the ratios they will demand.

To be more precise, we can use a numerical example to illustrate this reasoning. Let's take the case of a hypothetical investment project. Two lenders (Alfabank and Betabank) are willing to accept 1.3 and 1.6 DSCRs, respectively, for all years of the loan repayment plan.

Based on the DSCR formula, we know that:

$$\text{DSCR}_{\text{Alfabank}} = \frac{\text{OCF}_t}{K_t + I_t} = 1.3$$

$$\text{DSCR}_{\text{Betabank}} = \frac{\text{OCF}_t}{K_t + I_t} = 1.6$$

---

12. This result derives from the linear properties of the NPV. If an investment presents a sequence of flows that differs from another only by a constant multiplier (1.4 in our example), the NPV of the first investment is equal to the NPV of the second multiplied by the given constant. So we have $\text{NPV}(\varpi A) = \varpi \text{NPV}(A)$.

Rearranging the terms in the two equations, we get:

$$\frac{1}{1.3}\text{OCF}_t = K_t + I_t \quad \text{for Alfabank}$$

$$\frac{1}{1.6}\text{OCF}_t = K_t + I_t \quad \text{for Betabank}$$

At this point, note that in any given year of the loan amortization, the operating cash flows generated by the project are multiplied by a number between 0 and 1. In fact, we have 0.769 (or 76.9%) for Alfabank and 0.625 (62.5%) for Betabank. In other words, having requested a DSCR of 1.3, it is as if Alfabank were to weight each nominal flow produced by the initiative at approximately 77% of its value. Betabank, the more risk-averse lender, actually uses a weight of 62.5%.

We can easily see from this example that, in order to accept participation in the financing, the debt service for each year is equated to a percentage of the available cash flow that can be drawn from the project each year. Naturally, we use the same reasoning in considering the loan life cover ratio.

Uncertainty regarding the dynamic of flows expected from a project finance deal is measured by a coefficient (λ). This equals the inverse of the values of the cover ratios taken into consideration, so the lower this coefficient, the higher the value of the cover ratio in question.

Cover ratios can be interpreted as an application of the *method of certainty equivalents* for dealing with uncertainty in investment/financing decisions. According to this method, an investment/financing project characterized by a sequence of cash flows not known to the evaluator *a priori* must be accepted or rejected on the basis of the NPV criterion. In estimating this factor, the figures regarding expected project cash flows are weighted by coefficients representing the evaluator's aversion to risk. So we have

$$\text{NPV} = \sum_{t=1}^{n} \frac{F_t \lambda}{(1+i)^t}$$

with λ falling between 0 and 1.

5.4   Sensitivity Analysis and Scenario Analysis

Once a balance is struck that makes it possible to achieve all the objectives of the contract counterparties (sponsors' and lenders' IRR and minimum levels of DSCR and LLCR), the next step is to verify the project's robustness in the face of negative scenarios. The result of these tests involves the following:

- The generation of various scenarios, each of which will show the project's performance when a series of parameters change (scenario analysis)
- The use of simulation techniques (such as Monte Carlo simulations) applied to a set of key variable, and the creation of the probability distribution of output variables considered critical (usually the IRR for sponsors or DSCRs)

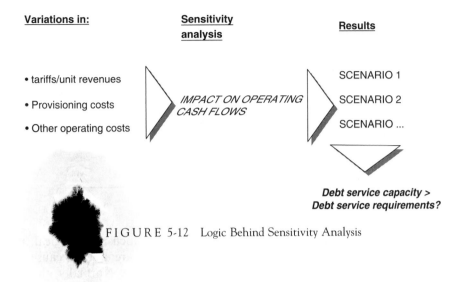

FIGURE 5-12   Logic Behind Sensitivity Analysis

Scenario analysis is part of the family of sensitivity analyses that serve to provide potential financers with a possible spectrum of cases (from a base case to a worst case). This is done to determine the level of project solidity when negative contingencies emerge.

Sensitivity analysis is based on logic illustrated in Figure 5-12.

Carrying out sensitivities, i.e., generating several equally possible scenarios, is not particularly complex. In fact, the same model used to draw up a base case is used again to produce scenarios. The difference lies in the input values, while obviously the algorithms for calculating and determining results are the same.

However, just as it is theoretically possible to generate an infinite number of scenarios, we must also limit this number to a manageable level. In fact, with too many scenarios we risk creating confusion for a potential participating bank or shifting the focus away from the evaluation of the real risk factors that impact the project.

For this reason, the sensitivity analyses conducted by the advisor are limited to a few alternative scenarios derived by manipulating only a small number of key variables. The logic behind sensitivity analysis is to verify the project's degree of resistance to adverse changes in the factors that determine cash flows. Instead of assigning a definite probability of verification to a given event, which is always rather subjective, sensitivity analysis should focus on coming up with the maximum possible variation in a key variable that still allows the *debt service capacity > debt service requirements* condition to be met. Then it is up to the individual intermediaries invited to participate in the project to decide if this extreme variation should be seen as likely or unlikely (on the basis of their own risk aversion).

5.4.1   Which Variables Should Be Tested in Sensitivity Analysis?

The guiding principle for advisors in generating scenarios is *relevance*. In fact, it makes no sense to offer scenarios produced by modifying variables with little

TABLE 5-21   Downside Scenarios in the Italy Water Case

1. Decrease in water tariffs	
Tariff on drinking water	−20%
Tariff on nondrinking water	−20%
2. Decrease in price of Green Certificates	−20%
3. Increase in operating costs	+20%
4. Increase in base tax	+100 basis points
5. Increase in investment costs	+10%
6. Decrease in public funding	−20%
7. Decrease in duration of concession	5 yrs

impact on the values of operating cash flows. It is much more logical, instead, to ascertain which values, when altered only slightly, are apt to cause significant variations in total available cash flows for debt service. Normally, these variables are the ones that determine the components of operating cash flow, such as sales revenues and operating expenses Consider, for example, inflation rates to which sales prices are indexed, or the cost of sourcing input that isn't covered by put-or-pay contracts.

Table 5-21 provides an example of variables that can be tested in sensitivity analysis. Naturally, though these variables are linked directly to the Italy Water Project, it is worthwhile to study them closely to give yourself a feel for conducting "what if" analysis.

Drop in Water Supply Tariffs: One of the most critical variables in choosing the preferred bidder in a call for public tender is the fee structure for the service offered, although this is the most effective tool in determining the profitability of the project. For this reason, the definitive fee structure is set up just before "the sealing of the envelopes" containing the offers presented to the public concession authority. In the Italy Water Project, the difference between the fee for water for nondrinking water (100 euro per 1000 mc of water supplied) and for drinking water (300 euro per 1000 mc of water supplied) is due to the cost variables for water treatment.

Drop in the Price of Green Certificates: The Italy Water Project also involves the production of around 106 GWh/year of hydroelectric power when the plant is fully functional. These facilities take advantage of the opportunity to sell Green Certificates for the first 8 years of operations at an estimated price; the actual value is contingent on market trends underlying the sales of these certificates. To compute the potential impact of a price reduction of Green Certificates in 2009, we arbitrarily decided on a percentage drop in the sales price.

Increase in Fixed Costs: Some fixed costs can be established in contracts; others, such as general expenses or personnel costs, are only estimates and as such are subject to change. The same considerations can be made as regards variable costs, in light of the fact that an increase in water treatment costs triggers a price hike for the supply of drinking water.

Variation in the Interest Rate: The Italy Water simulation is based on the assumption that interest rates will rise at the same rate as inflation. The outcome of the simulation depends largely on the coverage policy adopted for interest rate risk. If most of the debt is converted to a fixed rate, a rate increase would lead to an increase in the operating margin (assuming that costs and revenues rise proportionally to the same degree) along with a negligible upswing in interest expenses. Conversely, a drop in rates would cause the operating margin to shrink considerably, with a limited decrease in interest rates. The project tends to downslide as rates fall. The opposite occurs with variable-rate financing, for it is more likely that the growth in the operating margin will be more than compensated by the increase in interest payable.

Increase in the EPC Contract Price: Even though the EPC contract is normally a fixed-price agreement, conditions may arise that would necessitate raising the price during the construction phase. All parties might agree to an increase to pay for improvements on the initial project, for example. Or extra funds may be needed to contend with force majeure events (costs linked to implementing new safety standards, or new regulations on emissions, etc.). In any case, increases (debiting ancillary charges such as VAT and interest as well) have to be limited to the total available stand-by funds (stand-by equity and stand-by loan). If the cost increase exceeds available funds, a default event would result. Therefore, when this simulation is run, we have to make sure the stand-by facility is not entirely drained.

Cut in Public Grants: The variable that quite probably has the greatest influence on the concession authority in choosing an offer is the economic/financial equilibrium of the project. With BOT concessions for building and operating public services, private financing (meaning conferring of debt and equity) is not enough to guarantee an adequate return on investment and total reimbursement of the loan. For this reason, this type of sensitivity plays a key role in decision-making policies of private sponsors. A cutback in public grants during the construction phase has to be compensated by a step-up in financing, where financial ratios are adequately robust, and a bigger contribution from sponsors.

Decrease in the Duration of the Concession: The length of the concession is quite a significant variable for the public concession authority when choosing the winning proposal, though this factor does not greatly impact the financial/economic equilibrium of the project. In fact, in the case of concessions running over 20 or 30 years, extending or compressing the life span of the contract does not affect the rate of return on the project or on investment capital a great deal. As regards the project's financial sustainability, instead, despite the obvious condition that the final maturity of the loan must predate the expiration of the concession, limiting the duration of the concession increases the risk of the project. The reason is that if downside scenarios occur that call for additional funds, the possibility to refinance the loan is partly compromised.

Once variables are singled out, an accurate *range* of variation has to be set for each one. Whenever possible, common sense should be substantiated by assessments conducted by various consultants, for specific areas of expertise (how much operating costs could actually fluctuate, the lowest possible level of plant efficiency, the real risks of price increases for the EPC contract, etc.). Simulations on single variables should not show excessive sensitivity to results of the project initially measured by DSCR, LLCR, and IRR.

An even more important result emerges from simulations that take into account several downside conditions in the same scenario. This is done to test the project's robustness when adverse circumstances coincide. The combined downside scenario has to demonstrate that the project can repay the loan installments on the principal and interest. In terms of the model, this means that the minimum DSCR level has to be at least 1. A lower figure would imply that cash flows generated are not enough to repay the debt.

The scenario presented in Table 5-22 produces unacceptable financial results from a financial perspective and in terms of earnings (minimum DSCR 1.06x, minimum LLCR 1.08x, project IRR 7.75%, shareholders' IRR 6.47%). However, here it's crucial to understand the meaning of the analysis. A downside scenario has to be "validated" by the bank's technical consultant, and in any case it has to be properly mitigated through commercial contracts and the concession contract.

Moreover, in these circumstances the outcome of the model should be interpreted carefully. For example, suppose we come up with a minimum DSCR of 0.95x and an average DSCR of 1.30x. On average the project can readily repay the debt in full (with a margin of 30%). However, in at least one operating year the available cash flow is inadequate. This is easily dealt with by redefining the payback plan, as we see in Section 6.9. If the new plan is also appropriate in the "normal" situation established

TABLE 5-22   Combined Downside Scenario in the Italy Water Case

Variables	Base Case	%	Downside Scenario
Increase in Capex (keuro)	1,120,737	7	1,197,555.0
Decrease in Water Tariff			
Tariff on potable water (Euro/000 cubic meters)	338	−5	321.1
Tariff on non-potable water (Euro/000 cubic meters)	113	−5	107.4
Increase in Opex (keuro)	21,701	7	23,220.1
Green Certificate (Dec. 31, 2009) (Gwh/yr)	116	−5	110.2
Water Authority Fee (keuro)	5,000	10	5,500
Energy Authority Fee (keuro)	5,000	10	5,500
Public Grant (% on Capex)			
Section 1	55%	−2.50	52.5%
Section 2	55%	−2.50	52.5%
Senior Facility Base rate	4.50%	1.50	6.00%
Results			
DSCR			
Min	1.48		1.06
Average	1.51		1.09
LLCR			
Min	1.53		1.08
Average	1.55		1.09
IRR			
Project	9.54%		7.75%
Equity	12.42%		6.47%

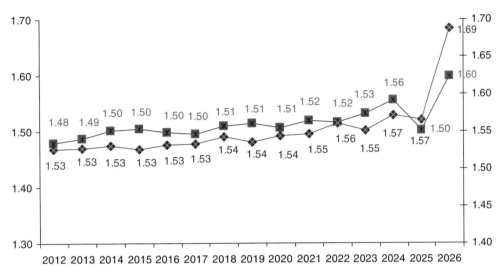

FIGURE 5-13   DSCR and LLCR Trends in the Italy Water Project

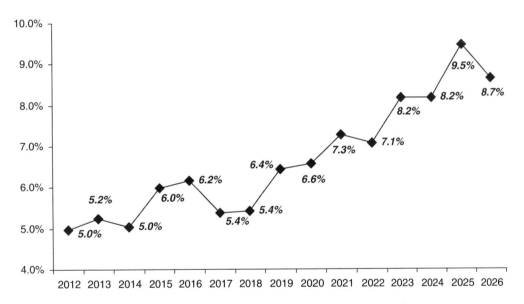

FIGURE 5-14   Reimbursement Trend for the Senior Facility in the Italy Water Project

in the base case, it can be adopted; otherwise, contract terms can be considered that allow for a certain margin of flexibility (albeit limited) in the repayment plan.[13]

An alternative and complementary method for verifying a project is to change each relevant variable until we find the value that gives us a minimum DSCR of 1,

13. Modeling the optimal payback plan can be done by calculating the loan installment beginning with the available cash flow estimated by the model, rather than by carrying out endless trials. Assuming a minimum DSCR of $1.30x$, the loan installment (principal + interest) should be proportional to the available cash flow by a ratio of 1:1.30. Subtracting interest due from the figure obtained by this calculation, we get the installment on capital. See Section 6.9.7 for more information.

which is inherent to the situation described earlier of a missed installment payment (assuming an optimal repayment plan). If the variation needed to trigger a project default is so extreme as to be highly improbable, the project would prove sufficiently robust in the face of events that could give rise to such changes. On the other hand, if the variable stays at a plausible value, this signals the need to find adequate structures to mitigate this risk. For example, if the project tends toward default when quite plausible interest rate increases are considered, hedging policies should be reviewed, and the fixed-rate component of financing should be given more weight.

In designing the model, we should keep in mind the importance of visualizing the economic factors of the project through images and graphs. Often this makes it possible to understand the problem quickly.

The DSCR and LLCR profiles (such as the ones shown in Figure 5-13) provide a snapshot of possible inefficiencies of the payback plan.

By visualizing the repayment plan itself, instead, we can clearly see if the profile is excessively back-ended, i.e., if the final installments are too heavy. See, for example, Figure 5-14.

CHAPTER • 6

Financing the Deal

Introduction

Funding a project finance deal is extremely complex. In both the case of bank loans and recourse to the capital market (bond issues), the size of projects means that a large number of banks or very many bond investors must participate. For an example, see the tombstone in Figure 6-1.

This chapter reviews how syndicated loans and bond issues are organized and also analyzes the various alternatives sponsors have for obtaining funds to invest in their projects. The first three sections investigate the structure of syndicated loans, the most common form of funding used for project finance deals. The analysis covers the activities of advisors, arrangers, and other roles and the various fees paid for organization of the pool itself. International projects syndicates often include multilateral banks (MLBs) and export credit agencies (ECAs) (Sections 6.4 and 6.5). Their involvement means private banks can enjoy privileged creditor status; this has considerable advantages from the standpoint of credit risk and equity absorption. Section 6.6 gives a summary of other financial intermediaries who may participate in a project finance deal, whereas Sections 6.7 to 6.11 analyze the various forms of funding. Section 6.7 covers equity provided by sponsors; Section 6.8 analyzes mezzanine financing and subordinated debt; senior debt and refinancing are covered in Section 6.9; and leasing is covered in Section 6.10.

The chapter ends with Section 6.11, which examines the project bond market and the process for issuing these securities.

6.1 Advisory and Arranging Activities for Project Finance Funding

Services offered for project finance deals by financial intermediaries fall into one of two major categories: advisory services or financing services. The first category

FIGURE 6-1   Tombstone for a Refinancing Project Finance Facility

includes soft services used to define the risk profile for a deal, its time schedule, and its size in order to make it bankable, that is, to model the deal so that it can be proposed to potential lenders. Because such services don't require huge amounts of capital, they can be provided by parties not represented by financial intermediaries: consulting firms, auditing firms, large-scale constructors, engineering firms, and individual professionals who often play an important role in terms of consultancy for structuring deals. In certain cases the sponsors themselves carry out a large part of the studies concerning technical, legal, and financial aspects. They then contact the arranger bank for the sole purpose of organizing financing terms and conditions.

The second category of services concerns lending activities and consists of granting loans and, sometimes, providing equity based on indications in the feasibility study prepared by consultants. Because this activity requires the availability of capital, clearly it is a business area in which financial intermediaries—particularly commercial banks—play a leading role.

TABLE 6-1   Types of Services Proposed by Financial Intermediaries

Advisory (consultancy services)	• Analysis of technical aspects (together with technical advisors)
	• Analysis of regulatory and legislative aspects (together with lawyers)
	• Due diligence reporting as regards parties involved in the deal
	• Development of assumptions for risk allocation
	• Preparation of the business plan and performing sensitivity analyses
	• Establish financial requirements and methods to fund these
	• Identify methods to obtain debt and equity capital
	• Organize and negotiate terms of financing (arranging)
	• Organize and negotiate terms of bond issues (global coordination)
Lending (financing services)	• Grant bridge financing
	• Underwrite bank financing
	• Grant pool financing (lending)
	• Grant leasing for plant
	• Contribute to equity
	• Contribute to mezzanine finance
	• Issue guarantees and suretyships
	• Manage technical relations with the SPV
	• Act as agency, maintaining documentation and monitoring use of funds by the borrower

Table 6-1 shows the main types of activity for each of the two major service categories.

Advisory and arranging services are mainly provided by commercial and investment banks. Although for many years there has been deep division between commercial banks and investment banks in many countries—with the exception of European countries in the German-speaking bloc and Japan, where the universal banking model has always prevailed—today this clear-cut division between commercial and investment banks has all but disappeared, given that constraints posed by legislation have been removed.

However, the division does in effect still exist, owing to years of specialization in certain types of financial services. Investment banks have found and still find it more convenient and profitable to specialize in the advisory field, namely, business areas marked by a high service level that are more similar to consultancy than financial intermediation in a strict sense. This is why sponsors of international project finance deals traditionally use the services of British merchant banks or American investment banks for advisory support during the initial phases of structuring a deal. On the other hand, the financial intermediation and lending services area is the preferred field for commercial banks, given that they have more stable, low-cost deposits. Because some of these banks are present at an international level, this makes them particularly well suited to provide international arranging services, whether in the form of syndicated loans or bond issues.

6.1.1   Advisory Services

Advisory services include all studies and analyses required to make a preliminary valuation of the financial feasibility of a project and also to outline an initial assumption as to how the funding required to sustain a SPV can be obtained.

The advisor's tasks are:

- To understand fully the sponsors' objectives and then to identify alternative solutions to achieve these
- To evaluate risks inherent in the project and to attempt to find strategies to mitigate, manage, and allocate these risks
- To assist sponsors in preparing and negotiating major contracts concerning the project
- To assist sponsors as regards certification of all permits, licenses, and authorizations obtained
- To assist sponsors in preparing the business plan or by reviewing the plan already prepared by them
- To highlight problems sponsors have not considered but that must be resolved to ensure the deal's success

Advisory services in the initial stages concern gathering technical, legal, and fiscal information regarding the project, the parties involved, the localization of the venture, and political and administrative factors it involves. This activity is frequently performed in association with a team of advisors from different organizations who have the necessary expertise as regards the legal, technical, and insurance aspects concerned (as seen in Chapter 4).

The gathering and initial processing of basic information forms the foundation of input for the business plan. In essence the advisor must translate information gathered into figures to evaluate what impact the many variables will have on cash flows, profitability, and the equity structure of the SPV. The business plan must enable the advisor, together with the sponsors, to devise the mix of financing sources to be set up to ensure that the project has the financial support it requires (see Chapter 5).

The final outcome of the financial advisor's work is the information memorandum, that is, the document with which the advisor contacts potential lenders and begins to negotiate the credit agreement and loan documentation with the arrangers until the financial close is reached (see Chapter 7). The advisory stage has a heavy service content and doesn't require a commitment for lending from the party conducting the activity.

The factors that sponsors focus on when selecting an advisor are usually the organization's reputation, competitive standing, expertise in specific sectors or specific geographical locations, and possibly already existing relations with the sponsors (except, of course, in cases where they are able to prepare the business plan without needing assistance from external parties).

Figure 6-2 shows a league table for the top twenty advisors worldwide for the period 2001–2004. Considering the entire period analyzed, this represents more than 90% of total mandates awarded. In fact, the market shows quite a high level of concentration, even though the trend for this percentage is decreasing as a result of a progressive fragmentation in the sector.

At a world level, PricewaterhouseCoopers is the leader figuring in one of the two top places in the league table during the four-year period considered. Also the second and third positions are almost always occupied by Ernst & Young and Macquarie, although the latter was overtaken in 2004 by KPMG. As for the remaining positions, they show a much greater turnover, with a presence of both pure advisors (typically the corporate finance divisions of major auditing firms) and integrated commercial banks, as in the case of ABN Amro, Société Générale, Royal Bank of Scotland, or ING.

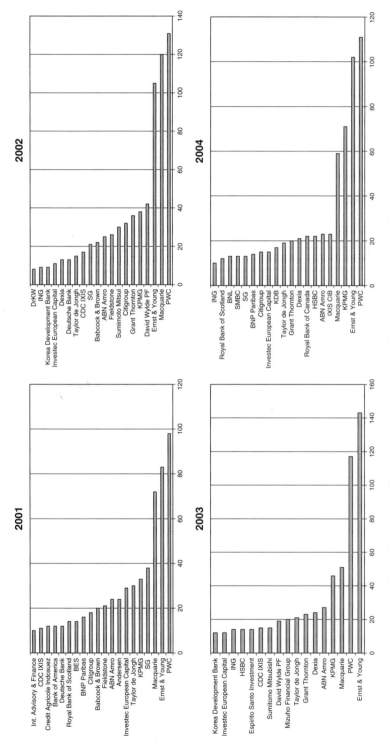

FIGURE 6-2 Global Advisors by Number of Project Finance Deals (2001–2004)
Source: Project Finance International.

Trends seem to be reasonably clear:

1. The progressive leadership of the corporate finance divisions of major consultancy and auditing firms (PricewaterhouseCoopers, KPMG Corporate Finance, and Ernst & Young) as credible competitors to financial intermediaries;
2. Leading names in the international investment banking (Morgan Stanley, JPMorgan, Lehman Brothers, Credit Suisse First Boston, Merrill Lynch), who figured in league tables in the first half of the 1990s, have been overtaken by the group of large, integrated commercial banks. This situation would seem to confirm the competitive superiority of the "integrated" intermediary model illustrated later in Section 6.1.3.

6.1.2   Arranging Services

As opposed to advisory services, which represent a business area open to a wide range of competitors, arranging services is a competitive area covered exclusively by commercial banks that:

- Have good international coverage (this helps when structuring loan pools involving banks from different countries);
- Have considerable financial strength and a huge amount of equity: in project finance there is a symmetry between the size of the project and the size of the intermediary that structures and negotiates the financing pool. And so it is evident that even in smaller projects (but that still will involve tens of millions of dollars) a bank must have a solid financial standing.

Arranging consists of a mandate from the SPV borrower to structure and manage the financing contract. The arranger (or mandated lead arranger—MLA—as it is often known) must therefore be able to contact the widest possible number of banks interested in participating in the deal and must then be the coordinator representing all lenders. In technical language this is referred to as *syndication,* and project finance loans are a special category of the wider group of syndicated lending (SL). When the deal isn't very large, common practice is to grant the mandate to a sole arranger. But when the deal is sizeable and has an international scope it is certainly more usual to create a team of arrangers, each of which has a specific role (contacts with lawyers, handling tax matters, gathering and updating documentation, etc.).

Arranging always means that sponsors are given an underwriting guarantee of availability of funds, even if no lenders are found who are interested in supporting the project. In order to grant an underwriting guarantee, the arranger bank must have significant financial strength: If the arranger should fail to place the loan in the market, the weight of the entire commitment would have to be borne by its financial statements, with the consequence that it would have to back it up with equity.

Furthermore, underwriting all or part of the financing is also a guarantee much appreciated by banks asked to provide funds for the SPV, inasmuch as it implies that the arranger has confidence in the SPV's venture.

Sponsors select arrangers based on factors similar to those used to choose the advisor:

- Experience gained in previous deals
- Reputation and track record

- Flexibility as regards both unforeseen events arising after the mandate has been given and possible needs to revise the basic conditions (refinancing) underlying the financing contract during the life of the project
- Cost of the financing

For many years this last point was certainly considered the major discriminating factor. However, competition in the sector has recently been very heavy, and so pricing differences have tended to be just a few basis points. Given this situation it is the remaining factors that make the difference when selecting an arranger.

Market data for the top twenty arrangers worldwide classified in terms of amount of arranged loans[1] indicate that they have a market share ranging from 53% to 73% of the total market for the period 2001–2005 (Figure 6-3). This share, however, is dropping and confirms the fact that there is progressive fragmentation under way for lending, as was already seen for advisory services. This may indicate that the market is growing faster than traditional lenders are capable of expanding their activities, which means conditions are right for new competitors to enter the market. It should be noted that, as opposed to the situation in the case of advisors, the group of best arrangers is highly homogeneous, inasmuch as the large majority are clearly commercial banks, in addition to the investment banking divisions of large banking groups. As would be expected, there are no corporate finance divisions of large consultancy and auditing firms.

Citigroup is the market leader; it was number one three years out of four and was still among the top five arrangers in 2001. However, European banks are firmly entrenched in the top part of the league and are greater in number than the American intermediaries.

6.1.3   Integration of Advisory and Arranging Services

We have analyzed the roles of financial advisors and arrangers separately. It is now time to clarify if the same bank (whether an investment bank or commercial bank) can simultaneously be both the financial advisor and the arranger of the deal, provided, of course, that the advisor has the financial strength to take on the task of organizing the pool of lenders.

As for the SPV-borrower, there are three alternatives.

1. The first is to maintain a clear-cut division between the roles of financial advisor and arranger: The borrower decides not to allow its financial advisor to participate in the loan pool once this is structured (specialization model).

---

1. This criterion was preferred to the alternative of using loan amounts effectively disbursed. The reason is that each project necessarily has a mandated lead arranger (or more than one if the size of the deal warrants this), who later sells more important or less important shares of the syndicated loan to other participants. Classification by amount of arranged financing leaves total resources effectively invested unchanged but offers the advantage of highlighting the more active intermediaries in the most important role for the success of the deal. It could be said that a classification by amount financed distorts perception of competitive interaction in the international syndicated loan arranging business field. In fact, the risk would be to find banks with only modest expertise in arranging but with massive balance sheet capabilities—pure lenders—toward the top of the league, whereas less "robust" banks from a financial standpoint but with the necessary expertise to structure deals would be way down the list.

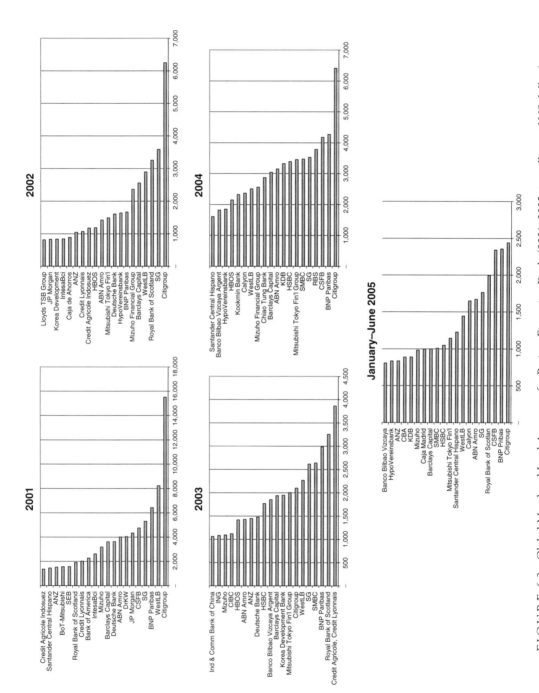

FIGURE 6-3 Global Mandated Lead Arrangers for Project Financing Deals (2001–2005; in millions of US dollars)
Source: Project Finance International.

2. The second alternative is exactly the opposite, in which case the borrower decides beforehand that the chosen financial advisor will also be the arranger in the second phase (integration model).
3. The third situation lies somewhere between the previous two, namely, where the borrower decides to allow its financial advisor to compete with others for the role of arranger.

The advantages and disadvantages for each alternative are clearly exactly opposite in the case of total separation between advisor and arranger or integrated management of the two mandates.

Separating roles between two different intermediaries has the major merit of reducing potential conflict of interest between the party assigning the mandate (the SPV) and the party receiving it (the bank). The pure advisor simply provides a consultancy service where the aim is to get the project off the ground in order to earn the associated success fees. In this case the advisor has no interest in setting a price for the financial package that would be more remunerative in the absence of competitive offers—which might happen if the two roles are integrated. In essence the advisor should in principle ensure impartiality so as to guarantee a balance between the SPV's interests and those of lenders who will later disburse funds to the project company.

However, the specialization model has its significant drawbacks. First of all the pure advisor doesn't invest money in the deal, and so banks called on to support the project have no credible points of reference, such as an underwriting commitment. For this reason banks may fear that the advisor is trying to sell them an excessively risky deal. This in turn means the borrower will find it difficult to source the necessary funds. Furthermore, the advisor may handle the mandate in a particularly prudent manner and structure the security package in favor of lenders, with the aim of making it easier to sell participation in the loan during the syndication phase. This would naturally be a disadvantage for the borrower because the cost of borrowed funds would be higher, making the deal less profitable for sponsors. As a third point, the decisive disadvantage of the specialization model is that duplication of roles is in any event costly for borrowers, even if the issues mentioned earlier were to be resolved.

Once the advisor has completed the mandate, the entire documentation is delivered to the arranger. Before making contact with lenders, the arranger must review all the legal, fiscal, technical, and administrative aspects, which will often require further opinions on specific issues. Clearly this leads to additional costs that could be avoided if the roles of advisor and arranger were combined within a single organization. The question of increased initial costs is a very touchy issue in smaller projects, for which cash flows generated in the operations stage may not be sufficient to absorb structuring costs and at the same time provide an acceptable return on the share capital put up by sponsors.

For all these reasons, data available indicate that a growing number of banks operate in the dual role of advisor and arranger, offering their clients convenient one-stop-shopping solutions and abandoning more extreme forms of specialization. In Table 6-2, prepared based on ProjectWare's Dealogic data, information in the advisor and arranger league tables are cross-matched to verify the number of arrangers who figure among leaders in the advisory market. For the first twenty positions, excluding 2002, the match between advisory and arranging roles is always in the 50–60% range. The group of integrated intermediaries comprises a more or less

TABLE 6-2   Strategic Groups of Financial Intermediaries in the
Project Finance Business (2001–2004)

Number of Top 20 Arrangers in Position of Top 20 Advisors			
2001	2002	2003	2004
8	5	5	8

Integrated Intermediaries
JPMorgan Chase & Co
Citigroup Inc
Bank of America Corp
Deutsche Bank AG
Société Générale
Credit Suisse First Boston (CSFB)
Barclays plc
ABN Amro Holding NV
Dresdner Kleinwort Wasserstein (DKW)
Australia & New Zealand Banking Group Ltd
Toronto-Dominion Bank

Focusing on Arranging Services
Canadian Imperial Bank of Commerce
Credit Lyonnais
National Australia Bank
WestLB AG
BNP Paribas
ING Groep
Royal Bank of Scotland

Focusing on Advisory Services
Macquarie Bank Ltd
Merrill Lynch & Co. Inc.
Morgan Stanley
Rothschild
Lehman Brothers Inc

Source: Authors processing of Project Ware's Dealogic data.

stable nucleus of 10–12 banks that respectively account for a significant 50% and 55% of the total worldwide advisory and arranging markets. Integration between commercial and investment banking also seems to be beneficial for capital market activities. Many integrated operators also figure in leading league positions for project bond bookrunners (see Section 6.11) and so are making inroads on a market segment traditionally dominated by investment banks, which tend to have much more experience in the bond market.

Narrowing the gap between the advisory and arranging business areas appears to be much more appealing to banks with a strong commercial background, traditionally focused on lending and therefore relatively more competitive in arranging services. In fact, it is understandably less costly for the latter banks to extend their range of activities to include advisory services than it is for an investment bank to increase its lending potential.[2]

6.2   Other Roles in Syndicated Loans

Compared to advisory and arranger roles, there is very little to say about other roles played by banks in project finance deals. The reason is that these participants only lend money to the SPV or merely have a cash management and agency role. It must be said that not all roles mentioned will necessarily be found, especially in smaller deals, and many times the same roles are referred to by a different name from deal to deal, depending on the MLA. In any event, the tombstone for the deal shows the name chosen for a given category of lender: The precise role played by each party is indicated in the credit agreement (see Chapter 7).

- **Lead manager, manager, and comanager:** These are banks that grant part of the loan structured by the arranger. The difference between the various categories is based on the amount of participation. Usually a minimum lending commitment (ticker) is established to acquire the status of lead manager, manager, or comanager. A further difference—but only in some cases—is that lead managers and managers can be called on to underwrite part of the loan together with the arranger.
- **Participant:** This is a bank or financial intermediary that lends an amount below the threshold established for the lending commitment. It plays no other role than to make funds available in accordance with the agreed contractual terms.
- **Documentation bank:** This is the bank responsible for the correct drafting of documents concerning the loan (of course, produced by legal firms) as agreed by the borrower and arranger at the time the mandate was assigned. This role is very delicate indeed. Whereas many documents are drafted in a relatively standard manner, others, like those concerning covenants in favor of lenders or default by the borrower (see Chapter 7), must be drafted ad hoc. It is essential that the latter guarantee lenders adequately and cannot be impugned by sponsors or other participants in the deal in the event of changes in the market or the borrower's situation.
- **Agent bank:** This is the bank responsible for managing the SPV's cash flows and payments during the project lifecycle. Normally the loan agreement establishes that cash flows received are credited to a bank account from which the agent bank draws funds based on priorities assigned to payments.

6.3   Fee Structure

When a syndicated loan pool is organized, sponsors of the SPV agree to pay fees to banks participating in the funding in addition to interest on the funds used. Sponsors basically pay two fees in a project finance deal: one for the advisory services and one

---

2. In addition to this, the abolition of the Glass-Steagall Act in the United States, which for years had prevented commercial banks from operating in the investment banking field, has led to a reform of regulations and thereby accelerated the trend toward integration as regards U.S. intermediaries.

for arranging services. These fees are only paid to the advisor/arranger, who then transfers part of them to other banks participating in the pool based on their role. So sponsors only have to make payments to two parties—the financial advisor and the MLA—unless of course both roles are covered by the same bank, in which case fees are paid to only one party. The lead arranger then pays other banks in the pool by returning part of the fees received to them. The terms governing this procedure are established by the lead arranger in a fee letter that, if accepted, is returned countersigned by each bank participating in the pool.

6.3.1 Fees for Advisory Services

The structure of fees payable by sponsors to the financial advisor (apart from sums reimbursed for expenses incurred) includes retainer fees and success fees.

- **Retainer fee:** This covers the advisory's costs during the study and preparation phase of the deal. Justification for the advisor's request for a retainer fee is based on the need to use analysts' time to study the feasibility of the deal and maintain contacts with parties initially involved in planning it. In certain cases, however, preliminary studies can take a long time, and this leads to costs that will not be paid if the project cannot be funded. The retainer fee is intended to cover such costs partially; market standards for this fee call for a monthly payment by sponsors ranging from 15,000 to 25,000 euro, established on a lump-sum basis.
- **Success fee:** This fee is paid by sponsors once the study and planning mandate has led to a successful conclusion. As opposed to the retainer fee, the success fee is established on a percentage basis, to provide an incentive for the advisor not only to structure the deal but also to organize it based on the most favorable terms and conditions for sponsors. As for market standards, success fees range from 0.5% to 1% of the debt value—not the project value.

There are two possible explanations for this practice.

1. Intuitively, it wouldn't make sense for sponsors to pay a fee on funds they contribute themselves, which would be the case if the percentage were calculated on the total investment. It is much more logical to base the success fee on the loan value.
2. Linking the fee to the loan amount gives incentives to the advisor to plan deals with the highest possible debt-to-equity ratio, with obvious benefits on the rate of return for the SPV's sponsors.

The percentage negotiated between the advisor and the sponsors will depend on various factors. The size of the project and the degree of innovativeness of the venture will be two determining factors. The level of the success fee will be inversely proportional to the size of the project; a smaller project will command a higher percentage. The degree of innovation inherent to the project will, in contrast, affect the fee directly; an extremely innovative venture will require a greater effort by the advisor and therefore will justify the request for a more generous fee.

If advisory and arranging services are provided by the same intermediary, then there will be a single fee structure to remunerate both roles. Again in this case there will be reimbursement of expenses and a retainer fee for the study and preliminary planning phase. However, the success fee will be established as a single percentage. Furthermore, it is normal practice for the arranger to discount part of the retainer fee (usually the equivalent of fees for two/three months) from the success fee agreed on with the sponsors of the venture.

6.3.2 Fees for Arranging Services

Sponsors pay a one-time arranging fee to the MLA as compensation for activities to finalize structuring of the financing. In certain cases a retainer fee is paid too, although this doesn't happen very often. Again, in this case the arranging fee is established as a percentage of the debt (for the same reasons discussed with reference to advisory fees). Market standards range from 0.7% to 1% of the syndicated debt.

The arranging fee can in turn concern the following.

- **A pure arranging fee:** In this case the MLA operates on a best-effort basis. The arranger commits to sponsors that best efforts will be made to syndicate the loan but without guaranteeing a market response sufficient to cover fully the financing requirements for the project.
- **A fee for underwriting and arranging services:** In this case the mandated lead arranger operates on a committed basis. That is, as in the previous case, every effort will be made to syndicate a pool of lenders. However, in this case there is the guarantee that the necessary funds will be made available in the event it becomes impossible to find intermediaries interested in participating in the deal. This guarantee is undoubtedly beneficial for the borrower but has a cost in the form of a higher arranging fee.

After the sponsors pay the arranging fee, the mandated lead arranger returns part of it to other banks participating in the pool. If the deal calls for other arrangers (coarrangers), then they are paid part of the arranging fee, usually proportional to the amount underwritten. The percentage, however, is usually lower than that earned by the lead arranger (on average between 0.5% and 0.8% of the part of the loan underwritten). In essence the lead arranger earns a percentage of the arranging fee, calculated on the amount it has underwritten, and the spread between the percentage paid by sponsors and that recognized for coarrangers, calculated on the part not underwritten by the lead arranger.

6.3.3 Fees to Participants and the Agent Bank

Participating banks (lead managers, managers, and comanagers) receive an up-front management fee ranging from 20 to 40 basis points on the amount each of them lends. The up-front management fee also comes out of the arranging fee paid by sponsors to the MLA.

Participants are also entitled to a commitment fee, calculated on the basis of time, with reference to the difference between the maximum amount made available to the SPV (committed amount) and the amount disbursed at the beginning of each reference period (for instance, a half-year). This means

$$\mathrm{CF} = (\mathrm{CL} - E_t) \times \mathrm{cf} \times \frac{t}{360}$$

where CF is the commitment fee paid, CL is the maximum committed loan to the borrower, cf is the percentage of the annual commitment fee, E_t is the amount disbursed at the beginning of period t, and t is the number of days for calculating the reference period. In essence, the SPV pays lenders interest calculated at the agreed rate on that part of the loan effectively used, whereas it pays a commitment fee on the amount committed but not used. The reason for this payment is that while lender banks may not have materially disbursed certain funds, they are required to set aside part of their capital for committed loans based on equity coefficients established by each country's banking supervisory authority (see Chapter 8). Given that the bank's equity capital should be remunerated, the commitment fee should enable lenders to obtain compensation to cover part of this notional cost. The SPV pays the commitment fee periodically to the agent bank, which then returns it to banks participating in the pool based on funds each of them has committed. Lastly, the agent bank receives a fixed annual payment ranging from 40,000 to 100,000 euro. The amount of this agency fee will depend on the number of banks participating in the pool because this is the variable determining the intermediary's administrative task.

6.3.4   Example of Fee Calculation

Table 6-3 shows salient information as regards the structuring and syndication of a project finance loan for an amount of 200 million euro. The deal has been organized by an advisor (Bank A) as a syndicate in which Banks B and C are respectively mandated lead arranger and coarranger on a committed basis (so the latter jointly underwrite the entire loan amount). Banks D, E, and F participate in the role of managers for an amount of 150 million euro. This means that after the selling process, the mandated arranger and coarranger will participate as lenders for the remaining 50 million euro (subdivided based on the underwriting agreement for an amount of 25 million each).

Amounts recognized for each participant are calculated as follows. The advisor receives a success fee of 75 basis points calculated on 200 million, therefore

TABLE 6-3   Participating Intermediaries and Structure of the Deal

Syndicated amount	200,000,000.00 euro
Advisor success fee	0.75%
Arranging fee	1%
Coarranging fee	0.80%
Up-front management fee	0.20%

Members of the Syndicate	Role	Fee	Underwritten Amount (euro)	Financed Amount (euro)
Bank A	Advisor	Success fee	n.a.	n.a.
Bank B	Lead arranger	Arranging fee	100,000,000.00	25,000,000.00
Bank C	Coarranger	Arranging fee	100,000,000.00	25,000,000.00
Bank D	Manager	Up-front fee	n.a.	40,000,000.00
Bank E	Manager	Up-front fee	n.a.	50,000,000.00
Bank F	Manager	Up-front fee	n.a.	60,000,000.00

TABLE 6-4   Return of the Arranging Fee (in euro)

Fee	Bank B	Bank C	Bank D	Bank E	Bank F
Arranging fee	2,000,000.00				
Coarranging fee	800,000.00	800,000.00	n.a.	n.a.	n.a.
Up-front management fee	350,000.00	50,000.00	80,000.00	100,000.00	120,000.00
Total fees	850,000.00	850,000.00	80,000.00	100,000.00	120,000.00

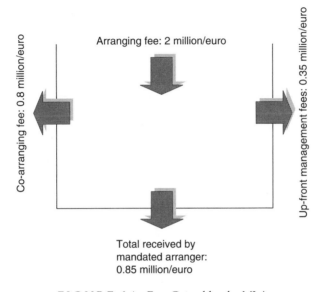

FIGURE 6-4   Fees Gained by the MLA

1.5 million euro. The mandated lead arranger receives a total of 2 million euro (1% of 200 million) and then proceeds to return the fee to the other participants as indicated in Table 6-4.

In essence the arranger's position is as outlined in Figure 6-4.

Clearly the percentage return on capital invested (calculated in Table 6-5) is certain for managers, whereas it depends on the amount of the loan financed by participants for the arranger and coarranger. This can be seen by comparing amounts in the last line of Table 6-4 with those shown in the column "Financed Amount" in Table 6-3.

It should also be noted that the mandated lead arranger's strong negotiating position means it can return lower percentages for coarranging fees and up-front management fees, respectively, to coarrangers and managers. In the preceding example, the sum of coarranging fees and up-front management fees is exactly 1%.

TABLE 6-5   Percentage Return on Capital Invested for Members of the Pool

Bank B	Bank C	Bank D	Bank E	Bank F
3.40%	3.40%	0.20%	0.20%	0.20%

TABLE 6-6   Allocation of Fees in the Event of a Low Return of the Coarranging and Up-Front Management Fees (in euro)

Fee	Bank B	Bank C	Bank D	Bank E	Bank F
Arranging fee	2,000,000.00				
Coarranging fee	700,000.00	700,000.00	n.a.	n.a.	n.a.
Up-front management fee	262,500.00	37,500.00	60,000.00	75,000.00	90,000.00
Total fees	1,037,500.00	737,500.00	60,000.00	75,000.00	90,000.00
	Bank B	**Bank C**	**Bank D**	**Bank E**	**Bank F**
	4.15%	2.95%	0.15%	0.15%	0.15%

And so the MLA's return on the deal is exactly the same as that of the coarrangers if their bargaining power is so strong that they manage to wrest the entire 1% from the lead arranger. Using the same example, but in this case assuming that only 0.7% is returned to coarrangers as their fee and that the up-front management fee is 0.15%, the distribution of income and percentage returns would be as shown in Table 6-6.

6.4   International Financial Institutions and Multilateral Banks

A special category of bank that often participates actively in international syndicated loans is the international financial institution (IFI), which plays a leading role in project finance deals in developing countries. There are many of these institutions, diversified in terms of their role, function, mission, investment capacity, and area of activity. But before illustrating the part they play, it is necessary to describe briefly the role of IFIs and how they have evolved.

A glance at data prepared by the World Bank (see Table 6-7) shows that the role of IFIs, including those formed in 1944 on the wave of Bretton Woods, have changed over time. Support for development has seen a decrease in official financial flows toward poor countries in favor of flows coming from the private sector. In 1990 official flows accounted for 56% of flows to developing countries; in 2004 the World Bank estimate indicates a marginal weight of around 7%.

TABLE 6-7   Net Capital Flows to Developing Countries, 1970–2004 (in US$ billions)

	1970	1980	1990	1996	2000	2004e
Net flows of resources	11.17	82.81	99.14	311.80	201.10	323.80
Official net flows (subsidies and loans granted)	5.38	34.99	55.60	30.50	23.00	22.50
Net private flows (equity and loans)	5.79	47.82	43.55	281.30	178.10	301.30
Official flows (% of total flows)	48.2%	42.3%	56.1%	9.8%	11.4%	6.9%
Private flows (% of total flows)	51.8%	57.7%	43.9%	90.2%	88.6%	93.1%

Source: Global Development Finance, various years.

TABLE 6-8 Net Official Financing to Developing Countries, 1990–2003 (in US$ billions)

World Bank Institute	1990	2000	2001	2002	2003e
Grants (subsidies and aid)	27.70	28.70	27.90	31.20	34.30
Net financing	26.50	−5.90	26.90	4.10	−6.30
Multilateral organizations*	15.50	0.90	34.60	14.70	6.50
Concessional	6.7	5.6	7.3	7.5	6.4
Nonconcessional	8.8	−4.7	27.3	7.2	0.1
Bilateral organizations	11.0	−6.8	−7.7	−10.6	−12.8
Concessional	8.5	0.7	1.6	−1.8	−1.0
Nonconcessional	2.5	−7.5	−9.3	−8.8	−11.8
Total	54.20	22.80	54.80	35.30	28.00

*International Monetary Fund (IMF) included.
Source: Global Development Finance, various years.

The reason for the lower weight of official flows compared with a growth for private-sector flows is due to budget problems in industrialized countries and much stronger resistance by the U.S. Congress as regards the financing and management of international agencies that have questioned financing for international aid organizations.[3] The effect of this drop in availability of funds for bilateral and multilateral banks has been to make cooperation policies more selective, and at the same time it has reduced the amount of funding available for this purpose. This modified scenario has led to a change in the role of banks, whereas the financial needs of developing countries have remained stable over time: Banks no longer lend directly but instead promote investments coming from the private sector by means of guarantees granted by the latter (Table 6-8).

As we can see in Table 6-8, disbursements by official sources (including grants) dropped from $55 billion in 2001 to $28 billion, based on the World Bank estimate for 2003. This drop reflects rapid swings in multilateral loans in order to provide rescue packages to countries facing crises and not a reduction of funds destined for loans to developing countries.

Rapid growth of project finance in developing countries in the 1990s was facilitated by direct aid in the form of loans, guarantees, and insurance from bilateral and multilateral agencies. At that time, an official agency participated in the majority of project finance deals, even though the amount of official aid varied according to the project sector and country concerned. In response to the growing conviction that private projects are what really fuels development, many bilateral and multilateral organizations have changed their objective, moving away from financing governments of developing countries and toward financing private deals. Their willingness to invest in high-risk countries and sectors has certainly contributed to the growth of project finance in recent years.

3. A criticism made of IFIs (even bilateral ones) concerns their role, which ought to focus more on financing sustainable development. As opposed to their private counterparties, these organizations base their decisions on political pressures as opposed to financial return on the investment. When the Bretton Woods organizations were set up, their "tasks" were to participate in large-scale, risky projects. Today their role has changed, both as a result of increased flows of private financing and because of the realization that large infrastructure projects are not the best way to achieve sustainable development. See Pearce and Ekins (2001).

6.4.1   Multilateral Organizations

Multilateral financial organizations play a very important role in project financing for developing countries, for three reasons.

- Their institutional mandate allows taking on financial commitments even in countries with a high political risk.
- They have played a leading role in privatization policies.
- They continue to promote financing in the private sector and private investment in the infrastructure sector.

In principle, multilateral financial organizations should counterbalance the trend for private financial flows by increasing loans in periods of reduced interest from the financial market. Among the multilateral financial organizations, the most important in terms of political weight and financing volume is the World Bank Group. It comprises four major agencies through which the World Bank contributes to development in member countries in a wide variety of ways, working together with both private and public parties: the IBRD (International Bank for Reconstruction and Development), IDA (International Development Association), IFC (International Finance Corporation), and MIGA (Multilateral Investment Guarantee Agency). In addition to the World Bank, which operates at global level, there are other international multilateral financial organizations (major regional development banks) that focus their activities on a specific geographical area. Some have a continental scope and mission (European Investment Bank in Luxembourg, Asian Development Bank in Manila, African Development Bank in Abidjan, Inter-American Development Bank in Washington). Then after the fall of the Berlin Wall, the European Bank for Reconstruction and Development (EBRD), based in London, was added. The regional bias of these banks is also seen in their governing bodies, given that stakeholders reflect the continental focus of their activities.

Table 6-9 shows the financial contribution of multilateral financial organizations at the end of 2004. The differences between the various agencies are quite evident. From the standpoint of amounts, the most exposed are the World Bank and EIB, whereas in terms of investment in the private sector IFC (100%) and EBRD (75.6%) play a leading role.

TABLE 6-9   Financial Contribution of Multilateral Banks, 2004 (in US$ billions)

Bank	Portfolio	Amount Invested in Private Sector	% Invested in Private Sector
IBRD and IDA	104.40	n.a.	17.00%
IFC*	8.90	8.90	100.00%
Asian Development Bank	5.30	0.53	10.00%
African Development Bank**	1.26	n.a.	6.00%
EBRD	6.19	4.68	75.62%
EIB	98.32	n.a.	12.50%
Inter-American Development Bank	5.46	0.19	3.48%

* Refers to FY ending Dec. 31, 2005.
** Loan approvals.
Source: Multilaterals' Annual Reports, various years. Where data are missing, estimates have been made by the author.

TABLE 6-10   Multilateral Bank–Committed Funds for Infrastructure Works, 1995–2002 (in US$ billions)

	1995	1996	1997	1998	1999	2000	2001	2002
Total funds committed	52.38	74.07	45.95	43.17	44.22	43.93	43.02	42.34
Total funds for Infrastructure works	17.8	18.3	16.6	17.7	13.8	15.0	14.7	16.5
% of total committed funds	33.98	24.71	36.13	41.00	31.21	34.15	34.17	38.97
Asian Development Bank	3.42	2.85	1.90	2.33	1.75	2.66	2.26	2.88
African Development Bank	0.17	0.08	0.21	0.37	0.28	0.16	0.37	0.46
EBRD	1.40	1.63	1.07	0.87	0.92	0.79	0.16	1.46
EIB	2.66	2.43	3.06	3.48	2.99	3.74	3.55	4.40
IBRD/IDA	7.38	7.95	6.61	6.67	5.28	4.29	4.98	4.60
Inter-American Development Bank	2.22	2.67	2.80	3.11	1.78	1.70	0.99	1.00
IFC	0.33	0.36	0.49	0.39	0.29	0.47	0.32	0.49
Islamic Development Bank	0.21	0.15	0.29	0.26	0.35	0.47	0.48	0.45
MIGA*	0.14	0.15	0.14	0.18	0.20	0.75	0.57	0.86

* Political risk insurance coverage.
Source: Global Development Finance, 2004.

In contrast, Table 6-10 shows multilateral bank commitments for loans to developing countries concerning investments in infrastructures.

The table reveals that funds committed for infrastructure works saw a slowdown in 1999 but then grew progressively in terms of both amount and percentage incidence. A further aspect the table highlights is that as opposed to the early 1990s, when the World Bank was the major source of multilateral financing to emerging countries, in recent years the major regional development banks taken together have provided about the same level of resources as the World Bank.

6.4.1.1   World Bank Group

The World Bank was founded in 1944 at Bretton Woods during a conference that saw the participation of the governments of 45 countries. Originally called the International Bank for Reconstruction and Development (IBRD), it was set up primarily to finance postwar reconstruction in Europe. However, compared to the early days, the aim to reduce poverty in the world has taken on greater importance.[4]

The World Bank Group includes five interlinked agencies in which the stakeholders are governments of member countries that have power to make final decisions. Every agency has a distinct role in the common mission to fight poverty and promote sustainable growth in less developed economies, even though from the standpoint of project finance the two most significant are IFC and MIGA, because they focus

4. The World Bank's most recent strategic goals were agreed on in 2002 by 189 countries during the Millennium Summit of the United Nations, at which the Millennium Development Goals were defined. More precisely these were: (1) to eliminate the roots of poverty and hunger; (2) to ensure universal primary education; (3) to promote equality between men and women and give more power to women; (4) to reduce infant mortality; (5) to combat AIDS, malaria, and other diseases; (6) to ensure a sustainable environment; (7) to develop global cooperation for growth.

TABLE 6-11   Target for Intervention of World Bank Group Agencies

Agency	Year Founded	Number of Member Countries	Main Activity Categories	Target for Intervention
IBRD: International Bank for Reconstruction and Development	1944	184	Loans, guarantees, equity investments, consultancy	Developing countries with average income and high credibility
IDA: International Development Association	1960	164	Loans at heavily subsidized conditions	Poorest developing countries
IFC: International Finance Corporation	1956	175	Loans, equity investments, arranging of loan syndicates, indirect methods of support	Entirely private projects in developing countries
MIGA: Multilateral Investment Guarantee Agency	1988	163	Stimulates foreign investment in developing countries by offering guarantees against political risks	Potential investors in developing countries
ICSID: International Center for Settlement of Investment Disputes	1966	139	Developing foreign investments in emerging markets by means of legal advice and settling disputes on investment questions at international level	Target investment countries for foreign operators

mainly on private investment. Table 6-11 gives a summary of certain elements that help understand the mission of the different agencies.

IBRD (International Bank for Reconstruction and Development): IBRD is, effectively speaking, the World Bank because both share the same mission and intervention strategy.

Specifically with regard to project finance deals, the agency operates by means of:

- Direct loans
- Partial risk guarantees
- Partial credit guarantees
- Enclave guarantees

Direct loans encourage the private sector by means of cofinancing deals, known as B-loans. In direct loan schemes the private sector makes loans to developing country governments together with IBRD (which grants an A-loan) and benefits from the privileged status of the bank's loans. To finance projects directly in the private sector the bank must use governments as intermediaries: IBRD and private banks (respectively with the A- and B-loans) finance governments that, in turn, finance private parties. An alternative is that IBRD and private banks lend directly to the SPV after obtaining guarantees from the host government. Operations of the SPV are partly conditioned by limits and rules imposed by IBRD, in conformity with international competitive bidding (ICB) procedures.

The partial risk guarantee covers political risks and is available for all countries entitled to receive World Bank loans, with the exception of very low-income countries that can be insured by guarantees proposed by MIGA (see later in this chapter). The guarantee is available for investors that enter into financing contracts directly with host governments (in other words, the borrower is a government body) or with SPVs guaranteed by the host government or with counterparties of the SPV backed by government guarantee.

These conditions explain why this facility is used in very few project finance deals. Wherever possible the World Bank tries to use instruments made available by its other agencies (above all IFC and MIGA), thereby avoiding direct intervention, which only occurs in the form of a guarantee of last resort if:

- No private financing is available
- Financing from IFC or risk coverage from MIGA is insufficient

So the projects concerned are very large and complex and intervention of the World Bank is indispensable in order to structure the total financial package. The guarantee is granted to the SPV's lenders and covers the following risks (see Chapter 3):

- Currency convertibility risk
- Transferability and expropriation risk
- Change in law
- Breach of contract risk

Instead the partial risk guarantee doesn't cover the risk of political violence, war and expropriation, which must be handled directly with the host government by means of rules defined in the government support agreement.

The partial credit guarantee is a facility used to resolve a significant problem in the syndicated loan market for financing infrastructure projects. Some, especially very complex ones, require very long repayment plans that private banks find very difficult to finance. In this case, the World Bank can operate as the guarantor for capital repayments and interest due in periods beyond those that credit committees of private banks consider acceptable, given constraints imposed by their internal credit policies. The same guarantee can also cover bullet capital repayments (namely, a single repayment at the end of the loan period) that the SPV intends to refinance. Despite its importance as a catalyst for private capital investment, only limited use has been made of this instrument.

The enclave guarantee is a facility reserved for so-called *enclave projects*, that is, project finance deals set up to realize projects focusing on exports (frequently seen in the oil and gas sector for realization of pipelines to export natural gas or oil production in offshore sites). Revenue flows for these projects are in foreign currency from a source outside the host country (for instance, from an escrow account outside the country or from an SPV domiciled outside the host country boundaries) and so protect the project from two basic risks.

- Foreign currency is never transferred to the host country, and therefore there is no possibility to limit its transfer to countries where the sponsors and creditors are resident; furthermore foreign exchange available outside the country can be withheld directly to service the debt (transferability risk).

• Revenues are stated in foreign currency, and so sponsors and lenders have no currency risk. Because both currency risk and transfer risk are covered, the enclave guarantee can be requested to cover additional risks, such as expropriation, civil war, or changes in regulations.

IDA (International Development Association):   IDA provides financial support for poorer countries that fail to meet criteria for access to World Bank-IBRD financing. Development finance support is in the form of very long-term loans (35–40 years), with long grace periods (up to 10 years) and with no interest payment, which is replaced by an annual servicing fee of 0.75%. The scope of interventions is development of human capital, basic infrastructures, support for setting up stable political structures, and institutions in very poor countries in order to promote sustainable growth. The main aim is to reduce inequalities between countries and within countries themselves, particularly as regards primary education and availability of water and health services. IBRD and IDA are managed based on the same guidelines, share the same staff and facilities, and use the same criteria when evaluating projects. The only difference is that they are financed by different sources. Whereas the World Bank obtains funding in international financial markets, most of IDA's operating resources come from contributions made by the governments of developed countries.

Bearing in mind the target countries and sectors concerned, IDA's role in the project finance field is limited to indirect loans, similar to those offered by IBRD, and a guarantee program for projects that fail to qualify for enclave guarantees. IDA also provides private investors with guarantees against currency convertibility risk in the event such guarantees for investments are unavailable.

IFC (International Finance Corporation):   IFC is the multilateral agency that provides financing (loans and equity) for private projects in all sectors in developing countries. Of all World Bank agencies, this is the only one that doesn't require the direct intervention (or a guarantee) of the host government to proceed with financing a venture. Even though IFC focuses mainly on private projects, it can also provide financing for a company that has a public-sector partner, provided there is a private investor involved and that the company is managed as a profit-making venture. It can finance 100% locally owned companies or joint ventures with local and foreign partners.

IFC promotes sustainable growth in the private sector mainly by doing the following:

• Financing private projects in developing countries
• Helping private companies in developing countries to obtain financing in international financial markets
• Providing consultancy and technical assistance services to companies and governments.

As far as project finance deals are concerned, IFC offers a series of financial products and services to companies in member developing countries, it helps to structure financial packages, to coordinate financing from foreign banks, from local banks, from companies, and from export credit agencies (ECAs; see Section 6.5.2). To be eligible for IFC financing, projects must be profitable for investors, generate benefits for the host country's economy, and observe environmental and social guidelines imposed by the agency.

Services offered to investors are:

- Loan programs
- Equity investments
- Derivatives to set up hedging policies
- Guarantees

Loan programs involve IFC cofinancing with private funding. To ensure participation of private investors and creditors, IFC caps the share of financing it makes available for each project: On average, for every $1 financed by IFC the other investors put up over $5. The current limit is a cap of $100 million per individual project, and with a limit of 25% of total costs for new projects, 35% for smaller projects, and 50% for expansion of preexisting projects. IFC finances are based on market conditions. (There are no subsidies for borrowers.) Moreover, there is no requirement for direct guarantees from the host country government, as opposed to other World Bank agencies. The term of loans can be up to 20 years.

In addition to financing by means of direct loans, IFC also has a B-loan program. (B-type loans are syndicated loans.) This is based on similar principles to the World Bank program discussed earlier in this section. In B-loan programs IFC sells shares of the loan to commercial banks but continues to act as if it were the lender of record, administering the loan and being the recipient of guarantees. In this way a borrower cannot pay IFC and declare default as regards other members of the pool, given that all payments are divided proportionately between A-loans (granted directly by IFC) and B-loans. Default on a B-loan equates to breach of contract with IFC. The fact that IFC is lender of records as far as B-loans are concerned has positive effects for members of the pool, inasmuch as privileged creditor status applies to loans granted as part of the B-loan program. In this way banks can avoid setting up risk provisions if the country in which the project is financed is insolvent, given the privileged status assigned to such lenders.

In addition to direct loans and cofinancing in A- and B-loan programs, IFC can hold a minority stake (usually between 5% and 15%, up to a maximum of 35%) in the equity of SPVs as a passive investor according to the private equity investor approach (equity investment program). In other words, IFC doesn't intervene in the SPV's strategic and operating decisions. The average duration of investments is longer than in the private equity market and can extend up to 8–15 years. Preferably sale of equity takes place on the stock exchange in the country where the SPV is set up. Equity investment is rather conservative and usually requires payment for shares at par value without any share premium reserve to repay sponsors for study, initial development, and start-up costs. There is always a potential conflict of interest in deals where IFC is both an equity investor and lender of record for a B-loan program for the same project. Sponsors and lenders clearly have opposite interests as regards the amount of equity in a project's financial structure: The former want to minimize it, whereas the latter subordinate high financial leverage to perfect mitigation of project risks. If IFC were an equity investor, it could propose a more aggressive debt-to-equity ratio and lower cover ratios (see Chapter 5) to banks participating in the B-loan program.

The third type of assistance, which IFC began offering in the early 1990s, concerns derivatives. These involve swaps to hedge interest and exchange rate risks, options, forward contracts, and other derivative products to help clients manage financial risks in the best possible manner. Derivatives are offered because SPVs in developing countries find it difficult to access international capital markets. IFC acts as an intermediary. It mobilizes participation of commercial banks in these deals by sharing risks and promoting development of local capital markets.

The fourth type of aid provided by IFC is the guarantee program. In fact, partial credit guarantees are given similar to those issued by the World Bank, which cover all credit risks during a specific period of the loan and can therefore be used to extend the repayment period of private-sector loans.

As can be seen in Table 6-12, even today the majority of IFC's financial activities concerns loans, which account for over 70% of total funds allocated in the years analyzed. Commitments in terms of equity contribution have instead decreased progressively as a percentage of the total committed portfolio. Furthermore, starting in 2003 there has been a constant increase in the number of projects.

MIGA (Multilateral Investment Guarantee Agency): MIGA contributes to the World Bank's mission by providing political risk coverage to lenders and investors; in this way it makes investment in developing countries more attractive for private foreign capital.

MIGA offers coverage for all 163 World Bank member countries. Its own capital is for the most part provided by members and a smaller proportion by the World Bank as a contribution to capitalize MIGA. Within the World Bank Group, and including regional development banks, it is the only agency that offers coverage for investments against political risks. In addition to this main activity, MIGA has a special section dedicated to consultancy (IMS, Investment Marketing Services), the aim of which is to help developing countries attract foreign investment. In this area MIGA offers both consultancy services on request and investment information and tries to help companies in member countries by developing necessary skills.

As a World Bank Group agency, MIGA only offers coverage based on an agreement with the host country. In line with its aims to promote economic growth and development, investment projects must be financially and economically viable. Coverage for political risks includes both debt financing and equity investments, up to a maximum coverage of 95% of debt service (principal repayment plus interest) and equity investment, with a maximum limit of US$200 million per project and US$420 million per country. The insurance premium ranges from 0.5% to 1.75% of the insured sum, and the contract has a duration of 15 years, with a possibility of up

TABLE 6-12   IFC Intervention in the Private Sector by Type of Facility, 2001–2005 (in US$ billions)

	2001	2002	2003	2004	2005
New projects committed	205	204	204	217	236
Total financing committed	3.90	3.60	5.00	5.63	6.45
Financing committed for IFC's own funds	2.70	3.10	3.90	4.75	5.37
Total committed portfolio*	5.4	5.8	5.4	17.9	19.3
Equity as % of portfolio	25%	23%	21%	20%	17%
Loans as % of portfolio	75%	71%	71%	74%	77%
Structured finance products (including guarantees) as % of portfolio	n.d.	5%	6%	5%	5%
Risk management products as % of portfolio	n.d.	1%	2%	1%	1%

* Includes off-balance-sheet products such as structured finance and risk management products.
Source: IFC, *Annual report*, various years.

to 20 years in exceptional cases. The insured party has an option to cancel the coverage after 3 years.

In addition to direct insurance, MIGA manages the so-called CUP (Cooperative Underwriting Program). This program is very similar to the B-loan programs managed by IBRD and IFC, with the difference that it concerns insurance contracts and not loans. MIGA cooperates with private insurance companies by taking on risks itself and then reinsuring them with private insurers. Given that MIGA provides coverage for political risks, the following are the negative events covered.

- **Currency convertibility and transferability:** If convertibility becomes impossible, the investor can deliver the nonconvertible currency to MIGA, for which the agency pays in a guaranteed currency. Damage caused by delays in transferring funds can also be covered.
- **Expropriation:** If equity investments are expropriated, MIGA reimburses the net book value of the insured investment. As for expropriation of funds, MIGA pays the amount insured for blocked funds. In the case of loans and loan guarantees, MIGA insures the outstanding principal and interest due but not paid. However, MIGA guarantees do not cover measures taken by host governments acting in good faith and relating to a legitimate right to regulate and control its own country.
- **War, civil war, terrorism, sabotage:** Should such events occur, MIGA insures both physical damage to the project and damage caused by business interruption that can compromise the project's viability. In these cases MIGA reimburses the net book value of the equity investment and the value of the outstanding principal and interest due not paid as a result of the damaging event.
- **Failure to pay damages awarded by arbitration:** If the host government causes a breach of contract and the SPV has been awarded damages by a court or in international arbitration proceedings, in some cases the host government challenges the award and payment of damages is delayed. In such cases MIGA can pay compensation and also an advance while awaiting the final outcome of litigation.

6.4.2 Regional Development Banks

Regional development banks are also multilateral financial agencies, but they operate in a more restricted geographical area than the World Bank. They focus on one geographical area only (usually a continent), and their share capital is held by governments of countries in the area concerned.

6.4.2.1 European Investment Bank (EIB)

The European Investment Bank, the European Union's (EU's) financial agency, was set up in 1958 by the Treaty of Rome. Members of the EIB are EU member countries that subscribed to the bank's equity capital. The agency is both legally and financially independent from the European Union, but its mission is to promote the EU's objectives by offering long-term financing for specific projects meeting strict criteria in terms of evaluation and selection of the ventures concerned. In this way, it contributes to economic integration within Europe and greater economic and social cohesion.

EIB participation in financing investment projects is based on a preliminary evaluation and ongoing monitoring of the venture concerned; therefore, EIB operates according to best practices in the private banking sector. To receive EIB support, projects must be viable from the economic, technical, environmental, and financial standpoints. EIB loans are essentially financed by funding on capital markets. Given its special ownership structure, it has a maximum (AAA) international bond market rating, and so the bank can propose advantageous pricing to project companies. Furthermore, as in the case of IFC, EIB continually seeks to involve private capital in projects it finances, acting as a catalyst for private lenders in order to expand available funds.

The scope of EIB's activities can best be explained by dividing them into two categories:

- Ventures within the European Union
- Ventures outside the European Union

Ventures Within the European Union: As regards EU countries, EIB finances projects that contribute to economic growth and benefit cohesion within the EU. Guidelines for financing are very precise: Participation can cover up to 50% of the total project cost for a duration of up to 12 years for industrial projects or 20 years for infrastructure projects. In the case of PPP projects (public–private partnerships; see later), the duration can exceed 20 years (a common situation in the social infrastructure sector, such as hospitals) and even extend to 30 years for urban development and local transport projects. At the end of 2003, PPP projects with a duration exceeding 25 years accounted for about one-quarter of the Bank's PPP portfolio.

Conditions proposed to SPVs are more favorable than those offered by the private banking sector, thanks to EIB's ability to obtain funds in the bond market at a lower cost. A further feature of these loans is that there is no arranging fee, as is normally the case with syndicated loans, but only an agency fee to cover the bank's operating costs. As in the case of private banking-sector loans, the bank can lend at a variable or fixed interest rate.

While there are clearly financial advantages, borrowers obtaining funds from EIB have to accept some very stringent conditions.

- Projects undergo an in-depth preliminary analysis to determine whether they are technically sustainable and what benefits can be obtained from the venture, even when there are guarantees from the private banking sector.
- Projects must meet EU environmental standards and follow the EU's procurement rules and procedures.
- As opposed to private banks, EIB doesn't take on project completion risk, in other words, risks associated with extra costs, delays, or performance before completion of the project and its start-up phase (see Chapter 3). The bank may, however, accept risks in the project's postcompletion stage, although not immediately after operations begin and after an evaluation of initial performance. The only exception from these guidelines is the Structured Finance Facility (SFF), created in 2000 for the purpose of providing senior debt, mezzanine debt, and derivative instruments to hedge risks. Under the terms of this facility and depending on funds set aside, the EIB can take on precompletion risk and also operating risk during initial project start-up phases.

- To cover this very restrictive policy as regards risk-taking, EIB requests commercial bank guarantees to cover its own commitments at risk. These guarantees must cover outstanding debt at a certain date, interest payments for 6 months, and a figure to cover breach-of-contract risk. Banks must be able to meet eligible criteria based on a minimum rating level or provide cash guarantees.

Ventures Outside the European Union: Outside the EU, EIB finances projects based on mandates received from the EU defining the maximum amount that can be financed in every area. These mandates concern:

- Future member-states of the EU
- Certain countries in the Mediterranean area, developing countries, and the Balkans

For loans outside the EU, EIB takes on the political risk in its most restricted sense, namely, the risk of currency convertibility and transferability, political violence, and expropriation risk. Instead it doesn't cover breach-of-contract or creeping-expropriation risk (see Chapter 3). So the bank requires complete bank guarantees to cover business risks. Furthermore, EIB doesn't cover subsovereign risks and so requests a guarantee from the host government or lends directly to that government (in which case it can have a direct interest in the project), which in turn loans the funds to the SPV.

EIB Participation in Public–Private-Partnership (PPP) Projects: As part of its policy to provide support for growth of EU member states, starting in the second half of the 1990s the bank increased its participation in public infrastructure projects financed with private capital, with the aim of enabling the public sector to benefit from advantages deriving from EIB's participation in financing these types of projects. For PPPs the bank applies the same valuation and selection criteria used for other projects. Ventures must be financially sound, economically and technically viable, and compatible with the bank's EU environmental guidelines, and procurement contracts must be awarded based on competitive procedures and rules established by the EU. In fact the bank participates right from the early stages by working with potential bidders during the competitive phase running up to award of contract so that bidders can pass on part of the benefits deriving from EIB's participation as a lender to the public sector.

As far as lending policies are concerned, however, a PPP project has to comply with the same rules applying to a 100% private project. PPPs financed by EIB need to present guarantees from the banking or monoline insurance sectors (see Chapter 4), excluding precompletion and early operating stage risks (except projects financed by a Structured Finance Facility), which must pass stringent tests in terms of cover ratios. The involvement of the public sector as the final debtor is considered very important. In many PPPs, in fact, the public sector is the sole purchaser of the product or service (take, for instance, the case of hospital or school construction), and so there is no market risk. It should also be noted that the average amount of participation in PPPs is not very significant; this means the bank is able to limit concentration risk as regards its loan portfolio.

6.4.2.2 AfDB (African Development Bank)

AfDB is a multilateral regional development bank whose stakeholders are the 53 African nations and 24 non-African countries from the Americas, Europe, and Asia.

It was set up in 1964 and began operations in 1967 to promote the economic growth and social progress of its regional members, both individually and collectively. The bank promotes projects in the infrastructure field and with a particular emphasis on PPPs, for which it provides financial support in the form of loans and equity investments. It also provides:

- Advisory services to private parties as regards structuring deals
- Advisory and support services to public bodies to help them create a favorable institutional environment from the legal and regulatory standpoints and to ensure that they are capable of managing their relations efficiently with private parties

As with other multilateral agencies, the bank's role is to integrate rather than replace sources of private capital. It stimulates and provides support for industrial investors and private lenders by supplying financial assistance to financially sound projects. In this way the bank acts as a catalyst to obtain resources from the private sector (particularly from multilateral and bilateral partners).

Loans: In the project finance field AfDB mainly participates as a lender in its own right, as regards both infrastructure and PPP projects and those in which no public body is involved. The Private Sector Department (OPSD) handles direct loan deals without a sovereign guarantee and provides technical assistance services. Direct financing, which includes senior debt financing and providing guarantees, has been used to finance important private infrastructure projects in Africa in the power, telecom, and wind-farm sectors.

In the project finance field the bank can approve loans to create, expand, and modernize plant in various sectors (excluding the real estate and commerce sectors). The total amount of assistance for each SPV, including loans, guarantees, and underwriting, doesn't normally exceed one-third of the total project cost, whereas the bank's equity investment will usually not exceed 25% of the SPV's capital stock. Furthermore, it will not act as the sole large lender for the project. Total project costs must not be less than US$9 million; the only exception is if smaller projects have high growth potential and produce significant spin-offs for the rest of the economy.

The bank can lend long-term in hard currency. Loans are available in U.S. dollars, euro, pounds sterling, and yen. There is also a growing number of loans in local currency, especially the South African rand. Interest rates (established with reference to LIBOR or Euribor interbank rates) and other fees are established based on market conditions in accordance with the risk level of the project being financed. Fees include those usually applied in the case of syndicated loans (see Sections 6.3.1 and 6.3.2). Loans granted by the bank are guaranteed to limit credit risk. The standard security package (see Chapter 7), represented by mortgages on plant, pledges, and floating charges on the SPV's cash balances, inventories, and other current assets, is normally requested and evaluated case by case according to the risk level of the venture. Guarantees can also be requested from lenders or sponsors of the SPV. Maturities generally range between 5 and 15 years, with adequate grace periods consistent with trends for project cash flows. Longer maturities are an exception and mainly involve complex infrastructure projects.

Guarantees: The bank can issue guarantees to lender banks or business partners (domestic and international) to cover servicing the debt. Claims are settled by the bank in currencies available for direct lending activities.

Equity: The bank can invest in an SPV with an equity contribution for common or preferred stock or other participating securities, mainly in local currency. As with other multilateral and bilateral agencies, the bank acts as a passive stockholder and doesn't intervene in the management of the SPV's business. Right at the outset, however, it does establish the way to exit from the investment, which is preferably by selling stock held on the local market and only after the project becomes operational and shows a good track record in terms of performance.

6.4.2.3 IDB (Islamic Development Bank)

The Islamic Development Bank was founded in 1973 to promote economic growth and social progress in member countries and Islamic communities, both individually and jointly. The bank must abide by principles of Islamic law, which prohibits the charging of interest on loans; for this reason it has a limited range of action compared with other development banks. The bank participates in its own capital and in subsidies for projects in addition to offering other forms of financial assistance to member countries to further their economic and social growth. It offers technical assistance by financing preinvestment studies and valuations and feasibility studies in less developed countries. Financing is provided in the form of a grant up to a maximum of 300,000 Islamic dinars[5] or in the form of a zero-interest loan for a maximum period of 16 years, with a 4-year grace period.

Various forms of participation are available as regards project financing.

Loans: Long-term loans are offered for projects that will have a strong impact from the economic and social standpoints (even if they are not particularly profitable). Loans are granted to private companies, governments, and public bodies, and though they are zero-interest loans they do carry a fee of up to 2.5% to cover the bank's administrative costs. Loans cannot exceed 7 million Islamic dinars per project and have a maturity ranging from 15 to 25 years, with a grace period from 3 to 7 years.

Leasing (*ijara*): Leasing is used to finance capital investments in profitable projects. The bank acquires the asset and then allows the beneficiary to use it based on a leasing agreement for a given period of time during which the latter pays 6 monthly installments. At the end of the period ownership is transferred to the beneficiary. The maximum amount financed in leasing is 35 million Islamic dinars.

Installment Sale (*murabaha*): This is used to finance fixed assets. The bank purchases an asset (up to 90% of the total project value) that the beneficiary repays by installments. The amount repaid is the asset cost plus a profit margin of 6%; there is no commitment fee or penalty in the event of late payment. Total duration of the installment sale (from purchase of the asset to the end of the repayment period) can be as long as 15 years. Similar to the *murabaha* is the *istisna'a,* a structure whereby the lender pays for the availability of an asset (for instance, an industrial plant) before it is built. The maximum loan period is 15 years.

Equity: The bank can participate in a member-country company's equity, provided the terms and conditions are compatible with Islamic law. Maximum participation is one-third of the company's capital. In addition, the bank can set up joint ventures with the sponsors of an SPV (*musharakah*).

---

5. The Islamic dinar is a fictitious unit of account equivalent to an International Monetary Fund SDR (special drawing right) (approximately US$1.50).

6.4.2.4 ADB (Asian Development Bank)

The Asian Development Bank was founded in 1966 as a regional development bank. Starting in 1983 with the creation of a PSOD (Private Sector Operations Department), the bank began to provide direct assistance for investments in the private sector that have a strong social and economic impact in member countries.

As with other multilateral agencies, the role of the bank is to act as a catalyst for private capital for investments in areas where it is active. Furthermore, the bank plays a promotional role toward governments in countries that are stakeholders in the bank, to encourage them to introduce favorable political and institutional frameworks that can attract private capital. In addition, as in other cases, the action of a regional bank like ADB provides a guarantee for private lenders, which in turn means long-term loans are easier to set up and also increases the amount of funding available. In the project finance field the bank focuses on strategic sectors such as telecommunications, power and energy, water, and transport infrastructures (ports, airports, and toll roads), often in favor of SPVs that have BOOT or BOT concessions.

There are various forms of support for private investors, for instance, equity investment, loans, guarantees, and credit enhancement. A preferential condition for obtaining ADB support is that projects be compliant with procurement rules established by the bank; in particular, sponsors must be selected by a competitive bidding type of process. In any event the maximum financial support for a single project is limited to the lesser of 25% of total project cost and US$75 million.

Loans: Loans to the private sector are granted at conditions that reflect the risk level of the project concerned. Pricing is based on a spread above LIBOR or Euribor, although fixed-rate loans can also be made at the fixed rate quoted at the time of financing for swaps against floating rate. In addition, standard fees for syndicated loans are applied (front-end fee 1%–1.5% and commitment fee 0.5%–0.75%). The bank can ask for guarantees for the loan based on a case-by-case analysis. There are no rigid guidelines as regards duration. Normally there is a grace period of 2–3 years, while final maturity is established based on the project's cash flow profile. As in the case of IFC, ADB offers a B-loan program (syndicated loans) known as complementary financing schemes (CFS), in which the bank acts as lender, lender of record, and agent bank. In this way a private lender obtains the same privileges and immunity guaranteed for a loan disbursed directly by ADB (for instance, exemption from withholding taxes or extension of restrictions imposed by the host government on capital and interest payments) and also preferred creditor status in the event of sovereign risk.

Guarantees: ADB offers private investors credit enhancement schemes to improve the ability to attract private capital. The first type of guarantee is a partial credit guarantee (PCG), which provides coverage for both business and political risks. The guarantee covers that part of debt service maturing beyond the normal tenor of a private lender and all instances of failure to pay capital and interest. This is especially useful (1) for projects that require very long-term funding and (2) in countries with more severe capital rationing conditions.

The second type of guarantee is a political risk guarantee (PRG), which aims to facilitate investment of private capital in cases where there are sovereign or political risks. This provides coverage for risks of breach of contract, expropriation and nationalization, nonconvertibility or nontransferability of currency, and political violence. The PRG can be issued without counterguarantees from the host government for an amount not exceeding a minimum of US$150 million and 50% of the project cost.

Equity investments: ADB can make private equity investments up to a maximum of 25% of the SPV's capital stock. Divestment of shares occurs once the project has entered the operating stage and can entail either a sale to the other sponsors or listing on the local stock exchange.

6.4.2.5 European Bank for Reconstruction and Development (EBRD)

The EBRD was set up in 1991 and operates in 26 countries in central and eastern Europe plus countries that were once part of the Soviet bloc. As with other international financial agencies, its role is to promote infrastructure systems in target countries. The bank also stimulates target countries to improve their regulatory, institutional, and political framework. In the large-scale project sector EBRD is involved in those with a value ranging from 5 million to 250 million euro, with an average in the area of 25 million. The bank finances up to 35% of the total project cost (in the case of Greenfield projects) or up to 35% of long-term investments in the case of already-existing companies. Projects must be localized in one of the bank's target countries and be sufficiently profitable to be adequately capitalized with equity from sponsors (at least one-third of the cost must be equity financed). Furthermore, projects must have externality within the economy and conform to the bank's environmental standards. Its forms of intervention are, again, loans, equity investments, and issuing guarantees.

Loans: Loans are granted based on a valuation of a project's ability to generate cash flow. The amount can range from 5 million to 15 million euro and apply to either fixed- or variable-interest loans. Maturities vary between 5 and 15 years and can also include grace periods negotiated on a case-by-case basis. The bank can also establish subordination clauses or grant mezzanine or convertible debt. Loans are without recourse; however, the bank can ask sponsors to provide specific performance or completion guarantees, as is normally the case in limited-recourse project finance deals. Similarly, sponsors must stipulate insurance contracts and provide the usual security package, which may include mortgages, pledges, floating charges, and assignments in favor of creditors. The bank has also set up an A-/B-loan program similar to the IFC's, in which EBRD acts as lender of record for private lenders involved in the pool, who also benefit from preferred creditor status granted to international financial agencies.

Guarantees: The bank provides both all-risk guarantees against default as a result of whatsoever cause and partial risk–specific contingent guarantees that cover default originating from specific events.

Equity Investments: EBRD can provide equity for projects—directly or through its own investment funds—acting as a minority stockholder and with a clear exit strategy. It can invest in ordinary stock or special categories of instruments; however, the specific terms of the investment depend on the nature of the project financed.

6.4.2.6 Inter-American Development Bank (IADB)

The IADB was founded in 1959 and operates in South America and the Caribbean, participating in the private sector with loans and guarantees. However, equity participation is through funds (MIF—Multilateral Investment Fund—and IIC—Inter-American Investment Corporation).

Loans: Loans are granted at market conditions to the private sector without sovereign guarantees, in key sectors such as power, transport, health, and telecommunications. Also, IADB has an A- and B-loan program similar to that offered by IFC that aims to promote involvement of private capital in financing infrastructure.

Guarantees: The bank can provide guarantees for loans granted by third-party creditors, denominated in either U.S. dollars or local currency. Guarantees can apply to all or only some of a loan's maturities and can be issued alongside guarantees from other multilateral agencies or private banks. Conditions are established case by case but in general have a maturity ranging between 8 and 15 years. Political risk guarantees are provided against breach of contract, currency transferability and convertibility, and political violence, for an amount not exceeding the lesser of 50% of the project cost and US$150 million. IADB also provides a credit guarantee against all risks run by commercial banks as regards loans. In this case the limit is the lesser of US$75 million and 25% of the total project cost. For smaller countries or those with less developed capital markets, coverage can reach as much as 40% of the total project cost.

6.5   Bilateral Agencies: Developmental Agencies and Export Credit Agencies (ECAs)

Bilateral agencies are those linked to governments of individual countries for economic policy purposes and commercial and international promotion of the countries businesses. In this category it is normal to distinguish between developmental agencies and export credit agencies.

6.5.1   Developmental Agencies

These are agencies that pursue industrial and financial development aims based on market principles and practices, as opposed to the concessional aid model. They are referred to as *bilateral* because they must pursue aims linked to foreign economic policy or commercial promotion and internationalization of businesses in the agency's home country. They act as financial investment houses that grant loans (even when not linked to exports of plant or equipment) and invest in the equity capital of companies (often joint ventures promoted by sponsors resident in countries in which the developmental agency operates) in developing countries when these are of special interest to domestic industry.

The following are some of the more active developmental agencies.

AB (Sweden):   Swedfund International is owned by the Swedish government and provides its equity and debt capital to joint venture projects in which there is a Swedish partner.

Abu Dhabi Fund for Development (Abu Dhabi):   This is an autonomous public body that provides direct loans, subsidies, and its own capital to Arab, African, and Asian developing countries. Loans range from 7 to 25 years and offer favorable interest rates.

CDC—Commonwealth Development Corporation (United Kingdom):   Up until 2000 this was a state-owned company. Now it has been transformed into a mixed public–private company. Previously it invested in projects aimed at development in emerging countries; now it focuses on investing in equity capital.

DEG (Germany): *Deutsche Entwicklungs Gesellschaft* is a German government financial institution that provides long-term debt and equity.

FMQ (the Netherlands): *Nederlandse Financiering-Maatschappij voor Ontwikkelingslande* is 51% government controlled, whereas the remaining stakeholders are major Dutch banks and several private investors. It focuses its activity on Asia and Latin America.

Kuwait Fund for Arab Development (Kuwait): This fund operates in a similar manner to the Abu Dhabi fund.

OECF (Japan): The Overseas Economic Cooperation Fund is the Japanese government's bilateral development agency that reinvests the majority of its balance sheet surplus abroad. As a development agency it grants loans at aid conditions to governments based on intergovernmental agreements. It can also grant loans and take equity positions in the private sector. Geographically it focuses on Asia.

PROPARCO (France): The *Société de Promotion et de Partécipation pour la Cooperation Economique* is 71% owned by AFD (*Agence Française de Developpement*), and the remainder is in private hands. It offers equity and debt capital for projects in developing countries that don't require the presence of a French partner.

Saudi Fund for Development (Saudi Arabia): This agency provides loans and guarantees for projects in developing countries.

SIMEST (Italy): The *Società Italiana per le Imprese all'Estero* is a state-controlled finance agency founded in 1990. It lends to commercial banks and provides loans and equity to companies controlled by Italian investors.

Table 6-13 gives a list of bilateral agencies that in terms of volume have the most impact on development in emerging countries. However, IFC makes a greater contribution and is more incisive in this field.

6.5.2 Export Credit Agencies (ECAs)

If the SPV is based in a developing country and imports plant or equipment necessary to construct and operate the project, ECAs can provide political risk coverage, total coverage, or direct loans to exporting companies operating in their home country. ECAs can also provide financial support by means of interest rate equalization to commercial banks. By providing direct loans or subsidized interest rates, ECAs enable exporters to be competitive in international procurement processes or to participate in projects in which the element of risk would otherwise not be sustainable. ECAs also insure equity investments against political risks.

TABLE 6-13   Financial Contribution of the Major Bilateral Development Agencies, 2005 (in US$ millions)

	Investment Volume	% in Private Sector	Portfolio of Investments
CDC (United Kingdom)	367	100%	1,738
DEG (Germany)	698	100%	3,090
FMO (Netherlands)*	750	100%	1,290
PROPARCO (France)*	229	22%**	616

* Data referred to FY 2004.
** Author's estimates.
Source: Company web sites and www.edfi.be

TABLE 6-14   Activity for Berne Union Members (in US$ billions)

	1995	1996	1997	1998	1999	2000	2001	2002	2003
Export credits	398	407	349	373	465	491	442	473	576
% medium/long-term	87	79	64	61	62	73	60	56	66
Outstanding amounts of export credits at year end*	570	561	469	482	446	471	430	450	623
Investment insurance**	10	15	9	12	14	13	16	14	15
Insured/guaranteed amount of investments at year end	36	43	40	43	61	57	65	65	69

* Not yet due for repayment.
** Includes new amounts of foreign investments insured/guaranteed against political risks.
Source: Berna Union Yearbook, Various years.

These agencies utilize the various forms of financing made available to them by their governments to encourage exports of goods and services and also to pursue their mission by offering political and/or business risk insurance and a mix of insurance and lending activities (a model above all used by British agencies). All major ECAs (together with MIGA and some private insurers) are members of the Berne Union (International Union of Credit and Investment Insurers), which promotes international coordination and exchange of information in this sector. As can be seen in Table 6-14, the majority of ECA portfolios focus on short-term business and are therefore not particularly significant for project finance. Exposure for export credits as regards Berne Union members at the end of 2003 stood at around 30% of the over $2.3 trillion of debt in developing countries in that same year.

6.5.2.1 Financing Activity

The ECAs use three different methods of financing: direct lending, intermediary (or indirect) lending, and interest rate equalization. *Direct lending* is the simplest, most traditional structure: The importing project company is the borrower of funds, whereas the ECA is the lender. The loan is, of course, granted exclusively for the purchase of goods or services from the agency's country of origin, a condition that also applies to the other financing methods employed.[6] This method is used by countries such as the United States, Canada, and Japan, and loans are made at a fixed subsidized interest rate. *Indirect lending* is in the form of financial intermediary loans (bank to bank): The agency lends funds to a financial intermediary (for instance, a commercial bank), which in turn lends to the SPV importer at a low fixed interest rate. This technique is used by the Italian (ISACE), French (COFACE), and British (ECGD) export credit agencies. Lastly, *interest rate equalization* means that the loans are made to importing companies by commercial banks at lower-than-market interest rates. The difference is reimbursed to the banks concerned by the export credit agency.

The entire financing activity of ECAs is regulated by a document signed by OECD members and is known as the *OECD Consensus*.[7] The aim of this document

---

6. Loans not subject to this purchase agreement, used, for instance, by other bilateral or multilateral agencies, are referred to as *untied*.

7. The Arrangement of Guidelines for Official Export Credits dates from 1978 and was signed by the world's major exporting countries: Australia, Canada, European countries, Japan, Korea, New Zealand, Norway, Switzerland, United States.

is to ensure an orderly export credit market by avoiding competitive battles between various countries seeking to offer the most favorable financial conditions for exports. Thus, competition between ECAs is limited to the quantity of credit support available, that is, how much credit risk an ECA is willing to accept in order to finance a specific project in a given country. The main guidelines for the OECD Consensus are as follows.

- Export credit granted is limited to 85% of the contract value, and therefore a cash down payment is required for the remaining 15%.
- The maximum duration of the loans is 8.5 years from the start of the project (COD, commercial operating date) for Category 1 countries[8] and 10 years for Category 2 countries. Loans for projects concerning power plant construction can be repaid over twelve years.
- Repayment must be by constant, at least six monthly, installments that must begin no later than the sixth month after performance tests on the SPV's structure.
- In 1998 a more flexible temporary agreement was decided on for project finance that allows for longer repayment terms.
- The interest rate applied cannot be lower than that calculated every month by the OECD. This rate is known as the CIRR (commercial interest reference rate) and is equal to a 1% spread on the return of long-term government bonds in the same currency. The spread is the same for every currency, regardless of the country providing the financing.

Given the complicated mechanisms with which one must contend to obtain support from an ECA (compliance with the Consensus limits; greater complexity when there is an additional player in the project finance structure; high initial premiums to be paid to the ECA), it is worth resorting to these agencies only if there is no other way to attract commercial banks to finance the project. Recourse to ECAs offers two main advantages.

- The CIRR interest rate is subsidized and fixed.
- Participation of an ECA offers a certain intangible political support for the project and therefore makes lenders and investors feel more secure.

6.5.2.2 Insurance Activity

Although all ECAs adopt the common guidelines dictated by the OECD Consensus, their activities differ from many standpoints. Certain ECAs only offer their services to national banks; others make services available to all banks operating in the target country (therefore also to branches of foreign banks) or even to any bank wherever located. Following are highlights of different policies in the insurance field as regards:

- Percentage of risk coverage (maximum coverage and exemption payable by the insured party)
- Risk coverage during the construction phase
- Business risk coverage

---

8. Category 1 countries are those with a per capita GDP in excess of US$5,685 (World Bank data for 2004); all other countries belong to Category 2.

- Political risk coverage
- Direct agreements with most governments
- Level of insurance premiums payable by insured parties
- Environmental risk coverage

Percentage of Risk Coverage: Some ECAs don't cover the entire risk they are insuring, the aim being to avoid moral hazard on the part of the insured party. For instance, if 85% of the contract value is financed by a commercial bank with coverage by an ECA, the insurance could cover only 90% of this 85%, thus leaving the commercial bank with a 10% exposure, or 8.5% of the contract value. This is a way of making sure commercial banks (or lenders in general) take the ECA's interests in the project into account, as opposed to ignoring them because of protection provided by the insurance. Instead, other ECAs cover 100% of the risk. In the case of projects in developing countries, the residual percentage not covered by ECAs (e.g., 8.5%) can be too risky and therefore unacceptable for a bank. In such cases a possible solution is to force the project company to deposit the exposed percentage in cash in a collateral account and thereby guarantee the bank (cash collateralization). Obviously, this guarantee is also subdivided so as not to disturb the equilibrium in terms of ratios of responsibility for the bank and the ECA: The ECA takes 90% of the guarantee and the bank 10%.

Completion Risk: Some ECAs don't accept project completion risk. In fact this risk is under control of the exporter if the latter is the EPC contractor and insurance cannot affect the exporter's performance. So during the construction phase, ECAs only guarantee political risk and expect commercial banks to assume the completion risk, namely, the risk of poor performance by the SPV's business partner. When they make a direct loan, ECAs ask commercial banks to lend directly in the construction phase (ECAs cover political risk in this phase), and then later they refinance the loan once the construction phase is complete. Regarding the construction phase, some ECAs can also insure interest capitalized up to the end of construction.

Business Risk: Some ECAs only offer coverage for political risk, some for all risks run by lenders during the entire project life and, therefore, also for business risks (so-called *full cover*); others, in contrast, cover 95% of the political risk and 85% of the business risk. Lately ECAs have tended to offer full cover because it is difficult to distinguish between political risk and business risk. Clearly an ECA that provides a direct loan takes on both risks.

Political Risk: The various ECAs also have different policies as regards political risk.

- All ECAs cover standard political risks: currency availability and transferability, expropriation, and political violence.
- Some ECAs don't cover creeping expropriation.
- Effects of a change in law are usually covered indirectly by including indemnification clauses in one or more of the major project contracts.
- Some ECAs cover contract risk if the host government has made commitments in a government support agreement.

Direct Agreements with the Host Government: When the offtaker is an organization controlled by the host government, some ECAs require signature of a direct contract with the host country government. Based on this contract the government agrees to accept a commitment for any payment to lenders made by the ECA in cases in which the counterparty of the SPV is considered to have low creditworthiness.

Premium Level: Insurance premiums to be paid to the ECA for risk coverage can be costly. They must be paid on the financial close date but cover risks for the entire life of the project; a one-time payment representing the NPV of all future annual insurance premiums must therefore be made immediately. Premiums vary depending on the risk level of the country concerned and type of coverage required. For typical coverage in a developing country the premium can be as much as 10% of the sum guaranteed.

Environmental Risk Coverage: Some ECAs only cover risks as regards compliance with certain environmental protection standards. The American ECAs (U.S. Exim and OPIC) require an Environmental Impact Assessment (EIA) for projects they finance; others are less strict except in cases where the host country imposes specific rules.

Table 6-15 shows factors differentiating the various export credit agencies, which, as can be observed, have quite a variety of policy guidelines even though they all comply with the OECD Consensus guidelines. This leads to what are often significant differences in the way they operate.

In terms of competitiveness, offering greater coverage can be the determining factor for ECAs. In Europe the only agency to offer total cover is the ECGD. A further factor that can be a plus in terms of an agency's competitiveness is coverage for completion risk. In 2002 COFACE decided to offer this coverage in order to be able to compete with other agencies.

In addition, ECAs often work together closely in cases where exports come from various countries and therefore several agencies are involved in the same project. In such situations the typical structure is to appoint a lead ECA (usually the one linked to the major project contractor) that provides all the financing and guarantees. All other ECAs involved then reinsure the lead ECA for their share of the risk. In this way the structure of the deal is not excessively burdened and the SPV has to deal with only one agency. An example was the Russian Blue Stream project, in which ISACE reinsured with ECGD in 1999.

6.6   Other Financial Intermediaries Involved in Project Finance

A final remark is dedicated to the remaining categories of financial operators often involved in project finance deals and who frequently participate in real-life business deals.

Leasing Companies: While leasing is a product that can be offered by both commercial and investment banks (either directly or by subsidiaries within the same group), banks have been kept separate from intermediaries operating in leasing, given that for SPVs this represents an alternative source of financing to bank loans or bond issues. Leasing as one of the funding options is covered again in Section 6.10.

Insurance Companies: Private insurance companies and insurance brokers and advisers (as opposed to insurance activities performed by multilateral and bilateral banks and by ECAs) play a key role in project finance deals. As seen in Chapter 4, insurance companies come into play when none of the SPV's contractual counterparties wants to remain exposed to a risk. The request for insurance coverage can pertain to a

TABLE 6-15 Comparison of the Major ECAs

	U.S. Exim	OPIC	EDC	NEXI/JBIC	COFACE	ISACE	ECGD
Legal status	Private	Public	Public	Private	Private	Public	Public
Loans							
Direct lending	Yes	Yes	Yes	Yes	No	No	No
Intermediary lending					Yes	Yes	Yes
Interest rate equalization							
Insurance activity							
% of project cost coverage	Lesser of 85% of contract value and 100% of U.S. share	50% for new projects 75% for expansion projects	—	—	50%	35%	60%
Completion risk	No	No	No	No	Yes (case by case)	No	Yes
% of risk covered							
Business risk	Yes		Yes	Yes	Yes	Yes	Yes
% of risk covered			90%	80%	95%	95%	100%
Political risk	Yes	Yes	Yes	Yes	Yes	Yes	Yes
% of risk covered	100%	100%	90%	97.5%	95%	95%	100%
Currency availability	Yes	Yes	Yes	Yes	Yes	Yes	Yes

	Also non-U.S. banks	U.S. investors or lenders	Canadian and other banks	—	Banks operating in France	Commercial banks within and outside Italy	Banks operating in the UK
Currency transferability	Yes	Yes	Yes	Yes	Yes	Yes	Yes
Expropriation	Yes	Yes	Yes	Yes	Yes	Yes	Yes
Political violence	Yes	Yes	Yes	No	Yes	Yes	Yes
Creeping expropriation	Yes	Yes	No	No	No	No	Yes
War		No	No	Yes	No	No	Yes
Civil war	No	No	No	Yes	No	No	Yes
Revolution	No	No	No	Yes	No	No	Yes
Change in legislation	No	No	No	No	No	No	No
Breach of contract	No	Yes	No	No	No	No	No
For bonds	Yes	Yes	Yes	No	No	No	
Eligibility	Also non-U.S. banks	U.S. investors or lenders	Canadian and other banks	—	Banks operating in France	Commercial banks within and outside Italy	Banks operating in the UK
IDC	Yes	No	No	No	No	No	No
Untied guarantees	No	No	No	Yes	No	No	No
Untied loans	No	No	No	Yes	No	No	No
Equity insurance	No	Yes	Yes	No	Yes	Yes	No
% of risk coverage	—	90%	—	—	—	—	—

very wide range of risks, although it can rarely eliminate every possible risk for the insured party.

Institutional Investors: The last category of financial intermediaries considered is institutional investors with asset allocation policies to invest in securities issued by parties realizing deals marked by a medium-to-high risk level and long duration. These are mutual funds that invest savers' funds mainly in infrastructure works and in bonds and equity issued by an SPV operating in the large-scale project field or in securities issued by securitization vehicles of large infrastructure project portfolios. Frequently these investments focus on a very specific sector; today, for instance, it is quite common to find mutual funds investing in new projects in the power sector or in asset-backed securities (ABS) issued in securitizations of PPPs ventures.

However, involvement of institutional investors is not a significant part of funding for project finance deals. As we see in Section 6.11, financing projects by issuing high-yield bonds (known in America as *junk bonds*), that is, securities with a low rating to be sold to institutional investors, represents a much lower figure than the volume financed by banks loans. This is particularly true as far as Europe is concerned.

6.7   Funding Options: Equity

The remaining pages of this chapter cover the various forms of funding that define the deal's debt-to-equity ratio, starting with equity provided by sponsors.

The question of equity is often overlooked when discussing project finance. Yet the role of share capital in the initial stages of the deal is very important.

- It is the means to support and finance the planning, study, and feasibility analysis stages up to preparation of the business and financial plans to be submitted to lenders. Costs for initial development are recorded as project costs and so contribute to increasing the initial amount of investment for the venture.
- It makes the project safer for lenders. The greater the equity, the higher the risk borne by sponsors; this means less risk for lenders. An increase in equity improves the cover ratio level required by lenders, although it has a negative impact on the sponsors' internal rate of return (IRR).

6.7.1   *Timing of the Equity Contribution and Stand-by Equity and Equity Acceleration*

Typically an SPV is a corporation or limited partnership in which the sponsors put up equity. Our aim now is to clarify when shareholders must pay in equity to the project company. The law in many countries requires a minimum amount of initial capital that sponsors must confer when the SPV company is formed, but normally this is a rather small amount. But there are three alternatives to pay in the majority of the equity, each of which must be negotiated beforehand with the pool of lenders:

1. Paying in the remaining capital before starting to draw on the loan granted by banks
2. Paying in the remaining capital after the loan facility has been fully utilized
3. A clause establishing pro-rata payments.

Whereas the first alternative is easy to understand, the second and third need to be reviewed more carefully.

The second alternative is used only when sponsors are of the highest creditworthiness (otherwise lenders would bear an excessive level of credit risk) and only when sponsors provide lenders with a backup guarantee in the form of a letter of credit or other form of insurance bonding. Since such guarantees have a cost that must be paid until the equity is not provided, sponsors must assess the trade-off between an early equity contribution and the opportunity cost of alternative foregone opportunities plus the cost of the guarantee.

The third alternative can be analyzed by means of an example. Let us assume a project with a value of 1,000 is financed for 15% by equity and 85% by borrowed capital. It will also be assumed for simplicity's sake that payment for the construction is made in four equal installments of 250 at the end of each year during the construction period. The stage-payment clause establishes that each payment will be subdivided into borrowed capital and risk capital in a proportion corresponding to the weight of each source in total financing. In this case the creditors ask the sponsors to make stage payments and to issue a letter of credit to cover future payments.

Table 6-16 gives a comparison of the timing for paying in equity according to the three alternatives mentioned.

Each of the three alternatives implies a different advantage for sponsors. Final payment means shareholders only have to pay in capital after a certain period of time, but this also forces them to incur higher financing costs for use of credit lines and letters of credit in the initial years of the project. On the other hand, initial payment means saving on interest paid but generates an opportunity cost because the funds concerned are not available for investment for other purposes. Compared with the previous solutions, the use of a stage-payment clause represents a compromise falling between the two extremes.

Apart from the question of advantages for sponsors, the different timing for conferring equity is dictated by the lenders' inclination as regards risk. The latter will always push for an initial equity contribution to limit risk inherent to the venture. This consideration also explains why only those sponsors with a strong bargaining power and high creditworthiness can propose financing solutions to banks that call for paying in capital after credit lines have been fully exploited. In all other cases, the stage-payment solution is the one that partially reduces conflict of interests between shareholders and creditors.

As we will see in Section 6.9, in project finance deals a standard business practice is the subdivision of the debt into an initial tranche, or base facility, and an additional tranche, or stand-by facility, only utilizable on fulfillment of certain condition precedents. In cases where share capital has been defined on a stage-payment basis and the

TABLE 6-16 Alternative Ways of Paying in Equity

Year	Stage Payment			Initial Payment			Final Payment		
	Debt	Equity	Payments	Debt	Equity	Payments	Debt	Equity	Payments
1	212.5	37.5	250	100	150	250	250	0	250
2	212.5	37.5	250	250	0	250	250	0	250
3	212.5	37.5	250	250	0	250	250	0	250
4	212.5	37.5	250	250	0	250	100	150	250

SPV were also to use the stand-by facility, then the debt-to-equity ratio would change. The borrower could then use the additional debt without making further equity contributions. This problem is resolved by the stand-by equity clause. This states that if the stand-by facility is used, then more shareholders' equity must be paid in so that the SPV's debt-to-equity ratio remains unchanged.

Lastly, mention must be made of the equity acceleration clause, a self-explanatory term indicating the condition that allows lenders to ask sponsors to pay in the full amount of the SPV's equity immediately. This is an exceptional measure that can arise if the project is in default and is limited to certain events of default established in the credit agreement as indicated in Chapter 7.

6.7.2   Can Shares in an SPV Be Listed on a Stock Exchange?

It is important to clarify whether the SPV's shares can be listed on a stock exchange. Whenever possible, a stock exchange listing is an opportunity not to be missed, for it means turnover of shareholders involved in the venture is easier. In addition, listing facilitates both access to funding and a greater quantity thereof from institutional and retail investors for the future. Usually, however, the ownership group comprises a stable nucleus of nonfinancial shareholders (constructors, buyers, suppliers, and operators). In such cases, listing is not very likely and the SPV's ownership structure remains stable throughout the life of the project. Furthermore, in the case of a PPP, public authorities in a country may impose further restrictions on the circulation of SPV shares or even forbid their listing on the stock exchange.

However, in certain cases it can happen that a sponsor withdraws or the shareholding structure for one or more sponsors changes. Such events are considered as default for the project itself because if a key party sells its share in the SPV's capital to third parties then there is less incentive for the project to be performing (see Chapter 4). The only real change in the ownership structure could be a change in the SPV's financial shareholders, typically private equity funds, when present.

Clearly a combination of industrial and financial parties would considerably broaden the range of deals that can be financed using the project finance approach. Industrial shareholders would remain the stable nucleus throughout the life of the project, whereas financial shareholders could change as a result of stock exchange transactions. However, the investment horizon for institutional investors interested in these ventures hardly ever exceeds 10 years (and is more often 5–6 years), while investment projects financed by project financing on average last for 20 years or more. This means it would be reasonable to list the SPV's shares 5–6 years after the venture becomes operational so that institutional investors can launch a secondary offer to sell the securities in their portfolio.

6.8   Funding Options: Mezzanine Financing and Subordinated Debt

When a sponsor puts up equity, remuneration is in the form of a residual flow—represented by dividends. Sponsors are paid only after the rights of all other parties involved in the deal have been satisfied. The right of creditors, however, is unequivocal. The SPV has made an irrevocable commitment to them to service the debt as established in the credit agreement. We know that cover ratios guarantee creditors a certain margin of flexibility in the event the deal should produce lower cash flows than indicated in the budget. Lenders' rights as creditors are certain. However, they don't enjoy the benefits of performance improvements that the project may achieve during the operating phase. Such improvements, in fact, are entirely for the benefit of the SPV and, therefore, its shareholders.

Debt and equity capital offer their contributors opposite frameworks as regards incentives and remuneration. The former is a combination of low risk and low return; the latter is closer to a high-risk/high-return type of approach. An intermediate solution between these two extremes is mezzanine financing, which can also attract lenders who are more open to risk but whose investment guidelines or articles of incorporation don't allow them to contribute equity. But mezzanine finance can also be used by sponsors themselves to reduce their equity commitment partially. This form of financing was launched on the U.S. market in the mid-1970s. It came on the wave of merger and acquisition (M&A) deals achieved by massive recourse to debt and took the form of a subordinated loan. This debt can also take the form of a bond issue and is characterized by the fact that it is reimbursed after senior debt has been repaid. In essence, operating cash flows are applied immediately to service nonsubordinated debt, then for subordinated loans, and lastly for paying dividends to sponsors.

Mezzanine financing can be structured and adapted to suit the specific needs of the project and can, as necessary, incorporate larger "share-type" or loan contract components. An example can be debts that pay a minimum guaranteed interest and pay subordinated creditors a share of project cash flows available for sponsors. So the role played by mezzanine financing is more similar to that of share capital than to that of debt capital. On the one hand, in fact, the guarantee level for pure lenders is higher (given that the denominator in the ratio of debt to equity plus quasi-equity increases). On the other, lenders who are more willing to take a risk will receive a fixed and certainly attractive remuneration and will, above all, profit from the enhanced project value if it should perform really well.

Examples may prove useful to better understand the advantages shareholders and creditors can obtain from mezzanine financing or subordinated debt. The first example (Table 6-17) compares a project with a value of 100 financed by two different

TABLE 6-17   Advantages of Mezzanine Financing—Shareholders' Position

Capital Structure 1		Capital Structure 2	
Assets	100	Assets	100
Senior debt	75	Senior debt	75
Junior debt	0	Junior debt	15
Equity	25	Equity	10
EBIT	10.00	EBIT	10.00
Interest on senior debt	6.00	Interest on senior debt	6.00
Interest on junior debt	0.00	Interest on junior debt	1.50
Earnings before taxes (EBT)	4.00	Earnings before taxes (EBT)	2.50
Taxes @ 50%	2.00	Taxes @ 50%	1.25
Net income	2.00	Net income	1.25
ROE	**8.00%**	**ROE**	12.50%

Cost of senior debt (K_d): 8%.
Cost of mezzanine debt (K_{sub}): 10%.

financing structures. The first consists of senior debt only, the second calls for lower equity and use of subordinated (junior) debt. Junior debt has a subordination clause and therefore requires a higher remuneration (10% instead of 8% paid on the senior tranche). The project generates an EBIT (earnings before interest and taxes) of 10 and is taxed at a rate of 50%. Table 6-17 shows that the return for shareholders assuming financial structure 2 (accounting ROE) is higher than that obtained when adopting structure 1. The reduction in net profit, in fact, is more than offset by the equity saving. Note that the shareholders' advantage would be the same even if the shareholders themselves also contributed to the junior debt. In this case, in fact, the sum of gross cash flows received would be equal to the sum of interest on junior debt and net profit ($1.5 + 1.25$) to be divided by the total capital employed. The return on the deal is 11%, as opposed to 8% when only senior debt is used.

In contrast, the second example considers the advantages for senior creditors as a result of releverage of the company by means of a subordinated loan. Let us assume the initial situation of the company was as indicated in the left-hand side of Table 6-18. Then a calculation is made of the loss incurred by senior creditors if company assets were to be sold off at different values, corresponding to the book values of these assets. As we can note, the only case when creditors do not incur a loss is when the sales value for assets is greater than 75% of their book value. Now consider a new project with a value of 10 financed entirely by a new subordinated loan of the same amount and then recalculate the outcome. In this case, it is easy to see that senior creditors are fully repaid if the value realized for assets is lower than in the previous case. Assets need only be sold off at about 68% of their book value to ensure that the senior creditors' loans are repaid in full. This is the case because the subordinated loan is the first to absorb losses from the unfavorable business situation.

Very often sponsors of a project finance deal use mezzanine and subordinated debt. There are a number of reasons why they prefer to finance the project by means of a combination of debt and equity.

- A subordinated loan requires payment of interest after senior debt service but before dividends. This means the sponsors' remuneration is more certain than just relying on dividends and also reduces volatility of returns on total funds contributed to the project.
- Interest paid on subordinated debt is tax deductible in many countries. Greater financial leverage generates a higher tax saving that benefits sponsors of the venture directly. It should also be noted that in some countries when the subordinated loan is made by sponsors/shareholders in the company, the tax shield on interest due can be limited to a certain degree based on thin-capitalization, or thin-cap, regulations.
- Especially during the initial years of the project's life, recourse to subordinated debt means the so-called "dividend trap" can be avoided.

A simplified example will clarify the dividend trap concept. Let us assume that sponsors must finance a total investment of 4,000, with a senior debt/equity ratio of 4 to 1. In addition the following information is known:

- The investment can be amortized over 10 years in equal annual installments, each amounting to 10%.
- For tax purposes, sponsors can use accelerated depreciation with a rate of 20% during the first 3 years.

TABLE 6-18　Mezzanine Financing—Advantages for Senior Creditors

Financial Structure 1

Assets	100
Senior debt	75
Junior debt	0
Equity	25

% Liquidation Value	Liquidation Value	Payoff for Senior Creditors	Payoff for Junior Creditors	Shareholders' Payoff	Loss for Senior Creditors
20%	20	20	0	0	−73%
30%	30	30	0	0	−60%
40%	40	40	0	0	−47%
50%	50	50	0	0	−33%
60%	60	60	0	0	−20%
70%	70	70	0	0	−7%
80%	80	75	0	5	0%
90%	90	75	0	15	0%
100%	100	75	0	25	0%

Financial Structure 2

Assets	110
Senior debt	75
Junior debt	10
Equity	25

% Liquidation Value	Liquidation Value	Payoff for Senior Creditors	Payoff for Junior Creditors	Shareholders' Payoff	Loss for Senior Creditors
20%	22	22	0	0	−71%
30%	33	33	0	0	−56%
40%	44	44	0	0	−41%
50%	55	55	0	0	−27%
60%	66	66	0	0	−12%
70%	77	75	2	0	0%
80%	88	75	10	3	0%
90%	99	75	10	14	0%
100%	110	75	10	25	0%

Cost of senior debt (K_d): 8%.
Cost of mezzanine debt (K_{sub}): 10%.

TABLE 6-19 Base Case—Project Financing Using Only Senior Debt

						Year					
	0	**1**	**2**	**3**	**4**	**5**	**6**	**7**	**8**	**9**	**10**
Depreciation %		20%	20%	20%	10%	10%	10%	10%	0%	0%	0%
Depreciation		800	800	800	400	400	400	400	—	—	—
Accumulated depreciation		800	1,600	2,400	2,800	3,200	3,600	4,000	4,000	4,000	4,000
Residual book value		3,200	2,400	1,600	1,200	800	400	—	—	—	—
Principal repayment		10%	10%	10%	10%	10%	10%	10%	10%	10%	10%
Principal repayment		320	320	320	320	320	320	320	320	320	320
Loan repaid	3,200	2,880	2,560	2,240	1,920	1,600	1,280	960	640	320	—
Interest expenses		256.0	230.4	204.8	179.2	153.6	128.0	102.4	76.8	51.2	25.6
Revenues		1,125.0	1,175.0	1,225.0	840.0	855.0	865.0	885.0	895.0	925.0	925.0
− Operating costs		175.0	175.0	175.0	175.0	175.0	175.0	175.0	175.0	175.0	175.0
− Depreciation		800.0	800.0	800.0	400.0	400.0	400.0	400.0	—	—	—
= EBIT		150.0	200.0	250.0	265.0	280.0	290.0	310.0	720.0	750.0	750.0
− Interest expenses		256.0	230.4	204.8	179.2	153.6	128.0	102.4	76.8	51.2	25.6
= *EBT*		106.0	30.4	45.2	85.8	126.4	162.0	207.6	643.2	698.8	724.4
− Taxes		—	—	14.9	28.3	41.7	53.5	68.5	212.3	230.6	239.1
+ Tax credit		106.0	30.4	—	—	—	—	—	—	—	—
Loss carryforward			14.9	28.3	41.7	51.5	—	—	—	—	
= Net Income		106.0	30.4	45.2	85.8	126.4	160.0	139.1	430.9	468.2	485.3
EBIT		150.0	200.0	250.0	265.0	280.0	290.0	310.0	720.0	750.0	750.0
− Taxes		—	—	—	—	—	2.0	68.5	212.3	230.6	239.1
− Depreciation		800.0	800.0	800.0	400.0	400.0	400.0	400.0	—	—	—
= Free cash flow		950.0	1,000.0	1,050.0	665.0	680.0	688.0	641.5	507.7	519.4	510.9
− Interest expenses		256.0	230.4	204.8	179.2	153.6	128.0	102.4	76.8	51.2	25.6
− Principal repayment		320.0	320.0	320.0	320.0	320.0	320.0	320.0	320.0	320.0	320.0
= Cash flow to equity		374.0	449.6	525.2	165.8	206.4	240.0	219.1	110.9	148.2	165.3

- The senior principal is repaid over 10 years in 10 equal installments; interest at 8% is paid annually, calculated on the outstanding debt at the end of the prior year.
- Any losses can be carried forward to future years and so reduce tax liability. (This is normal practice, with various limitations and conditions, in numerous countries.)
- The tax rate is 33%.

Table 6.19 presents data for the project's first 10 years of life. The upper section of the table shows calculations for depreciation, debt repayment, and interest. The middle and lower sections, respectively, refer to income statement and cash flows generated by the project. Observing the data, it will be noted that depreciation is very high in the first 3 years because the sponsors use the accelerated method and this generates a loss in the first 2 years. So depreciation has two effects:

1. It leads to losses that can be carried forward to future years and thus reduce the SPV's tax liability.
2. The income statement is affected by this cost, which, however, is not a cash outlay. This means the project shows a loss on an accrual basis but not on a

cash basis. In fact, the table shows that right from the very first year the project is able to generate a positive cash flow for sponsors.

Effect 2 clearly is created only when depreciation is higher than debt service (interest on senior debt and subordinated debt), whereas the effect is opposite (profits are higher than cash flows) when debt service is greater than depreciation. In theory, therefore, sponsors could receive dividends right from the first year. However, legislation in many countries clearly establishes that dividends cannot be distributed if the company makes a loss, even if there are positive cash flows available for shareholders. This situation is known as the *dividend trap*. In the example, shareholders can only receive dividends starting from year 3. But dividends distributed will not be equal to profits, given possible allocations to the debt reserve or legal requirements to make a minimum reinvestment in the project. (In Italy, for instance, the mandatory figure is 5% of profits until such time as the reserve reaches 20% of the company's share capital.) So, given the same equity contribution, the dividend trap penalizes their IRR. Table 6-20 summarizes the sponsors' payoff if only senior debt is used.

The dividend trap can be avoided by using subordinated debt provided by the SPV's sponsors. Suppose the same project value of 4,000 is financed by a structure calling for senior debt of 3,200 and also subordinated debt of 500, which means equity can be reduced to 300. The subordinated debt is repaid in ten equal installments after the senior debt has been repaid, and pays interest at a fixed rate of 15%. This interest is tax deductible. Table 6-21 summarizes the data used and shows calculations for profits and cash flows.

Clearly, in this case the project income statement shows a loss for the first three years. However, the figure for depreciation is higher than debt service for the senior plus subordinate debt, and so cash flows are positive right from the first year. But in this case the dividend trap is avoided, given that interest on subordinate debt is deductible in the income statement and is paid before dividends. Sponsors can therefore start to recover their investment from the first year and improve their IRR, given the same figure contributed for equity plus subordinated debt. Table 6-22 shows the subordinated debt/dividend payoff.

While subordinated debt is a good solution for the dividend trap problem, using it can cause the further problem of negative equity. Interest on subordinated debt is a cost that generates losses, which, in turn, must be covered by sponsors' capital. If it is assumed that the sum (equity plus subordinated debt) of the investment required remains fixed, then a higher amount of subordinated debt will mean a lower equity value. However, higher subordinated debt will also mean that interest costs rise and that there will be lower profits/higher losses, and so erosion of the sponsors' capital base will

TABLE 6-20 Sponsors' Payoff If Only Senior Debt Is Used

					Year					
	0	1	2	3	4	5	6	7	8	9	10
Begin with year equity		800.0	694.0	663.6	665.9	670.2	676.5	684.5	691.4	713.0	736.4
Net income/loss		106.0	30.4	45.2	85.8	126.4	160.0	139.1	430.9	468.2	485.3
5% reserve provision		—	—	2.3	4.3	6.3	8.0	7.0	21.5	23.4	24.3
Dividends to shareholders		—	—	42.9	81.5	120.1	152.0	132.1	409.4	444.8	461.1
End year equity		694.0	663.6	665.9	670.2	676.5	684.5	691.4	713.0	736.4	760.7

TABLE 6-21 Financing the Project with a Mix of Senior Debt and Subordinated Debt

	Year										
	0	1	2	3	4	5	6	7	8	9	10
Depreciation %		20%	20%	20%	10%	10%	10%	10%			
Depreciation		800	800	800	400	400	400	400			
Accumulated depreciation		800	1,600	2,400	2,800	3,200	3,600	4,000			
Residual book value		3,200	2,400	1,600	1,200	800	400	—			
Principal repayment		10%	10%	10%	10%	10%	10%	10%	10%	10%	10%
Principal repayment		320	320	320	320	320	320	320	320	320	320
Senior outstanding	3,200	2,880	2,560	2,240	1,920	1,600	1,280	960	840	320	—
Subordinated repayment		—	—	—	—	—	—	—	—	—	—
Subordinated outstanding	500	—	—	—	—	—	—	—	—	—	—
Interest expenses senior		256.0	230.4	204.8	179.2	153.6	128.0	102.4	76.8	51.2	25.6
Interest expenses subordinated		75.0	75.0	75.0	75.0	75.0	75.0	75.0	75.0	75.0	75.0
Revenues		1,125.0	1,175.0	1,225.0	840.0	855.0	865.0	885.0	895.0	925.0	925.0
− Operating costs		175.0	175.0	175.0	175.0	175.0	175.0	175.0	175.0	175.0	175.0
− Depreciation		800.0	800.0	800.0	400.0	400.0	400.0	400.0	—	—	—
= EBIT		150.0	200.0	250.0	265.0	280.0	290.0	310.0	720.0	750.0	750.0
− Interest expenses		256.0	230.4	204.8	179.2	153.6	128.0	102.4	76.8	51.2	25.6
− Interest expenses subordinated		75.0	75.0	75.0	75.0	75.0	75.0	75.0	75.0	75.0	75.0
= EBT		181.0	105.4	29.8	10.8	51.4	87.0	132.6	568.2	623.8	649.4
− Taxes		—	—	—	3.6	17.0	28.7	43.8	187.5	205.9	214.3
+ Tax credit		181.0	105.4	29.8	—	—	—	—	—	—	—
				—	3.6	20.5	49.2	93.0	280.5	486.4	700.7
Loss carryforward			—	3.6	17.0	28.7	43.8	187.5	35.7	—	
= Net Income		181.0	105.4	29.8	10.8	51.4	87.0	132.6	568.2	453.6	435.1
EBIT		150.0	200.0	250.0	265.0	280.0	290.0	310.0	720.0	750.0	750.0
− Taxes		—	—	—	—	—	—	—	—	170.2	214.3
+ Depreciation		800.0	800.0	800.0	400.0	400.0	400.0	400.0	—	—	—
= Free cash flow		950.0	1,000.0	1,050.0	665.0	680.0	690.0	710.0	720.0	579.8	535.7
− Interest expenses		256.0	230.4	204.8	179.2	153.6	128.0	102.4	76.8	51.2	25.6
− Interest expenses subordinated		75.0	75.0	75.0	75.0	75.0	75.0	75.0	75.0	75.0	75.0
− Principal repayment		320.0	320.0	320.0	320.0	320.0	320.0	320.0	320.0	320.0	320.0
Subordinated repayment		—	—	—	—	—	—	—	—	—	—
= Cash flow to equity		299.0	374.6	450.2	90.8	131.4	167.0	212.6	248.2	133.6	115.1

be heavier. Table 6-21 shows that losses in the first three years lead to negative equity. Legislation in many countries does not allow this, and so the investment must be liquidated. When sponsors and arrangers define the capital structure and combination of subordinated debt and equity, they must bear in mind the trade-off between avoiding the dividend trap and the negative equity problem.

6.9 Funding Options: Senior Debt

This section reviews the issue of senior bank debt in depth; the alternative of recourse to bond capital markets is covered in Section 6.11. First the review covers the various

TABLE 6-22   Sponsors' Payoff If Subordinated Debt Is Used

	Year										
	0	1	2	3	4	5	6	7	8	9	10
Beginning year equity		300.0	119.0	13.6	16.2	15.7	13.1	8.7	2.1	26.3	49.0
– Net income/loss		181.0	105.4	29.8	10.8	51.4	87.0	132.6	568.2	453.6	435.1
5% reserve provision		—	—	—	0.5	2.6	4.4	6.6	28.4	22.7	21.8
Dividends to shareholders		—	—	—	10.3	48.8	82.7	126.0	539.8	431.0	413.3
End year equity		119.0	13.6	16.2	15.7	13.1	8.7	2.1	26.3	49.0	70.7
Payoff subordinated + dividends		75.0	75.0	75.0	85.3	123.8	157.7	201.0	614.8	506.0	488.3

tranches of senior debt made available by the pool of banks, after which an analysis is made of refinancing the debt already granted.

6.9.1 The Base Facility

To speak of senior debt in a general manner oversimplifies project finance deals, given that banks make available various tranches to the SPV. Each of these tranches is intended to finance part of the project's needs and is utilized and repaid in different ways. The majority of the financing constitutes the base facility. This is debt granted to the SPV to finance construction and will be repaid from cash flows the project generates in the operating phase. Clauses covering utilization and repayment of the base facility are very strict, and therefore the SPV is left with very little discretion. Uses of the base facility concern SPV payments to the constructor. Payments are made after invoices presented covering progress for the works have been checked and approved by the pool's agent bank. Interest due will then start to mature on the part utilized, whereas the SPV will pay the commitment fee on the unutilized part. Instead, repayments are structured based on the cash flow trend forecast in the financial plan. Each repayment reduces the SPV's debt to the pool, and so the base facility is not a revolving credit. The two options for repayment—variable capital installments and a given percentage are analyzed in Section 6.9.7.

6.9.2 Working Capital Facility

The second tranche of debt that banks make available to the borrower is intended to finance any cash deficit arising as a result of the cash collection cycle, that is, the difference between the average collection period for trade receivables plus average age of inventories and the average payment period for supplier accounts payable. The amount of working capital will depend on the type of project. In PPPs, for instance, the working capital facility covers the period necessary for the SPV to receive payments from the public administration. In projects in the power sector, working capital may be needed to finance the average collection period of receivables from the offtaker.

Clearly this type of facility can be used at the SPV's discretion and is a revolving credit, so every repayment made by the SPV means this credit line granted to the borrower is again available. Furthermore, given the predictability of an SPV's operations compared to that of an already-operating company, the trend for use of the working capital facility will see an initial drawdown of funds in the early stages of operation and then stabilization throughout the entire life cycle of the project. Full repayment normally takes place in the final stages of the project's life cycle.

6.9.3 Stand-by Facility

This is a tranche of additional debt made available to the SPV to cover contingencies arising during the project's life cycle. The tranche can only be used if specific events occur. There are two possibilities:

- A stand-by loan only utilizable to cover additional costs to those estimated in the budget
- A stand-by loan utilizable to cover additional costs compared to those budgeted after the base facility has been completely used (the more frequent case)

Clearly this is the riskiest part of the loan for lenders because it will be used only if contingencies arise. For this reason a higher spread is requested for this facility than the one applied for the base facility and the working capital facility.

6.9.4 VAT Facility

The early years of the project will concern the construction stage, during which initial development costs are incurred. If the project takes place in a country where VAT is in force and VAT reimbursement times are long, then the SPV will be entitled to a tax credit but will not be able to recover it from VAT on sales (given that the project will start to produce revenue only after the construction stage and not before). And so cash will be needed to finance VAT paid on construction and development costs. A specific VAT facility is granted by the pool to the SPV to cover VAT requirements during the construction phase. Clearly the VAT facility will be repaid from VAT receipts during the operating phase. For instance, if during the first year of operation the project generates sales of 100 with a VAT rate of 20%, then cash flow from sales will be 120, of which 20 will be used to repay the VAT facility. So the higher the sales, the sooner the VAT facility will be repaid. The spread requested for the VAT facility is lower than that applied for the previous tranches.

6.9.5 Loan Remuneration

The tranches analyzed are granted at a cost equal to the interbank market rate plus a spread, which can be fixed for the entire tenor of the loan repayment period. However, the most frequent practice is to establish a variable spread linked to time or depending on the level of cover ratios for each year (especially the loan life cover ratio). As regards the spread–time relationship, the most used solution is to provide for an increasing spread: Low increases to the base rate are applied during the construction phase (and therefore to capitalization of interest). After the start of the operations phase (and for a period ranging from 1.5 to 2 years), spreads begin to increase; starting from the fourth/fifth operating year the spread is fixed at its definitive level. As far as spread–cover ratios are concerned, on the other hand, in certain projects interest is established based on the level reached by cover coefficients: The higher the coefficients (and therefore the higher the project's performance), the lower the spreads applied to the base rate, and vice versa.

6.9.6 Loan Currency

Loans can be disbursed in the currency of the SPV's home country or in one or more foreign currencies. The latter case is referred to as a *multicurrency agreement*, according to which the project company can choose the currency in which to draw down the funding required based on a comparison of convenience in terms of the interest rate differential and the differential between spot and forward exchange rates. We should bear in mind that, in terms of loan cost, recourse to currency swap contracts (see Chapter 3), in certain cases, will enable a borrower to obtain better cost conditions by contracting debt in one currency and then transforming the original currency to the home country currency by means of a currency swap.

Apart from certain contracts involving nonresident counterparties that invoice their services in foreign currency (in which case a decision to finance itself in foreign currency would be taken for purposes of matching), the sponsors' advisors will always tend to set up loans in the SPV's accounting currency so as to avoid exchange rate risk. These problems should not be underestimated, given that it is difficult to set up forward cover or use derivatives for a time frame exceeding 18 months, a very short period as compared with the project's life cycle.

6.9.7 Repayment Options

The main component of a syndicated loan—the base facility—includes the methods of utilization and repayment defined beforehand with lenders in the credit agreement. Repayment methods for the base facility are critical given that the ratio of debt capacity to debt requirement is a direct function of the period over which the loan is amortized. The longer this period is, the more likely that the first figure will be higher than the second. Simulation models can be used to test various alternative repayment plans for the capital amount borrowed (see Chapter 5). Examples of two plans are given. However, we should mention that it is rare to find fixed installment or equal principal repayment plans as in the case of normal industrial loans inasmuch as these plans always contain clauses that change loan repayment. The reason for this is that fixed repayment plans don't fit in well with the volatility of operating cash flows.

The alternatives are:

1. A tailor-made loan repayment plan
2. A dedicated percentage loan repayment plan

In the first case, the advisor estimates operating cash flows and then establishes a timetable for loan repayments in which the percentage to be repaid year by year also takes into account assumptions as regards future interest rate trends. However, the percentages defined may not match operating cash flow trends perfectly. This situation leads to debt service cover ratio (DSCR) values below the minimum threshold acceptable by lenders or that cannot satisfy the average level required. If such is the case, then the percentages are revised down to reallocate repayments to years when positive cash flow is higher.

In the case of the dedicated percentage option (which, as we see shortly, assumes the defining of a constant DSCR), the capital repayment is in proportion to operating cash flow for the year because a constant percentage is established at the outset. The higher the cash flow, the larger the repayment made to lenders. The equation for this is

$$DS_t = FCO_t \times DP$$

where:

$$
\begin{aligned}
OCF &= \text{Operating cash flow for year } t \\
DS &= \text{Debt service to be paid in year } t \\
DP &= \text{Percentage of operating cash flow established for repayment} \\
&\quad \text{(dedicated percentage)}
\end{aligned}
$$

To illustrate the difference between these two alternatives, consider the following example, in which it is assumed that outstanding debt at the start of operations is 1,000, for which the minimum debt service cover ratio is 1.3. In the case of repayment of a variable capital amount, the advisor set up the loan with 16 half-yearly deferred installments, initially for an amount equal to 6.25% of the total debt at the beginning of the operating phase. In this case it is easy to see that repayment of the loan will proceed in exactly the same manner as in the equal principal method. Based on this, the model will generate the results shown in Table 6-23.

Clearly, the assumption for the repayment plan is sustainable based on the project's operating cash flows (shown in the OCF column): All DSCRs are higher than the minimum ratio of 1.3 (even though they are very close in the early years). Given this situation, the advisor revises the repayment plan by modifying the percentage of debt to be repaid in terms of capital. As we can see from the cash flow trends, in later years the cover ratio is considerably higher than the minimum value and so can support higher debt service amounts. Assuming the advisor reduces the first three installments by 50 basis points and reallocates the 150 points to the last three installments, then the situation will be as shown in Table 6-24. After the change in the repayment plan it is clear that all DSCRs reach an acceptable level in terms of the required minimum. This can be a valid solution the advisor could propose to banks invited to participate.

Let us now consider repayment based on a dedicated percentage. In this case the terms of the problem are reversed. Whereas in the first case the principal amount was established and as a consequence the interest and debt service were determined, in this case it is the latter value mentioned that is established first. Clearly this has two effects.

1. The debt service cover ratio will be a function of the dedicated percentage decided. If the percentage is stable throughout the entire repayment period, the DSCR will remain constant. In effect, given a certain level of DSCR, the dedicated percentage will immediately be equal to the inverse of the DSCR.
2. The tenor of the repayment plan will depend on the dedicated percentage decided by the advisor. The greater the percentage, the faster the loan will be repaid, and vice versa.

TABLE 6-23   Repayment with Variable Capital Installments: The Advisor's First Assumption

Installment	Base Rate Value	Spread (b.p.)	Current Rate	Capital Repayment %	Capital Repayment	Interest	Debt Service	Outstanding Debt	Repaid Loan	OCF	DSCR
0	6%	120	7.20%					1,000.00			
1	6.25%	120	7.45%	6.25%	62.5	37.25	99.75	937.50	62.50	131.67	1.32
2	6.35%	120	7.55%	6.25%	62.5	35.39	97.89	875.00	125.00	130.19	1.33
3	6.50%	120	7.70%	6.25%	62.5	33.69	96.19	812.50	187.50	134.66	1.4
4	6.60%	120	7.80%	6.25%	62.5	31.69	94.19	750.00	250.00	133.75	1.42
5	6.60%	135	7.95%	6.25%	62.5	29.81	92.31	687.50	312.50	133.85	1.45
6	6.80%	135	8.15%	6.25%	62.5	28.02	90.52	625.00	375.00	131.25	1.45
7	6.85%	135	8.20%	6.25%	62.5	25.63	88.13	562.50	437.50	129.54	1.47
8	6.85%	135	8.20%	6.25%	62.5	23.06	85.56	500.00	500.00	125.78	1.47
9	6.75%	150	8.25%	6.25%	62.5	20.63	83.13	437.50	562.50	124.69	1.5
10	6.75%	150	8.25%	6.25%	62.5	18.05	80.55	375.00	625.00	121.63	1.51
11	6.75%	150	8.25%	6.25%	62.5	15.47	77.97	312.50	687.50	120.85	1.55
12	6.65%	150	8.15%	6.25%	62.5	12.73	75.23	250.00	750.00	116.61	1.55
13	6.60%	150	8.10%	6.25%	62.5	10.13	72.63	187.50	812.50	116.20	1.6
14	6.55%	150	8.05%	6.25%	62.5	7.55	70.05	125.00	875.00	112.08	1.6
15	6.55%	150	8.05%	6.25%	62.5	5.03	67.53	62.50	937.50	106.70	1.58
16	6.55%	150	8.05%	6.25%	62.5	2.52	65.02	—	1,000.00	102.72	1.58

TABLE 6-24 Repayment with Variable Capital Installments: The Advisor's Simulation

Installment	Base Rate Value	Spread (b.p.)	Current Rate	Capital Repayment %	Capital Repayment	Interest	Debt Service	Outstanding Debt	Repaid Loan	OCF	DSCR
0	6%	120	7.20%					1,000.00			
1	6.25%	120	7.45%	5.75%	57.5	37.25	94.75	942.50	57.50	131.67	1.39
2	6.35%	120	7.55%	5.75%	57.5	35.58	93.08	885.00	115.00	130.19	1.399
3	6.50%	120	7.70%	6.00%	60	34.07	94.07	825.00	175.00	134.66	1.431
4	6.60%	120	7.80%	6.25%	62.5	32.18	94.68	762.50	237.50	133.75	1.413
5	6.60%	135	7.95%	6.25%	62.5	30.31	92.81	700.00	300.00	133.85	1.442
6	6.80%	135	8.15%	6.25%	62.5	28.53	91.03	637.50	362.50	131.25	1.442
7	6.85%	135	8.20%	6.25%	62.5	26.14	88.64	575.00	425.00	129.54	1.462
8	6.85%	135	8.20%	6.25%	62.5	23.58	86.08	512.50	487.50	125.78	1.461
9	6.75%	150	8.25%	6.25%	62.5	21.14	83.64	450.00	550.00	124.69	1.491
10	6.75%	150	8.25%	6.25%	62.5	18.56	81.06	387.50	612.50	121.63	1.5
11	6.75%	150	8.25%	6.25%	62.5	15.98	78.48	325.00	675.00	120.85	1.54
12	6.65%	150	8.15%	6.25%	62.5	13.24	75.74	262.50	737.50	116.61	1.54
13	6.60%	150	8.10%	6.25%	62.5	10.63	73.13	200.00	800.00	116.20	1.589
14	6.55%	150	8.05%	6.50%	65	8.05	73.05	135.00	865.00	112.08	1.534
15	6.55%	150	8.05%	6.75%	67.5	5.43	72.93	67.50	932.50	106.70	1.463
16	6.55%	150	8.05%	6.75%	67.5	2.72	70.22	—	1,000.00	102.72	1.463

So, again considering the loan of 1,000 of the previous example and maintaining the same interest rates, if the advisor opts for a dedicated percentage of 70% of the operating cash flow, then repayments to lenders will be structured as shown in Table 6-25.

Of course, acting in the interest of sponsors, the advisor will attempt to secure the lowest possible dedicated percentage. Each reduction in the amount applied to service the debt will, in fact, increase dividend flows earned in the early years of operation, which will benefit the sponsors' IRR. So if, for instance, the dedicated percentage is reduced to 60% and we assume a flat yield curve from the seventh year onward and a constant operating cash flow from that same year, then the repayment period will increase from 16 to 21 half-yearly payments and generate the flows shown in Table 6-26.

6.9.8 Refinancing Loans Already Granted to the SPV

The pool of lenders may change after the loan has been structured, given that some banks may opt out of the deal and be replaced by others. In these circumstances, can terms and conditions for the funding be revised? Actually, it is rather common practice to refinance an already-granted loan or to increase it to reduce the sponsors' equity commitment or to change the contractual terms and conditions of the debt. Usually the project sponsors themselves launch discussions to renegotiate the debt. However, it is not unusual for a bank (perhaps the arranger of the original financing package) to propose refinancing in order to obtain a new assignment and in doing so earn the relevant compensation (the so-called *work fee*). The refinancing is structured with the aim of improving the NPV and the internal rate of return for the deal's sponsors. In fact their objectives are:

- To free up cash blocked to service reserve accounts (especially the debt reserve)
- To reduce spreads paid above base interbank interest rates
- To extend the tenor of the debt
- To introduce a new form of funding alongside the bank loan, based on a bond issue, which will mean diversifying the group of lenders
- To reduce the severity of certain covenants

Refinancing can be broken down into two categories:

- Soft refinancing (often known as a waiver)
- Hard refinancing, or refinancing in the true sense

6.9.8.1 Soft Refinancing (Waiver)

The waiver is the easiest and fastest way to refinance a deal. In reality it would be more correct to speak of renegotiating conditions, inasmuch as this approach doesn't involve changing the financial leverage decided for the project and the tenor of the loan. In effect, the waiver is an amendment. Increasing financial leverage (so-called *regearing*) or extending the tenor would, in fact, increase the project's risk profile. This would necessarily mean discussing participation again with each of the banks in the pool, considerably lengthening the time required to come to a new agreement.

TABLE 6-25   Repayment Based on a Dedicated Percentage

Installment	Base Rate Value	Spread (b.p.)	Current Rate	Capital Repayment %	Capital Repayment	Interest	Debt Service	Outstanding Debt	Repaid Loan	OCF	DSCR
0	6%		7.20%					1,000.00			
1	6.25%	120	7.45%	70.00%	54.92	37.25	92.17	945.08	54.92	131.67	1.428571
2	6.35%	120	7.55%	70.00%	55.46	35.68	91.14	889.62	110.38	130.19	1.428571
3	6.50%	120	7.70%	70.00%	60.01	34.25	94.26	829.61	170.39	134.66	1.428571
4	6.60%	120	7.80%	70.00%	61.27	32.35	93.62	768.34	231.66	133.75	1.428571
5	6.60%	135	7.95%	70.00%	63.16	30.54	93.70	705.19	294.81	133.85	1.428571
6	6.80%	135	8.15%	70.00%	63.14	28.74	91.87	642.05	357.95	131.25	1.428571
7	6.85%	135	8.20%	70.00%	64.36	26.32	90.68	577.69	422.31	129.54	1.428571
8	6.85%	135	8.20%	70.00%	64.36	23.69	88.04	513.33	486.67	125.78	1.428571
9	6.75%	150	8.25%	70.00%	65.11	21.17	87.28	447.23	552.77	124.69	1.428571
10	6.75%	150	8.25%	70.00%	66.69	18.45	85.14	380.54	619.46	121.63	1.428571
11	6.75%	150	8.25%	70.00%	68.90	15.70	84.60	311.64	688.36	120.85	1.428571
12	6.65%	150	8.15%	70.00%	68.93	12.70	81.63	242.71	757.29	116.61	1.428571
13	6.60%	150	8.10%	70.00%	71.51	9.83	81.34	171.20	828.80	116.20	1.428571
14	6.55%	150	8.05%	70.00%	71.56	6.89	78.45	99.64	900.36	112.08	1.428571
15	6.55%	150	8.05%	70.00%	70.68	4.01	74.69	28.96	971.04	106.70	1.428571
16	6.55%	150	8.05%	70.00%	28.96	1.17	71.91	—	1,000.00	102.72	1.428571

TABLE 6-26 Lowering the Dedicated Percentage

Installment	Base Rate Value	Spread (b.p.)	Current Rate	Capital Repayment %	Capital Repayment	Interest	Debt Service	Outstanding Debt	Repaid Loan	OCF	DSCR
0	6%	120	7.20%					1,000.00	—		
1	6.25%	120	7.45%	60.00%	41.75	37.25	79.00	958.25	41.75	131.67	1.666667
2	6.35%	120	7.55%	60.00%	41.94	36.17	78.12	916.31	83.69	130.19	1.666667
3	6.50%	120	7.70%	60.00%	45.52	35.28	80.80	870.79	129.21	134.66	1.666667
4	6.60%	120	7.80%	60.00%	46.29	33.96	80.25	824.50	175.50	133.75	1.666667
5	6.60%	135	7.95%	60.00%	47.54	32.77	80.31	776.96	223.04	133.85	1.666667
6	6.80%	135	8.15%	60.00%	47.09	31.66	78.75	729.87	270.13	131.25	1.666667
7	6.85%	135	8.20%	60.00%	47.80	29.92	77.73	682.07	317.93	129.54	1.666667
8	6.85%	135	8.20%	60.00%	47.50	27.96	75.47	634.57	365.43	125.78	1.666667
9	6.75%	150	8.25%	60.00%	48.64	26.18	74.81	585.93	414.07	124.69	1.666667
10	6.75%	150	8.25%	60.00%	48.81	24.17	72.98	537.13	462.87	121.63	1.666667
11	6.75%	150	8.25%	60.00%	50.35	22.16	72.51	486.77	513.23	120.85	1.666667
12	6.65%	150	8.15%	60.00%	50.13	19.84	69.97	436.64	563.36	116.61	1.666667
13	6.60%	150	8.10%	60.00%	52.04	17.68	69.72	384.61	615.39	116.20	1.666667
14	6.55%	150	8.05%	60.00%	51.76	15.48	67.25	332.84	667.16	112.08	1.666667
15	6.55%	150	8.05%	60.00%	50.62	13.40	64.02	282.22	717.78	106.70	1.666667
16	6.55%	150	8.05%	60.00%	50.28	11.36	61.63	231.94	768.06	102.72	1.666667
17	6.55%	150	8.05%	60.00%	52.30	9.34	61.63	179.64	820.36	102.72	1.666667
18	6.55%	150	8.05%	60.00%	54.40	7.23	61.63	125.24	874.76	102.72	1.666667
19	6.55%	150	8.05%	60.00%	56.59	5.04	61.63	68.65	931.35	102.72	1.666667
20	6.55%	150	8.05%	60.00%	58.87	2.76	61.63	9.77	990.23	102.72	1.666667
21	6.55%	150	8.05%	60.00%	9.77	0.39	61.63	—	1,000.00	102.72	1.666667

The waiver can help sponsors achieve three of the objectives mentioned previously:

1. To free up cash from the debt service reserve account
2. To reduce spreads paid on the loan
3. To reduce restrictions imposed by covenants

As regards the first point, it is quite normal practice to allow sponsors to use cash in reserve accounts, which is replaced by a bank guarantee (bond or letter of credit); the second and third objectives, instead, are achieved in negotiations with all the other banks in the pool, carried out by the arranger of the refinancing. Once the pool has given approval, the arranger's legal advisor then amends the financing agreement, introducing the new conditions negotiated with the SPV. In terms of cost, a soft financing renegotiation requires payment of a work fee (or waiver fee) to the arranger amounting to around 10/20 basis points. In addition to this are costs for revising the legal documentation and fees for legal, technical, and insurance consultancy. Market standards indicate that soft refinancing can be set up in a period of 1.5 to 2 months.

6.9.8.2   Hard Refinancing

True refinancing concerns the agreements between the sponsors and pool of lenders, and leads to a change in the level of leverage for the deal or the tenor of the loan, two conditions that can increase considerably the risk factor for the pool of lenders. Hard refinancing doesn't present any problems from the standpoint of logic. Again, in this case it is a question of modifying some of the basic project financing conditions, exactly as in the case of the waiver costs or covenants change. Here, however, the problems are of a legal nature and a tax nature. Refinancing is worthwhile if can minimize the following two effects that depend on tax regulations and laws in the country concerned.

- **Tax costs:** In some countries, new long-term financing is subject to the payment of tax on the debt amount and guarantee amounts for the debt itself.
- **Clawback action:** In some countries, refinancing is considered a new debt and therefore cancels out time allowed to creditors to avoid falling foul of a clawback action in the event of default of the project.

Takeover: Takeover is the first method of hard refinancing. It involves acquisition of the loan by a new pool of lenders, who replace the old pool as regards relations with the SPV. The takeover can involve either maintaining the same loan amount and tenor or changing both (the more frequent case). In several countries, regulations usually require that the takeover be approved unanimously by all creditors, which is the major obstacle to overcome with the takeover technique.

Takeover combined with regearing of the deal deserves special mention. In this case, the deal is structured in two tranches. The first concerns replacement of the old creditors by the new ones; the second, in contrast, is to grant funding up to the new, higher level of debt (lower level of equity) agreed with the SPV's sponsors, who can immediately draw this additional amount of cash. This second tranche is guaranteed but with a lower level of seniority than the refinanced tranche. This solution can be a way of avoiding tax on the new financing and guarantees. The greater procedural complexity of the takeover technique as compared to the simple waiver is also reflected in the cost, which includes not only the work fee and costs for legal advice but also the underwriting fee on that part of new debt that is required to increase leverage. The significant change in loan risk, furthermore, means that renegotiation of terms with banks in the pool and with new lenders requires more time. In practice, it takes from 3 to 5 months to complete the deal.

New Financing (or New Lending):   Many loan agreements give the debtor the option to repay the pool in advance, although this usually requires giving notice. It is therefore possible to set up a deal in which the following occurs.

1. A pool of new lenders advances a sum to the SPV that is sufficient to repay creditors in the old pool completely.
2. The new lenders grant a new loan tranche to increase the leverage level, guaranteeing this increased funding with a lower level of seniority than for the first loan. The reasons for creating a second tranche are exactly the same as those mentioned for the takeover solution.
3. The SPV's sponsors immediately draw down the additional cash.

When the deal is structured in the form of new financing (or new lending), the debtor borrows a sum to pay off another debt and can also decide to replace the old creditor with a new one, even without the consent of the former. A diagram showing the structure of such a deal is shown in Figure 6-5. Costs and time required to structure refinancing using this method are very similar to those mentioned for the takeover solution.

Bond Issue at the End of the Construction Phase: The three methods analyzed previously don't lead to a change in debt structure because the funding continues to be provided to the SPV by a pool of banks, whether the old or the new group. At the end of the construction phase, this method of refinancing calls for a project bond issue and credit enhancement guarantee scheme (for instance, recourse to monoline insurers using the wrapped bond technique; see Section 6.11.2). This can increase the

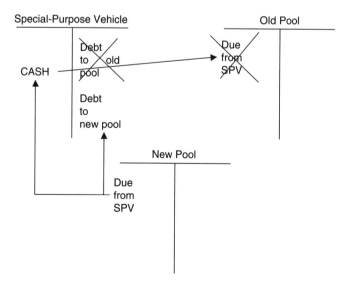

FIGURE 6-5   Refinancing Using the New Financing Option

rating level for the issue in order to achieve a private placement with a preselected group of institutional investors. The funds raised by the bond issue can be used to repay the banks that funded the project during the construction phase. Issue of project bonds usually means that better conditions can be achieved in terms of tenor: An issue can have a tenor of up to 20 years. Furthermore, these bonds are quite appealing to professional investors in times when rates are dropping or when they are low on securities from issuers with a high standing.

The advantage of refinancing using bonds can be illustrated by the following example. Let's assume a project has a cost of 300 and is financed 75% by a senior loan (tenor 3 years and swapped cost 5%) and the remaining 25% by equity. Interest during the construction phase is capitalized up to the end of year 2. Refinancing of the senior loan is planned at the end of year 2 (end of the construction period) by means of a bond with a 4-year maturity and interest rate of 4.75%.[9] Table 6-27 gives an analysis based on a syndicated loan

The project has cover ratios ranging from a minimum of 1.08 to a maximum of 1.19, a project IRR of 8.63%. and IRR for sponsors of 13.9%. The extension of the tenor and lower interest rate on bond refinancing clearly improves the sponsors' position. See Table 6-28.

The costs of organizing a bond issue are similar to those for a takeover and new lending; but in addition there is a rating fee to pay to the rating agencies (see

TABLE 6-27   Refinancing the Deal—Standard Syndicated Loan

	Construction Period			Operating Period			
	0	1	2	3	4	5	6
Project EBITDA	0	0	0	100	100	100	100
Project Investment	100	100	100	0	0	0	0
= Unleveraged free cash flow	−100	−100	−100	100	100	100	100
Interest costs @ 5%	0	0	0	12.03	8.02	4.01	0.00
Debt withdrawals	75	75	75	0.00	0.00	0.00	0.00
Capital repayment (old loan)	0	0	0	80.19	80.19	80.19	0.00
Equity contribution	25	25	25	0.00	0.00	0.00	0.00
Free cash flow to equity	0	0	0	7.78	11.79	15.80	100.00
Flows to sponsors	−25	−25	−25	7.78	11.79	15.80	100.00
DSCR				1.08	1.13	1.19	n.m.
Project IRR	8.63%						
Sponsors IRR	13.9%						
Old loan repayment schedule							
Outstanding (year end)	75	157.69	240.57	160.38	80.19	0.00	0.00
Capitalized interests	7.69	7.88	0.00				
Principal repayment	0	0	0	80.19	80.19	80.19	0.00
Interest costs				12.03	8.02	4.01	0.00

9. The longer tenor and lower interest rate for the bond compared to the senior loan are by no means a matter of good fortune. If a project overcomes the construction phase, then many of the risks that could have affected it have already been overcome. A bookrunner (an arranger of bond issues) can therefore propose more aggressive conditions to potential investors.

TABLE 6-28   Refinancing Using a Bond Issue

	Construction Period			Operating Period			
	0	1	2	3	4	5	6
Project EBITDA	0	0	0	100	100	100	100
Project Investment	100	100	100	0	0	0	0
= Unleveraged free cash flow	−100	−100	−100	100	100	100	100
Interest costs on loan	0	0	0	0	0	0	0
Debt withdrawals	75	75	75	0	0	0	0
Capital repayment (old loan)	0	0	240.57	0	0	0	0
Bond issue	0	0	240.57	0.00	0.00	0.00	0.00
Bond repayment	0	0	0	60.14	60.14	60.14	60.14
Bond interests	0	0	0	11.43	8.57	5.71	2.86
Equity contribution	25	25	25	0	0	0	0
Free cash flow to equity	0	0	0	28.43	31.29	34.14	37.00
Flows to sponsors	−25	−25	−25	28.43	31.29	34.14	37.00
DSCR				1.40	1.46	1.52	1.59
Project IRR	8.63%						
Sponsors IRR	16.9%						
Old loan repayment schedule (+) bond issue							
Outstanding (year end)	75	157.69	240.57	180.43	120.29	60.14	0.00
Capitalized interests	7.69	7.88	0.00	0.00	0.00	0.00	0.00
Old debt repayment	0	0	240.57	0.00	0.00	0.00	0.00
Bond issue	0	0	240.57	0.00	0.00	0.00	0.00
Bond principal repayment	0	0	0	60.14	60.14	60.14	60.14
Bond interest costs	0	0	0	11.43	8.57	5.71	2.86

Section 6.11.5.1) and the listing fee if the issue is to be listed on a stock exchange (in Europe, this is normally done on the Luxembourg stock exchange). The time required to organize a bond issue ranges from 3 to 5 months. However, it is advisable for sponsors to define the refinancing strategy to be adopted right from the start (bank loan or Eurobond) so that the arranger is able to evaluate the best timing for the issue. The main difficulty in this type of transaction in some countries is incompatibility of limits for issuing bonds with the high debt-to-equity ratio of a project finance deal. A possible solution is recourse to an issuing vehicle incorporated in a foreign country.

Mixed Solutions—New Lending and Bond Issue: The single solutions analyzed can also be combined. For instance, the combination of a new financing and a bond issue can involve two phases:

1. An initial phase, in which the arranger/underwriter lends the SPV the necessary funds to repay the old loan and, if necessary, the additional funds for regearing (in effect the arranger becomes the 100% lender for a predefined period)
2. A second phase, in which the arranger proceeds with the bond issue and places the residual part of the new contractual conditions with a pool of banks that can include both old and new member banks

Clearly this is only an option for very large intermediaries who can cover 100% of the SPV's existing debt without infringing regulatory limits as regards large borrowings and risk concentration. Furthermore, the higher degree of risk assumed by the arranger (who could fail to place the bond issue or refinance the deal with a new pool) means that structuring takes longer, making costs higher for sponsors. But given that the mandate for the two deals is assigned to the same arranger, the fees will be lower than if the mandate had been given to two different intermediaries.

6.10   Project Leasing

An alternative to a syndicated loan (but less widespread) is the use of leasing, which in some cases offers interesting opportunities in countries with favorable tax regimes. Leasing has been used in the UK in several PFI projects involving the construction of different kinds of real estate investments (schools, social housing, prisons, and hospitals).

In a project leasing contract, the leasing company (lessor) provides the asset to the SPV (lessee) after purchasing it from the supplier (contractor). In turn the SPV commits to pay the lessor installments (either fixed or floating) for a given period of time according to a preestablished timetable. There is also a provision for redemption when the contract expires.

While the contract does not differ from a regular leasing contract, some complications must be kept in mind when comparing project leasing to a normal finance leasing contract:

- The type of asset obtained in leasing by the project company
- Relations with lenders as regards the debt (essentially with the pool of banks that materially disburses funding to complete the structure to be assigned in leasing)

The asset assigned in leasing can be a plant or sometimes a very complex structure that is assigned to the SPV on a turnkey basis after construction and initial testing. So the SPV transfers the problems of organizing and monitoring the construction phase to the leasing company. Because the lessor/leasing company is the owner of the asset right from the start of the construction phase, it obviously must assume the risks of this phase and negotiate all the guarantees that enable it to cover all risks adequately.

6.10.1   *Valuing the Convenience of a Project Leasing*

A financial evaluation to establish whether using project leasing techniques is opportune isn't different from the case of financing by means of a syndicated loan but shows certain significant differences.[10] An important difference now is that the lessor, in addition to banks and sponsors, must obtain an acceptable rate of return given the degree of risk assumed for the deal. The IRR for the lessor is obtained by comparing construction costs and financial expenses that arise from borrowing to fund structure implementation and incoming cash flows from leasing installments paid by the SPV

---

10. To investigate in depth aspects concerning construction of financial simulations for leasing contracts in project finance, see Bull (1995), p. 131.

(lessee) and received by the lessor during the operations phase. When speaking of leasing during the construction phase, the industrial and financial organization remains with the leasing company, which contracts out the construction work concerned.

Furthermore, the lessor, like the banks, must also evaluate if the leasing installments effectively match positive cash flows generated by the project by calculating cover ratios similar to those already seen in the case of a loan.

Cover ratios concerning the lessor are easy to calculate. The debt service cover ratio will equal the result of dividing operating cash flow of the SPV by the leasing installment, whereas the loan life cover ratio will be the present value of the sum of operating cash flows of the SPV throughout the life of the leasing contract and the outstanding at the time of valuation.

Figure 6-6 summarizes the variables which influence the convenience of a project leasing. Here it is assumed that the lessor and the constructor are two different parties. The alternative is when constructor and lessor are the same party (as in the case of operating leasing).

Figure 6-6 shows the life cycle of the project and indicates that during the construction phase the leasing company (lessor) pays the contractor with funds borrowed from banks and used based on a preagreed milestones schedule. The investment of the leasing company is then repaid during the operation phase by the SPV-lessee with the cash flows generated by the project. It becomes clear that this financing alternative is feasible when:

1. SPV sponsors get a satisfactory equity IRR calculated as discussed in Chapter 5.
2. The leasing company gets an acceptable level of IRR. In this case, the lessor IRR can be calculated as

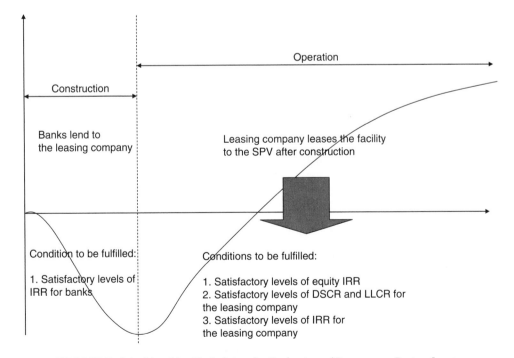

FIGURE 6-6   Variables Underlying the Evaluation of Recourse to Project Leasing

$$CC_j = \sum_{t=j}^{n} \frac{LI_t}{(1 + IRR_{lessor})^t}$$

where:

CC_j = Construction cost plus interest expenses incurred by the leasing company until year j (COD, commercial operating date) LI_t

= Leasing installment cashed in at time t

n = Number of leasing installments agreed with the SPV-lessee.

3. The leasing company gets acceptable levels of DSCR and LLCR, calculated as follows:

$$DSCR_{lessor}(t) = \frac{OCF_t}{LI_t}$$

$$LLCR_{lessor}(t) = \frac{\sum_{t=1}^{n} \frac{OCF_t}{(1 + i)^t} + DR_t}{OL_t}$$

where:

OCF_t = Operating cash flow generated by the SPV in year t

LI_t = Leasing installment in year t

DR = Debt reserve available at time t

i = Discounting rate of interest (corresponding to the leasing IRR)

OL_t = Outstanding amount of leasing to be repaid by the SPV at time t

6.10.2   The Tax Effect

Other differences between project leasing and syndicated loans concern the measure of certain key project investment variables that change radically when moving from a loan to a project leasing approach:

- The potentially different interest rate for the SPV's debt from the rate obtained from a leasing company
- The impact of the tax variable

As regards the interest rate, while the SPV lacks credit standing in its own right and cannot count on total recourse to sponsors, the lessor is often an established company already operating in the market that has a business history and can be evaluated by lenders based on its past performance. If the leasing company has a good credit rating, the interest rate charged to the SPV on debts with the lessor may

TABLE 6-29   Calculation of Recoverable and Nonrecoverable Losses

	0	1	2 (j)	3	4	5 (m)	Recoverable Losses	Nonrecoverable Losses
Assumption 1								
Loss/Profit	−10	−10	−10	+5	+5	+5	15	15
Assumption 2								
Loss/Profit	−10	−10	−10	+5	+10	+20	30	0

sometimes be lower than the cost of direct bank funding to the SPV, which basically depends on risk analysis and risk allocation.

The tax variable plays a critical role in the use of leasing. If the SPV owns the structure, then in its first few years of life it may fall foul of the dividend trap discussed in Section 6.8 due to depreciation effects. In several countries tax regulations don't allow losses to be carried forward or only allow this for a limited number of years. In such cases it can become convenient to resort to a leasing contract solution. For instance, if m is the maximum period for carrying forward losses and j is the year in which SPV operations move from a net loss to a net profit situation, then the SPV can completely benefit from a tax shield on losses if

$$\sum_{k=j}^{m} \text{EBT}_k \geq \sum_{k=0}^{j} L_k$$

where:

$$\text{EBT} = \text{Earnings before taxes for year } k$$
$$L = \text{losses in the balance sheet referred to year } k$$

The equation indicates the amount of losses recoverable and, therefore, by difference, the amount of losses that cannot be used to reduce tax liability. Assuming that the SPV benefits from a loss carryforward for direct tax purposes over a period m equal to a maximum of 5 years and a period 0–2 (j therefore equals 2) for negative income, given two different assumptions for earnings before taxes, the situation from a tax standpoint would be as shown in Table 6-29.

In the case of financing using project leasing, the problem of nonrecoverable losses is almost always overcome. In fact, if the leasing company makes a profit (which is likely because the company is already operative) and has other deals already in place, it will be able to benefit from tax savings immediately, given that the EBT and therefore taxes will be reduced. As a consequence, the tax saving that is not lost can in part be transferred to the SPV in the form of lower leasing installments while still ensuring that the lessor achieves a satisfactory IRR level.

6.11   Project Bonds

A project bond issue is an alternative that an SPV can use to obtain funding. As in the case of bank loans, the principal and interest on project bonds are also repaid to investors from the project's cash flows. Because many bank syndicates finance project loans granted to SPVs on the interbank market or by issuing bonds themselves, it would seem quite reasonable for SPVs to approach the bond market directly. From an SPV's standpoint, issuing bonds is similar to contracting debts with banks. The borrower, in fact, obtains resources in the form of a long-term debt. The main difference between a project loan and a project bond is that a bond issue can count on a much wider base of parties potentially interested in financing the deal (so-called *bond purchasers* or *bondholders*). As is seen in Section 6.11.1, this group will include not only banks but also institutional investors such as pension funds and insurance companies or mutual funds specialized in infrastructure investments.

Apart from the foregoing difference, project loans and project bonds are similar. First, quite frequently the SPV's bonds are purchased by a pool of banks (a so-called *bought deal*; see Section 6.11.5.4). Second, bonds are securities that can be traded on financial markets between an investor and another buyer, although in reality project bonds can show lower liquidity than usual corporate bonds. Often they are sold to groups of institutional investors by private placement (Section 6.11.2) and are held in portfolio right up to maturity. The international market for project bonds is much smaller than the project loan market, which still constitutes the normal form of project financing (see Table 6-30).

However, the growth rate for the bond market has been quite significant in recent years. Furthermore, issues are concentrated in well-defined geographical areas; in fact, the United States, western Europe, and Asia account for almost all issues during the years considered. Data available as regards quality of issues (measured by ratings for issuers) also show that the market certainly prefers use

TABLE 6-30   Project Bond Issues by Country, 2002–2005 (US$ millions)

	2002	2003	2004	2005
Americas	7,043	17,521	14,926	16,663
United States	3,422	10,432	8,794	12,582
Canada				956
Argentina				
Brazil	250	1,900	852	
Chile	405	1,213	1,280	
Mexico	2,966	3,000	3,912	3,000
Western Europe	1,853	9,076	7,035	4,669
U.K.	1,330	5,769	6,500	4,669
Central Europe and CIS				
Middle East and North Africa				
Sub-Saharan Africa		252		
Asia	2,008	2,418	2,183	4,528
Indonesia				
Malaysia	1,904	1,917	1,519	2,278
South Korea				
Australasia	2,884	2,897	3,043	841
Total	**13,788**	**32,164**	**27,187**	**26,701**

Source: Adapted from *Project Finance International*, issues 257 (January 22, 2003), 281 (January 21, 2004), 305 (January 26, 2005), 329 (January 25, 2006).

TABLE 6-31   Project Bond Issues by Rating Class, 1996–2004

S&P Rating	June 1996	June 1997	August 1998	August 1999	June 2000	June 2001	August 2002	December 2003	December 2004
AAA	2%	1%	2%	7%	9%	9%	10%	10%	10%
AA+, AA, or AA−	4	4	2	4	2	2	2	1	3
A+ or A	7	5	4	6	6	7	7	12	4
A−	9	6	8	7	7	6	6	4	5
BBB+	4	5	4	3	4	4	3	10	5
BBB	7	14	11	12	12	12	10	6	17
BBB−	50	42	32	28	23	25	28	14	23
BB+	2	4	5	6	12	10	7	4	3
BB	7	6	11	14	9	10	10	3	6
BB−	5	9	11	5	5	6	4	2	6
B+	0	1	2	1	1	1	2	9	6
B	1	1	2	2	2	2	2	16	3
B−	0	1	2	1	0	1	1	1	4
CCC and below	2	1	4	4	8	5	8	8	5
Total	100%	100%	100%	100%	100%	100%	100%	100%	100%
Total rated volume (US$ billions)	$19.6	$27.6	$37.5	$50.4	$62.5	$81.3	$106.3	$120.6	$146.0
Number of bonds	57	78	113	152	161	196	230	221	288
% Investment grade	83%	77%	63%	67%	64%	65%	66%	64%	66%
% Rated B+ or lower	5%	5%	9%	5%	6%	5%	5%	15%	18%

Source: Adapted from Standard & *Poor's Project & Infrastructure Finance: Criteria and Commentary* 9/98, 9/99, 10/00, 10/01, 10/02, 10/03, and 11/04; *Global Project Finance*, 7/96, 10/05.

of project bonds for safe projects. Data in Table 6-31, processed based on Standard and Poor's data, indicate a percentage of investment-grade issues of at least 60% for the period 1996–2004.

There are various reasons for the growth of the project bond market.

- Growth in demand for infrastructure development and upgrading requires heavy investments, whereas governments have been increasingly less willing or unable to intervene directly in order to finance them.
- Expertise and interest from institutional investors is increasing for alternative investments meeting their requirements for medium-, long-term assets with specific combinations of risk and return.
- International rating agencies are taking on a more central role in evaluating project finance deals, which represents an important and low-cost source of information for investors in securities.
- Experience in the U.S. market (particularly in the power sector) has been positive for project sponsors and relevant lenders.

From the standpoint of sectors in which bond issues are used most often, Table 6-32 shows that power and oil and gas account for almost all issues in the 2000–2005 period. Also note the increase in use of project bonds for PFI ventures in the last year of the period under review.

TABLE 6-32   Project Bond Issues by Sector, 2000–2005 (US$ millions)

Sector	2000	2001	2002	2003	2004	2005
Power	11,920	17,273	4,315	12,346	11,376	7,261
Infrastructure	3,394	2,430	6,471	11,931	11,082	3,621
Oil gas	3,285	3,813	2,632	7,023	5,159	9,677
Telecom	2,036	1,487	0	864	0	0
Petrochemical	0	0	0	0	734	400
Industrial	176	0	250	0	128	0
Mining	0	0	0	0	168	718
Leisure	0	0	120	0	0	0
Social infrastructure/PFI	0	0	0	0	0	5,024
Total	**20,811**	**25,003**	**13,788**	**32,164**	**28,647**	**26,701**

Source: Adapted from *Project Finance International*, issues 209 (January 24, 2001), 233 (January 23, 2002), 257 (January 22, 2003), 281 (January 21, 2004), 305 (January 26, 2005), 329 (January 25, 2006).

6.11.1   Investors in Project Bonds

Bonds issued by SPVs are purchased by institutional investors with a long-term asset allocation profile—mainly pension funds and insurance companies. Project bonds are, in fact, alternative investments to government or corporate bonds with specific risk–return combinations. As regards life insurance companies, only the largest ones have the necessary ability to analyze credit and other risks associated with a project finance deal. Small ones almost always rely on assessments of rating agencies as regards the quality of bonds issued by SPVs (see Section 6.11.5.1). Given the nature of the life insurance business, these companies can count on a relatively predictable annual cash flow and must invest for very long periods, given the nature of their liabilities toward policyholders. This requirement finds a match with the needs of SPVs that issue project bonds. This match is also found as regards the size of investments, which for the majority of life insurance companies is around $5 million, whereas only the largest insurers invest higher amounts. It should be mentioned that the main factor influencing a life insurance company's investment decision is credit risk, an aspect that is often regulated by law. For instance, in the United States the National Association of Insurance Commissioners (NAIC) has specific rating systems to evaluate these investments, which means American insurance companies tend to select bonds with a rating higher than the Standard and Poor's BBB– investment grade or Moody's Baa3 grade (corresponding to NAIC-2) (see Section 6.11.5.1).

The second category of investors interested in project bonds is pension funds. In the United States there are both public pension funds for government and public administration employees and private corporate funds, although only the latter are important potential purchasers of project bonds. This, because they are subject to fewer constraints as regards credit risk for their investments, which must have a Standard and Poor's rating of at least A. These investors are mainly attracted by the return offered and liquidity of the securities and, in particular given their mission, project bond issues with protection against inflation risk (see Section 6.11.4.4).

Among other categories of investor interested in investing in project bonds are the following.

- *Investment funds specialized in financing infrastructure projects in certain sectors or geographical areas*: Often many of these funds are the arms of multilateral development banks (see Section 6.4);
- *Investment banks, commercial banks, damage insurance companies, and foundations*: In this regard, an interesting survey was conducted by Randolph (2001) of the project finance market in the liquefied natural gas (LNG) sector that analyzed their involvement in project bond investment.

6.11.2 Various Categories of Project Bonds

As mentioned, project bonds are issued by the SPV to a series of investors to whom it commits to pay periodic coupons and to repay the capital sum at maturity or according to a predefined amortization schedule. The general definition can, however, be adapted to cover a wide range of financial instruments that can be issued for purposes of project finance deals. And in fact project bonds can be classified based on various characteristics:

1. Nationality of the issuer in terms of issue currency for securities and placement market
2. Target investors
3. Existence of capital and interest payment guarantees or otherwise
4. Subordination clauses
5. Interest calculation method
6. Capital repayment method

6.11.2.1 Nationality of the Issuer in Terms of Issue Currency for Securities and Placement Market

An SPV could issue bonds in its domestic currency and then place the securities with institutional or retail investors in its own country. In such a case, this funding instrument is referred to as *domestic bonds* and is appropriate for small-scale projects concentrated in a well-defined geographical area. In the case of a large-scale project, however, a single geographical market may not be able to supply sufficient funding to finance the deal. In such circumstances, the solution is to place the bonds in a broader market with greater liquidity than the domestic one. Furthermore, the SPV could decide to issue the bonds in other than its domestic currency to take advantage of a preference of investors to employ their funds in a given currency (the most popular currencies are the U.S. dollar, the pound sterling, the Japanese yen, and the euro). Currency swaps against the domestic currency (see Chapter 3) are then used to avoid exchange rate risk. If bonds are issued by an SPV in other than its domestic market and in the currency of the placement market, they are referred to as *foreign bonds*. If the SPV issues bonds in a currency other than that of the placement market they are referred to as *Eurobonds*. Examples of foreign bonds are so-called Yankee bonds (issued in U.S. dollars on the American market, registered with the Securities and Exchange Commission (SEC) by nonresident issuers); samurai (or shogun) bonds, namely, issues in yen of the Japanese market, registered with the Japanese Ministry of Finance; bulldog bonds—issues in pounds sterling by issuers not resident in the UK; kangaroo bonds, Australian dollar securities issued in Australia by a nonresident SPV.

6.11.2.2 Target Investors

An SPV and the intermediary handling the bond issue (the so-called *bond bookrunner*; see Section 6.11.5) must decide which investors they want to be buyers of their bonds. The two alternatives available are a tender offer to retail investors and a private placement restricted to institutional investors. In the case of a tender offer to the retail market, the SPV must comply with regulations that the relevant authority in the country concerned has issued to protect investors (in the United States this function is fulfilled by the SEC). The fact of being regulated by a national authority means the issuer must publish a prospectus satisfying requirements concerning transparency and periodic disclosure, and in certain cases there may be a requirement to obtain ratings. All of these requirements can add up to a disadvantage for issuers in terms of costs (much higher) and timing (much longer) than for an offer made only to institutional investors. Issues offered to retail investors can, on the other hand, reach a much broader investor base and might achieve a saving on cost of funding, especially when market conditions are particularly favorable (so-called *hot issue markets*) and because of greater liquidity for securities as a result of their listing on a secondary market. The cost–benefit ratio for an issue aimed at the retail market is normally less than 1. This is why the majority of bonds issued as part of project finance deals are placed with institutional investors using the private placement mechanism. In the case of private placement, an SPV instructs its bond bookrunner to identify a well-defined group of professional investors interested in purchasing the bonds and holding them in portfolio until maturity. Insurance companies, banks, and mutual funds specialized in infrastructure finance are, in fact, on the lookout for medium- to long-term investment opportunities with a good return/risk ratio and are less interested in the instrument's liquidity because in reality the bonds will never be traded and will be held until maturity. The advantages of private placement are many:

- Lack of strict regulatory constraints applying in the case of tender offers to the retail market
- Speed of structuring the deal and therefore the possibility to exploit better the time-to-market factor
- Possibility to structure the characteristics of the bond to suit the requirements of investors
- Cost of funding—placing bonds with a limited group of investors is less risky for the bookrunner, which means underwriting fees are lower than for issues aimed at the retail public.

A very clear example of private placement is represented by the Rule 144A Placement market in the United States. Up until April 1990, stocks and bonds purchased in a private placement on the American market couldn't be sold for at least 2 years. During this period an investor was therefore unable to liquidate the investment, and this led to a request for a higher return for investors as a premium for the security's lack of liquidity. In April 1990 the SEC introduced Rule 144A and eliminated this time restriction for trading these securities. Stocks and bonds, even those issued by nonresidents, which are not registered with the SEC (because they were purchased by private placement), can be traded between so-called QIBs—qualified institutional buyers. These are institutions with security portfolios exceeding a value of $100 million. The introduction of Rule 144A represented an important innovation for the project bond market, facilitating security issues by both domestic and nonresident

SPVs on the American market, which is the world's largest and most liquid. This precludes the costly registration procedure for issues with the SEC and requirements for periodic disclosure. Project bonds issued pursuant to Rule 144A are usually issued with the help of a pool of underwriter banks or purchasing banks (in a bought deal; see Section 6.11.5.4) that subsequently sell the bonds to a target of QIBs. So this excludes small-scale issues; in fact, the market range is between $100 million and $200 million.

6.11.2.3 Capital and Interest Payment Guarantees

Payment of principal and interest on an SPV's bonds can be guaranteed by the project assets. In this case they are referred to as *secured* (or *collateralized*) *bonds*. When there are no such guarantees, then the bonds are defined as *unsecured*. Such bonds are more difficult to place with investors, even if they are professionals. For instance, some of the latter are bound by articles in their memorandum of incorporation that prohibit investment in securities with ratings below S&P's BBB– or Moody's Baa3 (so-called *speculative grade;* see Section 6.11.5.1). To avoid this problem, a special form of guarantee can be set up for the bond issue with an insurance company (so-called *monoline insurer*; see Section 4.3.6) that unconditionally and irrevocably "loans" its own rating to the SPV—creating what are known as wrapped *bonds*—in exchange for payment of an insurance premium. This means that if the SPV should default on principal and interest payments to investors, then the monoline insurer steps in and pays but then has the right to demand repayment of the sums concerned by the SPV (see Figure 6-7).

Participation of a monoline insurer often means the bond obtains an investment-grade rating from the rating agencies. Given that only leading insurers operate in this line of business, ratings obtained are usually high, even as high as the maximum AAA/Aaa, although wrapping by a monoline insurer is costly and premiums paid diminish cash flows available to sponsors. As a result, evaluation of recourse to a monoline insurer requires careful comparison of benefits and costs. The benefits are as follows.

- It reduces the cost of funding for project bonds issues.
- Covenants as regards debt reserve requested by investors in the bonds are likely to be less stringent.
- Consequently, the sponsors IRR improves, all other conditions being equal.

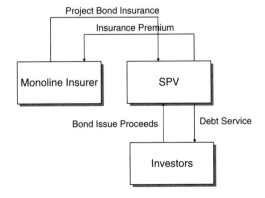

F I G U R E 6-7   Issue of Bonds with Recourse to Monoline Insurers

The main disadvantage of recourse to monoline insurers is the higher cost represented by insurance premiums paid. Project performance as seen from the sponsors' standpoint improves only if benefits exceed costs.

The most active monoline insurers in the international financial market are American, for instance, FGIC (Financial Guarantee Insurance Corporation), FSA (Financial Security Assurance), AMBAC, MBIA, and XL. Recourse to monoline insurers is very popular in the UK, where it has been used in numerous PFI projects, and in the United States, where in the 1970s it was used for municipal bond issues (see Section 6.11.3).

6.11.2.4 Subordination Clauses

Project bonds can include subordination clauses providing for rights over other categories of creditor (rights for senior lenders, usually banks that have formed the syndicate to finance the loan to the SPV). In this case, these are known as junior bonds and the subordination clause calls for repayment of the principal on one of two conditions:

- Only after full repayment of the senior loan (the most frequent case)
- Only on the condition that debt service of the senior loan and interest on the junior bonds have been fully satisfied

In the latter case, if the remaining cash doesn't have to be allocated to debt reserve or O&M reserve account, then the junior bonds can be repaid with the residual funds available.

Junior bonds are hardly ever placed with institutional investors because of the higher level of risk involved when compared to senior bonds. As seen in Section 6.8, junior bonds are usually purchased by the sponsors themselves. Such instruments represent a hybrid form of capitalization used to prevent blocking of funds available to sponsors in the event of lower annual net profits (dividend trap).

6.11.2.5 Interest Calculation Method

Project bonds can be issued with a fixed coupon (fixed-rate bonds) or, as is the case with syndicated loans, with a variable interest rate (floating-rate bonds using the base rate plus a spread). This solution can facilitate sale of these securities to investors, especially when bonds have a very long tenor. CPI (consumer price index) bonds are similar to floating-rate bonds. In the case of these securities the yield (or more often repayment of principal) is linked to a consumer price index. This type of instrument has been used in the UK, where CPI bonds have financed hospitals, prisons, and gas and water pipelines.

6.11.2.6 Capital Repayment Method

The most widespread form for bonds is total repayment of the principal at maturity (*bullet payment* or *balloon payment*). This method is entirely logical in the case of corporate bonds destined to be refinanced at maturity, given the ongoing nature of business operations. However, it is not the best in the case of project finance, given that the deal has a closed life cycle. For this reason, bonds provide for the gradual repayment of the principal that is directly linked to the timeline for the specific project's cash flows. The final maturity of project bonds is usually fixed. This is also another difference from corporate bonds, which in certain cases include put options in favor of investors themselves that make bonds easier to sell to investors. Call option clauses allowing the SPV to repay the bonds before maturity are not very common either.

6.11.3   Municipal Bonds

Municipal bonds are a special category of bond issued by public bodies in order to finance projects linked to the mission of local authorities. While these are not part of the project bond category discussed in previous sections, they are worth mentioning because they are structured in the same way as project bonds. The term *municipal bonds* refers to bonds issued by public bodies such as states, governments, provinces, municipalities, or other bodies in order to finance operating expenses or specific projects. These bonds can be sold either by public placement to retail investors or by private placement targeting institutional investors.

Many operators consider this method of financing the forerunner not only of bond project financing but of project finance itself as the term is intended today. In fact, the U.S. municipal bond market has existed and grown over more than one century (the first issue was made by the City of New York in 1812) and has become the world's largest market.

Their widespread popularity is due to the fact that interest is tax-free (which reduces returns requested by the market), and normally the issues are for a relatively low value (around $10 million) and therefore also utilizable for small-scale projects. Other countries have also started to use these instruments, for instance, East European countries (Poland, Czech Republic, Bulgaria, Hungary, Estonia, etc.) and those in South America (Brazil, Argentina, Colombia, etc.), which often issue them on the Euromarket.

These instruments can be classified into the following categories:

- General obligation bonds
- Project revenue bonds
- Dedicated revenue bonds

General obligation bonds are securities for which debt service is guaranteed by "full faith and credit," namely, by the issuer's creditworthiness, which depends on its power to impose taxes on the public.

Project revenue bonds are very similar to project bonds. In fact, debt service for the loan is guaranteed by the cash flows generated by a specific project. The essential difference from a project bond is that the issuer is a public body instead of an SPV. These bonds are named according to the sector for which funding is being raised and so there can be airport revenue bonds, highway revenue bonds, hospital revenue bonds, public power revenue bonds, resource recovery revenue bonds, sport revenue bonds, water and sewer revenue bonds, and industrial revenue bonds. Funds from issues are transferred by the public body to a private company for purchase of plant and structures, and revenues from the latter will be used to guarantee repayment of the bonds. A variation can be the case where the public body purchases the necessary structures and then leases them to the company. A typical contractual framework is shown in Figure 6-8).

Lastly, *dedicated revenue bonds* are a special category of bond in which debt service is guaranteed by a specific cash flow generated by revenues collected by the

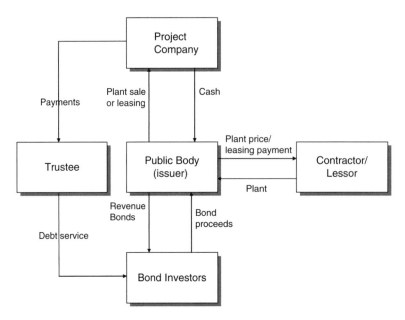

FIGURE 6-8   Contractual Framework for a Project Financed by Project Bonds

public body concerned. However, these flows are not normally linked to the specific project in question. For instance, there can be bonds issued based on cash flows from tax receipts (such as taxes from production of alcoholic beverages, natural gas, gasoline, etc.) to which the public body is entitled or funds transferred to it by the central government.

6.11.4   When Should Project Bonds Be Used?

Project bonds represent a form of funding for an SPV as an alternative to the more frequent form of a syndicated loan. However, this is a valid alternative only in certain well-defined situations and markets. It should be remembered that whereas syndicated loans are contracts an arranger structures according to sponsors' needs in a tailor-made manner, project bond issues are based on securities that are much less easy to personalize. In effect, a project bond bookrunner knows it will be more difficult to find investors willing to hold project bonds in their portfolio if they have a large number of special characteristics, unless these investors have been identified in advance as targets for a private placement. If, instead, the issue is to be listed on secondary markets, it must have standard characteristics that won't form a perfect match with the specific needs of a project finance deal. A further aspect to consider is that bond investors (unlike banks) are less inclined to run risks associated with the construction phase, preferring to assume risks only in the operating phase. Also, country risk can be a handicap for a bond issue when the SPV is located in a country where this type of risk is particularly high. This is why, whenever possible, bond issues are more appropriate for refinancing deals that have already overcome the construction phase (see Section 6.9.8) because in this case the bonds are more similar to an asset-backed securitization than a project finance deal.

Certain factors will now be reviewed to distinguish between project bonds and project loans and that can influence sponsors and their advisors' decision as regards one of the two alternatives available.

6.11.4.1 Investor Target

Only a few countries have a well-developed domestic capital market in which the financing needs of an SPV can be satisfied by investors qualified to evaluate the risks and forecast return. If the corporate bond market (in which project bonds are a subcategory) is not very well developed and lacks availability of funds, then this will represent an obstacle for a project's ability to draw on capital markets directly. In the case of syndicated loans, arrangers can structure the pool either on a domestic basis (inviting only domestic banks) or on an international basis, therefore overcoming the constraints of the corporate bond market in the country where the project is located. As already mentioned, a real turning point for overcoming similar obstacles was the introduction of Rule144A in the U.S. capital market, which essentially encourages bond issues by nonresident project companies.

6.11.4.2 Tenor of Financing

Probably the greatest advantage of project bonds as opposed to syndicated loans is that a bookrunner can structure an issue with a longer tenor than in the loan option. Sometimes project bonds can bridge the tenor gap with the bank loan market because the project bond investor market manages to assume longer-term risks than are acceptable to banks. Tenors of 20–25 years can easily be reached, especially in mature markets, although even maturities of 35 years and longer have been tested with success.[11] This is possible mostly thanks to the types of investors interested in project bonds. Life insurance companies and pension funds certainly like long-term/very long-term assets to back up their liabilities so as to optimize their ALM (asset and liability management) strategies. Generally speaking, banks find it quite easy to propose loans up to 15 years. However, internal restrictions based on the type of relative liabilities and external restrictions imposed by the regulatory environment mean that this limit cannot easily be exceeded. The effect of maturity also plays an even more important role after the implementation of Basel II (see Chapter 8), inasmuch as longer maturities mean that banks must absorb more capital, all other conditions being equal.

6.11.4.3 Preservation of the Sponsors' Financial Flexibility

A bond issue can mean that sponsors don't have to use their own credit lines for this reserve, which would otherwise deplete the unusual portion of credit facilities with banks. The fact of being able to access a different investor base makes project bonds more independent than bank lending, which is certainly an advantage.

6.11.4.4 Inflation-Linked Bonds

As seen in Chapter 3, one of the risks inherent to projects is the unpredictable trend in inflation, especially when costs and revenues are not tied to the same price

---

11. Based on a sample of 176 syndicated loans and project bonds, Esty reports that 24% of the bond loans issued for project finance deals have a tenor of more than 20 years, compared with 8% for project bank loans. The average duration for bank loans was 9.4 years (median 8.0) against 13.6 years for project bonds (median 13.3). See Esty (2005).

index. While floating-rate syndicated loans are granted at a variable interest rate (linked as regards the base rate component to the inflation trend reflected in the nominal interest rate), project bonds can explicitly incorporate the inflation effect if structured in the form of inflation-linked bonds. These are bonds for which payment of interest and/or capital is tied to a consumer price index (CPI), all the better if this index is the one to which the SPV's costs and revenues are linked. Inflation-linked bonds are particularly popular with institutional investors with long-term-maturity financial portfolios, as is the case with life insurance companies and pension funds.

6.11.4.5   Structure for Utilization and Repayment of Funding

The inflexibility of project bonds compared with syndicated loans becomes evident when considering utilization of funds and subsequent method of repayment. As seen in Section 6.9.7, with project loans, sponsors and banks structure the loan so that project trends for unleveraged free cash flows and debt service (in the operations phase) and covering outgoings for start-up and construction costs by withdrawals from credit facilities are made as compatible as possible. Project bonds, on the other hand, mean that funds from the issue are received immediately and so the SPV has to reinvest the proceeds until the funds are required. If, as often happens, the return on liquidity is less than the IRR on project bonds (so-called *negative arbitrage*), the project bond issue is inefficient compared to a project loan.

6.11.4.6   Credit Policies and Market Sentiment

Bank credit departments tend to define credit policies and guidelines based on long-term growth objectives. Recourse to project loans is therefore almost always a possibility. In contrast, bond markets are much more sensitive to short-term macro-economic and company trends (so-called capital market short-termism). In such cases, a currency crisis or bond default by a private or sovereign state issuer can cause a generalized loss of confidence and, as a result, the impossibility to finance projects with bond issues. Cases like the Asian crisis in the 1990s and the more recent crisis in Argentina show that the bottom can drop out of the bond market when investors lose confidence and panic.

6.11.4.7   Fixing the Financing Terms and Conditions

Once an arranger has a mandate to syndicate a project loan, conditions for the spread and fees can probably be indicated to sponsors right from the early stages of syndication, even though this would not become a formal commitment from the banks until confirmed at the time of the financial close. This clearly means more accurate financial forecasts can be prepared from the start. As is seen in the following section, the contractual terms and conditions for project bond issues are fixed at a much later stage. Except in cases of bought deals, the effective interest of investors and their willingness to accept a given yield on bonds can only be discovered later as a result of road shows. Sponsors are therefore unsure of the final price throughout the period of preparing to launch the bonds on the market.

6.11.4.8   Confidentiality

Contractual terms for a bank loan are strictly confidential. The series of contracts signed by the SPV and included in the information memorandum cannot be disclosed and can only be used by parties involved in the deal, so fewer lenders in the pool ensures greater confidentiality. The case of bond issues is different. If the issue is aimed at retail investors, then the law in many countries requires publication of a prospectus and disclosure of certain contractual terms. This may not be acceptable to one or more sponsors, for business reasons. For instance, a general contractor might not want to disclose information concerning guarantees given for building a plant. In the case of private placement, this problem is less critical. As we saw previously, the introduction of Rule 144A means that registration with the SEC and other related formalities are no longer required, which has helped reduce problems associated with disclosure of confidential information.

6.11.4.9 Covenants and Monitoring Management of the Project

One of the essential features of project loans is the inclusion of a series of extremely detailed covenants and commitments binding the SPV in the credit agreement. These commitments make monitoring easier and avoid moral hazard on the part of the SPV's management. In this way lenders have an incentive to monitor their investment, and this is facilitated because commitments are clearly defined.

Project bonds don't usually have such precise, strict covenants as project loans, for two reasons. First, the investor public in project bonds is numerically larger than the banks participating in a pool. This generates problems of free riding, given that no individual bondholder is interested in monitoring the SPV or, rather, sustaining the costs of this and sharing the benefits with other investors. Secondly, the inclusion of extremely precise contractual conditions makes the bond very much tailor-made and therefore difficult to replace with other forms of investment. All other factors being equal, this means the security has a lower liquidity in the market.

6.11.4.10 Renegotiation of Contractual Conditions and Refinancing

Sponsors tend to prefer financing methods that enable them to change the original contractual terms and conditions negotiated for the deal. This is the case both when the SPV's performance exceeds the forecast and when it is less favorable and breaking covenants means the debt must be refinanced to avoid default of the project. If the project generates a higher cash flow than forecast, the sponsors could use this excess liquidity to repay the debt in advance. In the case of bank syndicates, early repayment is an option that normally calls for payment of a penalty, although not an excessive one (around 0.5–1% of the outstanding debt at the time of repayment).[12] Inclusion of a call option for early repayment in a project bond is also possible, but investors usually want a higher rate of return in such cases. In effect, if sponsors repay a bond in advance, an investor could run a reinvestment risk (also known as *prepayment risk*), that is, the risk of not finding an alternative investment on the market with a similar interest rate to that of the bond repaid in advance. The prepayment risk must therefore be compensated by a higher return (a higher coupon or lower placement price) than that of a normal bond without a prepayment option.

One of the major weaknesses of project bond issues is renegotiation of financing when project performance falls short of the forecast or when certain covenants have been broken. In fact, a project that runs into trouble requires significant changes in contractual terms in order to ensure survival; however, it is very difficult to establish a direct dialogue with bondholders. This is especially true when there are a large

---

12. See Yescombe (2002).

number of bondholders, each of which holds just a small number of the bonds issued. Intuitively, it is easy to see that the cost and time required to renegotiate a loan increases the higher the number of creditors involved.[13] In such cases interest to organize refinancing actively is very low and the temptation for free riding is higher. Furthermore, passive investors normally have a short-term mentality. So, after downgrades in ratings, they tend to sell the security concerned quickly to recover the investment, which in turn accelerates default of the project. In this regard, it should be noted that the trustee of a bond issue (see Section 6.11.5.2) represents the bondholders' interests but cannot take decisions on their behalf, whereas having decision-making powers would facilitate and speed up the renegotiation process with the SPV's creditors. All that the trustee can do is to call a bondholders' meeting. On the other hand, it is much easier to negotiate with a small number of banks in a pool than with a larger number of bondholders.[14] Especially in cases of public project bond issues, the process of amending all the bond documents is extremely long and complex and, therefore, inappropriate in a crisis situation requiring a solution as fast as possible. The difficulty of managing restructuring in the case of project bonds also explains why bonds are only preferred when refinancing syndicated loans in performing projects that have already overcome the critical construction phase. (There is less likelihood such projects will run into difficulties.)

6.11.5 Procedure for Issuing Project Bonds

As we saw in Section 6.11.2, the form used most frequently when issuing project bonds is private placement with a group of clearly identified investors. Issuing project bonds by private placement is a somewhat similar procedure to organizing a syndicated loan by one or more mandated lead arrangers (see Sections 6.1.2 and 6.2). The parties involved in the deal and cash flows deriving from it are summarized in Figure 6-9. Compared with a syndicated loan, however, Figure 6-9 indicates certain parties that are only found in the case of bond issues: rating agencies, the bond trustee, and the paying agent. The roles played by these parties are covered next, before describing the issuing procedure itself.

6.11.5.1 Rating Agencies

Even though investors in project bonds have departments that can analyze an SPV's ability to pay interest and capital over time, they tend to base their investment decision on both the project bond bookrunner's certification of the quality of the issuer and, above all, on the assessment of creditworthiness issued by rating agencies. This rating refers to an issuer's intention and ability to repay its debts punctually both in the short term and the medium to long term. As far as project finance is concerned, meaningful ratings are those referring to medium-/long-term credit-worthiness. Table 6-33 shows the scales used by the world's three major rating agencies (Standard and Poor's, Moody's and Fitch IBCA). Here, we can clearly see that distinction is made between the so-called investment grade (bonds having a

---

13. See Gilson, John, and Lang (1990). Troubled debt restructuring: an empirical study of private reorgan-ization of firms in default. *Journal of Financial Economics*, and Asquith, Gertner, and Scharfstein (1994). Anatomy of financial distress: an examination of junk bond issuers.*Quarterly journal of Economics.*

14. Esty and Megginson (2003). Furthermore, it is easier to restructure fast if the pool of banks comprises a limited number of lenders.

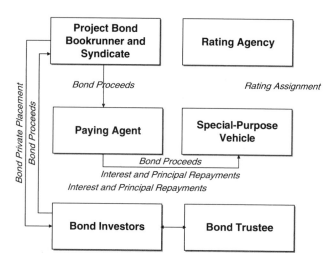

FIGURE 6-9   Parties and Cash Flows Involved in a Project Bond Issue

limited risk of insolvency) and speculative grade (bonds with an increasing risk of insolvency up to actual default).

Rating agencies play a key role with regard to bond issues, including project bonds. Often even the charters of some institutional investors, such as pension funds, forbid the purchase of these securities if they lack this credit assessment. One of a project bond bookrunner's main tasks (also chronologically speaking) is to present the project to one or more rating agencies. Completing the procedure for assigning a rating is extremely time consuming; this is why the project bond bookrunner contacts agencies almost immediately after receiving the mandate for a private placement. See Figure 6-10.

The rating procedure follows a very precise timetable that includes all phases leading up to publication of the rating by the agency. A simplified overview of the procedure is illustrated in Figure 6-11.

The preliminary discussion doesn't represent a commitment for the sponsors. This is an exploratory meeting with the agency during which information is given concerning the criteria for assigning a rating and requirements to obtain a final rating. If the sponsors accept the conditions, then a mandate is given to the agency concerned. The first stage in the procedure is to prepare a credit assessment, namely, a preliminary indicator of creditworthiness expressed by means of a rating grade or in

Decision to request rating										
Initial contacts with agency										
File rating application										
Set up meeting										
Prepare data										
Submit data										
Meeting with agency										
Rating given										

FIGURE 6-10   Standard Timetable for Assigning a Rating
Source: Moody's

TABLE 6-33   Rating Grades Used by the Major International Rating Agencies

Standard and Poor's *		Moody's**		Fitch	
Invest. Cat.	**Description**	**Invest. Cat.**	**Description**	**Invest. Cat.**	**Description**
Invest. grade					
AAA	Extremely high ability to pay interest and repay capital	Invest. grade	Notes with the lowest investment risk: payment of both interest and capital is safe thanks to very high and extremely stable margins. Changes in economic conditions will not affect the safety of the notes.	Invest. grade	Maximum creditworthiness
AA	Very high ability to honor payment of interest and capital—only marginally different from issues in the highest grade	Aa	High quality notes. They have a lower rating than the previous grade inasmuch as they have lower or less stable margins or, over the long term they are exposed to greater dangers.	AA	Very high creditworthiness
A	High ability to pay interest and capital, but a certain sensitivity to unfavorable changes in circumstances or economic conditions	A	Medium-high quality notes. Elements guaranteeing the capital and interest are adequate but factors exist that raise doubts as to whether these elements will also persist in the future.	A	High creditworthiness
BBB	Sufficiently high capability to pay interest and capital, however, unfavorable economic conditions or a change in circumstances could have a greater effect on the ability to honor the debt normally	Baa	Medium quality notes. Payment of interest and capital appear to be adequately guaranteed at present but the same cannot be said for the future. These notes have both speculative and investment features.	BBB	Good creditworthiness

Speculative grade

BB	Less vulnerability to risk of insolvency in the short-term than other speculative issues, however, considerable uncertainty and exposure to adverse economic, financial and sectoral conditions	Ba	Notes featuring speculative elements; they cannot be said to be well guaranteed over the long term. The guarantee for interest and capital is limited and may no longer exist in the event of future unfavorable economic conditions.	BB	Speculative
B	More vulnerable to adverse economic, financial and sectoral conditions, however, currently able to honor its financial commitments	B	Notes that cannot be termed as being desirable investments. Guarantees for interest and capital or timely performance of other contractual conditions are low over the long term.	B	Very vulnerable
CCC	Currently vulnerable and dependent on favorable economic, financial and sectoral conditions in order to honor its financial commitments	Caa	Low quality notes. May be in default or there can be elements of danger as regards payment of capital and interest.	CCC, CC, C	Extremely vulnerable
CC	Currently extremely vulnerable	Ca	Highly speculative notes. They are often in default or risk other significant losses.		
C	Proceedings for bankruptcy or similar have been filed, although payments and financial commitments are being maintained	C	Notes with extremely low prospects of payment.	DDD, DD, D	In default
D	Insolvency (default)				

* Ratings from AA to CCC inclusive can be modified by adding a + or − notch to better define the position within the rating grade.

** Ratings from Aa to Caa inclusive can be modified by adding the numbers 1, 2, or 3 in order to better define the position within an individual rating grade (1 equals the highest quality, 3, the lowest).

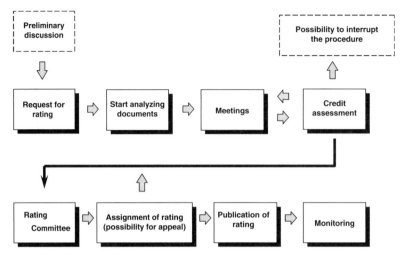

FIGURE 6-11   Procedure for Assigning a Rating
Source: Standard and Poor's

descriptive terms. This evaluates the issuer or financial structure's strengths and weaknesses. This evaluation isn't subject to monitoring and is usually confidential. The credit assessment is based on an analysis of contracts stipulated by the SPV, by reviewing the term sheet, financial model, and sensitivities, and also makes use of draft reports prepared by independent advisors. This assessment leads to the establishment of a preliminary rating based on information received to date and assumptions developed by the agency's analysts concerning points still outstanding. The preliminary rating is issued to facilitate publication of the presale report, that is, the document circulated among investors so that they can evaluate how an assessment concerning a given project finance deal was arrived at. Then once all the documents and opinions have been signed off by the SPV, independent advisors, and contractual counterparts, the agency publishes the final rating. The preliminary rating, in fact, is only modified to become the final rating when the debt has been issued and all information has been received and analyzed. Usually the final rating coincides with the preliminary rating; if, however, there have been substantial changes in terms of forecasts and assumptions incorporated in the preliminary rating, then the two assessments may differ.

6.11.5.2   Bond Paying Agent and Trustee

Funds deriving from placement of the issue with investors are only transferred to the SPV indirectly. First they are channeled to the bond-paying agent, usually a bank, which then transfers them to the SPV. It is also this party's task to receive sums due from the SPV to cover payments on the debt and to credit them to the bondholders. And so it could be said that this role equates to that of an agent bank in the case of a bank loan (see Section 6.2). The task of the trustee is basically to represent bondholders and their interests (checking, for instance, that the SPV issuer complies with covenants and all other commitments included in the trust indenture), to hold the securities on their behalf, and to call meetings to vote on specific decisions (for instance, renegotiation in the case of restructuring). Sometimes these two parties (bond-paying agent and trustee) can be the same institution.

6.11.5.3   Choice of the Project Bond Bookrunner

Investors in project bonds don't tackle the due diligence procedure that is fundamental for evaluating the project (or at least not in depth). Instead they rely on the review performed by the investment bank selected by the project company (project bond bookrunner or lead manager) and above all on assessments made by rating agencies. Usually sponsors assign an investment bank or large commercial bank the role performed by the financial advisor in more traditional project finance frameworks based on bank loans. The role of this advisor is, in effect, to study various aspects of the project, prepare the bond issue, and establish contacts with possible final investors. The choice of this advisor can be fundamental for the success of the entire deal. Normally the selection process entails the progressive screening of candidate banks based on the sponsors' priorities. Cost and ability to establish correct pricing are clearly the basic points. However, in certain cases importance is also given to the range of services the bank can offer, its degree of sophistication in terms of support, the existence of a solid relationship with the issuer, or ability to distribute bonds to final investors.

The choice of a bookrunner marks the beginning of the process to outline and plan a bond issue. In the initial stages the sponsors and bookrunner first define underlying assumptions in order to sound out the potential investor market. Following this, as we describe later, the offer is progressively defined in detail. The book-running services market is highly competitive, and only banks with specific expertise figure as leaders in international league tables. Table 6-34 indicates major investment and commercial banks involved in the bond placement business in 2005.

6.11.5.4   Setting Up the Syndicate: Managers and Selling Group

As in the case of syndicated loans, the bookrunner sets up the syndicate with which to share the underwriting risk for the entire issue, possibly with assistance from one or more comanagers. Today, in fact, it is normal market practice to organize bought deals, that is, bond issues bought by the syndicate and then sold to interested investors. Bought deals cost more for the issuer in terms of higher fees; however, they prevent the risk of undersubscription by the market, which is a risk in the case of placements based on a best-efforts clause. The banks in the pool that also underwrite the issue are known as the *managers*.

TABLE 6-34   Major Lead Managers of Project Bond Issues, 2005

Manager	Country	$million	No. of Issues
Credit Suisse	Switzerland	2,517.4	8
Mizuho Financial	Japan	2,209.5	9
Citigroup	U.S.A.	1,599.4	11
West LBAG	Germany	1,478.4	13
SG (Société Générale)	France	1,151.4	7
RBS (Rojal Bank of Scotland)	Great Britain	1,039.4	6
Banco Bilbao Vizcaya Argentaria	Spain	919.90	12
Goldman Sachs	United States	889.3	4
Calyon	United States	803.9	10
Mitsubishi UFJ Financial	Japan	788.5	11

Source: Adapted from *Project Finance International*, issue 329 (January 25, 2006).

In issues that are not structured as bought deals, the syndicate is extended to include banks forming the selling group, that is, banks whose task is to sell the bonds to their customers. This group will be responsible for placement with final investors. As opposed to bookrunners and managers, the selling group doesn't give any underwriting guarantees and therefore isn't exposed to risks if they don't manage to sell bonds assigned to them. To inform potential members, the bookrunner prepares a preliminary bond prospectus that includes the same data as in the information memorandum for a syndicated loan. This facilitates evaluation of the project by financial institutions that are candidates to become managers. Already in this phase the intermediaries involved start to contact investors and inform their customers who could potentially be interested in purchasing the bonds.

In certain cases meetings are also organized to present the issue.[15] These meetings—known as *road shows*—involve structured presentations in major international financial centers during which lead managers and sponsors illustrate the project to interested investors so that they can evaluate the deal. (This valuation, obviously, is also very much based on the rating assigned in the presale report.)

6.11.5.5   The Subscription Agreement

Just as in the case of negotiating credit agreements for syndicated loans, negotiations between the issuer and the bookrunner concern services the bank will provide to the issuer and rules for risk sharing and underwriting among members of the syndicate set up by the bookrunner. This structure determines the compensation due to the lead manager from the SPV. This compensation will be the difference between the price at which the lead manager buys the securities from the issuer and the price at which they are resold (so-called *gross spread*). The gross spread covers the following fees.

- **Management fee:** This is the amount paid to the lead manager for setting up the syndicate. It therefore depends on the complexity of the issue transaction, its size, and the effort required to structure it. Part of this fee is returned by the lead manager to any comanagers involved.
- **Underwriting fee:** This is the fee recognized for the underwriting service. If, in fact, the issue is entirely underwritten by the syndicate, then the latter bears the risk that it is not completely resold or sold at the planned conditions. In any event, the issuer will always be certain of obtaining the necessary resources. The underwriting fee is divided between the bookrunner and the managers and of course isn't paid for bond issues on a best-efforts basis (without guaranteed placement).
- **Take-down (or selling) fee:** This is the sales commission paid to compensate the syndicate for the sales effort. Except in the case of bought deals, the banks comprising the selling group receive part of the gross spread returned by the lead manager.
- **Expense reimbursements:** These include all expense items incurred by the syndicate, for instance, preparation of road shows. It therefore depends on the range of services contracted.

15. To a large degree, the road show is superfluous in the case of issues aimed at specific categories of investor (private placements). It is only necessary in the case of large issues to be placed in several markets. In such cases the bookrunner accompanies the sponsors for a series of meetings (road shows) with the financial community to evaluate the potential investors' appetite for the project bond issue.

All terms and conditions concerning relations between issuer and lead manager, including the characteristics of the securities themselves, are established in the sub-scription agreement. Efforts of members of the underwriting syndicate (managers and other bank underwriters) in terms of individual quotas underwritten are detailed in the underwriting agreement. In contrast, the selling group agreement covers relations between the underwriting syndicate and the group of banks that have the task of selling the securities to final investors.

6.11.5.6 The Final Bond Prospectus

In the final stages of preparing the issue, all the various details must be established and included in the final bond prospectus, also known as the *bond offering circular* in the Eurobonds market. In specific terms, the offering circular includes the following information.

- **Price (under/at/above par):** The choice from among these options will determine directly the issue proceeds and the level of the coupon. Given the same IRR, a sale under par will in fact lead to a lower coupon than that required for a sale at or above par. The decision will have to take into account the trends for forecast cash flows during the construction and operating phases.
- **Variable or fixed coupon:** The inclination to choose a variable coupon (like LIBOR or Euribor plus spread) is justified by the long-term nature of these issues and consequent interest rate risk run by bondholders, who therefore require that this be limited.
- **Maturity:** The characteristics of the project are reflected in the final maturity of the bonds, which is usually quite long.
- **Yield (or internal rate of return):** This is perhaps the key point because it must express the return required by investors. The yield is fixed on the basis of a market benchmark to which a spread is added based on the forecast rate for bond default. For an investment in project bonds, the investor requires a yield equivalent to that for an investment with the same tenor but free of risk (so a risk-free benchmark yield is used, like that on government bonds). A spread is then added to this, reflecting the risk inherent in the specific project (which is derived directly from the rating assigned to the issue). Lastly, adjustments are made to take into account the degree of liquidity forecast for the security or performance of similar projects.
- **Covenants:** As in the case of syndicated loans, project bonds can include positive, negative, and financial covenants. It should also be mentioned that covenants are used much more in cases of private placements. They are used much less for bonds to be listed on retail markets or to be listed on the secondary market, given that these clauses limit the security's liquidity, making it very specific and not easy to replace by other investments.

CHAPTER ◆ 7

Legal Aspects of Project Finance*

Introduction

This chapter is devoted to the legal aspects of project finance. The purpose here is to identify legal issues raised by project finance transactions and the solutions that are normally developed and adopted by operators.

The project finance technique makes it possible to raise the financial resources needed to develop an economic initiative primarily through a bank loan that is repaid from the cash flows generated by the project itself. (In this sense repayment is secured by these flows.) Describing the legal aspects of project finance means outlining how financial and economic/industrial planning for the development of the project is reflected in a system of legal/contractual relationships that are binding for the participants. If this system is not possible or is not reliable, the project finance deal itself is not possible.

The observations that follow in this chapter will overlap somewhat with issues that have already been addressed in previous chapters. This is unavoidable. A project finance deal is, in fact, a complex system in which every element is interconnected.

However, it is probably fair to say that the legal issues inherent to project finance essentially revolve around two basic concepts or groups of concepts:

1. The project company and its economic/legal function
2. The network of contracts (first and foremost, the credit agreement) that regulate the relationship between the different players in the project

Addressing legal issues also means contending with (or at least delineating) an initial structural complication. The legal framework of project finance originated in common law systems. Within the framework of codified legal systems (i.e., the civil

* This chapter is by Massimo Novo.

233

law systems), the legal construction of project finance becomes a search for the available legal instruments that are fit for the purpose of project finance. This means taking notions born in contexts other than project finance and adapting them to the specific needs of this technique. In many circumstances this is just not possible, and, as a consequence, market practice has come to accept financing projects on the basis of "legal structures" much less suited to the purpose than what would be possible in a common law context. This is a sign of the vitality of this financing technique, for it rises above and beyond the possible structural rigidity of the legal environment to which it has to be adapted.

Fundamentally, project finance is a financing technique or a financing structure as opposed to a legal concept in the strict sense. This is true in the jurisdictions that conceive of such institutions and regulate (or codify) them as a conceptual fact prior to actual utilization and in noncodified jurisdictions as well, where conceptualization of legal notions comes (if at all) after actual implementation.

A legal analysis of project finance, therefore, basically consists of studying a specific example of a typical project finance deal (the kind of project that might only be found in textbooks) and how it takes shape around:

- The project company
- The contracts relating to the project and their interconnections

The remainder of this chapter is organized as follows: Section 7.1 focuses on the special characteristic of the project company, the reasons for its incorporation and the relative corporate documentation. Section 7.2 is dedicated to the contract structure of the deal. More specifically Section 7.2.1 analyzes the due diligence report and the term sheet. Section 7.2.2 is centered on the classification of project documents, further examined in Sections 7.2.3 (credit agreement), Section 7.2.4 (security documents), Section 7.2.5 (equity contribution agreement, intercreditor agreement, and hedging agreements), and Section 7.2.6 (project agreements). Section 7.3 concludes the chapter with some indications about the refinancing of existing project finance deals.

7.1   The Project Company

In project finance, an initiative is developed "in" or "through" a project company, which is actually the borrower of the financing. This is common knowledge for anyone familiar with the definition of this financing technique.

To be clear, *project company* usually refers to a legal entity, i.e., the company that is formally responsible for a specific project finance deal. For reasons explained in the following pages, this company must be a newly organized entity. It is "born" along with the project and does nothing but develop, build, and operate the project. From this perspective, the project company is defined as a *newco* and a special-purpose vehicle (SPV). This latter expression is not exclusive to project finance and in fact is normally used in all structured finance deals that require a company for a single purpose (for reasons that are in part the same as those regarding project finance).

There is no particular reason why the project has to be developed in an SPV, either in terms of the economic or the industrial nature of the project or the bankability of the investment in abstract terms. A possible exception is a project with several sponsors, which would give rise to the opportunity and/or the need to create a joint venture company in which sponsors participate as shareholders. Choosing a corporate structure in which to develop an investment project could entail applying the "usual" standards of corporate and tax optimization, which is normally how it is done.

7.1.1 Reasons for Incorporating the Project in a Project Company

To begin with, we briefly address the legal implications of what it means to develop a project "in" or "through" a project company. Fortunately, the reason is simple. The project company acts as the formal entity that runs and is the owner of the project: Civil law systems normally use the notion of "entrepreneur" to describe this position with respect to the project. The project company owns, develops, and operates the project (or at least these activities are legally attributable to it).

Therefore, the project company is entitled to use the site (as owner or lessee), the industrial plant and its several assets, and all legal relationships with third parties needed to build and operate the project.

There are generally two categories of reasons why a project has to be developed in a special-purpose company so that it can be financed on a without-recourse basis: defensive reasons and positive reasons.

7.1.1.1 Defensive Reasons

A given project could be developed by the sponsor in a preexisting legal structure, presumably a company in the group in question most compatible with the project (in terms of available resources).

However, this strategy runs into a nearly insurmountable obstacle: the principle of general liability of any person. This principle is recognized in all advanced legal systems, without exception (though the nature, extension, and applicability of exceptions may vary depending on the legal system). Based on this principle, people are liable for their debt obligations with all its present and future assets. No limitations or exceptions are allowed, beyond those cases specifically established by the law. (The main such exception is the possibility to create security rights in favor of a specific creditor.)

The repercussions of this principle on project finance are clear. If previous or ongoing activities have nothing to do with the project, then there is a risk that liabilities deriving from or connected to such activities could contaminate the assets of the borrower company (see Section 1.5.1). On the one hand, without recourse lenders would be exposed to risks unrelated to the project, which would create an imbalance in the financial structure of the project. On the other hand, nonproject lenders would benefit from the liquidity injection and project-related investments added to the assets of their borrower. Note that mixing together project and non-project receivables and liabilities has no consequences that are necessarily adverse for lenders. It would simply be incompatible with project finance. Outside the legally protected circle of the legal entity that is the project company, financing spills over into corporate financing, where, by definition, borrowers make all their assets, without exception, available to lenders as security (unless specific additional security is requested). We simply find ourselves in a different legal and financial area. In this sense, the term *ring fencing* is used, which means protecting the project company from external factors that could distort the correlation between the financial model and the project company's legal relationships.

7.1.1.2 Positive Reasons

Underlying any legal analysis of project finance are the positive reasons why the project company and the project finance transaction have to coincide. Just as the project has to be defended from liabilities that predate the financing and that would alter the financial base case, without recourse lenders have to be able to establish the allocation area of the cash flow generated by the investment project *a priori*. This way they can implement the most suitable legal mechanisms to ensure that these funds are allocated and applied in accordance with the financial model.

The customary solution is to give the project company a single purpose. This ensures that the cash flow generated by the project can be totally controlled (at least in theory) and that it will be channeled in the order of priority set down in the financial model.

This is why the project company is called an SPV. It coincides with the project itself, in the sense that the entire cash flow related to the project has to be entirely attributed to the company. At the same time the company has to be protected against any possible external interference that might jeopardize the economic, financial, or legal management of the project in any way. The purpose of the project company is essentially to make the project and its cash flow coincide as perfectly as possible with the entity that is liable for servicing the debt toward lenders. Ring fencing, then, is the technique (consisting mainly of legal instruments) by which lenders establish and give substance to the project as a financial structure in formal legal terms. The entire project (and its assets) is available to lenders as a debtor, as an entrepreneurial entity destined to produce revenues and cash flows; only the project has any liability toward lenders.

7.1.2   The Project Company as a Joint Venture: Another Reason to Develop a Project in an SPV

There is, in fact, another reason why positioning a project in a special company is standard procedure in the development of a project finance initiative. A project with a single sponsor is possible, in theory, but does not often happen in actual practice. Normally a number of entrepreneurs join forces to develop a project (see Section 1.3). Creating a company through a joint venture then becomes the most obvious strategy, one that would probably be adopted to develop the investment project, aside from the intention to apply without-recourse financing to such a project.

Under these circumstances, the joint venture traits of the project company intersect with those strictly connected with its financing. The agreements among sponsors, which are documented in the shareholders' agreement (or joint development agreement), have to be structured in such a way as to reflect (or at least not jeopardize) the project's bankability. According to normal market procedures, potential investors are informed of agreements among sponsors, but these agreements are not usually part of the project agreements or project contracts. In most cases, this is the compromise struck between the autonomy of the sponsors and the financial and legal analyses carried out by the arrangers and their need to control the project from a contractual standpoint.

7.1.3   *The Project Company and Groups of Companies*

At first glance it might appear that developing a project within a specific company is no different than what usually takes place in groups of companies, where it is normal for different business units to be organized into separate legal entities (though they are coordinated within the context of the group). Of course, one or more project companies can be members of a group of companies. But what we must realize is that a project company is inherently different in terms of financing. In fact, the companies in a group are run with a comprehensive strategy; the interests and needs of the group are coordinated from the industrial, commercial, and financial standpoints. The project company, in contrast, has a different kind of legal separation. This separation (1) is essential for obtaining without-recourse financing for the project company but (2) exempts it from the management and coordination activity of the group (i.e., of the holding company) because the project company is managed with an entrepreneurial approach entirely focused on financing the project.

Ring fencing assets and liabilities, mentioned earlier, prevents group interests from prevailing over the structure of the project company in any way.

7.1.4   *Corporate Documentation: Articles of Incorporation*

Drawing up the constitutional documents of a project company is not generally a difficult exercise and creates no major obstacles in negotiations between sponsors and arrangers. There is no specific set of articles of incorporation for a project company, but there are provisions that these articles of incorporation could commonly include that run counter to without-recourse financing. More specifically, certain provisions may be incompatible with the security interests that lenders will want to take over the project company's shares, and possible enforcement thereof, as set out in greater detail later.

The project company's capital has to be secured to lenders (normally through a pledge over the shares). The articles of incorporation of the project company cannot include any provision prohibiting such security, nor can the granting of the security interest be subject to constraints such as approval of the board of directors or other sponsors. Though under normal circumstances these limitations can be overcome, they could hinder the security interest on shares issued after the financial close on the financing. As a result, such restrictions are not acceptable to lenders.

As discussed in Section 6.7.2, due to the very nature of the project company, its capital will have limited circulation. The credit agreement delineates the circumstances in which the sponsors are allowed to transfer their ownership in the project company, either all or in part, to third parties. Clearly, the participation of sponsors in project company capital is seen by lenders as an indirect warranty of the robustness of the project, at least from a technical/industrial perspective. Despite this, project lenders normally object to limits to the circulation of capital set out in the articles of incorporation. The problem here, in fact, is possible enforcement of a pledge on the company shares that would lead to their sale. Any restrictions on the circulation of capital would diminish the scope and the function of taking security over the project company's shares in this situation. Therefore, limits on the transferability of shares must remain a contractual matter between the project company and lenders and, when applicable, between the project company and sponsors. Restrictions in the articles of incorporation on circulation, in contrast, have a negative impact on the bankability of the project, for they represent an impediment to the possible enforcement of the security interest.

7.1.5 Outsourcing the Corporate Functions of the Project Company: How the Company/Project Is Actually Run

At this point we may be led to the wrong conclusion about the nature and function of the project company. If from a legal standpoint a given project is an entrepreneurial initiative and therefore an enterprise, the project company is the owner of such initiative and, therefore, in formal terms, the entrepreneur.

This statement is not incorrect, but for the most part its correctness belongs only to the formal sphere of things. Two very distinct ideas coexist in the project company that may seem contradictory (and in some ways actually are). On one hand, every effort is made to enclose the project in the project company from the financial and legal standpoints. So, once again, the project company contains the entire project and nothing else. It is necessarily the point where legal responsibilities for all relationships relating to the project converge so that every legal relationship passes through and is controlled by the project company (and consequently every financial relationship as well, regarding both assets and liabilities of the project).

But we have to remember, as we said before, that this is correct only from a formal legal standpoint. In other words, it is true insofar as it means that the responsibility for legal relationships relating to the project centers exclusively and necessarily on the project company.

In practice, as we saw in Section 1.4, the project company in turn contracts out all activities pertaining to its operations to third parties; later we turn our attention to the key contracts used to implement this. The reasons underlying this outsourcing are easy to explain.

- Internal costs, which are variable and hard to control, can and must be transformed into costs that are fixed or that vary only within certain preset parameters (often linked to the performance of the contracting party who would benefit from a cost increase).
- Predetermined objectives can be applied for outsourcers in terms of economic results or performance targets.
- Consequently, the contract can be terminated if these objectives are not achieved, and the outsourcer in question can be replaced with an alternative, more efficient, and/or less expensive service supplier.

This is the only way that the project can be financed with extremely aggressive debt-to-equity ratios. The resulting corporate structure in the financed company is minimal; every corporate function is assigned to third parties through a preestablished network of legal relationships needed to run the project. The nature and degree of outsourcing costs and risk are perfectly transparent and subject to monitoring and direction.

Bearing this in mind, the project company becomes a fictitious creation to some extent—a mere shelter set up to place the financing and the cash flow needed to repay it. A project company can be described as a box used to make money move: First it comes in (the money from the bank loan and contributions from the sponsors) and then it goes out (the money is spent to finance the development and construction of the plant) and then it comes in again (revenues from the project plant are collected by the project company from the day commercial operations begin), with binding obligations established to give priority to servicing the loan as far as possible.

From this perspective, the nature and functions of the project company have to be interpreted with critical realism, being well aware of what these terms actually mean.

7.2   The Contract Structure

The remainder of this chapter focuses on the system of contracts by which the project finance deal is organized and a description of their structure and content. The key legal problems linked to drafting these agreements are also identified.

7.2.1   Before the Financing: The Due Diligence Report and the Term Sheet

Two documents are particularly important in the context of project finance: the due diligence report and the term sheet of the credit agreement. These items have appeared sporadically in these pages, especially in Chapters 3 and 6, and deserve a brief summary here. We should stress that these documents come before the project finance contract system is put in place, so they are preliminary and instrumental to it.

7.2.1.1   Due Diligence Report

This report is a summary of the project from a legal standpoint. A complete and exhaustive due diligence report is an essential tool for lenders in valuing a project. Any and all its critical aspects have to be described and explained in this document. In addition, the essence of the project finance transaction—risk analysis/risk mitigation—is systematically outlined for the benefit of potential lenders.

The due diligence report constitutes the basic document of analysis for the project and for its bankability on a without-recourse basis. In light of this purpose, the due diligence report is actually made up of two documents, each with distinctive characteristics and objectives, but that are combined on every single page of the report: a description of the legal context of the project and an analysis of its risk.

The first document simply provides information that could actually be had from other sources (e.g., a description of the legislative and/or regulatory framework in a given sector, such as the energy sector; rules on urban waste disposal; permits for building and operating infrastructures for use by the general public) or gleaned from other project documents (e.g., corporate documents of the project company or the sponsors; see Section 7.2.6). These data are compiled in a brief, systematic way to facilitate the bankability analysis carried out by arrangers and lenders.

The second component of the legal due diligence report constitutes the document's real added value: a risk analysis, which involves describing the project's weaknesses. More precisely, the aim of such analysis is to illustrate the aspects and instruments that give legal form to the lenders' expectations of future project revenues. In addition, where this proves to be unreliable, lenders learn what measures are available to them to mitigate these project weaknesses.

Here a basic example is useful. Let's say that national legislation where the project is to be developed adopts the "supervening hardship principle," i.e., a principle—common to many legal systems—pursuant to which a party to an agreement is released from its obligations arising under such agreement if the performance of such obligations becomes excessively onerous and this circumstance is not attributable to that party. Now let's see what impact this would have as applied to a fuel supply contract for a power plant that has been project financed (see Section 3.2.2). We easily realize that this rule conflicts with the underlying principles of project finance. The point of a long-term fuel supply contract is to guarantee the project both a constant supply (obviously, a constant supply is ensured if the supplier is reliable; but this is counterparty risk and not a legal problem and has no legal solution other than replacing the supplier) and a fixed price for the entire duration of the contract. From the perspective of risk analysis, this means that the project outsources the risk linked to this variable. (In this case, the project transfers this risk to the long-term supplier.) The hardship principle would invalidate all this. If fulfilling an obligation became excessively onerous, the supplier would have the right to reverse the risk back onto the project and would be fully entitled to refuse to supply fuel (or obtain an increase of the price; see later). This would create a major problem for project operations, with three possible solutions:

1. Interrupt operations due to lack of the raw material contracted in the fuel supply agreement. (This is unacceptable, because it would inflict serious damage on the project and cut off its cash flow.)
2. Look for alternative suppliers. This could work, but the project would face the risk relating to finding a long-term supplier and the market price that the project company would have to incur at that time. Note that the cause of the supervening excessive hardship for the original supplier is probably due to general market conditions (e.g., a surge in the price of crude oil). Under these circumstances, the entire market would apply prices that by definition would be "excessively onerous" (for the buyer, not for the supplier). Moreover, these new market conditions would probably make suppliers reluctant to sign any long-term contract with the project company. The price risk and the availability of fuel would once again be the burden of the project company at the most inopportune time.
3. Offer the original supplier a higher price and maintain the original fuel supply agreement. This appears to be the simplest solution in most cases, but it clearly entails a cost: however much it takes to make the contract "fair value" again.

Therefore, what needs to be ascertained is whether the supervening hardship principle can be waived, i.e., whether a party to a contract can relinquish this right, taking on the relative risk. If such is the case, mitigating this problem is quite simple. Project participants only have to peruse the project agreements to see if project counterparties have waived hardship in favor of the project company. But it is in the due diligence report that the arrangers' legal team states specifically whether this waiver has been made. This is true for the hardship principle as well as a myriad of other issues pertaining to the project's bankability; the due diligence report provides a definitive summary.

In practice, the due diligence report is organized by descriptive areas rather than risk-related concepts or legal issues (such as hardship), combining information and risk analysis. (Lenders normally prefer a descriptive approach to a systematic one based on legal concepts.)

Box 7-1 provides an example of how a typical due diligence report is set out.

Box 7-1   Structure of a Typical Due Diligence Report

Generally speaking, the due diligence report contains the following essentials.

- Summary and very institutional observations on the key legal problems linked to project finance in general and to the project in question specifically. This is a sort of a readers' guide to the topics found in the analysis carried out in the report. The legal issues described here (such as contract termination and the determination of contract damages or supervening hardship) are briefly discussed at the end of Section 7.2.6.
- An analysis of project agreements to determine project bankability, in other words the existence of factors that expose the project company to risks that could preclude the financing for the project. Arrangers are normally asked to comment on the project agreements during negotiations. (There is some leeway here, unless the public administration, monopolies, or quasi-monopolies are involved, in which case there is hardly any room for negotiation.) However, the project agreements are controlled by the project company, both when they are executed and beyond in terms of how they are managed. The lenders are asked to verify compatibility with project finance and its characteristics.
- A section on administrative and environmental issues; more importantly permits and authorizations required to build and operate the project in its various stages. The purpose of this analysis is twofold. (1) On one hand, it's meant to verify the state of the project from this perspective, ensure its correct project development from an administrative standpoint, and establish how soon building construction of the project might begin. Clearly, a project that needs a particular administrative permit is not yet bankable if this permit has not yet been (and may not be) granted. (2) On the other hand, it aims to build the basis for drafting the annex to the credit agreement containing a list of permits that the project company will be required to obtain according to the specified timetable and to maintain pursuant to the terms of the credit agreement corresponding to specific obligations and conditions in the agreement.
- A section intended to provide information on the corporate structure of the project company and, in some cases, of the sponsor companies. Any peculiarities that might obstruct the project's bankability are highlighted. (A typical example is if the articles of incorporation prohibit the granting of security over project company shares.) In any case, this kind of problem is almost always addressed and resolved long before the stage of the transaction at which the due diligence report is produced, given the timing and development methods in the arranging stage of the financing.

Because this is an extremely complex document that is essential to the realization of the project, work on the due diligence report begins in a very preliminary stage (and an initial draft is circulated among the arrangers). This report usually ends up as one of the documents that constitutes conditions precedent for the first drawdown on the loan. (We discuss this concept more thoroughly in Section 7.2.3, on the credit agreement.)

The due diligence report is also an essential document for loan syndication (see Section 7.2.3.15). In fact, participating banks normally learn about the project through this document (at least initially). For clarity, keep in mind that the legal due diligence is only one of the reports that must be prepared when structuring a project finance deal.

7.2.1.2 The Term Sheet

The term sheet can be described in much simpler terms. It is a document containing a schematic summary of the key terms of a contract document and is agreed on by the parties in light of the forthcoming drafting of the same document by legal advisors.

Technically speaking, a term sheet can be drawn up for any contract (even a corporate or commercial agreement). But in financial deals the term sheet is used systematically as a documentary outline that forms the basis for a specific operation. Sponsors and arrangers negotiate the term sheet, which is the starting point for the arranging mandate. This document summarizes the key aspects of the loan and therefore lays the documentary groundwork for building the contract structure of the financing itself. In this sense, it is a summary of what shall be included in the contract; it does not summarize a contract that has already been drafted.

The term sheet of the credit agreement sets down the basic conditions of this contract in a short format (using schematic concepts, without detailing specific contract clauses that will be drafted in due course and included in the final agreement). This encompasses economic terms and basic contract provisions (such as conditions precedent, covenants, events of default, and so on). Certain essential questions pertaining to the overall financing system are also clarified, such as security interests (security documents; see Section 7.2.4) and direct agreements that may be requested by lenders (see Section 7.2.4.8). In some cases, certain specific points are addressed that are particularly relevant within the framework of the project finance deal in question and that the parties consider essential in order to progress the development of the deal.

7.2.2 Classification of Project Documents

At this point, we provide an initial general list of the legal documents on which a project finance deal is actually built. These need to be classified for various reasons, none of which is linked to any theoretical legal doctrine. Clearly, most of these documents vary a great deal, from a legal standpoint; the following classification is based on their function and emerges from actual practice.

- Finance documents
- Security documents
- Project agreements

Even though this classification is substantially consolidated, it comes from practice and may vary on a case-by-case basis.

Finance documents include the credit agreement (often referred to as the *facilities agreement*) and other documents closely related to it. Actually, there is a primary finance document (the credit agreement) and a series of contract documents that are instrumental and correlated to it. Finance documents are drawn up by the lenders' lawyers; documents that are complementary and accessory to the credit agreement are regulated by the same law governing the credit agreement, as far as possible. (At times this is not possible, as we see shortly.)

The purpose of the *security documents* is to create a system of security interests that assist lenders (essentially the participating banks in the pool of lenders in the financing deal). Due to technical/legal requirements, the laws of the jurisdiction where the assets are located normally regulate these security interests. This is one reason why security documents are kept separate from finance documents in the strict sense.

Project agreements are the project company's operational contracts. The nature of project finance is such that the list of project contracts is a closed one, in theory. In fact, the project company cannot have any relationship or responsibility that is not strictly associated with structuring the financing, in financial and legal terms. Lenders are not parties to these contracts, but acquire certain rights as regards these agreements through the security documents (either by pledging or assigning the credits deriving from these contracts by way of security) and on occasion through direct agreements (see Section 7.2.4.8). Lenders come to an agreement on the form and content of the project agreements. The project company cannot depart in any way from the contract system agreed on with lenders, even though the latter are not technically party to it, or the project itself will no longer be bankable.

At this point, we turn to a separate analysis of each contract, along with the legal problems that arise with each of them.

7.2.3   The Credit Agreement

If a project finance deal is made up of a complex, articulated system of contracts, with provisions for a myriad of interrelations among its components, the credit agreement is the center of the system. All aspects that characterize a project finance deal are regulated, directly or indirectly, in this document.

In Europe, common practice is for the credit agreement to be subject to English law. This choice is practically an obligatory one if the deal is to be syndicated in the international banking market. However, cases where the credit agreement is subject to "local" law (i.e., the law of the country where the project is located) seem to be increasing in number.

7.2.3.1   Overview

By means of the credit agreement, lenders agree to make financial resources available to the project company up to a preset maximum amount and on request. (The banks assume this obligation severally; in other words each bank severally commits to a quota of the total financing and is not responsible for the obligations of any other bank.) The loan is granted exclusively for the purpose specified in the agreement itself (to cover the cost of building and operating the plant, including development costs); the project company is not allowed to use these funds in any way that is not strictly associated with this purpose.

The credit facility will be a medium- to long-term one (see Section 6.9). The final maturity of the loan is strictly a financial question, but due to the nature of project finance (where reimbursement comes from revenues generated by project operations) loans have to be granted for a time span that allows the resources needed for reimbursement to be generated.

The project company is granted the option of prepayment, as we will see. However, the banks might force the borrower to make early repayments if events occur that show or forewarn that the borrower won't be able to fulfill its obligation to repay the loan.

7.2.3.2   Interpretation

As a rule, every finance document begins by setting out certain provisions on how it should be interpreted. A definitions section is included in the contract (normally at the beginning) for the purpose of simplifying the process of drawing up and consequently reading and interpreting the document.

Here an example proves useful. *Bank* can refer to each of the banks that are lenders in a credit agreement (and *banks* are all of them taken together). This is different than *bank* (lowercase), which simply indicates a bank in the common sense of the word. There is nothing complicated here from a conceptual viewpoint, but when examining project documents (and not only the credit agreement) the drafting technique should be taken into account and always kept clearly in mind. What's more, after overcoming some initial reluctance, this drafting technique has become common contract practice even in countries where English is not spoken (and, obviously, where English law does not apply). There are also other general provisions on the interpretation of the document, which are extremely specific and have become standard in the market.

7.2.3.3   The Credit Facilities

A project finance loan is always divided into different credit lines, called *credit facilities* or simply *facilities*.

Formally speaking, every facility is a separate credit transaction, with a distinct purpose and a distinct contractual treatment. We could say that though they are functionally connected, the facilities of a project finance loan are separate credit lines. In theory, there could be different lenders for every facility or only for some. In practice, however, this does not happen except, in some cases, for a specific facility used to cover the costs of VAT. The purpose, nature, and terms of repayment of this facility are completely different from the project facilities in the strict sense, and so the lenders can also be different.

As seen in Sections 6.9.1 to 6.9.4, a project finance loan normally involves at least the following facilities: a base facility, a stand-by facility used to cover construction costs that were not included in the original budget (cost overruns), and a VAT facility. Generally, this last facility has a shorter maturity, due to the possibility of either obtaining a refund on VAT paid to the contractor or offsetting this VAT against VAT to be paid to the tax authorities during the operations phase. If a refund request is filed, lenders usually ask that the relevant claims for refund toward the tax authorities be pledged or assigned by way of security in their favor for repayment of the VAT facility. Since a VAT facility has a shorter maturity, it either is not included or is only partially included in the security package set up for the other project facilities. On occasion, though more and more rarely, the VAT facility is kept separate and is not even included in the credit agreement. This might be the case when the bank or banks that grant the VAT facility are not the same lenders in the credit agreement, as mentioned earlier.

The base facility can be broken down further into separate facilities when project construction is divided into distinct, autonomous sections. Clearly, the lenders want the project company to complete construction of the project plant, since this provides the only possible source of revenue for repaying the loan. Therefore, breaking down the loan into separate facilities makes sense in cases when construction can be split into distinct phases that the lenders may wish to keep separate. (This might be the case if the lenders want drawdowns on the loan relating to a specific construction phase to be conditional on the completion of the previous phase.) An example is wind farm projects: These plants can be divided into separate fields that are completely autonomous in functional terms and have different timing and characteristics as far as construction is concerned. In such a case, breaking down the project loan into distinct facilities would be the recommended solution.

Separate facilities (and the individual drawdowns under each facility) may also be consolidated in a single facility at the end of the construction phase. This simplifies financial management and administration of the deal. In such cases, an additional facility is sometimes built into the credit agreement, which can be used at the end of construction solely to refinance the existing facilities for the amounts actually utilized.

Within each separate facility, the lending commitment of the banks involved is divided up pro quota on the basis of their respective participation. Depending on the circumstances, each bank may take on an equal share, or the loan syndication might be set up to allow various levels of participation for different lenders (see Sections 6.1 to 6.3). In this way, first-level lenders participate with a higher percentage than lower-level lenders.

In any case, participation of lenders in the financing involves no joint liability. In other words, if one bank does not respect its obligation to make advances, the other banks are not held to compensate for the shortfall in the funds to be made available to the borrower.

7.2.3.4   Conditions Precedent: Availability of Drawdowns

We have described and classified the facilities included in the credit agreement by which the lenders make financial resources available to the borrower. However, this should not lead to the conclusion that the loans granted are freely accessible to the borrower. All the conditions that have been described in the course of this book for financing the project with no (or limited) recourse are reflected in the credit agreement as the *conditions precedent*.

From a technical/legal standpoint, most conditions precedent can be defined as provisions that suspend the obligations of the lenders to make the funds granted in the credit agreement available to the borrower project company. In practical terms, conditions precedent represent the contractual mechanism that entitles lenders to check that the transaction meets all the substantial and formal criteria we have outlined in the previous pages before these funds are actually advanced to the project company. The characteristics of project bankability, reflected in the credit agreement, are verified here as a prerequisite for utilizing the loan, right before the first (and each successive) drawdown.

Normally the term *financial close* refers to the moment when conditions precedent for initial utilization of the loan are met. The first drawdown (specifically on the base facility) is clearly a major event in the development of the project finance deal and certainly not (or at least not purely) for symbolic reasons. First of all, with the initial drawdown the development costs incurred up to that point in time are refinanced by the project company; this is normally a considerable sum. Secondly, this marks a boundary line for lenders and the risk they take on. Before the first drawdown, this risk is of a merely professional nature: Time and resources may be wasted (and reputations tainted) from evaluating a project that proves unbankable. After the first drawdown, instead, lenders move into the sphere of credit risk; as a result their vision of the project changes: From external players, lenders are now involved in the specific risk of the project as members of the group of entities that have put money into the project.

Consequently, conditions precedent for the first drawdown or conditions for the financial close and conditions precedent for later drawdowns are normally differentiated, as is the approach of whoever has to verify them: censorial and conservative for the first drawdown and overtly more participatory for later ones.

Usually it is the agent bank (see Section 7.2.3.13) that receives the conditions precedent and confirms to lenders that these have been met.

Box 7-2 lists a typical set of conditions precedent for a project finance deal.

Not all the conditions precedent are future and uncertain events beyond the control of the parties involved in a project. An example is the first item in the second list in Box 7-2, the drawdown request, which if anything is the responsibility of the project company. The question here is strictly a technical/legal one: Every document required in order to utilize the loan is the responsibility of the borrower. It is the

---

Box 7-2   Conditions Precedent to the Financial Close

Conditions precedent to the financial close are usually various kinds of documents the agent bank has to receive from the borrower or from third parties:

- Copy of corporate documents (e.g., articles of incorporation, certificate of registration in the Registrar of Companies) of the borrower and other entities that are of fundamental importance for the project (sponsors, counterparties to key project agreements)
- Copy of the corporate resolutions that are mandatory to authorize the borrower and the "key" parties referred to in the previous point to execute the finance documents and/or the project agreements
- Specimen of borrower's authorized signatures, a typical request that is part of normal banking procedures
- Copy of the finance documents
- Copy of the security documents (see Section 7.2.4), with evidence that all formalities for their perfection have been carried out and that they are enforceable against third parties
- Copy of the project agreements (see Section 7.2.6)
- Project reports: normally from the technical advisor and the environmental expert, the insurance advisor, the advisor responsible for the financial model; legal due diligence report
- The first set of financial documents and information requested from the borrower and other finance documents relative to sponsors and key counterparties
- Documentary evidence that the sponsors have injected the initial equity requested in the credit agreement
- Copy of administrative permits required to build the plant
- Copy (in paper and/or software form) of the financial model, updated with the latest available data
- Legal opinions, normally from the lenders' lawyers (as regards both local law and the law regulating the credit agreement and other project contracts, if the two are different) and the borrowers' lawyers. "Special" legal opinions may also be requested relating to other parties involved in the project (generally sponsors and, if possible, the contractor and operator) and referring exclusively to aspects regarding the involvement in the project of these parties

The specific nature of each project can obviously lead to the formulation of ad hoc documents; the availability and delivery of these papers to the agent bank represent a condition precedent to the financial close.

In addition to the foregoing points, other conditions are usually set for all drawdowns on the loan:

- The drawdown request (in the agreed form) sent from the borrower to the agent
- Indication of the drawdown date, which must fall in the availability period set down in the credit agreement
- Satisfaction of the debt-to-equity ratio as regards the project company's situation after the drawdown in question
- Verification that there are no events of default or any other circumstances lenders would consider serious enough to block the project company's ability to drawdown the loan
- Confirmation that representations under the credit agreement are true (see Section 7.2.3.10)
- Documentation on the use of the requested funds, such as a certificate from a technical advisor or a statement from the borrower confirmed by this advisor, as regards the actual costs incurred for realizing the project (see Section 4.2).

Here, too, the circumstances of a given project can lead to the formulation of other specific conditions precedent to each drawdown under the credit facilities agreement.

borrower who bears the risk of satisfying these requirements, even when this company has no direct control over the specific item (as is the case with legal opinions of the lenders' lawyers).

The project company takes on the responsibility for and the risk of satisfying conditions precedent in order to utilize the loan, as we said. The lenders can waive these requirements at any time and advance the loan even if some of these conditions precedent are not met.

7.2.3.5   Interest on Drawdowns

From a legal standpoint, not much can be said about interest on a project finance loan, at least in an institutional framework. Interest is determined by adding a margin to the rate the banks advancing the loan can get when raising the capital on the interbank market (usually Euribor for loans in euro or Libor in other cases; see Section 6.9.5).

Since the margin is affected by the credit worthiness of the borrower, it may vary during the different stages of project development. (The margin could be higher during the construction phase, which by definition carries higher risk with respect to the operating phase.) It may also change depending on the financial ratios that are periodically calculated as required in the credit agreement itself. (In Sections 7.2.3.11 and 7.2.3.12 we refer to these with regard to covenants and events of default.)

The interbank rate applied to the drawdowns requested by the borrower is normally computed on the basis of rates listed by international financial information services. Specific clauses in the credit agreement provide for alternative ways to determine the interest rate when it is not possible to follow the normal procedure.

In extreme circumstances, there may be no way to come up with the applicable rate because there is no active market in that given moment. (So, realistically, lenders cannot raise capital to cover the drawdowns according to the credit agreement.) This is a case of market disruption, which triggers a temporary suspension of the banks' obligation to advance funds to the borrower.

Every single drawdown triggers a separate interest rate calculation (and periodic interest payment) from the date it is advanced (and financed by lenders). This is one of the administrative complications of managing the financing that would prompt lenders to consolidate all drawdowns at the end of the construction period (i.e., after the availability period, as described earlier).

The borrower has to pay a higher interest rate on amounts that are overdue and have not yet been repaid. This is called a *default interest rate*, which is usually computed by using the rate the borrower would have normally paid plus 100–200 basis points (more in some cases). Specific provisions in the credit agreement regulate how relative time periods are defined and what default interest rate is charged, but here we are moving into a situation of a financial crisis of the project. Due to the very nature of project finance, the response instruments available to lenders and described in the security documents (specifically the step-in option) count much more than applying a higher interest rate (probably a very theoretical course of action). We detail this point further on.

7.2.3.6 Repayment of the Loans: Canceling the Facility

Repayment of project finance loans takes place over a relatively long time horizon. After construction is complete, the project company must be given the time to generate cash flows, which are used primarily for repaying the loan. Only when operations are under way can the loan amortization schedule start, and no sooner. How quickly the debt is repaid depends on the financial model, which allows room for an adequate safety margin.

In some clearly defined cases, apart from crisis situations, the amortization schedule can be modified or payment can be made before the preset maturity date. This might be the result of the borrower's decision (voluntary prepayment) or a specific contract provision (mandatory prepayment). Let's take a quick look at these two possibilities.

All structured financing credit agreements explicitly provide for the borrower's option to prepay all or part of the debt, on advance notice to the agent bank. Specific contract provisions outline how prepayments are to be allocated in the case of partial reimbursement. (The options would be pro quota allocation on all future installments or allocation on final installments, which take place at the latest date and as such are riskiest for lenders.)

In any case, consider the following.

- During the construction phase the project company has no self-generated financial resources and can only count on funds from the loan and equity contributed by sponsors.
- During the operational phase, the repayment plan (i.e., the amortization schedule) is based exclusively on the project company's business plan.

For these two reasons, it seems understandable that in market practice the prepayment option is actually an opportunity for the sponsors to refinance the project, closing one financing transaction and opting for another one (which may or may not be without recourse; see Section 6.9.8). Another possibility, less likely in the real world but possible in theory, is that sponsors/the project company might decide to not to take their share of revenue from project operations to accelerate repayment of the loan (in part). We talk about refinancing project finance deals in Section 7.3.

Cases of mandatory prepayment are very limited. Here, we should make it clear that we refer to something different from crisis situations, when an acceleration of the financing is required due to circumstances defined as events of default (see Section 7.2.3.12).

As a rule, mandatory prepayment on the loan arises in cases when there are insurance indemnities due to damages incurred by the project or if the project company collects other types of extraordinary financial resources. The lenders in such cases can be beneficiaries of these payments, preventing this money from going to the sponsors. Therefore, the mandatory prepayment mechanism is the contract provision with which lenders "intercept" these financial resources that are made available to the project company and claim this money for themselves.

The borrower is given the chance to cancel undrawn funds made available through the credit agreement. This is usually called the *right to cancel the loan*, by which the lenders' commitment decreases proportionally. Note that equal treatment, and therefore proportionality, toward lending banks is a necessary rule. (Remember that lenders can participate in the financing by contributing different amounts.) In fact, the borrower is exempt from this rule only in certain specific cases (which we discuss later) when particular circumstances affect the position of only one or a few lenders. It may be advantageous to the borrower to cancel a portion of the loan not yet advanced if there is no need for these funds in order to avoid paying the commitment fee.

However, cancellation is usually subject to one condition: The project company must show it has adequate resources to complete the project. Otherwise, canceling the credit line would amount to abandoning the project, which would be unacceptable to lenders. The financing and contract system of project finance is a fixed and rigid one, in which the financial model must be fully funded in order to be bankable. Restrictions on voluntary cancellation of the loan by borrowers are one of the contractual methods for ensuring that this principle is respected.

7.2.3.7   Credit Agreement Costs

The economy of a project encompasses all expenses involved in developing and building it, including costs relating to the financing itself. Therefore, it is normal for the project company to be charged for the tax costs of executing the credit agreement as well as for the costs triggered by possible detrimental changes in the tax regime applicable to the financing deal. Additional tax charges may take the form of withholding taxes that the borrower has to pay in lieu of the lenders as a substitute taxed entity. This is done by means of a gross up mechanism, which calls for recalculating every sum owed by the borrower so lenders are paid the net total provided in the credit agreement.

As regards execution of the credit agreement, two indirect taxes could apply: registration duties and stamp duties. Based on the principle referred to earlier, even when technically these taxes should be for the account of the lenders, in the credit agreement these charges are transferred to the borrower, who has to pay them back to the lenders. (Usually the corresponding sum is withheld directly from the loan advances.)

The project company is also responsible for paying supplemental charges, when applicable, that may fall due after execution of the credit agreement in relation to this or the drawdown of the loan. The underlying principle here is that, in the international banking system, credits granted in various jurisdictions must be equivalent and comparable from the financial and economic standpoints. Therefore, legislative or regulatory changes that could generate a cost or lower profits for lenders result in an indemnity charged to the borrower in favor of lenders who are damaged by this burden or added cost. (A classic example is a modification in capital requirements that would make the loan in question less profitable for some lenders.)

These provisions are called *increased cost clauses*, which at first glance may seem quite unfair to the borrower. But they can be understood in light of the operating procedures of international banks, which have to be as neutral as possible with respect to the various jurisdictions where banking activities are carried out. Note also that if increased cost clauses are implemented, the borrower usually has a prepayment option, which would give it the right to yank the bank that requested the higher payment or indemnity out of the operation. As mentioned previously, this is one of the few cases of voluntary prepayment by the borrower (who by doing so can avoid the added charges of activating these mechanisms) that does not benefit all lenders equally. Instead this prepayment is channeled toward repaying the specific lender who incurred an increased cost and by availing itself of such provisions asked that this cost be transferred to the borrower.

One principle, similar to some extent to the one just described, forms the basis of contract provisions normally referred to as the *illegality clause*. A situation may present itself in which one of the lenders is unable to maintain the financing stipulated in the credit agreement due to legislation in the home country or the regulations of the central bank. The typical example is a commercial (or lending) embargo of one country, which would ban the banks of this country from entering into or maintaining credit transactions with another country. Consider three factors: (1) the international dissemination of project finance, (2) the use of this technique in developing countries (very often for infrastructure works and with the support of the government and/or supranational credit institutions; see Sections 6.4 and 6.5), (3) the duration of project finance initiatives. In light of these considerations, it is not hard to imagine that these provisions can potentially be applied much more often than one would initially expect.

In these circumstances, the banks affected by supervening illegalities are released from their lending obligations, and the borrower is required to prepay what it owes to these banks. (The principle of equal treatment of lenders does not apply here either, but this is a case of an obligation, not an option, of the borrower.)

Note that in all cases of increased cost or illegality when a lender withdraws from the financing and the loan is canceled, it is very likely that, in practice, this lender's quota would be acquired by one or more of the other lenders, if possible. (This could be done with the assignment mechanism, which is discussed further on.) By doing so, there would be no interruptions in the project development or its relative financing. Other solutions may also be found (such as transferring the lending office of the loan from one jurisdiction to a jurisdiction where the relevant problem does not exist).

7.2.3.8   Information Flow from Borrowers to Lenders: Financial Ratios

Lenders need to monitor the progress of the project continually; this plays out in two different directions:

1. Monitoring the technical/industrial progress of the project, in the construction phase and the operations phase (which correspond to different level of risk, as we saw earlier)
2. Monitoring the borrower and its economic results.

As regards the first point, a number of information requirements are normally included in the covenants of the credit agreement (see Section 7.2.3.11) and in some cases directly in the project contracts.

Very specific obligations regarding the supply of documents and financial data ensure that the financial conditions of the project company can be monitored. These requirements go from the obvious commitment to send annual and semiannual balance sheets, the budget and budget updates, and other accounting and financial documentation, to the generic commitment to provide additional data and information when agent banks make "reasonable" requests.

Project company financial statements must be duly kept in respect of strict standards of accuracy; obligations also apply as regards the accounting criteria adopted. The information provided to the agent by the project company is covered by specific representations on its true nature and completeness (see Section 7.2.3.10).

Financial ratios play a special role in enabling lenders to monitor the project company and the project. The financial meaning and the economic rationale of these ratios are outlined in Section 5.3. Here it is worth mentioning that a typical credit agreement establishes financial ratios and sets specific dates for verifying that the project company is actually respecting these ratios. This may happen when the annual or semiannual accounting statements are prepared or at the end of each fiscal quarter. Such verification might also be required in exceptional circumstances, for example, when construction has been completed or when distributions are made to sponsors.

Verification of financial ratios is generally included in the credit agreement for the following contractual purposes.

- *To set conditions for drawdowns on the loan:* A downslide in certain ratios is normally penalized by prohibiting additional drawdowns. Clearly, this mechanism works only during the plant construction phase, corresponding to the availability period of the loan that is used (primarily) to pay for the project construction disbursements.
- *To modify the interest rate:* The risk on the loan granted for the project in question changes if the creditworthiness of the borrower deteriorates, a situation that is typically revealed by financial ratios.
- *To set down conditions for making distributions to sponsors* (see Section 7.2.3.9): This becomes relevant exclusively during the operations phase, which is the only period when distributions may occur.
- *To establish events of default:* A substantial drop in certain financial ratios constitutes an event of default (see Section 7.2.3.12).

7.2.3.9   Distributions

Sponsors get involved in a project to make a profit, obviously. With corporate financing, the borrower's right to distribute profits to its shareholders is not normally questioned. In fact, if the terms of the loan are respected (including financial ratios, if applicable), there is no conflict between the rights of the lenders and the distribution of profits to sponsors, in theory, even though lenders would no doubt prefer that profits not be distributed, so as to consolidate their borrower's equity.

In project finance the question is radically different, and Section 7.1, addressing the nature and function of the project company, certainly helps us see why. A project company is a container created to develop the project and delineate its legal boundaries. Lenders rely solely on the cash flow generated by the project. Distribution of profits means taking something away from this company to which the lenders, in theory, are entitled with priority over the sponsors.

As a result, there may be a total ban on the distribution of profits generated by the project to sponsors until the loan has been entirely repaid. This is clearly extremely penalizing—and in fact unacceptable from a business standpoint—for sponsors.

Normally, therefore, the solution lies in a compromise. The cash flow generated by the project can be distributed (clearly during the operations phase; before that there is simply no cash flow) only if certain conditions are met. These requisites pertain to the absence of any critical situation involving the project or the project company (i.e., circumstances that would constitute an event of default) and other conditions that prove that the project is solid from the financial and industrial standpoints. (These usually include compliance with required levels of financial ratios.)

In discussing the distribution of the project's cash flow, we do not mean, strictly speaking, a distribution of dividends as defined in company law. The concept of distributions does not coincide with that of the distribution of dividends. In fact, distributions do not involve resources that can be called "dividends" by law or in accounting terms (despite the fact that often we refer to "dividend" lockups when describing conditions that prohibit making distributions).

Now, it is clear that the nature of the project company is such that its flow of payments is regulated in the credit agreement on the basis of cash flow. Every sum collected by the project company during project operations must be used to pay suppliers for the necessary goods and services and to cover other payments, such as taxes, which are required for the very existence of the project and/or the project company. In other words, the project company has to pay all amounts due according to the credit agreement. What is left over are "profits," clearly not in the accounting or corporate sense, but in the project finance meaning of the word. To put it another way, if the conditions mentioned previously are met (and, again, these are contractually stipulated with lenders), the funds in question can be distributed to sponsors.

The overall structure of a project company has been outlined in the previous paragraphs. Now we can see that a considerable distance separates the financial and legal structure of project finance from corporate loans. The project company truly (and consistently) is an instrument created to make financing possible without recourse. With this vehicle we create creditworthiness (i.e., the possibility to receive credit from the banking system) that would not exist otherwise or that would require quite a different credit standing if the corporate loan logic were to be adopted.

Therefore, the concept of regulated distribution in project finance does not correspond (except perhaps incidentally) with dividend distribution to shareholders.

This is only one way for the project company to make distributions to sponsors (and certainly not the most common one or the easiest to implement, given the restrictions in company law normally placed on distributing dividends to shareholders). Other possibilities are for the project company to disburse interim dividends, where possible, and repay subordinated debt, which constitutes a component of the project company's equity (again, in the project finance sense of the word), as seen in Section 6.8. Making prohibited distributions is a clear breach of the obligations taken on by the project company in the credit agreement, and it is therefore an event of default pursuant to the credit agreement. Clearly, the inverse restriction also applies: The project company cannot make distributions to sponsors if the applicable law does not allow it.

7.2.3.10 Representations

The term *representations* refers to a corpus of provisions that are always included in structured credit agreements; as such they are by no means unique to project finance contracts.

An analysis of the nature and the legal meaning of representations clearly goes beyond the purpose of this chapter. Here we will simply attempt to provide a definition and a generic description in the context of project finance and try to explain the "mechanical" purposes of representations in a project finance credit agreement.

Representations are specific statements by the borrower, who warrants their truth for the benefit of lenders. These declarations may address a vast and diverse number of issues. This makes it complicated to come up with a summary classification of representations; we next give a brief description of the key representations included in a project finance credit agreement. Obviously, this list is not exhaustive, and other representations can be found in actual practice with reference to specific issues affecting each individual project finance transaction.

- Representations that relate to the borrower company itself: that it has been incorporated and exists in accordance with applicable law; that all necessary corporate resolutions have been made and correctly passed to duly execute the credit agreement and the other project documents
- Representations on the validity of the undertakings by the borrower in the project documents, confirming *inter alia* that no conflicting undertaking toward third parties exists
- Representations on the nature of the borrower's obligations toward lenders in accordance with finance documents, with specific reference made to the absence of rights granted to third parties that would subordinate these obligations (except, obviously, rights established directly by the law)
- Representations on the validity of security interests granted by the borrower or by third parties (sponsors as far as pledges on the borrower's shares are concerned) as security for the credit agreement
- Representations on the existence and validity of all administrative authorizations needed to develop the project
- Representations on the absence of litigation or situations that could results in litigation involving the project company
- Representations on the absence of any event of default, as defined by the credit agreement itself
- Representations on project documents, specifically verifying the absence of any situation of nonperformance or irregular performance of the obligations under these documents

- Representations as to the correctness and reliability of the borrower's accounting statements
- Representations referring to the execution and validity of insurance policies pertaining to the project and the plant
- Representations on the ownership of the borrower's shares
- Representations regarding the ownership of the site where the project plant will be built and every other right required to undertake its construction
- Representations on possible environmental issues that may affect the site and the project in general
- Representations on the truth of the information that the borrower has provided or will provide to lenders concerning the project, with specific reference to the data used for the purpose of the information memorandum
- Other representations of a more legal nature, such as the valid choice of a foreign law as governing law of the credit agreement, the absence of withholdings on payments made according to the law in question, the due completion of every legal or tax formality in relation to the finance documents and the validity of the obligations assumed in accordance with these documents, and the absence of sovereign immunity situations or similar.

Some representations are repeated at various points in time, usually at the financial close and on every drawdown. The truth of these representations has to be ascertained at these times as well.

If a representation is incorrect, this constitutes an event of default under the credit agreement. However, normally such an occurrence is only such if the event and/or its consequences are material in light of the interests of the project.

7.2.3.11   The Project Company's Covenants

A somewhat narrow view of lending activity could lead us to conclude that in a credit agreement the only thing the borrower is expected to do is to pay lenders their dues at maturity. In fact, nothing can change the fact that this is and always will be the primary obligation of every borrower. In a project finance context, however, it is completely normal, and indeed necessary, for the borrower to take on a complex, detailed set of obligations toward lenders that are ancillary to both the obligation to repay and to the financing in general. These obligations may be either correlated to loan repayment (if the project company does not take certain actions, by definition it will not be able to repay the loan at the schedule maturity dates) or required by lenders in order to monitor their credit investment and verify that it is being managed properly.

Here too we will look at a typical set of covenants for a project finance transaction, keeping in mind that, as with conditions precedent and representations, specific circumstances can result in specific covenants beyond the standard ones usually seen on the market. Normally, the credit agreement differentiates between positive covenants and negative covenants, which refer to things that must and must not be done. Covenants are designed as supplemental obligations of the borrower, in addition to the basic obligation to repay to the lenders the amount due on the scheduled maturity dates.

Positive Covenants:

- Obligations relating to building and operating the plant and the project according to sound industrial and business criteria. Therefore, beyond going to build the project plant and make it operational, the financing in question involves a specific obligation to build and operate the project. Clearly, the wording of relative clauses varies greatly, depending on the project in question, and may be quite detailed as regards criteria and objectives that in fact constitute this obligation.

- Obligations to use the funds made available through the credit agreement solely for the purposes set out in that document.
- Obligations to keep the insurance policies required for the project in force. Normally, the list of these policies (or a more general "insurance policy" to be complied with by the project company) is included in an annex to the credit agreement.
- Obligations to implement the interest rate risk coverage policy (and, when applicable, exchange rate risk) as agreed with lenders. This is sometimes specified in a detailed annex to the credit agreement or in a separate document.
- Obligations to obtain the administrative authorizations listed in the relative annex to the credit agreement and every other administrative authorization needed to build and operate the project.
- Obligations to duly execute and perform obligations under the project agreements.
- Obligations to comply with reserved discretions. A brief description of this concept, and in fact an explanation of this covenant, is given in the following pages.
- Obligations to comply with laws and regulations applicable to the project and the activity of the project company in general.
- Obligations to comply with environmental laws and regulations and to act prudently with respect to environmental matters.
- Obligations duly and accurately to keep the project company's accounting documents.
- Obligations to open and maintain the project bank accounts specified in the credit agreement (or in a separate, specific contract). We outline the project account structure further on in this chapter.
- Obligations to create and maintain security interests as security for the financing and to provide security on the additional future assets of the project company.

Negative Covenants:

- Obligations not to modify or jeopardize the rights of the project company under the project agreements. The contractual formulation of these covenants is much more extensive, but we can sum them up in the obligation not to alter the contractual position of the project company without lenders' approval. As we have seen and will more fully elaborate, the overall structure of project agreements is a key element in the structure of the project finance. For this reason, "managing" project agreements is not left to the discretion of the project company, but instead is monitored and restricted in favor of lenders. If project agreements are modified or incorrectly executed, the project is no longer a project finance initiative; it becomes a different operation, one that can no longer be financed on a without-recourse basis.
- Obligations of the borrower not to dispose of its assets (except in specific circumstances, such as for obsolete assets).
- Obligations not to incur, create, or permit to subsist any other financial indebtedness (unless contemplated in the project contracts). Any supplemental

financial resources made available to the borrower would increase indebtedness toward third-party lenders, who would enjoy the same level of credit rights as the original project finance lenders. Clearly, the original lenders can allow a waiver to this prohibition, and occasionally further indebtedness is allowed if the rights of the new financiers are subordinated to those of the original lenders.

- Obligations that prohibit the creation of other security in favor of third parties (with minor exceptions); this covenant is referred to as the *negative pledge clause*. Such obligations are usually included in ordinary credit agreements as well, but in project finance they play a fundamental role in light of the logic underlying the financing itself.
- Obligations not to undertake any other activity except for building and operating the project. As we said before, this covenant is a key element with respect to the structure and functions of the project company. In fact, this company coincides with the project from the entrepreneurial and financial standpoints, and the project is the only activity it is allowed to perform.
- Obligations not to buy assets or sign contracts not included in the list of project contracts or approved by lenders. This covenant is based on the same principle as the previous one.
- Obligations not to abandon the construction and/or operation of the project. This covenant corresponds to the obligation to realize the project, which we saw earlier. Since the resources for repaying the loan will come (exclusively) from operating the project, the realization of the project is not left to the discretion of the project company; instead it is a specific contract obligation of the project company toward the lenders.
- Obligations not to undertake any merger, demerger, or other corporate reconstruction and not to buy shares in other companies. (In general, all extraordinary corporate operations are prohibited.) Along with the previous point, this is another aspect of the principle that the project company has binding legal constraints in relation to its corporate existence and operations.
- Obligations not to decrease the equity capital and not to issue shares that are not pledged in favor of the lenders. In normal circumstances all the project company's share capital is granted as security to lenders, so the purpose of this covenant is to protect this security. We get back to this when we specifically address the security package.
- Obligations not to grant credit to third parties or guarantees to third parties. (Security is prohibited by the negative pledge prohibition.)

Violation of a covenant in the credit agreement constitutes an event of default. However, there may be mitigations, such as (1) a grace period allowing the project company the chance to cure the breach in question and (2) the concept of materiality of the breach, i.e., the breach is an event of default only if its is material.

Now it is time to explain and analyze an expression used a number of times in the previous pages: events of default.

7.2.3.12   Events of Default and Their Consequences: The Financial Crisis of the Transaction

As already stated, the main obligation of the borrower is to repay the amounts owed to lenders at the stated maturities. However, just as the project company has a series of ancillary and complementary covenants contemplated in the credit agreement, there are also a number of circumstances that lenders see as symptomatic of a crisis situation of the project and of the loan. In such situations, the lenders would be justified in terminating the financing transaction ahead of schedule. These circumstances, normally called *events of default*, are specifically described in the credit agreement.

As before for conditions precedent and covenants, here we look at typical events of default package included in a project finance credit agreement. Note that here too the specific characteristics of each project can lead the parties to make provisions for other instances classified as events of default and in some (less common) cases exclude a few that are listed next.

1. Nonpayment of amounts due at maturity in accordance with the credit agreement. This is clearly the main event of default. A grace period is often allowed, necessarily a quite short one. In such a case, failure to pay the amount due only becomes an event of default (a term that is always clearly defined, see earlier), for example, five days after the stated maturity date.
2. Nonfulfillment of other obligations by the borrower (other than repayment obligations) as set out in the credit agreement. Normally such a breach has to pass a materiality test in order to be considered an event of default. In other words, it has to be significant in light of the project and the financing. We give a brief description of what this means in the following pages.
3. Nonfulfillment of an obligation stipulated in a project agreement by a sponsor or another party to such an agreement. Here, too, the breach in question normally must pass a materiality test. Of course, the language in a given contract may be extremely detailed in describing and classifying these cases of default by third parties. It is fairly common practice to identify who among the counterparties to a project contract is "relevant" for the purposes of the project and therefore for the purpose of this event of default. For example, it is completely normal and usually uncontested to consider the turnkey contractor and the operator "key" counterparties; in fact, nonperformance on their part is material for the purpose of the occurrence of an event of default.
4. Representations made in the credit agreement prove materially untrue. (In some cases, representations in other finance documents are also relevant for the purpose of this event of default.) If initially the system of representations and warranties is a "snapshot" of the project as depicted to lenders, the lack of truth of this system represents, by definition, a seriously adverse situation and as such an event of default.
5. The borrower is subject to liquidation or insolvency procedures that prevent the project from going forward.
6. Some other key counterparty to some project agreement is subject to liquidation or insolvency procedures making it impossible to duly fulfill its obligations set down in said agreement.
7. Some sponsor, party to some project agreement, is subject to liquidation or insolvency procedures.

Please note that the situations mentioned in points 6 and 7 become events of default at the point in time when the parties with potential interest in the project are subject to project contract obligations. Conversely, such events are no longer relevant, for example, if a contractor goes bankrupt after having fulfilled all obligations set down in the construction contract or if a sponsor does the same after having made all relevant equity contributions (though this is clearly a more delicate situation, and as such the lenders may want to consider this an event of default at all times). Another exception might be a case where the contractual counterparty in question, within a certain preset period of time, is replaced by a different entity that lenders consider reliable in the context of the project.

8. A significant decline in one or more of the project's financial ratios (see Section 7.2.3.8).
9. Expropriation, nationalization, or similar actions that impact the project company, the project, or a significant part of it or its assets.
10. Loss of the rights relating to the project or any significant part of it by the project company. This can happen without distinction either, due to an action by the project company (clearly in contrast with the undertaking taken on in the loan covenants; see the earlier section on covenants) or for reasons beyond the control of the project company.
11. Claims of project assets by third parties. This is very similar to point 10.
12. Plant construction is not finished on time. Clearly this event of default can have several detailed specifications, according to the stages of the outsourcing contract for project construction.
13. A project agreement or finance document is terminated or ceases to exist for any reason. This event of default is sometimes mitigated by the possibility that the relevant agreement or document is replaced by another, equivalent agreement.
14. Cross default (i.e., default of other financial obligations).
15. The agreed insurance coverage expires or is not implemented.
16. The project company loses or does not obtain a required administrative authorization to build or operate the project.
17. A transfer of shares in the project company takes place that is not allowed by the credit agreement, or the security over such shares is released and is not regranted in a timely fashion.
18. The entire plant or a significant part of it is destroyed or irreparably damaged (regardless of whether this is due to any fault of the project company).

In describing the typical events of default package, several references have been made to the materiality test. This tool can qualify instances identified as events of default and can actually apply to many other such cases as well.

The materiality test, as the term implies, means that the consequences of what is classified as an event of default have to be material. Very often legal procedures build a specific definition, so the materiality test is that the event in question has a "material adverse effect" (or similar). It is clear that the materiality test for the borrower represents the final defensive barrier against the possibility of lenders' declaring an event of default.

In any case, normally the notion of material adverse effect has to involve an event that either hinders the ability of the borrower (or some other relevant entity) to fulfill its contract obligations or jeopardizes the rights of lenders as established in the finance documents. But here, thanks to the creativity of project finance legal experts, definitions and concepts have been formulated that diverge from the typical notion to take into account specific situations found in individual projects.

As we mentioned before, if an event of default occurs, by definition this is a pathological situation in the context of the loan. As a condition precedent to draw-downs and distributions, the credit agreement normally requires that no events of default have occurred or are outstanding. But the key point is that if an event of default were to occur, this would trigger the option for lenders to cancel any part of the loan that is still available for drawdown and demand immediate repayment of the loans made up until that moment. Normally repayment cannot be made unless sponsors inject their own equity; in fact, the company has no other resources except those generated by the project, so by definition it cannot comply with the demand to repay the loan immediately. In this case, lenders can enforce security interests and take possession of the project, if they think this is the only way to recover all or part of their money.

In the remainder of this section we examine the mechanics of the consequences of an event of default on a credit agreement. In Section 7.2.4, on security documents, we look more closely at step-in rights, i.e., the legal instruments that allow lenders to replace sponsors and/or the project company in running the project.

Effects of Default: Let us imagine that an event of default has occurred. First, for clarity, we look back at the concept referred to earlier: An event of default does not coincide with the borrower's failure to perform its obligations. Certain breaches of the facilities agreement by the project company are not considered events of default; even though these may be violations of contractual obligations, they are not subject to the remedies described later. Likewise, some events of default do not result from breaches of the finance documents by the project company.

Quite often the provisions of the credit agreement require that the event of default in question be not only verified but actually in existence when lenders exercise the options described shortly. In fact, normally, the event of default has to be continuing when lenders exercise their contractual remedies. These options are no longer valid if in the meantime the negative circumstance has been remedied or no longer exists (or if, usually on the request of the borrower, the lenders "forgive" the borrower the event of default and agree to waive their relevant rights under the credit agreement).

If an event of default occurs and is continuing, lenders have the following options:

- To cancel their available commitment on the credit facilities in the credit agreement, or, in other words, to revoke their commitment to advance moneys under the credit facilities, and/or
- To declare the loans payable on demand, and/or
- To declare all amounts due under the loans immediately due and payable, which is normally called the *lenders' right of acceleration.*

If the second option is exercised, lenders can demand immediate repayment of the amount due at any later date, simply by making this demand. In practice, this is seen as an interim solution. The amounts in question become payable on demand, and in the meantime participants ascertain whether recovering the deal is possible (perhaps by changing the terms) or if instead there is no way to remedy the situation. In the latter case, the only remaining option is to demand acceleration on the loan.

What we have just described, in a strict sense, is how the system of events of default works (in addition to enforcing security interests and exercising step-in rights, which we examine further on). In summary, this system centers on three concepts that are the potential consequences of an event of default, at the lenders discretion:

1. Cancellation
2. Loan payable on demand
3. Acceleration

Note that these concepts are not exclusive to project finance but are customarily found in any financing initiative syndicated according to market standards. What is typical in project finance is the logical framework that all of this slots into and the specific conception of many of the events of default, as we have briefly seen. To avoid any misunderstanding, we want to clarify that the consequences of an event of default listed earlier are merely options for lenders. But nothing is preventing them from taking no action or even formally waiving these rights as regards a specific event of default, either before or after such a circumstance arises. (As already mentioned, these are cases of lenders waiving a specific right or option.)

7.2.3.13   Role of the Agent

Up to now we have referred generically to lenders as parties to the credit agreement with rights, options, and obligations. Formally speaking this is true, but it neglects the fact that project finance initiatives are not actually managed by each lending bank directly but by an agent bank that acts for all the banks that participate as lenders in the deal. Note that the agent's role is a normal part of all syndicated financing and not just project finance transactions. In fact, due to the nature of project finance and the risk inherent to any project finance deal, it is not realistic to imagine that such a financing transaction could be bilateral (i.e., involving only one lending bank) and not syndicated. Due to this and the technical and financial complexity of project finance, it is evident that in some respects the agent plays an essential role in project finance, one that is often more complicated and demanding than the role played by the agent in a normal syndicated financing deal. As a rule, the agent (or agent bank) handles the following activities in relation to the financing.

- Managing the flow of funds granted by lenders to the project company; receiving payments, which are then distributed to lenders depending on their level of participation in the loan or according to their competency. In a way, the agent plays the role of a bank teller who gives the project company access to the loan.
- Managing the communication flow between the project company and lenders (including requests for drawdowns). In this sense, the agent is the lenders' domiciled office for the purpose of the project finance loan transaction.
- Typically exercising all rights and options to which lenders are entitled to according to the credit agreement. This is done in strict conformity with the conditions set down in this contract, which are respected not only in substance but also from a formal and procedural standpoint. For example, the credit agreement may stipulate that a given option can be exercised by the agent with no additional conditions or exclusively on instructions from the lenders who together hold a majority participation in the financing. We look at what this entails shortly.

Up until this point the role of the agent has actually been a question of administrative convenience (a very considerable convenience, perhaps even a need). But another issue is at stake here. The project and its financing constitute a single entity that has to be managed as such, both for lenders and for the project company. As we described earlier, though lenders do not take on joint responsibility for the obligations that they assume in the credit agreement, every other action they take in terms of the financing is necessarily collective, which is also to the borrower's advantage.

The instrument used to achieve this result is to concentrate relationships with the project company in the figure of the agent bank. A meticulous system has to be developed detailing circumstances in which the agent can and cannot take the initiative for lenders. Also, regulations must be drawn up, in part in the credit agreement and in part in the intercreditor agreement, specifying how these initiatives and actions are decided on and carried out.

From a legal standpoint, we can consider the agent a representative of the lenders. This person is commissioned and empowered to manage the financing (including transferring funds to and from the project company) and to send and receive all communications relative to the financing.

We should specify that the agent is entrusted with exercising the rights and options of the lenders as need be, in compliance with the specific conditions set down in the credit agreement. For example, it is common practice for the agent to declare an acceleration following an event of default if the majority banks (those that have the majority quota of participation in the financing) deem this necessary and give the agent corresponding instructions. In fact only these conditions can legally trigger an acceleration of the loan; none of the lenders exercises this option independently. Likewise, the credit agreement always includes clauses that regulate the substitution of the agent, if need be. In addition, a single lender acting alone cannot revoke the authority jointly assigned to the agent. (By the same token, the financing deal must have an acting agent appointed to carry out relative duties.)

The borrower also has an interest in nominating the agent and the duties that are to be performed. What's more, the borrower can object to exercising rights and options lenders are entitled to if such action does not conform to the provisions that regulate the responsibilities of the agent. Be that as it may, the agent acts not independently but in the name of the lenders, except for those rights granted specifically to the agent, such as paying a fee normally charged to the borrower to remunerate the agent (agency fee; see Section 6.3.3.).

7.2.3.14   The Account Bank: Brief Comments on the Account Structure and Monitoring Payments

The agent is given responsibility for managing the cash inflows and outflows relating to the financing. Consequently, in a way the agent acts as the bank teller for the project company. However, this does not necessarily mean that the bank accounts used for the financing and the project are opened with the agent bank. Normally, in a project finance deal an account bank is appointed (which can be the agent, though this is not necessarily the case). This is the only bank where the project company is allowed to open and maintain its bank accounts.

Project finance involves setting up an account structure, so we need to examine what this entails. The credit agreement (or in some cases a separate contract) contains a list of bank accounts that the project company is obliged to open and maintain with the account bank. This system is based on the fact that the project company has to maintain these accounts and must not have any other bank account in any other bank. So the list is a closed one, confirming once again that project finance is, in financial terms, inherently a preestablished, binding, and—to a certain extent—rigid system.

Each of the project's accounts has a specific function, and the borrower has to operate on each one exclusively in accordance with the provisions that regulate the account structure. Basically, the account structure and the different project accounts have three distinct purposes:

1. To give lenders the chance to monitor the project company's money collections and payments (through the account bank and the agent, obviously) and to channel them by the preestablished order relative to the project finance deal. This preset order or priority is called the *payment waterfall*, which the project company has to respect in accordance with the credit agreement during the entire life of the loan.
2. To create a reserve of value secured in favor of the lenders.
3. To create a security in favor of the lenders over the cash of the project company.

Point 2 shouldn't be confused with point 3. The latter is simply dictated by the need to identify specifically where the cash of the project company will be deposited, so as to secure it in favor of the lenders (see Section 7.2.4). This is not a method for controlling how the cash assets of the borrower are managed (which is done directly or indirectly through other mechanisms in the credit agreement) but only a way to monitor the borrower's "containers." The aim of point 2 is different: It calls for maintaining accounts in which the project company has to keep cash on hand, for example, in the form of a reserve account (see Section 5.2). If there were no contract provisions to this effect, the project company would use these funds for different purposes, without holding them in a bank account in order "artificially" to create value to secure in favor of the lenders.

Now we look at a possible model of a project finance account structure (albeit a necessarily simplified one).

Normally a general account is set up for all of the project company's cash inflows; this is usually called the *proceeds account* or the *revenues account*. All payments coming from third parties, with a few specific exceptions, should be deposited in this account. This allows the agent to keep the financial performance of the project company under control by monitoring the cash inflows. The revenues account also has a secondary function: Every inflow that is not specifically mentioned in the credit agreement is credited to this account.

There are two possible ways to monitor the flow of payments from the project company to third parties. The simpler one is to make such payments directly from the proceeds account, which functions as a general account for deposits and withdrawals (except for flows specifically earmarked for other accounts). In more sophisticated structures, a separate account is set up, usually called a *disbursement account* or an *operating account*. Cash is withdrawn from this account and transferred to third parties to cover the project's operating expenses. In this case, withdrawals can be made periodically from the proceeds account to transfer the necessary resources to the disbursement account. As a rule, this is in compliance with the budget presented by the project company to the agent, who approves it if it conforms to the financial model.

In certain cases, the provisions in the credit agreement call for drawdowns on the loan by the project company to be deposited in the proceeds account or the disbursement account (if there is one). Some lenders would rather keep separate the resources that the project company receives from the loan and those that come from project operations because financial monitoring is simpler. During the operating phase, usually there is an overlap of the last drawdowns on the loan and the initial income from operations. In some circumstances it is preferable for these resources to be deposited into different accounts. But there does not seem to be a consolidated rule by which the clear majority of operators tend to prefer one solution over another.

The credit agreement requires some "special secured accounts" to be opened and maintained. The number of, function of, and amount deposited in these accounts depend a great deal on the specific circumstances of the individual project. Generalizations can be made only with ample reservations.

Normally, a debt service reserve account is set up (see Section 5.2); the amount kept in it is contingent on the debt. This is one of the accounts from which the project company is allowed to make withdrawals, according to the credit agreement, to cover the payments required in this same contract. Other reserve accounts are usually opened to cover unexpected expenses during the operational phase, such as damages to the project or extraordinary maintenance. Lastly, it is completely normal for the creation of a special reserve account to be one of the mitigations implemented for specific project risks (so that money is ready when a specific risk becomes actual damage to the project). However, there are no generalized rules regarding this matter.

Generally speaking, the list of project accounts also includes a compensation account, where possible insurance indemnities from damages to the project are deposited, as well as indemnity payments from third parties. The purpose is to set apart the indemnity payments that the project company receives. It is common practice to request the creation of security interests in favor of the lenders on the compensation account too, since, by definition, inflows (indemnity payments) materialize here if the project experiences some prejudice.

The last item on this basic list of project accounts is normally called the *distributions* or *dividends account*. The project company has the right to transfer cash here that it can distribute to sponsors, according to the terms of the credit agreement. Accordingly, this account is not secured in favor of the lenders, since the resources deposited here have already been freed up for sponsors. In fact, lenders have relinquished the right to these funds, which, as far as they are concerned, are no longer applicable to loan reimbursement. As long as it is deposited in the distribution account, this liquidity is still the property of the project company, legally speaking, but now the sponsors are rightly entitled to it according to the logic of project finance.

With this quick digression describing the project accounts from a "static" perspective, we can now conclude the discussion we began earlier on credit agreement provisions relating to managing cash flow in project operations. The flow of payments involving the project company is closely regulated by principles that, as we mentioned, provide for a waterfall, or in other words, establish how the cash flow generated by the initiative may be used and the ranking of payments to third parties (see Figures 5.2 and 5.6). The provisions of the credit agreement set forth the ranking of payments to be made by the cash flow generated by the project. At the top of the list are payments required by law and those that are essential to the very existence of the project company and the management of the project. Next come the service of the debt arising under the credit agreement and any other related payments. At the bottom of the waterfall are distributions to sponsors. These provisions regarding the project company's obligations for managing payments correspond to regulations relating to deposits and withdrawals allowed for each account. In this sense, the payment waterfall established in the credit agreement is not only a system of obligations for the project company, it corresponds in fact to the movement of cash in the project's accounts, which can actually be seen on each account and in each transaction. As such, two goals are ensured in the most rigorous possible way, as we mentioned earlier: to monitor the operations of the project company and adherence to the provisions in the credit agreement regarding managing liquidity; and to create security interests on the project cash flow.

7.2.3.15 Assignment of the Credit Agreement: Assignment After Syndication

We won't go into great detail on the possibility of substituting the parties to the credit agreement or assignment and transfer of this contract by a lender or a borrower. There simply are not many problems in this regard that pertain specifically to project finance. Generally speaking, the provisions of the credit agreement dealing with debt assignment are similar to those in all market-standard financing deals. The major difference (which does not apply to the credit agreement in the strict sense) is that debt assignment in a project finance deal means transferring a security package that is very articulated and complex, much more so than we would normally find in other types of bank loans.

Of course, debt assignment is out of the question for the project company under normal circumstances. The project *is* the project company, and the project is financed without the support of external economies, in other words, without recourse. The finance documents do not allow the borrower to be replaced. Realistically speaking, such a substitution can happen in the face of a crisis (in case of default on the loan), when security interests are enforced and step-in rights are exercised. But this would involve specific, extraordinary circumstances, which do not pertain to ordinary operations but to the financial restructuring world, when such is the case.

The matter is completely different with regard to lenders. In fact, substituting lenders typically comes into question at two times: at the outset of the financing during initial syndication and later when one of the lenders, acting alone, opts to dismiss its investment in the financing deal.

As detailed earlier and in Sections 6.1 and 6.2, the commitment to grant financing to a project finance deal is initially taken on by a small number of banks who are often also the arrangers of a given initiative. (These banks are referred to as the *underwriters*.) Only later, through syndication, is the deal assigned to other banks so that no single institution has excessive exposure on a single project. From a contractual perspective, this can be done either by having all banks in the syndicate underwrite the credit agreement directly (previously agreed on with the arrangers and the original underwriters) or by initially executing the credit agreement with the underwriters and later assigning it in part to other lending banks. This usually happens by executing a standard document annexed to the credit agreement between the assignor and assignee (commonly referred to as a *transfer certificate* or similar.)

These transfer certificates can be used when a single lender decides to leave the syndicate and finds a lending institution willing to replace it. Rather than impacting the financing deal as a whole, this would affect only one of the lenders. But the mechanism is the same, and in a broad sense this circumstance is also a case of assignment and transfer of a contract and the credits and obligations deriving from it.

Normally credit agreements do not require borrowers to agree to lenders' transferring the financing. As such, standard practice goes against the general rule, by which the assignment of a contract is permitted with the consent of the counterparty. (However, this right can usually be waived by the parties, since general consent of transfer can be granted ahead of time.) In any case, before the deal is finalized, arrangers and sponsors usually agree to a list of banks that are invited to participate in the loan, the banks that participate in the syndication.

7.2.3.16   Reserved Discretions

The project company runs the project by means of the project contracts, at least from a formal legal standpoint. We look more closely at these agreements in Section 7.2.6. The nature and content of these documents cannot be changed by the project company (in any substantial way) without prior consent of the lenders, as we saw in relation to covenants normally included in the credit agreement.

Additionally, project finance requires that restrictions be placed on the rights and options granted discretionally to the project company under the project agreements. These limitations benefit the lenders, for they ensure that the project company cannot exercise these rights and options in any way that goes against the interests of the lenders. Such restrictions are established in general terms and are preventive measures. They do not take into account whether or not exercising a given option by the project company constitutes an event of default. These clauses simply consist in a covenant of the project company not to take certain actions without the lenders' consent, as communicated through the agent.

These contract options that are subject to restrictions, called *reserved discretions*, can be positive or negative. The project company can be obliged to exercise a given contract option if and how the agent says it should do so. Or the company can be obliged not to exercise a given option without prior consent of the agent. Or both can be true (as is most often the case in actual practice): The same contract provision in the project agreement may give the project company an option it can exercise at its own discretion, but the project company cannot exercise this option without the authorization of the agent and will do so if so instructed by the agent.

Reserved discretions are a typical feature of project finance and should be interpreted in light of other clauses in the credit agreement that set certain limits on the discretion of the project company in running the project. In fact, reserved discretions are one of the points where lenders' involvement in the project is most advanced. As such, the same general perplexity applies regarding the risk that reserved discretions go beyond the threshold that separates the running of the project/enterprise by the project company, with the corresponding responsibilities, from the position of the lenders.

7.2.4   Security Documents: Security Interests and What They Do

We have defined the credit agreement as the system's center, which controls the entire financing deal. The security package, then, is the protection system, which is activated if the project or financing does not work properly.

7.2.4.1   Introduction to the System of Security in Project Finance

The underlying logic in structuring security for a project finance initiative is linked to a view of the financing package as a whole, as we have said before. If the project company faces a financial crisis, possible solutions should be seen as an overall package. As far as possible, the security interests securing the financing are closely interrelated. This is why we refer to structuring a security package, also to underscore the fact that we find ourselves in a vastly different context than with a normal secured bank loan, even if the security interests, taken individually, are actually the same.

Before analyzing the security that is normally a part of a project finance deal, it may prove useful to make a few preliminary and institutional comments on the rules and principles in effect regarding security interests and the purpose of a security package.

Security interests have the purpose of segregating a given asset as security for a credit: The asset in question is still the property of whoever secured it (the security provider or the grantor of the relevant security), whether this person is the borrower itself or a third party (third-party security provider). In any case, the lender acquires the following rights over the secured asset:

- The right to have it sold to a third party and to convert the asset into cash.
- The right of preemption, or the right to obtain priority over other potential creditors of the same borrower to collect the amount owed from the sale of the item.
- The right to enforce the security over an asset even if said asset is purchased by a third party. In other words, in theory a security interest "follows" the secured asset, and secures it throughout all its later sales until the debt is repaid in full.

It is important to note that the right to enforce security (i.e., to sell the secured asset) must be exercised in respect of the formalities established by law; in some cases this may call for judicial proceedings. Please note, however, that security is an area of law where civil law and common law are quite distant, and specific rules in any given jurisdiction may differ greatly from what we outline in these few pages.

Structuring a project's security package is done in compliance with the nature and function of the project company. Just as the project company contains and coincides with the project, in the same way the security package encompasses the project company itself (through the shares representing the capital) and all (or almost all) the assets it owns, in other words all the assets required for the project and (at least in theory) nothing more.

So the structural difference begins to emerge between security on traditional loans and the security package for project finance. In the first case, the security supports the obligation of the borrower to repay. Whether or not there actually is security depends on the credit worthiness of the borrower. Also, the security package is usually commensurate to the value of the secured assets, which whenever possible should be of equal or greater value than the loan in question. If the borrower does not pay, the security does, usually through the sale of the secured asset to a third party.

In project finance, the project company, by definition, does not own assets that have value comparable to the project finance loan; this is an essential fact for estimating value at risk (VaR) of a loan granted to an SPV (see Section 8.5).

First, the project company does not own any material assets whatsoever at the outset of the project; it buys or constructs assets with the proceeds of loans (for the most part). But even after plant construction is complete, the project company does not have any assets of sufficient value to secure the loan. Since in project finance the loan in question is backed by expected future revenues generated by project operations, it follows that single assets (just as the sum of their individual values) do not cover the value (or the costs) of the project. In fact, when the value of the security package is enough to cover total exposure to banks, we do not have a project finance transaction in the true sense of the term.

This is why identifying assets to be secured in favor of lenders does not (or should not, at least) constitute a contentious point between the parties. Shares that represent the project company's capital are always included in the security package, which also comprises the other rights of sponsors over the project company as regards equity (see Section 7.2.5.1) normally encompassing reimbursement credit for the subordinated loans granted to the project company as an alternative to subscribing to share capital. All assets of the project company, both tangible and intangible, must also be part of the security package. There is no logical reason why some of the project company's assets or categories of assets can or must be excluded from the security package, seeing as the lenders have security interests on the entire project. The only exception is the money available for distributions to sponsors (and credited to the distributions account; see earlier). Based on the mechanisms for managing project accounts and the payment waterfall (Section 7.2.3.14), sponsors are entitled to these funds, even if they are still formally the property of the project company. This is why the relevant bank account and the available cash deposited in it (which clearly the sponsors would want to withdraw as soon as possible) are excluded from the security package.

With the foregoing clarification, we can understand the analogy between the defensive and positive functions of the project company, described previously, and the functions of the security package, which are complementary to the role played by the special-purpose vehicle in which the project is developed.

The defensive function pertains to protecting the project and its property from the rights of third parties, who may be sponsors' creditors claiming settlement for their loans on the project company's corporate capital, which is actually pledged in favor of project lenders. Third parties might also be creditors to the project company itself. In this case project lenders need to have security interests directly on the project company's assets. This prevents these assets from being subject to enforcement by third parties who would otherwise have competing rights with lenders with respect to the project revenues and/or would be able to seize assets that are vital for running the project.

The "positive" reasons that justify the creation of the security package are related directly to a possible financial crisis the project may face. In this sense, these reasons are more similar to the traditional function of security: to make it possible to repay a loan in case of default, limiting the loss given default (LGD) for the lender as far as possible (see Section 8.5). But the fact is that the aggregate value of the secured assets is not enough to ensure economically acceptable coverage for the financing. The function of security interests inevitably becomes a consequence of the original function of the project company; security interests are an instrument lenders can use directly or indirectly to take possession of the entire project and continue to run it (or have someone else run it). In fact, this is their only hope that the loan will be reimbursed (although it will probably have to be rescheduled). Keeping the project operational must be the aim of any action taken by the lenders in case of project company default. Security interests are the primary instrument for doing so (though not necessarily the only one, as we will see). Lenders would have to take possession of the project to avoid the risk of interrupting operations, which would further damage the project and reduce the chances for loan reimbursement.

Only after every possibility for reestablishing an acceptable profit level for the project has been exhausted can security interests be used the way they are traditionally intended. At this point, these are likely to be enforced on an individual basis to get the highest possible sale price on every single asset. But this situation would be an extreme case when there is absolutely no other solution. Moreover, enforcing security interests is by definition the last tool lenders may want to utilize in the event the project faces a crisis. Long before this, lenders intervene, usually in conjunction with the project company and (if possible) with sponsors, implementing other "interference" tools that are sanctioned in the project documents discussed here. If the crisis at hand is the result of bad project management, this situation will have to be corrected either by substituting the operator or by changing the criteria for management practices, according to the O&M agreement. Lenders' defensive strategy, in this sense, can be implemented with instruments different from the security package. An example here is useful: Poor performance by the operator according to the terms of the O&M agreement (see Section 7.2.6.3) entitles the project company to terminate the contract itself. By means of reserved discretions, lenders will oblige the project company to exercise this right and appoint a different, and hopefully more efficient, operator.

The term *step-in right* refers to the mechanism lenders utilize to take total or partial control over the project or some of its components. We get back to this concept at the end of this section, after quickly reviewing security interests and giving a description of direct agreements with the counterparties of the project company.

7.2.4.2   Common Provisions in the Security Documents

Now we briefly discuss the common features of typical security interests in project finance.

We should mention that the provision of security is usually a condition precedent to the disbursement of the loan (see Section 7.2.3.4). In fact, whenever possible, the borrower is asked to complete all the perfection formalities before requesting the first drawdown. The reason for this is that every detail regarding security interests has to be finalized before the banks grant any portion of the loan secured by these security interests, including the formalities required by law to make the creation of security enforceable against third parties.

It is common practice for each contract or deed establishing security to appoint one representative for all lenders, who is usually the agent bank appointed in the credit agreement. This person is empowered by lenders for active and passive representation, even in litigation matters concerning the security package. This way, every right and option to which all lenders are entitled can be exercised by their common representative (including voting rights at the shareholders' meeting of the project company and the right to collect distributions as far as the security over shares is concerned). In common law systems, a trust is used. One person (here again usually the agent, in compliance with the credit agreement) acts as the security trustee of the lenders and holds the security interests for the financing on their behalf.

In the complex structures of project finance, security interests can be enforced only in the context and under the circumstances that regulate default situations and the remedies lenders can apply, according to the terms of the credit agreement. Consequently, the enforcement of security interests is normally limited to cases of events of default. Often an additional condition is set: that lenders have exercised the right to trigger an acceleration of the loan. The point at which security interests become enforceable represents the boundary line between the rights of sponsors to keep the project company running the project and the option of lenders to take every necessary action to protect their credits toward the project company.

Please note that the existence of a secured credit that is due, payable and unpaid, in these circumstances, does not necessarily coincide with these events. There may be an event of default and no loan unpaid on maturity. There can be a collectable and unpaid credit (which would undoubtedly be or soon become an event of default, according to the credit agreement) without lenders having declared an acceleration on the loan.

It is advisable for the validity of the security package to remain in place not only until all loans are repaid in full, but beyond. This extension normally coincides with the point in time when bankruptcy clawback action can no longer be made on payments relating to the loans in question. For further information on this topic, see Section 7.3.

7.2.4.3 Pledge on Project Company Shares

Security on the shares representing the project company's corporate capital is security par excellence. In summarizing the actual function of security interests in project finance, we confirm once again that when the project faces a crisis, the only realistic chance lenders have to safeguard their interests is to take over the project and/or project management. Since the project and the project company are, in substance, one and the same, having security interests on the project company's corporate capital is essentially a security on the entire project. The pledge on the shares of a company gives secured lenders the right to carry out forced sale of these shares. In other words, lenders can sell all or part of the pledged shares if the borrower defaults on the loan. The profit from the sale goes to repay first these lenders and then any others the borrower may have.

Rather than selling pledged shares to third parties, in many jurisdictions the secured lender can claim ownership over them in certain circumstances. If applicable, this is a very favorable provision in a project finance context. In fact, the market value of the shares representing the project company's corporate capital will no doubt be negligible when the security is enforced, because this would only happen when the project company is in trouble. Opting to sell to the highest bidder, in most cases, proves to be economically illusory.

Typically a pledge on the project company's shares has primarily a positive function, i.e., as we mentioned in the introduction of this section, an offensive one. It is typically positive, since this is the easiest security to enforce, and such enforcement is the most effective in terms of protecting lenders. Since company shares belong to the sponsors and not the project company itself, it is the sponsors' creditors who pose a threat to lenders, not other creditors the project company may have. In fact, sponsors' creditors are the ones who have the right to subject the company's assets to enforcement. Under normal circumstances, this risk is mitigated when lenders give a positive assessment of the sponsors' financial and corporate situations. In any case, since the project company's shares are pledged, they are certainly not the first assets that unsatisfied creditors of the defaulting sponsor will subject to enforcement. In this sense, the defensive function of the security comes back into question, to some extent.

Now that this has been clarified, the question arises as to the function of security created directly on assets owned by the project company and why this cannot be avoided.

The answer lies, first of all, in the defensive function of security interests: Lenders want to take every possible measure to defend the project company's assets, which they themselves have financed for the most part. Moreover, when lenders cannot or do not want to enforce security on shares, they will find themselves having to act directly on secured assets. The primary case is when the project company goes bankrupt; in such a circumstance the very notion of the company's capital and rights on relative shares loses any real meaning, in actual fact and in legal terms. The function of security interests on project company assets is most apparent in this context, when the pledge on company shares is worthless. The bankruptcy administration is the "third party" that lenders have to guard against by taking every precaution allowed by the law of the country where the project is developed.

7.2.4.4 Security on the Project Company's Receivables

If the cash flow generated from project operations is the source that provides the project company funds to repay the loan, security on the project company's credits toward third parties is the closest lenders will come to securing this flow.

As regards this type of security, first we have to describe the nature of the credits granted as security (pledged or, with an alternative but basically identical instrument, assigned by way of security) in a project finance initiative. These are (present or future) receivables deriving from contracts entered into by the project company, typically for payment and/or fees from the sale of goods or provision of services. Such credits also include future and contingent credits for reimbursement, restitution, compensation, indemnities, and credits arising from guarantees issued in favor of the pledgor relating to these contracts (such as performance bonds issued on the construction contract for the project plant on behalf of the contractor) and indemnity payments from insurance providers.

Each one of the project company's receivables from third parties is subject to a pledge or assignment by way of security in favor of lenders. The function of this security is immediately clear for single credits, such as possible future receivables with third-party guarantors (such as bank bonds issued in favor of the project company on the construction contact) or construction credits, such as indemnity payments from the counterparties to the project agreements, or indemnity credits from insurers.

Receivables from offtake agreements are revolving credits. They derive from the supply of goods or services by the project company to respective buyers (e.g., the buyer of the power generated by the project) and are payable according to the conditions set down in these agreements. These credits are paid periodically; the account is settled and the credit converted into cash and deposited in the bank account of the project company. Only in case of enforcement (i.e., following an event of default or, when applicable, an acceleration of the financing), lenders reserve the right to demand payment directly from third-party debtors.

7.2.4.5 Security on the Project Company's Bank Accounts

The need to create security on the project company's bank accounts can be explained in two ways. The first is simply the fundamental requirement that all assets of the project company must be subject to security. Clearly cash is the most attractive for a lender, for it does not have to be transformed to satisfy the secured credit, and it is not affected by market risk.

The second, mentioned previously, involves following a logical line that from receivables from third parties (subject to pledge or assignment by way of security) leads to a pledge on cash from the moment the project company collects a payment and turns a credit into cash or, rather, into funds in a bank account. This way the pledges on the project company's receivables (in particular, credits from offtake agreements) and the pledge on bank accounts taken together represent security on the overall cash flow of the project. All of the project company's bank accounts are pledged, the only exception being the account where cash available for distributions to sponsors is credited.

The enforcement of this security is regulated as per the other security and follows an event of default. However, as repeatedly seen in general and with reference to specific security on project company assets, lenders will decide to enforce the security over the project company's assets only if there is no possible way to keep the project running. Once again, "traditional" enforcement of security interests would mean the end of project operations and would obliterate that basic premise that the project loan will be repaid with revenues from project operations.

7.2.4.6 Mortgage on the Project's Property

Generally, building has not yet begun when the project company takes out a mortgage on the plant construction site. The object of the mortgage will be complete when plant construction is finished; the single components of the plant are immovables (if/because they are attached to the surface of the ground). Any project mortgage clearly specifies the extension of the mortgage to the future construction of the plant.

There are cases in which the project company does not own the site where the plant will be located. This is possible only if the project company holds an adequately reliable and irrevocable right (an alternative to property rights) so that the bankability of the project is unaffected.

In project finance initiatives that involve the public administration, the right to build and maintain an infrastructure developed through project finance is granted by means of a public authorization. The soundness of the right to build the project (the industrial structure or infrastructure) is verified on a case-by-case basis in the applicable jurisdiction. The possibility of creating a valid security interest in favor of the lenders over the right to build is also to be ascertained. The only insurmountable barrier would be if the project company's rights to the project real estate and the relative security interests in favor of lenders are unreliable or unsound to the point where the project is no longer bankable.

7.2.4.7 Security on Other Project Company Assets

The other assets of the project company, besides receivables, cash in bank accounts, and real estate, are also secured for the benefit of lenders. Here the defensive function comes to the fore, since it is highly unlikely that these assets have an economic value that would attract the interest of lenders.

As with security interests, the project location determines which law is applied to the security instruments relating to the assets in question. Among different jurisdictions, there is significant divergence relating to the possibility of securing these assets and the effectiveness of this security (and relative costs). On this point, we can only refer to specific analysis of the various legal systems.

7.2.4.8 Direct Agreements

A description of direct agreements in project finance in a section on security interests is a necessary incongruity. Direct agreements are recognized as a normal part of a project finance security package in standard practice. Most of these contracts, and the most substantial part of the contents of each, address situations where the project is in difficulty. As such, these agreements are part of the security package mentioned in describing the nature and function of security documents or security interests. Though direct agreements do not technically constitute security interests, the function of these agreements is strictly related to that of security interests and remedies available to lenders in case of a crisis of the project. Understanding these agreements is essential to getting a true picture of the project in case of default as well as lenders' step-in rights.

Direct agreements are contracts executed directly by the lenders and the key counterparties to the project agreements. Like reserved discretions, direct agreements can be numbered among the legal instruments that lenders use to reserve the right to interfere directly in the relationship between the project company and third parties. Bearing this out, customarily the counterparty in direct agreements recognizes that the project company is given certain discretions in the contract in question that are subject to the control or approval of lenders (in other words, reserved discretions, as we saw earlier).

Typically, the purpose of direct agreements is twofold: to safeguard the project agreements, on one hand, and to establish a sort of lenders' right to "take over" these agreements on the other. Let's look at each one separately.

In order for an investment initiative to be structured on the basis of project finance, one requirement is that there be bankable project agreements. In other words, these contracts must be compatible with the goals and the particular features of the financing, in economic and legal terms. So the project has to be "structured" on the basis of contractual relationships having certain distinctive legal and economic features, which have to protect the project company and its expected revenues. If the project agreement system adequately safeguards these expectations, the project is a suitable candidate for project finance: It is bankable.

Losing project contracts (which can happen in case of termination due to default by the project company) means jeopardizing the bankability of the project.

This explains why lenders want to be able to intervene directly with respect to counterparties to project agreements if the project company risks losing these contracts (i.e., termination by the counterparty or any analogous legal event having the same effect) due to its own nonperformance or for any other reason. Provisions in the project contract to which the direct agreement in question refers (which we will call the "relevant contract" here) have the purpose of mitigating the risk of termination because of default by the project company. In addition to these, the direct agreement normally gives lenders the right to be informed directly about any circumstances that would justify terminating the contract. Lenders are also entitled to intervene (or have third parties intervene in their name) to remedy the default situation so as to prevent termination of the relevant contract. In some instances this contract may go so far as to include the possibility of nominating an additional party who would assist the project company in contract execution and take on the relative obligations, on either a temporary or permanent basis, as the case may be.

Clearly, these rights can be explained in the context of a crisis situation for the project company: Lenders reserve the option to help the project company overcome such a contingency (at least temporarily) rather than allowing the crisis to deepen and cause the project irreparable damage.

The second typical function of direct agreements relates to the enforcement of security interests, which can be explained in the context of a characteristic feature of project finance: step-in rights of project lenders. Under certain conditions specified in the direct agreements, lenders can replace the project company with a third party as counterparty to the project agreements. These conditions usually entail circumstances that would justify terminating the relevant contract due to default by the project company or situations that would entitle lenders to enforce their security interests.

The purpose of these provisions is clear: Lenders reserve the right to replace the project company with a different party in the project contracts both to prevent the possibility that a default by the project company may trigger termination and to take control of the project if the need should arise. This would be the last possible resort in the face of a financial crisis. Lenders demand the right unilaterally to "divest" the project company of the project agreements (to assign them to a third party—a possible buyer of the project and/or the plant or the plant operator acting for the lenders). This is done in light of the possibility that lenders may find themselves forced to dispossess the borrower from the entire project to take over control and operations.

7.2.4.9   Enforcing Security Interest and Lenders' Step-in Rights

A project is financed without recourse not because it has an existing credit capacity, but because the initiative is set up to be bankable in light of particular conditions on the basis of the project finance technique. Project operations and the resulting revenues are the only source of loan reimbursement. If these are threatened, the chances of paying back the loan exclusively with the project company's resources are likewise jeopardized.

Due to the peculiarities of project finance, lenders actually find themselves in a rather weak position in the face of financial difficulties that the project company may come up against. This is true despite the impressive system of contract solutions and security interests that lenders can rely on.

With corporate financing, there is a clear and unquestionable logic behind loan acceleration. If an event of default occurs that lenders deem sufficiently serious, acceleration allows them to collect their due from the borrower's resources in advance, before these funds are lost or paid out to other creditors. In simpler terms, we can say that in normal situations, the borrower has the capacity to repay its debts, or, in other words, its financial resources are greater than its debt vis-à-vis the lenders. Consistent with this, the contractual system of the financing includes provisions that allow lenders periodically to monitor this situation.

In project finance, the acceleration solution is (almost by definition) an illusory one. Most of the project company's resources are applied in repayment of the loan. The account structure mechanism (see Section 7.2.3.14) is well suited to ensuring that liquidity available to the project company is channeled to repay lenders, except that which covers the costs essential to the survival of the project and the company. Acceleration of the loans does not generate the financial resources needed to repay the loan, and by definition the project company does not have any reserve funds that it would have to pay immediately to lenders in case of acceleration.

The option of enforcing security interests is also illusory, if taken in the traditional sense. To benefit from security means to have the right to sell the secured item and keep the proceeds of the sale. The beneficiary of security has priority over the asset and then proceeds from the sale of the asset itself.

All this makes sense if the security in question has its own independent value and was secured on the basis of that value. In project finance, the perspective is completely different. Security is created on everything that has to do with the project. The project has value only if it is up and running and can generate revenues, which are used to repay the project loan and to compensate sponsors. The individual economic value of the assets that are subject to security, if not negligible, is by no means commensurable to the amount of the loan. And this value shrinks even more if the project defaults, which is precisely when the question of enforcement comes into play.

These are the reasons why step-in rights emerge as the concrete solution available to lenders in case the project faces a financial crisis. By means of the legal instruments provided in the finance documents (security documents and direct agreements), lenders are entitled to take control of the project in order to remedy or make arrangements to remedy the causes of the default situation, as far as possible. In the first and most common situation, this is implemented by appropriating voting rights relating to secured shares and replacing the board of directors, enforcing the security on the shares themselves, and, if necessary, taking ownership of the project company's share capital. (Note that at this point in time the economic value of the project company's stock is likely to be negligible: The more serious the crisis at hand, the lower the value of the company.)

If lenders have completely lost control of the situation and the project company is subject to insolvency procedures, their position becomes more complicated. In this case, the security created directly over the company's assets takes on vital importance (the mortgage, pledges, and floating charge on assets and receivables). Step-in will probably be carried out by means of an agreement with the administrator in bankruptcy. Remember, in any case, that lenders represent the majority of the company's debts, but at the same time they have security interests on almost all the company's assets. Therefore, both in practice and in legal terms, they find themselves in an extremely peculiar position vis-à-vis the insolvency procedure under way. Step-in rights provided for in the direct agreements again prove useful if a third party buys or rents the plant from the insolvency procedures, most likely with the lenders' consent. In this kind of situation, the project agreements can be assigned to the new plant operator and the project will have safeguarded some of its value.

Only if there are no other possible solutions (realistically only when project operations or revenues are irremediably damaged) are security interests enforced in the traditional sense. Every single asset is sold for the highest possible price. But it is hard to imagine this kind of situation ever arising in the real world, since lenders are the ones who are most keen to avoid bankruptcy procedures for the project company.

7.2.5 Other Finance Documents

This section reviews the other finance documents that lawyers contribute to set up in a project finance deal:

1. The equity contribution agreement
2. The intercreditor agreement
3. The hedging agreements

7.2.5.1 Equity Contribution Agreement

In the equity contribution agreement (or equity agreement or similar), sponsors commit to contributing equity into the project company as required in the project model. In this contract the project company ensures that the debt-to-equity ratio is respected.

The notion of equity of the project company does not coincide with share capital. In fact, equity usually includes share premium reserves and contributions from sponsors whose credits against the project company are subordinated to the rights of bank lenders.

Subordinated debt, as we saw in relation to distributions and the dividend trap (see Section 6.8), presents the significant advantage that it can be repaid to the sponsors by the project company whenever distributions of project revenues are allowed. If, instead, equity contributions are made in the form of capital, this option calls for the distribution of dividends or the (often) more complex process of reducing and repaying the project company's share capital.

The mechanics of the equity contribution agreement are not inherently complex. The sponsors are required to confer equity on request by the project company. This request is made any time it becomes necessary to do so according to the terms of the credit agreement. This normally happens in order to satisfy the debt-to-equity ratio required by the terms of the financing. Normally project equity has to be entirely paid up if the project is in default. This is in compliance with the same principle that authorizes lenders to take over the project in such circumstances by enforcing security interests and taking any other action permitted in the finance documents. Once the project rights are lost to lenders, the last obligation sponsors have to fulfill toward the project company is to confer all residual equity.

Lenders do not necessarily have to be parties to the equity contribution agreement. In certain projects, this has even led to classifying the equity contribution agreement as a project agreement rather than a finance document, which would seem more appropriate given its purpose. In any case, there is no doubt that the equity contribution agreement is significant in relation to financing the project and the commitments taken on by the project company toward the lenders. It is completely normal within the framework of such a contract for the project company's credits toward sponsors to be assigned by way of security to the benefit of lenders. This makes any disposal of these credits that might be in violation of the covenants of the credit agreement not binding on the lenders. An additional contractual arrangement is also possible: to designate lenders as third-party beneficiaries of the equity contribution agreement, even when they are not parties to this contract.

Up until now we have described the equity contribution agreement as the instrument by which the sponsors formally assume their obligations to contribute financial resources to the project, as measured by the debt-to-equity ratio. But we should mention that this contract (or in some instances a parallel contract, with a similar structure) can include sponsors' commitment to confer additional resources to the project company, as regards certain specific risks previously identified during preliminary project risk assessment.

An initiative based on project finance consists of an investment project and an expected cash flow. This is exposed to a number of risks that are mitigated by means of instruments associated with the financing (contractual and otherwise). The purpose of this risk mitigation is to make the deal acceptable, or bankable, to its financial providers. A risk that is deemed excessive or that cannot be properly assessed and that cannot be mitigated in any way would make the initiative unsuited to the project finance technique.

With regard to such circumstances, in order to maintain without-recourse financing, whatever risk the project cannot ensure or mitigate internally must be covered externally. In some cases certain risks may not even be covered by insurance policies (which turn an uncertain cost into a fixed one that can be valued in terms of impact on the economics of the project). Sponsors are the natural candidates for taking on those risks that lenders consider incompatible with financing the project on a without-recourse basis; sometimes they're the only ones left if they want the initiative to move forward and be financed.

There are basically two technical methods by which external coverage of non-bankable risks is ensured by sponsors. The first is that the sponsors directly guarantee lenders repayment of the financing by the borrower; such a guarantee is capped to an amount equal to the potential impact of the risk in question on the project. In other words, the guaranteed amount is equal to the monetary damage that this risk could cause in a worst-case scenario. The second possibility would be to pay the same amount by way of an equity contribution.

The first solution (guarantee in favor of the lenders, which could result in a direct payment to them) is the one that lenders prefer because it creates a benefit that they enjoy directly, to the exclusion of anyone else. Covering the risk in question with an equity contribution is the solution that sponsors prefer, and objectively speaking it is more consistent with the structure and ultimate philosophy of project finance. Sponsors would rather reintegrate project resources with an additional equity contribution (it is still "their" project after all) than pay lenders directly, even if both options involve the same amount of money. That is why in these circumstances the equity contribution agreement becomes the contractual instrument to cover those risks that the lenders refused to leave with the project company.

7.2.5.2   Intercreditor Agreement

Describing the structures, contents, and contractual and legal complications that are typical of an intercreditor agreement is more complex than for all the other documents analyzed in this chapter. This agreement is, in fact, the least standardized of the key finance documents relating to a project finance transaction.

First, we have to clarify that the issues related to intercreditor arrangements are characteristic of all structured finance deals and are not exclusive to project finance. Basically, the purpose of this contract is to regulate the relationships among the lenders who participate in the deal. The intercreditor agreement is indispensable when there are different categories of lenders; the position of each one in relation to the borrower and to other creditors is regulated in order to achieve the financial structure adopted by the deal in question. Now we will try to give a general definition of the objectives of an intercreditor agreement in project finance.

Project finance initiatives are characterized by one category of financial creditors, the hedging contract counterparties (see Section 7.2.5.3), who normally benefit from the security package to a limited extent. The rights of lenders and the hedging contract counterparties (often called *finance parties*, not only in project finance) as regards the project company and the security package are typically addressed in the intercreditor agreement.

This contract usually also includes provisions relating to the pool of lenders and the decision-making procedures they will follow during the life of the loan. As we can easily imagine, despite meticulous regulations, a plethora of unforeseen circumstances arise in real project finance transactions. The project company interfaces continually with the lenders through the agent and often needs clarifications and waivers and occasionally may request amendments to the credit agreement. Typically the intercreditor agreement contains the decision-making rules for the lenders' syndicate (generally based on the vote of the majority of the economic participants in the financing).

Less frequently (though by no means to be neglected) we find situations in which different categories of lenders are involved in the same project (public bodies, supranational organizations, and subordinated or mezzanine creditors). All the issues regarding reciprocal relationships converge in the intercreditor agreement and are regulated by it.

An additional issue relating to the relationships among creditors is the subordination of shareholder loans by the sponsors. In order to make effective the subordination of their credits toward the project company with respect to lenders' credits, in many cases sponsors are required to be parties to the intercreditor agreement.

As we said before, the notion of equity as defined in the context of project finance extends to financing by sponsors, on the condition that these loans are subordinate to those of the lending banks. For sponsors the chance to contribute equity in the form of shareholder loans is extremely appealing (as opposed to capital contribution in the strict sense, as described in Section 6.8). This is why the deal is usually structured to provide for subordination agreements for sponsors' credits to the benefit of the finance parties.

7.2.5.3 Hedging Agreements

The need for hedging agreements in project finance represents a typical manifestation of risk mitigation. As we have seen, this logic is one of the cornerstones of project finance. Project finance is always granted on the basis of a floating interest rate, based on lending rates taken from the interbank debt market. This would create quite a significant variable cost for the project company, given the size of the loan in relation to the cost structure of the project company. Even if lenders are actually the beneficiaries of this cost (since they are the ones who collect floating interest on the borrower's loan), they do not want the economy of the project to be impacted by this cost increase. They would rather make the project company turn this risk into a fixed cost. This is why, as we saw in Section 3.1.3.3, the project company is normally required to implement a risk coverage policy on fluctuations in the interest rate (and the exchange rate as well, if the loan is not denominated in the project company's "home" currency). This is done by means of hedging agreements. Here we give a very brief overview of hedging agreements to provide some understanding of hedging deals in the context of project finance.

Hedging agreements are finance documents that are included among the conditions precedent of the loan, as we have seen. The hedging counterparty is normally, but not necessarily, one of the lenders; there may be more than one hedging counterparty.

Hedging agreements are contracts in which the parties voluntarily assume a risk, not determined in its maximum amount, in relation to the value of their respective obligations. Here the uncertainty reaches the point of providing for an exchange of a perfectly comparable consideration. (Both obligations are cash payments.) In fact, some contracts simply call for compensation of the difference between payments in one direction and the other.

Normally hedging operations benefit from the security package established to secure the financing. However, the hedging counterparties may be completely or partially excluded (often because they want to eliminate or reduce the fiscal costs of creating this security on hedging agreements, where the amounts at risk are clearly less than for the financing). This is a typical case where provisions of the intercreditor agreement take effect that grant hedging counterparties something to which they would not formally be entitled (for instance, the proceeds from enforcing a mortgage in which they are not named beneficiaries).

7.2.6   *Project Agreements*

7.2.6.1   **Brief Introduction**

The project company is a vehicle that has primarily a financial function. The project company is a corporate shell (necessarily a new company) that contains the project so that the project finance technique can be implemented. The project company has no entrepreneurial, corporate, or managerial resources of its own. If it did, it would not be suited for developing a project finance initiative. So the project company outsources every corporate and entrepreneurial function, and through contracts (for supply of goods and services) generically referred to as *project agreements*, it procures everything it needs to develop and operate the project.

Up to this point, there is nothing conceptually different here from any corporate vehicle used in structured finance deals. The difference lies in the quantity, if anything. Unlike a Property Company (or PropCo), used in real estate finance transactions, the project company owns an actual industrial development project, so the system of project agreements is particularly extensive and complex. What is more, the nature of project finance is such that project agreements have to address certain peculiarities that make it possible to apply project finance to the initiative in question. This requirement is defined as the *bankability* of the project agreements.

Here we offer a checklist of basic general rules that can be applied to all project agreements to verify their bankability. Obviously, exceptions and additional needs for individual project finance initiatives are nearly infinite. The financial aspects of these contracts were outlined in Chapter 3. It is advisable to refer back to that chapter for a cross-analysis of financial and legal aspects of each contract.

In order to be bankable on an individual basis and to make a positive contribution to the overall bankability of a project finance initiative, a project agreement must meet the following requirements.

- It must be entered into (by the project company) with a reliable counterparty, both from an industrial and a financial standpoint; failure by the counterparty to perform under the contract must be a fairly remote risk.
- When the project company has to make a cash payment, this must be fixed (or fixed in relation to the quantity—and quality, if applicable—of the good or service that the project company receives in exchange for this payment). The price indexing clauses the project company has to respect do not jeopardize the project bankability if the project company can pass on the higher cost to third parties (by means of contract instruments or mechanisms that are soundly built in to the relative market system). An example here proves useful: The project company buys the fuel it needs through a fuel supply agreement. The price of fuel is indexed (and this would be a weak point for the project). But if the price of fuel rises, the project company has the right to revise the price set down in its offtake agreements. In this case, the project company has the right to pass on the higher price of fuel to third parties (the pass-through right). As a result, the negative impact of a price rise is mitigated.
- In terms of contracts for the sale of goods or services from the project company to a third party, there must be a take-or-pay clause. As the term implies, the buyer has to pay the minimum set price (or at least an amount corresponding to a minimum quantity, which is consistent with the base case) even if the buyer

does not actually take the good or service for any reason other than nonprovision by the project company.

- If a construction contract is involved, the relative agreement has to specify clearly the physical and performance characteristics of the contracted work. With service provision, the contract stipulates the characteristics and the quality level of the service in question. Any time the project company gets something less than what was agreed on, there has to be a preestablished indemnity computed on the basis of the overall damage to the project caused by the nonperformance of the subcontractor.

- The agreement has to be subject to termination or withdrawal in favor of the project company in case of default by third parties; this also includes insufficient-performance levels in terms of quality or quantity. The project can replace a nonperforming supplier (the only exception being a case of legal or economic monopoly of the good or service supplied by that entity) with another supplier deemed capable of correctly fulfilling the project agreement in the place of the original supplier.

- Termination of the contract by the counterparty must be restricted. As mentioned before (see Section 7.2.4.8), losing a project agreement is a serious problem for the project. In fact, there may be no other way to source the good or service in the lost project agreement, or procurement may be impossible at the same price or under the same conditions or according to bankable contractual terms. The agreement must minimize the circumstances in which the counterparty would be entitled to invoke clauses or principles of supervening impossibility, force majeure, or supervening hardship that would allow the counterparty to be excused from performing its obligations toward the project company, either temporarily or permanently.

- The length of the contract should cover the entire repayment period of the credit agreement. During this period, the project has to maintain its bankable status, because the lenders are exposed to without-recourse credit risk and require that the project finance deal retains its characteristics.

7.2.6.2 Construction Contract

Now we will look at a more detailed description of the most common project agreements.

In a traditional project finance deal, the plant in question is built entirely with disbursements on the project loan and equity contributions by sponsors. When the credit agreement is signed, in most cases the project company owns or has a lease (which can also be legally acceptable) on the site where the plant is to be built, nothing more. The project starts from scratch, or from the green field.

However, this is not what usually happens in the real world of project finance. In fact, it is not uncommon for plant construction to be under way when the project company begins to make drawdowns on the project loan. In such a case, the first drawdown is usually used to refinance the resources spent by the project company till that time. These initial resources come from either equity or a bridge loan from sponsors or from one or more lending institutions (often the arrangers themselves) secured by the sponsors. This small-scale refinancing in the preliminary development stage of project development shouldn't be confused with the much more complex overall refinancing of a project finance initiative (Section 7.3).

In other circumstances, the project objectively has limited bankability. Since the construction phase is by definition the period characterized by the highest risk for the project and its lenders, the sponsors can opt to finance all or part of this phase and related costs on a full-recourse basis and then activate without-recourse financing at a later date.

If without-recourse project financing does not begin until plant construction is complete, the issues in this section are irrelevant, for the most part (but not entirely, for there is clearly the chance that the responsibility of the contractor could be called into question even after the plant is finished). Conversely, the construction contract must have the features that make it compatible with project finance. To clarify further the checklist given in the introduction to project agreements in general, let's look at legal and contractual aspects of a construction contract in project finance.

This is a work supply contract: One party, the contractor, commits to building the plant, using its organization and assuming the relative risks, in favor of the principal (usually identified as the owner). Due to the nature of project finance, the project company has to sign a turnkey contract. All operations relating to building the plant have to be subject to contractual obligations taken on by a third party with a solid technical reputation and financial status. The project has to assign a third party the risk of completing the work and ensuring that the expected plant specifications are met. This role is taken on by the contractor, whose function and responsibility is fundamental in the economy of project risks. In project finance, the term *EPC contract* is often used, in which the contractor ensures engineering, procurement (of materials, equipment, and machinery for the plant), and construction. In terms of project bankability, it is indispensable for a single organization to be charged with building the entire plant or infrastructure. Lenders want the project company to deal with one counterparty who is entirely responsible for building the project, one single point of responsibility.

Nonfulfillment by the contractor of its obligations is sanctioned by means of a comprehensive system of indemnities; the amount of relative payments in various circumstances is set down in the contract itself. This is a contractual mechanism for liquidation damages that has a specific purpose. The project company is granted a certain indemnity if it is prejudiced in any way (a delay in delivery or failure of the plant to meet the set standards). Lenders can look at the worst-case scenario and ascertain whether the maximum damage is acceptable in light of the chances that it will actually occur. Whatever the contractor does not provide in terms of timing on plant delivery and/or plant specifications (measured by production capacity below the standard set in the contract) is compensated by a cash indemnity.

Unlike what usually happens as regards finance documents, it is not yet a consolidated procedure to draw up project finance construction contracts under English law. At the same time, due to the connections to the jurisdiction of the country where the contract will be executed (i.e., where the project is to be developed) and in some cases because of contractors' preference for the law of their home country, very often the law that regulates the construction contract is the same as the law of organization of the project company. In some circumstances even a third legal system may be applied, different from that of the finance documents.

Normally the construction contract is signed well in advance by the constructor and the project company, which has to have the time to allow lenders to analyze its contents and finalize the financing. Consequently, what is actually signed might be better defined as a contract option granted by the contractor to the project company. The declaration of intent to proceed with the execution of the contract and, consequently, the communication to the contractor to start the performance of the works is given the moment the project company can count on adequate financing or when the sponsors decide to activate project construction and finance temporarily the related costs with their own resources, as mentioned earlier.

The contract price is a fixed price. In fact, a vital factor in the robustness of the project is that the highest possible percentage of building costs be fixed, and the contract price for building the plant is a fundamental cost item for the project. As said in our discussion of the basic features of the credit agreement, a specific facility is set up for unexpected costs that the project might have to face. The project company must not find itself unable to complete the project due to a lack of funds. In keeping with this, the provisions of the construction contract preclude the possibility of a revision of the contract price, as far as technically and legally possible. The project company normally reserves the right to request variations in the project and construction while the works are in progress. However, this option is subject to the approval of lenders (remember our explanation of the nature and function of reserved discretions) when additional costs are involved or if said modifications significantly alter the technical nature of the project. It is normal, instead, for contractors to assume the risk of fluctuations in construction costs, even if they would otherwise be entitled to demand a contract price revision.

The price of works is normally paid with an initial down payment and then in conjunction with subsequent milestones. From a legal standpoint, these are classified as advance payments on the total project price, not payments corresponding to final acceptance of single sections of the contracted work. As we will see, only when work is complete does the project company have to decide whether to accept the plant or reject it for nonconformity with preagreed specifications.

As is common practice in all major international construction contracts, usually the contractor is asked to issue bank or insurance bonds to cover possible payment obligations. These are usually for indemnities or reimbursement of the advance payments in case of early termination of the contract. As it slots into the framework of project finance, instead, the construction contract typically includes provisions for a third-party guarantee (in addition to bank bonds) in case the contractor's creditworthiness is not deemed adequate by lenders. This guarantee generally covers any payment obligations deriving from the construction contract that the contractor may have and is a typical aspect of contract bankability (as we saw earlier as regards the bankability of project agreements in general). The project company and consequently its lenders have to be able to count on reliable counterparties in terms of fulfilling the characteristic obligations of the project agreements. (Therefore, as we have reiterated several times, the contractor has to be a company with a solid technical and professional reputation.) Reliability also relates to paying possible indemnities.

Another typical feature of construction contracts in project finance is the presence and wide-ranging functions of technical consultants (see Section 4.2), who act as counterparties to the contractors. These experts are called on to intervene and approve of every issue pertinent to the execution of the contract (such as endorsing completion of a certain milestone or carrying out the tests, discussed later).

The basic terms of the contractors' obligations, and therefore the objectives of the construction contract, center on four key factors. These are closely linked to the requirements of the financial model so that the system satisfies profit requirements that ensure the ongoing bankability of the project.

Two of these factors are associated with the plant specifications as built and delivered by the project company, in other words, plant performance in terms of production output and reliability. The construction contract draws a distinction between *optimal performance* and *minimum performance*. The first is the objective of this agreement and an obligation of the contractor. As for the second, if the plant performs below this threshold, it will not be accepted by the project company. Building a plant that can achieve optimal performance is the obligation of the contractor, from a contractual standpoint; if this does not happen, the contractor is forced to pay an indemnity. This sum is calculated in proportion to the project company's loss of profit resulting from suboptimal plant output with respect to contract specifications. Under these circumstances, the financial model still stands if the project company receives an outside contribution that compensates for the lower-than-expected production performance. The principle is the same one underlying equity contributions by project sponsors, though the justification and the contractual mechanism are different, of course, because the latter involves liquidation of the indemnity due for nonfulfillment of a given obligation. This indemnity mechanism is triggered at the minimum-performance threshold set down in the contract. Below this line the economy of the project system is no longer acceptable. If the plant delivered by the contractor performs below this minimum level, the project company is entitled to refuse delivery of the work (*right of rejection*). In such a case, the contractor has to return the advance payments made up to that point plus pay the indemnities required in the given circumstances.

A similar structure is normally followed to determine the timeline for executing the works. Clearly, the timetable in the construction contract is closely linked to the availability period set down in the credit agreement for drawdowns on the loan, since most of the money borrowed by the project company is earmarked for paying the contractor.

The contractor must deliver the work (i.e., achieve mechanical completion) by a set date, and ideally at that time the plant begins functioning at optimal performance levels. If this is the case, the contractor has completely fulfilled all obligations in a timely fashion. However, if when tested the plant achieves minimum performance, it is accepted on a preliminary basis. From this point on the contractor has a set time interval in which this company can (or must, depending on the case) upgrade the plant and its performance to reach an optimal level, if possible. Compensation for the delay is an indemnity calculated in proportion to how much longer it takes to achieve acceptance of the plant with respect to the target date. Two indemnity systems intersect from the moment the plant is accepted, when the work is delivered, and operations begin.

1. One is based on the negative difference between the actual and optimal performance, as verified by tests (which the parties will have to conduct in collaboration with the technical advisor).
2. The other is determined on the basis of the delay in plant operations with respect to the contracted start date (and the financial effect of this delay on the model). If minimum performance isn't achieved by the deadline set down in the contract, the project company has the option to reject the work.

Rejection is the most extreme remedy possible. In such a case, the contractor would have to return all advance payments received up till that time, plus pay a penalty for damages, also established in the contract. Provisions may be made for compensation of the maximum damage, but the contractor is usually protected by a cap on the amount of mandatory compensation. From a contractual standpoint, this falls in the context of contract termination by breach. In theory, once the work has been rejected, the owner is entitled to damage compensation (as mentioned earlier), and the area where the works were carried out must be returned to its original state. In the context of project finance, the initiative will be declared "dead" even before reaching the operations phase, and clearly various events of default will come into play in this type of situation. In actual fact, a project finance initiative would most likely be refinanced on a corporate basis with contributions from sponsors. In fact, none of the parties involved would likely want to allow the worst possible scenario actually to happen.

The contractor is usually obliged to respect a warranty period that extends beyond the date of plant delivery and the beginning of operations by the project company. (But, as we see shortly, this actually involves the operator's taking control and running operations rather than the project company.)

7.2.6.3   Operations and Maintenance (O&M) Agreement

Once plant construction is complete, plant testing has given satisfactory results (according to the principles illustrated in the previous section), and the works have been accepted, the operational phase begins, i.e., the commercial operations of the plant. Plant ownership passes from the contractor to the project company on acceptance. As we have said before, the project company does not have its own technical or industrial resources to run the plant, and, according to project finance logic, these functions should be outsourced to third parties. Plant operations are commissioned to the *operator* (normally a company highly specialized in the sector).

From a technical/legal standpoint, the O&M agreement is a service supply contract by which the operator is commissioned by the project company to handle plant operations and maintenance. The operator may be assigned responsibility for a wide variety of services, since projects with O&M agreements can involve different kinds of plants and because the tendency is to leave everything up to the operator. The first essential question to answer is a general one: Why does a project plant have to be run by a third party, in other words through sourcing operations entirely (or as much as possible)? Though it is standard procedure to contract a third party for the specific functions relating to plant construction, including design and engineering, the same cannot be said for operations and maintenance. There is no technical or industrial reason why under normal circumstances the project company cannot take on the resources it needs to run the plant. Realistically speaking, in fact, one of the prerequisites for entrepreneurs in making an investment decision is the ability to run the new production facility themselves. Experts in management and business organization know exactly how to create a new company through a joint venture; they transfer or acquire the necessary human resources and know-how to this company.

The answer to this apparent paradox lies once again in the nature of project finance and the structure of the project company. In Section 7.1.5 we said that the company outsources every other function, as far as possible; what could be generated internally is acquired externally. Outsourcing gives clear financial advantages.

- Costs can be predetermined.
- The quality and quantity of services purchased can be established *a priori* in project agreements.
- The sourcer can be replaced if performance is not satisfactory.
- Structural costs are practically eliminated.

On this basis, understanding the structure of the O&M agreement is not particularly difficult. The operator commits to providing the project company with the operation and maintenance services outlined in the technical document annexed or referred to in the contract. In exchange, the operator receives an agreed fee (which is usually subject to periodic revision based on predefined parameters given the duration of the contract).

In running the plant, the operator is obliged to meet certain performance criteria, which are linked to the expected cash flow as set down in the financial model. Performance depends on the characteristics of the plant in terms of production output and reliability. This explains (or confirms once again) the principle of the substantial and legal connection that necessarily exists among project agreements. We also get a clearer picture of the importance of the system of plant performance and plant performance tests set out in the construction contract.

If plant performance is below the expected levels, the operator's responsibility for performance (and consequently indemnity requirements, where applicable) is downgraded as well.

Inadequate production performance by the operator triggers penalties in the form of indemnity payments as set down in the contract, unless external factors are the cause of this underperformance. This general principle applies: The project has to be supported externally if expected performance is not achieved. The related risk is transformed into a preestablished indemnity, which is enough to ensure respect for the financial model (in theory at least) and, in any case, service of the bank loan.

The general observations on bankability of project agreements also apply to O&M contracts.

7.2.6.4 Other Project Agreements

Categories are hard to establish and are less meaningful for any contracts beyond the basic ones required for a project finance operation. Due to the unique features of every project and the fact that each involves an industrial plant or a public infrastructure, the number and nature of additional project agreements are extremely variable.

We can infer the bankability requirements of this contract from the previous general discussion; specifically: a long-term, fixed price (or one protected from market price fluctuations) and a take-or-pay clause (see Section 3.2.4.1). An example of these contracts can be found in power plants, where the project finance technique is often applied. Typically these projects also necessarily entail fuel supply agreements for the essential raw material for the production process. In these agreements, the price is the key requisite for bankability. However, there are power production projects, like wind or solar power plants, where no fuel is needed. Other projects involve waste-to-energy facilities, where the fuel has a negative cost, and a part of the project and the plant actually are specifically designed to process this fuel.

There are major differences in the structure of offtake agreements for public infrastructure. In these cases, the source of revenue can come from fees for public use of the infrastructure, with or without subsidies by the public administration. Moving into this area, the complete list of project agreements for every single initiative becomes more and more heterogeneous. In fact, we can also count the contract for the purchase of the plant site as a project agreement as well as the conventions the project company may draw up with public bodies.

As regards classifying project agreements, it is important to remember that these contracts are carefully examined during the due diligence process. Moreover, they have a particular status, which basically entails the following:

- The project company commits not to modify them without the approval of lenders.
- Contingencies that have an adverse effect on these contracts can be considered events of default of the credit agreement (as when the contract becomes invalid, or in case of default or insolvency of the relevant counterparty).
- The project company's discretions relating to these agreements are subject to reserved discretions (as previously).
- Direct agreements are entered into with relative counterparties (which we described in relation to the security package).

7.3   Refinancing Project Finance Deals

Refinancing, like several other issues addressed in this chapter, is not exclusive to project finance. From a commercial standpoint, the possibility and/or opportunity for refinancing is inherent in every structured finance deal, beginning at a specific moment in the lifetime of the deal. In project finance this issue is magnified by the weight of the financial costs in the context of each individual transaction. The more aggressive the debt-to-equity ratio of the transaction, the more this weight increases. Another factor of magnification is the peculiar evolution of project risk, which makes the project extremely different as it goes through its various stages.

Generally speaking, as we saw in Section 6.9.8, refinancing means simply restructuring the existing debt by substituting it with another loan with more advantageous terms for the borrower. These amended terms might be a lower interest rate, a longer tenor, and/or more favorable contract terms for the borrower. Usually refinancing is requested by the borrower and is made up of a comprehensive package that includes a number of these features. In this section we refer specifically to *refinancing* as operations undertaken by borrowers to improve the terms of their loans when better conditions can be had from the banking system (perhaps by placing the debt entirely or partially in the capital markets). Refinancing in this sense does not include *debt restructuring* triggered by a financial crisis of the project (or loan rescheduling). The financial and legal contexts for these operations are completely different and are beyond the scope of this book.

In project finance, we typically see an extremely variable level of risk during the development of the initiative in question. Risk is highest during the construction phase, and for lenders the increase in risk is directly proportional to drawdowns, which occur when payments are made on construction contract milestones. From a conceptual perspective, for lenders the greatest uncertainty is just before plant performance testing, when the financing has been fully disbursed but the functionality of the plant has not yet been verified. Once the tests on plant performance and reliability are successfully carried out and operations begin, project risk is (almost) instantly transformed. From this point on, the borrower can consider the possibility of refinancing the project, in light of economic conditions that are no longer impacted by construction phase risk.

Infrastructure works involve a different aspect of risk. This is more controllable in relation to project milestones; the risk of overall performance is low. But the issues regarding refinancing are basically the same, though less evident.

Technically, refinancing can be done by modifying the terms of the existing loan. In theory, this is entirely possible from a legal standpoint as well. But common practice (not only in project finance) seems to show a consistent preference for setting up a completely new loan, organized by lending institutions that may not be the arrangers in the original financing initiative. With the proceeds from the new loan, the existing debt is repaid or "refinanced." Note that in current banking practice, every structured finance deal includes provisions that allow the borrower to prepay the loan, at its own discretion, with adequate prior notification.

The new loan is more advantageous than the previous one but normally keeps the same basic distinctive features and the same characteristics as without-recourse project financing. No sponsor would voluntarily give up without recourse. In fact, through refinancing sponsors may try to release themselves from the specific circumstances (if there are any) in which lenders can call on sponsors equity commitments (see earlier, in relation to the equity contribution agreement).

There are not many legal and contractual issues specifically relating to the topic of refinancing. Here we'll quickly review the most important ones.

The project company is bound by contract provisions relating to the existing financing, which have been the focus of most of this chapter. If the project company assumes additional obligations different from these, it would breach the commitments undertaken to the benefit of its existing lenders. The problem is usually solved by making the refinancing operation contingent on repayment of the existing loan. Alternatively, current lenders have to authorize the project company specifically to sign the contracts relating to refinancing, which require the existing loan to be paid in full when the new loan is opened.

A security package in favor of existing banks is incompatible with the security that the new lenders will demand. To solve this problem, existing security interests are immediately released on financial close of the refinancing (and on full repayment of the existing loan), and simultaneously security interests for refinancing banks are established. Alternatively (but only with the approval of banks in the existing syndicate) it is possible to create a second-ranking security package that becomes first ranking as soon as the current loan is fully repaid.

Lastly we turn to the issue of payment clawback, which in some legal systems takes on major significance because of the generous application of this instrument by courts. Every payment made by a borrower who later goes bankrupt is subject to bankruptcy clawback, under certain conditions. Normally the clawback action on payments is associated with safeguarding lenders who are jeopardized by the bankruptcy of their borrower. The aim is to prevent the borrower from favoring some of its lenders to the detriment of others in the face of impending bankruptcy. This is the basis of the right of the administrator in bankruptcy to revoke (or, essentially, to request reimbursement of) payments made by the bankrupt company during a certain period of time prior to declaring bankruptcy.

For the banks in the existing syndicate, refinancing entails prepayment of their loans; at the same time they are no longer subject to the requirements of the security package (which is entirely or partially reestablished in favor of the new lenders). Therefore, for these banks refinancing gives rise to the problem of exposure to clawback action risk; banks that participated in both the original financing and the refinancing are doubly exposed. If the project company goes bankrupt, they may find themselves:

- With exposure toward the project company, entitled to the refinancing and secured by the security package
- With a risk of clawback and/or ineffectiveness in relation to the amounts received to repay the original loan

This gives further proof that, due to the nature of project finance deals, it is in the best interest of lenders to prevent the project company from going bankrupt.

CHAPTER ✦ 8

Credit Risk in Project Finance Transactions and the New Basel Capital Accord*

Introduction

This chapter analyzes the problem of measuring credit risk in a project finance transaction from the lenders' viewpoint. As seen in previous chapters, a number of specificities are inherent to structured financing as compared to corporate financing. These features have as much to do with how the financing is structured as with the assessments creditors make in ascertaining the financial sustainability of a given transaction.

These unique traits are also reflected in a regulatory context. In fact, the Basel Committee notes that the family of structured transactions, or specialized lending (SL), is characterized by a series of specific features that suggest that such deals should be treated differently from corporate exposures. As we will see, valuing a project-financed initiative on a self-standing basis (not taking into account guarantees in the form of sponsors' assets) calls for a creative approach to the issue of quantifying and managing credit risk.

The chapter is organized as follows. After a review of the specialized lending (SL) deals in Section 8.1, Section 8.2 describes the field of study, highlighting typical characteristics of structured financing and how it differs from corporate financing. This is useful to provide a clearer frame of reference for the position taken by the Basel Committee. Section 8.3 focuses on the issue of evaluating and quantifying the risk of structured transactions. Though this section gives a general overview, a number of

* From Section 8.6 on, the chapter is based on Gatti, Rigamonti, Saita, and Senati (2007). I thank the publisher for having allowed the use of this article.

examples refer to project financing, where this issue is more open to debate. Section 8.4 outlines the Basel Committee's position on risk relating to specialized lending, underscoring the essential affinity between the approach proposed and that commonly found in international best practice as regards rating. Sections 8.5 to 8.9 center on the definition of value at risk (VaR) in project finance deals. Section 8.5 introduces the concepts of expected loss, unexpected loss, and VaR. Section 8.6 proposes a definition of default for project finance. Section 8.7 analyzes the cash flow modeling as a basis for estimating VaR with Monte Carlo simulations (Section 8.8). Lastly, Section 8.9 deals with the problem of defining project value in the event of default and the linked problem of estimation of the loss given default (LGD).

8.1   The Basel Committee's Position on Structured Finance Transactions (Specialized Lending, SL)

Within the framework of the New Capital Accord, in the very first version published in January 2001, the Basel Committee recognized the essential difference between corporate financing and structured financing. As for the former, the Committee gives priority to the ability of the current management of the beneficiary company to generate revenue and cash flow as a source of loan reimbursement. Regarding the latter (included in the SL category), the Committee acknowledges that repayment depends primarily on the cash flow generated by an asset or a project rather than by the quality of the borrower.

The difference between the two transaction categories is key, because from this distinction stem substantially different procedures for defining probability of default (PD), loss given default (LDG), and exposure at default (EAD) as delineated by the Committee. This is true for the standardized as well as the foundation and advanced IRB approach.

The Committee's indications on classifying a transaction as specialized lending are based on a series of common traits that closely correspond to those described in previous chapters of this book. More specifically, such deals must meet the following criteria.

1. The purpose of the loan is to buy or refinance a real asset or a pool of assets. In light of the precise reference to real assets, but not financial assets, the Committee opted to deal separately with financing granted on the basis of pools of financial assets in the context of securitization, without including such transactions in the category of specialized lending.
2. The loan is granted to a legal entity created specifically to finance and/or manage the project. This is the SPV, which will be the beneficiary of the financing in question.
3. This legal entity does not possess substantial assets beyond those earmarked for the project/initiative. For this reason, on its own the SPV can repay the loan only with revenue generated by the asset that is to be financed.
4. The loan conditions provide the lender a considerable degree of control over the assets and revenues generated by them.
5. Consequent to the previous point, the primary source of loan reimbursement is the revenue generated by the initiative rather than the overall ability of an already-in-place firm to pay back the loan.

The criteria for classifying a transaction as a corporate exposure (CE) or as specialized lending (SL) would seem to differentiate clearly between the two categories. In actual fact, however, there are some gray areas where the Committee does not take a clear-cut position and instead deliberately provides only generic suggestions. The difference between CE and SL is based on two criteria.

The first refers to whether a key counterparty is present within the framework of the transaction. Consider, for example, a case involving the financing of a large industrial plant. All production from this plant will be sold in bulk to one large buyer with solid creditworthiness who draws up a multiyear contract with the SPV like a *take-or-pay agreement*. In these circumstances, the second listed condition would be met, i.e., financing is granted to an SPV. However, this is the position of the Committee: Loan repayment depends first and foremost on the offtake contract and the soundness of the buyer. For this reason, the Committee recommends that the deal be classified as a corporate exposure and not as specialized lending (specifically project finance).

On the other hand, if the SPV is exposed to risks relating to construction, management, or sale of the product or service or if the offtaker has no sources of income other than those deriving from its operations, then the transaction can fall in the specialized lending category.[1] Note that the first interpretative criterion can be linked to whether or not there is a free market or a multiyear buying contract for the product. If such a contract exists, the Committee would classify the transaction as a corporate exposure. Proof of this assertion is the example the Committee itself provides: the construction of a building complex that generates cash flow respectively from renting space on the free market and renting to a large operator with a long-term contract.

The second criterion underlying the separation between corporate exposures and specialized lending centers on the relative size of the transaction with respect to the overall business of the borrower. If the deal involves a very limited financial commitment with respect to the assets of a heavily diversified company, again financing is based on the ability of the firm and not the initiative to repay the principal and interest. This would then be a case of a corporate exposure, not specialized lending. Conversely, if the transaction or the asset represents a significant financial commitment with respect to the overall size of the borrower, the deal is considered structured and is therefore classified as SL.

8.1.1 Classes of Transactions Included in Specialized Lending

The common characteristics described in the previous section apply to a fairly wide range of transactions. The Committee has chosen to utilize a definition of structured finance that follows international common practice to some extent, but with certain exceptions. Specifically, the classes of specialized lending are the following:

- Project finance (PF)
- Income-producing real estate (IPRE)

---

1. It should be noted that only in very rare cases would an SPV be exposed to construction, management, and market risks. Though it is quite possible and even common for coverage from market risk to be lacking (or impossible), very few instances of project finance deals do not include contractual provisions to cover construction and management risk. This is the main criticism made by rating agencies regarding the Committee's approach to distinguishing between corporate exposures and specialized lending. See Moody's (2001a and 2001b).

- Object finance (OF)
- Commodity finance (CF)
- High-volatility commercial real estate (HVCRE)

The first two classes have already been discussed. The third, object finance, consists in buying plants and machinery (in particular, big ticket), for which loan repayment is based mainly on cash flows generated by the financed asset. The most obvious example is that of big-ticket leasing, in which the borrower buys or builds and later leases the asset to the lessee. In terms of commodity finance, this involves structured transactions (normally short-term) to provide financing for buying stocks of raw materials based on the principle of self-liquidation. Revenues from the sale of commodities are the primary source of loan repayment.

Lastly, a brief mention of transactions labeled *high-volatility commercial real estate lending*. In actual fact, this is a subset of IPRE that was added to the first version of the Committee's Working Paper on Specialized Lending, October 2001, in response to comments from Quantitative Impact Study 2 respondents. The results of this study brought to light a higher volatility in PD rates typically found in the past with certain kinds of real estate financing in various countries. This class of transaction includes financing earmarked for the purchase of land and the subsequent construction of building complexes. However, the future sale of this real estate is uncertain as of the date of construction, or the flows generated by rent are in doubt because there are no signed rental agreements or the occupancy rate of the building complex is lower than average for the reference market.

Regarding the classes drawn up by the Committee, it should be said that in practice IPRE transactions are considered similar to project finance deals. Market procedures clearly demonstrate that intermediaries involved in structured finance apply the principles of risk assessment and risk allocation typical of project finance to transactions that also have a substantial real estate component, which are now handled by creating ad hoc companies. This implies that combining the first two categories could simplify successive implementation of Committee rules by intermediaries. Similar reasoning applies to object finance: big-ticket leasing deals are handled by the structured finance departments of the major financial institutions on the basis of principles similar to those utilized for project and real estate financing.

8.2   Rating Criteria for Specialized Lending and Their Application to Project Finance

Given the peculiarity of specialized lending transactions, it is not surprising that the Committee has set down a specific rating system to evaluate the creditworthiness of the five classes of transactions discussed in the previous section. Once the Accord is fully implemented, every lender must distinguish between corporate and specialized lending ex ante on the basis of the criteria just described and then assign a specific rating category to each exposure. During this phase, the rating assignment will be based on criteria provided by the Committee, which are linked to practices already used by intermediaries and rating agencies in terms of asset-backed lending programs. Later, the approach utilized for project finance deals is outlined. Given the similarities between these transactions and other types of specialized lending, the description can quite readily be extended to the remaining classes. Further information is provided in the documents drawn up by the Committee.

The Committee's final document, published in June 2004, takes up on what was outlined in Quantitative Impact Study 3, establishing four grades[2] in addition to default:

1. Strong
2. Good
3. Satisfactory
4. Weak

For each grade, quite detailed criteria are established that should enable lenders to rate different positions accurately: (1) financial strength, (2) political and legal environment, (3) asset characteristics/transaction characteristics, (4) strength of sponsors, (5) mitigants and security package. Next we briefly comment on each criterion with reference to project finance. We should clarify that for this type of transaction, the asset characteristics criterion is not applicable; instead, transaction characteristics is the category of reference.

8.2.1 Financial Strength

This category refers to market conditions (specifically whether there are competitive advantages to be had relating to cost, location, and a unique product that cannot easily be substituted) as well as financial conditions. In this regard, variables to consider when assigning one of the four grades listed earlier to a transaction are: the level of cover ratios, the degree of financial leverage utilized, the characteristics of the financing structure in terms of the project life (duration of the project) to loan life (tenor of the loan) ratio, the amortization schedule, the results of scenario analyses and/or stress tests, and the inclusion of clauses that oblige sponsors to build debt reserves, either in cash or with a counter-guarantee in the form of letters of credit for a sufficient amount of time.

8.2.2 Political and Legal Environment

Many project finance transactions take place in undeveloped or developing countries or in national contexts where existing legislation does little to guarantee the enforceability of lenders rights. In these circumstances, accurately assessing political and legal risk is vital to the rating process. Several factors should be taken into account: political risk, including transfer risk, risks of force majeure, government backing and the long-term importance of the project to the country, the stability of the legal and regulatory system (i.e., the risk of a potential change in law), possible permits and approval by the local government, and the enforceability of contracts and guarantees.

---

2. Grades 2 and 3 were established after the initial version of the document was published in October 2001. Originally, there were only three categories, with "fair" encompassing 2 and 3.

8.2.3   Transaction Characteristics

This criterion is based on the industrial and operational features of the transaction. Here is a list (albeit incomplete) of some important ones.

- The existence of factors that impact technological and planning risk
- Construction risks, as far as obtaining permits and licenses, and the type of construction contract in question
- Whether the contractor offers completion guarantees in the form of liquidated damages
- The track record and financial strength the contractor has demonstrated in the past in realizing similar projects
- The presence and scope of O&M contracts and the experience shown by the operator agent in comparable projects
- Whether there are offtake agreements at preset prices and, if so, the relative credit worthiness of the buyer
- Whether there is supply risk and, if so, coverage with long term contracts with suppliers

8.2.4   Strength of Sponsors

As we have seen, the soundness of sponsors is essential for the success of a structured transaction. To assign an accurate grade to a deal, the sponsors' track records on similar transactions should be evaluated, along with financial strength and experience in their respective business sectors, contract provisions regulating equity contribution, and standby capital that may be added in the form of equity or mezzanine finance. To complete the description of this parameter, one should keep in mind that though it overlaps the previous one in many ways, the sponsor is not necessarily a counterparty in the SPV. The standing of the counterparty is vital in order to assess transaction characteristics, but not the strength of sponsors if the counterparty is not a shareholder in the SPV. What is more, it is quite common for the sponsor and the counterparty to be one and the same; in fact, this situation is seen as a positive attribute by lenders in many project finance deals.

8.2.5   Mitigants and Security Package

A good security package enables lenders to have total control over the project's assets and should therefore lead to a higher rating for the initiative. Factors to consider when assigning a grade are whether there are provisions for assigning contracts and funds available on the SPV's accounts to creditors, establishing guarantees and mortgages on assets and credits claimed by the SPV, lenders' control over the SPV's cash flow by means of escrow accounts, and the strength and depth of covenant packages included in the credit agreement.

8.2.6   Summary of Grading Criteria

To clarify how the factors listed earlier contribute to determining a grade, Table 8-1 sums up the information provided within the framework of the Committee document

TABLE 8-1   Factors That Determine Grades: Comparison Between a Strong and a Weak Grade

Criterion	Strong	Weak
Financial strength		
Cover ratios	Solid compared to sector average	Weak compared to sector average
Financial levers	Solid compared to sector average	Weak compared to sector average
Results of stress analysis	Strong, sustained resistance to stress	Project destined to default if conditions do not improve
Duration of the project compared to duration of the credit	Tenor of loan much shorter than useful life of the project	Tenor of loan very close to useful life of the project
Amortization schedule	Amortizing debt	Balloon loan/debt not entirely amortized upon maturity
Political and legal environment		
Enforceability of contracts and guarantees	Enforceability strong	Enforceability uncertain
Risks of force majeure	Low exposure	High exposure, not fully mitigated
Government support	Project is of strategic importance for government	Project is not strategic, government backing weak
Transaction characteristics		
Project and technology risk	Fully proven technology and design	Issues with unproven technology/complex design
Construction risk	All permits obtained	Key permits not yet obtained
	Fixed-price date-certain turnkey contract	No turnkey contract
	Other completion guarantees from financially sound sponsors	Few or no completion guarantees
Operative risk	General contractor with excellent track record	General contractor with weak track record
	Long term O&M contracts with performance-based incentives	No O&M contract; risk of cost overrun not covered by guarantees
Market risk		
When there is a take-or-pay contract	Offtaker with excellent track record, buyer with excellent credit worthiness; tenor of contract much longer than maturity of the debt	Track record of offtaker weak or limited, buyer with low credit worthiness; tenor of contract life does not exceed maturity of the debt
When there is no take-or-pay	Output absorbed on stable, identified market at projected prices	Market restricted to only one or a few buyers; no organized markets
Supply risk	Long-term supply contracts with suppliers of excellent financial standing	Short-term supply contract; supplier's standing weak
Strength of sponsors		
Track record and financial standing	Excellent track record; solid sponsor	Sponsor with poor standing; questionable track record
Additional sponsor support (stand-by equity)	Credible support (project is strategic for the sponsor)	Limited support (project is not strategic for the sponsor)
Security package		
Reserve funds	Yes, longer than average coverage period; funds in cash or counter-guarantee with letters of credit from highly-rated banks	None or locked up shorter than average; funds fed by operating cash flow
Assignment to lenders	Fully comprehensive	Weak
Guarantees	Total and unconditional on project assets and key contracts	Little security for lenders; weak negative pledge clause

Source: Author's synopsis of Basel Committee (2004).

issued in June 2004. Strong and weak grades are compared for each of the variables mentioned above.

8.3   Rating Grade Slotting Criteria of the Basel Committee and Rating Agency Practices

The rating grade slotting criteria proposed by the Basel Committee do not significantly differ from common rating practices utilized by international agencies for project and infrastructure finance.[3] The project assessment process that international agencies implement is typically judgmental and is based on a multilevel structure. Every level is assigned a score according to the parameters included in the structure as compared to a benchmark, and the total score at each level is reviewed in the final stage of rating. According to the proposal of Standard & Poor's, for example, the five levels of analysis are:

- Project-level risks
- Sovereign risk
- Institutional risk
- Force majeure risk
- Credit enhancements

The first level addresses risks inherent to the project and the relevant field of business; this corresponds for the most part to the criteria of "financial strength" and "transaction characteristics" proposed by the Basel Committee. Specifically, the following factors are considered: the contract structure (whether there are offtake contracts, clearly defined security packages, tight controls over project cash flow), technology, construction, operations and maintenance risks, market risks (specifically whether there is a stable, predictable market or, conversely, a very competitive, volatile market that is difficult for the SPV to control), legal risk, counterparty risk if there is an offtake contact signed with a third party, and financing risk relating to the project's financing structure, cover ratio levels, and project performance in different scenarios and stress tests.

The second and third levels deal with assessing sovereign risk and institutional risk. This corresponds exactly to the "political and legal environment" criterion suggested by the Committee, discussed earlier.

The fourth level focuses on the specific quantification of "force majeure risk," as separate from risks classified under the political and legal risk category by the Committee. This involves risks relating to natural disasters or arising from exceptional human actions. Examples of the former are floods, storms, earthquakes, and other acts of God; the latter include terrorist attacks and sabotage, which are becoming increasingly important. Systematic coverage for these risks through insurance policies is key in order for the project to obtain a high credit rating.[4]

---

3. Standard & Poor's (2002b and 2002d).
4. Force majeure risks are not diversifiable with respect to individual projects, unlike in cases of corporate lending. An explosion resulting from an act of sabotage that damages an industrial plant will unavoidably undermine the capacity of a project to repay its debt. If the same event occurred in a corporate context, the firm might be able to stay in business if it had other production facilities.

The fifth and final level refers to the presence of mechanisms that increase the creditworthiness of the project. Essentially, this involves third-party guarantees (typically insurance coverage but also backing from multilateral organizations or coverage provided by export credit agencies (ECA's) or financial institutions), and the prevalence and timing of covenants that regulate the relationship between borrower and lender.

8.4 The Basel Accord: Open Issues

The focus of this section is the debate surrounding the position taken by the Basel Committee in its final document, dated June 2004, regarding project finance. As with corporate exposures, the Committee sets out differentiated solutions for quantifying the basic components of expected loss (EL).

For banks that use the standardized approach (PD and LGD are not estimated by the lender but, instead, are defined on the basis of standard weights defined by the Committee) or for banks that do not meet the requirements for estimating PD within the framework of the IRB approach for corporate loans, the Committee delineates five weights relating to the five rating grade slotting criteria outlined earlier (strong, good, satisfactory, weak, and default). As we show in the following section, the Committee itself acknowledges that these weights correspond to rating classes issued by external agencies. In this sense, too, we can observe the Committee's alignment with rating criteria utilized by the major international rating agencies for project finance.[5]

For banks that use the IRB Foundation approach, therefore meeting the criteria for estimating PD, the LGD is fixed at an average level of 45%. This is in line with IRB Foundation parameters for corporate exposures. Specifically, the function underlying the calculation of risk-weighted assets is the following:

$$\text{Correlation } (R) = 0.12 \times \frac{(1 - e^{(-50 \times \text{PD})})}{(1 - e^{(-50 \times \text{PD})})} + 0.24 \times \frac{1 - (1 - e^{(-50 \times \text{PD})})}{(1 - e^{-50})}$$

Maturity adjustment $(b) = (0.11852 - 0.05478 \times \ln(\text{PD})$

$$K = \text{LGD} \times N\left[(1 - R)^{0.5} \times G(\text{PD}) + \left(\frac{R}{1 - R}\right)^{0.5} \times G(0.999)\right]$$

$$\times [1 - 1.5 \times b(\text{PD})]^{-1} \times [1 + (M - 2.5) \times b(\text{PD})]$$

$$\text{RWA} = K \times 12.5 \times \text{EAD}$$

Lastly, banks that fulfill the requirements for internal estimates of PD, LGD, and EAD are permitted to use the advanced version of the internal rating system for corporate exposures. In the end, it seems the Committee's position is to treat project finance like corporate exposures in terms of models and algorithms utilized, at least

---

5. At the discretion of national supervisory bodies, the weights that correspond to each rating can be downgraded for exposures labeled as strong (50% in place of 75%) and good (75% instead of 100%). This exception to the norm is allowed in cases of deals with a residual life of less than 2.5 years and when the bank in question has a better risk profile.

as far as the two IRB approaches. However, this position might not be entirely acceptable. In fact, two pertinent issues are still open to debate:

- Why does the Committee consider project finance loans riskier than corporate loans? Is there any evidence that proves the opposite to be true?
- Though the Committee likens project finance and corporate finance from the standpoint of IRB approaches, no specific indications are given regarding parameters for measuring PD and LGD in a structured finance transaction. Essentially, the Committee provides no guidelines for estimating EL (expected loss) and UL (unexpected loss), hence value at risk, for a project finance deal.

The first issue is addressed in Section 8.4.1; the second requires a more in-depth analysis, which is found in the remaining part of the chapter.

8.4.1 Effects of the Basel Proposal on the Syndicated Project Finance Loan Market

Project finance still represents a very small portion of most banks' credit portfolios. For this reason, only recently the Basel Committee proposals have received the attention they are due. In fact, in light of the growth in the market in the last few years, in 2001 the Committee commissioned the Model Task Force (MTF) to analyze the qualitative characteristics and risk components of structured financing deals, with particular attention to project finance. This group had originally been established to implement the IRB approaches to corporate exposures.

The MTF's initial assumption was that specialized lending should be considered riskier than corporate lending, given that the regulatory estimates of LGD for SL exposures were higher than those required for traditional loans. Consequently, project finance loans should have a higher risk weight than corporate loans.[6] Table 8-2

TABLE 8-2 Risk Weights for Corporate and Project Finance Exposures

Obligor Rating Category	Probability of Default	Corporate Exposures Standardized Approach	Project Finance Exposures Basel Committee Supervisory Categorization	Basic Approach Risk Weights
AAA to A−	0.03%–0.09%	20%–50%	Strong	75%
BBB+ to BBB	0.25%	100%	Strong	75%
BB+	0.75%	100%	Good	100%
BB	1.00%	100%	Good	100%
BB−	2.00%	100%	Satisfactory	150%
B+	3.00%	150%	Satisfactory	150%
B to C	5%–20%	150%	Weak	350%
D (default)		N/A	Default	625%

Source: Authors' summary based on the Basel Committee on Banking Supervision (2001b).

6. "The MTF has reviewed some initial evidence on realized losses for each product line [including project finance]. For the [project finance] portfolios, our initial evidence suggests that realized losses during difficult periods may exceed those of senior, unsecured corporate exposures.... [However,] the MTF notes that data limitations on this area are particularly severe, and welcomes industry comment and evidence on the loss data for each of these product lines." See Basel Committee on Banking Supervision (2001b), p. 12.

shows the weighting coefficients in the standardized approach and the basic approach for corporate and structured finance exposures, based on their rating according to the initial provisions in the 2001 working paper.

According to this proposal, for a $100 million project finance transaction classified as "satisfactory," a bank adopting the basic approach would have to have a $4 million capital increase over financing the same transaction with a corporate loan [= (150% risk weight according to the basic approach − 100% risk weight according to the standardized approach) × $100 million × 8%]. Assuming the bank expects a ROE of 20%, the cost of capital for the project finance deal would see an increase of around 80 basis points [= ($4 million × 20%)/$100 million]. In applying such a penalizing risk weight to specialized lending exposures, serious negative effects may have resulted from the Committee's proposal on the syndicated project finance loan market.

First, higher capital requirements would make project-based financing less convenient for most banks. From the viewpoint of a price-maker bank, holding more capital (expected ROE being equal) would lead to an increase in debt pricing. From the perspective of a price-taker, higher capital requirements would dampen interest in undertaking new transactions. Another potential negative consequence of the initial Committee proposal was that when faced with higher loan prices, borrowers might opt for corporate rather than project financing.

Thirdly, in project finance deals, many intermediaries with limited size and capacity play a key role in creating a robust syndicated loan market. Such intermediaries could potentially suffer serious losses from the New Accord. While more expert banks could adopt the advanced approach, thanks to the analysis of historical performance data on their portfolios, the same option was not available to smaller banks. The increase in the cost of capital deriving from the proposed regulatory framework would drive smaller intermediaries out of the market. If the remaining lenders were not willing to increase their credit exposure to offset these changes, the ultimate risk would be a shortage of liquidity on the market.

Lastly, there would be yet another negative outcome for intermediaries who participate in syndicate loans. Due to the increase in loan pricing, in fact, borrowers would be free to turn to other financial creditors not subject to Basel regulations.[7]

8.4.1.1 The International Consortium of ABN AMRO, Citibank, Deutsche Bank, and Société Générale

To address the issues that emerged from the 2001 Basel Committee proposal, four banks (ABN AMRO, Citibank, Deutsche Bank, and Société Générale) established a consortium in 2002. They set out to perform a joint analysis of statistical data from their project finance loan portfolios and to create the first database relating to project finance transactions, this in response to the Committee's request for more information. Since these four players were well established in the market, the sample they

---

7. "The Model Task Force views project finance as very risky due to the perception that the probability of default is high and that it is highly [positively] correlated with loss given default. We don't believe either perception is correct and worry that the resulting capital requirements will force us to increase our loan spreads. In a market where loan pricing is important, we won't be able to price competitively with other sources of capital that are not subject to the new Basel Accord." See Esty (2004), p. 469.

analyzed represented the entire spectrum of loans granted on the basis of a project finance logic, in terms of both time horizon (Table 8-4) and sector (Table 8-5). In addition, Table 8-3 shows the market share of these four banks, which from 1997 and 2001varies from 17% to over 24%.

The definition of default accepted by the consortium was restrictive enough to incorporate the unique characteristics of project finance but at the same time sufficiently inclusive to be used in comparisons with corporate finance transactions. The consortium decided to adopt a broader definition, in line with that used by rating agencies for corporate lending. This designation encompasses situations in which banks might make recourse to debt restructuring before the borrower fails to make payment; at the same time a simple breech of covenant is not considered a default. Moreover, this definition was deliberately conservative so as to allow statistical analyses to be conducted on the database using more specific parameters for default than those required. In procedural terms (with an eye to the deadline set by the

TABLE 8-3   Volume of Syndicated Loans Granted by Consortium Members (US$ billions)

	Citigroup	ABN Amro	Société Générale	Deutsche Bank	Total for all Banks	Total Market	% of Market
1997	2.913	4.512	0.754	3.315	11.494	67.425	17.05
1998	2.514	2.35	1.998	4.091	10.953	56.651	19.33
1999	5.897	2.302	3.218	3.045	14.462	72.392	19.98
2000	11.927	7.875	9.616	6.487	35.905	110.885	32.38
2001	15.512	4.019	5.301	3.623	28.455	108.478	26.23
Total	38.763	21.058	20.887	20.561	101.269	415.831	24.35

Source: Adapted from Esty and Sesia (2004).

TABLE 8-4   Distribution of Project Finance Loans by Year of Origination

Origination Year	1988–1992	1993–1995	1996–1998	1999–2001	Total
Number of facilities	58	171	260	270	759
% of total	7.64%	22.53%	34.26%	35.57%	100.00%

Source: Adapted from Esty and Sesia (2004).

TABLE 8-5   Distribution of Project Finance Loans by Region and Sector

	North America	Europe	Asia Pacific	Latin America	Africa	Total	% of Total
Power	128	50	62	48	9	297	39.13
Oil, gas, and petrochemicals	22	16	42	25	26	131	17.26
Infrastructure	8	41	17	1	1	68	8.96
Metals and mining	6	9	16	15	15	61	8.04
Media and telecom	30	61	17	29	10	147	19.37
Other	10	14	23	8	0	55	7.25
Total	204	191	177	126	61	759	
% of total	26.88%	25.16%	23.32%	16.60%	8.04%		

Source: Adapted from Esty and Sesia (2004).

Committee for submitting comments on the 2001 document), the consortium first formulated estimates on LGD and later on PD.

As regards LGD, the consortium collaborated with Standard & Poor's Risk Solutions. After processing the data provided by consortium members, S&P computed recovery rates, i.e., the total amounts liquidated after the default event divided by the total debt owed at the time of default plus interest accrued and penalties. The LGD was defined as a complement of the resulting recovery rate.[8]

The four banks identified forty-three defaults. The average LGD of their combined portfolios was approximately 25%, with a recovery rate of 75%, while the median was 100%. Then Risk Solutions compared the result on project loans with the other four types of corporate exposures: leveraged loans,[9] secured debt, senior debt, and senior unsecured debt (Table 8-6). Though there were more data for other types of corporate loans, project financing transactions on average showed a higher recovery rate, except when compared to senior leveraged loans, or those with the same seniority as another existing debt.

As the consortium expected, the first part of the study verified that project finance loans, on average, have a lower LGD than traditional corporate exposures. This was an indication that in troubled situations, project finance transactions performed better post default recovery.

The second part of the consortium's work focused instead on analyzing PD. The method adopted by Risk Solutions was to take static groups of transactions at the start of every year and to calculate their default rate over time. First Risk Solutions examined PD using the more general definition of default; then it applied more restrictive parameters (i.e., excluding restructured debt with changes in the amortization schedule and maturities as well as defaulted debts in which the borrower makes payments within the relative grace period).

Following the same procedure used for LGD, Risk Solutions compared the two PD rates it obtained with default rates on corporate loans. The results showed that project finance loans had a lower probability of default. In fact, when considering the broader definition of default, the cumulative PD rate for 10 years on project finance loans was 7.63%, compared to 9.38% for corporate loans (Table 8-7).

TABLE 8-6   Comparative Data on Recovery Rates by Type of Exposure

| | Project Finance | Leveraged Loans* | | Secured Debt | Senior Debt | Senior Unsecured Debt |
		Rank 1	Rank 2			
Number	43	182	19	339	844	311
Average	75.40%	81.70%	51.30%	68.90%	67.30%	46.20%
Median	100.00%	100.00%	50.90%	78.90%	78.10%	40.40%
Std. Dev.	34.90%	26.60%	34.30%	32.70%	34.20%	36.30%

* Leveraged loans rank 1 are senior debt or pari passu with other existing debt. Leveraged loans rank 2 are debts subordinated to other existing debt.
Source: Adapted from Esty and Sesia (2004).

8. For example, if a bank recovers $97 million on a loan worth $98 million at the time of default plus $2 million in interest and penalties, the recover rate would be 97% (= $97 million/$100 million), while the LGD would be 3% (= 100% − 97%).

9. Leveraged loans include senior debt with a BB+/BA rating or less and all unrated loans priced at Libor plus 150 basis points (Esty, 2004).

TABLE 8-7   Cumulative Average Default Rates on Project Finance and Corporate Loans

	Year									
	1	**2**	**3**	**4**	**5**	**6**	**7**	**8**	**9**	**10**
Project finance	1.52%	3.13%	4.40%	5.58%	6.65%	7.09%	7.30%	7.63%	7.63%	7.63%
Corporate finance loans	1.49%	2.98%	4.30%	5.38%	6.27%	7.06%	7.75%	8.34%	8.87%	9.38%

Source: Adapted from Esty and Sesia (2004).

The outcome of the PD analysis further consolidated the opinion of the representative of the four banks, who considered project finance transactions to be higher performers than traditional loans to companies. The performance of project finance loans, in fact, was in line with that of corporate exposures rated from BBB to BB, but with a much higher recovery rate (75% for project loans, compared to around 50% for corporate loans). From these results, the consortium put forth a proposal to change the risk weights, recommending that the capital requirements for project finance be approximately half of that applicable to corporate exposures (Table 8-8).

8.4.1.2   International Finance Corporation Study

While the consortium was carrying out its work, the International Finance Corporation (IFC) began analyzing its project loan database. Like the consortium, the IFC was seriously concerned that the Committee's initial proposal would have an extremely negative impact on project finance deals.[10] In actual fact, since IFC does business exclusively in developing countries, it would be reasonable to assume that this multilateral institution had a higher-risk project loan portfolio than other organizations operating mainly in industrialized countries. To prove that this conclusion was unfounded, as was the assumption that project finance lending is a riskier activity than corporate lending, IFC conducted a study in 2001 on its loan portfolio (Table 8-9).

TABLE 8-8   Risk Weights Proposed by the Consortium

	Supervisory Rating Category							
	AAA to A−	**BBB+ to BBB**	**BB+**	**BB**	**BB−**	**B+**	**B to C**	**Default**
Corporate loans								
Basel Committee proposal*	19–35%	55%	90%	100%	130%	150%	186–376%	625%
Project finance loans								
Basel Committee rating slots	Strong	Strong	Good	Good	Satisfactory	Satisfactory	Weak	Default
Consortium proposal	10–18%	28%	46%	50%	65%	75%	93–188%	313%

* Assuming an LGD between 45% and 50%.
Source: Adapted from Esty and Sesia (2004).

10. At the time, the opinion of Suellen Lazarus, director of the Syndications and International Securities Department at IFC was as follows: "[T]he proposed approach would have the effect of increasing overall risk by shortening project finance tenors. More fundamentally, it would reduce long-term lending to emerging markets and have a harmful impact on economic development. We strongly recommend that project finance not be included in specialized lending as separate from corporate lending." See IFC (2001), p. 2.

TABLE 8-9   Performance of Project Loans in IFC's Portfolio (1956–2001)

	All Closed A and C Loans*	Project Finance Portfolio	% of Total
Number of projects	1,175	675	57.45
Total distributions (millions)	9,250	5,860	63.35
Average loan amount (millions)	7,870	8,630	
Net losses (millions)	284	123	
% of net losses	3.07%	2.10%	

* C loans cover a complete range of hybrid products (quasi-equity), including convertible loans, which require a preset repayment schedule; these loans are also used for project finance in developing countries.
Source: Adapted from IFC (2001).

The study involved 1,175 loans over a period of 45 years for a total value of $9.25 billion, of which $5.826 billion was used in project finance transactions. With these results, IFC demonstrated that the loss rate for project finance loans was 2.1%, compared to 3.1% on all loans taken as a whole. Figure 8-1, in contrast, shows that the default rates on IFC's entire loan portfolio from 1981 to 2001 ranged from a minimum of 4% to a maximum of 18%. (Peak rates were recorded during periods of crisis on emerging markets.) On the other hand, loss rates never exceeded 2% in any given year and normally remained below 1% annually.

The data gleaned from IFC's portfolio are comparable to what one would expect over a 21-year period from a solid corporate portfolio with a rating ranging from BB+ to BBB−.

8.4.1.3   Final Proposal of the Basel Committee (June 2004)

From 2002 to 2004, the few available empirical studies on PD and LGD levels contributed to reshaping the initial position of the Committee, which heeded the recommendations of market players in part. In the final version of the document, dated June 2004, the risk weights for the standardized approach were revised. They are listed in Table 8-10 and compared to corporate exposures with the same rating.

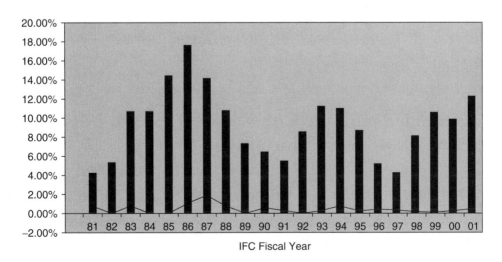

FIGURE 8-1   Performance of IFC's Loan Portfolio, 1981–2001

TABLE 8-10   Risk Weights for the Standardized Approach (June 2004)

	Corporate Exposures	Project Finance Exposures	
Obligor Rating Category	Standardized Approach	Basel Committee Supervisory Categorization	Basic Approach Risk Weights
AAA	20%	Strong	70%
AA+	20%	Strong	70%
AA	20%	Strong	70%
AA−	20%	Strong	70%
A+	50%	Strong	70%
A	50%	Strong	70%
A−	50%	Strong	70%
BBB+	**100%**	**Strong**	**70%**
BBB	**100%**	**Strong**	**70%**
BBB−	**100%**	**Strong**	**70%**
BB+	**100%**	**Good**	**90%**
BB	**100%**	**Good**	**90%**
BB−	100%	Satisfactory	115%
B+	**150%**	**Satisfactory**	**115%**
B or below B	150%	Weak	250%

It is clear that the original penalization of project finance loans carries over for transactions that fall in the highest rating classes (from AAA to A−), while there is less capital consumption for projects on the variable rating scale ranging from BBB+ to BB (for the most part taking into account the observations that emerged from the study run by the consortium of the four large international lenders mentioned in Section 8.4.1.1.) and for the B+ rating level.

Though conceding this important adjustment of the initial, more rigid approach toward project finance loans, the Committee has not changed its position in terms of the IRB approach. The rules applied to corporate exposures are extended to project financing with no adaptations. Moreover, there is no acknowledgment of the peculiarities of PD and LGD estimates for this type of transaction. The aim of the rest of the chapter is to provide some clarification of this important and still-unsolved issue.

8.5   Introduction to the Concepts of Expected Loss, Unexpected Loss, and Value at Risk

In the past few years, the topic of credit risk valuation from the perspective of bank lenders has been the focus of increased attention in the theoretical and empirical literature. Many models have been developed to measure value at risk for corporate borrowers, i.e., for already-in-place companies operating with an existing mix of real and financial assets. Value at risk is defined as the maximum potential loss that a portfolio or a financial institution may incur within a certain time interval and level of confidence; this loss can be exceeded only in a given percentage of cases (e.g., 1%).

The models of analysis are typically based on two key concepts: expected loss (EL) and unexpected loss (UL). Expected loss is the average amount that will not be repaid to the lender; this figure is computed as the product of the exposure at default (EAD), the probability of default (PD), and the loss given default (LGD). While expected loss identifies the average amount of money the bank is likely to lose, a lender should allocate enough capital to face potentially higher losses. In fact, this may occur in cases where either exposure at default is higher than expected (as when the counterparty has the chance to take full advantage of a standby facility before defaulting), default frequency is higher than expected, or loss in the event of default exceeds ex ante estimates. This extra loss the bank may face in the worst-case scenario at a given confidence level is identified as unexpected loss, and it coincides with the value at risk of the exposure.

Unfortunately, the models developed for valuing credit risk for existing borrowers cannot be applied directly to project finance transactions. In fact, these deals are actually characterized by a number of peculiar aspects that differentiate them from "normal" loans. The existence of an SPV, the absence of appreciable collateral, a valuation that places priority on cash flows, the fact that project loans are normally much larger than corporate loans, the higher debt-to-equity ratio, and the longer maturity as compared to corporate exposures—all these factors differ from loans usually granted to firms in operation.

These five specific traits of project finance have vital consequences for a lender. The contractual nature of project finance implies that the credit risk valuation must take into account both project performance and the soundness and creditworthiness of each counterparty linked to the SPV.[11] Separating these two aspects is always difficult and somewhat arbitrary. On the other hand, each project finance deal is in some way unique in terms of location and contractual complexity. The way in which each deal is structured, so as to allocate risks properly among different parties, can hardly be standardized. As a consequence, a lender would not do well to rely on the historical estimates of PD and LGD derived from its corporate loan portfolio. In fact, the empirical studies described in Sections 8.4.1.1 and 8.4.1.2 illustrate that project finance loans are *not* the same as corporate loans.

In this framework, we have seen that the New Capital Accord leaves banks the option of either applying the standardized approach or using their internal value at risk estimates, albeit with a clearly-defined set of qualitative and quantitative conditions and after a meticulous validation process by supervisory authorities.

The alternative solution proposed by the Committee allows banks to apply the internal ratings based (IRB) approach to calculate the probability of default (PD), the loss given default (LGD), and the exposure at default (EAD) of a project finance loan. In this case, the Committee suggests applying the internal rating solution used in the advanced approach for corporate exposures to specialized lending. However, the Committee's viewpoint raises some doubts as to whether the special features of project finance as compared to corporate exposures are recognized. These features should influence the definition of default and the estimates of PD, LGD, and EAD used to classify the risk of these transactions.

11. See Moody's (2001a, 2001b), Esty (2002b), Brealey, Cooper, and Habib (1996), and Dailami and Hauswald (2001).

The main objective of the following sections is to suggest a method for measuring value at risk in project finance deals based on Monte Carlo simulations. In particular, we:

- Show how default can be identified through a simulation of the project cash flows over a number of years
- Discuss how inputs can be estimated and describe the problems deriving from the existence of asymmetric information among different players
- Suggest how a synthetic value at risk measure can be derived so as to summarize the entire cash flow simulation in a number that might be consistent with VaR figures for corporate loans. While recent contributions have suggested adopting simulations to assess risk from the sponsors' viewpoint, we extend the method to the lender's position and address the specific issues that must be tackled to produce a value at risk estimate.

We begin in Section 8.6 by defining default events in project finance transactions and move on in Section 8.7 to analyzing how to model the uncertain cash flows of the project through a Monte Carlo simulation. Section 8.8 discusses the problem of estimating value at risk in a project finance transaction, while Section 8.9 describes how loss given default may be modeled.

8.6 Defining Default for Project Finance Deals

The first key step in quantifying default risk for project finance deals is to model the cash flows the project will generate. For firms, in keeping with various models developed according to Merton's (1974) approach,[12] the assumption is that default will occur when the value of corporate assets falls below a certain threshold. A similar analysis can be conducted with reference to a project's cash flow. Therefore, a default may take place when these flows are too low to repay the debt service in a given period. In any case, it could prove difficult to determine whether this condition has occurred. Typically, lenders try to reduce their risk by obliging the SPV to build cash reserve accounts (in the form of a debt service reserve accounts). Another option is to allow the project's cash flows to be tapped only on the condition that appropriate levels of DSCR and LLCR are maintained.

Default occurs when the debt cannot be serviced by the project's cash flows, be they generated from operations, outstanding debt reserves, standby equity, or standby credit lines. This check must be done according to the stepwise procedure shown in Figure 8-2.

This definition of default can be applied in the context of a simulation approach. In fact, though project scenarios are unknown and potentially infinite in number and size, they can be simulated so as to be consistent with the risk view of the bank that is financing the structured deal. By projecting the cash flows for the SPV, it is then possible to dynamically test if and when a default situation could arise during the life of the project. Section 8.7 describes how to replicate the input needed for the simulation. Naturally, all pertinent factors must be taken into consideration, such as market risk related to prices and interest rates, event risks that could impact the project, the correlation among income lines, the financing structure of the project.

Event risks are obviously a critical issue. Here the judgmental component has a major impact on risk assessments and probability of default estimations. The reason

---

12. Specifically, see Black and Cox (1976) and Crosbie and Bohm (2003).

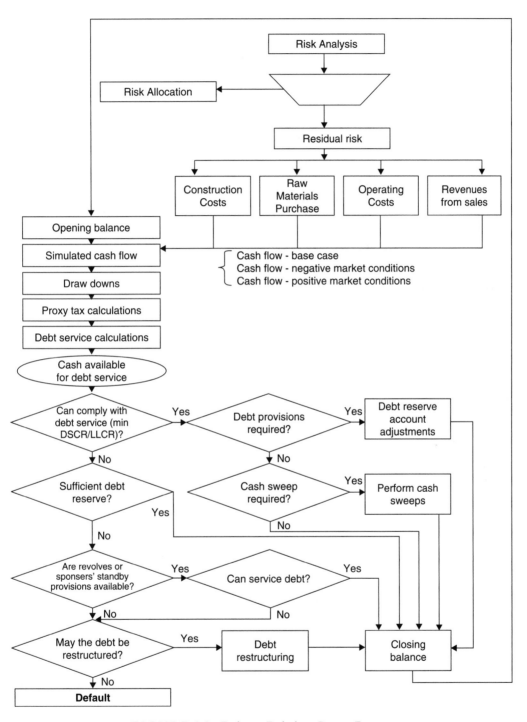

FIGURE 8-2 Defining Default in Project Finance

is that many events are difficult to model. For example, how does one quantify the possibility of a political downturn in a country? Other events, instead, may be correlated to the regular parameters used in risk management. Another example is the default probability of a sponsor that may be related to the standard rating scale that banks use to evaluate counterparties.

Generally speaking, experience in identifying project drivers and modeling their behavior is vital, since even in the simulation context that is suggested here, several parameters of the model cannot be derived by means of empirical evidence.[13]

Due to the complex nature of a default event in project finance deals, the simulation must carefully monitor DSCR, LLCR, and the ratio of EBITDA to senior or total debt. If preset minimum levels of these ratios are breeched, this does not necessarily or directly imply a default, but such a circumstance may be used as a trigger to impel sponsors to take appropriate steps to prevent credit deterioration (e.g., by an equity injection or an increase in mitigation requirements).

8.7   Modeling the Project Cash Flows

Creating a scenario in project finance deals can be viewed as a process (see again Figure 8-2) necessitating the following steps:

1. Defining a suitable risk assessment model (risk breakdown structure, or RBS)
2. Defining project variables and key drivers (project breakdown structure, PBS)
3. Estimating the input variables and respective value distribution; accounting for correlations among different variables
4. Modeling the project's cash flows, calculating outputs, and valuing results

8.7.1   Defining a Risk Assessment Model

The first step in this process is to identify the key risks inherent to the project (the risk assessment model) and to classify them in a consistent and hierarchical manner through the so-called risk breakdown structure (RBS). Risk valuation models can be either qualitative or quantitative.[14] An in-depth analysis of various models is beyond the scope of this book, but all models have one trait in common: They require subjective judgments by experts. Such opinions are needed because each project and its conditions of execution are unique, historical data are often not statistically sufficient to carry out historical analysis, and in some cases data on the project in question cannot be compared to other projects with different sizes or targets.

A simplified example of a risk breakdown structure can be obtained through the international project risk assessment (IPRA) model (Construction Industry

---

13. For oil and gas deals, for example, the fact that data are available can facilitate empirical estimates of parameter volatility (e.g., oil price volatility), while in other transactions time series are not available and experience and judgment prove to be indispensable (for instance, deals involving infrastructure or telecommunications).

14. Specifically, qualitative models include FMECA (failure mode effect and criticality analysis) and IPRA (international project risk assessment model). Quantitative models include deterministic models, such as sensitivity analysis or AHP (analytic hierarchy process; and probabilistic/stochastic simulation models (like Monte Carlo simulations).

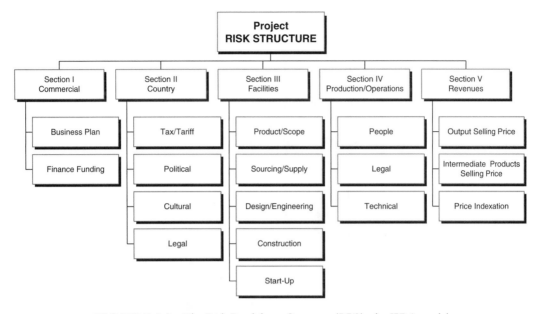

FIGURE 8-3   The Risk Breakdown Structure (RBS): the IPRA model

Institute, 2003), one of the most widely used qualitative models. The typical first level of the RBS has four sections (commercial, country, facilities, production/operations) plus a fifth section on revenues that is necessary for project finance deals.[15] Each section is then broken down to obtain a more detailed list of project risks (see Figure 8-3).

In the IPRA model, risk assessment is based on an estimate of the likelihood that each risk will occur and its relative impact. The result is a risk assessment matrix that helps to classify risks by relative importance, considering the chance that each will happen and the impact that each would have. The risk segmentation that emerges provides a support tool for identifying key risks and thus for developing a strategy to mitigate and allocate risk to third parties (if possible) and managing residual risk in order to reduce the volatility of cash flow components. The strategy of risk transfer and mitigation as well as the size and quality of residual risk are undeniably crucial for risk evaluation from the lender's viewpoint.

8.7.2   Identifying Project Variables and Key Drivers

Following the same strategy for risk assessment, the project breakdown structure (PBS) is a top-down hierarchical decomposition that aims to pinpoint all project variables that are key drivers of the project's performance/cash flows (Archibald, 2003). An example is shown in Figure 8-4.

Each of the main project variables is then broken down further in a detailed set of drivers that represent input variables of the cash flow model. A complete example of a project finance deal in the waste-to-energy industry is given in Table 8-11.

15. The fifth section on revenues does not belong to the standard IPRA model, since it normally covers project risk and project costs only.

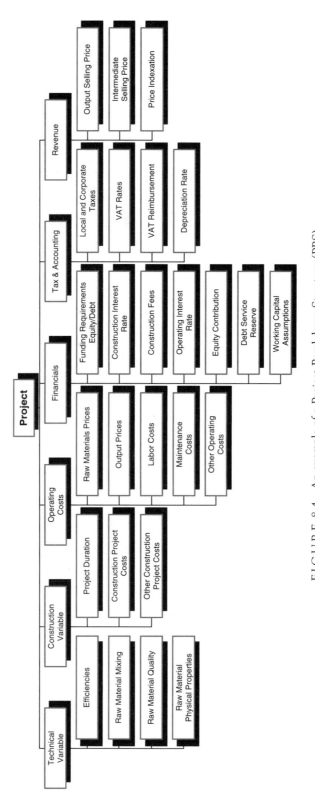

FIGURE 8-4 An example of a Project Breakdown Structure (PBS)

TABLE 8-11 Project Breakdown Structure—A Case of Waste-to-Energy Production Plants

Level II PBS Variable	Level III PBS Variable	Drivers	Notes
Technical variables	Efficiencies	Maximum capacity Waste disposal (tons/year) Power production (MW) Plant availability (% of maximum capacity) 1st year 2nd year Following years Energy yield of waste (kcal/Kwh depending on the quality of the waste employed for power production)	Control of agreements with the contractor for minimum performance standards
Construction variable	Project duration	Construction duration Operation timing Beginning construction (t) End construction (t) Beginning operation (t) End operation (t)	When a turnkey construction agreement is signed, timing is usually fixed. Penalties are paid by the contractor in case of delay.
Construction variable	Construction project costs	Turnkey construction contract amount Owner's costs Land purchase cost Development costs (consulting, opinions, etc.)	Consider VAT on all items and timing of payment (i.e., how much in percentage I will pay for every year/semester of construction) Consider depreciation percentage (needed to calculate operating and net income in P&L accounts)
Construction variable	Other project costs (additional investments)	VAT on project costs Capitalized interests during construction Capitalized commitment fees during construction Underwriting fee Taxes on debt	Consider spread over Euribor; percentage of commitment fee

(*Continues*)

TABLE 8-11 (Continued)

Level II PBS Variable	Level III PBS Variable	Drivers	Notes
Operating costs	Raw material Prices/contracts	Sources of purchase (put-or-pay with municipalities? free market?)	Existence of put-or-pay agreements with waste suppliers
		Minimum purchase volume (tons/year)	
		Revenue for every ton of waste processed	If part of the waste must be purchased on a free market, market risk may arise in terms of volume and prices
		Calorific yield of waste	
Revenue	Energy price	Tenor (number of years)	Existence of take or pay agreement
	Energy quantity	Volume of energy sold (MW)	
		Revenue components	
		Plant charge (€/KW)	
		Energy charge (€/KW)	
		Incentive for waste treatment (€/KW)	
	Price indexation	Indexation (index chosen to review the revenue components)	
Operating costs	Fixed costs	Fixed costs	Existence of an O&M agreement: If existent, some of the items in the column to the left are included in a service payment to the operator, which usually provides personnel and structures
	Labor costs	Personnel (number of employees and unit cost)	
	Maintenance costs	Maintenance insurance premiums general expenses	
	Contingencies	Contingencies	
	Labor costs	Variable costs	
	Raw material prices	Sodium bicarbonate (price/kg and kg for every ton of waste processed)	
		Active carbon (price/kg and kg for every ton of waste processed)	
		Water (price/kg and kg for every ton of waste processed)	
		Ash disposal and treatment (price/kg and kg for every ton of ashes disposed)	

Category	Subcategory	Detail	Notes
	Raw material indexations	Average price of methane (the most common parameter used for indexing the energy charge component of the energy sale)	
Tax and accounting	Taxation	% of taxes on revenue	
		Other taxes	
	VAT	VAT (%)	
	Macroeconomic variables	Inflation and inflation index	
Financials	Financial structure		Minimum equity IRR required: it is a trigger for the modelist. If not fulfilled, simulation must be run again after changing parameters
	Equity contribution	Base equity	Minimum DSCR, ADSCR; LLCR
		% equity (out of total investment cost)	
		Standby equity	
		Base facility	
		Committed amount (€)	
		Repayment period (years)	
		Frequency of repayment (x months)	
		Repayment schedule (% of loan repaid every x months)	
		Reference rate	
	Interest rates	Spread	
		During construction	
		Years 1–5	
		Remaining years	
		Underwriting fee (b.p.)	
		Commitment fee (b.p.)	
	VAT Rates	Similar drivers are set up for VAT facility, standby facility	

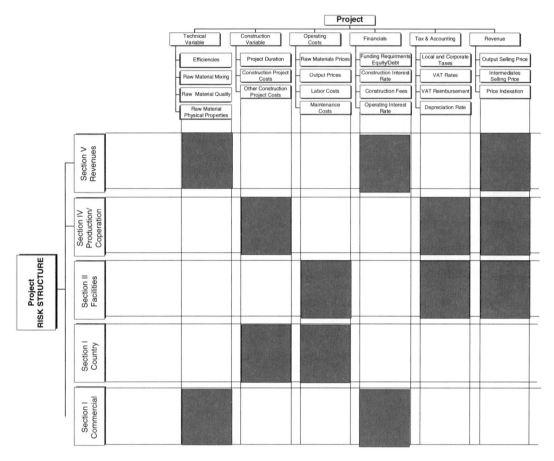

FIGURE 8-5   Identifying the Risk Package

The risk breakdown structure and project breakdown structure are then combined into the so-called risk package. This represents all key project variables derived through the PBS, identifies whether and how they may be affected by each of the risk categories identified in the RBS, and includes all information concerning the parameters of each input variable (see Figure 8-5).

The risk package is therefore the starting point for any kind of risk analysis on the project, from a simple sensitivity analysis aimed at assessing the impact of a single variable change on the project's performance to a more sophisticated stochastic analysis of the project cash flows. From the lender's viewpoint, the relevant risk package should only consider residual risks remaining after the risk allocation and mitigation treatment.

8.7.3   Input Variables: Estimation and Data Collection

After identifying the key input variables, the range of admissible values and their frequency distribution must be estimated and defined. Input data collection may be organized using three methodologies:

- Historical data analysis (when historical data about the required variable exist)

- Expert judgments, obtained with techniques such as range evaluation (Schuyler, 2001) or the event risk tree (Harrison, 1985)[16]
- Hybrid models (combining historical and expert judgments)

Hybrid models are the most widely used, since the analyst would like to use historical data whenever available, while many variables cannot be estimated only through historical and objective data. In hybrid models, the data for "risk variation range" and "variable probability distribution" are collected relying on both historical and expert information. Experts begin by estimating input variables through a qualitative model, assigning risk scores and also directly estimating the optimistic, pessimistic, and most likely values of input variables.

Judgments are obtained through a Delphi work session and are independent; averages and variances of most likely, pessimistic, and optimistic values and risk scores are calculated.[17] All available historical data are included, and risk variables are clustered in risk levels (see Figures 8-6 and 8-7). Risk levels define common probability shape distribution and range variation, applicable to all groups belonging to the same level for each risk category. In our example we included five levels, but in principle it is possible to define different levels for each single specific need. (In theory, a different distribution and/or fluctuation range could be assigned to each variable.)

The next step is to quantify the correlations between input variables, a task that is complex to analyze and ascertain. A series of historical data should be available to

RISK SCORE							
Impact	0.05	0.1	0.2	0.4	0.8		RISK
Probability							
0.9							Very
	0.045	0.090	0.180	0.360	0.720		High
0.7	0.035	0.070	0.140	0.280	0.560		High
0.5	0.025	0.050	0.100	0.200	0.400		Moderate
0.3	0.015	0.030	0.060	0.120	0.240		Low
0.1	0.005	0.010	0.020	0.040	0.080		Very Low

FIGURE 8-6 Matrix Risk Score—Risk level identification

16. Intuitively, range evaluation is the direct estimate of the most likely optimistic and pessimistic values of an input variable, which then leads to the identification of the variable distribution (often through simplifying assumptions). The event risk tree is an application of decision model support theories, in which the model considers the tree of decisions and events that may define the single variable and then reconstructs its distribution based on the probability of each sequence of events or decisions.

17. One problem here is trying to reduce the risk of potential return overestimation and risk underestimation that may intentionally or unintentionally be introduced by those who are too actively involved in the project. This problem is well known in the capital budgeting literature; see, for instance, Statman and Tyebjee (1985) and Pruitt and Gitman (1987).

Risk	Variation	Distribution Type
Very high	0%/+20%	PERT distribution
High	0%/+15%	PERT distribution
Moderate	–15/10%	PERT distribution
Low	–2%/6%	PERT distribution
Very low	–3%/3%	Normal distribution

FIGURE 8-7   Table of clusters

calculate correlation factors, and some back-test analysis should be done to establish their level of confidence. Moreover, additional hypotheses are needed to maintain the same correlation values throughout all the years of project life.

For some financial variables, correlations may be estimated through historical data. This is true, for instance, for the correlation between interest rates and inflation rates, between inflation rates and raw material prices or output selling prices. Some historical analyses are possible at times, even among certain project drivers, like erection time and construction costs. In any case, correlation analysis typically focuses only on those variables that have proven to have a material impact on the cash flow model, and even in this case one should clearly weigh the greater precision required by introducing correlation between a pair of variables against the extra model risk implicit in the estimation of correlation values.

The estimation of input variables and the correlation among them is a critical issue for outsiders, as for bank lenders. In the business of project finance, there are at least three different categories of outsiders who are subject to an increasing level of asymmetric information relative to sponsors: the structured finance or project finance team of the bank (in charge of the customer relationship), the risk management team, and the regulatory authorities who must decide whether an internal, simulation-based approach developed by the bank is compliant to substitute a standard approach in calculating minimum capital requirements for the project finance deal.

A project finance/structured finance team typically builds a complex worksheet to evaluate project cash flows in the base case and then applies deterministic, what-if scenario sensitivity analysis. This team, as least in part, may be in a position to define reasonable estimates for the random variables behind the cash flow model. They may do so both by using past experience in other projects and turning to external independent consultants (i.e., auditors or technical advisors), who are often involved in certifying the base case analysis. The bank's risk manager should then check the assumptions to guarantee that the project finance team has not underestimated the deal risk, either unintentionally or (worse still) deliberately for budgetary reasons. Supervisors, finally, should control whether the bank's internal value at risk estimate is adequate or whether either the project finance or risk management team have been overoptimistic in their evaluation.[18]

Of course, the efforts to develop an internal model for project finance deals require a sizeable investment in project evaluation skills. In fact, such skills must be found not only in the team responsible for evaluating the deal first (as would happen even if

18. In any case, this kind of interaction between decision makers and controllers is common to any complex lending decision, and the general rule at each subsequent step should be to adopt a very conservative approach while leaving to the counterparty the opportunity to prove that a more favorable evaluation is needed.

a standard approach for calculating capital charge were adopted) but also in the risk management unit, which should be able to question and revise the assumptions behind the risk assessment of the project finance unit inside the bank.

8.7.4 *Estimating Project Cash Flow and Valuing Results*

The cash flow model, if fed with appropriate inputs, defines the basis for supporting lenders' decisions in terms of risk valuation and pricing (spreads, fees, and minimum acceptable internal rate of return). Traditional risk valuation is based on a definition of a base case and a repeated output stress analysis or subjective scenario analysis. The base case analysis defines an integrated forecast of balance sheets, income statements, and cash flow statements for all the years in which the project is operational, conditioned on a number of assumptions. An example of cash flow statements is included in the Italy Water Case discussed in this book.

In a traditional repeated output stress analysis, a shock is applied to one project driver (within a predetermined range), while all the others are fixed. In the case of scenarios, a set of variables is changed and the effect of the behavior of project cash flow is then assessed. A stochastic analysis, in contrast, allows all (or at least most) of the input variables to vary simultaneously. For instance, in the example in Table 8-11, revenues from waste disposal may vary from year to year, depending on the usage of the plant's production capacity and on the potential variability of the fees for waste elimination, which may be indexed to inflation. Other cash flow components will vary according to the probability distributions specified by the analyst, and as a result a probabilistic distribution of all output variables will be obtained. This enables sponsors' and lenders' advisers to carry out a regression analysis of model inputs.

Figure 8-8 shows two examples of estimates of relative impact that key input variables have on a target variable (such as IRR), which can be obtained by a stochastic analysis. The first part illustrates the frequency distribution of IRR that emerged from a simulation, while the second part shows the results of a regression between key input variables and IRR.

This regression is relevant since it more clearly illustrates that variables have a substantial impact on the final performance of the project and that variables are less relevant. This may also require refining the analysis by challenging or further improving the estimates on those variables that appeared to have a major role after the simulation is run.

8.8 Estimating Value at Risk through Simulations

By developing a stochastic model of future cash flows, the lender may be able to determine how frequently the project might reach a situation that can be identified as a default, according to the stepwise process discussed in Figure 8-2. While the overall default probability throughout the life of the project may be relevant information for the risk manager, a bank is typically interested in determining a value at risk measure over a much shorter horizon (normally one year). It is therefore critical to clearly define which notion of "value" the bank is willing to adopt and how the deterioration of project cash flows could impact that measure. Value at risk would then be identified with the maximum potential loss the value of the project may face within a certain confidence level and time horizon (presumably one year).

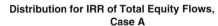

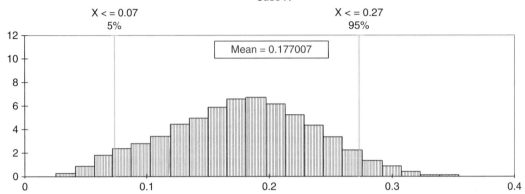

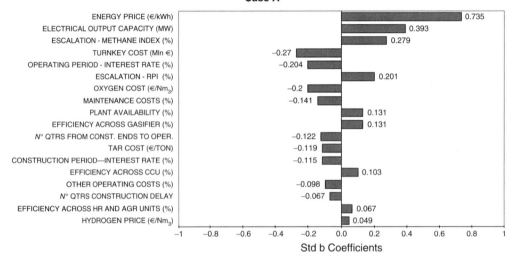

FIGURE 8-8   Estimate of the effects of input variables on the internal rate of return (IRR)

A first, simplified solution could be to adopt the approach of default-mode credit risk VaR models,[19] which typically assume that the value of the loan should be equal to its notional value, except in case of default. Therefore such models identify the risk over the one-year horizon only as the chance that the project may default during the first year. Yet, since the debt service could be distributed in many different ways along the life of the project provided that minimum DSCR and LLCR are satisfied, this approach could be misleading. When structuring the project, in fact, reducing debt service requirements in the early years would lower the first-year default probability of the project, almost irrespective of its true quality and probability of default in subsequent years. At the same time, VaR estimates would fluctuate from year to year only as a consequence of changes in debt service requirements from year to year[20] (assuming, of course, all else is equal). Consequently, this solution should be rejected.

19. For example, see Credit Suisse Financial Products (1997).
20. This risk could obviously be reduced if the project's financial structure is designed so as to have an almost constant debt service cover ratio from year to year and if actual cash flows are close to expected ones.

Another possible solution is to adopt a mark-to-market approach, where value at risk is identified as the difference between the loan's forward expected value and its forward value in one year's time in the worst-case scenario at the $\alpha\%$ percentile level. The critical issue here becomes how the forward value of the loan can be estimated. In a classic model *á la* CreditMetrics[TM,21] the forward value of the loan would be identified by discounting the value of future cash flows with forward zero coupon rates, incorporating a proper spread for credit risk. For a bond, for instance, the variability of the forward price derives from the fact that cash flows are discounted at different rates, depending on the rating class in which the issuer ends up at the end of the year, according to a predefined rating transition matrix. Trying to apply similar logic to project finance deals is not easy. For a bond, the proper discounting rate can be determined based on its rating class. For a project finance deal, modeling the relationship between theoretical credit spreads and the project's behavior is instead much more complex.[22]

Considering these problems, a third possible solution is to assume that the credit spread may remain the same for the next year. So one would model the distribution of the forward values of the project by simply discounting the cash flows for debt service repayment in each simulation run. Therefore, in all simulations where the project will default (according to the definition proposed in Figure 8-2), the present value of the cash flows will be lower than in nondefault scenarios. This implies that a distribution of loan values may be built that would enable lenders to calculate both the expected loss (i.e., the difference between the value of the loan in the case of nondefault and its expected value) and value at risk or the unexpected loss (i.e., the difference between the expected value and the worst-case scenario value within a given confidence level), plus any other risk measure (such as expected shortfall) that may be considered useful. This solution offers the advantage of linking the value of the loan to the timing of potential default, since a late default would imply a greater number of years with regular payments.[23]

A critical issue is how to model the project value in the event of default. This is important, since the left side of the distribution of the loan's forward present value would be determined precisely by the cases in which the project will be totally or partially unable to cover its debt service and will meet the conditions described earlier, in Section 8.6. This problem is discussed in the next section.

8.9 Defining Project Value in the Event of Default

Provided that the definition of the default event proposed in Section 8.6 is acceptable, it is necessary to estimate the loss given default (LGD) or, equivalently, the recovery rate for the banks financing the project. The recovery rate clearly depends on the value of the project in the event of default, which could be represented either by the

---

21. See Gupton, Finger, and Bhatia (1997).

22. Imagine the case of a project evaluated in its first year of life, where negative cash flows are higher than expected. While this is clearly bad news, it is hard to determine if or how this might impact the credit spread for the cash flows in subsequent years. Moreover, it is unclear how the different liquidity of a project finance deal against a traded bond could impact discounting rates.

23. In this way it should also be possible to account for the case of increases in the loan exposure due to loan commitment facilities, for instance. If, for example, contingencies not covered by standard contracts arise during the construction phase, the project may absorb a part of the undrawn portion of the standby facilities, increasing lenders' exposure. This could be modeled as a negative cash flow for the lender, entering the calculation of the loan's present and one-year forward value.

market value of the underlying asset (as, for example, in the case of a real estate or aircraft industry project) or by the present value of future cash flows. In a Monte Carlo setting, one could adopt different solutions, depending on the characteristics of the individual project and the degree of precision that sponsors or lenders wish to attain. In particular, there are three critical choices related to:

- Whether and how the random nature of loss given default is taken into account
- How the value of the project at default is modeled
- How to consider the case of debt restructuring

These three problems are analyzed in order next.

8.9.1   Deterministic vs. Stochastic LGD Estimates

When modeling the value of the project in the event of default, assuming a fixed LGD percentage value is clearly the easiest choice. However, the risk of the project finance deal may be underestimated, because there is frequently a positive correlation between probability of default and LGD. Since the value of the project often depends solely on the value of the future cash flows that will be produced (except in those cases when there is a redeployable underlying asset), a reduction in the value of future cash flows has the joint impact of increasing the probability of default (e.g., by falling below a certain critical threshold value in DSCR or LLCR or both, as discussed in Section 6) and decreasing the present value of the cash flows after default, thereby reducing the recovery ratio for the banks that financed the project. A fixed percentage LGD would instead ignore the risk deriving from LGD variability and its correlation with the event of default and could therefore underestimate actual risk.

The second solution would be to simulate a single random LGD value if default occurs, either by extracting a random value from the distribution modeling the market value of the redeployable underlying asset in case it exists or by continuing the simulation of the project cash flows after default and then summing their net present values. The recovery rate would then be represented by the ratio of either the market value of the underlying asset or the aggregate net present value of future discounted cash flows to the value of outstanding debt, and hence the loss given default would be easily determined. If this solution is adopted, the effect of the uncertain loss given default rate and the correlation between PD and LGD deriving from the reduction of project cash flows could be modeled. Yet for each default a single, albeit random, value of loss given default is considered. Therefore, reflecting the variability of LGD in value at risk estimates would probably require running a huge number of simulations, especially if default occurs very infrequently.

In order to solve this problem, a third possible solution is first to run a project simulation that identifies the scenarios when default occurs and then to run a set of sub-simulations for each default scenario aimed at building a distribution of LGD values.[24]

---

24. Imagine, for instance, that by simulating 1,000 random multiperiod cash flow projections in 40 simulations (i.e., 4% of cases), default occurs. One could then extract 100 random loss given default values for each of the 40 default scenarios. Using this procedure, the final values would come out as $960 + 40 \times 100 = 4,960$. When reconstructing the empirical distribution used to estimate value at risk, of course, the weight of the 960 nondefault scenarios would be equal to $1/1000 = 0.1\%$, while the weight of each of the 4,000 default-conditional scenarios would only equal $(1/1000) \times (1/100) = 0.001\%$. In this way, however, the picture of the extreme percentiles of the distribution could be much more precise than by running 5,000 "normal" simulations in which only 200 (i.e., $4\% \times 5,000$) paths would have been used to model the left tail of the loan value distribution.

This solution is more complex, and it is viable especially when either default is rare (so that the number of subsimulations is low) or the LGD is easy to model, as is the case when it can be derived directly by simulating the value of the underlying asset. Despite the effort required, this solution may be useful when the bank is interested in measuring VaR up to an extreme percentile of the distribution (e.g., 99.97%), which could also be more sensitive to the variability of the LGD rate.

8.9.2 LGD Drivers: The Value of Underlying Assets vs. Defaulted Project Cash Flows

The second issue related to the estimation of loan value in case of default concerns the drivers used to simulate one or more "recovery values" for the project. When the project has an underlying asset that could be sold in case of project default, the easiest way would be to model the recovery rate by extracting one or more random values from the distribution of the underlying asset values. A simple case is represented by real estate projects, for instance. Here, estimating the LGD value is faster, since one could extract a single value instead of running another a cash flow projection.

On the other hand, if there is no redeployable underlying asset, then the value in case of default could be modeled by continuing the cash flow simulation even beyond the default event. In this case, the underlying assumption is that the lenders would prefer to extract the (albeit insufficient) residual cash flows rather than terminate the project completely with a zero recovery rate. Yet it is critical to decide whether the credit spread used to discount the project's postdefault cash flows may still be assumed to equal the initial credit spread. If a different credit spread is adopted, then the project's value in the case of default would also depend on the changes in the discount rate that may be triggered by the default event.

8.9.3 Restructuring vs. Default

A third issue in modeling the distribution of the loan forward value is whether and how to deal with the possibility that the debt may be restructured. In fact, it is reasonable to assume that under certain circumstances the pool of financial institutions supporting the project might accept a debt restructuring rather than allow the project to default. This assumption, also confirmed in practice (Esty and Sesia, 2004), is consistent with the fact that practitioners consider the breach of covenants in loan agreements as a trigger forcing lenders to take proper measures to prevent the project's ability to generate cash from declining. When a default event included in the loan agreement occurs, the immediate cancellation of the loan—although possible in principle—would lead to a severe drop in the value of the project. The lenders, well aware of this consequence, will tend to take corrective actions aimed at keeping the project in operation as a "going concern."

For example, in the case of a step-in clause, which allows lenders to select another operator and substitute it for the existing one, continuation is safeguarded by avoiding the bankruptcy of the project. The maturity of the deal is obviously modified: Renegotiation can actually lengthen the terms of repayment of capital, interests, and fees.[25]

---

25. Debt restructuring may take place in several other forms, from a renegotiation of the debt terms and conditions (e.g., by delaying in part the debt service by increasing the debt maturity) to the block of dividend distributions and the destination of cash surplus to existing debt reserves, to a partial conversion of debt into equity, and could therefore affect substantially the cash flows for the lenders.

If this possibility is factored into the simulation, then one should try to model a sort of "loss given restructuring," since a refinancing agreement or the conversion of debt into equity could also imply a loss for the lenders.

Incorporating restructuring events into the simulation requires first determining (as in the case of default) reasonable "restructuring triggers" that can be based on DSCR and LLCR, as discussed in Section 8.6. Even if the triggers are set off, restructuring is not automatic, since it typically requires acceptance by all the lenders. So the likelihood of restructuring may also depend on the number of lenders and the strength of the arranger who acts as the leader of the refinancing. Then, provided that restructuring occurs, the forms it takes may vary so much that it is difficult to model them formally. Developing this feature in simulation experiments may also be a challenge for more sophisticated risk managers.

CASE STUDY ◆ 1

Cogeneration*

C1.1 Situation

"Listen, Gianfranco, they've just called me from American Investment Banking Co. saying that they have a very good project finance deal at hand. And one of the sponsors is Alfa, one of our most important clients." Giovanni Altieri, Director of the Large Corporate Department at Pieff Bank, is talking to his assistant, Gianfranco Arrigoni, on the phone.

"Very interesting, Boss," replies Gianfranco. "Did they tell you where they are with it?"

"No, Gianfranco, they were very vague. They told me that they are still in the preliminary phase, studying the operation, but they are interested in starting to contact some Italian banks to survey the market and evaluate their opinions regarding the viability of the initiative. They told me that in the next few days they'll send a very brief summary report on the main information. They've asked me to look it over carefully and give them feedback on our possible involvement during the debt syndication phase. I'll send you everything as soon as I get it."

"Ok, Boss, keep me informed."

Two weeks later, a package marked "American Investment Banking Co." arrives on Arrigoni's desk. On the envelope is a clearly visible message from Altieri: "Attn: Gianfranco Arrigoni. Prepare a review of the document highlighting the strong and weak points of the preliminary proposal. Crucial deal—Alfa is a sponsor, and for us it's important to get into the syndicate. Have it all ready by next Friday. Regards, Giovanni Altieri."

Arrigoni opens the envelope and takes out the contents; it is the summary report that Altieri had told him about during their phone call. He decides to read through it

---

* Since the deal was designed and closed in 1993, before the euro came into use, all data are kept in the original currency (Italian lira). The exchange rate is 1 euro = 1,936.27 Italian lira.

immediately, leaving himself time for reflection. He also wants to consult with other colleagues and some contacts in London.

C1.2   Production Process

The Cogeneration project involves the construction of a cogeneration plant in a municipality in the southern part of the Italian peninsula. More specifically, it is a structure that generates electric power and steam by burning by-products (essentially tar) from crude (oil) refining.

The plant is essentially structured on the following process: Tar is initially pretreated with solvents in a special "deasphalting" plant; subsequently, the treated tar (the base feedstock of the plant) is burned in combination with oxygen produced by special plants that favor a more efficient combustion of the raw material. This process produces steam, which is then injected into turbines; the movement of these turbines generates electric power. Part of this steam comes out of the process as a by-product of power generation and can be utilized either for industrial purposes or for domestic heating.

The electric power produced by the plant is transmitted to the national electric circuit through a high-voltage power line about 70 km long. The profile of the sparsely populated territory where the power line runs is rugged terrain covered with untamed forests; a large part of the zone is a tourist attraction for domestic and foreign visitors.

Buyers of the plant's output are:

- ENEL, the Italian national electric company, which buys the power production on the basis of an ESA/PPA contract (energy sale agreement/power purchase agreement), paying a contribution over the cost of energy production for the first 8 years of operation in accordance with the 1992 CIP6 Decree (Interdepartmental Committee on Prices).
- Alfa, which buys the steam produced by Cogeneration for industrial uses.

The treatment of the production waste is initially carried out in the same Cogeneration structure; afterwards, the pretreated residue is pumped to a treatment plant managed by a consortium of municipalities located in the immediate vicinity of the cogeneration plant. The consortium plant currently works on the basis of a temporary authorization.

A graphic model of the cogeneration process using tar as base feedstock is presented in Figure C1-1.

The two sponsors have already chosen the technology for deasphalting; it is therefore an unchangeable variable. In fact, they have already selected the supplier of the technological license on the basis of the efficacy of the proposed technology in the treatment of Alfa's tar.

The supplier of the deasphalting technological license is American Petroleum Co., one of the "Seven Sisters" of the international oil market.

C1.3   Sponsors of the Deal

There are two sponsors of the operation:

- Alfa SpA
- ME Energy Corporation

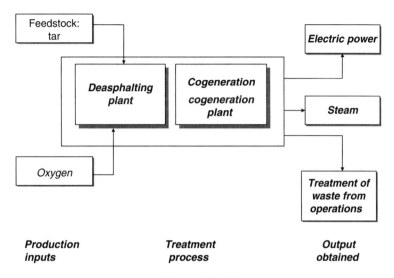

FIGURE C1-1   Graphic Model of the Cogeneration Process

The companies are committed to providing equity capital (51% and 49%, respectively) to a special-purpose vehicle company called Cogeneration. This SPV will be the owner of all the rights and contractual obligations arising from the venture.

Alfa SpA is one of the leading Italian oil companies. It operates in the crude oil industry and owns a network of petroleum stations located throughout the country. It has a refining capacity of 14 million tons of crude oil per year and runs around 2,000 distribution points, with a market share of about 6%.

ME Energy Corporation is an American utility. It is one of the most important players in the sector of power generation. Its company mission ranges from developing new power plants and cogeneration plants to acquiring power plants and cogeneration plants, from handling plant construction to providing maintenance services (operation and maintenance). In Europe it has won recognition in particular for two project finance deals in the UK involving cogeneration plants similar to Cogeneration.

C1.4   Agreements Underpinning the Deal

American Investment Banking Co. has studied the operation so as to evaluate the potential risks arising from the initiative and has concluded that the following agreements must be stipulated:

- Cogeneration turnkey construction contract
- Construction contract for the deasphalting plant
- Operation and maintenance agreement
- Energy sale/power purchase agreement
- Steam purchase agreement
- Feedstock supply agreement
- Oxygen supply agreement

C1.4.1   Cogeneration Construction Agreement

The construction agreement is signed with Gamma Italia SpA, the Italian subsidiary of the American Gamma Group, one of the most important developers in the design and construction of industrial plants in the world.

Gamma signed the construction agreement as lead manager of a consortium. The following companies, which are subcontractors for the supply of the turbines, are consortium members:

- Omega Progetti SpA
- Iniziative Industriali SpA

Both represent major engineering and plant construction firms in the Italian market. They have participated in different project financing initiatives at an international level in partnership with the largest world contractors.

The construction agreement includes the following provisions:

- A fixed, unchangeable turnkey price equal to about 1.100 billion lire
- Wraparound responsibility for the technology chosen by the sponsors and based on the license of American Petroleum Co.
- A guarantee on project performance (minimum performance standards)
- A guarantee on completion time (40-month construction period)

The performance guarantee refers to a minimum performance standard (MPS) of 95%. The first plant test can be carried out either with the feedstock produced by the deasphalting plant or with a number of alternative feedstocks compatible with the plant. An independent technical consultant will have to certify that the plant has passed the performance test, specifying the feedstock used.

The performance guarantee is backed up by a performance bond that covers 20% of the value of the works. In case of failure to reach the MPS, the constructors' consortium will pay penalties calculated proportionately to construction delays. The consortium guarantees that the operational conditions of the plant will be maintained after the plant performance tests, and this guarantee will be valid for the entire year following the end of plant construction.

The following expenses are not taken on by the contractors' consortium:

- The creation of the 70-km power line needed to connect the plant to the national power grid
- Construction permits
- Work authorization

Any delay in obtaining permits and authorization forces Cogeneration to allow the possibility of postponing plant delivery after the initially agreed-on termination date without paying liquidated damages.

C1.4.2   Deasphalting Plant Construction Agreement

The construction agreement for the plant to treat raw materials is also signed by the lead manager consortium, Gamma, at the same conditions relating to Cogeneration:

- Fixed price (100 billion lira)
- Performance guarantee
- Guarantee of completion time
- Clause specifying the coordination between completion of the Cogeneration structure and the conclusion of works on the deasphalting plant

Through the coordination clause, the constructors' consortium is committed to completing the deasphalting plant on time for the start of Cogeneration operations. This coordination implies that the deasphalting plant must be completed before (or simultaneously with) the cogeneration facility so as to enable Cogeneration to produce power with the tar provided by Alfa.

C1.4.3   Operation and Maintenance Agreement

This contract is signed between Cogeneration and Cogeneration Service SpA, an ad hoc company set up by Alfa and ME Energy Corp. with the same allocation of equity capital as Cogeneration.

The following guarantees given:

- Plant performance
- A step-in clause in favor of the financiers

Failure to reach the agreed-on performance level leads to the payment of penalties proportional to the damages caused to the vehicle company.

C1.4.4   Energy Sale Agreement/Power Purchase Agreement

The energy sale agreement will be signed by ENEL in a few months on a 20-year basis. This is a preliminary agreement; a definitive contract will be signed at a later date.

The price paid is based on a capacity charge and an energy charge (covering the avoided cost for the plant construction and the cost of fuel, respectively), to which an incentive is added for the first 8 years of operations on the basis of CIP6 regulation (CIP—Interdepartmental Committee on Prices of the Ministry of the Economy).

C1.4.5   Steam Purchase Agreement

Alfa SpA has agreed to buy the steam for a 20-year period and has contracted for the purchase of preset volumes of by-products at fixed prices.

C1.4.6   Feedstock Supply Agreement

Alfa SpA will serve as supplier of the tar to be treated in the deasphalting plant and is committed to supplying this feedstock for 20 years at fixed prices. Furthermore, anytime tar is not available, Alfa is obliged to provide an alternative feedstock chosen from among the following:

- Feedstock 1
- Feedstock 2
- Feedstock 3

The supply of alternative feedstock may be needed in two situations:

- When the initial test of the plant at the end of the construction period is carried out with the alternative feedstock instead of the tar (feedstock base)
- When, during the operational phase, Alf SpA is not able to supply the tar to Cogeneration

C1.4.7   Oxygen Supply Agreement

The oxygen supply agreement is signed by SIO SpA and provides for a multiyear supply of oxygen at fixed prices. The oxygen production plant that feeds the deasphalting plant is based on air liquid technology. The construction of this plant will be leased by SIO to a constructor yet to be defined. SIO's investment in the plant will be repaid through the sale of oxygen to Cogeneration.

C1.5   Financial Structure

American Investment Banking Co. proposes the financial structure for the project (data in billions of lira) shown in Table C1-1.

Equity will be provided by the sponsors at the end of the construction period.

Lenders are secured by the mortgage on Cogeneration plants, on all ancillary machinery, and by the pledge on the SPV shares as well.

The intention of American Investment Banking Co. is to structure a syndication with a strong presence of national intermediaries as coarrangers. The lead arranger, on the other hand, will have to be chosen from among banks operating at an international level that have the reputation and experience to give credibility to the operation.

TABLE C1-1   Sources and Uses of Funds for the Cogeneration Project (data billion lira)

Source		Use	
Total cost of structure	1,800	Equity	400
Cogeneration plant	1,100	Debt	1,400
Deasphalting plant	100		
Total sources	1,800		1,800

C1.6   Conclusion: In Arrigoni's Office

Arrigoni has analyzed the documentation that American Investment Banking Co. sent to Pieff Bank. He has consulted with some of his colleagues who work in the structured finance departments of big international banks in London.

Some elements are very clear to him; others are ambiguous. Also, support documentation is missing and some risk profiles are not well defined.

He is about to call Altieri, his director, and tell him that he doesn't totally agree with the summary report. His director needs to ask for some clarifications from the advisor.

CASE STUDY • 2

Italy Water System*

Introduction

In accordance with Article 37/bis of the Merloni-ter Law (the Italian law regulating public works and concessions to private partners), the sponsor XYZ—one of the leading construction companies in Italy—is bidding to be nominated concessionaire to design, build, operate, and finance the upgrading of the water supply and treatment adduction systems in southern regions of Italy.

C2.1 Business Plan of the Project

The business plan represents the basis for studying the financial feasibility of the project, taking into account the entire duration of the concession, which is 30 years, starting from the end of the construction period (2011–2040).

The project concerns the maintenance of the existing water system and the building and operation of two different sections (hereafter "1st section" and "2nd section"). The operational period starts by the first half of 2003 for the 1st section and at the beginning of 2011 for the 2nd section.

Life-cycle costs are planned during the entire concession.

The business plan contains the following parts:

- Summary sheet
- Capex analysis
- Water revenues sheet
- Energy revenues sheet
- Opex sheet

* This Case is by Stefano Gatti, Daniele Corbino, and Alessandro Steffanoni.

- Profit and loss
- Working capital sheet
- Cash flow statement
- Public grant sheet
- Senior facility sheet
- Balance sheet

C2.2   Assumptions

The business plan has been developed using assumptions based on Engineering Department estimates ("1st section" and "2nd section" Capex) and forecasts on the operational phase (water volume and tariffs, power generation and tariffs, O&M costs, and authority fees).

All the sheets and statements are compiled on an annual basis.

C2.2.1   Timing

The concession started on January 1, 2006, and runs for a period of 34 years, until December 31, 2040. See Table C2-1.

TABLE C2-1   Timing of the Italy Water Project

Capex	Construction Period	Operational Period
1st Section	2006–2009	2010–2011 (1st delivery level)
2nd Section	2006–2011	2012–2040 (2nd delivery level)

C2.2.2   Inflation Index

The model utilizes the consumer price index for workers (CPI-W) issued by the Italian Statistics Institute to increment the water revenues and opex, assumed equal to 2% per year. Capex are calculated on 2003 figures and incremented by 2% per year. Energy revenues are incremented by 1.5% per year.

C2.2.3   Depreciation

The costs capitalized during construction are depreciated on a straight-line basis over the term of the concession, as stated in the Italian Tax Code in relation to the costs capitalized in a build, operate, finance, and transfer scheme.

C2.2.4   Interests and Financial Costs

The interest and financial costs of the facilities are detailed in Table C2-2.

Interest and financial costs are also calculated for the guarantee facilities released to cover the VAT reimbursement and grants received.

All the interest and financial costs accrued during the construction period are depreciated on a straight-line basis over the term of the concession.

TABLE C2-2   Terms and Conditions of the Senior and VAT Facility

Facility	Base Rate	Margin	Commitment Fee	Up-Front Fee
Senior facility	IRS 21 years plus credit margin	150 b.p.	70 b.p.	100 b.p.
VAT facility	IRS 8 years plus credit margin	100 b.p.	50 b.p.	100 b.p.

C2.2.5   Interest on Positive Cash Balances

Interest on cash balances (1.5% per year) is calculated on the free cash flow and debt service reserve account balance.

C2.2.6   Value-Added Tax (VAT)

VAT rates applied in the model are detailed in Table C2-3.

TABLE C2-3   VAT Rates for the Italy Water Project

	VAT Rate
Capex	20%
Water revenues	10%
Energy revenues	20%
Opex	20%
Authority fee	10%

C2.2.7   Taxes

The tax assumptions are described in the following subsections.

C2.2.7.1   IRES (Corporate Income Tax)

IRES is calculated at a rate of 33%. The tax payable position is applied against earnings (EBT) in the profit and loss account.

Tax losses in the 3 years following the establishment of the concessionaire (January 1, 2006) are assumed to be available without restriction. Any tax losses incurred after this must be utilized within 5 years. It is presumed that any tax losses incurred after the initial 3-year period will be the initial source of tax losses used to offset taxable profit. Only after all the temporary tax losses have been exhausted, will the taxable profit in the period be reduced by losses eligible for indefinite carry-forward.

C2.2.7.2   IRAP (Regional Tax on Productive Activities)

IRAP is calculated at a rate of 4.25% and applied against earnings (EBT). The exception is that, unlike IRES, financial costs and personnel costs are not considered deductible expenses.

The loss calculations do not apply to the IRAP calculation.

Taxes are paid based on taxes calculated for the previous year.

C2.2.8   Working Capital

The model records the accrual position in order to capture accurately the cash balance of the concessionaire at the end of each year and makes an adjustment for the impact of accounts payable and receivables. The payment terms for each of the revenue and cost categories are set out in Table C2-4.

TABLE C2-4   Working Capital Assumptions for the Italy Water Project

	Term
Receivables	
Water revenues	60 days
Energy revenues	60 days
Existing water system	60 days
Payables	
Water opex (no personnel)	60 days
Authority fee	60 days
Energy opex	60 days

C2.2.9   Debt Service Reserve Account

Cash flows accrued after debt service are used to fund the debt service reserve account. Throughout the duration of the senior facility repayment period, the balance of the DSRA is maintained at a level equal to the forecast debt service requirement for the following year.

The opening balance of DSRA is funded with the final drawdown of the senior facility at the end of the availability period.

C2.3   Capital Expenditure

The total amount of the capital expenditure is 1,120,737 euro split in the two sections as follows:

- 1st section Capex (610,669 million euro)
- 2nd section Capex (506,068 million euro)

During the operational period there are 49.127 million euro of life-cycle costs, depreciated on a straight-line basis during the residual part of the concession period. The capital expenditure breakdown is detailed in Table C2-5.

C2.4   Financial Requirement and Sources of Financing

The construction costs timetable runs from 2006 to 2011.

TABLE C2-5   Capital Expenditures for the Italy Water Project

	Amount (keuro)	%
1st Section		
Capex 1	260,687	22.3
Doubling YYYY	134,551	11.5
Potable Water System YYYY	143,332	12.3
Design and other costs	64,445	5.5
Expropriation	11,653	1.0
TOTAL CAPEX 1st Section	614,668	52.5
2nd Section		
Capex 2	80,417	6.9
Doubling XXXX	91,414	7.8
Potable Water System XXXX	259,548	22.2
Design and other costs	51,352	4.4
Expropriation	23,337	2.0
TOTAL CAPEX 2nd Section	506,068	43.3
Total Capex	1,120,736	95.8
Life-cycle cost	49,127	4.2
Total investment	1,169,863	100.0

The financial requirement at the end of the construction period (2011) is set out in Table C2-6.

TABLE C2-6   Uses of Funds for the Italy Water Project

	Amount (keuro)	%
Capex		
1st section	614,669	43.6
2nd section	506,068	35.9
Total Capex	1,120,737	79.6
Financial fee	5,723	0.4
Capitalized interest	111,814	7.9
DSRA	19,039	1.4
Change in working capital	2,877	0.2
VAT (2006–2011)	148,269	10.5
Total uses	1,408,459	100.0

C2.4.1   Financial Sources

The financial sources are listed in Table C2-7.

C2.4.1.1   Debt Facility

Senior-term loan facility, a long-term facility of 361.729 million euro to finance part of the costs of the project (Capex, interest, and financial costs, development costs).

TABLE C2-7   Sources of Funds for the Italy Water Project

	Amount (keuro)	%
Loan		
Senior facility	361,729	25.7
VAT facility	22,370	1.6
Total Loan	384,099	27.3
Cash during construction	148,674	10.6
Public grant	616,405	43.8
Equity	133,382	9.5
VAT reimbursement (12/31/2011)	125,899	8.9
Total Uses	1,408,459	100.0

The availability period is from 2006 to 2011, and the facility is withdrawn according to the schedule given in Table C2-8.

The tenor of the facility is 21 years, and the repayment period is scheduled over 15 years, from 2012 to 2027.

The repayment schedule is tailored to the annual operating cash flow, net of taxes paid, the working capital requirement, and life-cycle costs of the period.

TABLE C2-8   Timing of the Senior Facility Withdrawals

Year						
2006	2007	2008	2009	2010	2011	Total
10%	25%	43%	9%	10%	3%	100.0%

C2.4.1.2   VAT Revolving Facility

The VAT facility is used to finance the VAT deficit incurred during the construction period.

VAT costs are offset by the VAT grant payables.

VAT on the capital spent is to be reimbursed in the 2 years following that in which the VAT capital expenditures are initially paid; all reimbursements are used to repay the VAT facility.

Interest and financial costs on the VAT facility are capitalized during the construction period.

C2.4.1.3   Guarantee Facility

- **Grant guarantee facility:** As stated in Article 37-quinquies of the Merloni Law, the concessionaire is obligated to provide a grant guarantee to cover all sums received by the authority pertaining to the concession. This facility is provided by the bank.
- **VAT guarantee facility:** Drawdowns are made on the facility during construction. Any VAT reimbursement during operations is also included in this calculation. Release of the guarantee facility is made 3 years after the reimbursement of VAT by the fiscal authority.

C2.4.1.4 Equity

Equity amount injected by the sponsor is about 133 million euro on a pro-rata basis with the senior facility. This covers 9.5% of the total capital expenses and is based on a gearing ratio of 26:84.

C2.4.1.5 Public Grants

Public grants represent 55% of the capital expenditures, equaling 616.405 million euro. The grant is drawn during the construction period on an annual basis and depreciated during the entire duration of the concession.

C2.4.1.6 Cash Flow During Construction

After the completion of the 1st section, the water system is able to deliver 120 mc of additional water. In this way, during the construction period (2009–2011) the concessionaire generates cash flow to reduce the financial requirement.

C2.5   Operational Period

The operational phase takes into account all the revenues and costs of operations of:

- The existing water system
- The new water supply and treatment systems
- The two hydroelectric plants

Starting from the end of the 2nd section, the EBITDA remains constant. Revenues and costs of the operation of the water system are incremented according to the annual ISTAT Index, while energy revenues are incremented 1.5% annually.

The breakdown of the EBITDA is given next.

C2.5.1   Operation of the Existing Water System

The concessionaire takes over operation of the existing water system during the first half of 2009.

The 1st level of nonpotable water delivered is 239 million mc per year instead of the 209 million mc currently delivered by the existing system.

The 1st annual level of potable water delivered is 213 million mc per year instead of the 123 million mc currently delivered by the existing system.

The tariffs applied are as shown in Table C2-9.

The operational expenses are 43 million (2011 value) euro per year, starting from 2009. The concessionaire must pay an annual fee of 5 million euro to the authority.

TABLE C2-9   Water Tariffs for the Italy Water Case

Potable water	0 €/1,000 mc (calculated on the Dec. 31, 2003, value)
Nonpotable water	200 €/1,000 mc (calculated on the Dec. 31, 2003, value)

C2.5.2   Operation of the New Water Supply and Treatment Systems

The project reaches its maximum water capacity at the end of the 2nd section construction period. In this phase, part of the water is delivered to the authority's offtaker (potable water), while the rest is delivered directly to industrial and agricultural users (nonpotable water).

Table C2-10 shows the level of water delivered and relative tariffs starting from the end of the 2nd section construction period.

Operational expenses for 2009 are listed in Table C2-11.

TABLE C2-10   Additional Water Delivered (million mc/yr) and Tariffs

	2009	2010	2011
Nonpotable water			
Tariff: 0 €/1,000 mc (Dec. 31, 2003)	30	30	40
Potable water			
Tariff: 300 €/1,000 mc (Dec. 31, 2003)	90	90	170
Total additional water delivered	**120**	**120**	**210**

Total Additional Water Delivered (million mc/year)

Potable	Nonpotable
293	249

TABLE C2-11   Operational Costs Breakdown

	1st Section Water System	2nd Section Water System
Personnel	100 employees	130 employees
Annual unit cost	€60.480	
Opex		
Drinkable system	60 euro per 1,000 mc of water delivered	
Maintenance	0.5% of Capex	
Other services	1.549 million euro per year	2.066 million euro per year
General expenses	5% of maintenance and personnel	

C2.5.3   Operation of the Two Hydroelectric Plants

The two hydroelectric plants produce about 84.89 GWh/year and sell energy at the tariffs listed in Table C2-12.

TABLE C2-12   Revenues from Sales of Energy from Hydroelectric Plants

Tariffs	Value 2009 (thousands of euro/GWh)	Power Generation (GWh/year)
1st component of the tariff	62	26.23
2nd component of the tariff	69	58.66
"Green Certificate"	82	84.89

"Green certificates"[1] are sold during the first eight years of power generation (2009–2016).

Operational expenses are 25.6 million euro per year beginning in 2009, and the concession holder must pay an annual fee of 5 million euro to the authority.

C2.6   Economic and Financial Ratios

- **Project IRR (Posttax):** This is calculated by comparing the value of the Capex (net of public grant contribution) and the operating cash flow of the project during the concession period (net of working capital requirement and tax paid).
- **Equity IRR:** This is calculated by comparing the equity injected by the sponsor, the dividends paid by the SPV to the shareholders, and the cash released at the end of the concession.

The financial feasibility of the project is calculated by using two significant ratios to verify the capacity of the cash flow to cover all the debt requirements during the life of the loan.

1. **Annual debt service cover ratio (DSCR):** This means, in relation to any given year, the ratio of:
   - Operating cash flow (net of tax paid)
   - Debt requirement (capital repayment plus annual interest and financial costs)

2. **Loan life cover ratio:** This means, in relation to any given year, the ratio of:
   - The aggregate of (1) the net present value of forecast operating cash flow (net of tax paid) from the calculation date to the final facilities repayment date, and (2) the balance of the debt service reserve account on the calculation date
   - Debt service (capital repayment plus annual interest and financial costs)

The results are as follows:

- Project IRR: 9.54%
- Equity IRR: 12.47%
- ADSCR (annual debt service cover ratio) has an average value of $1.51x$ and a minimum of $1.48x$.
- LLCR (loan life cover ratio) has an average value of $1.53x$ and a minimum of $1.51x$.

---

1. A *green certificate* is a tradable commodity proving that certain electricity is generated using renewable energy sources. Typically one certificate represents the generation of 1 megawatt/hour of electricity. Green certificates represent the environmental value of the renewable energy generated. The certificates can be traded separately from the energy produced. Italy uses green certificates as a means to make the support of green electricity generation closer to market mechanisms instead of relying on a heavier involvement of the public administration.

APPENDIX to CASE STUDY • 2

Structure and Functioning of the Simulation Model*

Introduction

This appendix serves as a user's manual for the financial model found on the CD-ROM included with the book. The file was designed as a support tool for the Italy Water case, presented in Case Study 2, and compiled on the basis of the variable values for the base case produced by the advisor.

The structure and breakdown of the financial model have been intentionally simplified with respect to real-life situations. Though assumptions are included that would not be found in actual transactions, readers can study the layout of the worksheets and slot in any variations to the model they consider appropriate. In this sense, the framework proposed here represents a takeoff point for constructing more sophisticated financial models.

This model was developed by using Excel 2000; the following procedure should be followed to set up this application.

1. Go to the *Tools* menu and click on *Add-ins*.
2. Activate the *Analysis tool pack* and the *Analysis tool pack—VBA* tabs.

Before opening the file of the model, readers should go to a blank Excel sheet and do the following.

1. Go to the *Tools* menu and click on *Calculation* under *Options*.
2. Activate *Iteration* and use the *Manual* tab.

---

* This Appendix is by Stefano Gatti, Daniele Corbino, and Alessandro Steffanoni.

341

This will prevent circular references from emerging, which otherwise would make it impossible to use the model. Also, relative results will be verified only after modifications are applied to sensitivities.

Every time a calculation is made, first press the F9 key.

A.1   Breakdown of the Financial Model

The model is divided into several interrelated worksheets. These can be classified as *input sheets* (where all technical, economic, and financial variables can be observed), *calculation sheets* (which break down and detail all input on a preset time horizon), *reports* (which give the results of the model), and the *balance sheets* of the project company. A graphic representation of the structure is provided in Figure A-1.

Readers can easily recognize the inputs for the model because they are written in *blue*. These data can be modified to run sensitivity analyses. Data in *black* and *green* (found only on the Assmpt. sheet) either are automatically calculated by the model or relate to input on project dates and can't be changed by readers. To prevent inadvertent deletion of a formula, the *black* and *green* cells are protected from accidental data entry.

The model is structured on a series of Excel sheets that readers can access by clicking on the corresponding tab located at the lower part of the screen. The sequence of the sheets is as follows.

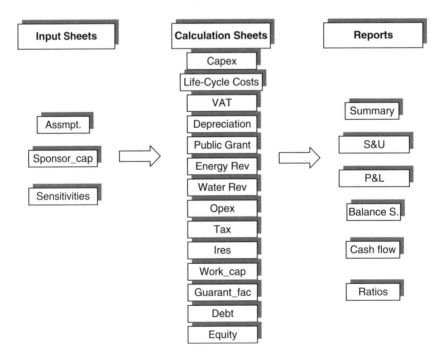

FIGURE A-1   Breakdown of the Model

A.1.1   Assmpt. (Assumption) Sheet

This sheet, accessed by clicking Input, contains all the main variables needed to compile consecutive sheets automatically. Readers simply modify the numbers in blue (after keying F9), and the model recomputes the figures in the other worksheets (Figure A-2).

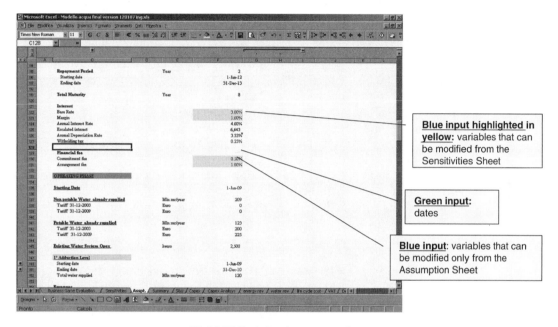

FIGURE A-2   Assumption sheet.

The inputs on the assumption sheet are presented in the following order.

- *Timing:* The duration of construction and operations can be changed as well as the start date for construction. The program automatically recalculates the completion date and start and end production dates. (In this case we recommend that readers verify that results are consistent with the new dates.)
- *Tax rates and macroeconomic variables:* Percentages of taxes (IRAP—regional tax on productive activities, IRES—corporate income tax) can be modified as well as figures relating to indices for inflation adjustments and revaluations on retail energy prices published by ISTAT, the Central Statistics Institute in Italy.
- *Data on direct and indirect investments:* As far as direct investments (turnkey plant, real estate, owner's expenses, and development costs), the amount and timing of payments can be changed. Capitalized financing charges, on the other hand, are computed automatically on the basis of values compiled in the sheets relating to cash flow loans and unsecured loans. Specific investment items are detailed in the *Sponsor_cap* sheet; the numbers on this sheet are automatically inserted in the Input sheet. *Therefore, readers can change the items on the Sponsor_cap sheet without modifying the figures on the Input sheet.*
- *VAT assumptions:* VAT rates can be modified with respect to investments, public grants, and concession fees, water and energy sold, and costs (excluding personnel). Moreover, the average time for VAT refunds can be changed. Next

the inputs relating to VAT financing are given, where only the pricing on the VAT Line can be modified.

- *Operations:* These are the key data that, through later reports, allow us to quantify the water supplied by the existing plant and the additional water resulting from the plant upgrade as well as the amount of energy produced yearly by the facility. Based on year-end 2003 figures, tariffs are estimated for water, both potable and nonpotable, and sales price of the energy produced and relative green certificates.

- *Data on fixed and variable costs of operations.* Readers can modify both fixed and variable costs pertaining to the water supply system (divided into the existing system, 1st water supply level, and 2nd water supply level) and the hydroelectric plants. They can also change concession fees for operating the water supply plant and the use of water for power production.

- *Working capital:* Assumptions were made pertaining to the average collection and payment time during operations.

- *Public grants:* The total amount of public funding is a percentage of the investment cost relative to the two sections of the works.

- *Equity:* The total equity injected on a pro-quota basis with the senior debt is a percentage of the financial requirements net of public grants.

- *Financing:* The total debt derives from the difference between the net financial requirement, the equity conferred, and the grants obtained. The pricing of financing can be changed, as can the annual percentage of loan reimbursement (from the Sensitivities sheet).

- *Unsecured credit line:* The total of the two unsecured credit lines (on grants collected by the concession holder and VAT refunds), issued by law, is a function of the investment curve in the case of grant guarantee and the refund profile for VAT credits. The pricing on the financing can be modified.

- *Debt service reserve account:* On the Assumptions sheet, we can change the percentage of cash available after payment on the senior debt earmarked for the debt service reserve account.

A.1.2 Sponsor_cap Sheet (Capex Analysis)

This is an input sheet which allows us to modify the timing and the total investments relating to the two sections (see Figure A-3).

Since investment costs are computed at 2003 prices, a capitalization rate is applied on the basis of inflation forecasts for the construction period. Clearly, any variation in these figures will also impact the total financial requirement.

A.1.3 Sensitivities Sheet

On this input sheet, readers can carry out sensitivity analyses on technical, economic, and financial input (see Figure A-4).

Where input is expressed in percentages (e.g., inflation, interest rates, public grants, equity) the sensitivity factor is added to the base case number. As regards other data (e.g., operating costs, the green certificate tariff), the sensitivity percentage represents the multiplier factor for the base case. We can also vary the debt repayment profile (in cells D131:D145) to ascertain the impact on the average loan life.

CAPEX ANALYSIS

Year			2006	2007	2008	2009	2010	2011	Total
Escalation Factor 2003			6.12%	8.24%	10.41%	12.62%	14.87%	17.17%	
1° Section									
CAPEX 1	keuro	238,914	23,891	95,566	119,457				238,914
Escalation (2%)	keuro	21,773	1,462	7,878	12,433				21,773
SAL %			*10%*	*40%*	*50%*				
Total	keuro	260,687	25,353	103,444	131,890				260,687
Doubling YYYY	keuro	123,313	12,331	49,325	61,657				123,313
Escalation (2%)	keuro	11,238	755	4,066	6,417				11,238
SAL %			*100%*	*10%*	*40%*	*50%*			
Total	keuro	134,551	13,086	53,391	68,074				134,551
Potable water System YYY	keuro	131,361	13,136	52,545	65,681				131,361
Escalation (2%)	keuro	11,971	804	4,331	6,836				11,971
SAL %			*100%*	*10%*	*40%*	*50%*			
Total	keuro	143,332	13,940	56,876	72,517	-	-	-	143,332
Design and other costs	keuro	59,231	14,521	19,991	19,990	4,730			59,231
Escalation (2%)	keuro	5,214	889	1,648	2,081	597			5,214
SAL %			*100%*	*25%*	*34%*	*34%*	*8%*		
Total	keuro	64,445	15,409	21,638	22,071	5,327	-	-	64,445
Expropriation	keuro	10,807	4,323	4,323	2,161				10,807
Escalation (2%)	keuro	846	265	356	225				846
SAL %			*100%*	*40%*	*40%*	*10%*			
Total	keuro	11,653	4,588	4,679	2,386	-	-	-	11,653
			6.12%	8.24%	10.41%	12.62%			
Total Capex	keuro	563,626	68,202	221,749	268,946	4,730	-	-	563,626
Escalation (2%)	keuro	51,043	4,174	18,279	27,992	597	-	-	51,043
TOTAL CAPEX 1° Section	keuro	614,669	72,376	240,028	296,932	5,327	-	-	614,669

FIGURE A-3   Layout of the Capex Analysis Sheet

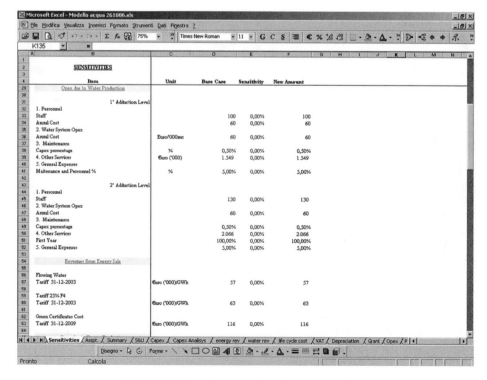

FIGURE A-4   Layout of the Sensitivities Sheet

A.1.4 *Capex Sheet*

This sheet summarizes investments, in terms of both costs relating to the construction phase and later investments (labeled *life-cycle costs*). See Figure A-5. On this sheet, if we wish to utilize cost increase sensitivity, we can verify the impact on costs.

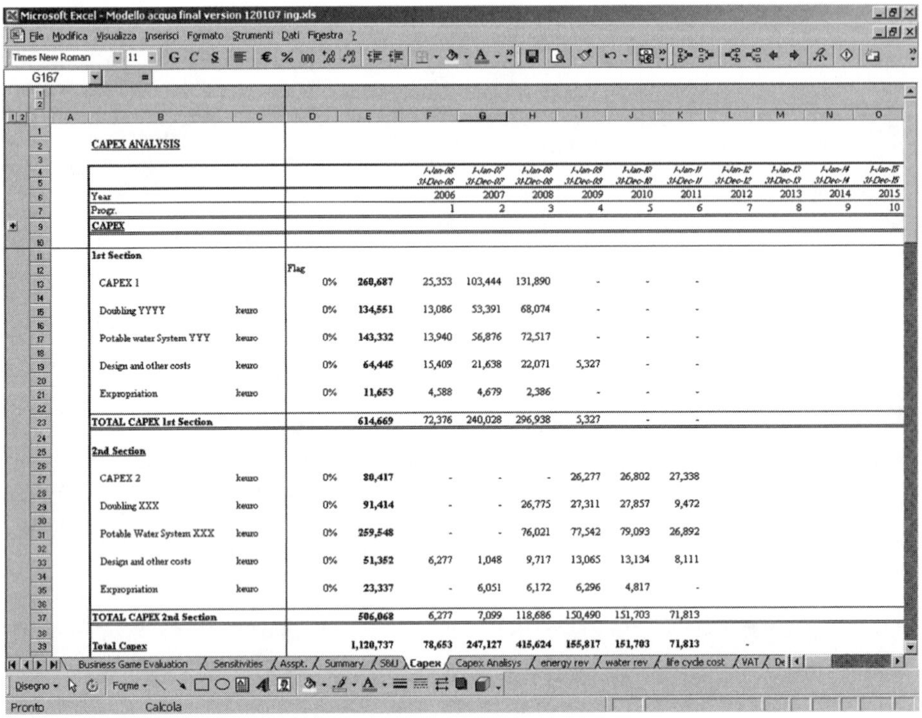

CAPEX ANALYSIS

				1-Jan-06 31-Dec-06	1-Jan-07 31-Dec-07	1-Jan-08 31-Dec-08	1-Jan-09 31-Dec-09	1-Jan-10 31-Dec-10	1-Jan-11 31-Dec-11	1-Jan-12 31-Dec-12	1-Jan-13 31-Dec-13	1-Jan-14 31-Dec-14	1-Jan-15 31-Dec-15
Year				2006	2007	2008	2009	2010	2011	2012	2013	2014	2015
Progr.				1	2	3	4	5	6	7	8	9	10
CAPEX													
1st Section		Flag											
CAPEX 1		0%	**268,687**	25,353	103,444	131,890	-	-	-				
Doubling YYYY	keuro	0%	**134,551**	13,086	53,391	68,074	-	-	-				
Potable water System YYY	keuro	0%	**143,332**	13,940	56,876	72,517	-	-	-				
Design and other costs	keuro	0%	**64,445**	15,409	21,638	22,071	5,327	-	-				
Expropriation	keuro	0%	**11,653**	4,588	4,679	2,386	-	-	-				
TOTAL CAPEX 1st Section			**614,669**	72,376	240,028	296,938	5,327	-	-				
2nd Section													
CAPEX 2	keuro	0%	**80,417**	-	-	-	26,277	26,802	27,338				
Doubling XXX	keuro	0%	**91,414**	-	-	26,775	27,311	27,857	9,472				
Potable Water System XXX	keuro	0%	**259,548**	-	-	76,021	77,542	79,093	26,892				
Design and other costs	keuro	0%	**51,352**	6,277	1,048	9,717	13,065	13,134	8,111				
Expropriation	keuro	0%	**23,337**	-	6,051	6,172	6,296	4,817	-				
TOTAL CAPEX 2nd Section			**506,068**	6,277	7,099	118,686	150,490	151,703	71,813				
Total Capex			**1,120,737**	**78,653**	**247,127**	**415,624**	**155,817**	**151,703**	**71,813**	-			

FIGURE A-5 Layout of the Capex Sheet

A.1.5 *Life-Cycle Costs Sheet*

This sheet provides a summary of investments during operations up to the year 2040 (see Figure A-6).

Life-Cycle Costs relating to the two work sections are shown in 4-year intervals and are recalculated with a "wear and tear" factor for the facilities and with the inflation rate applied to tariffs.

A.1.6 *VAT Sheet*

This sheet sums up VAT credit/debt management during the concession period (see Figure A-7).

During the construction phase, VAT credits are offset by VAT debts relating to collecting grants, while during the operational phase the company is in a position of deficit toward the VAT authority.

		E	F	G	H	I	J	K	L	M	N	O
	LIFE CYCLE COSTS											
		9	10	11	12	13	14	15	16	17	18	19
		2,014	2,015	2,016	2,017	2,018	2,019	2,020	2,021	2,022	2,023	2,024
1st Section												
	xxxx yyyy	895,536				895,536				895,536		
	Doubling YYYY	805,983				805,983				805,983		
	Potable water Syste	1,074,644				1,074,644				1,074,644		
2nd Section												
	Doubling XXX			559,030				559,030				559,030
	Potable Water System XXX			894,447				894,447				894,447
Total		2,776,163	-	1,453,477	-	2,776,163	-	1,453,477	-	2,776,163	-	1,453,477
cost increase for wear and tear 1,2%		1.012	1.02	1.04	1.05	1.06	1.07	1.09	1.10	1.11	1.13	1.14
	Sum	2,809,477	-	1,506,433	-	2,946,779	-	1,580,053	-	3,090,791	-	1,657,272
		-	-	-	-	-	-	-	-	-	-	-
Increase for revaluing by mc 2%		1.06	1.08	1.10	1.13	1.15	1.17	1.20	1.22	1.24	1.27	1.29
	Life Cycle Cost	2,981,439	-	1,663,223	-	3,384,922	-	1,888,310	-	3,843,010	-	2,143,858

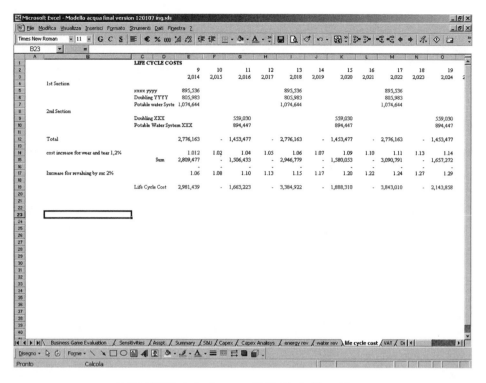

FIGURE A-6 Layout of Life-Cycle Costs Sheet

		E	F	G	H	I	J	K	L	M	N	O
VAT SHEET												
		1-Jan-06 31-Dec-06	1-Jan-07 31-Dec-07	1-Jan-08 31-Dec-08	1-Jan-09 31-Dec-09	1-Jan-10 31-Dec-10	1-Jan-11 31-Dec-11	1-Jan-12 31-Dec-12	1-Jan-13 31-Dec-13	1-Jan-14 31-Dec-14	1-Jan-15 31-Dec-15	1-Jan-16 31-Dec-16
Year		2006	2007	2008	2009	2010	2011	2012	2013	2014	2015	2016
Progr.		1	2	3	4	5	6	7	8	9	10	11
VAT Deficit												
CAPEX 1	keuro	5,071	20,689	26,378	-	-	-	-	-	-	-	-
CAPEX 2	keuro	-	-	-	5,255	5,360	5,468	-	-	-	-	-
Doubling YYYY	keuro	2,617	10,678	18,970	5,462	5,571	1,894	-	-	-	-	-
Potable water System YYY	keuro	2,788	11,375	29,708	15,508	15,819	5,378	-	-	-	-	-
Expropriation	keuro	918	2,146	1,712	1,259	963	-	-	-	-	-	-
VAT CAPEX	**keuro**	**11,393**	**44,888**	**76,767**	**27,485**	**27,714**	**12,740**	-	-	-	-	-
Design and other costs	keuro	4,337	4,537	6,358	3,678	2,627	1,622	-	-	-	-	-
GRANT VAT	keuro	(4,326)	(13,592)	(22,859)	(8,570)	(8,344)	(3,950)					
Operating VAT												
Grant Rate	keuro				2,478	3,043	4,856	4,953	5,053	5,154	5,257	5,362
Concession fee Rate	keuro				2,000	2,040	2,081	2,122	2,165	2,208	2,252	2,297
Water revenues Rate	keuro				(6,149)	(6,272)	(9,326)	(9,513)	(9,703)	(9,897)	(10,095)	(10,297)
Energy revenues Rate	keuro				(2,527)	(3,207)	(3,255)	(3,303)	(3,353)	(3,403)	(3,454)	(3,506)
Operating VAT position	**keuro**				**(4,198)**	**(4,396)**	**(5,644)**	**(5,741)**	**(5,839)**	**(5,939)**	**(6,041)**	**(6,144)**
VAT Receivables/(Payable)	-	**11,405**	**35,833**	**60,265**	**18,395**	**17,601**	**4,769**	**(5,741)**	**(5,839)**	**(5,939)**	**(6,041)**	**(6,144)**
VAT Reimbursement/(Cost)												
Average payment by VAT Authori	Year	2										
VAT Reimbursement/(Cost)	**keuro**	**0**	**0**	**11,405**	**35,833**	**60,265**	**18,395**	**17,601**	**4,769**	**(5,741)**	**(5,839)**	**(5,939)**
VAT FACILITY												
		1-Jan-06	1-Jan-07	1-Jan-08	1-Jan-09	1-Jan-10	1-Jan-11	1-Jan-12	1-Jan-13	1-Jan-14	1-Jan-15	1-Jan-16

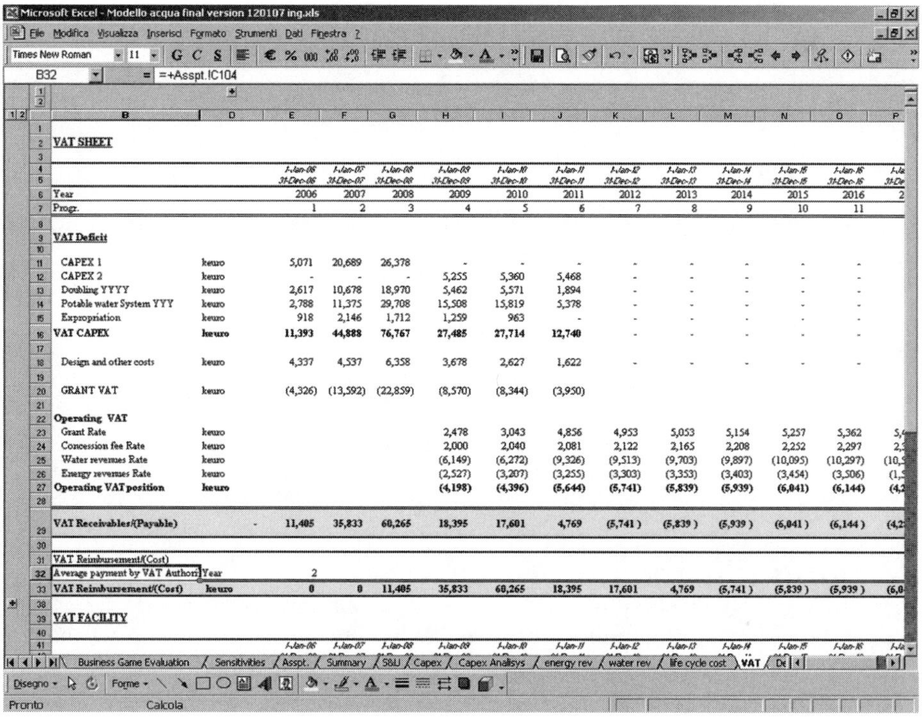

FIGURE A-7 Layout of VAT Sheet

VAT refunds are deferred for 2 years after the credit appears. In the second part of the sheet, the dynamic of VAT financing is shown; the use of these funds coincides with VAT credits accrued during the construction phase and reimbursements with relative income.

A.1.7 *Depreciation Sheet*

This sheet provides a summary of the concession amortizations (see Figure A-8).

The amortization of the total amount relating to the two sections begins at different times, there being two work phases, and ends when the concession expires. The same principle also applies for life-cycle costs, for which amortization starts the year after they emerge.

At the bottom of the sheet deferrals relating to public grants are reported.

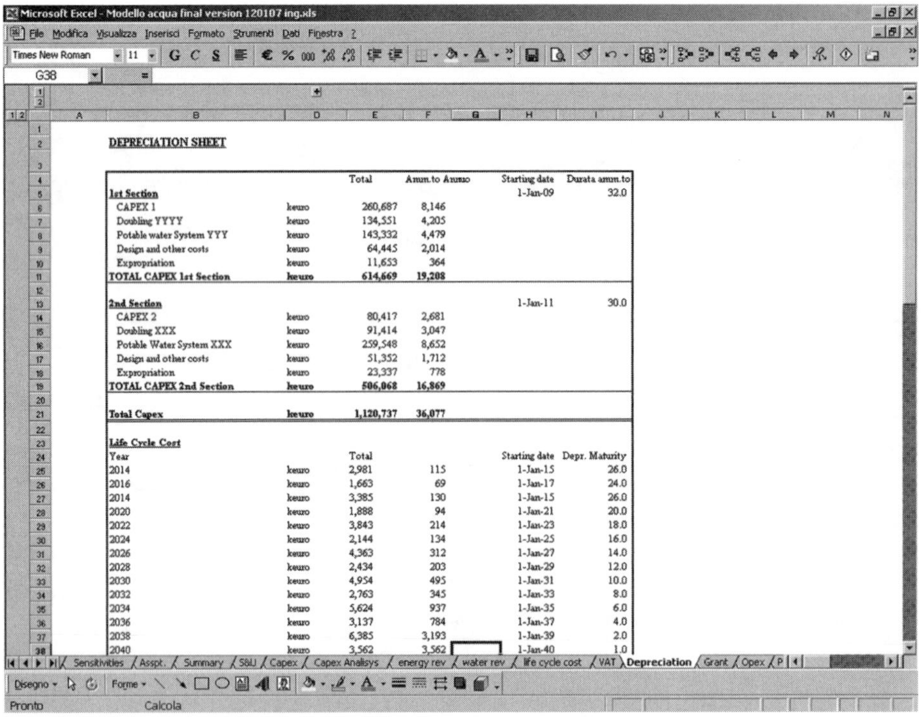

DEPRECIATION SHEET

		Total	Amm.to Annuo	Starting date	Durata amm.to
1st Section				1-Jan-09	32.0
CAPEX 1	keuro	260,687	8,146		
Doubling YYYY	keuro	134,551	4,205		
Potable water System YYY	keuro	143,332	4,479		
Design and other costs	keuro	64,445	2,014		
Expropriation	keuro	11,653	364		
TOTAL CAPEX 1st Section	**keuro**	**614,669**	**19,208**		
2nd Section				1-Jan-11	30.0
CAPEX 2	keuro	80,417	2,681		
Doubling XXX	keuro	91,414	3,047		
Potable Water System XXX	keuro	259,548	8,652		
Design and other costs	keuro	51,352	1,712		
Expropriation	keuro	23,337	778		
TOTAL CAPEX 2nd Section	**keuro**	**506,068**	**16,869**		
Total Capex	**keuro**	**1,120,737**	**36,077**		
Life Cycle Cost					
Year		Total		Starting date	Depr. Maturity
2014	keuro	2,981	115	1-Jan-15	26.0
2016	keuro	1,663	69	1-Jan-17	24.0
2014	keuro	3,385	130	1-Jan-15	26.0
2020	keuro	1,888	94	1-Jan-21	20.0
2022	keuro	3,843	214	1-Jan-23	18.0
2024	keuro	2,144	134	1-Jan-25	16.0
2026	keuro	4,363	312	1-Jan-27	14.0
2028	keuro	2,434	203	1-Jan-29	12.0
2030	keuro	4,954	495	1-Jan-31	10.0
2032	keuro	2,763	345	1-Jan-33	8.0
2034	keuro	5,624	937	1-Jan-35	6.0
2036	keuro	3,137	784	1-Jan-37	4.0
2038	keuro	6,385	3,193	1-Jan-39	2.0
2040	keuro	3,562	3,562	1-Jan-40	1.0

FIGURE A-8 Layout of the Depreciation Sheet

A.1.8 *Grant Sheet*

This sheet sums up the public grants collected during the construction phase pertaining to the two different sections (see Figure A-9). Construction costs are paid when relative grants are collected.

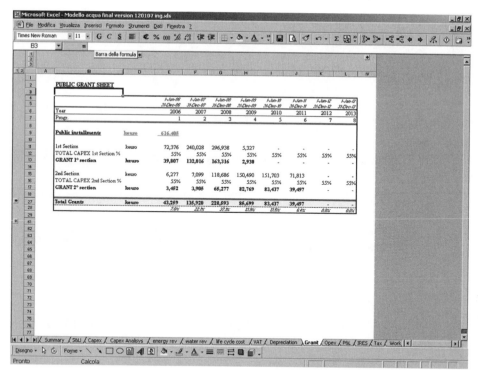

FIGURE A-9   Layout of the Grant Sheet

A.1.9   Energy_rev Sheet

This sheet provides a summary of revenues deriving from the sale of power generated by the two hydroelectric plants (see Figure A-10).

The revenue sheet is split up into three components, calculated as the product of energy produced, the tariff applied, and the annual escalation. During the first year of operations, the plants have a reduced production capacity of 80%.

A.1.10   Water_rev Sheet

This sheet summarizes the revenues deriving from the supply of potable and non-potable water (see Figure A-11).

The water revenue sheet is divided into two different types of water: potable and nonpotable. In addition, this sheet shows the different quantities and tariffs for water supplied by the preexisting system and by the supplementary plant. All tariffs are incremented annually on the basis of the forecast inflation rate.

A.1.11   Opex Sheet

This sheet provides a summary of operating expenses for the entire system. The revenue sheet is divided into two different cost items, relating to operating the water supply system and the hydroelectric plants (see Figure A-12).

ENERGY REVENUES

		1-Jan-06 31-Dec-06	1-Jan-07 31-Dec-07	1-Jan-08 31-Dec-08	1-Jan-09 31-Dec-09	1-Jan-10 31-Dec-10	1-Jan-11 31-Dec-11	1-Jan-12 31-Dec-12	1-Jan-13 31-Dec-13	1-Jan-14 31-Dec-14	1-Jan-15 31-Dec-15	1-Ja... 31-De...
Year		2006	2007	2008	2009	2010	2011	2012	2013	2014	2015	2...
Progr.		0	0	0	0	1	2	3	4	5	6	
Annual Escalation		0.0%	0.0%	0.0%	0.0%	1.5%	1.5%	1.5%	1.5%	1.5%	1.5%	1....
Tariff 1												
Energy	GWh/year	-	-	-	26.23	32.78	32.78	32.78	32.78	32.78	32.78	32.
Tariff 1	Euro ('000)/GWh	-	-	-	62.3	63.26	64.21	65.17	66.15	67.14	68.15	69.
Tariff 1 Revenues	keuro	-	-	-	1,635	2,074	2,105	2,137	2,169	2,201	2,234	2,2
Tariff 2												
Energy	GWh/year	-	-	-	58.66	73.33	73.33	73.33	73.33	73.33	73.33	73.
Tariff 2	Euro ('000)/GWh	-	-	-	68.89	69.92	70.97	72.03	73.11	74.21	75.32	76.
Tariff 2 Revenues	keuro	-	-	-	4,041	5,127	5,204	5,282	5,361	5,442	5,523	5,6
Green Certificate												
Energy	GWh/year	-	-	-	84.89	106.11	106.11	106.11	106.11	106.11	106.11	106.
Green Certificate	Euro ('000)/GWh	-	-	-	82.00	83.23	84.48	85.75	87.03	88.34	89.66	91.
Green Certificate Revenues	keuro	-	-	-	6,961	8,832	8,964	9,099	9,235	9,374	9,514	9,6
TOTAL ENERGY REVENUES	keuro	-	-		12,637	16,033	16,273	16,517	16,765	17,016	17,272	17,5

FIGURE A-10   Layout of the Energy_rev Sheet

WATER REVENUES

		1-Jan-06 31-Dec-06	1-Jan-07 31-Dec-07	1-Jan-08 31-Dec-08	1-Jan-09 31-Dec-09	1-Jan-10 31-Dec-10	1-Jan-11 31-Dec-11	1-Jan-12 31-Dec-12	1-Jan-13 31-Dec-13	1-Jan-14 31-Dec-14	3...
Year		2006	2007	2008	2009	2010	2011	2012	2013	2014	
Progr.		0	0	0	0	1	2	3	4	5	
Annual Inflation rate		0.0%	0.0%	0.0%	0.0%	2.0%	2.0%	2.0%	2.0%	2.0%	
Water supplied											
Total Non potable water	Mln mc/year	-	-	-	239	239	249	249	249	249	
Total Potable water	Mln mc/year	-	-	-	213	213	293	293	293	293	
Total	Mln mc/year	-	-	-	452	452	542	542	542	542	
Additional Non potable water	Mln mc/year	-	-	-	30	30	40	40	40	40	
Tariff	Euro	-	-	-	113	115	117	120	122	124	
Additional Non potable water revenues	keuro	-	-	-	3,378	3,446	4,687	4,780	4,876	4,973	
Additional Potable water	Mln mc/year	-	-	-	90	90	170	170	170	170	
Tariff	Euro	-	-	-	338	345	351	359	366	373	
Additional Potable water revenues	keuro	-	-	-	30,406	31,015	59,755	60,950	62,169	63,412	6
Non potable Water already supplied	Mln mc/year	-	-	-	209	209	209	209	209	209	
Tariff	Euro	-	-	-	-	-	-	-	-	-	
Non potable Water already supplied revenues	keuro	-	-	-	-	-	-	-	-	-	
Potable Water already supplied	Mln mc/year	-	-	-	123	123	123	123	123	123	
Tariff	Euro	-	-	-	225	230	234	239	244	249	
Potable Water already supplied revenues	keuro	-	-	-	27,704	28,258	28,823	29,399	29,987	30,587	3
TOTAL WATER REVENUES	keuro	-	-		61,488	62,718	93,264	95,129	97,032	98,973	10

FIGURE A-11   Layout of the Water_rev Sheet

Microsoft Excel - Modello acqua final version 120107 ing.xls

File Modifica Visualizza Inserisci Formato Strumenti Dati Finestra ?

Times New Roman 11 G C S € % ...

G167

OPEX SHEET

		1-Jan-06 31-Dec-06	1-Jan-07 31-Dec-07	1-Jan-08 31-Dec-08	1-Jan-09 31-Dec-09	1-Jan-10 31-Dec-10	1-Jan-11 31-Dec-11	1-Jan-12 31-Dec-12	1-Jan-13 31-Dec-13	1-Jan-14 31-Dec-14	1-Jan-15 31-Dec-15	1-Jan-16 31-Dec-16
Year		2006	2007	2008	2009	2010	2011	2012	2013	2014	2015	2016
Progr.		1	2	3	4	5	6	7	8	9	10	11
Annual Inflation rate		2.0%	2.0%	2.0%	2.0%	2.0%	2.0%	2.0%	2.0%	2.0%	2.0%	2.0%
Escalating Factor		100.0%	102.0%	104.0%	106.1%	108.2%	110.4%	112.6%	114.9%	117.2%	119.5%	121.9%
1° Adduction Level												
Personnel	keuro	-	-	-	3,209	6,547	-	-	-	-	-	-
Water System Opex	keuro	-	-	-	5,731	5,845	-	-	-	-	-	-
Maintenance	keuro	-	-	-	1,429	2,915	-	-	-	-	-	-
Other Services	keuro	-	-	-	822	1,677	-	-	-	-	-	-
					7,981	10,437						
General Expenses	keuro	-	-	-	560	849	-	-	-	-	-	-
Total Opex 1° level	keuro	-	-	-	11,750	17,832	-	-	-	-	-	-
					17580000							
2° Adduction Level												
Personnel	keuro	-	-	-	-	-	8,681	8,854	9,031	9,212	9,396	9,584
Water System Opex	keuro	-	-	-	-	-	11,262	11,487	11,717	11,951	12,190	12,434
Maintenance	keuro	-	-	-	-	-	5,355	5,462	5,571	5,682	5,796	5,912
Other Services	keuro	-	-	-	-	-	2,281	2,327	2,373	2,421	2,469	2,518
	keuro	-	-	-	-	-	18,897	19,275	19,661	20,054	20,455	20,864
General Expenses	keuro	-	-	-	-	-	1,379	1,406	1,435	1,463	1,493	1,522
Total Opex 2° level	keuro	-	-	-	-	-	28,957	29,536	30,127	30,729	31,344	31,971
Water opex												

Sensitivities / Asspt. / Summary / S&U / Capex / Capex Analysys / energy rev / water rev / life cycle cost / VAT / Depreciation / Grant / Opex / P

Disegno Forme

Pronto   Calcola

FIGURE A-12   Layout of the Opex (Operating Expenses) Sheet

In addition, the fees paid to the authority for operating the aqueduct and for energy production are shown. All costs are revalued annually on the basis of the forecast inflation rate.

A.1.12   P&L (Profit and Loss) and SP (Balance Sheet)

These sheets provide a synthesis of the annual profit and loss account and the balance sheet for the project (see Figure A-13).

Since all costs, interest and financial charges are capitalized for each section for the first three years of construction, the concession holder has a net profit of zero.

A.1.13   IRES (Italian Corporate Income Tax) and Tax Sheets

These sheets are used to calculate taxes paid by the concession holder on an accrual and a cash basis (see Figure A-14).

The IRES sheet allows us to compute the amount due from the concession holder for this tax based on the fact that since it is a newly founded company, for the first 3 years losses can be completely compensated. After that time, losses can be offset with taxable income only in the following 5 years.

Once the IRES due is computed on the previous sheet, the Tax sheet makes it possible to calculate accrued IRAP (regional tax on productive activities) and to frame the fiscal charges during the concession period.

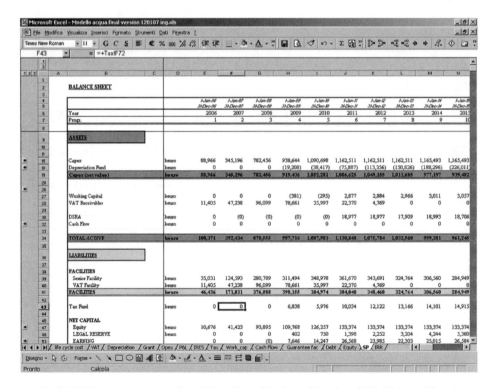

FIGURE A-13   Layout of the P&L Sheet (Profit and Loss) and SP (Balance Sheet)

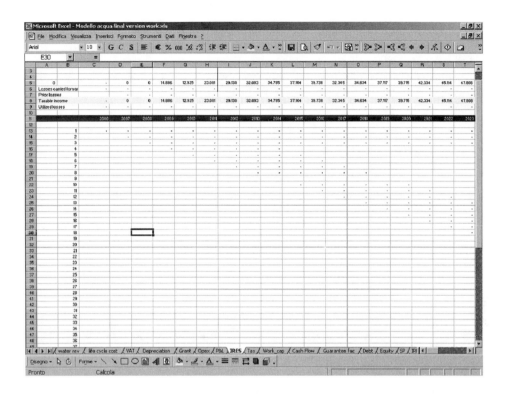

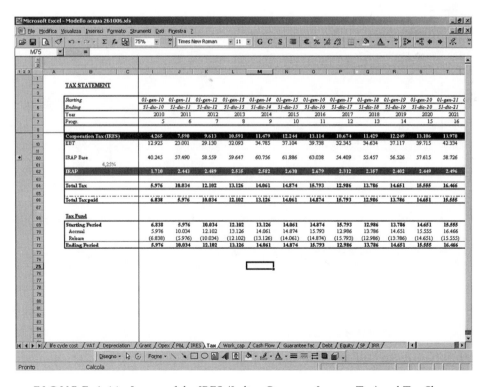

F I G U R E A-14   Layout of the IRES (Italian Corporate Income Tax) and Tax Sheets

As this is a model set up on an annual basis, for simplicity's sake we assume that the taxes accrued for the year in question are paid in full by the cash flow from the following year.

This is why at the bottom of the Tax Sheet the Tax Fund is calculated, representing the fiscal debts flows which rise at the end of the current year, and then ebb in the year they are paid off in cash.

A.1.14 *Work_cap Sheet*

This is the sheet that enables readers to ascertain the impact of fluctuations in working capital on the cash flow of the concession holder (see Figure A-15).

This calculation is based on policies regarding payments to suppliers and revenues for water supply and hydroelectric energy production. In fact, supply credits are reckoned on the basis of average payment time, and supply debts are figured on the timing for payment of operating costs (excluding personnel costs). The value of working capital is computed at the bottom of the Work_cap sheet. A positive (negative) variation would temporarily drain (confer) liquidity to the concession holder.

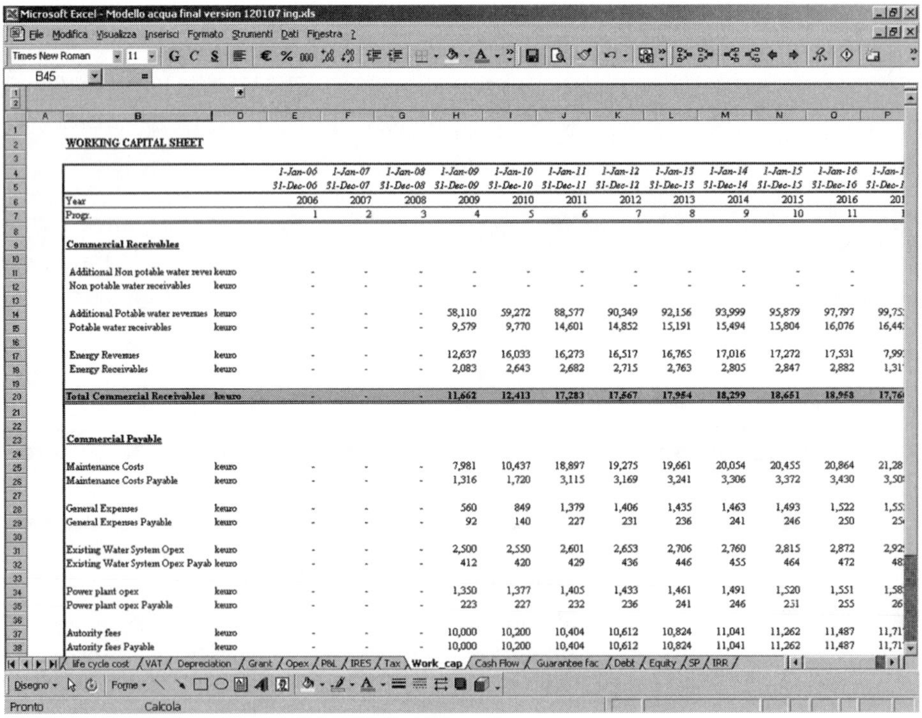

WORKING CAPITAL SHEET

		1-Jan-06	1-Jan-07	1-Jan-08	1-Jan-09	1-Jan-10	1-Jan-11	1-Jan-12	1-Jan-13	1-Jan-14	1-Jan-15	1-Jan-16	1-Jan-1
		31-Dec-06	31-Dec-07	31-Dec-08	31-Dec-09	31-Dec-10	31-Dec-11	31-Dec-12	31-Dec-13	31-Dec-14	31-Dec-15	31-Dec-16	31-Dec-1
Year		2006	2007	2008	2009	2010	2011	2012	2013	2014	2015	2016	201
Progr.		1	2	3	4	5	6	7	8	9	10	11	1
Commercial Receivables													
Additional Non potable water revei	keuro	-	-	-	-	-	-	-	-	-	-	-	
Non potable water receivables	keuro	-	-	-	-	-	-	-	-	-	-	-	
Additional Potable water revenues	keuro	-	-	-	58,110	59,272	88,577	90,349	92,156	93,999	95,879	97,797	99,75
Potable water receivables	keuro	-	-	-	9,579	9,770	14,601	14,852	15,191	15,494	15,804	16,076	16,44
Energy Revenues	keuro	-	-	-	12,637	16,033	16,273	16,517	16,765	17,016	17,272	17,531	7,99
Energy Receivables	keuro	-	-	-	2,083	2,643	2,682	2,715	2,763	2,805	2,847	2,882	1,31
Total Commercial Receivables	**keuro**	-	-	-	**11,662**	**12,413**	**17,283**	**17,567**	**17,954**	**18,299**	**18,651**	**18,958**	**17,76**
Commercial Payable													
Maintenance Costs	keuro	-	-	-	7,981	10,437	18,897	19,275	19,661	20,054	20,455	20,864	21,28
Maintenance Costs Payable	keuro	-	-	-	1,316	1,720	3,115	3,169	3,241	3,306	3,372	3,430	3,50
General Expenses	keuro	-	-	-	560	849	1,379	1,406	1,435	1,463	1,493	1,522	1,55
General Expenses Payable	keuro	-	-	-	92	140	227	231	236	241	246	250	25
Existing Water System Opex	keuro	-	-	-	2,500	2,550	2,601	2,653	2,706	2,760	2,815	2,872	2,92
Existing Water System Opex Payab	keuro	-	-	-	412	420	429	436	446	455	464	472	48
Power plant opex	keuro	-	-	-	1,350	1,377	1,405	1,433	1,461	1,491	1,520	1,551	1,58
Power plant opex Payable	keuro	-	-	-	223	227	232	236	241	246	251	255	26
Autority fees	keuro	-	-	-	10,000	10,200	10,404	10,612	10,824	11,041	11,262	11,487	11,71
Autority fees Payable	keuro	-	-	-	10,000	10,200	10,404	10,612	10,824	11,041	11,262	11,487	11,71

FIGURE A-15 Layout of the Work_cap (Working Capital) Sheet

A.1.15 *Guarantee_ fac Sheet*

Here we calculate the guarantees that the law requires the concession holder to provide contingent to collecting public grants during the construction phase and VAT refunds from the Tax Office on credit accrued during this same period (see Figure A-16).

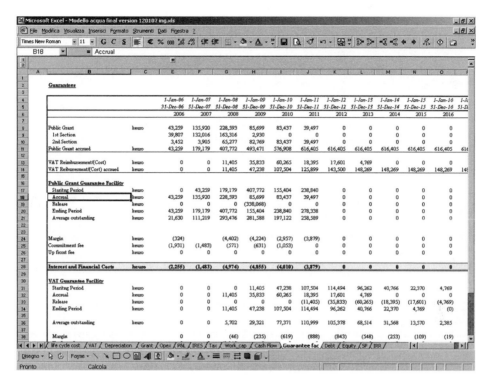

FIGURE A-16   Layout of the Guarantee_fac Sheet

The guarantee on the relative grants is partially decreased by 338 million euro at the end of the construction period for section 1 works, following partial acceptance of the works by the authority. Fiscal charges are also computed (margin + commitment fee in the case of the grant guarantee and margin + up-front for the guarantee on the collection of VAT credit).

A.1.16   Debt Sheet

This Excel sheet shows the dynamic of the senior debt; the time frame for the use and reimbursement of this money is based solely on project cash flows (see Figure A-17).

This debt is utilized over a period of 6 years (during the construction phase), while reimbursement, computed annually, spans the 15 years following construction.

Financial charges are calculated on the basis of the average debt for the period. This simplification is used because in project finance, drawdowns on the credit line are usually done monthly, while debt payments are made on a semiannual basis.

By using the average value, we attempted to moderate the temporal distortion that arises from the use of an annual model. The substitute tax is paid on every drawdown.

A.1.17   Equity Sheet

The Equity sheet is divided into two sections. The first serves to compute the equity injection by shareholders as a percentage of the total for works on the two

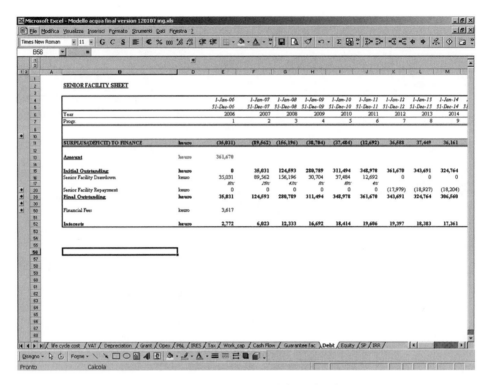

FIGURE A-17   Layout of the Debt Sheet

Sections.[1] In the second part a comparison is made between revenue that can be disbursed, net of that set aside for reserve funds as required by law, and cash available to shareholders, to ascertain the dynamic of the distribution of dividends (see Figure A-18).

The structure presented here shows no major cash trap problems, because until 2031 the concession holder can distribute the entirety of the cash generated by the project on an annual basis.

A.1.18   Cash Flow Sheet

The cash flow structure for the project is summed up on this sheet; the system of payments is called "cascade" or "waterfall." In fact, the project's operating cash flow is determined and then adjusted for the following: taxes to be paid in cash, any variation in working capital, the creation of a debt service reserve account, and the value of investments. Later, equity injections and public grants are taken into account and financial charges on cash credit and unsecured loans are subtracted. The next step is to identify the structure of the senior debt, which is used during the construction phase and reimbursed during project operations (see Figure A-19).

1. To calculate the level of the equity contribution made by shareholders, as a point of reference we also use the total cost of the works (net of grants), the total fiscal impact, and the effect of working capital, added to the total costs and financial charges attributable to the financial structure. Financial requirement = Capex − public grants + taxes ± change in WC + interest, financial costs, and debt service reserve account.

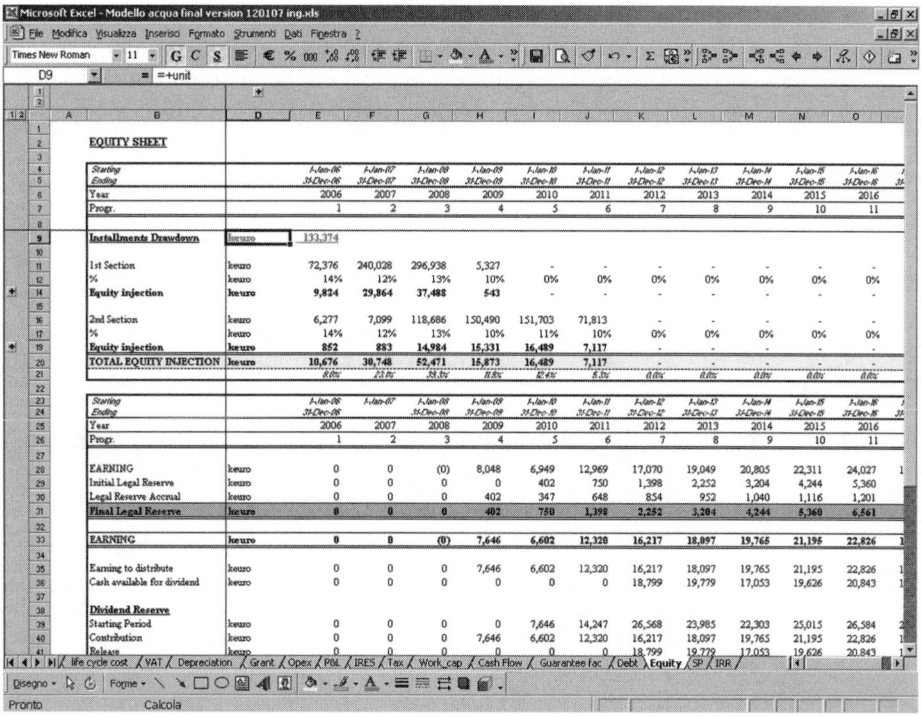

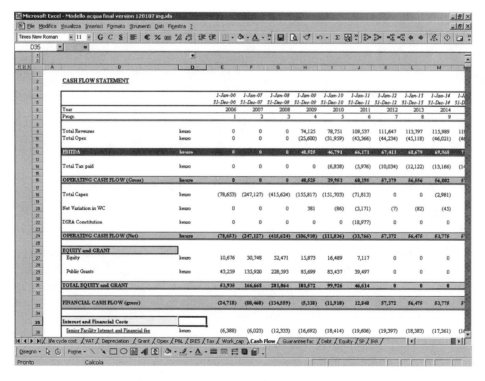

FIGURE A-18   Layout of the Equity Sheet

FIGURE A-19   Layout of the Cash Flow Sheet

After highlighting the dynamic of the debt service reserve account, the residual cash flow is earmarked for paying dividends to the concession holder's shareholders. When dividends cannot be distributed, this cash is put in reserve and released at the end of the concession, when the concession holder is dissolved.

A.1.19   IRR (Internal Return Rate) Sheet

This summary sheet details all the major economic and financial indicators for the project and the calculation methods for each. As regards project IRR (the internal return rate on the project), equity IRR (internal return rate for shareholders), ADSCR, and LLCR, refer to the section on Economic/Financial Indicators. (See Figure A-20.)

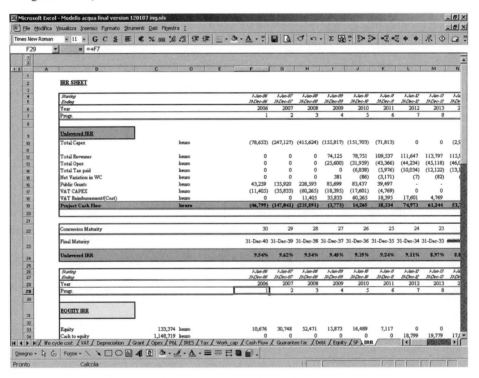

FIGURE A-20   Layout of the IRR Sheet

Two additional indices are calculated in the model.

- *Gearing ratio:* This represents the level of shareholder equity with respect to senior debt conferred by the banks during each period of the life of the loan.
- *PA calculator:* Our intention in using this indicator is to assess the return on investment for the public authority after cash outflows (public grants) and inflows (taxes and concession fees).

CASE STUDY • 3

Hong Kong Disneyland Project Loan*

We are investment bankers, not commercial bankers, which means that we underwrite to distribute, not to put a loan on our balance sheet.
—MATT HARRIS, Managing Director, Chase Securities

In 2000, Hongkong International Theme Parks Limited (HKTP), an entity jointly owned by The Walt Disney Company and the Hong Kong Government, began the process of raising HK $33 billion (approximately US $425 million) in the syndicated loan market to finance part of the construction and operation of its Hong Kong Disneyland theme park and resort complex. Syndicated loans involve two or more bank lenders united by a single set of legal documents for the purpose of providing credit to a borrower. In the case of HKTP, 32 banks participated in the syndicate and the deal was heavily oversubscribed. In this article, I discuss how Disney, acting on behalf of HKTP, awarded the mandate to lead the financing to Chase Manhattan Bank[1] as well as the bank's strategy for pricing and syndicating the loan among participating banks. Although I analyze a single transaction, it is representative of what happens in the global syndicated loan market, particularly the process Disney and Chase went through to raise the funds and the decision points they faced along the way.

The volume of global syndicated loans increased from US $413 billion in 1990 to US $2.195 trillion in 2000, making it not only the largest source of corporate funds in the world, but also one of the fastest growing. Yet despite the size of this market and its importance as a source of corporate funds, there has been relatively little research on syndicated lending or the intricacy underlying these deals. Most previous academic research into debt policy has focused on such topics as determining an optimal

* Reprinted with permission from Blackwell Publishing (2001). Structuring loan syndicates: A case study of the Hong Kong Disneyland project loan. *Journal of Applied Corporate Finance*, 14, 80–95.

1. At the time, Chase Manhattan and J.P. Morgan had not yet agreed to merge. They subsequently announced the merger on September 13, 2000, which eventually created J.P. Morgan Chase & Co.

capital structure, choosing between private bank debt (or private placements) and public bonds, or selecting among various loan features such as short vs. long term, fixed vs. floating rate, and cash pay vs. zero coupon debt.[2] Through this case study of the HKTP financing, I hope to move beyond the overly simplistic, albeit theoretically tractable, models of debt choice favored by academics and begin to explore the dynamics and consequences of various real-world debt structures. Rather than focusing on the credit analysis or documentation issues, I focus on structuring and distribution because they are less well understood and because they provide interesting insights into debt management. Before getting into the syndication process and strategy, I provide a brief introduction to the terminology and economics of syndicated lending.

C3.1   Background on Syndicated Bank Lending

Before delving into the details of the Hong Kong Disneyland financing, it is important to understand the generic process of loan syndication, acquire some basic terminology that will be used in the rest of the article, and describe the compensation of participating banks.[3] As mentioned above, syndication joins two or more banks under a common set of legal documents. The obligations are several in nature; individual banks are not responsible for other banks' obligations. Nor are commitment amounts necessarily equal across participating banks; instead, banks share funding, repayment, and certain fees on a prorata basis according to their original level of participation.

Banks participate in the syndicated loan market for different reasons. Arranging banks, which are typically more interested in generating fee income, seek to structure and lead transactions. Participating banks, those interested primarily in generating loan assets while staying within regulatory constraints on leverage and loan size, seek to diversify credit exposures to particular borrowers, industries, or countries as well as to make loans in markets where they lack origination capabilities. As one can see from this description, there are important differences between arranging banks and participating banks in a syndicated loan financing; this article focuses mainly on the arranging banks and their role in structuring transactions.

The syndication process itself consists of the following sequential events, and can take as little as one month in the case of an acquisition loan or as long as nine months in the case of certain structured loans such as a project financing. First, a prospective borrower selects a *lead arranger* to advise and manage the syndication process. In most cases, this *mandate* is awarded based on competitive bidding among the borrower's principal relationship banks or other banks with relevant expertise. At times, borrowers request that more than one bank share the lead mandate (*sole vs. joint mandates*) to maximize the chance of a successful syndication or to reward several banks with lead status and higher compensation. The lead arranger is responsible for negotiating key terms and covenants with the borrower, in addition to

---

2. See Barclay and Smith. "The Capital Structure Puzzle: Another Look at the Evidence." *Journal of Applied Corporate Finance,* Vol. 12, No. 1 (Spring 1999) and "On Financial Architecture Leverage, Maturity, and Priority," *Journal of Applied Corporate Finance,* Vol. 8, No. 4 (Winter 1996).

3. For a detailed overview of syndicated lending, see Rhodes, "*Syndicated Lending: Practice and Documentation,*" (London: Euromoney Books, 2000, 3rd edition).

analyzing credit quality—although each bank participating in the syndication is ultimately responsible for its own credit analysis and review of documentation.

When funding certainty is critical, borrowers often request *fully underwritten* bids, meaning that the lead arranger(s) must commit to provide the full amount of the loan on specific terms and pricing. The alternative is a *best efforts* bid in which the lead arranger agrees to underwrite some portion of the loan—typically the amount it is prepared to hold on its own balance sheet—and attempts to place the remainder in the bank market. The associated risks and returns are very different in these two kinds of deals. In a best efforts financing, also known as an *arrangement*, the borrower takes the risk that the market does not accept the deal and that it might have to pay higher fees or spreads to entice greater bank participation. In an underwritten deal, the lead arranger (also known as the *underwriter*) takes the risk that the market does not accept the deal and that it might have to book the entire loan amount. Although underwritten deals can be funded more quickly, the underwriting fee is generally higher to compensate the underwriter for greater credit and syndication risks. In practice, approximately 70% of deals are done on an underwritten basis. For "new money" deals—those that provide borrowers with new financing rather than refinance an existing loan—the rate is closer to 90%.

After awarding the mandate, the borrower and lead arranger execute a *commitment letter* that confirms key terms, duties, and compensation. The lead arranger then engages legal counsel to prepare an initial draft of the loan documentation. At this point, the lead arranger and borrower usually agree on one of two basic syndication strategies: a single-stage *general syndication* or a two-stage syndication with *subunderwriting*. In a deal with subunderwriting, the lead arranger and a small group of banks underwrite the full amount before offering shares to a broader group of banks. One can think of the subunderwriting as an optional, "wholesale" phase of syndication and the general syndication as the "retail" phase. The general syndication serves to distribute the loan to a bank group that is large enough to commit the desired amount but not so large that it becomes unwieldy. A supportive and cooperative bank group facilitates making changes to loan documentation when necessary, as when exceptions arise, which they almost invariably do during the life of a loan, or because financial problems create a need to restructure the loan.

Prior to general syndication, the lead arranger structures the syndicate in tiers according to commitment amounts, sets closing fees for each tier, and identifies which banks to invite to participate. Banks in each tier of the syndicate have titles based on their commitment amount. The most common titles are, in descending order of amount: mandated arranger, lead arranger, arranger, coarranger, lead manager, and manager. The banks invited to participate are not necessarily the borrower's relationship banks, but rather banks with syndication relationship banks, but rather banks with syndication relationships with the lead arranger. The lead arranger prepares and sends an "information memorandum" containing a detailed description of the borrower and the transaction to each bank. The lead arranger then holds a bank meeting to address questions about the deal, announce closing fees, and establish a timetable for commitments and closing. Invited banks are free to make commitments for any tier offered. The size of a bank's commitment is a matter of internal policy and varies based on factors such as the size of the bank, its internal credit policies on exposure to the particular client, country, or industry, and specific loan terms.

If the total commitments received equal the amount desired, the deal is said to be *fully subscribed*; if they exceed or fail to reach the target amount, the deal is said to be *oversubscribed* or *undersubscribed*, respectively. In either case, the lead arranger, often in consultation with the borrower, determines the *final allocations*. The commitments are based on credit approvals by each bank, and as such, the lead arranger cannot increase the amounts. However, the lead arranger has the right to scale back commitments at its discretion. Following closing, banks can and often do sell their positions. Such trading in the secondary market for bank loans is becoming more common as the pool of available loans grows over time.

Most large banks have a syndicated finance group that specializes in these deals. The syndicated finance group performs two key functions: *structuring*, which involves designing and negotiating deals with borrowers, and *distribution*, which involves marketing deals to other banks. The two functions must be closely coordinated because the deal that is presented to the borrower (structuring) has to reflect terms that are acceptable to the market (distribution).

The competition among banks to lead syndicated financings has prompted several financial publications to compile rankings, commonly referred to as league tables, to track leadership in the field. The market assigns the most importance to the Lead Arranger and Bookrunner titles. Usually the lead arranger also takes the bookrunner title, a title that refers to the activities in the later stages of the syndication process such as managing the prospective lenders through the credit approval process, setting the closing fees, and making the final allocations. These titles appear prominently on the cover of the information memorandum, in the financial press "tombstones" after closing, and in the lucite deal mementos that each lender receives. In addition to tracking arranger status (volume or number of deals arranged), league tables also track provider status (dollars lent).

Lender compensation comes in three forms. When the loan documents are signed, lenders receive *closing fees*—also known as *up-front* or *participation fees*—to compensate them for the work involved in due diligence and credit approval. Closing fees typically range from 20 to 200 basis points, with larger and/or riskier transactions commanding higher fees. Generally, project finance deals have higher closing fees than other loan types because they require more credit analysis and involve riskier positions given the non-recourse nature of the loans. After closing, borrowers pay *commitment fees* on any loan amount that is committed, but unborrowed, plus interest on the amount that is borrowed. Bankers refer to these loan amounts as the undrawn and drawn amounts, respectively. Commitment fees are typically 50 basis points or less per year. The loan's interest rate, at least for U.S. dollar loans, is usually set in terms of a spread over published inter-bank rates such as six-month LIBOR (London Inter-Bank Offered Rate). For loans denominated in other currencies, bankers sometimes use local interest rates. For example, Hong Kong dollar loans are often based on the Hong Kong Inter-Bank Offered Rate (HIBOR). In either case, the interest rate varies over time as the benchmark rate changes, even though the spread typically remains constant. Usually, one bank acts as the *administrative agent* for the syndicate, keeping track of borrowings and repayments as well as serving as the clearinghouse for interim cash flows. While the bank acting as the administrative agent can be one of the lead arrangers, it does not have to be one of them.

Arranging banks also receive compensation for structuring deals. In a best efforts deal, the borrower pays the lead arranger an arrangement fee for its services. At a minimum, banks charge approximately $100,000 to arrange a deal, though the average fee is more like $500,000. For larger and/or more complex deals, banks charge even more. In an underwritten deal, the borrower pays a single underwriting fee to the lead arranger/underwriter, which then retains some portion as compensation for its services and uses the rest as closing fees for banks participating in the syndication. The retained underwriting fee is usually quite substantial in relation to the underwriter's ultimate exposure as a lender in the deal. If the deal involves a subunderwriting phase, the underwriter keeps a portion of the fee and shares the rest with the subunderwriters; the subunderwriters, in turn, keep a portion of their fee (the subunderwriter fee) and use the rest to compensate participating banks with closing fees.

Table C3-1 describes the calculation of deal fees for a sole-mandated loan with subunderwriting. The example assumes a loan of HK $3.3 billion (the size of the Hong Kong Disneyland loan) and is based on an underwriting fee of 125 basis points as well as a subunderwriting fee of 125 basis points and top-tier closing fees of 70 basis points. (These are *not* the actual fees, which were not disclosed to protect confidentiality.) With these assumptions, total fees are based on the underwriting fee and equal HK $41.25 million (HK $3.3 billion × 125 bp). If Chase is the sole-mandated lead arranger and there is a group of four subunderwriters, the fees are broken down as follows. Participating banks receive 50 basis points for Lead Manager commitments of HK $100 million, 60 basis points for coarranger commitments of HK $150 million, and 70 basis points for "top-tier" Arranger commitments of HK $250 million or more. The subunderwriters, including Chase, receive closing fees of 70 basis points on their final hold positions plus underwriting fees of 25 basis points on the amount they underwrite (five banks each underwrite HK $660 million for a total of HK $3.3 billion). Chase keeps the difference between the underwriting fee charged to the borrower and what is paid to the subunderwriters. In this case, the difference is 30 basis points (125 bp underwriting fee – 25 bp subunderwriter fee – 70 bp closing fee) on the entire HK $3.3 billion.

The most complicated part of the compensation scheme is the calculation of "pool" income, even though it usually represents a relatively small fraction of total fees. The HK $1.0 million of pool income in this example represents the difference between fees available to pay participating banks, assuming all banks receive top-tier closing fees of 70 basis points (HK $23.1 million), and the actual fees paid to participating banks, which range from 50 basis points to 70 basis points (totaling HK $22.1 million). For example, the 20 basis point difference between the top-tier closing fee of 70 basis points and the 50 basis points actually paid to Lead Managers accrues to the pool and is split evenly among the subunderwriters. By adjusting the fee levels and commitment amounts, the subunderwriters try to attract enough banks to participate so that the loan clears the market. With this description as background, I now turn to the actual events surrounding the syndication of the Hong Kong Disneyland project loan.

C3.2   The Hong Kong Disneyland Project Loan

In December 1999, Disney and the Hong Kong Government signed a comprehensive agreement for a new theme park and resort complex to be located on the northeastern end of Lantau Island. According to the agreement, the project would have three phases. Phase I would include a Disneyland-style park with several themed "lands" featuring Disney rides and attractions, as well as one or two hotels and a retail, dining, and entertainment complex. Phases II and III were less well defined, but

TABLE C3-1   Calculation of Fees for a Sole-Mandated Loan with Subunderwriting

Loan amount ($HK millions) =	$3,300		Mandate =				Sole
Underwriting fee (assumed) =	1.25%		Subunderwriting =				Yes
Subunderwriting fee =	0.25%		$HK/$US exchange rate =				7.80
Top-Tier closing fee =	0.70%		Total underwriting fees ($HK millions) =				$41.25

		Initial UW		Sub UW	General Syndication					
	No. of Banks	Commit Amount (HKM)	Total Commit (HKM)	Alloc (HKM)	Invitation Amount (HKM)	Total Commit (HKM)	Percent Scaled Back	Final Alloc (HKM)	Total Alloc (HKM)	Alloc/ Bank (USM)
Chase	1	$3,300	$3,300	$660		$660	54.5%	$300.0	$300	$38.5
No. other mandated banks	0	$0	$0		$0	$0	0.0%	$0.0	$0	$0.0
Lead arrangers (Sub UW)	4			$2,640		$2,610	54.5%	$300.0	$1,200	$38.5
Arrangers	4				$250	$1,000	0.0%	$250.0	$1,000	$32.1
Coarrangers	4				$150	$600	0.0%	$150.0	$600	$19.2
Lead managers	2				$100	$200	0.0%	$100.0	$200	$12.8
TOTAL	15		$3,300	$3,300		$5,100			$3,300	

CALCULATION OF FINAL HOLD POSITIONS

HKM = Millions of Hong Kong dollars; **USM** = Millions of US dollars; **UW** = Underwriting.

Number of banks: Describes the number of banks at each syndicate tier. Chase, as the mandated Lead Arranger, has agreed to fully underwrite the HK $3.3 billion loan. In this scenario, there are four other banks with Lead Arranger titles with approved subunderwriting commitments (see below). The arrangers, coarrangers, and lead managers represent three descending levels of participation amounts in the general syndication.

Initial Underwriting: First stage of the syndication. Commitments held by the bank(s) initially responsible for underwriting the loan. Here, Chase underwrites the full loan amount.

Subunderwriting (optional): An intermediate stage of syndication in which the sole underwriter(s) subdivides the full underwriting amount among a small group of banks. The four Lead Arrangers each agree to subunderwrite $660 million. The exhibit shows Chase's subunderwriting commitment, and the total amount committed by all of the Lead Arrangers collectively.

General syndication: The final stage in which the underwriter(s) obtains commitments from additional banks in order to reduce the subunderwriting exposures to final hold positions. The columns show, in order from left to right:

• **Invitation amount per bank:** Chase invites the general syndication banks to offer loan commitments in defined ranges, from a maximum of HK $250 million down to a minimum of HK $100 million. The general syndication banks must get credit approval for a specific amount and submit formal commitment letters to Chase requesting participation at a specific level.

• **Total commitment for all banks:** Equals the number of banks times the Invitation Amount for general syndication banks; and the number of banks times the subunderwriting commitment for Chase and the other subunderwriters (Lead Arrangers).

• **Percent scaled back:** In the event a deal is oversubscribed, the commitment submitted or offered by any bank may be reduced or "scaled back" to reach the target loan amount. In this case, the HK $660 million subunderwriter commitments are scaled back to HK $300 million final hold positions. Other banks get the requested amounts with no scale-back.

• **Final tier allocation:** The per-bank commitment amount that has been accepted for each tier in the syndicate. This amount will be reflected in the final loan documentation and is the amount on which closing fees are calculated.

• **Total allocation:** This column shows the final allocations for each tier in the syndicate.

• **Allocation per bank:** The final allocations expressed in $US.

TABLE C3-1   (*Continued*)

	UW Fees	Closing Fees	UW Spread	Sub-UW Spread	Closing Fee Income	Poo Income	Total Per Bank (HKK)	Total Per Bank (USK)	Total for All Banks (HKK)	Total for All Banks (USK)
					Per Bank Income (HKK)					
Chase	0.30%	0.70%	$9,900	$1,650	$2,100	$200	$13,850	$1,776	$13,850	$1,776
No. other mandated banks			$0	$0	$0	$0	$0	$0	$0	$0
Lead arrangers (Sub UW)	0.25%	0.70%		$1,650	$2,100	$200	$5,950	$506	$15,800	$2,026
Arrangers		0.70%			$1,750		$1,750	$224	$7,000	$897
Coarrangers		0.60%			$900		$900	$115	$3,600	$462
Lead managers		0.50%			$500		$500	$64	$1,000	$128
TOTAL FEES									$41,250	$5,288

CALCULATION OF FEE INCOME

HKK = Thousands of Hong Kong dollars; **USK** = Thousands of US dollars; **UW** = Underwriting.

• **Fees:** This example assumes that Chase charges the borrower an underwriting fee of 1.25% (total fees equal the product of the 125 bp underwriting fee times the HK $3.3 billion loan amount or HK $41.25 million) and allocates fees to syndicate members based on their commitment levels. As the underwriter, Chase keeps 30 bp and gives 95 bp to the subunderwriters (including itself). The subunderwriters keep 25 bp on their subunderwriting allocation and give 70 bp for top-tier (arranger) commitments.

• **Underwriter spread:** This amount is Chase's primary compensation for acting as the sole mandated bank and underwriter. The HK $9.9 million equals 30 bp times the total loan amount (HK $3.3 billion).

• **Sub-underwriter spread:** The five subunderwriters (including Chase) each earn HK $1,650,000, or 25 bp times the subunderwriter allocation of HK $660 million.

• **Closing fee Income:** Equals the amount received by each bank based on its final commitment amount. See below for further information.

• **Pool income:** See below.

Calculation of Pool Income	General Syndication Closing Fees	Final Allocation (HKM)	Closing Fees per Bank (HKK)	Total Closing Fees All Banks (HKK)
TOTAL CLOSING FEE INCOME AVAILABLE	0.70%	$3,300		$23,100
Chase	0.70%	$300	$2,100	$2,100
Other mandated banks			$0	$0
Lead arrangers (Sub UW)	0.70%	$300	$2,100	$8,400
Arrangers	0.70%	$250	$1,750	$7,000
Coarrangers	0.60%	$150	$900	$3,600
Lead managers	0.50%	$100	$500	$1,000
TOTAL CLOSING FEE INCOME PAYABLE				$22,100
POOL INCOME (TOTAL AVAILABLE—TOTAL PAYABLE)				$1,000

CALCULATION OF POOL INCOME

Chase agrees with the subunderwriters to share equally in a pool consisting of any difference between the total closing fees available to be paid to member banks and the actual amount of closing fees paid member banks.

HKM = Millions of Hong Kong dollars; **HKK** = Thousands of Hong Kong dollars.

• **General Syndication Closing Fees:** The fees offered to each syndicate tier.

• **Total Closing Fee Income Available:** Equals the closing fee of 70 bp times the full loan amount of HK $3.3 billion.

• **Total Payable Closing Fee Income:** Equals the actual fees paid to each tier times the final allocation amounts for that tier. All banks earn the 70 bp closing fee or less in the general syndication.

• **Pool Income:** The difference between the Total Available Fee Income and the Total Payable Fee Income is split equally among the five subunderwriters (HK $1.0 million divided by five banks equals HK $200,000 per bank).

included options to develop adjoining sites at some point in the future.[4] Jon Headley, Disney's Director of Corporate Finance, described the development strategy this way:

> *Learning from our experience with Disneyland, the strategy for Hong Kong was to start small and then to add capacity over time as demand grew. In fact, Phase I included plans to double capacity within the first ten years of operations. The real keys to success are having the land available for growth and the ability to finance this growth out of operating cash flow.*

Because most of the construction site was currently ocean, the sponsors had to reclaim land. The Hong Kong Government agreed to pay for land reclamation and infrastructure development at a cost of HK $14 billion. According to the target dates, land reclamation would begin at the end of 2000, resort construction would begin in 2002, and the park would open for business in 2005. The Government supported the project because it expected the park to generate sizable public benefits. One local economist estimated that land reclamation and construction would generate 16,000 new jobs, while the resort would generate 18,000 jobs at opening and up to 36,000 jobs within ten years.[5]

A new corporation, Hongkong International Theme Parks Limited (HKTP), was created to construct, own, operate, and finance the project. It planned to raise the HK $14 billion construction cost from four sources (see Table C3.2)—this sum does not include an additional $14 billion of land value and associated infrastructure development contributed by the Hong Kong Government. The Hong Kong Government and Disney agreed to provide equity shares of HK $3.25 billion (57% share) and HK $2.45 billion (43% share), respectively. In addition, the Hong Kong Government agreed to provide HK $6.1 billion of subordinated debt with a 25-year maturity and repayments starting 11 years after opening day. This left a shortfall of HK $2.3 billion (16% of total capital), which the Hong Kong Government hoped to fill with some kind of external finance. Inclusion of private sector financing would not only show that the project was viable in the eyes of the international banking community, but would also provide independent oversight of construction as well as monitoring of ongoing operations. Eventually, HKTP decided to raise HK $2.3 billion through a 15-year, non-recourse term loan for construction and HK $1.0 billion in a 15-year, nonrecourse revolving credit facility for postconstruction working capital needs.

Because HKTP did not need significant construction funds until after the land reclamation was complete, it had the option of waiting until 2002 before raising the bank debt. By waiting, it could delay paying the commitment fees charged by the banks. Jon Headley noted:

> *Although we had two years in which to place the commercial loan, the Asian loan market was showing signs of recovery by early 2000. Knowing the structuring and syndication process could take six to nine months, we decided to start the process sooner rather than later. Our fear, given the recent volatility in the Asian banking market, was that if we waited until 2002, we might not be able to get a loan, never mind a loan with attractive pricing.*

---

4. The value of staged commitment in the context of venture capital organizations is illustrated in W. Sahlman, "Aspects of Financial Contracting in Venture Capital," *Journal of Applied Corporate Finance*, Vol. 1 (1988). The same benefits sometimes apply to large projects.

5. Tracy Yu of Standard Chartered Group, reported by Knight Ridder Tribune Bridge News, Sept. 11, 1999.

TABLE C3-2   HKTP Sources of Cash

		Amount (HK$ millions)	Percent of Total
Debt	Bank term loan	$2,275	16.2%
	HK government loan	6,092	43.3
	Subtotal	8,367	59.5
Equity	HK government	3,250	23.1
	Walt Disney	2,449	17.4
	Subtotal	5,699	40.5
TOTAL		$14,066	100.0%

Source: Chase et al., Hong Kong International Theme Parks Limited Offering Circular, September 2000. Excludes the estimated HK $14 billion cost of land reclamation and infrastructure development to be contributed to HKTP by the Government in exchange for non-participating, convertible stock.

Here Headley refers to the sharp economic contraction and credit crunch experienced in Southeast Asia beginning in late 1997: Hong Kong's GDP fell 5.2% in 1998, its unemployment rate doubled from 2.2% in 1997 to 4.7% in 1998, consumer prices fell, and the outstanding balance of commercial bank loans dropped by almost one-half. HIBOR, the Hong Kong inter-bank rate, spiked up from 6% in mid-1997 to 15% at year-end, and did not return to the 6% level until the second half of 1998. It was against this backdrop that HKTP, under Disney's leadership, set out to raise HK $3.3 billion of bank debt.

In April 2000, the Disney team developed a term sheet for the bank financing and contacted the company's primary relationship banks as well as other banks it viewed as having expertise in the HK syndicated loan market. In these discussions, Disney hoped to get a preliminary expression of interest and an assessment of current conditions in the Hong Kong bank market. Disney explained that they wanted to raise HK $3.3 billion in a nonrecourse loan package on a fully underwritten basis, and expected to select up to three lead arrangers for the transaction. They wanted a 15-year term, which was a potential stumbling block given that most banks prefer maturities of less than five years on emerging market loans. Finally, Disney wanted to use operating cash flow for expansion purposes and to pay its management fees and royalties ahead of debt service. Even though these two stipulations might pose credit issues for certain lenders, Disney was adamant that they be included in the term sheet.

It was highly predictable that Disney would contact Chase Manhattan Bank. In addition to being one of Disney's top ten relationship banks, Chase was the third largest bank in the U.S. and a leader in the third largest bank in the U.S. and a leader in the field of syndicated finance. The financial press had recognized Chase's leadership with numerous awards: Best Loan House of the Last 25 Years 1974–1999 (*International Finance Review*), Best at U.S. Syndicated Loans—1999 (*Euromoney*), and Best Project Finance Arranger in the U.S.—1999 (*Project Finance*). Disney met with Chase and 16 other banks to discuss the proposed term sheet in early May, and set May 16th as the deadline for first-round proposals.

Following these meetings, the Chase team had to decide how to bid on this mandate. Managing Director Matt Harris described their logic:

> *There are three ways to approach a deal: bid aggressively to win, bid less aggressively without fear of losing, and no bid. Although Disney is an important global client, the deal did not seem that attractive to us initially. It had a long tenor (15 years) which banks don't like, we had to contend with the problems at Disneyland Parts, the sponsors wanted to mandate as many as*

three lead arrangers which hurts our economics, and our competitors, especially the local banks like Bank of China and Hong Kong Shanghai Banking Corporation (HSBC), were likely to bid aggressively. And so, we decided to bid less aggressively without fear of losing. Yet to protect our reputation, we wanted to bid aggressively enough to make the short list for this high-profile deal. If we happened to win the mandate, it would have to be on terms that met our earnings thresholds.

Chase submitted its package on schedule and learned on May 25th that it, along with five other banks (HSBC, Bank of China, ABN-Amro, Citibank, and Fuji Bank), had been short-listed for the mandate. Disney instructed each bank to submit final proposals by July 19th.

As economic conditions in Hong Kong improved, with liquidity returning to the bank market, and as Government commitment to the project became clearer—the loan appeared more like "quasi-sovereign" credit rather than a pure corporate exposure—Chase became more interested in winning the mandate. The deal team knew, however, that they had to address several key credit and syndication issues before they could feel comfortable leading a fully underwritten transaction. With regard to the credit issues—long tenor, lack of collateral, no subordination of management fees, and an ability to use cash flows for project expansion rather than debt repayment—the team became comfortable with the credit risk after running various financial models. A key factor in their willingness to accommodate some of the unusual terms was the loan's seniority relative to other claimants and the fact that it represented only 16% of total capital. Based on an analysis of comparable transactions,[6] much the same way investment bankers price acquisitions, the team decided on a loan spread for the deal. Initially, the spread would be 100 basis points over HIBOR, stepping up to 125 basis points in year six, and to 137.5 basis points in year 11. Step-up pricing, a common feature on project loans, appeals to borrowers who want lower expenses in the early years and who plan to refinance before the step-ups take effect. It also appeals to lenders, who view the increases as compensation for longer maturities and greater future uncertainty.

The team also reviewed the syndication risks. The most critical decisions were whether to agree to fully underwrite the deal and how much to charge. Although a fully underwritten deal exposed the bank to greater risk, the team decided to seek senior management approval for a full underwriting as requested by Disney. Such a proposal would show Chase's support for the client, signal its confidence in the deal, and provide greater profit for the bank. It might also set Chase apart from other banks that were unable to commit to underwrite the full amount. As for the fee, they thought something in the range of 100 basis points to 150 basis points would be appropriate—for simplicity and confidentiality reasons, I assume the fee was 125 basis points. Harris commented:

If anything, we thought our fee might be on the high end, but we didn't feel bad about this for two reasons. First, we were not afraid to lose this deal on up-front pricing—we care about deal quality and profitability, not deal volume. Second, if properly marketed, borrowers viewed the up-front fees in terms of their annual cost, not the nominal first-year cost.

6. The benchmark transactions were two quasi-sovereign deals (Airport Authority of Hong Kong, 7/99; Mass Transit Railway Corp., 9/99), two project finance deals (Hutchinson Telephone Corp., 3/00; Asia Container Terminals, 1/00), and a corporate finance deal (Cheung Kong Finance Co., 12/99). In addition, they studied a number of regional deals that had closed before the Asian crisis.

As part of their final proposal, Chase did three things to improve the chances of winning. First, they added several creative elements to the deal. For example, they suggested splitting the revolving credit facility into two parts, a HK $250 million portion that would be available for construction cost overruns and a HK $750 million portion that would not be available until construction was completed. While the "available" portion would carry a market-based commitment fee of 37.5 basis points per annum, the unavailable portion would carry a discounted fee of 15 basis points per annum. Second, Chase provided regular market updates to Disney. And third, they presented two possible syndication strategies, one with and one without subunderwriting. In addition, they presented a list of target banks to show how the syndication was likely to play out and to illustrate their knowledge of the local banking market. Vivek Chandiramani, a member of the Chase deal team, described this process:

> The key to success in this business is being close to the market. This means being in touch with banks on a weekly, if not daily, basis. We started with a universe of approximately 90 banks and created a target lender list that might be interested in this deal. We then partitioned the target list into commitment size categories and assigned participation probabilities for each category. This process gives us a sense of liquidity and an indication of whether the deal will clear the market. Based on our analysis for the Disney deal, we expected it would be oversubscribed by 57%. This kind of analysis illustrates our closeness to the market and our confidence in the deal.

As instructed, Chase submitted its final proposal on July 19th, and was notified by Disney that it had won the lead mandate on August 10th. Jeff Speed, Disney's Vice President of Corporate Finance and Assistant Treasurer, said:

> We chose Chase because its pricing was competitive, it agreed to underwrite the full amount, and they showed a high degree of flexibility on structuring, particularly their willingness to permit ongoing capital expenditures without burdensome covenants.

Having won the sole mandate, Chase met with Disney to negotiate a commitment letter with final terms, discuss the syndication strategy, and map out a syndication timetable. As with any legal document, the content of a formal commitment letter invariably requires negotiation. From experience, Chase knew its standard "market flex" provision was likely to be one source of contention. The market flex clause that was presented to Disney read:

> Chase shall be entitled, after consultation with Disney and the Borrower, to change the structure, terms, amount, or pricing of the Facility if the syndication has not been completed due to a change in the Hong Kong Dollar market and if Chase determines, after consultation with Disney and the Borrower, that such changes are advisable to ensure a successful syndication of the Facility.

Although borrowers dislike the provision, Chandiramani argued for its inclusion particularly in the volatile Asian market:

> Chase was the pioneer in the use of market flex terms. It makes good business sense to include this clause, even though our competitors sometimes use it against us in competitive mandates, because things can change between the time you sign a deal and the time you try to close it. Unlike the "material adverse effect" (MAE) or "material adverse change" (MAC) clauses,

which allow us to pull a commitment, the market flex provision is not an out. Instead, it provides room to maneuver, to adjust key terms as with a bond issue. But to date, we have never invoked the market flex clause in Asia. Nor did we invoke the MAC clause, even during the Asian financial crisis of 1997–1999, and we tell this to clients.

Disney, like many borrowers, countered with the argument that they were paying for a fully underwritten deal expressly to avoid syndication risk. After several weeks of negotiations over this one clause, they reached an agreement limiting the extent of the flex. Typically, borrowers permit some flex in pricing, say 25 basis points, as well as in certain covenants, but are less willing to permit flex in amount. With this issue resolved, Chase turned its attention to the syndication strategy.

C3.3   Designing a Syndication Strategy

The determinants of syndicate structure are many and varied, ranging from project type and sponsor to project location and loan size. Any attempt to draw lessons from this case study must confront two problems. First, observed structures do not always reflect intended structures, due to uncertainty in the bank market. To deal with this problem, I have relied on personal interviews with the participants. Second, the Hong Kong Disneyland project, like all projects, had idiosyncratic features that influenced the loan structure. What is representative, however, is the process Chase went through and the issues it confronted during the syndication. This section describes several of these key issues and the trade-offs Chase faced in designing a syndication strategy for the loan.

The first issue Chase had to address was whether to proceed with a one-stage, general syndication or a two-stage syndication with subunderwriting. From Chase's perspective as the underwriter, there was a risk/return trade-off. Proceeding directly into general syndication involves greater syndication risk and greater credit risk if the deal is undersubscribed, but entails greater returns. With the subunderwriting approach, in contrast, the underwriter shares the risk but also the fees with other banks. Of course, involving more banks and especially prominent banks as lead arrangers or underwriters can facilitate the syndication. Here, I simply intend to illustrate how syndicate structure affects compensation and exposure.

Table C3-3 presents the economics for six possible syndication strategies assuming a HK $3.3 billion loan and a 125 basis point underwriting fee. The strategies differ by whether they have a sole or joint mandate, a subunderwriting or not, and a large or small number of banks. Comparing Strategy #1 (a sole-mandated deal with subunderwriting—the economics correspond to the example shown in Table C3-1) against Strategy #3 (a sole-mandated deal with general syndication), we see that the general syndication does, indeed, have higher risk and higher returns. The risk, defined here as the maximum exposure in the general syndication, is HK $3.3 billion compared to only HK $660 million when the HK $3.3 billion is divided evenly among five subunderwriters, while the return, Chase's total fee income, is HK $23.26 million compared to HK $13.85 million. Note that a jointly mandated deal with subunderwriting (Strategy #6) has even less risk but an even lower return. The only dominated strategy is Strategy #2, which involves a joint mandate with general syndication: Strategy #1 offers higher fees and lower risk in terms of exposure.

TABLE C3-3   Comparison of Possible Syndication Strategies

	Hold Amounts (HK$ mn)	Syndication Strategy					
		#1	#2	#3	#4	#5	#6
Type of mandate for Chase (sole vs. joint)		Sole	Joint	Sole	Sole	Sole	Joint
Type of underwriting (sub vs. general)		Sub	General	General	General	General	Sub
No. of banks by syndicate tier							
• Chase (mandated arranger)	$300	1	1	1	1	1	1
• Coordinating arrangers (other mandated banks)	$300	0	2	0	0	0	2
• Lead arrangers (subunderwriters)	$300	4	0	0	0	0	3
• Arrangers	$250	4	4	4	12	0	4
• Coarrangers	$150	4	6	8	0	0	2
• Lead manager	$100	2	5	8	0	30	2
• Total no. of banks		15	18	21	13	31	14
Chase maximum exposure (HK$ millions)		$3,300	$1,100	$3,300	$3,300	$3,300	$1,100
Chase fees[a]							
HK$ in millions		$13.85	$8.78	$23.36	$20.25	$26.25	$6.90
US$ in millions		$1.78	$1.13	$3.00	$2.60	$3.37	$0.88
Chase exposure in the general syndication							
HK$ in millions		$660	$1,100	$3,300	$3,300	$3,300	$550
US$ in millions		$85	$141	$423	$423	$423	$71
Chase fees/Chase gen.syndication exposure		0.021	0.008	0.007	0.006	0.008	0.013
No. banks needed to control 60% of the loan		7	8	10	8	18	7

[a]Assuming an underwriting fee of 1.25%, subunderwriting fee of 25 bp (where applicable), top-tier closing fees of 70 bp, and a final hold position for Chase of HK $300 million.
Source: Based on author's estimates.

An underwriter's desire to subunderwrite a deal is directly proportional to the expected difficulty of syndication, which is higher with either an especially aggressive deal or a tight credit market. Because subunderwriting can expedite the process but does not cost the borrower anything extra, most borrowers are amenable to it. Even when the underwriter expects a successful general syndication and, therefore, sees little need for a subunderwriting, the borrower may still request a subunderwriting so that its relationship banks will have the benefit of senior status and increased compensation. In this case, Chase knew it was important to accommodate Disney's preferences for a subunderwriting group that included several short-listed banks as well as other qualified banks with expertise in syndicated lending and project finance, particularly in Asia. In commenting on this decision to use a subunderwriting, Chase's Matt Harris said:

> *Relationship considerations, while not the only consideration, are the most important considerations in deciding on a syndication strategy. Accordingly, we decided not to oppose Disney's preference for a sub-underwriting with specific banks. As the sole mandated bank, we knew we were going to make more than we had initially expected. We just had to resist the temptation to be too greedy.*

Next, Chase had to select a target lender group, a decision that depended on the characteristics of the local market and three interrelated issues: how big a final hold position Chase ultimately wanted to take, how many banks to invite. Chase's standard practice is to hold 10% of loans it arranges, a target equal to HK $330 million in this case. With larger or riskier loans, its preference is to hold smaller shares, although bankers readily admit that they often have to hold larger shares of riskier loans. Because of the higher-than-average credit risk (mainly due to the 15-year final maturity), Chase set a target final hold position of HK $300 million (9.1% of the total loan). Consistent with this target final hold position, Table C3-4 shows that the largest bank lender typically holds 20% of the average syndicated loan but only 10% of the largest project finance loans. Whereas these figures represent shares at closing, it is important to remember that after closing, banks can and sometimes do sell down their positions in the large secondary market for bank loans. Increasingly, banks are bundling their project finance loans into portfolios and selling them through collateralized bond obligations (CBOs). As a practical matter, however, Chase sells its position down to zero in only very rare instances.

In selecting a final hold position for risky loans, a bank must evaluate two sets of conflicting objectives, On the one hand, diversification motives argue for holding smaller positions. On the other hand, agency or incentive conflicts can force the bank to retain larger positions. For example, a bank might have to retain a larger share of a

TABLE C3-4   Comparison of Syndicated Loan Structures

	All Syndicated Loans	Syndicated Project Finance Loans		Syndicated Loans for General Corp. Purposes
		Loans > $75 m	Loans > $500 m	
Average size (US$ millions)	$146	$304	$948	$108
Average maturity (Years)	4.8	9.4	10.2	4.5
COMPENSATION (bp)				
Spread over LIBOR	134	131	108	113
Commitment fee	31	32	29	28
Up-front fee	37	53	48	31
DEBT OWNERSHIP CONCENTRATION (%)				
Largest single share	19%	20%	10%	19%
Share of top 5 banks	59%	61%	37%	62%
Number of banks	16	14	28	13

Source: Kleimeler and Megginson, "Are Project Finance Loans Different from Other Syndicated Credits?," *Journal of Applied Corporate Finance*, Vol. 12, No. 1 (Spring 2000); Esty and Megginson, "Legal Risk as a Determinant of Syndicate Structure in the Project Finance Loan Market," Harvard Business School mimeo (2001); Esty and Megginson, "Credit Risk as a Determinant of Syndicate Structure," Harvard Business School mimeo (2001).

riskier loan to assuage concerns about the credit, and thereby induce other banks to participate. Similarly, as the chief monitor of borrower repayment, the lead arranger should hold a larger position than other banks to demonstrate a clear incentive to monitor the loan. Evidence shows that lead banks hold larger shares of riskier loans both in the project finance market and in other syndication markets.[7]

With a 9% final hold position, Chase then had to decide how to syndicate the other 91% of the loan, which leads to the question of syndicate size. Ignoring for the moment the difference between invitations and acceptances—the underwriter might want 20 banks but get only ten acceptances in the general syndication—the question is really about the advantages and disadvantages of smaller syndicates. From the borrower's perspective, smaller syndicates ensure greater confidentiality, concentrated voting control, and administrative convenience. Confidentiality can be important because sponsors do not want key information such as their project's cost structure widely known. Similarly, host governments are reluctant to share information on the extent of public assistance (as in the discussions surrounding government support in the form of "launch aid" for Airbus' new A380 jet). With regard to voting control, loan documents usually specify that waivers and amendments, which invariably occur in project loans, require approval from banks holding a defined majority of the total commitment. In this case, a group of banks known as the "instructing banks" holding at least 60% of the loan had to approve such changes. Table C3-4 shows that the five largest banks often control 60% of the total loan, except for the largest loans. In default situations, it is easier to restructure with a smaller syndicate and pari passu treatment across banks.

Whereas most of the benefits of small syndicates accrue to the borrower, most of the benefits of large syndicates accrue to the underwriters. For example, underwriter compensation generally increases as syndicate size increases. Comparing Strategies #4 and #5 in Table C3-3 (both are sole-mandated deals with general syndication), we see that the larger syndicate structure (31 banks vs. 13 banks) results in more fee income to the underwriter (HK $26.25 million vs. HK $20.25 million) for the same level of risk. Another benefit of larger syndicates is that they more effectively deter strategic default because the group can credibly threaten to withhold all future lending.[8] A third reason that underwriters may prefer larger syndicates is that they lead to greater competition among investor banks and, therefore, better execution and pricing. Finally, by including more banks, underwriters can avoid disappointing banks that might otherwise be excluded from the deal. Of course, a syndicate of 31 banks instead of 13 banks involves higher administrative costs and additional coordination problems; with more banks in the syndicate, restructuring becomes more difficult and more costly. And participating banks prefer smaller syndicates because they involve greater revenue and allow them to have more voice in amendments and waivers.

7. Project finance loans are studied by B. Esty and W. Megginson in "Legal Risk as a Determinant of Syndicate Structure in the Project Finance Loan Market," Harvard Business School mimeo (2001), syndicated loans are studied by K. Simons in "Why Do Banks Syndicate Loans?", *New England Economic Review* (January/February 1993) and S. Dennis and D. Mullineaux, "Syndicated Loans," *Journal of Financial Intermediation*, Vol. 9 (2000); loan sales are studied by G. Gorton and G. Pennachi, "Banks and Loan Sales: Marketing Non-Marketable Assets," *Journal of Monetary Economics*, Vol. 35 (1995); and venture capital syndications are studied by J. Lemer, "The Syndication of Venture Capital Investments," *Financial Management*, Vol. 23 (1994).

8. Models of costly default are presented in P. Bolton and D. Scharfstein, "Optimal Debt Contracts and the Number of Creditors," *Journal of Political Economy*, Vol. 104 (1996), D. Diamond, "Monitoring and Reputation: The Choice Between Bank Loans and Directly Placed Debt," *Journal of Political Economy*, Vol. 99 (1991); and B. Chowdry, "What Is Different About International Lending," *Review of Financial Studies*, Vol. 4 (1991).

Academic research shows that both monitoring and renegotiation incentives are important determinants of syndicate size. Smaller syndicates comprising banks with larger loan shares are more effective monitors of borrower performance.[9] Firms that borrow from smaller syndicates experience larger abnormal stock returns upon the announcement of a new bank loan.[10] And in situations with extensive credit or sovereign risk, underwriters prefer smaller syndicates, apparently to ensure low-cost renegotiation in settings where default is more likely.[11]

Besides selecting a desired final hold position and a target syndicate size, Chase had to create a target invitation list. Again, this decision is based in part on the specific bank market where the project is located—some emerging markets have few banks. More generally, however, this decision focuses on the inclusion of relationship banks and the choice between domestic and foreign banks.

Disney had its own preferences on which banks to include, but Chase augmented these with banks that would increase the likelihood of a successful syndication. Because the project was located in Hong Kong dollars, local banks were the natural choice. They had better information about the project and the country, would not be exposed to currency risk, and could add a level of political protection.[12] Chase was particularly attuned to the importance of getting local support for the deal and wanted local banks such as HSBC, Bank of China, and Standard Chartered, each of which has an important regional presence, involved in senior roles. Their participation and endorsement would send a strong signal to the credit committees of both the smaller Hong Kong banks as well as the larger European and American banks. For these reasons, Chase decided to invite the major banks in the region to be subunderwriters and to target the smaller local banks for participation in the lower tiers.

In deciding how to structure the tiers, Chase followed a fairly standard procedure. The selection of invitation amounts, titles, and fees depends in part on the universe of available banks and in part on minimum compensation levels. Chase knew that there was a large group of local banks that could hold positions ranging from HK $100 million to HK $250 million (US $12.8 to US $32.1 million) and that each bank would need a closing fee of at least US $50,000, if not US $75,000, to cover the internal costs of reviewing the loan. The bankers then worked backwards to calculate a minimum closing fee. With a target hold position of HK $100 million, a 50 basis point closing fee would generate HK $500,000 or US $64,103 in fee income, which was in the desired range. To induce banks to take larger positions, Chase would have to offer more in fees. In the end, they decided on three participation levels: an arranger tier for commitments of HK $250 million with a closing fee of 70 basis points, a coarranger tier for commitments of HK $150 million with a fee of 60 basis points, and a lead manager tier for commitments between HK $75 million and HK $100

9. Evidence on the disadvantage of larger syndicates is presented in D. Preece and D. Mullineaux, "Monitoring, Loan Renegotiability, and Firm Value," *Journal of Banking and Finance,* Vol. 20 (1994).

10. See G. James, "Some Evidence on the Uniqueness of Bank Loans," *Journal of Financial Economics*, Vol. 19 (1987).

11. Syndicate size declines in moderate and high-risk countries; see B. Esty and W. Megginson, "Legal Risk as a Determinant of Syndicate Structure in the Project Finance Loan Market," Harvard Business School mimeo (2001).

12. Some argue that governments are less likely to expropriate from domestic lenders while others argue that governments are less likely to expropriate from foreign lenders, especially lenders from countries that conduct trade with or give aid to the host country.

million with a 50 basis point fee. While it might have been possible to squeeze the fees and pay 40 basis points for lead manager commitments, and 60 basis points for arranger commitments, Chase decided to go with higher compensation to guarantee a successful syndication.

C3.4 Executing the Syndication Strategy

Chase launched the subunderwriting in mid-September by sending invitations to seven banks: HSBC, Bank of China, Fuji Bank, Bank of America, BNP Paribas, Credit Agricole, and Standard Chartered. HSBC, Bank of China, and Fuji Bank had originally been short-listed for the arranger mandate; Bank of America and Standard Chartered had expertise in the Hong Kong syndicated lending market and had lending relationships with Disney in the U.S.; and BNP Paribas and Credit Agricole had senior roles in the Disneyland Paris financing. Chase asked the banks to make underwriting commitments of HK $600 million in return for lead arranger titles and subunderwriting fees of 25 basis points. When all of the banks except one agreed to participate, Chase scaled back their exposures to HK $471 million each (HK $471 million × 7 subunderwriters = HK $3.3 billion). Chase hoped to reduce these commitments to final hold positions of HK $300 million or less in the general syndication.

Chase launched the general syndication in early October with invitations to 67 banks requiring pro rata commitments for the HK $2.3 billion construction term loan and the HK $1 billion revolving credit facility. With high confidence due to the successful subunderwriting, Chase set a very strict deadline for commitments of October 25th, reserving the right to close the syndication early and reiterating its right to make final allocations at its discretion. The general syndication generated commitments totaling HK $5.3 billion from 25 banks. Counting the original HK $4.2 billion in commitments from the seven subunderwriters, Chase had received credit commitments totaling HK $9.5 billion, an oversubscription of close to three times. Of the 42 banks that declined to participate, 25 cited concerns about the tenor (final maturity), eight cited concerns over pricing, three cited concerns about funding a Hong Kong dollar loan, three cited concerns over Hong Kong exposure or credit, and three could not get internal credit approval for the deal.

With an oversubscribed deal, Chase had to scale back each bank's commitment based on five criteria. First, the total amount had to equal HK $3.3 billion. Second, the minimum closing fee had to be at least US $50,000. Chase's Matt Harris described the other three criteria:

> We determine the final takes based on three criteria: fairness—giving the banks as close to what they committed as possible; consistency—making sure the scale-back is consistent for all banks within a given tier; and client considerations—giving appropriate weight to the client's preferences on such things as final allocations for specific banks or voting rights within the bank group.

In this case, client considerations regarding composition of the subunderwriting group and voting control were the most important.

Table C3-5 shows the final allocations for the Hong Kong Disneyland loan. The scale-back percentages ranged from a low of 30% for the Lead Managers to a high of 72% for the subunderwriters. In terms of the five criteria for determining success.

Chase appears to have met two or three of them depending on one's assessment of the criteria:

1. total amount raised = HK $3.3 billion: met
2. minimum closing fee = US $50,000: not met (banks in the Lead Manager tier earned less)
3. fairness: not met (most banks received substantially less than their original commitments)
4. consistency: met (scale-back percentages are constant within tiers)
5. client considerations: met/unmet (while Chase invited the banks Disney requested in the subunderwriting, the lending group was larger than Disney originally wanted; it contained 32 banks, of which 17 were needed to reach the 60% threshold for approving waivers).

In judging this performance, one can argue that this deal, like most deals, had elements of both success and failure. There are several reasons to argue that it was a success. From the project's perspective, the heavy oversubscription was a show of confidence in the project and in Hong Kong. Second, the deal closed in a timely fashion, with the terms and pricing desired by Disney. From the bank's perspective, all banks that wanted to participate received shares of the loan. Especially pleased were the three subunderwriters (Credit Agricole, BNP Paribas, and Standard Chartered Bank) that were not on the short list yet received subunderwriter compensation. And finally, it was a success from the perspective of Chase, who won the sole mandate on a marquee deal, one of the most important financings since the start of the Asian crisis in 1997. In addition, Chase earned substantial fees as well as lead arranger status—Table C3-5 shows it earned an estimated $1.55 million in fees from the transaction. (Again, this is based on my hypothetical fees, which may or may not reflect actual compensation.)

Nevertheless, there are aspects of the deal that appear less favorable. For example, one can interpret the heavy oversubscription as an indication that either Disney overpaid Chase for the underwriting risk or that Chase overpaid the market. (Alternatively, Disney could have requested more favorable loan terms.) The magnitude of the oversubscription also indicates that a subunderwriting was probably not

TABLE C3-5   Final Allocations for the Hong Kong Disneyland Loan

Syndicate Tier	Number of Banks	Original Commitments (HK$ Millions)	Scale-back (Percent)	Final Hold Per Bank (HK$ Millions)	Total Amount All Banks (HK$ Millions)	Total Fees Per Bank (US$ 000)
Mandated arranger (Chase)	1	$471	72.4%	$130.0	$130	$1,551
Lead arranger (subunderwriters)	6	471	72.4	130.0	780	281
Arranger	18	250	58.0	105.0	1,890	94
Coarranger	3	150	43.3	85.0	255	65
Lead manager	2	100	30.0	70.0	140	45
Lead manager	2	75	30.0	52.5	105	34
Total	32				$3,300	

Source: Company documents, author's estimates; assumes an underwriting fee of 125 bp.

necessary, and that Chase could have retained a larger fraction of the fees by proceeding directly to a general syndication. Nevertheless, Chase led a very successful deal. It was able to mobilize the Asian bank market when it had to, which should bode well for future business. Viewed from this perspective, Chase erred on the side of conservatism. Rather than risking its reputation by leading an undersubscribed or failed syndication, Chase chose to pay larger fees to a larger investor bank group to ensure the success of the syndication.

The general syndication closed on October 25, 2000, and Chase made the scale-backs described in Table C3-5. Some conclusions can be drawn by comparing the actual syndication results with Chase's projections in its final proposal to Disney in mid-summer. The general syndication produced commitments of HK $5.3 billion, 16% more than what Chase predicted it could raise. Chase's projected bank response rate in its final presentation to Disney was 34%; the actual response rate was 37%. In terms of bank identities and nationalities, only four of the 32 banks were not on the target list in Chase's final presentation. Taken as a whole, the outcome shows that Chase's confidence in its ability to distribute the loan was well founded. It knew its investor base well and had the ability to mobilize the Hong Kong market for its clients. Of course, Chase benefited from the fact that the Hong Kong bank market continued to improve during the period—perhaps more than expected.

The parties signed the loan agreement, and up-front (underwriting and closing) fees were paid, on November 15, 2000. Financial closing (the date when all conditions precedent to borrowing have been met and the loan can be drawn) occurred in March 2001. Disney does not expect to borrow much under the construction facility until the reclamation work is finished sometime in the next two years. Nevertheless, it has a committed loan with favorable terms and attractive pricing in its possession.

C3.5   Conclusion

Besides illustrating the process, terminology, and economics of loan syndication, this case study reveals several important features of syndicated lending. First, it shows the importance of two kinds of banking relationships. There are borrower/creditor relationships such as those between Disney and its relationship banks. Disney made sure to invite them to bid for the lead mandate and pushed hard to make sure that qualified banks were invited to participate in the subunderwriting. There are also arranger/investor relationships such as those between Chase and its universe of investor banks. Harris described these relationships as follows:

> *Chase takes its relationships with investor banks very seriously. We don't simply view them as "stuffee" banks, but rather partner investors with whom a close relationship built on trust is critical. While we could often keep a larger slice of the pie, we don't want to expend any goodwill with our investors by leaving them with the impression that we had gouged them on fees or denied them an opportunity to acquire a meaningful earning asset. We view having paid more in fees than we really needed to as an investment in our relationships with other banks that are active in the market.*

Even though Chase had an opportunity to earn more than twice as much as it did on this transaction—up to US $3.4 million under certain syndication strategies compared to an estimated US $1.55 million on this deal—it chose to satisfy client preferences for a subunderwriting with specific banks.

This article also illustrates the different forms of debt ownership. At one extreme, small syndicates of two or three banks resemble the standard academic models of single-bank, private debt lending. At the other extreme, large syndicates of 100 to 200 banks begin to resemble the models of numerous independent public bondholders. The majority of bank lending, however, falls somewhere in the middle, with syndicates of 10 to 30 banks as typical. For this reason, syndicated lending can be viewed as an intermediate form of financing, replete with interesting governance and structuring issues. Selecting an optimal capital structure involves not only how much and what type of debt but also the nature of debt ownership. Issues like how many banks, which banks, and ownership concentration can all affect the value of a banking relationship and, therefore, the value of the issuing firm. As academics, we need to recognize this continuum and the consequences of various ownership structures, as we have done with equity ownership, and begin to develop the next generation of theoretical models. Because these models will more closely reflect actual lending practice, they should have greater predictive power and provide more useful guidance on capital structure and corporate governance decisions.

Glossary and Abbreviations

accelerated depreciation: The possibility allowed by the tax authority in various countries to accelerate the schedule of depreciation of a firm's assets in order to benefit from tax shields.

acceleration clause: Condition that allows lenders to demand immediate payment of the total debt outstanding of the SPV. This is an exceptional situation that can arise when the project defaults and only when certain events of default stipulated in the credit agreement occur.

ADB: Asian Development Bank

administrative risk: Possible consequences for the project due to nonfulfillment, delays, or decisions by the public administration.

advisor: Specialist hired by sponsors to provide consulting services with the aim of establishing the size, schedule, risk profile, and financing mix of a deal so as to make it acceptable to all lenders.

advisory: See *advisor*.

AfDB: African Development Bank

agent bank: The bank in charge of administering a deal in terms of actually issuing the financing and dividing debt repayment among the intermediaries who are members of the syndicate. Therefore, the agent bank is the player who takes responsibility for all administrative aspects of the financing and handles contacts with the SPV management and the lending banks.

all-in cost: The total cost of a financing, including the interest rate and all other accessory expenses charged on the loan (fees to the syndicate, commitment fees, etc.).

arranger: The bank or group of banks (joint arrangers) that play a key role in organizing the loan. Arranging entails establishing the amount and contract conditions of the financing and syndicating the loan on the market.

arranging: See *arranger*.

arranging fee: A fee paid to a mandated lead arranger (MLA) or group of banks (lead arrangers) for arranging a transaction. It includes fees to be paid to participating banks.

average debt service cover ratio (ADSCR): Mathematical average of debt service cover ratios recorded in each year of project operations. In the credit agreement, a request for a minimum level of cover ratios (DSCR) is usually also accompanied by an explicit condition regarding the average level (ADSCR)

balloon payment: A final debt installment that is substantially larger than the preceding payments.

base facility: The largest portion of the financing granted to the SPV to cover plant construction and start operations.

basis point: One-hundredth of a percentage point. 100 basis points equals 1% (100 b.p. = 1%).

bid price: In the power market, the price that generators/producers offer for power; the bid price is based on prices set by the authority that controls that market.

bilateral agency (BLA): An institution established by one country to promote trade with other countries, such as an export–import agency or an export credit agency (ECA).

bond/bonding: Bank or insurance security of a third party with acceptable financing standing; bonds are issued to make the debt liability of a given party bankable. This liability usually refers to damages or reimbursement of advance payments.

bond paying agent: Party that carries out the same functions as the agent bank where the SPV is financed by the issuance of a project bond.

BOO (build, own, and operate): Project finance technique by which a joint venture or private company is granted a concession to build and operate an infrastructure. When the concession expires, it can be extended, or the works can be definitively transferred to the concession holder in cases where the physical life of the project coincides with the concession period. Specifically, if there is a transfer of ownership, the acronym becomes BOOT (build, own, operate, and transfer).

bookrunner: The arranger in projects financed by the issuance of project bonds.

BOOT (build, own, operate, and transfer): See *BOO*.

borrower: The loan recipient, normally the project company/SPV.

BOT (build, operate, and transfer): Project finance technique by which a public body grants a concession to a joint venture or private company to build and operate an infrastructure. This technique allows the concession holder to build the plant, repay loans through plant operations, and then transfer the plant to the public authority that granted the concession.

bought deal: Method for issuing bonds issue where securities are bought by a syndicate and later sold to interested investors.

bullet payment: A one-time debt repayment, often after no or little amortization of the loan.

business disruption: The risk that third parties may suspend their business activity and the consequent impact this may have.

business plan: An integral part of the information memorandum, with this document the advisor translates the set of collected data into numbers to assess the impact of different variables on cash flows, revenues, and the asset structure of the project company.

buydown damage: Penalty charged to the contractor if the plant does not guarantee maximum expected output. The value of buydown damages corresponds to the difference in actual revenue as compared to projected performance at 100%.

buyer: Counterparty who purchases output from the SPV. There may be generic buyers, i.e., the retail market, or a single buyer (offtaker) who agrees to buy all of the SPV's output wholesale.

cap (option): Interest rate option by which the project company sets a maximum limit on the cost of debt when future rate rises are expected.

Capex (capital expenditure): Long-term expenditures for property, plant, and equipment.

cash flow statement: Document in which cash flows deriving from the project are calculated.

certainty equivalent method: Method for valuing an investment/financing project characterized by a sequence of financial flows that are not known to the evaluator a priori. The certain equivalents method determines whether the project should be accepted or rejected on the basis of the net present value criterion. In estimating this measurement, the numbers representing expected cash flows of an initiative are weighted by coefficients representing the evaluator's risk aversion.

cogeneration: Production process by which energy and steam are generated by burning a given fuel (generally renewable energy).

coinsurance effect: The phenomenon whereby a surplus of cash flows from one or more assets or divisions is used to cover the financial cash shortage of another asset or division inside the same firm.

collar (option): Interest rate option that is a combination of a cap and a floor. With a collar, there is both a lower and an upper bound on the interest rate, so this rate can fluctuate only within a range whose width is defined by the preset cap and floor rates.

collateral deprivation risk: Risks relating to the loss of assets or to the concession authority's not repurchasing the plant.

commitment document: Letter attesting to the commitment of the arrangers before syndication to underwrite the financing they are to organize.

commitment fee: A per annum fee applied to undrawn funds that lenders are committed to lend; this fee is charged until the end of the availability period.

completion risk: Risk pertaining to construction, development, or cost overruns.

condition precedent: Prerequisite included in the credit agreement establishing that events allow material disbursement of funds to the borrower. Conditions precedent differ in content and purpose depending on whether they apply to the first or successive drawdowns.

construction period: The phase of the project life when the plant is built and tested for the first time.

construction risk: See *completion risk*.

construction schedule: Detailed timetable of works, requested to monitor project milestones.

contamination risk: The possibility that the results from a new project could impact a party's overall solvency.

contract frustration risks: Risks associated with wrongful calling of guarantees and failure to deliver parts or pieces that are instrumental to realizing the project.

contract of differences: In the UK, mechanism by which local power producers, distributors, and regional electric companies (RECs) mitigate the risk of the buying/selling price of power. The parties to this contract create coverage on the basis of a strike price: If the price paid by the REC to the power pool exceeds the strike, the producer refunds the REC; if the opposite occurs, the REC pays the difference to the producer.

contractor (and main contractor): The company or consortium of companies that wins the bid for designing and building the plant in question on the basis of a turnkey construction contract. Contract obligations are assumed by the main contractor, which commits directly to the SPV; later these obligations are passed on to consortium members.

corporate loan: Financing granted to an up-and-running company that is often used for generic purposes, with no direct correlation between the loan in question and how these funds are invested.

cost overrun: Unforeseen increase in the project's cost structure due to erroneous forecasts or the occurrence of unexpected events during the project.

country risk: Narrowly defined, it refers to cross-currency and foreign exchange availability risks. More broadly defined, it can also include the political risks of doing business in a given country.

covenants: Limitations placed by lenders on borrowers that the latter must respect in order to draw down the funds in question. Positive covenants oblige the project company to do certain things; vice versa, negative covenants prohibit the project company from doing others.

cover ratios: Indicators of financial feasibility that make it possible to recognize the sustainability of the capital structure chosen for a project finance initiative. These ratios can show the extent to which a project's operating flows match those linked to the dynamic of financial items (debt service).

credit agreement: A financial accord summed up in a legal document that contains the contractual conditions negotiated with lenders. Drawing up the credit agreement is the final stage of the arranger legal advisors.

credit enhancement: Any kind of guarantee that a third party provides to a borrower in order to increase its creditworthiness. Very often used in the form of a monoline guarantee for asset securitization deals.

credit risk: The possibility that one of the parties involved in a project finance initiative cannot fulfill its commitments.

currency swap: With this contract, two parties agree to exchange cash flows according to a preset contractual model with reference to given currencies, amounts, and dates. Over time, the use of currency swaps makes it possible to separate the currency in which the funding is denominated from the real needs of the project company.

debt capacity: The capacity of a project's cash flow to satisfy debt requirements. If the project's debt capacity is greater than its debt requirements, the project's financial model can be considered feasible; if not, the model is rejected.

debt requirements: See *debt capacity* and *all-in cost*.

debt service: Principal repayments plus interest payable; usually expressed as the annual amount due per calendar or financial year.

debt service cover ratio (DSCR): Ratio of the operating cash flow over the principal and interest on the loan, calculated during each year of the operating life of the SPV. This indicator is used to verify that the financial resources generated by the project (numerator) can service the debt toward lenders in every year of operations (denominator).

debt tenor: Maturity of a loan.

debt-to-equity ratio: A ratio of a company's debt to its equity capital. The higher this ratio, the greater the financial leverage of the company.

dedicated percentage repayment: When capital repayment on a loan is made proportional to the operating cash flow for the year in question.

delay damages: Penalty payments charged to the contractor if the plant does not pass the minimum performance standard tests. The amount of delay damages paid to the SPV is based on lost revenues caused by the delay.

design, build, finance, and operate scheme: Model of project financing by which the public administration becomes a pure buyer of the service provided by a given project, after contracting out the design, building, financing, and operation of a public work. This technique is widely used in Private Finance Initiatives in the UK.

developmental agency: Financial institutions that grant financing and buy shares in companies (often joint ventures promoted by resident sponsors in the countries where the agency operates) that are key industrial players in developing countries.

dividend trap: A restriction on a project company's ability to pay dividends, despite having cash available to do so, because of a mismatch between net income and cash flow available to shareholders.

documentation bank: The bank responsible for correctly drawing up documents pertaining to a given loan.

due diligence: Control and analytical verification of the formal aspects contained in the documentation of an initiative, as well as preliminary corroboration of the economic/financial and equity standing of participants. Given the diversity of the factors considered during due diligence, this analysis is usually carried out by technical, financial, and legal advisors.

due diligence legal report: A summary report drawn up by the arrangers' lawyers for their clients on the project and its bankability, in formal and substantial terms. This report describes every constituent element of the initiative, to include the nature and characteristics of the project company, the project contracts, administrative concessions and permits, and the overall regulatory context of the project.

early completion bonus: Additional payment made to the main contractor if a project is finished ahead of schedule.

EBRD: European Bank for Reconstruction and Development

EIB: European Investment Bank

engineering procurement and construction (EPC): A contract in which the contractor ensures engineering, procurement (of materials, equipment and machinery for the plant), and construction; this is a way to assign a third party the risk of completing the work and ensuring that the expected plant specifications are met.

Environmental Impact Assessment (EIA): A study conducted by the independent engineer during due diligence. This consists of simulating different possible emergency scenarios, which are then used to estimate the probability that catastrophic events will occur, and their potential impact both in terms of damage to facilities and to the surrounding environment.

environmental risk: Economic or administrative consequences of slow or catastrophic environmental pollution.

equity contribution agreement: Documentation relating to the stipulations that regulate equity contributions by sponsors to the project company.

equity injection: Equity that project sponsors are called on to contribute when economic/financial parameters are not respected.

event of default: An act, fact, or event that entitles lenders to withdraw from their contract commitments toward their borrower. These events are listed in the project's term sheet, always along with provisions for remedies that lenders can implement.

evergreen clause: Method for utilizing a credit line made available to the SPV by lenders. In this case, drawdowns can be made at the SPV's discretion.

exchange rate risk: This rate risk emerges when some or all of the project's financial flows are stated in currencies different from that of the SPV's account.

export credit agencies (ECAs): Organizations that assist in supporting exports from their country through the use of direct loans and insurance policies provided to importers.

feasibility study: Document that defines unequivocally all aspects of a given project to allow a comprehensive assessment of whether it can actually be realized. Normally this document is drawn up by engineering companies and refers solely to the technical side of the project finance initiative.

fee: A fixed amount or a percentage of an underwriting or principal charged as part of a financing.

Final Acceptance Certificate (FAC): Document issued by an independent engineer when initial plant testing is complete. Once the final acceptance certificate is issued, the SPV takes charge of the plant.

finance documents: Documents defining the legal aspects of the deal. Finance documents are drawn up by the arrangers' lawyers and negotiated with the project company's lawyers.

financial closing: The phase in which all contract conditions of the financing established between the arranger bank and the pool of lenders are definitively closed.

financial package: Section of the information memorandum dedicated to the financial structure of the project in question. The financial package specifies the mix of capital that is consistent with the project's financial flows and the economic structure.

fixed-price turnkey contract: Construction contract for a plant based on payment of a fixed price. This is a way for sponsors and lenders of the SPV to transfer construction risk to the contractor.

floor option: Interest rate option that is structured with a lower limit (floor rate) on the interest on a variable-rate loan.

force majeure risk: The risk that contractual nonperformance is due to events beyond the control of all parties. These events are either "acts of God" (floods, fires, or other natural disasters) or political risks (war, strikes, riots, expropriation, breach of contract, etc.). Contractual performance is forgiven or extended by the period of force majeure.

fuel supply agreement: Contract for the purchase of fuel in the context of power generation projects.

Gantt chart: The graphic output of a software-supported grid analysis technique. It shows the project activities schedule and the activity sequencing.

hard refinancing: Technique for refinancing a loan by which all the original conditions included in the credit agreement are renegotiated with the original or a new bank syndicate.

heat rate: The thermal output of a power plant.

hedging agreement: Documentation pertaining to contracts covering risk of fluctuations in interest, exchange rates, or other economic variables.

IADB: Inter-American Development Bank

IBRD: International Bank for Reconstruction and Development. Member of the World Bank Group.

ICSID: International Centre for Settlement of Investment Disputes. Member of the World Bank Group.

IDA: International Development Association. Member of the World Bank Group.

IFC: International Finance Corporation. Member of the World Bank Group.

independent engineer: Technical consultant who plays a *super partes* role in a project finance deal. The independent engineer is asked to express an opinion as to the project's feasibility, make a project assessment, and act as controller during operations to safeguard the project. Usually the independent engineer conducts due diligence analysis, monitors the progress of the project, assists in plant acceptance, and oversees operations.

independent technical advisor: See *independent engineer*.

inflation risk: Risk that emerges when the inflation rates used for cash flow calculations in the business plan are different from actual values recorded during the life of the project.

information memorandum: A document that forms the basis of every project because it summarizes all the key elements of a deal. This memorandum provides all general information on the project and financing and outlines the content of the project agreements. Based on the information memorandum, the advisor contacts potential lenders and begins negotiating the terms of the financing.

intercreditor agreement: See *credit agreement*.

internal rate of return (IRR): The interest rate that makes the net present value of a project's positive operating cash flows equal to the net present value of its negative operating cash flows. In a project finance deal, three IRR can be calculated: equity IRR, lenders (senior or subordinated) IRR, and project IRR.

interest rate risk: The impact on project cash flow from higher-than-expected interest costs.

investment grade: An investment rating level of BBB– or better from Standard & Poor's Corporation or Baa3 or better from Moody's Corporation. When a borrower is below the investment-grade level, it is said to be speculative grade.

investment risk: Risks relating to currency convertibility, expropriation without indemnity, and war or other political upheaval.

joint venture: Agreement between firms by which a new company is established whose resources are provided by the partners. The strategic importance of such an agreement is high for all partners involved, who pursue the same business objectives through the new company.

junior debt: See *subordinated debt*.

k_d: Cost of debt capital.

k_e: Cost of equity.

lead arranger (or mandated lead arranger): The banks who wins the mandate to syndicate a loan facility for the SPV.

lead manager: A bank that participates in a bank syndicate and lends an amount higher than a preset threshold (ticker).

league table: A ranking of lenders and advisors according to the underwriting, final take, or number of project finance loans or advisory mandates completed during a given period.

legal opinion: Conclusive documentation in the setup phase of a financing that certifies the legal validity of the key features of the project. A very formal document, the presentation of the legal opinion represents a condition precedent to granting the loan in question.

legal risk: The risk that a party to a contract will not be able to enforce security arrangements, enforce foreign judgments, have a choice of law, or refer disputes to arbitration.

lending commitment: Promise by lenders to provide a given amount of debt capital.

lessee: See *project leasing*.

lessor: See *project leasing*.

limited-recourse financing: Financing deals in which recourse can be taken on SPV shareholders or third-party guarantors by lenders for only part of their credit risk exposure and only under certain previously contracted conditions.

liquidate, or make good: If a plant meets minimum performance standards but does not operate at 100% of expected potential, the contractor chooses one of two options: liquidate or pay the SPV the difference between actual revenues and projected 100% output (buydown damages); to make good, in other words spend whatever's necessary to bring the plant up to maximum output by a set date.

liquidated damages: Penalties paid by the contractor or other project counterparties to the project company when contractual obligations are not met.

loan drawdown schedule: Sequence of actual borrowings on a loan facility. In project finance, the loan drawdown schedule is often contingent on plant construction milestones.

loan life cover ratio (LLCR): The present value of operating cash flows produced from the calculation date to the final year the debt will be repaid, plus existing debt reserve, divided by outstanding debt at the same calculation date. Lenders use this ratio to evaluate the debt servicing capacity of the project's operating cash flows.

loss carryforward: The possibility of offsetting the current year's net loss against future years' net incomes.

main contractor: Lead company in the consortium that wins the bid to design and build a given plant on the basis of a fixed-price turnkey contract. Within the consortium, the main contractor plays a key role in terms of operations and responsibility toward the SPV.

main items purchasing list: Purchasing plan including essential orders and suborders for pieces and parts needed to realize the structure in question.

manager bank: A bank that participates in a bank syndicate and lends an amount lower than the ticker set for the lead managers but above the minimum participation ticker.

mandate document: Letter appointing arrangers to organize a given financing.

mandated bank: The bank given the authority to proceed into the marketplace on behalf of the borrower on the basis of the terms and conditions set out in the mandate letter. The mandated bank is often referred to as the *arranger* in the Euromarkets and the *administrative agent* in the United States.

market risk: Changes to the amounts sold or the price received that affect total revenue.

mechanical completion: Certificate attesting to finalization of construction works that represents the final verification of all interim payments. Mechanical completion provides for random testing of the execution and adequacy of works and confirms the accuracy of the statements by the main contractor and the sponsors' technical advisor.

merchant plant: A power plant that sells electricity without a long-term power purchase agreement.

mezzanine finance: Financing whose features are hybrid (neither pure equity nor pure senior debt). Usually mezzanine financing is a subordinated debt with possible equity kicker in the form of warrants or option to convert debt into equity.

MIGA: Multilateral Investment Guarantee Agency, a member of the World Bank Group.

minimum performance standard (mps): Lowest acceptable level of productivity that a plant must attain in order for the building consortium to avoid paying penalties. This standard refers to specific features of the plant (e.g., energy and steam, emissions and heat rate).

mitigation: In project financing terminology, this identifies any sort of contract that limits the impact of a potential risk on the SPV and indirectly on certain project participants (usually lenders).

MPL (maximum probable loss): The worst possible loss that could be incurred in case damaging events occur. MPL is important when analyzing project risks and identifying the best strategy for their coverage.

multicurrency agreement: Financing agreement between the SPV and lenders. Through a multicurrency agreement, the project company has the option to choose the currency in which it draws the loan, depending on comparative convenience in terms of the differential between interest rates and between spot and forward exchange rates.

negative equity: A problem arising when the use of subordinated debt results in more substantial interest payable, lower profits/higher losses, and thus greater erosion of the sponsors' equity capital.

net present value (NPV): Present value of cash flows generated by a project. This is an indicator of the incremental wealth produced by the initiative. A positive net present value demonstrates the project's capacity to generate enough cash to pay off initial expenses, compensate capital utilized in the initiative, and have residual resources for other uses.

nonpayment risks: Risks that arise for political or commercial reasons. Normally, such risks involve short- or medium-long-term loans, leasing contracts, and other documentary credits.

offtake agreement: An agreement to purchase all or a substantial part of a project's output, which typically provides the revenue stream for a project financing initiative.

Offtaker: See *buyer*.

operating cash flow: The difference between cash inflows and outflows before financial items are taken into account (principal and interest payments, reserve account contributions, and dividends to sponsors).

operating risk: Risk that arises when the plant functions but technically underperforms during tests following the initial trial run.

operations and maintenance (O&M) agreement: Contract between the operator/maintenance contractor and the SPV relating to the management and maintenance of the plant.

operations and maintenance contractor: See *operator*.

operator: The company or consortium of companies (in a joint venture) that takes over the plant from the contractor at the end of the construction period and handles plant operations for a set number of years. The operator has to guarantee the SPV efficient operations under preagreed output conditions.

opinion documents: Documents containing legal opinions.

outstanding capital: Residual debt at a given date of project life.

participant bank: A member of the bank syndicate that lends a minimum amount of money (minimum ticker).

payback period: Moment in time when project outflows and inflows are equal. Once the drawdown period is over (which usually coincides with the construction phase), the payback period is inversely proportional to the quantity of the operating cash flows generated by the plant.

payment curve: Sequence of drawdowns and repayments that the SPV is obliged to make during project operations.

performance bond: Guarantee issued by a bank on behalf of the contractor in favor of the project company to secure payment of a penalty if the plant does not supply the contracted output. The guaranteed amount generally corresponds to a percentage of the value of the output supply.

performance deficiency: Situation when a plant does not fulfill minimum performance standards.

performance test: Test run when plant construction is complete, to verify that certain production standards have been met (minimum performance standards).

permitting plan: In project finance, plan of permits and authorizations.

planning risk: The possibility that the structure that enables the SPV to generate cash flows during operations is not available.

political risk: It encompasses eight risks associated with cross-border investment and financing: currency inconvertibility, expropriation, war and insurrection, terrorism, environmental activities, landowner actions, nongovernmental activists, and legal and bureaucratic approvals. Usually, the first three are insurable. Political risk overlaps with the political component of force majeure risk.

power pool: The energy exchange in the UK; producers sell electricity to the power pool and then local distributors buy from the same pool.

power purchase agreement (PPA): With this contract for the purchase of electricity generated by a given plant, the price the buyer pays has to cover both the fixed costs of the project (including debt service) and the variable costs of the fuel used to produce energy.

private finance initiative (PFI): Economic policy implemented in the UK since 1992 by which the public administration has moved from owning assets to buying private services in public–private partnerships (PPPs). Each year, a special office of the Treasury sets down planning guidelines for works that may draw on private capital and how this should come about.

private placement: Method for placing securities that are sold to a predefined group of banks or institutional investors. The characteristics of the securities are structured after initial contact with financial institutions that are interested in participating in the project finance initiative.

progress curves: In project management, the graphic representation of the physical development of the project.

progress report: Periodic brief issued by the contracting party or the general contractor on the status of the project.

project bond: Bond issued by the SPV to finance the project; a financing alternative to syndicated loans.

project company: See *special-purpose vehicle.*

project counsel: Legal advisor for the project who has a formal joint mandate from project company sponsors. Being the project lawyer, this person is responsible for drawing up the project documents.

project documents: A set of contracts, permits, and other legal documentation needed to build and operate the project plant. The project company's lawyers are typically responsible for drawing up, executing, and obtaining these documents.

project leasing: Contract agreement by which the leasing company (lessor) supplies a good to the SPV (lessee) after having acquired ownership from the supplier (contractor). The SPV, in turn, commits to paying the lessor fixed or adjustable fees for a given time period at preagreed intervals. Once the leasing contract expires, the SPV is given the option to purchase the property rights to the good in question.

project management: Methodology whose aim is the determination of the timing and resources needed for various interrelated activities in a process that leads to a defined result within a preset time frame.

Provisional Acceptance Certificate (PAC): Document issued by an independent engineer after the first phase of plant testing certifying that preestablished minimum performance standards have been met.

public–private partnership (PPP): See *private finance initiative*.

punch list: Document listing the details regarding plant construction that have not yet been fully completed.

purchaser: See *buyer*.

put-or-pay agreement: See *put-or-pay contract*.

put-or-pay contract: Unconditional supply contract by which the supplier sells preagreed volumes of input to the SPV at preset prices. If supply is lacking, the supplier is required to compensate for the higher cost incurred by finding another source of input.

rating: A measure of the borrower's willingness and possibility to repay its outstanding debts, or, in other words, a measure of the borrower's risk of default. Major international agencies use one or more alphanumeric codes to rate any given bond.

recovery plan: Plan for emergency intervention in case of accidents impacting the building site or the project.

reserve account: Account that the SPV is obliged to set up to the benefit of lenders as coverage in case of unforeseen circumstances.

restructuring: Revision of the conditions of a loan. This procedure is necessary when the project proves unable to generate the expected cash flows.

retainer fee: A portion of the fees paid to the advisor that covers the cost incurred when the initiative is being analyzed and the proposal drawn up.

revamping: Substitution of obsolete machinery or facilities with the aim of bringing a power plant back up to its original efficiency (or better).

revolving financing: Line of credit that the SPV can tap at will and that can be reintegrated with later positive cash flows.

risk management: A process activated in the initial stages of a deal based on identifying risks and allocating them to the players who are best suited to cover against them.

S-curve: The graphic representation of the cumulative value of the resources used in a project at a given time. The S-curve sums the costs relating to the resources as a function of time and sequencing of activities; this curve is determined by applying critical path method scheduling.

security agreement: See *security package.*

security documents: Documents that constitute the security package granted on the loan, included among the finance documents.

security package: A set of contractual commitments and security interests that constitute the rules of conduct underlying the project financing initiative. The security package includes the commitments taken on by the SPV toward lenders, the security interests of the latter, binding obligations on the project company' assets, and procedures for recovery in case of default.

selling group: Pool of banks that commit to selling the securities in a bond issue of the project company. Unlike bookrunners and managers, the selling group does not provide an underwriting guarantee.

senior debt: The part of debt financing with first claim on project cash flows. Senior debt is given priority over subordinated debt and equity in terms of paying interest and principal repayment.

sensitivity analysis: Technique used to grasp the reactivity of project cash flows with respect to basic project variables and consequent repercussions on the debt service capacity.

shareholders' agreement: Contract relating to the agreements between sponsors and the distribution of project risks and profits.

syndication: The process through which the mandated lead arranger divides the loan it and other joint arrangers have initially underwritten among a number of lenders. Lenders are classified into different groups (lead managers, managers, comanagers) based on the loan amount they accept to lend.

soft refinancing (waiver): Refinancing technique by which some loan conditions are renegotiated but not the financial leverage or the tenor.

special-purpose vehicle (SPV): Ad hoc legal entity established to realize a given project. The primary roles of the SPV are: borrower toward lenders; counterparty to contracts underpinning the initiative; owner of project cash flows.

sponsor: A party wishing to develop and finance a project (with equity or a mix of equity and subordinated debt/mezzanine financing). Shareholders of project companies (SPVs) are known as sponsors.

standby clause: Method for utilizing the credit line made available to the SPV by lenders. In this case the borrower can make drawdowns on the loan within preset time periods.

standby facility: Tranche of additional debt made available to the SPV to cover contingencies that arise during the life of the project.

standby financing: See *standby clause.*

start-up: This is when the testing phase begins, followed by operations once plant construction is complete.

step-in clause/step-in right: By exercising this right, which is stipulated between the pool of lending banks and one of the counterparties of the project company (direct agreement), banks can literally step in, replace the counterparty, and take over project operations directly.

subordinated debt: Debt that is repaid after senior debt. Subordination usually refers to capital repayment. The subordinated debt will be repaid only after senior debt complete amortization.

subscription agreement: Contract that regulates the relationships between the project bond issuer and the bookrunner.

success fee: Variable (in rare cases fixed) compensation linked to the positive outcome of an activity. In the context of a project finance initiative, this is the fee paid to the advisor and the arranger for successfully designing the project and syndicating the loan.

summary report: A summary of the preliminary project feasibility study. On the basis of this report, the sponsors and their financial advisors contract with lending banks for the contribution of debt equity and relative contract conditions.

suppliers: Parties who provide the project company with input needed for the plant to function; supply is based on long-term contracts relating to transporting and storing raw materials.

supply-or-pay contract: See *put-or-pay contract*.

supply risk: This risk arises when the SPV is not able to obtain the needed production input for operations or when input is supplied in less than optimal quantity or less than the quality needed for the efficient utilization of the structure. Or the SPV might find input, but at a higher price than expected.

tail: In PPPs, it indicates the difference between the life of the concession and the tenor of the loan. It is the number of years that remain after the project financing has been repaid.

tailor-made repayment: Repayment on a loan made in variable installments.

take-or-pay contract: Contract that stipulates unconditional purchase of preagreed volumes by the buyer of a product or service at preset prices. The buyer commits to making periodic payments in exchange for the supply of a given product and must pay even if the item in question is not delivered (though only under certain conditions).

technology risk: The possibility that technology may be valid in theory but inapplicable in a working plant.

technology supplier: The counterparty that provides the technology needed for the plant to function in exchange for a royalty. The technology supplier is not always the contractor.

term sheet: Operational document that summarizes the key terms and conditions of the financing to be contained in the information memorandum pertaining to a given investment initiative.

thin capitalization: In many countries it is the rule that doesn't allow the SPV to deduct interest expenses for tax purposes when the firm debt-to-equity ratio is particularly high and/or is above a preset threshold.

throughput agreement: See *put-or-pay contract*.

tolling agreement: An agreement under which a project company imposes tolling charges on each project user as compensation for processing raw material.

tombstone: An advertisement including the borrower's name, the amount raised, financing institutions (participants), and key roles played by the participants.

transportation risk: Risk that can arise during transportation of pieces or parts of the project.

trustee: An independent or nominated third party who administers corporate or financial arrangements.

turnkey contract: A construction contract that provides for the complete engineering, procurement, construction, and start-up of a facility by a certain date, for a fixed price, and at guaranteed performance levels.

underperformance: See *performance deficiency*.

underwriting: A commitment by one or more banks (underwriters) to fund a project by which the availability of funds is guaranteed to the SPV even if underwriters don't find lenders interested in backing the project.

underwriting agreement: Contract that defines the relationships between members of the syndicate who underwrite a project bond issue.

up-front fee: Fee paid to the lead manager, manager, and comanager. It comes out of the arranging fee.

WACC (weighted average cost of capital): The weighted average of cost of equity (k_e) and net cost of debt (k_d). The weights are represented by the ratio obtained from net market value of equity and the sum of market values of debt and equity (for k_e) and market value of debt and the sum of market values of debt and equity (for k_d). Adopting weights calculated by using book values is not entirely accurate from a methodological standpoint; however, given that in project finance deals the value of assets depends on cash flows generated as opposed to the asset values themselves, this is an acceptable simplification.

VAT facility: Loan granted by the syndicate to the SPV to cover VAT expenses during construction.

vehicle company: See *special-purpose vehicle*.

waste-to-energy: In the context of cogeneration plants, this term refers to facilities specializing in producing electric power by burning waste.

without-recourse financing: Financing with no right of recourse over sponsors. This calls for the constitution of a project company to completely separate the sponsors, the project, and the financial needs associated with the project. Since relative loans are in the project company's name, the project itself has no impact on the balance sheet of the sponsors (off-balance-sheet deal).

work breakdown structure (WBS): Project management technique used to determine exactly which activities are needed to realize a project and the resources to be utilized to complete it.

work fee: Commission for soft refinancing.

working capital facility: Portion of a loan that banks make available to the borrower that is earmarked for financing the cash deficit that can emerge from the cash collection cycle.

wraparound responsibility: See *wrapping*.

wrapping: Guarantee provided by the main contractor on the performance of the technology incorporated in the construction contract. Since wrapping implies that the contractor is knowledgeable of the technology in question, this guarantee is not applicable in cases of completely new technology.

References

ADB—Asian Development Bank. (various years). *Annual report*. Manila, Philippines: ADB Editions.

ADB—Asian Development Bank. (various years). *Private-sector operations—catalyzing private investments across Asia and the Pacific*. Manila, Philippines: ADB Editions.

AfDB—African Development Bank. (various years). *Annual report*. Abidjan: AfDB Editions.

Alchian, A. A., and Demsetz, H. (1972). Production, information costs, and economic organization. *American Economic Review, 62,* 777–995.

Altunbas, Y., and Gadanecz, B. (2004). Developing country economic structure and the pricing of syndicated credits. *Journal of Development Studies, 40,* 143–173.

Archibald, R. D. (2003). *Managing high-technology programs and projects* (3rd ed.). New York: John Wiley & Sons.

Basel Committee on Banking Supervision. (2001a). *Consultative document—the internal ratings-based approach*. Basel, Switzerland: Bank of International Settlements Editions.

Basel Committee on Banking Supervision (2001b). *Working paper on the internal ratings–based approach to specialized lending exposures*. Basel, Switzerland: Bank of International Settlements Editions.

Basel Committee on Banking Supervision. (2004). *International convergence of capital measurement and capital standard—a revised framework*. Basel, Switzerland: Bank of International Settlements Editions.

Beale, A. L. (2002). Credit attributes of project finance. *Journal of Structured and Project Finance, 8,* 5–10.

Berkovitch, E., and Kim, E. H. (1990). Financial contracting and leverage induced over- and underinvestment incentives. *Journal of Finance, 45,* 765–794.

Berne Union. (various years). *Yearbook*. Berne, Switzerland: Berne Union Editions.

Black, F., and Cox, J. C. (1976). Valuing corporate securities: some effects of bond indenture provisions. *Journal of Finance, 31,* 351–367.

Bolton, P., and Scharfstein, D. S. (1996). Optimal debt contracts and the number of creditors. *Journal of Political Economy, 104,* 1–25.

Brealey, R. A., Cooper, I. A., and Habib, M. A. (1996). Using project finance to fund infrastructure investments. *Journal of Applied Corporate Finance, 9,* 25–38.

Brealey, R. A., Myers, S., and Allen, F. (1996). *Principles of corporate finance*. New York: McGraw-Hill.

Bull, P. (1995). Capital leasing in project finance. In H. Shaughnessy (ed.). *Project finance in Europe*. London, John Wiley & Sons.

Burch, T. R., Nanda, V., and Wather, V. (2005). Does it pay to be loyal? An empirical analysis of underwriting relationships and fees. *Journal of Financial Economics, 77*, 673–699.

Casolaro, L., Focarelli, D., and Pozzolo, A. F. (2003). *The pricing effect of certification on bank loan: Evidence from the syndicated credit market*. Working paper, Bank of Italy.

Clifford Chance. (1991). *Project finance*. London: IFR.

Chemmanur, T. J., and John, K. (1996). Optimal incorporation, structure of debt contracts and limited recourse project finance. *Journal of Financial Intermediation, 5*, 372–408.

Chen, A. H., and Kensinger, J. W. (1993). Uncommon equity. In D. Chew (ed.). *The new corporate finance*. New York, McGraw-Hill.

Chowdry, B. (1991). What is different about international lending? *Review of Financial Studies, 4*, 121–148.

COFACE. (various years). *Annual report*. Paris COFACE Editions.

Collin-Dufresne, P., and Goldstein, A. S. (2001). Do credit spreads reflect stationary leverage ratios? *Journal of Finance, 56*, 1929–1957.

Construction Industry Institute. (2003). Risk assessment for international projects. *Implementation Resources, 181* (Special Issue).

Cook, D., Schellhorn, C. D., and Spellman, L. J. (2001). *Lender certification premiums. Journal of Banking and Finance, 27*, 1561–1579.

Copeland, T., Koeller, T., and Murrin, J. (1990). Valuation: measuring and managing the value of companies. New York: John Wiley & Sons.

Credit Suisse Financial Products. (1997). *CreditRisk®. A credit risk management framework*. Technical document. London, NY, CSFB.

Crosbie, P., and Bohm, J. (2003). *Modeling default risk*. White paper. London, NY: Moody's & KMV.

Dailami, M., and Hauswald, R. (2001). *Contract risks and credit spread in determi-nants in the international project bonds markets*. Working paper. Washington, DC: World Bank Institute.

Dailami, M., and Hauswald, R. (2003). *The emerging project bond market: covenant provisions and credit spreads*. Policy research working paper no. 3095. Washington, DC: World Bank Institute.

Dailami, M., Lipkovich, I., and Van Dyck, J. (1999). *Infrisk: a computer simulation approach to risk management in infrastructure project finance transactions*. Policy research working paper no. 2085. Washington, DC: IBRD.

Damodaran, A. (1997). *Corporate finance: theory and practice*. New York: John Wiley & Sons.

Damodaran, A. (2006). *Applied corporate finance: a user's manual*. Hoboken, NJ: John Wiley & Sons.

Dennis, S. A., and Mullineaux, D. J. (2000). Syndicated loans. *Journal of Financial Intermediation, 9*, 404–426.

Department of Trade and Industry. (2001). *Communications liberalization in the UK*. London: Department of Trade and Industry Editions.

EBRD—European Bank for Reconstruction and Development. (various years). *Annual report*. Brussels, Belgium: EBRD Editions.

ECGD. (various years). *Annual report*. London Editions.

EDC. (various years). *Annual report*. Ottawa Editions.

EIB—European Investment Bank. (various years). *Annual report*. Brussels, Belgium: EIB Editions.

EIB—European Investment Bank. (2004). *The EIB's role in public–private partnerships*. Brussels, Belgium: EIB Editions.

EIB—European Investment Bank. (2005). *Evaluation of PPP projects financed by the EIB*. Brussels, Belgium: EIB Editions.

Emerick, D., and White, W. (1992). The case for private placements: how sophisticated investors add value to corporate debt issuers. *Journal of Applied Corporate Finance, 3*, 241–266.

Erb, C. B., Harvey, C. R., and Viskanta, T. E. (1996). Political risk, economic risk and financial risk. *Financial Analysts Journal, 52*, 28–46.

Esty, B. C. (2001). Structuring loan syndicates: a case study of Hong Kong Disneyland project loan. *Journal of Applied Corporate Finance, 14*, 80–95.

Esty, B. C. (2002a). Returns on project-financed investments: evolution and managerial implications. *Journal of Applied Corporate Finance, 15,* 71–86.

Esty, B. C. (2002b). *An overview of project finance—2002 update.* Cambridge, MA: Harvard Business School.

Esty, B. C. (2003). *Modern project finance: a casebook.* New York: John Wiley & Sons.

Esty, B. C. (2004). Why study large projects? An introduction to research project finance. *European Financial Management, 10,* 213–224.

Esty, B. C. (2005). *An overview of project finance—2004 Update.* Cambridge, MA: Harvard Business School.

Esty, B. C., and Megginson, W. L. (2003). Creditors' rights, enforcement and debt ownership structure: evidence from the global syndicated loans market. *Journal of Financial and Quantitative Analysis, 38,* 212–246.

Esty, B. C., and Sesia, A. (2004). *Basel II: assessing the default and loss characteristics of project finance loans (A). Case study no. 9-203-035.* Cambridge, MA: Harvard Business School.

Esty, B. C., and Sesia, A. (2007). *An overview of project finance and infrastructure finance—2006 update.* Cambridge, MA: Harvard Business School Teaching Note 9-207-107.

European Commission. (2003). *Guidelines for successful public–private partnership.* Brussels, Belgium: EU Editions.

Eurostat. (2004). *Long-term contracts between government units and nongovernment partners (public–private partnerships).* Luxembourg: Office for Official Publications of the European Communities.

Everhart, S. S., and Sumlinski, M. A. (2001). *Trends in private investment in developing countries. Statistics for 1970–2000 and the impact on private investment of corruption and the quality of public investment.* Discussion paper no. 44. Washington, DC: International Finance Corporation.

Fabozzi, F., and Nevitt, P. K. (2006). *Project financing* (7th ed.). London: Euromoney.

Fisher, G., and Babbar, S. (1999). *Private financing of toll roads.* Discussion paper no. 117, Washington: RMC—World Bank Institute.

FITCH-IBCA. (2003). *A survey of multilateral development banks and their responses to successive emerging market crises.* Special report. Loudon, NY: FITCH-IBCA.

Fitch Ratings. (2003). *Basel II: refinements to the framework. Special report—Credit Policy,* London, NY: Fitch Ratings.

Fox, J., and Tott, N. (1999). *The PFI handbook.* London: Jordan.

Freshfields, Brukchaus, & Deringer. (2002). *The Italian power market.* Unpublished mimeo.

Gatti, S., Kleimeier, S., Megginson, W., and Steffanoni, A. (2007). *Arranger certification in project finance.* Working paper. Milan, Italy: Bocconi University.

Gatti, S., Rigamonti, A., Saita, F., and Senati, M. (2007). Measuring VaR in project finance transactions. *European Financial Management, 17,* 135–158.

Grossman, S., and Hart, O. (1986). The costs and benefits of ownership: a theory of vertical and lateral integration. *Journal of Political Economy, 94,* 691–719.

Gupton, G., Finger, C., and Bhatia, M. (1997). CreditMetrics®. Technical Document. New York: JPMorgan & Co.

Habib, M. A., and Johnsen, D. B. (1999). The financing and redeployment of specific assets. *Journal of Finance, 2,* 96–131.

Harrison, E. The managerial decision making process, Boston, MA: Houghton Mifflin, 1975.

Harrison, F. I. (1985). *Advanced project management.* Aldershot, UK: Gower Press.

Heinz, C., and Kleimeier, S. (2006). *Project finance: managing risk in international syndicated lending.* Working paper, University of Munich.

IADB—Inter-American Development Bank. (various years). *Annual report.* Washington, DC: IADB Editions.

IDB—Islamic Development Bank. (various years). *Annual report.* Jeddah: IDB Editions.

IFC—International Finance Corporation. (various years). *Annual report.* Washington, DC: IFC Editions.

IFC—International Finance Corporation. (1996). *Financing private infrastructure*. Washington, DC: IFC Editions.

IFC—International Finance Corporation. (1999). *Lessons of experience 7—Project finance in developing countries*. Washington, DC: World Bank Publications.

IFC—International Finance Corporation. (2004). *Comments on the working paper on the internal ratings–based approach to specialized lending exposures* (November).

ISACE. (various years). *Annual report*. Rome: ISACE Editions.

Ivashina, V. (2005). *Effects of syndicate structure on loans spreads*. Working paper. New York: Stern Business School.

Jensen, M. C., and Meckling, W. H. (1976). Theory of the firm: managerial behavior, agency costs and ownership structure. *Journal of Financial Economics, 3*, 36–78.

John, T., and John, K., 1991. Optimality of project financing: theory and empirical implication in finance and accounting. *Review of Quantitative Finance and Accounting, 1*, 51–74.

Kensinger, J. W., and Martin, J. (1988). Project finance: raising money in the old-fashioned way. *Journal of Applied Corporate Finance, 3*, 69–81.

Kleimeier, S., and Megginson, W. L. (2000). Are project finance loans different from other syndicated credits? *Journal of Applied Corporate Finance, 13*, 75–87.

Klompjan, R., and Wouters, M. J. F. (2002). Default risk in project finance. *Journal of Structured and Project Finance, 8*, 131–176.

La Porta, R., Lopez de Silanes, F., Shleifer, A., and Vishny, R. (1998). Law and finance. *Journal of Political Economy, 106*, 1113–1150.

La Porta, R., Lopez de Silanes, F., Shleifer, A., and Vishny, R. (2002). Investor protection and corporate valuation. *Journal of Finance, 57*, 1147–1170.

Leland, H., and Skarabot, J. (2003). *Financial synergies and the optimal scope of the firm: implications for mergers, spin-offs and off-balance-sheet finance*. Mimeo. Berkeley: CA: Haas School of Business, University of California.

Lessard, D., and Miller, R. (2001). Understanding and managing risks in large engineering projects. Working paper no. 4214-01. Cambridge, MA: MIT Sloan School of Management.

Lipton, J. D. (1996). Project financing and the environment: lender liability for envi-ronmental damage in Australia. *Journal of International Banking Law, 1*, 12–36.

Kleimeier, S., and Megginson, W. L. (2000). Are project finance loans different from other syndicated credits? *Journal of Applied Corporate Finance, 13*, 75–87.

Merton, R. (1974). On the pricing of corporate debt: the risk structure of interest rates. *Journal of Finance, 29*, 449–470.

Mills, S. (1994). Project financing of oil and gas fields development. *Journal of International Banking Law, 9*, 213–315.

Mills, S. (1996). Project financing of oil and gas fields development: balancing the interests of investors and lenders. *OLGTR Review, 4*, 145–169.

Moody's. (2001a). *Weaker credit trends ahead for project companies lacking third-party surety for construction obligations*. Special comments. London, NY: Moody's Investors' Service.

Moody's. (2001b). *Moody's response to the Basel Committee proposal on an internal rating–based capital adequacy approach for project finance*. Special comments. London, NY: Moody's Investors' Service.

Moody's. (2000c). *Project finance recognizes benefits of bank loan ratings*. Working paper. London, NY: Moody's Investors' Service.

Myers, S. (1977). Determinants of corporate borrowing. *Journal of Financial Economics, 5*, 147–175.

NEXI/JBIC. (various years). *Annual report*. Tokio: NEXI/JBIC Editions.

OPIC. (various years). *Annual report*. Washington, DC: OPIC Editions.

Pearce, B. and Paul Ekins. International Financial Institutions. Enhancing their role in promoting sustainable development, London, Royal Institute of International Affairs, 2001.

Project Management Institute. (1996). *A guide to project management body of knowl-edge*. Sylva, NC: PMI Communications.

Pruitt, S. W., and Gitman, L. J. (1987). Capital budgeting forecasting biases: evidence from the Fortune 500. *Financial Management, 3,* 46–51.

Rajan, R., and Winton, A. (1995). Covenants and collateral as incentives to monitor. *Journal of Finance, 50,* 1113–1146.

Randolph G., "Financing LNG Projects: the role of capital markets going forward," GOLDMAN SACHS, London, 2001.

Rose, P. D. (1996). Petropower® project financing in Chile: a sponsor's perspective on approaching the market. *Journal of Project Finance, 2,* 16–41.

Ross, S. A., Westfield, R. W., and Jaffe, J. F. (1993). *Corporate finance.* Homewood, IL: Irwin.

Saaty, T. L. Fundamentals of Decision Making and Priority Theory with Analytic Hierarchy Process. Pittsburgh, PA: RWS Publications, 2000.

Schuyler, J. R. Risk and decision analysis in projects. Newton, PA: Project Management Institute, 2001.

Shah, S., and Thakor, A. V. (1987). Optimal capital structure and project financing. *Journal of Economic Theory, 42,* 209–243.

Smith, A. J. (1999). *Privatized infrastructure—the role of government.* London: Telford.

Smith, C. W., and Warner, J. B. (1979). On financial contracting: an analysis of bond covenants. *Journal of Financial Economics, 7,* 117–161.

Sorge, M., and Gadanecz, B. (2005). *The term structure of credit spreads in project finance.* Working paper. Basel, Bank for International Settlements.

S&P-Standard and Poor's. (2002a). Project and infrastructure finance 2002: beyond the crisis. *Project and Infrastructure Review.* New York, S&P.

S&P-Standard and Poor's. (2002b). Project collateralized loans and bonds: rating considerations. *Project and Infrastructure Review.* New York: S&P.

S&P-Standard and Poor's. (2002c). Credit implications of traffic risk in start-up toll facilities. *Project and Infrastructure Review.* New York: S&P.

S&P-Standard and Poor's. (2002d). *Ratings Direct—Basel II: no turning back for the banking industry.* New York: S&P.

Statman, M., and Tyebjee, T. T. (1985). Optimistic capital budgeting forecasts: an experiment. *Financial Management, 3,* 27–33.

Stulz, R. M. (1985). An analysis of secured debt. *Journal of Financial Economics, 14,* 501–521.

Sufi, A. (forthcoming). Information asymmetry and financing arrangements: evidence from syndicated loans. *Journal of Finance.*

Tinsley, R. (2000a). *Advanced project financing: structuring risks.* London: Euro-money Books.

Tinsley, R. (2000b). *Project finance in Asia Pacific: practical case studies.* London: Euromoney Books.

U.S. Exim Bank. (various years). *Annual report.* New York: Exim Bank Editions.

Williamson, O. E. (1988). Corporate finance and corporate governance. *Journal of Finance, 43,* 567–591.

Willis, J. R., and Clark, D. A. (1989). An introduction to mezzanine finance and private equity. *Journal of Applied Corporate Finance, 2,* 131–152.

Wood, P. R. (1995). *Project finance, subordinated debt and state loans.* London: Sweet & Maxwell, 1995.

World Bank Institute. (various years). *Annual report.* Washington, DC: World Bank Editions.

World Bank Institute. (2002). *Global development finance.* Washington, DC: World Bank Editions.

Yescombe, E. R. (2002). *Principles of project finance.* San Diego, CA: Academic Press, 2002.

Index

Page numbers followed by "f" denote figures; those followed by "t" denote tables

Date Due

IL53817074	due	6/5/09
IL5814237		NOV 24 09
IL58161496		11-4-09
IL140002374		1.20.15

BRODART, CO.   Cat. No. 23-233-003   Printed in U.S.A.